# The Changing Portrayal of Adolescents in the Media Since 1950

# The Changing Portrayal of Adolescents in the Media Since 1950

*Edited by*
Patrick E. Jamieson
Daniel Romer

THE ANNENBERG
PUBLIC POLICY CENTER
OF THE UNIVERSITY OF PENNSYLVANIA

Robert Wood Johnson Foundation

OXFORD
UNIVERSITY PRESS

2008

**OXFORD**
UNIVERSITY PRESS

Oxford University Press, Inc., publishes works that further
Oxford University's objective of excellence
in research, scholarship, and education.

Oxford   New York
Auckland   Cape Town   Dar es Salaam   Hong Kong   Karachi
Kuala Lumpur   Madrid   Melbourne   Mexico City   Nairobi
New Delhi   Shanghai   Taipei   Toronto

With offices in
Argentina   Austria   Brazil   Chile   Czech Republic   France   Greece
Guatemala   Hungary   Italy   Japan   Poland   Portugal   Singapore
South Korea   Switzerland   Thailand   Turkey   Ukraine   Vietnam

Published by Oxford University Press, Inc.
198 Madison Avenue, New York, New York 10016

www.oup.com

Oxford is a registered trademark of Oxford University Press

Library of Congress Cataloging-in-Publication Data
The changing protrayal of adolescents in the media since 1950 / edited
by Patrick Jamieson, Daniel Romer.
p. cm.
ISBN-13: 978-0-19-534295-6 (pbk. : alk. paper)
ISBN-10: 0-19-534295-X (pbk. : alk. paper)
1. Youth in mass media. 2. Mass media and youth. I. Jamieson,
Patrick E., 1973– II. Romer, Daniel, 1946–
P94.5.Y72C43   2008
302.230835—dc22      2007052293

9 8 7 6 5 4 3 2 1
Printed in the United States of America
on acid-free paper

To my daughter, Sylvia Jane, for teaching me what really matters.—P. E. J.

To my wife, Lauren B. Alloy, who keeps my spirits up
when it really matters.—D. R.

# Preface

This volume grew out of a project jointly sponsored by the Annenberg Public Policy Center (APPC) and the Robert Wood Johnson Foundation to gain a greater understanding of the media's influence on adolescents since World War II. The Coding of Health and Media Project (CHAMP) that began in 2006 has undertaken this objective by first examining the portrayal of health risk behaviors in major motion pictures since 1950. Because not much is known about these and other historical trends in the media, the APPC convened a conference in March 2007 of scholars who have been studying various media influences on youth. This meeting highlighted several themes that paved the way for this volume.

The first theme discussed in the Introduction to this volume and by Bill Osgerby (Chapter 1) was the increased interest in the teenage market following the war. Indeed, the discovery of the "teenager" as a demographic segment was a distinct postwar phenomenon. The emergence of this market was an inevitable by-product of the increasing affluence of the postwar period that permitted young people to control more disposable income than their parents had only a few years earlier. The increasing affluence also brought with it a consumer culture that celebrates what Bill Osgerby calls a youthful hedonism. The expansion of the media, especially the introduction of television, undoubtedly played a role in promoting this new ethos of immediate gratification. And the baby boom generation, the largest cohort of adolescents in the country's history to that point, came of age and helped fuel the new culture.

A second theme related to the rise of a youth culture is the growing influence and presence of adolescents in the media. Andy Bennett (Chapter 2) describes the development of this trend in regard to the most prominent form of expression, music, as carried on recordings and played on radio and in live performances. The music business provided a voice for young people to express their concerns and to start new cultural trends. As television matured and cable provided more outlets for youth content, music videos also evolved into a popular vehicle of youth expression. Michael Rich (Chapter 3) explores the development of this form of expression and its likely evolution on the Internet.

Related to the theme of a growing culture of youthful hedonism is the increasing concern about the effects of media portrayals on adolescent socialization. As the media expanded during the postwar period, they played an increasing role in facilitating the new culture of hedonism. This influence, which was evident in both advertising and entertainment, promoted immediate gratification as the route to personal fulfillment. As noted in the Introduction, most of the harmful influences of the media that came to be identified in research had their roots in this ethos. Furthermore, these influences were likely to be particularly harmful to adolescents who are still forming their identities and are more subject to impulsive behavior than adults. Hence, a major question raised by this volume is whether trends in media portrayals matter enough to be a concern of public policy, and if so, how those concerns should be addressed?

In the second and largest section of the volume, we explore the growing recognition of the influence of the media as a socializing agent on adolescents. The Introduction to the volume summarizes the many mechanisms of media influence that have been isolated in research. In Part II, several authors review the changes (or lack thereof) that have occurred in how the media portray behaviors that are influential in adolescent development. The adolescent of today as well as the culture in which he or she is raised have changed dramatically since 1950. This section explores what is known about these changes and how they are influencing adolescent development.

The opening chapter by Patrick E. Jamieson, Eian More, Susan S. Lee, Peter Busse, and Daniel Romer presents findings from a large-scale analysis of behavior trends in top-grossing films since 1950. Although the portrayal of some risk behaviors, such as tobacco and alcohol use, has steadily declined since 1970, other behaviors such as violence, suicide, and sex have increased in explicitness. Furthermore, youthful representation in these behaviors has either increased or remained the same. The authors also discuss the role of the Motion Picture Association of America rating system as a mechanism to reduce exposure to harmful content.

In Chapter 5, Jennifer L. Walsh and L. Monique Ward review what appear to be very slowly evolving changes in portrayal of gender roles of young men and women in both advertising and entertainment. This is somewhat surprising given the enormous changes that have occurred in the representation of women in higher education and the workplace. In Chapter 6, Kristen Harrison describes dramatic changes that have occurred in the body ideals and eating habits of the culture as represented in advertising, entertainment media, and marketing. Many of these trends can be linked to unhealthy eating habits in youth and the adult population in general. In Chapter 7, Carolyn A. Stroman and Jannette L. Dates review the increased representation of African Americans and other nonwhite groups in the media. Although largely invisible in the early years of television, these groups have grown to more closely approximate their representation in the population. Nevertheless, stereotypical portrayals remain a legacy in many media.

In Chapter 8, W. James Potter examines the voluminous literature on the portrayal of violence in the media, especially on television. This behavior is certainly the most heavily studied of the media influences on youth, and it poses some of the most difficult policy questions about the role of free expression and profit-maximization in the media business. A surprising finding is the increase in verbal aggression, particularly on television, along with its likely effects on our culture. Potter carefully examines the policy conundrums raised by the findings. In Chapter 9, Timothy Dewhirst examines another difficult problem, the advertising and portrayal of tobacco use in the media. He examines how this portrayal has changed over the years since the behavior was first discovered to be a major source of disease. He also reviews some policy questions that remain to be answered as we continue to grapple with the sale and advertising of this product.

Another difficult issue for media policy discussed by Jennifer Horner, Patrick E. Jamieson, and Daniel Romer (Chapter 10) is the portrayal and marketing of alcohol. Although the purchase of alcohol has been illegal since the 1980s for persons under age 21, advertising and promotion continue to reach adolescents. The authors examine trends in beer advertising since the 1950s and identify emerging themes that appear to speak to young people's difficulty in obtaining alcoholic beverages. They also review recent developments in the marketing of alcopops that appear to appeal to adolescents, especially girls.

In the final chapter in this section, Susannah Stern and Jane D. Brown review the dramatic changes that have occurred in the portrayal of sex across the media. These changes reflect the greater openness to experience and youthful hedonism that characterize our culture since the 1950s. Although sexual explicitness has increased, portrayal of safeguards against pregnancy or disease seldom receive much attention. Stern and Brown discuss the emergence of the Internet as a forum for young people to learn about and communicate about sex, a development that might actually help to balance the absence of helpful information on television or in films.

In Part III, we move to the emergence of two very powerful forces in the media world of young people: computerized video games and the Internet. James D. Ivory (Chapter 12) describes the dramatic growth and future direction of these games from both a technological and social perspective. He also reviews both the favorable and potentially harmful effects of these games, especially in regard to those that feature violent action. Linda A. Jackson (Chapter 13) reviews the major controversies surrounding the use of Internet content by young people, including the digital divide, the overall effects on social and cognitive behavior, and potential harmful effects on adolescents. She concludes with a relatively favorable assessment of the Internet's effects as established so far, but encourages further research to determine future policy directions for this evolving medium.

In Part IV, we conclude with two chapters on the potential policy implications of the growing and important role of the media in the socialization of adolescents. C. Edwin Baker (Chapter 14) reviews the various government strategies that might be employed to influence media content and finds many of them either difficult to implement (e.g., mandatory content rating) or unwelcome to a free society (e.g., censorship). He finds many of the problems raised by harmful media content to be an example of larger concerns about our media industries, such as their failure to provide products the public wants at a cost it can afford, and he suggests some alternatives that might increase the availability of content that is both attractive and healthy.

In the concluding chapter, the editors are joined by another conference participant, Amy Jordan, in a discussion of the major themes of the volume and their policy implications. A number of these policy options are raised for various actors, such as schools, parents, and the media industry, that could improve the media environment and provide a healthier socialization experience for young people.

We thank all the authors of the volume not only for providing thought provoking chapters but also for willingly reading other authors' chapters and providing helpful suggestions for improvement. We also thank Joan Bossert, our editor at Oxford University Press, for attending the initial conference and for encouraging the development of this volume. We finally thank the Robert Wood Johnson Foundation and the Annenberg Foundation for providing the funding that made the initial conference and this book possible. Nevertheless, the views expressed herein do not necessarily reflect those of the funders.

Patrick E. Jamieson and Daniel Romer
Adolescent Risk Communication Institute
Annenberg Public Policy Center
University of Pennsylvania

# Contents

Contributors   *xiii*

Introduction: Mass Media and the Socialization of Adolescents
Since World War II   *3*
>    *Daniel Romer*

### Part I   The Emergence and Evolution
### of a Youth Culture in the Media

1   Understanding the "Jackpot Market": Media, Marketing,
and the Rise of the American Teenager   *27*
>    *Bill Osgerby*

2   "Still Talking About My Generation!" The Representation
of Youth in Popular Music   *59*
>    *Andy Bennett*

3   Music Videos: Media of the Youth, by the Youth, for the Youth   *78*
>    *Michael Rich*

### Part II   Portrayal of Adolescents and Influential Behaviors

4   It Matters What Young People Watch: Health Risk Behaviors
Portrayed in Top-Grossing Movies Since 1950   *105*
>    *Patrick E. Jamieson, Eian More, Susan S. Lee, Peter Busse,
>    and Daniel Romer*

5   Adolescent Gender Role Portrayals in the Media: 1950
    to the Present   *132*
        *Jennifer L. Walsh and L. Monique Ward*

6   Adolescent Body Image and Eating in the Media: Trends
    and Implications for Adolescent Health   *165*
        *Kristen Harrison*

7   African Americans, Latinos, Asians, and Native Americans
    in the Media: Implications for Adolescents   *198*
        *Carolyn A. Stroman and Jannette L. Dates*

8   Adolescents and Television Violence   *221*
        *W. James Potter*

9   Tobacco Portrayals in U.S. Advertising
    and Entertainment Media   *250*
        *Timothy Dewhirst*

10  The Changing Portrayal of Alcohol Use in Television
    Advertising   *284*
        *Jennifer Horner, Patrick E. Jamieson, and Daniel Romer*

11  From Twin Beds to Sex at Your Fingertips: Teen Sexuality
    in Movies, Music, Television, and the Internet, 1950 to 2005   *313*
        *Susannah Stern and Jane D. Brown*

**Part III   Evolving Forms of Media Influence**

12  The Games, They Are a-Changin': Technological Advancements in
    Video Games and Implications for Effects on Youth   *347*
        *James D. Ivory*

13  Adolescents and the Internet   *377*
        *Linda A. Jackson*

**Part IV   Policy Implications for Healthy
Adolescent Development**

14  Policy Interventions   *415*
        *C. Edwin Baker*

15  Conclusions   *446*
        *Patrick E. Jamieson, Amy Jordan, and Daniel Romer*

    Index   *459*

# Contributors

C. Edwin Baker, JD
Nicholas F. Gallicchio Professor
University of Pennsylvania Law School
University of Pennsylvania
Philadelphia, PA

Andy Bennett, PhD
Professor
Department of Cultural Sociology
Director, Centre for Public Culture
    and Ideas
School of Arts
Griffith University
Southport, Queensland
Australia

Jane D. Brown
James L. Knight Professor
School of Journalism and Mass
    Communication
University of North Carolina–Chapel
    Hill
Chapel Hill, NC

Peter Busse, MA
Annenberg School for Communication
University of Pennsylvania
Philadelphia, PA

Jannette L. Dates, PhD
Professor and Dean
Department of Radio, Television and Film
Johnson School of Communications
Howard University
Washington, DC

Timothy Dewhirst, PhD
Assistant Professor
Department of Marketing and
    Consumer Studies
College of Management and Economics
University of Guelph
Guelph, Ontario
Canada

Kristen Harrison, PhD
Associate Professor
Department of Speech Communication
    and Division of Nutritional Sciences
University of Illinois
Urbana, IL

Jennifer Horner, PhD
George Gerbner Postdoctoral Fellow
Annenberg School for Communication
University of Pennsylvania
Philadelphia, PA

James D. Ivory, PhD
Assistant Professor
Department of Communication
Virginia Polytechnic Institute and State
  University
Blacksburg, VA

Linda A. Jackson
Professor
Department of Psychology
Michigan State University
East Lansing, MI

Patrick E. Jamieson, PhD
Associate Director
Adolescent Risk Communication
  Institute
Annenberg Public Policy Center
University of Pennsylvania
Philadelphia, PA

Amy Jordan, PhD
Senior Research Investigator
The Annenberg Public Policy Center
University of Pennsylvania
Philadelphia, PA

Susan S. Lee, BA
Administrative Coordinator
Adolescent Risk Communication
  Institute
University of Pennsylvania
Philadelphia, PA

Eian More, MLA
Research Coordinator
Adolescent Risk Communication
  Institute
University of Pennsylvania
Philadelphia, PA

Bill Osgerby, PhD
Professor
Department of Applied Social
  Sciences
London Metropolitan University

London
United Kingdom

W. James Potter, PhD
Professor
Department of Communication
University of California at Santa
  Barbara
Santa Barbara, CA

Michael Rich, MD, MPH
Director
Center on Media and Child Health
Children's Hospital Boston
Boston, MA

Daniel Romer, PhD
Adolescent Risk Communication
  Institute
Annenberg Public Policy Center
University of Pennsylvania
Philadelphia, PA

Susannah Stern, PhD
Associate Professor
Department of Communication Studies
University of San Diego
San Diego, CA

Carolyn A. Stroman, PhD
Associate Professor
Department of Communication and
  Culture
Howard University
Washington, DC

Jennifer L. Walsh, MA
Department of Psychology
University of Michigan
Ann Arbor, MI

L. Monique Ward, PhD
Associate Professor
Department of Psychology
University of Michigan
Ann Arbor, MI

The Changing Portrayal of Adolescents
in the Media Since 1950

# Introduction

## Mass Media and the Socialization of Adolescents Since World War II

DANIEL ROMER

There is little doubt that U.S. society experienced significant change over the last half of the twentieth century. After emerging from World War II with a reinvigorated economy and little competition from other industrialized powers, the United States entered a period of massive social and economic change. Indeed, the new prosperity and affluence that the country experienced is perhaps unprecedented in its scope and influence. Not only did Americans free themselves from the constraints of economic insecurity, they slowly but persistently pursued what Lindsey (2007) termed a new ethos of "mass hedonism" displayed most prominently in enhanced consumption of consumer goods. As seen in Figure I.1, household incomes rose dramatically following World War II, and the proportion of that income devoted to basic needs such as food, clothing, and housing declined continuously (Figure I.2). The proportion of the population that could be classified as poor in 1959 (20%) was less than half of what it had been (50%) in 1929 (H. Miller, 1964). The new prosperity also provoked increased interest in what Maslow (1954) termed higher-order needs, such as the quest for social status and self-actualization. The satisfaction of these needs was evident in ever-larger proportions of income spent on status products, such as cars, single-family homes, and higher education (Offer, 2006).

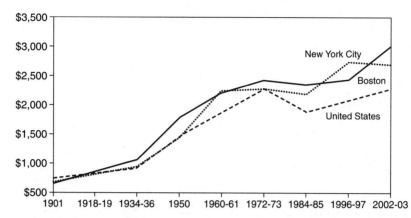

Figure I.1. Trends in household income (deflated to 1901 prices) from 1901 to 2003 for total United States, New York City, and Boston. (*Source*: U.S. Department of Labor, 2006.)

In this chapter, we examine the social and economic changes that occurred during the postwar period and how these forces, in combination with technological advances, have permitted the media to play an ever-increasing role in the lives of Americans and to assume ever-greater influence in the socialization of youth. We propose that the new affluence that emerged after the war changed the culture in dramatic ways that ultimately were transmitted to the first large cohort of baby boomers that grew up under the influence of the new media environment. The media were not responsible for the new age of affluence and its culture of consumption, but they

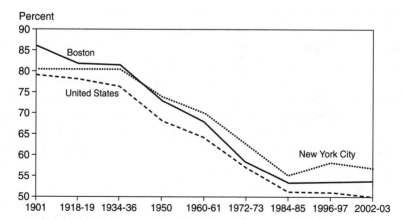

Figure I.2. Trends in shares of income devoted to necessities from 1901 to 2003 for total United States, New York City, and Boston. (*Source*: U.S. Department of Labor, 2006.)

played a large role in support of its growth and consequently in the socialization of each succeeding cohort of young people.

## POSTWAR PROSPERITY AND THE CULTURE OF CONSUMPTION

The new culture of consumption that emerged in the postwar period was made possible by many changes that originated in the first half of the century but that did not come to fruition until the prosperity and associated technological advances of the postwar period (Bell, 1976). By 1960, more Americans were employed in white collar than blue collar professions (43% versus 37%), a trend that has continued unabated (French, 1997). This change was facilitated in part by the growth of the modern corporation. Although often characterized as a stifling influence on American ingenuity in both fictional (e.g., Wilson's *The Man in the Gray Flannel Suit*) and social science accounts (Whyte's *The Organization Man*), the corporation also became a source of openness, acceptance of difference, and career opportunity (Lindsey, 2007). No longer could employees of large corporations hold onto provincial beliefs about working only with people known to them since childhood. Employees were ever more frequently working alongside persons from different backgrounds and regions of the country. The business model of the modern corporation did not include room for provincial prejudices (Galbraith, 1972). The new values in this environment encouraged what Riesman (1950) called the "other-directed" personality who paid more attention to others' opinions than the "inner-directed" person who was beholden to parental teachings.

The modern corporate environment also opened doors to women workers, albeit not in very high-level jobs. Over the course of the 1950s, married women with school-aged children increased their participation in the job market from 28% to 39% (French, 1997). Indeed, the proportion of women in the workforce who were married (52%) outnumbered those who were single (32%) or divorced/widowed (16%) for the first time (French, 1997). However, the large numbers of women who were now being educated in colleges and universities were often disappointed by the opportunities they found in the economy. The emergence of a modern feminist movement, spurred in part by the publication of Friedan's (1963) *The Feminine Mystique* and the earlier *The Second Sex* by de Beauvoir (1949), added impetus to the drive for equality in both the workplace and the home. In addition, the birth control pill, which was approved for sale in 1960, made it all the more possible for women to pursue both a career and childbirth on a schedule of their choosing.

The civil rights movement also dramatically changed the country's practices in regard to African Americans who properly felt left out of the new prosperity despite having fought (largely in segregated units) in the war. Indeed, the military was the first institution to socially integrate African Americans (1951) three years after President Truman outlawed segregation in the military by executive order. The subsequent hard fought abolition of segregationist laws in the South, unequal access to schools in both North and South, as well as greater voting rights, produced dramatic change in the legal status of African Americans and slowly but surely opened the door to greater participation in society. By 1963, 85% of Americans agreed that black persons "should have as good a chance as white people to get any kind of job" compared to only 45% in 1944 (Schuman, Steeh, Bobo, & Krysan, 1997).

A new generation of youth, the baby boomers, was the first generation to be socialized and to come of age in this new environment. It is not surprising that this large youth cohort first embraced so many of the novel features of this new culture, including greater acceptance of racial and ethnic differences, openness about sex, recognition of equality between the sexes, and reduced concern about economic security. Indeed, the new cohort soon came to recognize itself as a distinct demographic segment with consumer clout never before seen in young people (see Chapter 1). As early as 1956, the average teenager had as much to spend on disposables as the average family of the 1940s (Halberstam, 1993).

Another major change in youth socialization, namely extended adolescence, was also emerging. As the new business environment required ever more sophisticated expertise, the need for education through high school and beyond took hold. The increasing enrollment of youth in high schools had been a trend since the beginning of the century. However, starting in the 1950s, more than half of adolescents completed high school and ever-increasing percentages of young people also attended college, a trend that extended the period of dependency and delay of adult responsibility further into the third decade of life. This extension also increased young people's exposure to peers rather than the rapid introduction to the workplace or marriage that had been commonplace for most teens in previous generations (Epstein, 2007). These transformations helped to bring about a distinct youth culture that was ready to absorb the new messages that were transmitted in the mass media.

## MASS MEDIA IN THE POSTWAR ERA

It is not surprising that the mass media would play a role in the development of this new environment. As we argue below, the introduction of television was particularly important, not only because it replaced and competed with the use of other media, but also because it relied almost totally on advertising sponsorship. Driven by the needs of advertisers, television producers increasingly relied on entertainment with violent content (Hamilton, 1998). To remain competitive, film producers turned increasingly to violence and sexual content, especially after the constraints of long-standing censorship were lifted in the 1960s (see below). In addition, television helped to facilitate the culture of consumption by relentlessly exposing Americans to novel consumer goods and services.

It is noteworthy that this conclusion was not foreshadowed by the impressive study of media influence undertaken by Katz and Lazarsfeld shortly after the war in 1945 but before the age of affluence had emerged. Their study, appropriately titled *Personal Influence* (2006) downplayed the role of the media, especially films, magazines, and radio, as sources of direct influence in Americans' lives. It was not the media per se that influenced people, but rather how one's peer leaders reacted to and relayed media messages (the two-step flow of influence). Although the role of personal influence has undoubtedly remained important, especially for adolescents, this study could not anticipate the enormous changes that were soon to occur in the new age of affluence. We outline these changes for films, radio, and television.

## Films

Despite the small role that Katz and Lazarsfeld attributed to the media, they did note that young people were particularly avid consumers of films. The importance of film was not surprising given that the medium had drawn large audiences to local theaters and movie houses for some time. The importance of films as a source of role models undoubtedly rested on their national distribution, which permitted youth in all strata of society to see (mostly adult) movie stars play exciting parts in far-off places. However, starting in the 1930s, the content of films was tightly controlled by national censors using the strictures of the Production (or Hays) Code. The Code was designed to reduce imitation of violence, sex, drug and alcohol use, and to uphold traditional norms of behavior (F. Miller, 1994). Indeed, even the influential film about a troubled youth *Rebel Without a Cause* (1955), starring the popular teen role model James Dean, had very little explicit sexual content.

Two postwar rulings by the Supreme Court helped to end the power of the Code (F. Miller, 1994). One ruling in 1952 overturned earlier decisions that upheld the use of the Code and extended First Amendment protection to the film industry. In addition, an antitrust ruling by the Court in 1948 made it difficult for the industry to control the distribution of films to theaters—especially foreign films, which were not subject to the Hays code. As the 1960s approached, it was increasingly difficult for censors to control the showing of films with sexual, violent, or other antisocial content, especially (as noted) foreign films shown in art houses. In 1968, the Motion Picture Association of America formally abandoned the Code and adopted a rating system that could be used by parents and other gatekeepers to shield children from unacceptable content. From the 1960s onward, films provided ever-greater opportunities to portray both adult and youth behavior that violated previous standards of propriety not only in regard to sex but also violence (see Chapter 4).

## Radio

Radio had been a fixture on the American scene since the 1930s. Two major networks, the National Broadcasting Corporation (NBC) and the Columbia Broadcasting System (CBS), sent signals to the entire country with news and entertainment programming. The medium also introduced Americans to national brands of consumer products. Radio stations were mainstays of entertainment in their markets and increasingly played popular music. It was not surprising that recorded music provided the first major medium to recognize the unique voices of adolescents in the 1950s, permitting the new youth music inspired by African American influences, such as rock and roll and soul, to be played on radio and reproduced on vinyl recordings (see Chapter 2). Indeed, the new affluence permitted teens to own their own radios and record players, enabling them to consume music apart from the control of parents (Halberstam, 1993). As described in Chapter 2, recorded music played on radio has been an ever-changing outlet for the expression of young people's concerns. Music has also been a major avenue of youthful rebellion against adult norms and practices.

## Television

Despite the importance of radio and films during the postwar period, the rapid adoption of television in the 1950s provided a new platform to sell products to a population with ever-increasing means to acquire them. Introduced as a consumer item shortly after the war, by 1960 nearly 90% of U.S. households owned a set (Offer, 2006). According to time-use studies that began in the 1950s (Robinson & Martin, 2007), television had more impact on people's daily time budgets than "any other household technology in the last century." The adoption of television crowded out previous media activities such as radio listening, movie attendance, and reading. It also took time away from other domestic activities such as gardening and sleep. Time spent watching television as recorded in time-use diaries steadily increased from an average of ten hours a week among adults in 1960 to over twenty hours in recent years. As is also well-known, children and adolescents spend considerably more time exposed to television than adults (as much six hours per day).

Television was an ideal mechanism to encourage greater consumption, a project that the government saw as a remedy to the previous economic slowdown of the Great Depression. The landmark Employment Act of 1946 committed the government to policies that would stimulate demand for consumer products and that would keep unemployment in check (Santoni, 1986). The new agenda of consumer demand was quickly exploited by television networks that pitched the new medium to advertisers as a "selling machine in every living room" (Lindsey, 2007). It was not long before people were buying a product called the TV dinner that would allow them to prepare a meal quickly without missing any of the entertaining fare on the tube. Products such as these were, not surprisingly, first introduced on television as well. Hence, television became the preferred medium for introducing the ever-evolving range of new products that the consumption economy required.

With the economic need for ever-increasing consumption, the central role of advertising, especially on television, became ever more apparent. Galbraith (1969), among others, bemoaned the role that advertising played to maintain demand for increasingly redundant products. The newly emerging practice of consumer credit, a euphemism for debt, permitted Americans to buy products they could not immediately afford on the faith that they would repay the loans in the future (Halberstam, 1993). In a remark attributed to Robert Hutchins, American prosperity depended on "our patented way of getting rich, which is to buy things from one another that we do not want at prices we cannot pay on terms we cannot meet because of advertising we do not believe" (President's Commission for a National Agenda for the Eighties, 1980). Other commentators, such as Daniel Bell (1976) in his *Cultural Contradictions of Capitalism*, noted that the new era of immediate gratification actually clashed in fundamental ways with the foundations of the capitalist economy that required persistence and self-discipline for its ultimate success.

One of the ways that this contradiction played itself out was in opportunities that the new medium provided to socialize young people to the emerging ethos of immediate gratification. It is one thing for society to slowly incorporate a consumer mentality into its adult behavior; however, the rapid transmission of these practices to young people was a new phenomenon. With adolescents further removed from the assumption of adult responsibility and locked into longer periods of peer contact in schools (Epstein, 2007), the messages sent by the media accentuated adolescent impulsiveness all the more. It should not be overlooked that as adults were working harder to enjoy the fruits of the new prosperity, they were simultaneously adopting the characteristics of typical adolescents, in what Osgerby (Chapter 1) has termed *youthful hedonism*. As we find in our review of media influences, most of the harmful effects of the media involve the adoption of impulsive behavior patterns that maximize short-term reward at the expense of long-term gain. The media's evolving role must be considered in the context of the new culture of consumption.


## MEDIA INFLUENCE IN THE NEW CULTURE OF CONSUMPTION

With the ever-increasing ethos of immediate gratification in the media, it was not surprising that the cohort of youth growing up in the postwar period would absorb these media messages. Because adolescents are more impulsive than adults and willing to experiment with new behaviors, they are vulnerable to a host of adverse outcomes (Chambers, Taylor, & Potenza, 2003; Moffitt, 1993). Indeed, some of the unexpected consequences of the new adolescence that emerged in the 1960s included several signs of maladaptive behavior, including rising rates of suicide (Murphy & Wetzel, 1980) and homicide (Holinger, Offer, Barter, & Bell, 1994), increased depression (Ryan et al., 1992) and eating disorders (Lucas, Crowson, O'Fallon, & Melton, 1999), high rates of out-of-wedlock births (Luker, 1996), and massive cycles of drug use (Johnston, O'Malley, Bachman, & Schulenberg, 2005). Although the increases in homicide and out-of-wedlock births were more prevalent in poor youth, all of these signs of dysfunction had roots in adolescent impulsivity. Many observers of these trends felt that the media were at least partly responsible for these outcomes (Bushman & Huesmann, 2001; Strasburger, 2001). Indeed, the media found themselves enmeshed in what would eventually be dubbed the "culture wars" between social conservatives and more liberal factions who preferred free expression to government (or other forms of) censorship (Lindsey, 2007).

Despite the intensity of the culture wars, no simple dichotomy distinguished those who became concerned about the media's influence. Many professional organizations otherwise regarded as liberal in their views about child rearing expressed deep concerns about the media's role in socializing children, especially in regard to violence (Anderson & Bushman, 2002).

Indeed, research on the effects of media portrayals on young people sup-ported the views of those who advocated control over media content. Early research by Bandura found that exposure to mediated models display-ing violent behavior could influence young children's imitative behavior (Bandura, Ross, & Ross, 1963). An enormous body of subsequent research examining the long-term effects of exposure to violent television content in children and adolescents found that early exposure was linked to later violent behavior in adolescents and young adults (Comstock & Paik, 1991; Huesmann & Taylor, 2006).

Other research on the introduction of television in different parts of the country found that even if it did not increase violence, it may have encour-aged theft and other antisocial behaviors (Hennigan et al., 1982). Research on the introduction of television in other countries, however, found more evidence of effects on violence (Centerwall, 1992). And content analyses of television conducted over several years by Gerbner and colleagues found that the violence that was a staple of television content may cultivate a view of the world as dangerous and inhospitable among both heavy adult (Gerb-ner, Gross, Morgan, & Signorielli, 1980) and adolescent viewers (Gerbner, Gross, Signorielli, Morgan, & Jackson-Beeck, 1979). This "cultivation" analy-sis greatly influenced other research on the content and effects of television. We now move to a review of the other major mediating mechanisms that such research uncovered.

## Disinhibition

Berkowitz was an early investigator who tested the idea that filmed mod-els portraying otherwise disapproved behavior, such as violence, can serve to disinhibit similar behavior in observers otherwise provoked to anger (Berkowitz & Geen, 1967). He later interpreted this as an instance of se-mantic priming, whereby violence cues in the media unconsciously activate related beliefs and behaviors in observers, producing a short-term disin-hibition effect (Berkowitz, 1984). For example, Leyens and Parke (1975) showed that merely exposing persons to pictures of weapons was sufficient to increase their tendency to punish another person.

Bandura (2002) had a major influence on the interpretation of the ef-fects of television in his expanded versions of social cognitive theory ap-plied to the mass media. He treated the disinhibition effect as an instance of media prompting, whereby behaviors that have been learned in the past are activated by exposure to media models. Prompting would include not only the largely unconscious and short-lived effects of primes, but also the longer-lasting and less subtle effects of actors using or supporting violence to achieve their ends. Such prompts would not need to depict novel forms of behavior; they would only need to remind media consumers about ways of behaving they have learned in the past. The most prevalent of these influences would be efforts to spur consumers to buy products. Indeed, a good deal of advertising simply reminds viewers to use a product that they have consumed in the past, such as soft drinks. However, Bandura noted that this phenomenon may extend to more insidious forms of influence, such as the incitement to violence by prompting of aggressive cues.

Bandura also identified several other sources of disinhibition resulting from media portrayals. In particular, he noted that vicariously experienced rewards for otherwise punished behavior can serve to disinhibit the behavior. When models of aggression succeed in gaining their objectives with few negative consequences, observers may feel justified in using similar means to solve their problems. If these rewards are repeatedly delivered in the media, as Gerbner's research on television programming suggested, then observers may come to view these methods as normative (see Chapter 8). Indeed, this form of influence could extend to other disapproved behaviors, such as pornography. For example, Zillman and Bryant (1982) showed large amounts of filmed sexual behavior to research participants who later judged unusual sexual practices as more normative and acceptable. Hence, steady portrayal of successful but otherwise disapproved behavior can have both short-term disinhibiting and longer term normative effects.

Adolescents and young adults appear to be particularly susceptible to the disinhibiting effects of media portrayals. One particularly troublesome example of disinhibition is the phenomenon of behavioral contagion, whereby a spectacular event transmitted by the media can cause far-flung imitation of the behavior. Gabriel Tarde (1912) first noted the possibility of these occurrences, especially in regard to well-publicized instances of homicide, such as the case of Jack the Ripper. However, recent research has documented this phenomenon most clearly in regard to suicidal contagion (Gould, Jamieson, & Romer, 2003). The studies undertaken by Phillips (1974; Phillips, Leysna, & Paight, 1992) were particularly important in identifying the effects of newspaper reports of suicide as a source of contagion with the well-publicized death of Marilyn Monroe often cited as an example. Other research has extended the phenomenon to fictional portrayals in films and on television (Hawton et al., 1999) and to local television news (Romer, Jamieson, & Jamieson, 2006).

A persistent finding in this research is that young people are disproportionately influenced by exposure to suicides in the media (Phillips & Carstensen, 1986; Stack, 1991). This increased susceptibility is attributable to at least two factors. Young people experience higher levels of suicidal ideation than adults (Gould et al., 2003), and they tend to be more impulsive than adults (Zuckerman, 1994). The former condition makes suicides in the media more relevant to such youths who are presumably already considering the act. The second condition facilitates disinhibition by enhancing the likelihood that any temporary reduction in constraints will be acted upon.

## Desensitization and Normalization

A related effect of repeated displays of otherwise disapproved behavior is desensitization of emotional reactions to such behavior. Many forms of unacceptable behavior, such as violence, create unpleasant emotional reactions in audiences. However, when shown repeatedly and with muted consequences for either the victims or perpetrators, the behaviors may elicit less intense emotion and may increase tolerance for similar behavior in other situations (Berkowitz, 1984). For example, Thomas, Horton, Lippincott, and Drabman (1977) exposed 8- to 10-year-old children and college students to either a violent television police drama or an exciting but nonviolent volleyball game. Those exposed to the violent drama exhibited less emotion, as assessed by skin conductance, when subsequently viewing an age-relevant video of realistic aggression. Furthermore, those youth who reported watching more violent programming on television exhibited the lowest levels of emotional reactivity to the realistic aggression.

## Learning New Rules of Behavior

Bandura and others also enlarged the study of media influences by considering the role that media models play in teaching novel behaviors and the generative rules for imitating them. According to Bandura, modeling is not a simple case of mimicry. For example, seeing a woman supervising others in an office not only gives young viewers a model of such behavior but also the idea that a woman can assume a professional role with all the supporting beliefs, skills, and attitudes that this entails. Using these tools, viewers can learn to generate similar behavior on their own. This powerful socializing role has to be considered in evaluating the media as a major source of cultural transmission. Indeed, television increasingly came to be used for socially beneficial purposes with such innovations as educational programming for children. Furthermore, research began to identify the many favorable socializing influences of television, such as the encouragement of empathic and altruistic behavior in children (Mares & Woodard, 2005). However, it has not been difficult to observe high levels of risky behavior portrayed on prime-time television, such as failure to use seatbelts or protection during sex (Will, Porter, Geller, & DePasquale, 2005).

Modeling of new behavior was especially worrisome in regard to antisocial behaviors such as violence. By exposing children and adolescents to the use of violence as a solution to interpersonal and social problems, the media, especially television and other screen-based media, implicitly inculcate scripts that employ violence as a problem-solving technique, whether the behavior is portrayed as successful or not. In addition, by featuring violence at high rates, the media can give young people the impression that the world is a hostile place, an effect that has been linked to greater use of aggressive solutions to problems in children (Dodge, 1985). In a demonstration of the short-term effects of television on the behavior of children in grades 3 and 4 (ages 9 to 11), Robinson, Wilde, Navracruz, Haydel, & Varady (2001) showed that reducing exposure to television and violent video games for a period of six months resulted in a noticeable decline in reports of peer aggression and in behavioral observations of verbal aggression on the school playground.

All of the media influences identified in experimental research can be invoked to explain the apparent long-term influences of childhood and adolescent exposure to violence, especially on television, to later violent behavior (Levesque, 2007). Numerous long-term studies have found that early repeated exposure to violent programming on television predicts later antisocial and violent behavior (Huesmann & Taylor, 2006). A recent study of over 700 adolescents and young adults (Johnson, Cohen, Smailes, Kasen, & Brook, 2002) found that exposure to television at age 14 (in 1983) predicted various forms of aggressive behavior at age 22, including physical fights, robbery, and use of a weapon to commit crime. The study also found that exposure to television at age 22 predicted similar forms of aggressive behavior at age 30. This study controlled a number of additional factors that might also predict violent behavior, including family income, IQ, childhood neglect, psychiatric symptoms, and neighborhood violence. Hence, the study provides strong evidence that heavy exposure to television during adolescence is linked to significant forms of violent behavior in young adulthood and beyond (Anderson & Bushman, 2002).

A particularly troubling new form of screen violence, interactive video games, provides an even more engrossing experience that has drawn the attention of media researchers (Anderson, Gentile, & Buckley, 2007). These games now command a larger market than gross revenues for films. With this technology, players are invited to harm make-believe characters (or friends represented by on-screen avatars) without considering the consequences to others or to themselves. Many of the same media effects cited here may underlie the effects of such experiences on adolescents (Anderson et al., 2007). Advances in technology may also permit this form of screen play to evolve into a still more potent socialization influence on adolescents (see Chapter 12).

## MASS MEDIA ADVERTISING AND IMPULSIVE BEHAVIOR

Nearly all of the deleterious effects of media portrayals involve some form of inducement to behave impulsively. Disinhibition, desensitization, normalization, and learning of new rules of unacceptable behavior all encourage the use of harmful solutions (e.g., violence and suicide) to social and personal problems that could be avoided with more effective decision making. Other forms of influence encourage attraction to immediately rewarding but potentially maladaptive behaviors, such as sex and consumption of fattening foods. Although these effects may not influence all consumers of media, they may be particularly powerful in young people who, removed from the constraints of adult responsibility and under significant conformity pressure from peers, are more prone to act impulsively without regard for long-term consequences.

The impulse-enhancing function of the media does not necessarily suppose a simple causal path from message to receiver. In many cases, this function may merely reinforce marketing efforts that are at work independently of the media. The media nevertheless facilitate the consumption of an ever-evolving array of products that serve to cultivate a culture of immediate gratification. The U.S. economy spends over 2% of its GDP on advertising, the highest proportion of the advanced economies (Offer, 2006). This does not include the many activities involved in developing marketing and other plans to increase consumer acceptance of products (Galbraith, 1972). To put advertising expenditures in perspective, the amount spent on it is equivalent to approximately one-quarter of the total spending on all forms of education (Offer, 2006). An example of such influence is in the realm of food consumption.

At the dawn of the new era of affluence, Americans devoted about a quarter of their income to food. However, expenditures for food continuously declined as a proportion of the family budget, reflecting the ever-increasing ability to purchase discretionary items. As part of this trend, the proportion of the food budget devoted to eating outside the home steadily increased (see Figure I.3). Early innovators in the delivery of fast food, such as McDonalds, had to consider how to entice consumers to visit their restaurants on a regular basis. The now famous tag line, "You deserve a break today," was already an adaptation of the original line: "Give mom a break!" that

Percent of disposable income

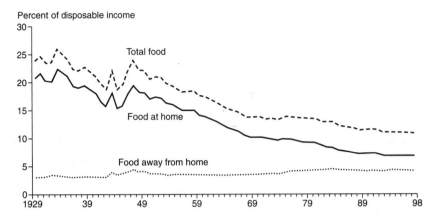

Figure I.3. Percent of disposable income spent on food at home and away from home from 1929 to 1998. (*Source*: U.S. Department of Agriculture, 2000.)

was used in the 1950s when the company first started in California. These early slogans were designed to remove the guilt of indulging in the now commonplace activity of eating out (Halberstam, 1993).

As the era of affluence advanced, the average weight of Americans steadily increased (Offer, 2006), a change that also registered in children and adolescents (Ogden, Flegal, Carroll, & Johnson, 2002). This trend has been attributed to many factors, but the increased availability of cheap eating-out options was a clear contributor (Offer, 2006). Analyses of obesity changes from 1984 to 1999 indicated that the density of nearby restaurants as well as the prices of neighborhood fast food outlets were the largest predictors (Chou, Grossman, & Saffer, 2004). The dramatic increase in the number of easily prepared food items available for purchase in supermarkets that are open at all hours of the day is undoubtedly another influence. Advertising to children and adolescents on television tends to feature food items, most of which are high in calories (Gamble & Cotugna, 1999; Kunkel & Gantz, 1992). With the help of such advertising, Americans of all ages have found it hard to resist the continual enticement to sample easily consumed but highly fattening foods. The inability of Americans to exert control over food choices became increasingly evident as the average number of calories consumed per day grew without a concomitant increase in physical activity (see Figure I.4).

Considerable evidence links children's long-term exposure to television advertising to being overweight (Kaiser Family Foundation, 2004). Indeed, experiments with children ages 9 to 12 have found that reducing time spent watching television and encouraging exercise and healthier diets can lead to reduced body weight (Gortmaker et al., 1999; Robinson, 1999). Although

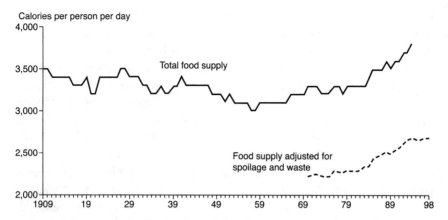

Figure I.4. Per-capita food calories available for consumption from 1909 to 1998. Estimates correcting for spoilage shown since 1969 indicate that the trends are similar whether spoilage is considered or not. (*Source*: Adapted from U.S. Department of Agriculture, 2000; available at http://www.ers.usda.gov/publications/foodreview/jan2000/.)

these studies do not pinpoint the source of television's influence, other studies have found that exposure to television advertising can influence the foods that children request of their parents (Galst & White, 1976; Taras, Sallis, Patterson, Nader, & Nelson, 1989); similar effects are presumed to be at work as children age into adolescence and determine their own food choices.

Although the media may have played a role in the increased consumption of food during the latter half of the last century, they also were able to come to the rescue when health warnings were issued by medical and other advocacy communities. The clearest example of this was in regard to the health risks of cigarettes. As evidence built that cigarettes were harmful, the media not only helped to transmit the story but also were increasingly required to refuse to carry advertising for the product (see Chapter 9). The film industry also began to reflect the increasing health concerns about cigarettes by showing fewer scenes of smoking in their most widely seen films (see Chapter 4). Advocacy groups and the government began to sponsor public service advertising campaigns to counteract adolescent behaviors such as drug use (Delaney, 2003), smoking,[1] and teenage pregnancy.[2]

It is also noteworthy that the media, reflecting society's interests and values, would transmit many inconsistent messages regarding health risks. While helping to promote the behaviors that encouraged overeating, the media were simultaneously featuring increasingly thin women on television shows and films (see Chapter 6). An intriguing study of the introduction of television to the Fiji Islands in the late 1990s found an increase in disordered eating and dieting among adolescent girls heavily exposed to the new medium (Becker, Burwell, Gilman, Herzog, & Hamburg, 2002). Interviews with girls indicated that the women they had seen in television programs accentuated the desirability of thinness, an ideal that had not previously been promoted in the local culture. A recent longitudinal study with girls ages 5 to 8 in Australia (Dohnt & Tiggemann, 2006) found that exposure to certain "appearance-focused" television shows (such as *Friends*) increased concerns about their own appearance. This thin body ideal could help to promote the dieting industry, but it also might create body dissatisfaction among girls, thereby increasing the prevalence of eating disorders. Hence, although the media send many helpful messages to youth, these influences are often counterbalanced by much less helpful but more frequent content that supports opposing tendencies.

## THE EVOLUTION OF ADOLESCENT PORTRAYAL IN THE MEDIA

Despite the increased study of media influence on adolescent development, there has been no systematic study of change in portrayal of adolescents or the behaviors that might influence their socialization since the advent of the new age of affluence. Because the media have undoubtedly played a role in socializing adolescents, it is of great interest to learn how that role has evolved since the 1950s. Indeed, it was evident to us that the ability of adolescents to learn about themselves in the media has increased greatly since 1950. In the beginning of television, there were only three channels (NBC and CBS, followed by ABC) with very limited opportunities to show anything with adolescent content. However, by the early 1980s, a new network (Fox) appeared on the scene with more youth-oriented programming. Soon thereafter, there were increasing opportunities for youth programming on cable channels such as MTV and BET (see Chapter 3).

To test the prediction of increasing adolescent presence in the media, we examined the number of television shows with top-thirty Nielsen ratings since 1950 that had an adolescent character and the number of such characters per year. As seen in Figure I.5, the presence of adolescents has increased quite steadily since 1950 both in number of shows and number of characters. The recent drop in adolescents most likely reflects the advent of more reality television shows (e.g., *American Idol*) that were not coded as containing regular adolescent characters. In addition, recent years

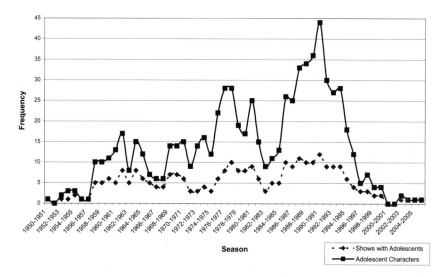

Figure I.5. Number of shows and characters described as adolescent in program summaries found on http://www.tv.com and http://www.imdb.com, 1950 to 2005.

have seen the advent of more niche programming directed to adolescents that would not register in the top-thirty ratings (e.g., *The OC*, *Dawson's Creek*). Hence, even restricting attention to the most popular shows on television, we find that the prevalence of young characters has steadily increased since 1950.

Other technological developments have greatly expanded the universe of screen-based media so that today there is even the opportunity for young people to communicate directly with each other on the Internet in venues such as Facebook and YouTube (see Chapters 11 and 13). Music in digital format has completely revolutionized the transmission of songs and transformed the focus of MTV in the process. These latest forms of media content essentially remove the role of traditional intermediaries and permit an almost unlimited range of youthful expression. The enormous expansion of alternative digital media and ways to consume them begs for enlightened consideration of their future role in adolescent socialization.

The question we ask in this volume is how portrayals of adolescents and the behaviors that might influence their socialization have changed over this period. We then ask whether media portrayals pose socialization risks for the future and what enlightened policy alternatives present themselves regarding media influence in the continuing era of media-saturated socialization. Controlling the media's socialization of children poses particularly difficult legal and ethical issues that will not be easily resolved (Levesque, 2007). However, in the two concluding chapters, some potential alternatives based on both legal theory (Chapter 14) and social science (Chapter 15) are considered.

## NOTES

1. See http://www.americanlegacy.org
2. See http://www.teenpregnancy.org

## REFERENCES

Anderson, C. A., & Bushman, B. J. (2002). The effects of media violence on society. *Science, 295,* 2377–2378.

Anderson, C. A., Gentile, D. A., & Buckley, K. E. (2007). *Violent video game effects on children and adolescents: Theory, research, and public policy.* New York: Oxford University Press.

Bandura, A. (2002). Social cognitive theory of mass communication. In J. Bryant & D. Zillman (Eds.), *Media effects: Advances in theory and research* (pp. 121–153). Mahwah, NJ: Erlbaum.

Bandura, A., Ross, D., & Ross, S. (1963). Imitation of film-mediated aggressive models. *Journal of Abnormal and Social Psychology, 66,* 3–11.

Becker, A. E., Burwell, R. A., Gilman, S. E., Herzog, D. B., & Hamburg, P. (2002). Eating behaviors and attitudes following prolonged exposure to television among ethnic Fijian adolescent girls. *British Journal of Psychiatry, 180,* 509–514.

Bell, D. (1976). *The cultural contradictions of capitalism.* New York: Basic Books.

Berkowitz, L. (1984). Some effects of thoughts on anti- and prosocial influences of media events: A cognitive-neoassociation analysis. *Psychological Bulletin, 95*(3), 410–427.

Berkowitz, L., & Geen, R. G. (1967). Stimulus qualities of the target of aggression: A further study. *Journal of Personality and Social Psychology, 5*(3), 364–368.

Bushman, B. J., & Huesmann, L. R. (2001). Effects of televised violence on aggression. In D. G. Singer & J. L. Singer (Eds.), *Handbook of children and the media* (pp. 223–254). Thousand Oaks, CA: Sage.

Centerwall, B. S. (1992). Television and violence: The scale of the problem and where to go from here. *Journal of the American Medical Association, 267,* 3059–3063.

Chambers, R. A., Taylor, J. R., & Potenza, M. N. (2003). Developmental neurocircuitry of motivation in adolescence: A critical period of addiction vulnerability. *American Journal of Psychiatry, 160,* 1041–1052.

Chou, S.-Y., Grossman, M., & Saffer, H. (2004). An economic analysis of adult obesity: Results from the Behavioral Risk Factor Surveillance System. *Journal of Health Economics, 23*(3), 565–587.

Comstock, G., & Paik, H. (1991). *Television and the American child.* San Diego, CA: Academic Press.

de Beauvoir, S. (1949). *The second sex*. New York: Knopf.

Delaney, B. (2003). Adolescent risk behavior research and media-based health messages. In D. Romer (Ed.), *Reducing adolescent risk: Toward an integrated approach* (pp. 203–209). Thousand Oaks, CA: Sage.

Dodge, K. A. (1985). Attributional bias in aggressive children. In P. C. Kendall (Ed.), *Advances in cognitive-behavioral research and therapy* (Vol. 4, pp. 73–110). San Diego, CA: Academic Press.

Dohnt, H., & Tiggemann, M. (2006). The contribution of peer and media influences to the development of body satisfaction and self-esteem in young girls: A prospective study. *Developmental Psychology, 42*(5), 929–936.

Epstein, R. (2007). *The case against adolescence; rediscovering the adult in every teen*. Sanger, CA: Quill Driver Books.

French, M. (1997). *U.S. economic history since 1945*. New York: Manchester University Press.

Friedan, B. (1963). *The feminine mystique*. New York: Norton.

Galbraith, J. K. (1969). *The affluent society*. Boston: Houghton Mifflin.

Galbraith, J. K. (1972). *The new industrial state*. New York: Mentor.

Galst, J., & White, M. (1976). The unhealthy persuader: The reinforcing value of television and children's influence attempts at the supermarket. *Child Development, 47*, 1089–1096.

Gamble, M., & Cotugna, N. (1999). A quarter century of TV food advertising targeted at children. *American Journal of Health Behavior, 23*(4), 261–267.

Gerbner, G., Gross, L., Morgan, M., & Signorielli, N. (1980). The "mainstreaming" of America: Violence profile no. 11. *Journal of Communication, 30*, 10–29.

Gerbner, G., Gross, L., Signorielli, N., Morgan, M., & Jackson-Beeck, M. (1979). The demonstration of power: Violence profile no. 10. *Journal of Communication, 10*, 177–195.

Gortmaker, S., Peterson, K., Wiecha, J., Sobol, A., Dixit, S., Fox, M. K., et al. (1999). Reducing obesity via a school-based interdisciplinary intervention among youth. *Archives of Pediatrics and Adolescent Medicine, 153*(4), 409–418.

Gould, M., Jamieson, P. E., & Romer, D. (2003). Media contagion and suicide among the young. *American Behavioral Scientist, 46*(9), 1269–1284.

Halberstam, D. (1993). *The fifties*. New York: Fawcett Columbine.

Hamilton, J. T. (1998). *Channeling violence: The economic market for violent television programming*. Princeton, NJ: Princeton University Press.

Hawton, K., Simkin, S., Deeks, J. J., O'Connor, S., Keen, A., & Altman, D. G. (1999). Effects of a drug overdose in a television drama on presentations to hospital for self-poisoning: Time series and questionnaire study. *British Medical Journal, 318*, 972–977.

Hennigan, K. M., Del Rosario, M. L., Heath, L., Cook, T. D., Wharton, J. D., & Calder, B. J. (1982). Impact of the introduction of television on crime in the United States: Empirical and theoretical implications. *Journal of Personality and Social Psychology, 42*, 461–477.

Holinger, P. C., Offer, D., Barter, J. T., & Bell, C. C. (1994). *Suicide and homicide among adolescents*. New York: Guilford.

Huesmann, L. R., & Taylor, L. D. (2006). The role of media violence in violent behavior. *Annual Review of Public Health, 27*, 393–415.

Johnson, J. G., Cohen, P., Smailes, E. M., Kasen, S., & Brook, J. S. (2002). Television
viewing and aggressive behavior during adolescence and adulthood. *Science, 295*,
2468–2471.

Johnston, L. D., O'Malley, P. M., Bachman, J. G., & Schulenberg, J. E. (2005). *Monitoring the future national survey results on drug use, 1975–2004: Vol. I, Secondary
school students* (No. NIH 05–5727). Bethesda, MA: National Institute on Drug
Abuse.

Kaiser Family Foundation. (2004). *The role of the media in childhood obesity.* Menlo
Park, CA: The Henry J. Kaiser Family Foundation.

Katz, E., & Lazarsfeld, P. F. (2006). *Personal influence: The part played by people in the
flow of mass communications.* New Brunswick, NJ: Transaction Publishers.

Kunkel, D., & Gantz, W. (1992). Children's television advertising in the multichan-
nel environment. *Journal of Communication, 42*(3), 134–152.

Levesque, R. J. R. (2007). *Adolescents, media, and the law: What developmental science
reveals and free speech requires.* New York: Oxford University Press.

Leyens, J., & Parke, R. (1975). Aggressive slides can induce a weapons effect. *European Journal of Social Psychology, 5*, 229–236.

Lindsey, B. (2007). *The age of abundance: How prosperity transformed America's politics and culture.* New York: Harper Collins.

Lucas, A. R., Crowson, C. S., O'Fallon, M., & Melton, L. J. I. (1999). The ups and downs
of anorexia nervosa. *International Journal of Eating Disorders, 26*, 397–405.

Luker, K. (1996). *Dubious conceptions: The politics of teenage pregnancy.* Cambridge,
MA: Harvard University Press.

Mares, M.-L., & Woodard, E. (2005). Positive effects of television on children's social
interactions: A meta-analysis. *Media Psychology, 7*, 301–322.

Maslow, A. (1954). *Motivation and personality.* New York: Harper & Bros.

Miller, F. (1994). *Censored Hollywood.* Atlanta, GA: Turner Publishing.

Miller, H. (1964). *Rich man, poor man.* New York: Signet Books.

Moffitt, T. E. (1993). Adolescence-limited and life-course-persistent antisocial behavior: A developmental taxonomy. *Psychological Review, 100*, 674–701.

Murphy, G. E., & Wetzel, R. D. (1980). Suicide risk by birth cohort in the United
States: 1949–1974. *Archives of General Psychiatry, 37*, 519–523.

Offer, A. (2006). *The challenge of affluence: Self-control and well-being in the United
States and Britain since 1950.* Oxford: Oxford University Press.

Ogden, C. L., Flegal, K. M., Carroll, M. D., & Johnson, C. L. (2002). Prevalence and
trends in overweight among U.S. children and adolescents, 1999–2000. *Journal
of the American Medical Association, 288*, 1728–1732.

Phillips, D. (1974). The influence of suggestion on suicide: Substantive and theoretical implications of the Werther effect. *American Sociological Review, 39*,
340–354.

Phillips, D., & Carstensen, L. L. (1986). Clustering of teenage suicides after television
news stories about suicide. *New England Journal of Medicine, 315*, 685–689.

Phillips, D., Leysna, K., & Paight, D. J. (1992). Suicide and the media. In R. W. Maris, A. L. Berman, & J. T. Maltsberger (Eds.), *Assessment and prediction of suicide* (pp. 499–519). New York: Guilford.

President's Commission for a National Agenda for the Eighties. (1980). *The quality of American life in the eighties.* Washington, DC: U.S. Department of Health and Human Services.

Riesman, D. (1950). *The lonely crowd: A study of the changing American character.* New Haven, CT: Yale University Press.

Robinson, J. P., & Martin, S. (2007). *Of time and television.* Paper presented at The End of TV Conference, Annenberg School for Communication, University of Pennsylvania.

Robinson, T. (1999). Reducing children's television to prevent obesity: A randomized control trial. *Journal of the American Medical Association, 282,* 1561–1567.

Robinson, T. N., Wilde, M. J., Navracruz, L. C., Haydel, K. F., & Varady, A. (2001). Effects of reducing children's television and video game use on aggressive behavior. *Archives of Pediatrics and Adolescent Medicine, 155,* 17–23.

Romer, D., Jamieson, P. E., & Jamieson, K. H. (2006). Are news reports of suicide contagious? A stringent test in six U.S. cities. *Journal of Communication, 56,* 253–270.

Ryan, N. D., Williamson, D. E., Iyengar, S., Orvaschel, H., Reich, T., Dahl, R., et al. (1992). A secular increase in child and adolescent onset affective disorder. *Journal of the American Academy of Child and Adolescent Psychiatry, 31*(4), 600–605.

Santoni, G. J. (1986, November). The employment act of 1946: Some history notes. *Review of the Federal Reserve Bank of St. Louis,* pp. 5–16.

Schuman, H., Steeh, C., Bobo, L., & Krysan, M. (1997). *Racial attitudes in America.* Cambridge, MA: Harvard University Press.

Stack, S. (1991). Social correlates of suicide by age: Media impacts. In A. Leenaars (Ed.), *Life span perspectives of suicide: Time-lines in the suicide process* (pp. 187–213). New York: Plenum.

Strasburger, V. (2001). Children, adolescents, drugs, and media. In D. G. Singer & J. L. Singer (Eds.), *Handbook of children and the media* (pp. 415–445). Thousand Oaks, CA: Sage.

Taras, H., Sallis, J., Patterson, T., Nader, P., & Nelson, J. (1989). Television's influence on children's diet and physical activity. *Journal of Developmental and Behavioral Pediatrics, 10,* 176–180.

Tarde, G. (1912). *Penal philosophy.* Boston: Little, Brown.

Thomas, M. H., Horton, R. W., Lippincott, E. C., & Drabman, R. S. (1977). Desensitization to portrayals of real-life aggression as a function of exposure to television violence. *Journal of Personality and Social Psychology, 35*(6), 450–458.

U.S. Department of Agriculture. (2000, May). Major trends in U.S. food supply, 1909–99. *Foodreview* (p. 231).

U.S. Department of Labor. (2006). *100 years of U.S. consumer spending: Data for the nation, New York City, and Boston* (No. 991). Washington, DC: U.S. Department of Labor.

Will, K. E., Porter, B. E., Geller, S. E., & DePasquale, J. P. (2005). Is television a health and safety hazard? A cross-sectional analysis of at-risk behavior on primetime television. *Journal of Applied Social Psychology, 35*(1), 198–222.

Zillman, D., & Bryant, J. (1982). Pornography, sexual callousness, and the trivialization of rape. *Journal of Communication, 32*, 10–21.

Zuckerman, M. (1994). *Behavioral expression and biosocial bases of sensation seeking.* New York: Cambridge University Press.

Part I

The Emergence and Evolution of a Youth
Culture in the Media

# 1

# Understanding the "Jackpot Market"

## Media, Marketing, and the Rise

## of the American Teenager

BILL OSGERBY

## "A CASTE, A CULTURE, A MARKET": TEENAGE
## SPENDING IN POSTWAR AMERICA

"It's 'Terrif,'" proclaimed *Business Week* in a 1946 feature that trumpeted
the rise of a new "jackpot market"—the American teenager. Whetting commercial appetites, the journal described how "the going is high, wide and
handsome with this market whose astounding responsiveness and loyalty
endear it to any manufacturer's heart" (*Business Week*, 1946, pp. 72–73).
Trends across the ensuing decade bore out this buoyant confidence. Indeed,
in a two-part special feature that appeared in *The New Yorker* magazine in
1958, cultural critic Dwight Macdonald drew readers' attention to the phe-
nomenal increase in American youth's commercial muscle. "Teenagers," he
affirmed, were now "not just children growing into adults but a sharply dif-
ferentiated part of the population." "Economically," Macdonald advised his
readers, teenagers constituted "the latest—perhaps the last—merchandising
frontier" (Macdonald, 1958a, p. 58). Before the year was out, he estimated,
America's seventeen million teenagers would have spent at least $9.5 bil-
lion, an annual spending that was set to rise by a further $5 billion by 1965
(p. 64). Proclaiming the advent of a "teenage revolution," he argued that
American youth had "a style of life that was fast becoming *sui generis*"
(p. 57). In these terms the 1950s had seen youth emerge as both a potent

economic force and a compelling cultural influence, Macdonald opined that the American teenager had now taken discrete and distinctive shape as "a caste, a culture, a market."

After 1945, then, teenage spending emerged as a mainstay in the U.S. economy, and this chapter surveys the major social, economic, and political changes that combined to bring this about. Particular attention is given to the relation between U.S. youth culture and the mass media and the ways in which the advertising and marketing industries worked both to crystallize and to popularize the distinct imagery and lifestyles that became synonymous with teenage America.

But youth also acquired powerful symbolic significance. Authors Joe Austin and Michael Willard highlight the important emblematic connotations that invariably surround popular debates about young people. "The youth question," they argue, acts as "an important forum where new understandings about the past, present, and future of public life are encoded, articulated and contested" (Austin & Willard, 1998, p. 1). This was especially true of America in the decades that followed World War II. Commentators made recurring use of the themes and images of youth as a vehicle for comment on broader patterns of social change, with young people both celebrated as the exciting precursor to a prosperous future and (sometimes simultaneously) vilified as the most deplorable evidence of woeful cultural decline. As well as charting the rise of the teenage market, therefore, this paper also emphasizes the way the "youth question" has operated as an "ideological vehicle," with postwar debates about American youth serving as a symbolic medium through which fundamental shifts in the nation's social boundaries and cultural relationships were explored, made sense of, and interpreted.

## "FLAMING YOUTH": THE RISE OF
## THE COMMERCIAL YOUTH MARKET

The commercial youth market certainly experienced spectacular growth during the 1950s and 1960s, but teen culture was not a phenomenon unique to the postwar era. During the late nineteenth century, U.S. cities had quickly grown into bustling centers of entertainment and consumption, and youth was a significant force in the transformation. Kathy Peiss (1987), for example, shows how young working women were pivotal to the development of commercial leisure in fin de siècle America, young women representing a major segment of the audience for dance halls, amusement parks, and movie houses. Young men were also a notable consumer group. In the mid-nineteenth century, for instance, the Bowery area of New York City was home to dandified street toughs known as "B'hoys." According to the socialite Abraham Dayton, "[t]hese 'B'hoys'…were the most consummate dandies of the day," and paraded the streets with lavishly greased front locks, broad-brimmed hats, turned-down shirt collars, black frock-coats with skirts below the knee, embroidered shirts, and "a profusion of jewelry as varied and costly as the b'hoy could procure" (Dayton, 1897, pp. 217–218).[1] Middle-class young men were also an important consumer market, Howard Chudacoff (1999) showing how an extensive "bachelor subculture" developed around the network of eating houses, barber shops, tobacconists, tailors, city bars, theaters, and an array of other commercial ventures that thrived on the patronage of affluent, young "men about town."

The 1920s saw a more fully formed, youth-oriented leisure culture take shape. Partly, the development was indebted to the expansion of American education. Between 1910 and 1930, enrollment in secondary schools increased nearly 400%, and peer cultures began to play a more central role in shaping young people's experience of adolescence as high school became a universal step in the path to adulthood. But the period's consumer boom was also important and saw American business steadily focus its attention on young people's spending power. As Stanley Hollander and Richard Germain (1993) argue, "entrepreneurs, consultants and marketing scholars expounded the significance of the youth market," while "special youth promotion, special youth pricing, and special youth distribution [was] applied to a wide range of products such as automobiles, apparel items, personal hygiene products, typewriters, and cigarettes, and services provided by such establishments as hotels, inns, dance halls and barber shops" (Hollander & Germain, 1993, pp. 114, 155). For Kelly Schrum, young women played an especially important role in these developments. "As girls entered high school from 1920 to 1945," she argues, "they exhibited strong interest in commercially defined ideals of fashion and beauty" and "eagerly consumed mass-produced fashions, beauty advice and products, music, and movies, responding to industries that attempted to cater to their desires and establishing their own relationships with industries that did not" (Schrum, 2004, p. 170).

The expansion of higher education also helped forge new peer cultures and their attendant industries. Once the preserve of a small elite, colleges and universities saw a threefold increase in enrollments between 1900 and 1930, nearly 20% of the college-age population attending some kind of educational institution by the end of the 1920s. Young, relatively well-to-do, and free of family responsibilities, students were an attractive market for American business and attempts to court youth spending were invariably focused on the college sector (Hollander & Germain, 1993, pp. 24–25). In turn, the products of the youth market fed back into the development of what Paula Fass identifies as "the first modern American youth culture"—a collegiate universe that formed around student fraternities, dance halls, cinemas, cafeterias, and other campus hangouts (Fass, 1978, p. 122). This hectic, leisure-oriented youth culture caught the imagination of a wave of American authors. The mood of zestful affluence was captured most obviously in F. Scott Fitzgerald's novel *This Side of Paradise* (1920), the tale of a Princeton undergraduate who rebels against his staid, Midwestern upbringing in a quest for sexual and intellectual enlightenment. Percy Marks in *The Plastic Age* (1924) and Floyd Dell in his autobiographical trilogy (*Moon-Calf*, 1920; *The Briary-Bush*, 1921; and *Souvenir*, 1929) also struck a chord with their depictions of young lives of hectic leisure, while respectable opinion was shocked by *Flaming Youth* (1923), Warner Fabian's tale of torrid passions among the young of upper-class suburbia.

American youth was hard hit by the Great Depression that followed the stock market crash of 1929. Young people represented 27.5% of those unemployed in 1930, and by 1937 16% of the total youth population remained out of work (Reiman, 1992, p. 143). The campus culture chronicled by Fass, however, weathered these lean years and remained an attractive market for manufacturers. Student fashion, for example, was still big business. From the 1890s sportswear had became popular for students' casual attire and shirt styles previously worn for sports replaced more formal garb as a new, leisure-oriented aesthetic surfaced within young men's fashion. An identifiable collegiate or Ivy League style of dress also took shape as clothing firms such as Campus Leisure-wear (founded in 1922), together with the movie, magazine, and advertising industries, gave coherence to a smart-but-casual combination of button-down shirts, chino slacks, letter sweaters, cardigans, and loafers. Throughout the 1930s, campus culture remained a key market for clothes firms such as Campus, Arrow, and Hart Schaffner & Marx—whose advertisements evoked an image of college life as a world of natty fashions and fraternity high jinks.

*Esquire* magazine also jumped on the bandwagon. *Esquire* had been launched in 1933 as an up-market style magazine geared to the fashion-conscious man of means. But *Esquire* also carefully cultivated a younger readership through its attention to students' tastes and lifestyles. *Esquire* kicked off its coverage of campus culture in its very first issue, with a feature spotlighting the "elegant indolence" of undergraduates at Princeton—"the fountainhead of young men's fashions" (*Esquire*, 1933a, p. 69)—together with a double-page spread of college fashion that featured camel hair polo coats, snap-brim homburgs, polka-dot bow ties, and the full wardrobe of clothes and accessories that were "dominant on every campus where attention to the niceties in the matter of dress is the rule rather than the exception"

(*Esquire*, 1933b, p. 58). The magazine's attention to the finer points of student style continued with fashion spreads that appeared throughout the 1930s. Every autumn, meanwhile, *Esquire* would include a "Going Back to School" feature that previewed the latest trends for the dapper undergraduate returning to his studies—sometimes accompanied by a section on "University Liveables," where advice was offered on the other requisites essential to a successful academic semester (phonographs, portable radios, closet-sized refrigerators, and so on).

## FROM ZOOT SUITS TO BOBBY SOCKS: YOUTH CULTURE IN WARTIME

The 1940s saw the American youth market further galvanized by the labor demands of wartime. The economic pressures of the war drew increasing numbers of young people into the U.S. workforce, partially reversing earlier trends toward extended schooling and dependency on parents. In 1944, for example, U.S. Census Bureau statistics showed that more than two in five young men between the ages of 16 and 17 were gainfully employed, with 35% of these having left school altogether to enter full-time work (Modell, 1989, pp. 165–166). As a consequence, greater disposable income was delivered into young hands and by 1944 American youth accounted for a spending power of around $750 million (Adams, 1994, p. 127).

Government moves against segregation also gradually opened up opportunities for young African Americans in both industry and the military. Racial inequalities and tensions, however, remained pronounced and sometimes erupted into violence. The summer of 1943, for example, saw a series of racist attacks that the press dubbed "zoot suit riots." Zoot suits—flamboyant outfits featuring broad tapered jackets and pleated baggy trousers, tight at the ankle, and sometimes accompanied by a wide-brimmed hat and gold watch chain—had been sported by young Mexican Americans (as well as some black and a scattering of poor white youths) in several American cities from the start of the 1940s. The style was loaded with cultural meaning. Loud and proud, the zoot suit represented a badge of defiance for socially and economically marginalized youths who "refused to concede to the manners of subservience" (Cosgrove, 1984, p. 78). Hence the brazenness of the zoot suit roused enmity among working-class whites, who were affronted by the flaunting of ostentatious consumption by those they regarded as social inferiors. With the introduction of wartime clothing restrictions, the zoot suit incited particular bitterness—its rebellious connotations exacerbated by (in white eyes) an outrageous lack of regard for the war effort. In June 1943, white anger boiled over. For over a week gangs of off-duty servicemen roamed the streets of Los Angeles assaulting zoot-suited Mexican Americans. The youths were brutally beaten and ritually stripped of their garb in a series of attacks that spread throughout California; similar incidents were reported from as far afield as Detroit, New York, and Philadelphia.[2]

The sensational news coverage surrounding these zoot suit riots fed into a wider climate of wartime anxiety prompted by a perceived upsurge in levels of juvenile crime. The media ran lurid stories about the violence of urban street gangs, and official statistics seemed to confirm an epidemic of juvenile lawlessness. Young women's sexual behavior also occasioned unease, which cohered around popular archetypes of Victory- or V-girls—young women whose free and easy liaisons with servicemen were interpreted as evidence of a breakdown in national morality. But the reliability of statistical data suggesting a wartime explosion of delinquency is questionable. Anticipated and watched for by expectant social agencies, the wartime "rise" in juvenile crime was duly identified—a classic example of self-fulfilling prophecy. Indeed, in 1944 a Senate subcommittee investigating the causes of delinquency concluded that, although juvenile crime was a serious issue, there was little hard evidence of a wartime escalation (Gilbert, 1986, p. 36).

## POSTWAR OPTIMISM AND AMERICA'S YOUTH

Youth, however, was not universally vilified. As the war drew to an end, the American media conjured more optimistic, upbeat images of a young generation that had coped stoically with the challenges of wartime and held promise for the peaceful future. In June 1945, for example, "Teen-Age Boys" was the cover story in *Life* magazine. A grinning, clean-cut adolescent graced the magazine's front page and the accompanying story painted a picture of cheerful, well-adjusted youngsters who boasted healthy appetites for home cooking and a penchant for loud flannel shirts (*Life*, 1945, p. 92). A few months earlier young women had received similar treatment. That time a *Life* photo-essay spotlighted a generation of girls characterized by "their energy, originality and good looks." "Moving through the awkward age," the magazine mused, "they eventually become—in the judgement of almost every Western nation—the most attractive women in the world" (*Life*, 1944, p. 91). Significantly, the *Life* feature also drew attention to the impact of teenage girls on American commerce. "American businessmen," the magazine noted, "have only recently begun to realize that teen-agers make up a big and special market":

> Department stores have organized teen-age clubs to exhibit and sell special teen-age fashions. Half a dozen radio programs are aimed at homes where a daughter will cut off her father's news to follow the fictional adventures of a contemporary. Every afternoon after

school lets out, music stores across the land bulge with girls listening to the singers and bandleaders they have made into national figures. The movies and the theater make money turning a sometimes superficial and sometimes social-minded eye on teen-agers. No one has even tried to estimate the teenage contribution to the hamburger, coke and juke-box business. (*Life*, 1944, p. 91)

Consumer industries ministering to youth had existed since the beginning of the century. But with the wartime boost in young people's spending power the commercial youth market shifted up a gear. As Schrum (2004) notes, fashion and entertainment businesses that focused on teenage girls underwent particular growth. During the 1940s the media coined the phrase "bobby-soxer" to denote adolescent girls who sported a new style of sweaters, full skirts, bobby socks, and saddle shoes, and who jitterbugged to the sounds of big-band swing or swooned over show business stars such as Mickey Rooney and Frank Sinatra. The "Swoonatra" phenomenon attracted particular attention. Though already in his mid-20s, Sinatra was promoted as the boyish kid from Hoboken, the singer capturing thousands of young hearts in 1942 as he sold out a monthlong residency at New York's Paramount Theater—his return to the venue, two years later, bringing Manhattan to a standstill as thousands of amorous fans besieged Times Square.

The runaway success of *Seventeen* magazine provided especially clear evidence of the growing scale of the American youth market. Conceived as a publication geared to college girls, *Seventeen* was launched in 1944. Its premier edition selling out within two days, *Seventeen*'s circulation had shot up to over a million a month by 1947 and by 1949 was touching the two-and-a-half million mark (Schrum, 1998, p. 139). *Seventeen*'s business strategies, moreover, were indicative of the increasingly sophisticated methods through which commercial interests were tapping into youth spending. Keen to maximize the magazine's economic potential, Helen Valentine, *Seventeen*'s first editor, hired a professional research team, Benson and Benson from Princeton, New Jersey, to survey her readership's buying habits. With this data at their disposal, *Seventeen*'s editorial team could tempt advertisers with valuable information on the tastes and desires of a group that was shaping up as one of the most lucrative consumer markets in America (see Figure 1.1).

## "THE TEEN-AGE TIDE": THE YOUTH MARKET AND AMERICAN MEDIA DURING THE 1950s AND EARLY 1960s

By the late 1950s the scope and scale of the American youth market seemed spectacular. The growth was partly a consequence of demographic trends,

Figure 1.1. Cover art from an early issue of *Seventeen* magazine (May 1957). (Photograph: Dan Wynn). Reprinted by permission.

with wartime increases in the birth rate and a postwar baby boom rocketing the U.S. teen population from ten million to fifteen million during the 1950s, eventually hitting a peak of twenty million by 1970. A postwar expansion of education, meanwhile, further accentuated the profile of youth as a distinct generational cohort (Modell, 1989, pp. 225–226). The proportion of U.S. teenagers attending high school, for example, rose from around 60% in the

1930s to virtually 100% during the 1960s. College and university enrollment also spiraled. In 1950 about 41% of high school graduates went on
to college, but by 1960 this had risen to 53%, the trend giving a new lease
on life to the campus culture that had surfaced between the wars (Modell,
1989, p. 266).

The vital stimulus behind the growth of the commercial youth market,
however, was economic. The proliferation of adolescent consumption—what
*Time* magazine dubbed "The Teen-Age Tide" (1964, p. 58)—was constituent in the wider postwar boom that saw the United States develop into
the world's largest consumer-oriented economy. National output of goods
and services doubled between 1946 and 1956, and doubled again by 1970,
with expenditure on private consumption accounting for two-thirds of the
gross national product throughout the period (Cohen, 2003, p. 121). Young
people, particularly, benefited from these shifts.

Peacetime saw a decline in full-time youth employment, but the wartime rise in youth spending was sustained by a combination of part-time
work and parental allowances—some estimates suggesting that young Americans' average weekly income rose from just over $2 in 1944 to around $10
by 1958 (Macdonald, 1958b, p. 60).[3] For some, the purchasing power of
American youth had become an astonishing phenomenon, and throughout the late 1950s and early 1960s the growth of teen spending provoked
open-mouthed commentaries from the American media. In 1956, for example, *Time* magazine estimated that "allowances and earnings give the
teenage boy an average weekly income of $8.96, compared to only $2.41 a
dozen years ago" (*Time*, 1956, p. 72). In 1957, meanwhile, a "Special Teenage Issue" of *Cosmopolitan* magazine proclaimed the 1950s as "the Time of
the Teenager." According to *Cosmopolitan*, it was "not at all uncommon for
teenagers to earn upwards of forty dollars a week at part-time jobs," with
American youngsters wielding a collective spending power of over $9 bil-
lion a year (Gehman, 1957, p. 72). According to *Life* magazine in 1959, the
magnitude of teen spending was even greater. Announcing the arrival of
"A New $10-Billion Power: the U.S. Teenage Consumer," an awestruck edi-
tion of *Life* explained that American youth had now "emerged as a big-time
consumer in the U.S. economy.…Counting only what is spent to satisfy
their special teenage demands, the youngsters and their parents will shell
out about $10 billion this year, a billion more than the total sales of GM
[General Motors]" (*Life*, 1959, p. 78).

During the 1960s the growth continued unabated. "There's a boom
coming in the youth market in this decade," prophesied the advertising journal *Printers' Ink* in 1962, with teen purchasing power "expected to reach
$14-billion annually by 1965" (*Printers' Ink*, 1962, p. 43). By 1964 *Time*
was already reporting that through a combination of parental allowances

and part-time work, American teenagers boasted an income of around $12 billion a year, so that "today's teenager pulls down three times more money than his counterpart right after World War II" (*Time*, 1964, p. 58). *Newsweek* was also bowled over, and in 1966 reported that "The high-school set has graduated from the ice-cream, soda fountain and bicycle circuit into the big leagues of U.S. consumption":

> Most studies, in fact, estimate that rising allowances and swelling incomes from part-time and summer jobs this year will put a whopping $12 billion into the jean pockets of the nation's high-school boys and girls. This about equals the total output of South Africa and adds up to an income of $670 per teen per year. (*Newsweek*, 1966, p. 45)

*Esquire* was equally impressed and, in 1965, dedicated a special "Teen Time" edition to coverage of the burgeoning world of contemporary youth culture. A double-page photo spread saw a beaming youngster sprawled across the trunk of a sports car, surrounded by piles of gleaming leisure goods, as *Esquire* estimated that teenagers wielded an annual disposable income of around $13 billion a year and that "in the time it takes to read these lines the American teen-ager will have spent $2,378.22" (Hechinger & Hechinger, 1965, p. 65).

American business was quick to grasp youth's commercial potential. Following in the footsteps of Helen Valentine and *Seventeen* magazine, a host of marketers developed strategies to zero in on adolescents' wallets. A young entrepreneur from Chicago led the field. Nineteen-year-old Eugene Gilbert was working as a shoe store clerk in 1945 when he noticed that despite stocking the latest styles, the shop attracted few young customers. Persuading the owner to advertise more directly to young buyers, Gilbert was struck by the sudden rise in sales and began to develop market research among his peers as a viable business proposition. By 1947 Gilbert's research organization, Youth Marketing Co., was flourishing, with plush offices in New York and accounts with such prestigious clients such as Quaker Oats, Studebaker, and United Airlines. Gilbert was especially proud of his innovative style of market research. Rather than relying on number-crunching and quantitative surveys, he favored a more qualitative approach. Recognizing that young people themselves were best placed to gauge the attitudes of the teenage market, Gilbert recruited an army of students to interview their friends, canvass opinions, and provide feedback on their consumer preferences. Gilbert's enterprise also neatly illustrated the way media interest in young people as a commercial market, in itself, helped consolidate the emergence of youth as a distinct consumer group. Indeed, Gilbert himself was celebrated as a figurehead of youth consumption. Profiled by magazines such as *Newsweek, Cosmopolitan,* and *Harper's,* he was hailed as a leading authority on modern youth. Pronouncements in his syndicated newspaper column—"What Young People Think"—charted the caprices of the young, while his book *Advertising and Marketing to Young People* (1957) became a manual for those chasing adolescent cash. With missionary zeal Gilbert evangelized youth as a commercial market of unprecedented importance. As he explained to *Advertising Age* in a 1951 interview,

> Our salient discovery is that within the past decade teenagers have become a separate and distinct group within our society, enjoying a degree of autonomy and independence unmatched by previous generations. (*Advertising Age,* February 26, 1951, p. 1)

It was hardly surprising, then, that commercial interests scrambled to stake a claim in the teenage goldmine. The range of media and products geared to the young was legion, consumer industries interacting with and reinforcing one another as they wooed young consumers. Of the $10 billion in discretionary income wielded by American youth in 1959, *Life* estimated that 16% (roughly $1.5 billion) went to the entertainment industries, the remainder being spent on everything from fashion and grooming products to cars and sporting goods (*Life,* 1959, p. 83).

Exemplifying the growth of the teen market was the rise of rock and roll—a genre of popular music tied much more closely than its predecessors to processes of mass marketing, media dissemination, and youth demand.[4] The roots of the new music lay in black rhythm and blues (R & B), where the phrase *rock and roll* was coined as a euphemism for sex. With African American migration during the 1940s, the popularity of rhythm and blues had spread to northern and western cities where black radio shows regularly featured R & B records produced by Atlantic, Chess, Sun, and a growing number of independent labels. The music was geared to a black audience, but it also picked up a significant white market as young radio listeners tuned in to late-night shows.[5]

The crossover of R & B into the white youth market was further galvanized by entrepreneurs such as Alan "Moondog" Freed, a Cleveland disc jockey whose playlists began to feature R & B records during the early 1950s. Moving to a bigger station in New York in 1954, Freed continued to champion the original black R & B performers but, in being pitched to a mainstream youth market, the music was steadily "whitened" and reconfigured as rock and roll.[6]

Through a process of hybridization rock and roll fused (black) R & B with elements of (white) country and western music. In the process, rock and roll retained a rebellious aura, but the sexual overtones characteristic of rhythm and blues were toned down as the major labels recruited white performers to produce acceptable covers of R & B standards. Decca, for example, enjoyed early success with "whitened-up" interpretations of R & B by Bill Haley, who scored hits with "Shake, Rattle and Roll" in 1954 and "Rock Around the Clock" the following year. A bigger commercial triumph, however, came in 1956 with RCA Victor's signing of Elvis Presley. The singer had enjoyed small-scale success on Sam Phillips's independent Sun label but, with the backing of a major company, Elvis became a cultural phenomenon, selling over eight million records within six months and representing a $20 million industry within a year (see also Chapter 2).

Presley's fertile cinema career ("the King" made thirty-one features) also pointed to the cross-media character of the youth market. Quickly contracted to a lucrative movie deal with MGM, Presley's prolific film appearances were indicative of Hollywood's growing interest in young cinema goers. As Thomas Doherty (2002) shows, a decline in adult cinema audiences during the 1950s prompted the American film industry to focus more attention on youth demand. Alongside MGM's Presley movies, for instance, Columbia Pictures also capitalized on the rock and roll boom by backing Alan Freed and Bill Haley in the films *Rock Around the Clock* and *Shake Rattle and Rock!* (both released in 1956), while *Don't Knock the Rock* (1957) and many others quickly followed. Rather than the major studios, however, it was the independent sector that most successfully exploited teen demand. Leader of the pack was American-International Pictures (AIP). Founded in 1954, AIP cashed in on the youth market and the flourishing drive-in circuit, the "teenpic" industry coming of age as AIP cranked out a glut of quickly made, low-budget sci-fi, horror, and romance features (Doherty, 2002, p. 29).[7]

Young audiences were also addressed by the budding medium of television. During the 1950s teenage life was a firm feature in many American TV soap operas and family-based sitcoms. As Mary Celeste Kearney (2004) observes, TV shows such as *The Adventures of Ozzie and Harriet* (ABC, 1952–1966), *Father Knows Best* (CBS, 1954–1955; NBC, 1955–1958; CBS, 1958–1962), and *Leave It to Beaver* (CBS, 1957–1958; ABC, 1958–1963) all featured teenage characters who became increasingly central to storylines over the course of the 1950s. The launch of the sitcom *The Many Loves of Dobie Gillis* (CBS, 1959–1963), meanwhile, saw the arrival of the first prime-time TV show focused on teenage characters, the series chronicling the hapless adventures of young Dobie and his beatnik buddy, Maynard.

The rise of American teen TV was the result of broadcasters' attempts to pull in advertisers through developing new program formats that would appeal to young audiences. This was especially true of the ABC network, which began broadcasting in 1948. Since its bigger, more established rivals (CBS and NBC) were best placed to exploit the mass TV audience, the younger and smaller ABC network sought to compete by courting more specialized markets, and the network developed a reputation for programming aimed at youth and young families with children. During the 1950s local stations also played their part in the growth of teen TV. Shows featuring pop performers and their fans became a staple of local TV stations' afternoon and Saturday morning schedules, examples being *Teen Twirl* (WNBK–Cleveland, 1955) and *Teen Club Party* (WGN–Chicago, 1957). Most famous, however, was *American Bandstand*. Launched by WFIL–Philadelphia in 1952, the show's success was so ensured that in 1957 it transferred to the ABC network, where its audience figures could touch twenty million.

The delights of teenage consumption, however, were not equally available to everyone. The teen market that emerged in the United States after the World War II was preeminently white and middle class. A rise in African American high school enrollment brought black and white youth together as never before,[8] while the emergence of rock and roll bore witness to important processes of interethnic cultural exchange. Nevertheless, as Grace Palladino has observed, embedded racism and economic inequality ensured that throughout the 1950s "black teenagers remained invisible as far as mainstream society was concerned" (Palladino, 1996, pp. 175–176).

Generally, the growth of teenage spending during the 1950s and early 1960s was concentrated in the white, middle-class suburbs. American society as a whole benefited from the postwar consumer boom, but it was the middle class who made the greatest gains. Between 1947 and 1957 the number of salaried workers increased by 61% as white-collar career opportunities multiplied among the expanding business corporations. The number of solidly middle-class families (with an annual income of between $4,000 and $7,500) grew from twelve-and-a-half million to eighteen million between 1947 and 1953, while the percentage of those earning between $7,000 and $10,000 per year rose from 5% to 20% between 1947 and 1959 (U.S. Bureau of the Census, 1975, pp. 289–290). This prosperity formed the bedrock for "The Teen-Age Tide," allowing the American middle class the ability to afford their children a life of material comfort with little financial responsibility. In 1947, for example, market research produced for *Seventeen* testified to the middle-class character of the magazine's readership—with 63% of readers' fathers working as company executives, professionals, or owning their own business (cited in Schrum, 1998, p. 139).

Of course, the styles, fashions, and music of American youth culture were not the exclusive province of the white middle class. Throughout the 1950s and early 1960s working-class (together with African American and Mexican American) youth generated their own, highly visible styles and cultural identities that fed into (indeed, were a crucial influence on) the wider constellation of modern youth culture.[9] However, the teenage merchandise and media churned out in the United States during the 1950s and 1960s were chiefly targeted at a white, middle-class market. As sociologist Jessie Bernard observed in 1961, "teen-age culture" was essentially the culture of a "leisure class":

> Youngsters of lower socioeconomic classes are in the teen-age culture only in their early teens. They are more likely than children of higher socioeconomic class to enter the labor force or the armed forces or to get married soon after high school and, thus, to disappear into the adult world. This exit from the teen-age world by youngsters of lower-class background means that those who remain are disproportionately from higher socioeconomic class background. (Bernard, 1961, p. 2)

## THE GROWTH OF THE TEEN MARKET OVERSEAS

At home, American business eagerly chased the spending power of this young "leisure class." The European market, however, was viewed with skepticism. Visiting Britain in 1954 and again in 1956, for example, Eugene Gilbert decided no potential existed for a permanent marketing office in London. Dwight Macdonald agreed. In his 1958 survey of the teen market, the cultural commentator averred that "Teenagers in England haven't enough freedom, or enough money, to be commercially interesting" (Macdonald, 1958a, p. 61). But Macdonald was a little rash in his verdict. The war's greater economic destruction on the other side of the Atlantic ensured that the development of modern consumer economies in Europe was slower, partial, and more uneven than in the United States (Mort, 1997). As a consequence, the rise of European teenage spending was more hesitant than in America. Nevertheless, by the late 1950s a distinctive youth market was being increasingly championed in a welter of books, magazines, and newspaper articles. In Britain, for example, the widely reported market research of Mark Abrams suggested that since 1945 British youngsters' real earnings had risen by 50% (roughly double that of adults), representing an annual expenditure of around £830 million (Abrams, 1959, p. 9). This, Abrams boldly declared, had laid the way for "distinctive teenage spending for distinctive teenage ends in a distinctive teenage world" (p. 10).

The global circulation of U.S. media also allowed the fads and fashions of teenage America to circulate worldwide. Rather than adopting American youth culture indiscriminately, however, European youngsters borrowed from, reconfigured, and creatively "re-embedded" U.S. teen style in local cultures and identities. In Britain, for example, the zoot suit was adopted by London youths during the 1940s, the style subsequently evolving into the long, draped jackets that were the badge of 1950s toughs known as Teddy boys. As Steve Chibnall suggests, for British youngsters this adoption of American style "offered a sense of worth, individuality and empowerment" (1996, p. 155). The Teddy boys' drape jacket, he argues, represented a "blasphemous mixture of orthodox British dandyism and Yank style," and was recognized by both brash young tearaways and upstanding authority figures as an emblem of "fundamental disrespect for the old class modes and manners—a disrespect born of a romance with an alien culture" (Chibnall, 1985, pp. 74, 69).

Behind the iron curtain, too, postwar youngsters re-embedded American teen style. In Russia, for example, from the 1950s *stiliagi* (or *stilyagi*) youth showed little interest in officially sanctioned forms of popular culture and instead defied the Soviet authorities by adopting Western forms of music and fashion, developing their own distinctive image—*stil'*—a (re)interpretation of American rock and roll styles.[10] Indeed, rather than being resented as an unwelcome instrument of U.S. cultural imperialism, American goods and media have often been embraced by young people around the world as positive symbols of freedom and modernity. The concept of *cultural imperialism* first emerged during the late 1960s and 1970s to denote the way some commentators saw the transglobal flow of the media as driven by the economic and political interests of powerful, capitalist countries—especially the United States.[11] More recently similar arguments have been voiced by Naomi Klein (2000), who sees the growing power of global business conglomerates as blunting the radical edge of youth subcultures, turning young people into brand-obsessed "walking, talking, life-sized Tommy [Hilfiger] dolls" (p. 28). Such arguments, however, overlook the way cultural artifacts are often appropriated and made meaningful by different audiences around the world. As Chibnall observes, for youngsters in many countries buying Levi's jeans or Coca-Cola "can take on the status of a personal political statement because the symbolic association of these objects with freedom, individuality and the 'American way' is underwritten in countless cinematic and televisual texts which relate product aesthetics to social attitudes, personal aspirations and nationality" (1996, p. 150).

Of course, global business corporations have wielded enormous power in the world of youth media and style, just as they have in the wider cultural universe. The 1980s and 1990s, especially, saw marked trends toward the conglomeration of global media corporations, so that by the beginning of the twenty-first century a handful of multinational companies accounted for a considerable slice of the world's media output.[12] The global scale of advertising and marketing, moreover, ensured that Western products—and, with them, Western cultures and lifestyles—diffused to all corners of the world. As a consequence, Western configurations of youthfulness have taken root in regions that hitherto had little experience of a commercial youth market (Wallace & Kovatcheva, 1998, p. 153). Nevertheless, while inequalities of power and control have to be acknowledged in these processes, notions of a linear and unilateral cultural imperialism (or, for that matter, Americanization) oversimplify and distort the flows of media production, distribution, and consumption.

Media theorists have increasingly drawn attention to the diverse and multifaceted nature of transglobal media flows—and, in the youth market, the complexity of these processes has been especially evident. The American share of the global market for popular music, for example, shifted during the 1990s as the relatively low cost of making and distributing recordings (compared to films and TV programs) made it possible for a wide range of national music industries to prosper. In some instances, indigenous output came to overshadow American products. For instance, Luciana Mendonca (2002) showed how sales of American pop music in Brazil declined significantly during the 1990s, while Brazilian music came to constitute around 80% of recordings broadcast on the country's radio. The computer games market saw similar trends. In 2006, for example, China's General Administration of Press and Publication announced that the preceding year had seen Chinese-designed products account for more than 60% of the country's computer game market (Welsh, 2007). The global spread of youth-oriented media, then, should not been seen as a coherent, unitary process of cultural imperialism, but as a much more elaborate syncopation of international business interests.

Account must also be taken of the way young people around the world reconfigure the meanings of cultural forms and media texts, integrating them within local cultures and identities. As Pam Nilan and Carles Feixa argue, "Youth cultures are always emphatically local, despite globally-derived details, since youth are embedded in immediate and embodied economic and political relations":

> Their reflexive engagement—choosing or rejecting, transforming or synthesizing—with global youth cultural products and practices—music, subcultures, fashion, slang—is shaped by their habitus: income, religion, language, class, gender and ethnicity, to create almost inevitably something which has not existed before. (Nilan & Feixa, 2006, p. 8)

Thomas Wee (1999), for example, shows how youth culture in Singapore is not simply a derivative of a "global teenage lifestyle," but is a complex fusion of Western consumer brands and local products and value systems. And research by Melissa Butcher and Mandy Thomas demonstrates how second-generation Middle Eastern and Asian youth in Australia are creative and selective "merchants of style" (Butcher & Thomas, 2003, 2006). The cultural expressions of these youngsters, they argue, are not only informed by mainstream Western culture and readily available global youth styles, but also draw on diasporic connections with their parents' homeland. This dynamic synthesis of cultural elements, Butcher and Thomas suggest, allows these youngsters "to negotiate a hybrid place between, and within, their family home, their friendship networks, mainstream Australian society, and global influences" (Butcher & Thomas, 2006, p. 68).

Globally circulating media forms, then, are consumed creatively and selectively by local youth audiences, and are given new inflections and meanings as they are spliced together with cultural elements derived from local and diasporic cultures. As a consequence of these ongoing processes of fusion and interconnection, modern youth cultures have a distinctly "hybridized" or "syncretic" character, operating across (and within) multiple cultural sites—so that young people's identities are constituted through the intersection of crisscrossing discourses of age, nationality, ethnicity, gender, class, and sexuality.[13]

## THE COOL AND THE CRAZY: THE SYMBOLIC RESONANCE OF TEENAGE CULTURE

Youth culture has always been surrounded by powerful symbolic connotations. In the United States, the sense of optimistic promise that had characterized many popular images of youth toward the end of World War II gave way to a growing sense of anxiety during the 1950s. Juvenile crime became a particular cause for concern and by the mid-1950s America was gripped by the perception that delinquency was spiraling out of control. In 1953 the anxieties prompted the appointment of a Senate subcommittee to investigate the problem's cause. Headed by Estes Kefauver, the official enquiry continued until the early 1960s, and its very existence helped confirm perceptions that juvenile delinquency—or the JD phenomenon as it was often dubbed—was a major social problem. Fears were further fueled by a torrent of media exposés in magazines, newspapers, and newsreels, all purporting to depict a wave of juvenile crime frighteningly new in its severity.[14]

It seems likely, however, that postwar perceptions of an exponential growth in youth crime exaggerated the problem. Notions of a quantum leap in delinquency seemed borne out by a relentless rise in crime statistics, yet James Gilbert has shown that this "juvenile crime wave" was largely a statistical phenomenon produced by new strategies of law enforcement and changes in the collation of crime data (Gilbert, 1986, pp. 66–70). As Gilbert argues, rather than being a response to a genuine eruption of adolescent vice, the postwar fears surrounding delinquency served as "a symbolic focus for wider anxieties in a period of rapid and disorienting change," with the concerns about youth crime articulating "a vaguely formulated but gnawing sense of social disintegration" (p. 77).

The topicality of delinquency, however, ensured it was a recurring theme in the popular media of the day. At the cinema, for instance, dysfunctional adolescence loomed large in a spate of JD movies, as they became known.[15] In 1955, for example, Warner's *Rebel Without a Cause* catapulted James Dean to stardom as the prototypical teen rebel, while the same year saw MGM's *Blackboard Jungle* paint a sobering portrait of teenage violence in an inner-city high school. But not all JD movies were straightforward homilies on the dangers of wayward youth. Whereas the major studios' films usually saw straitlaced adults moralizing to errant youngsters, the movies produced by independent studios such as AIP were more libertine. Typically, AIP films such as *The Cool and the Crazy* and *I Was a Teenage Werewolf* (released in 1958 and 1957, respectively) pitted autonomous, sexually aggressive teenagers against conformist and inhibited authority figures. Superficially, then, JD movies purported to preach against the evils of reckless adolescence— *The Cool and the Crazy*, for example, ended with a disclaimer proclaiming the producers' hopes the film would "raise the guard of teenagers and their parents against the awful perils of narcotic addiction"—but, at the same time, they gloried in the spectacle of the daring and the sensational. Indeed, much of their box office pull lay in the way they offered young audiences the vicarious thrills of delinquent rebellion.

The tastes and caprices of young Americans, however, were themselves a topic for concern. These anxieties were constituent in a broader climate of unease. Although postwar economic growth had brought prosperity for many, the 1950s saw a wide body of academic and popular opinion revile what was regarded as the malignant cultural fallout of the consumer boom. Across the political spectrum authors decried the rise of a debased mass culture they perceived as the corollary of modern consumerism, with processes of cynical marketing and mass consumption delivering a cultural life bereft of meaning and individuality.[16] For the mandarins of mass culture theory the flourishing youth market offered the starkest evidence of the consumer society's blanket of oppressive uniformity. For example, in 1950 (the same year that he lamented the "other-directed" conformism of *The Lonely Crowd*) David Reisman condemned a pop music industry that had the power "to mold popular taste and to eliminate free choice by consumers" (Reisman, 1950b, p. 361).

Dwight Macdonald, too, saw the young generation as falling easy prey to the wiles of commerce. "These days," he dolefully explained in his 1958 commentary for *The New Yorker*, "merchants eye teenagers the way stockmen eye cattle, thinking in terms of how much the creatures will cut up for" (1958a, p. 63). And, even though avid fascination was the underlying tone of *Esquire*'s 1965 special edition on "The Affluent Teen," a distinct sense of unease also crept in. Profiling the new movers and shakers of the youth market, *Esquire* seemed especially ambivalent. The magazine was spellbound by their business acumen but, gathered together in a group portrait, the grandees of teen marketing seemed to be presented in a more sinister light. Shot against a dark, shadowy background, Helen Valentine, Eugene Gilbert, and their confederates cast a somber gaze at the camera—configured, perhaps, as the manipulative Pied Pipers of teenage consumption.

Others were more forthright in their hostility. In its 1957 special issue on youth, for example, *Cosmopolitan* magazine rhetorically asked "Are Teenagers Taking Over?"—the inside copy only half jokingly conjuring images of "a vast, determined band of blue-jeaned storm troopers forcing us to do exactly as they dictate" (Geham, 1957, p. 72). But probably the most outspoken critique of the commercial youth market came in *Teen-Age Tyranny*, Grace and Fred Hechinger's 1962 best-selling book. Denouncing popular dance crazes such as the twist as "bump-and-grind exhibitionism" and a "flagrant example of a teen-age fad dominating the adult world" (1962, pp. 112–113), the Hechingers lamented the way Americans seemed to be "growing down rather than growing up," the nation standing "in such awe of its teen-age segment that it is in danger of becoming a teen-age society, with permanently teen-age standards of thought, culture and goals" (p. x).

Social responses to youth culture, however, were never unanimously negative. As Dick Hebdige (1988) has argued, a recurring duality has characterized popular debate about youth, with pessimistic accounts of delinquency and the "banality" of the teen market coexisting alongside celebrations of teenage consumption as the vanguard of a new era of affluence and modernity. This Janus-like quality has seen young people both vilified as the most deplorable evidence of cultural bankruptcy and celebrated as the exciting precursors to a prosperous future. During the 1950s the intensity of social change and the political tensions of the cold war ensured that more negative archetypes of youth held sway. By the end of the decade, however, a more positive set of representations was coming to the fore. The Kefauver subcommittee's investigation into the causes of juvenile crime lumbered into the 1960s, but the intensity of the delinquency panic was dissipating. Rates of juvenile crime were still rising, but by the end of the 1950s more positive perceptions of youth were emerging as young people were portrayed (celebrated even) as an invigorating and inspiring social force. Ideals of youth, for example, were powerfully mobilized by John F. Kennedy in both his public persona and in his optimistic vision of America's

New Frontier.[17] But commercial interests were also central to this upbeat re-branding of youth. As James Gilbert has argued, the rise of more positive social responses to young people during the early 1960s was "derived from a further extension of the market economy in American cultural life" (1986, p. 214). With the growing profitability of the teen market, the media and consumer industries feted young people as never before and youth became enshrined as the signifier of a newly prosperous age of freedom and fun.

Above all, it was the concept of the teenager that embodied this positive, uplifting iconography of youth. Since the 1600s it had been common to refer to an adolescent as being someone in their teens, yet it was only in 1941 that an article in *Popular Science* magazine featured the first published use of the word *teenager*, and the term increasingly leaked into popular usage (Hine, 1999, pp. 8–9). The advertising and marketing industries were especially crucial in popularizing the concept, marketers using the term *teenager* to denote what they saw as a new breed of affluent, young consumer who prioritized fun, leisure, and the fulfillment of personal desires. By the early 1960s, then, the term teenager did not simply describe a generational category but also denoted a new brand of conspicuous, leisure-oriented consumption. Teenagers were configured as the sharp end of the new consumer society, an exciting foretaste of affluent good times that promised soon to be within everyone's grasp.

Critics such as the Hechingers may have derided teenage culture as the worst example of commercial massification, but they were increasingly out of step with the times. Media and advertising rhetoric of the early 1960s typically promoted the teenager as an essentially classless avatar of pleasure and universal abundance. Here, Kirse May (2002) argues, images of California youth culture were in the forefront. During the early 1960s, the Golden State—home to surfing, hot rods, and pop groups such as the Beach Boys—set the pace for America's New Frontier in teenage leisure, pleasure, and good living. As media images of monstrous delinquents slipped into the background, therefore, they were superseded by archetypes of "well-behaved, well-meaning, middle-class teenagers" as films, TV series, and pop records all "packaged California's kids as a beautiful and wholesome generation living it up on the coast" (May, 2002, p. 119).

By the early 1960s, then, "youth" had become media shorthand for an America in which the sheer pace of economic growth seemed set to engender a new era of consumer abundance and social harmony. Taken as the quintessence of an exciting social transformation, teenagers were configured as the vanguard of this new consumer culture—a social group distinguished not simply by their youth, but by a particular style of conspicuous, leisure-oriented consumption.[18] Nowhere were these symbolic associations better exemplified than in the developing ad campaigns for Pepsi-Cola. In the 1950s, Pepsi had struggled with its reputation as "the kitchen cola," a consequence of its long-time positioning as a bargain brand. But, through a series of campaigns that relentlessly associated the drink with young, fashionable consumers, Pepsi successfully reconfigured itself as a hip and happening brand of the moment. First, 1958 saw Pepsi marketed as the drink of "The Sociables" who "do lively things with lively people." A more concerted bid for the youth market followed in 1961, with a campaign that proclaimed "Now It's Pepsi, For Those Who Think Young." Finally, in 1963, the strategy reached fruition as Pepsi identified itself not so much with youth as a chronological age, but with youth as a state of mind—a lifestyle with an onus on individuality, autonomy, and freewheeling hedonism. As the company's campaign slogan succinctly put it, "Come Alive! You're in the Pepsi Generation!"

## COUNTERCULTURE, CONSUMPTION, AND THE "ETHIC OF FUN"

Consumer pleasure in an age of swinging modernity, then, was the central theme in configurations of the 1960s teenager. By the end of the decade, however, the social and economic conditions on which this archetype was predicated seemed to be unraveling. During the late 1960s the U.S. economy was faltering and liberal optimism was crumbling in the face of racial violence, urban disorder, and the quagmire of the Vietnam War. Against this backdrop, the iconography of youthful high spirits began to give way to more negative representations of youth, with students and countercultural radicals attracting particular media venom.

The 1960s counterculture, however, was never a homogeneous movement. Rather, it was a network of loosely affiliated groups, with a disparate membership drawn from a variety of social backgrounds.[19] Responses from the media were also diverse. While political radicalism invariably prompted criticism and reproach, the counterculture's aesthetics and lifestyles often elicited fascination, sympathy, even a degree of admiration. Rather than being universally reviled, then, the 1960s counterculture could also be a source of fascination. Indeed, the libertine ethos of self-expression and "doing your own thing" proved widely attractive at a time when cultural values were rapidly changing. As traditional ideals of restraint and respectability gave way to an emphasis on hedonism and personal consumption, the fashions, hairstyles, music, and attitudes of the counterculture all percolated into mainstream social life. In fact, rather than representing the antithesis of modern consumerism, the 1960s counterculture is better seen as a developmental phase in its evolution.

As Thomas Frank has suggested, the counterculture was not the nemesis of the consumer society but "may be more accurately understood as a stage in the development of the values of the American middle class, a colorful instalment in the twentieth century drama of consumer subjectivity" (Frank, 1997, p. 120). For advertisers, especially, the countercultural scene offered images of youthful pleasure and freedom commensurate with consumerist agendas. As one American adman affirmed in a 1968 editorial for *Merchandising Week*, "Everywhere our mass media push psychedelia with all its clothing fads, so-called 'way-out' ideas etc. Youth is getting the hard sell" (cited in Frank, 1997, p. 120).

Through its appeal to particular consumer values, therefore, the youth market expanded well beyond its generational base to embrace consumer groups in their late 20s, 30s, and older. Effectively, youth culture was no longer the exclusive preserve of the young, but had become a particular kind of consumer lifestyle whose attitudes and spending patterns won wide appeal. As *Business Week* noted in 1970, "'youth' needs a new definition." "The 1970s," the magazine observed, "promise to be the decade when youth becomes a state of mind and overflows all traditional age boundaries." As one executive explained, the "youth market" was no longer limited just to the young—"My 35- and 40-year-old teenagers are my best customers" (*Business Week*, 1970, p. 34).

The growth of this "greying youth" market can, perhaps, be seen as a facet of new modes of adulthood and lifestyle developing among specific social groups. Here, the work of Pierre Bourdieu is illuminating. In *Distinction* (1984), his study of changes in the fabric of bourgeois culture in modern France, Bourdieu argued that after 1945 there began to emerge a new form of capitalist economy in which power and profits were increasingly dependent not simply on the production of goods but also on the continual regeneration of consumer desires (Bourdieu, 1984, p. 310). Associated with this new economic order was the emergence of new, middle-class groups who championed the cause of commodity consumption and judged people "by their capacity for consumption, their 'standard of living' [and] their life-style, as much as by their capacity for production" (p. 310). Above all else, Bourdieu argued, the new class faction conceived of themselves as connoisseurs in "the art of living," breaking away from the traditional bourgeois "morality of duty" (with its ideals of probity, reserve, and restraint) and embracing instead a new "morality of pleasure as a duty," in which it became "a failure, a threat to self-esteem, not to 'have fun'" (Bourdieu, 1984, p. 367).

Bourdieu's analysis was focused on cultural shifts in postwar France, but the United States underwent similar transformations.[20] Like Bourdieu's "new petite bourgeoisie," the ascending middle class of postwar America defined their social status and cultural identity through distinctive, consumption-driven lifestyles that prioritized autonomy, stylistic self-expression, and (to use Bourdieu's terminology) an "ethic of fun." Expressive and liberated, this hedonistic art of living embraced a new world of narcissism and leisure—a world in which young cultural tastes and youthful modes of consumption found a natural home.

## TEENAGE SPENDING: "THE LAST MERCHANDISING FRONTIER"?

The 1960s and 1970s also saw other changes in the U.S. youth market. African American youngsters, in particular, became a more prominent consumer force. Although racism and economic inequality remained entrenched, the combination of civil rights activism and greater employment opportunities improved living standards for many African Americans, who gradually emerged as a significant consumer market. As a consequence, TV executives and advertisers began to pay more attention to black youth culture and African American audiences. In 1970, for example, the Chicago TV station WCIU launched *Soul Train* as a black counterpart to *American Bandstand*, the show's success leading to its syndication the following year, while youth-oriented TV dramas such as *Room 222* (ABC, 1969–1974) and situation comedies such as *What's Happening!!* (ABC, 1976–1979) began to focus on the experiences of young African Americans.

The soul music boom of the 1960s also testified to the growing market influence of African American youth culture. The success of Detroit's Tamla-Motown record label was indicative. Founded by musician and producer Berry Gordy, Jr. in 1959, Motown broke into the commercial mainstream in 1962, scoring six top-ten hits on the Billboard Music Charts. Further success saw Motown emerge as the most successful independent record company in the United States, and by 1973 Gordy was chairman of Motown Industries—a multimillion-dollar company that boasted record, motion picture, television, and publishing divisions.[21]

The disco phenomenon of the early 1970s was equally significant. Originating in the black and gay clubs of New York, disco's pulsating rhythms filtered into the mainstream to become the defining sound of 1970s clubland, and went on to influence the development of dance music genres throughout the 1980s and 1990s.[22] But perhaps even more impressive was the hip-hop and rap music explosion. Emerging from the New York underground of the late 1970s, rap became a mammoth entertainment industry during the 1980s and 1990s, and turned hip-hop impresarios such as Russell Simmons and Sean "Puffy" Combs into moguls who presided over multimillion-dollar business empires.[23]

More generally, however, the 1970s and 1980s saw the commercial confidence that had characterized the youth market's earlier jackpot years shaken by a combination of demographic trends and economic recession. Decreasing birth rates brought a decline in the teenage population and the baby boomers made way for the baby bust generation, as the proportion of the U.S. population under age 18 dropped from 36% in 1960 to 28% in 1980 (Department of Health and Human Services, 1998, p. 16). At the same time, the favorable economic conditions that had paved the way for the postwar explosion of youth consumption—economic growth, full employment, and rising living standards—gradually crumbled. Advanced capitalist economies slid into a long downturn punctuated by particularly severe recessions in the mid-1970s, the early 1980s, and the early 1990s. Youth employment was a major casualty of the slump, and in the United States the jobless rate for teenagers hovered at around 15% throughout the late 1980s (Stern, Finkelstein, Latting, & Dornsife, 1995, p. 5). In this context, many young people faced bleak prospects and researchers such as Donna Gaines (1991) revealed the existence of a "teenage wasteland"—an alienated substratum of American youth who struggled with the hardships of social and economic disenfranchisement.

In the face of these shifts, many commentators were pessimistic about the youth market's future. Hollander and Germain, for example, observed that during the 1980s "emphasis on the youth market declined somewhat," with "fewer marketing research and advertising agencies claim[ing] to specialize in the youth market during that decade than was true during the 1960s" (1993, p. 110). Reports of the youth market's death, however, were greatly exaggerated. Despite rising levels of youth unemployment, the 1980s were still a time of relative prosperity for many youngsters. Dennis Tootelian and Ralph Gaedeke, for example, calculated that although the U.S. teenage population had dropped by 15.5% during the 1980s, their collective spending power actually increased by nearly 43%, with individual consumer spending rising from $1,422 to $2,409 per capita (1992, p. 35).

By the beginning of the new millennium, moreover, demographic shifts and economic trends seemed to signal a return to the jackpot days of the 1950s and 1960s. Although the long-term decline in birth rates continued, the youth populations of most Western countries were set to grow during the early twenty-first century as the "echo" of the baby boom worked its way through the demographic profile. Indeed, by 2000 the U.S. teenage population stood at 31.6 million, nearly 6% higher than the baby boomer peak of 29.9 million in 1976 (U.S. Bureau of the Census, 2001), and business eyed the potential market excitedly. Aired in February 2001, a PBS TV special spotlighted the army of market analysts and advertisers eagerly chasing "the hottest consumer demographic in America"—the "largest generation of teenagers ever" who "last year…spent more than $100 billion themselves and pushed their parents to spend another $50 billion on top of that."[24] The following year, meanwhile, commercial enthusiasm reached fever pitch as, in a widely publicized report, youth market analysts Teenage Research Unlimited (TRU) announced that since 1996 teen spending in the United States had climbed from $122 billion to $172 billion a year—TRU estimating that between 1998 and 2001 the discretionary spending of the average American teen had increased from $78 to more than $104 a week (TRU, 2002).

For some, the inexorable growth of teenage consumption was a depressing reality. Echoing the pessimism of 1950s critics such as David Reisman and Dwight Macdonald, many commentators lamented what they saw as a modern youth culture dominated by vulgar, shallow commercialism. Alissa Quart (2003), for example, deplored what she saw as a constant corporate battering designed to reduce teenagers' individuality and creativity, while Sharon Lamb and Lyn Mikel Brown (2006) presented girls as besieged by a manipulative media that pedaled stereotypical images of "cute, sweet, hot, little shoppers" (Lamb & Brown, 2006, p. 3).

Others, however, have argued that it is misleading to see young consumers as simply the hapless dupes of a cunning commercial machine. Instead, British theorists such as Paul Willis have highlighted dimensions of agency in youngsters' consumer practices. For Willis, young people should be seen as actively generating their cultures and forms of self-representation by "creatively selecting and appropriating the raw texts and artefacts made available by the commercial market" (Willis, 1990, p. 157). Drawing illustrative examples from a range of rich ethnographic studies, Willis argued that a variety of cultural activities and media forms (TV soap operas and advertisements, movie going, teen magazines, pop music, fashion, and hairstyles) were used by young people as raw materials for creative expression, youth's patterns of consumption representing "a kind of self creation—of identities, of space, of cultural forms—with its own kind of cultural empowerment" (p. 82). According to Willis, then, media industries might invite young audiences to understand and make sense of their products in specific ways, but they had no control over the way young people often appropriated, reinterpreted, and even subverted a text's meanings.

For critics such as Jim McGuigan (1992), however, the kind of approach advocated by Willis drifted dangerously close to an unqualified celebration of consumerism. Subsequently, other theorists have called for renewed attention to the political economy of the culture industries and to the "interplay between the symbolic and the economic" (Murdock, 1997, p. 68). This, however, should not entail sliding into notions of marketing Svengalis leading passive and undiscriminating youngsters by the nose. Instead, Steven Miles characterizes the relationship between youth culture and the commercial market as "mutually exploitative"—young people appropriating, transforming, and recontextualizing the meanings of media texts, although always within boundaries set by commercial interests:

> The proposition that young people actively engage with the mass media and to a degree forge it in their own image is a sound one, but is only ever partially realized. Ultimately, the parameters within which young people are able to do so, are set down for them by a mass media that is inevitably constructed first and foremost on the need to sell magazines, programmes and what is essentially a consumerist way of life. Young people are therefore liberated and constrained by the mass media at one and the same time—it provides them with the canvass, but the only oils they can use to paint that canvass are consumerist ones. (Miles, 2000, p. 85)

Whatever the tensions and contradictions that characterize young people's relationship with the popular media, the teenage market is set to remain a commercial force for the foreseeable future. Published in 2007, *The Teens Market in the U.S.* synthesized a range of market research data in a report that plotted the likely trajectory of American youth spending. Produced by the market analysts Packaged Facts, the report estimated that, despite an estimated 3% decline in the 12- to 17-year-old age group between 2006 and 2011, the value of the teen market would maintain its growth. The continued rise in teenage spending, the report predicted, would be funded by a combination of earnings from jobs and generous allowances from parents which, together, would raise aggregate teen income from $79.7 billion in 2006 to $91.1 billion in 2011 (Packaged Facts, 2007).

Perhaps even more important is the way the youth market has broadened its generational appeal. In 1958 Dwight Macdonald had speculated that the growth of teenage spending might mark "the last merchandising frontier." Fifty years later, the rise of the teenage market looks more like the prologue than the finale to the development of modern consumerism. With its emphasis on leisure, hedonism, and "hip" nonconformity, the teenage phenomenon of the 1950s and 1960s initiated new consumer values that laid the basis for a rising middle-class lifestyle—a mindset and culture that resists the trappings of encroaching middle age, and favors instead the tastes and pursuits (pop music, fashion, fast cars, drugs) once the preserve of the young.

## NOTES

1. See also Swiencicki (1998, p. 786).
2. Full accounts of the history and significance of the wartime "zoot suit riots" are provided in Cosgrove (1984), Escobar (1996), and Mazón (1984).

3. See also Gilbert (1957, p. 21, Tables 1–6).
4. Innumerable books chronicle the development of rock and roll; Gillett (1983) provides one of the fullest accounts.
5. See Lipsitz (1989) for an account of how radio allowed white youngsters to expand their cultural tastes during the 1950s.
6. Jackson (1991) gives an evocative portrait of Alan Freed's career and the early days of rock and roll.
7. A full history of American-International Pictures can be found in McGee (1984).
8. In the United States, the percentage of African American students finishing high school virtually doubled between the early 1940s and the late 1950s (Gilbert, 1986, p. 19).
9. Rizzo (2005) shows how successive generations of middle-class youngsters have appropriated the styles of working-class white and nonwhite youth as a symbol of "class otherness" that expresses discontent with conventional forms of middle-class identity.
10. See Pilkington (1994, pp. 66–71).
11. The concept of *cultural imperialism* was originally popularized by Herbert Schiller who, in *Mass Communication and American Empire* (1969), argued that American capitalism was consolidating its position of global domination through its media exports.
12. For a critical overview of these trends, see Hesmondhalgh (2007, pp. 84–89, 109–136).
13. For discussion of the "hybrid"/"syncretic" character of modern youth cultures, see Back (1996) and Gilroy (1993, 1997).
14. The extent to which the American public shared these fears is debatable, although Gilbert cites Gallup poll surveys suggesting a peak of popular concern in 1945, followed by a more sustained period of anxiety between 1953 and 1958 (Gilbert, 1986, p. 63).
15. A historical survey of the JD movie genre can be found in McGee and Robertson (1982).
16. Pells (1985) provides a valuable overview of critiques of mass culture and conformity in postwar America.
17. For a discussion of the aura of youthful idealism that surrounded the Kennedy presidency, see Hellmann (1997, p. 105).
18. Further analysis can be found in Osgerby (2001, pp. 87–119).
19. There exist innumerable histories of the 1960s counterculture. Gitlin (1987) provides one of the classic narratives, but other useful accounts are offered by Braunstein and Doyle (2001), Echols (2002), and Gair (2007).
20. While Bourdieu's account offers a useful framework for understanding general shifts in American middle-class culture, there remain some important differences between the French experience and that in the United States. In France, for example, Bourdieu highlighted cultural and socioeconomic resources as key markers of bourgeoisie cultural boundaries, but Michèle Lamont (1992) has suggested that in America a more significant role has been played by moral imperatives based around the qualities of honesty, hard work, and personal

integrity (Lamont, 1992, pp. 4–5). More generally, Lamont contends that cultural perimeters are more strongly demarcated in France than in America, where the presence of powerful ideologies of egalitarianism has meant that such boundaries are weaker and more loosely defined.

21. Nelson (2003) provides the definitive account of the rise of Tamla-Motown, while Early (2004) places the development of the Motown sound within its broader historical context.
22. For exhaustive histories of the 1970s disco phenomenon, see Jones and Kantonen (1999), Lawrence (2003), and Shapiro (2005).
23. Full accounts of the rise of hip-hop culture and rap music can be found in Chang (2005), Nelson (2000), and Rose (1994).
24. "The Merchants of Cool," a PBS *Frontline* documentary, was originally screened February 27, 2001.

## REFERENCES

Abrams, M. (1959). *The teenage consumer*. London: Press Exchange.

Adams, M. (1994). *The best war ever: America and World War II*. Baltimore: Johns Hopkins University Press.

*Advertising Age*. (1951, February 26). Interview with Eugene Gilbert, p. 1.

Austin, J., & Willard, M. (1998). Angels of history, demons of culture. In J. Austin & M. Willard (Eds.), *Generations of youth: Youth cultures and history in twentieth-century America* (pp. 1–20). New York: New York University Press.

Back, L. (1996). *New ethnicities and urban culture: Racisms and multiculture in young lives*. London: UCL Press.

Bernard, J. (1961). Teen-age culture: An overview. *The Annals of the American Academy of Political and Social Science, 338*, 1–12.

Bourdieu, P. (1984). *Distinction: A social critique of the judgment of taste*. London: Routledge.

Braunstein, P., & Doyle, M. (2001). *Imagine nation: The American countureculture of the 1960s*. New York: Routledge.

*Business Week*. (1946, June 8). Teen-age market: It's "Terrif," 72–73.

*Business Week*. (1970, December 12). Why "youth" needs a new definition, 34–35.

Butcher, M., & Thomas, M. (Eds.). (2003). *Ingenious: Emerging youth cultures in urban Australia*. Sydney: Pluto.

Butcher, M., & Thomas, M. (2006). Ingenious: Emerging hybrid youth cultures in western Sydney. In P. Nilan & C. Feixa (Eds.), *Global youth? Hybrid identities, plural worlds* (pp. 53–71). London: Routledge.

Chang, J. (2005). *Can't stop, won't stop: A history of the hip hop generation*. London: Ebury.

Chibnall, S. (1985). Whistle and zoot: The changing meaning of a suit of clothes. *History Workshop*, no. 20, 56–81.

Chibnall, S. (1996). Counterfeit Yanks: War, austerity and Britain's American dream. In P. Davies (Ed.), *Representing and imagining America* (pp. 150–159). Keele, UK: Keele University Press.

Chudacoff, H. (1999). *The age of the bachelor: Creating an American subculture.* Princeton, NJ: Princeton University Press.

Cohen, L. (2003). *A consumers' republic: The politics of mass consumption in postwar America.* New York: Knopf.

Cosgrove, S. (1984). The zoot suit and style warfare. *History Workshop,* no. 18, 77–91.

Dayton, A. (1897). *The last days of Knickerbocker life in New York.* New York: G. P. Putnam's Sons.

Dell, F. (1920). *Moon-calf.* New York: Knopf.

Dell, F. (1921). *The briary-bush.* New York: Knopf.

Dell, F. (1929). *Souvenir.* Garden City, NY: Doubleday.

Doherty, T. (2002). *Teenagers and teenpics: The juvenilization of American movies in the 1950s* (2nd ed.). Philadelphia: Temple University Press.

Early, G. (2004). *One nation under a groove: Motown and American culture.* Ann Arbor: University of Michigan Press.

Echols, A. (2002). *Shaky ground: The sixties and its aftershocks.* New York: Columbia University Press.

Escobar, E. (1996). Zoot-suiters and cops: Chicano youth and the Los Angeles Police Department during World War II. In L. Erenberg & S. Hirsch (Eds.), *The war in American culture: Society and consciousness during World War II* (pp. 284–312). Chicago: University of Chicago Press.

*Esquire.* (1933a, Autumn). Princeton undergraduate, 69.

*Esquire.* (1933b, Autumn). For the college lower class man or senior prep / For the college upper class man or younger grad, 58–59.

Fabian, W. (1923). *Flaming youth.* New York: Boni and Liveright.

Fass, P. (1978). *The damned and the beautiful: American youth in the 1920s.* Oxford: Oxford University Press.

Fitzgerald, F. S. (1920). *This side of paradise.* New York: Scribner's.

Frank, T. (1997). *The conquest of cool: Business culture, counterculture and the rise of hip consumerism.* Chicago: University of Chicago Press.

Gaines, D. (1991). *Teenage wasteland: Suburbia's dead end kids.* New York: Pantheon.

Gair, C. (2007). *The American counterculture, 1945–1975.* Edinburgh, UK: Edinburgh University Press.

Gehman, R. (1957, November). The nine billion dollars in hot little hands. *Cosmopolitan,* 72–78.

Gilbert, E. (1957). *Advertising and marketing to young people.* Pleasantville, NY: Printers' Ink.

Gilbert, J. (1986). *A cycle of outrage: America's reaction to the juvenile delinquent in the 1950s.* Oxford: Oxford University Press.

Gillet, C. (1983). *The sound of the city: The rise of rock and roll.* London: Souvenir.

Gilroy, P. (1993). *Small acts: Thoughts on the politics of Black cultures.* London: Serpent's Tail.

Gilroy, P. (1997). Diaspora and the detours of identity. In K. Woodwood (Ed.), *Identity and difference* (pp. 296–343). London: Sage.

Gitlin, T. (1987). *The sixties: Years of hope, days of rage.* New York: Bantam.

Hebdige, D. (1988). Hiding in the light: Youth surveillance and display. In D. Hebdige, *Hiding in the light: On images and things* (pp. 17–36). London, Routledge.

Hechinger, G., & Hechinger, F. (1962). *Teen-age tyranny*, New York: Morrow.

Hechinger, G., & Hechinger, F. (1965, July). In the time it takes you to read these lines the American teen-ager will have spent $2,378.22. *Esquire*, 65–68, 113.

Hellmann, J. (1997). *The Kennedy obsession: The American myth of JFK.* New York: Columbia University Press.

Hesmondhalgh, D. (2007). *The cultural industries* (2nd ed.). London: Sage.

Hine, T. (1999). *The rise and fall of the American teenager*, New York: Avon.

Hollander, S. C., & Germain, R. (1993). *Was there a Pepsi generation before Pepsi discovered it? Youth-based segmentation in marketing.* Chicago: American Marketing Association.

Jackson, J. (1991). *Big beat heat: Alan Freed and the early years of rock and roll.* New York: Schirmer.

Jones, A., & Kantonen, J. (1999). *Saturday night forever: The story of disco.* Edinburgh, UK: Mainstream.

Kearney, M. C. (2004). Teenagers and television in the United States. In H. Newcomb (Ed.), *Encyclopedia of television* (2nd ed., pp. 2276–2281). Chicago: Fitzroy Dearborn.

Klein, N. (2000). *No logo: No space, no choice, no jobs—Taking aim at the brand bullies.* London: Flamingo.

Lamb, S., & Brown, L. M. (2006). *Packaging girlhood: Rescuing our daughters from marketers' schemes.* New York: St. Martin's Press.

Lamont, M. (1992). *Money, morals, and manners: The culture of the French and American upper-middle class.* Chicago: University of Chicago Press.

Lawrence, T. (2003). *Love saves the day: A history of American dance music culture, 1970–1979.* Durham, NC: Duke University Press.

*Life.* (1944, December 11). Teen-age girls: They live in a wonderful world of their own, 91–99.

*Life.* (1945, June 11). Teen-age boys: Faced with war, they are just the same as they have always been, 91–97.

*Life.* (1959, August 31). A new $10-billion power: The U.S. teenage consumer, 78–85.

Lipsitz, G. (1989). Land of a thousand dances: Youth, minorities, and the rise of rock and roll. In L. May (Ed.), *Recasting America: Culture and politics in the age of the Cold War* (pp. 267–284). Chicago: University of Chicago Press.

Macdonald, D. (1958a, November 22). A caste, a culture, a market, I. *New Yorker*, 57–94.

Macdonald, D. (1958b, November 29). A caste, a culture, a market, II. *New Yorker*, 57–107.

Marks, P. (1924). *The plastic age.* New York: Grosset & Dunlap.

May, K. G. (2002). *Golden state, golden youth: The California image in popular culture, 1955–1966.* Chapel Hill: University of North Carolina Press.

Mazón, M. (1984). *The zoot-suit riots: The psychology of symbolic annihilation.* Austin: University of Texas Press.

McGee, M. T. (1984). *Fast and furious: The story of American International Pictures.* Jefferson, NC: McFarland.

McGee, M. T., & Robertson, R. J. (1982). *The J.D. films: Juvenile delinquency in the movies.* Jefferson, NC: McFarland.

McGuigan, J.(1992). *Cultural populism.* London: Routledge.

Mendonca, L. (2002). The local and the global in popular music: The Brazilian music industry, local culture, and public policies. In D. Crane, N. Kawashima, & K. Kawasaki (Eds.), *Global culture: Media arts, policy and globalization* (pp. 105–117). London: Routledge.

Miles, S. (2000). *Youth lifestyles in a changing world.* Buckingham, UK: Open University Press.

Modell, J. (1989). *Into one's own: From youth to adulthood in the United States 1920–1975.* Berkeley: University of California Press.

Mort, F. (1997). Paths to mass consumption: Britain and the USA since 1945. In M. Nava, A. Blake, I. MacRury, & B. Richards (Eds.), *Buy this book: Studies in advertising and consumption* (pp. 15–33). London: Routledge.

Murdock, G. (1997). Cultural studies at the crossroads. In A. McRobbie (Ed.), *Back to reality? Social experience and cultural studies* (pp. 58–73). Manchester, UK: Manchester University Press.

Nelson, G. (2000). *Hip hop America.* London: Penguin.

Nelson, G. (2003). *Where did our love go? The rise and fall of the Motown sound.* London: Omnibus Press.

*Newsweek.* (1966, March 21). Pleasures of possession, 45–46.

Nilan, P., & Feixa, C. (2006). Introduction: Youth hybridity and plural worlds. In P. Nilan & C. Feixa (Eds.), *Global youth? Hybrid identities, plural worlds* (pp. 1–13). London: Routledge.

Osgerby, B. (2001). *Playboys in paradise: Masculinity, youth and leisure-style in modern America.* Oxford: Berg.

Packaged Facts (2007). *The teens market in the U.S.* New York: Market Research Group.

Palladino, G. (1996). *Teenagers: An American history.* New York: Basic Books.

Peiss, K. (1987). *Cheap amusements: Working women and leisure in turn-of-the-century New York.* Philadelphia: Temple University Press.

Pells, R. (1985). *The liberal mind in a conservative age: American intellectuals in the 1940s and 1950s.* New York: Harper & Row.

Pilkington, H. (1994). *Russia's youth and its culture: A nation's constructors and constructed.* London: Routledge.

*Printers' Ink.* (1962, August 31). Teen agers: Half again as many by '70, 43–45.

Quart, A. (2003). *Branded: The buying and selling of teenagers.* Cambridge, MA: Perseus.

Reiman, R. (1992). *The New Deal and American youth: Ideas and ideals in a Depression decade.* Athens: University of Georgia Press.

Reisman, D. (1950a). *The lonely crowd: A study of the changing American character.* New Haven, CT: Yale University Press.

Reisman, D. (1950b). Listening to popular music. *American Quarterly, 2,* 359–371.

Rizzo, M. (2005). *Consuming class, buying identity: Middle-class youth culture, "lower-class" style and consumer culture, 1945–2000.* Ann Arbor: UMI.

Rose, T. (1994). *Black noise: Rap music and black culture in contemporary America.* Middletown, CT: Wesleyan University Press.

Schiller, H. (1969). *Mass communications and American empire.* New York: Beacon.

Schrum, K. (1998). "Teena means business": Teenage girls' culture and *Seventeen* magazine, 1944–50. In S. Inness (Ed.), *Delinquents and debutantes: Twentieth century American girls' cultures* (pp. 134–163). New York: New York University Press.

Schrum, K. (2004). *Some wore bobby sox: The emergence of teenage girls' culture, 1920–1945.* New York: Palgrave Macmillan.

Shapiro, P. (2005). *The secret history of disco: Turn the beat around.* London: Faber and Faber.

Stern, D., Finkelstein, N., Latting, J., & Dornsife, C. (1995). *School to work: Research on programs in the United States.* Bristol, PA: Falmer Press.

Swiencicki, M. A. (1998). Consuming brotherhood: Men's culture, style and recreation as consumer culture, 1880–1930. *Social History, 31,* 773–808.

*Time.* (1956, August 13). Bobby-soxers' gallup, 72–73.

*Time.* (1964, October 9). The teen-age tide, 58.

Tootelian, D., & Gaedeke, R. (1992). The teen market: An exploratory analysis of income, spending and shopping patterns. *Journal of Consumer Marketing, 9,* 35–44.

TRU. (2002, January 25). Teens spent $172 billion in 2001. Teen Research Unlimited Press Release.

U.S. Bureau of the Census. (1975). *Historical statistics of the United States: Colonial times to 1970.* Washington, DC: U.S. Government Printing Office.

U.S. Bureau of the Census. (2001). *Census 2000.* Washington, DC: U.S. Department of Commerce, Economics and Statistics Administration.

U.S. Department of Health and Human Services. (1998). *Trends in the well-being of America's children and youth.* Washington, DC: Department of Health and Human Services.

Wallace, C., & Kovatcheva, S. (1998). *Youth in society: The construction and deconstruction of youth in East and West Europe.* Basingstoke, UK: Macmillan.

Wee, T. (1999). An exploraton of a global teenage lifestyle in Asian societies. *Journal of Consumer Marketing, 16,* 365–375.

Welsh, O. (2007). Chinese game market explodes. *GamesIndustry.Biz.* Retrieved May 4, 2007, from http://www.gamesindustry.biz/content_page.php?aid=24773

Willis, P. (1990). *Common culture: Symbolic work at play in the everyday cultures of the young.* Milton Keynes, UK: Open University Press.

# 2

# "Still Talking About My Generation!"

## The Representation of Youth in Popular Music

ANDY BENNETT

Since the mid-1950s, popular music has been primarily defined as "youth" music. Successive genres of popular music—from rock and roll in the 1950s; through beat, psychedelic, and countercultural rock scenes of the 1960s; 1970s glam and punk music; to more contemporary styles such as rap, metal, and grunge—have each produced youth icons, that is, performers who speak to and for youth through their style, image, and music. The purpose of this chapter is to historically chart the way in which youth has been represented in popular music since the post–World War II era. I begin with the 1950s, when songs of teen romance, rebellion, and frustration signaled the emergence of "youth" and heralded it as a sociocultural category distinct from the parent culture, and go on to chart the increasingly militant overtones of popular music during the 1960s, when youth anthems such as "My Generation," by British beat group The Who, and the Rolling Stones's "Let's Spend the Night Together," paved the way for the more radical, countercultural stance of political rock and hippie youth during the second half of the decade. I then turn my attention to the early 1970s when songs such as David Bowie's "Rebel Rebel" and Lou Reed's "Walk on the Wild Side" vividly documented youth experimentation with gender identity and sexuality. In the following section of the chapter I focus on punk and new wave's dramatic statements concerning the erosion of young people's life chances, hopes, and aspirations due to the economic downturn and social instability in the late 1970s. I then examine how, during the 1980s, the impact of socioeconomic decline and its implications for youth were critically reassessed according to criteria of race and ethnicity by African American rap artists—the basic messages of rap subsequently being appropriated and reworked by artists around the globe in ways that established dialogues with youth audiences in specific local contexts. Finally, I consider how more recent youth musical styles such as grunge and extreme metal have provided their own commentary on the state of youth in an age of increasing risk and uncertainty.

## A SOUNDTRACK FOR YOUTH

Since the mid-twentieth century, popular music has frequently been referred to as a "soundtrack" for youth. In order to understand properly the significance of this statement it is important to consider briefly the context that initially inspired it. From the 1950s onward popular music was marketed primarily to a youth audience as part of a new teenage consumer market that also included fashion items (Osgerby, 1998), film (Lewis, 1992), and various forms of popular literature. Following the end of World War II, the rapid population growth in the West (more typically referred to as the baby boom) combined with the need to replenish the labor force produced a critical mass of affluent teenagers. Still living in the parental home and without the domestic constraints and financial commitments of marriage and family life to contend with, the postwar teenage generation commanded a significant amount of disposable income which they were free to spend on themselves. As Chambers (1985) observes, with the postwar consumer boom, youth became a credible, and readily targeted, consumer market. The growing significance of youth fashion, film, literature, and music figured centrally as aspects of youth consumption. Within this, popular music—more specifically rock and roll—played a pivotal part.

Coined by Cleveland-based DJ Alan Freed, the term *rock and roll* refers to a rhythm and blues–derived music first performed by African American artists such as Fats Domino, but made commercially popular by white artists like Bill Haley and Elvis Presley (Gillet, 1983; Palmer, 1976). In many ways the impact of rock and roll in the 1950s is synonymous with the cultural construction of the teenager as a distinct lifestage and with the demarcation of youth as the cultural space in which collective identity of teenagers was worked out and articulated (Shumway, 1992). Rock and roll made little sense to the parent generation. Indeed, it effectively drove a wedge between teenagers and the parent culture, the visible disgust often exhibited by adults making rock and roll all the more endearing to young fans and further marking it out as a "youth" music. This identification between rock and roll and its youth audience was further consolidated by the artists at the center of the rock and roll explosion who were, for the most part, the same age as their youth audience and often from similar socioeconomic backgrounds (Plasketes & Plasketes, 1987).

But rock and roll was more than just a platform for the cultural practice of youth; it also critically represented youth both in its musical and in its lyrical content. For the first time, popular music songs made open reference to youth with titles such as "Leader of the Pack," "Lonely Boy," and "The Young Ones." Visually, too, the impact of rock and roll on youth was significant. The image of popular rock and roll artists like Elvis Presley and Gene Vincent was eagerly emulated by male fans, to the extent that such artists achieved iconic status, becoming the bedrock for visually distinctive youth groupings variously theorized as "gangs" (Patrick, 1973) and "subcultures" (Hall & Jefferson, 1976; Hebdige, 1979). Such developments in music and its impact on young listeners did not go unnoticed by the parent generation. If the parent culture of the 1950s and early 1960s typically claimed not to understand rock and roll (see, e.g., Johnson, 1964), the sanctions imposed by the media and institutions of social control clearly illustrate the deeply felt concern regarding the emergence of rock and roll and its apparent resonance with a developing shift in the sociocultural sensibilities of youth (Mutsaers, 1990; Shumway, 1992). Commenting in 1964 on the impact of Beatlemania on British youth, Paul Johnson describes the Beatles as "grotesque idols" performing to a "pathetic and listless" audience with "sagging mouths and glazed eyes, the hands mindlessly drumming in time to the music" (1964, p. 327).

The discourse of youth espoused by rock and roll revolved largely around teenage rebellion against the parent culture. This was not communicated in any organized political way, which would emerge later during the latter part of the 1960s. Rather, rock and roll worked to oppose the mundane day-to-day organization of adult society. Rock and roll was essentially a fun type of music that encouraged participation through dance and in the repetition of its sing-along choruses. Songs such as "Rock Around the Clock" evoked the importance of leisure over work, study, and other activities promoted by the parent culture. Rock and roll, and the various musical styles that grew from it, created a ubiquitous association of leisure with youth, leisure being unequivocally represented as "the" domain of the young and a "natural" right of passage. Such messages are clearly heard in tracks such as the Beach Boys's "Surfin' USA" (which helped transform the California beach scene into an idealized mythscape for a global media audience) and Chuck Berry's "No Particular Place to Go," a song that also worked to champion the burgeoning car culture of the United States and its ready associations with youth, male bravado, and sexuality. The fact of leisure as the logical domain of the young was further reinforced through the tongue-in-cheek critiques of the establishment by artists such as Eddie Cochran, whose

"Summertime Blues" underscored the low value placed on the views, opinions, and frustrations of youth by parents, employers, and politicians.

Within all of this the ultimate renegade of the rock and roll era was Elvis Presley. If rock and roll was the music of youth, and if the icons of rock and roll were youth icons, then Presley was the personification of such cultural symbolism. Taking his inspiration directly from African American rhythm and blues artists, Presley took the vital ingredients of this black style and introduced them to white teenage audiences. Censored by media moguls such as Ed Sullivan (Shumway, 1992), Presley was nevertheless an instant hit with white teenagers who saw in his music an element of excitement and abandon absent from the work of previous white rock and roll singers. When Presley sang about love and heartache, it was with a rawness and sensuality that resonated intimately with the teenage psyche.

## TEENAGERS IN LOVE

Although rock and roll brought a new sense of excitement to popular music for youth, in many respects the subject matter of its lyrics was not at all dissimilar from that of popular music genres in the pre–rock and roll era. Themes such as love, romance, heartbreak, and remorse—staples of rock and roll artists such as Buddy Holly and Elvis Presley—had also been a mainstay in songs by pre–rock and roll artists such as Bing Crosby and Pat Boone. The key difference was, of course, that with rock and roll the previously taboo topic of love and romance among adolescents was squarely broached. Although not effectively documented until a number of years after the fact—and then primarily in fictional accounts such as the early 1960s nostalgia film *American Graffiti* (1973)—the discourse of teen romance presented in popular song permeated and informed the everyday life of teenagers during the 1950s and early 1960s at a variety of levels. The high school prom and the burgeoning car culture of middle America were among the more typically documented examples of music's interface with teenage patterns of courtship and romance during this period (see Lewis, 1992).

Teen romance has remained a constant topic in popular music since the rock and roll era. During the early 1970s, artist Donny Osmond's top ten hits "Puppy Love" and "Young Love" took rock and roll's narrative of teen romance as an unspoken and taboo topic and replayed it for a new "teeny-bopper" audience (McRobbie & Garber, 1976)—girls in their early teens whose music consumption practices were supplemented with the reading of teen magazines such as *Jackie* in the UK or *YM*, *Teen*, and *Seventeen* in the United States and watching television shows such as *Shang-a-Lang*, featuring the early 1970s prototype boy band Bay City Rollers (whose closest comparison in the United States was probably the Osmonds). As Frith and McRobbie (1990) observe, the boy-next-door image of such artists, combined with romantically tinged lyrics of their songs, presented an alternative representation of male sexuality to the machoistic and often misogynistic images and lyrics of rock and heavy metal artists that were also becoming increasingly popular at the time. According to Frith and McRobbie, in the context of teenybopper music, "male sexuality is transformed into a spiritual yearning, carrying only hints of sexual attraction. [The teenybopper needs] a sensitive and sympathetic soulmate, someone to support and nourish the incompetent male adolescent as he grows up" (1990, p. 375). By the early 1990s, the equation of teen romance topics with the songcraft of the boy band had become almost a cliché, as a succession of manufactured groups such as Take That and East 17 re-rehearsed what had by this time become a tried-and-tested formula.

## MY GENERATION

The above accounts begin to illustrate why, in a post-1950s context, popular music came to be labeled as a soundtrack for youth. There are, however, a number of other significant moments in postwar popular music history that have also played their part both in culturally aligning music with youth and also facilitating popular music's role in the representation of youth as a distinctive cultural category.

Fundamental in this respect were the socio-musical developments that took place during the 1960s. The decade saw a definite sea change in the relationship between youth and music. If rock and roll had functioned as a cultural beacon for youth, alerting them to their distinctive sociocultural status and serving as a means to vent their frustrations at the lack of attention paid to them by the parent culture and the establishment, during the 1960s popular music and its youth audience assumed a more discernibly political edge. The first stirrings of this came in 1965 with the release of "My Generation" by British beat band The Who. Musically speaking, the song comprises a simple two-chord structure (although it was also one of the first rock songs to feature a bass guitar solo, the latter proving highly inspirational for future generations of rock bass players). Lyrically, however, "My Generation" registers clearly as a song about youth and, more importantly, for youth. Through a series of age-related references dealing candidly with the perceived "coldness" of the adult generation to their misunderstanding of the nuances of everyday youth language, the song's most cutting rebuttal is delivered in a line in which lead vocalist Roger Daltry professes a wish to die before he gets "old." The cutting, lyrical sentiments of "My Generation" afforded it an instant symbolic currency among youth and the song was ultimately to become a template for a variety of critical attacks on the parent culture and the broader establishment that would be explored in popular music throughout the 1960s.

Such narratives of youthful discontent in the popular music of the time were given extra gravity through the emergent hippie movement, also referred to as the counterculture (see Hall & Jefferson, 1976), in which the derision of youth was played out through a series of critiques on various aspects of Western capitalist society, including the patriarchal nature of the family (Reich, 1970), the increasing reliance on technocratic progress (Roszak, 1969), and the foreign policy of corrupt governments (Snowman, 1984). A cornerstone of such explorations of youth's discontent with the machinations of Western capitalism in popular song was the emergence of rock, a style attributed to the song writing craft of artists such as Bob Dylan and the post-1966 Beatles. Heralded by serious music critics such as Lester Bangs and Griel Marcus of *Rolling Stone* magazine, rock was considered to mark an important departure from the hitherto chart-orientated nature of postwar popular music (Shuker, 2001). Indeed, Frith (1981) goes so far as to suggest that rock became the basis for a new ideological community among youth. Similarly, Reich (1971) suggests that rock acted as a musical message of hope, truth, and togetherness for youth in an age when the morality of the parent culture appeared increasingly corrupt. Harnessing the new developments in studio and public address system technology, rock was considered a new art form—a music for serious connoisseurs interested in the cultural and political statements deemed inherent in the rock text (Zak, 2001).

Certainly some of the more hard-edged critical engagements with a number of the more burning social issues of the late 1960s—war, poverty, and racism—are to be heard in the music of rock artists such as Jimi Hendrix and the Doors. Similarly, the price paid by youth for direct engagement with the political and military forces of government are poignantly documented in songs such as Buffalo Springfield's "For What It's Worth" and Crosby, Stills, Nash, and Young's "Ohio," both of which focus on National Guard shootings of young anti–Vietnam War demonstrators.

In truth, however, the oppositional messages of hippie culture were by no means confined to rock music, but permeated popular music at all levels during the late 1960s, a clear example of this being Scott McKenzie's "San Francisco (Be Sure to Wear Some Flowers in Your Hair)." Released in the summer of 1967 at the height of the hippie movement, this song, together with the Beatles's "All You Need Is Love," became signature tunes of the moment. However, if "All You Need Is Love" focused on love and peace as integral aspects of the hippie message, "San Francisco (Be Sure to Wear Some Flowers in Your Hair)" offered a lyrical imagery that focused pointedly on the people at the center of the hippie movement—the young hippies themselves and their purported quest for an alternative social order to that adhered to and endorsed by the parent culture. At a time when San Francisco, and in particular the city's Haight-Ashbury district, was attracting considerable national and international attention as the alleged center of the hippie movement, "San Francisco (Be Sure to Wear Some Flowers in Your Hair)" functioned as a globally mediated celebration of this unique, youth-centered carnival. Underscoring the gentle manner of the new hippie youth and its peaceful intentions, the song undoubtedly played a signature role in drawing the attention of the media to the counterculture movement and shaping its perception of the hippie youth at its center.

Another song from the late 1960s that functioned as an anthem was the Small Faces's "Itchycoo Park." If hippie youth's intention was to unlock the "doors of perception" and find a new level of truth and understanding in the world, then drug culture was considered an integral part of this. Mind-expanding drugs such as marijuana and the synthetically produced lysergic acid diethylamide (LSD) became a staple of hippie culture and were often used in conjunction with listening to rock music. Indeed, according to Willis the tonal textures and sound effects used in rock music were such that they practically invited the use of drugs on the part of the listener: "electronic effects, such as echo, feedback, stereo [and] loudness itself...[giving] the impression of space and lateral extension" when listened to under the influence of drugs (Willis, 1978, p. 167). "Itchycoo Park" tantalizingly combined open references to drug culture—at least among those familiar with hippie argot—with a musical score that featured heavy use of phasing, a then-new electronic effect that creates a swirling sensation in the music. Used in the bridging section between the verse and chorus, the phasing effect brings an ethereal quality to "Itchycoo Park" and evokes a shimmering feel that could be construed as attempting to evoke the experience of exposure to images and music while under the influence of LSD.

For many, the swan song of the hippie era was the 1969 Woodstock Music and Art Fair. By that time, the belief that rock music was key to changing the world was firmly ingrained in hippie discourse, a sentiment effectively captured in Michael Wadleigh's film documentation of the event, *Woodstock*, when festival co-organizer Artie Kornfeld proclaims during an interview that the message is in the music (Bell, 1999). Held at a greenfield site in upstate New York over a three-day period, at its height the Woodstock festival brought together half a million young people. The professed significance of this moment and its resonance with a new sensibility of youth at large in the wider world is poignantly documented in the Joni Mitchell song "Woodstock." Written as a tribute to the event by an artist who did not herself perform at the festival, Mitchell's song weaves a fictional first-person account of a journey to Woodstock (having heard about the festival from a fellow traveler) with a series of reflections on the event's significance as a symbol of cultural change—and the dawning of a new age of spirituality and awareness (more popularly broadcast in the subsequent hippie musical *Hair*'s signature theme, "The Age of Aquarius").

In hindsight, it is clear that the counterculture and its associated values were fundamentally flawed. As Palmer (1976) observes, the project of alternativism proffered by the hippies was weakly formulated and, ultimately, hippie culture became as commodified as any other youth culture before or since. Indeed, not all of the music of the late 1960s uncritically celebrated the hippie movement. Notable in this respect is the Beatles's "Revolution," a song that pointed to the confused narrative of a movement that promoted peace on the one hand but appeared to endorse the actions of totalitarian regimes on the other (Marcus, 1972).

Nevertheless, McKenzie's song remains something of a period piece, a musical statement of a particular youth-cultural era and an attempt to communicate this to a wider public via the ever-expanding range of the developing global media. Music's significance as a soundtrack for youth was probably never more stridently promoted than during the hippie era—music itself being promoted as a world-changing force that could harness and promote the view of hippie youth to the wider society.

### HE'S A SHE

In contrast to the late 1960s, the early to mid-1970s are generally regarded as a low period in terms of popular music's political significance and/or its impact on youth. Conventionally speaking, the early 1970s tend to be equated with the rise of soft rock and AOR (album-oriented rock) characterized in the United States by groups such as the Eagles and in Britain by the emergence of progressive rock and its more commercial spin-offs such as The Moody Blues and the Electric Light Orchestra. Occasional references to youthful angst and opposition emerging in early 1970s popular music—for example T-Rex's "Children of the Revolution," the Sweet's "Teenage Rampage," and Mott the Hoople's "All the Young Dudes"—were in many ways nostalgic commentaries on the late 1960s. Other popular music artists of the era delved back even earlier in time for musical and lyrical inspiration, with the likes of Roy Wood's Wizzard and Alvin Stardust producing music that embodied a distinctly 1950s rock and roll aesthetic.

Only with the advent of punk, in the mid-1970s, argued many music critics and other observers, did popular music regain a culturally meaningful edge and an authentic significance for young, disempowered (and, increasingly, dispossessed) audiences (see, for example, Savage, 1992). To be sure, the significance of punk as both a voice for and a representation of youth during the mid- to late 1970s cannot be denied (and the topic of punk is returned to later in this chapter). That said, however, to focus on punk at the expense of pre-punk music of the early 1970s glosses over some critical developments in popular music during this period (see Bennett, 2007).

Thus, if it is unquestionably true that the politicized countercultural rock project of the late 1960s had all but faded from view by the end of that decade, it is equally the case that new political questions came to the fore in popular music during the early 1970s, particularly in relation to issues of gender and sexuality. If such issues had already begun to figure in the late 1960s, notably through the work of artists such as Lou Reed and the Velvet Underground, during the early 1970s gender bending, cross-dressing, and experimentation with conventional understandings of sexuality assumed a more mainstream platform for expression in the form of glam rock.

Significantly, glam had an important crossover appeal, many performers associated with the glam style commanding both album-oriented rock and teenybopper audiences. It was in this respect that artists such as Roxy Music, the New York Dolls, and in particular David Bowie were to have their most influential impact as new youth icons. As Hebdige observes, "Bowie was responsible for opening up questions of sexual identity which had previously been repressed, ignored or merely hinted at in rock and youth culture" (1979, p. 61). Using heavy makeup, hair dye, and an array of ornate stage costumes, Bowie's Ziggy Stardust character presented as a truly androgynous figure on the stage, in publicity shots, and in interviews (Bennett, 2001). According to Hebdige, "Bowie's meta message was escape—from class, from sex, from personality, from obvious commitment" (1979, p. 61). As Taylor and Wall (1976) observe, among British working class youth, if Bowie's professed bisexuality was initially met with a negative or, at best, indifferent reaction, Bowie's challenge to traditional working class norms governing issues of gender and sexuality was clear.

In Bowie's music, too, clear intimations of a blurring boundary between male and female sexuality could be heard. His 1974 hit "Rebel Rebel," featuring a hard-edged, repetitive guitar riff that, in hindsight, was a clear precursor to punk, broached the gender-bending issue with lyrics that made open references to cross-dressing among youth and its troubling impact on the parent culture. Bowie's cover version of the Rolling Stones's "Let's Spend the Night Together," which had already registered as a highly controversial song during the 1960s due to its blatant promotion of premarital sex among young people, rearticulates the edginess of the song through a camp and sexually ambiguous interpretation that sees Bowie prying open the teasing narrative of the original and dropping in an unaccompanied, spoken vocal vignette in which the artist makes a literal and unmasked reference to "making love" with an unspecified partner.

Perhaps the quintessential musical statement of youth's experimentation with gender-bending and sexuality was Lou Reed's 1973 hit, "Walk on the Wild Side," a song that escaped radio censorship despite its open references to oral sex and heroin use. Although gender-bending had been a facet of urban life for many years, the repression that individuals exhibiting such sensibilities had been forced to endure began to break down during the 1970s. Reed's song is a celebration of this emergent shift in social tolerance and awareness in the urban metropolis, while simultaneously documenting the influx of young misfits into the city from the provincial towns and peripheral places in order to properly realize their preferred identities. Glam's representation of new youth sexualities was to retain an impact throughout the punk years; while not as overtly camp as some of the glam artists, both male and female punk performers challenged gender stereotypes, presenting alternative images to the macho male rocker, and to the female artist as sexualized object of the male gaze (see Frith & McRobbie, 1990).

Following the demise of punk, the British new romantic scene of the early 1980s produced a range of artists whose music revitalized glam's playful blurring of sexual identities. The early 1980s also saw the dawning of a new tolerance toward homosexuality, and this too was reflected in the world of popular music—a notable example being Boy George, lead singer with the British group Culture Club and one of the first pop artists to openly admit to being gay (see Rimmer, 1985). As the 1980s progressed the first open references to homosexual love were heard in chart music, notably in The Communards's 1987 cover version of "Never Can Say Goodbye (Boy)," a song written by Clifton Davies and previously recorded by disco artist Gloria Gaynor during the late 1970s. A decade earlier, disco itself had played a significant part as a platform for the emergence of a gay club and dance scene. Though ostensibly heterosexual in its lyrical and stylistic content (as portrayed in the film *Saturday Night Fever*), disco was quickly appropriated by gay culture with a number of its artists, notably Donna Summer, achieving iconic status.

## TEENAGE WASTELAND

In the minds of many observers, the emergence of punk in the mid-1970s was as pivotal as rock and roll had been some twenty years earlier in asserting the significance of popular music as youth music. Like rock and roll, punk was despised by the parent culture and subject to censorship by the media and the authorities (Laing, 1985). Moreover, as with rock and roll, punk emerged at a particularly volatile moment in twentieth century history. However, if rock and roll had signified a new frontier of affluence and hope, in which the youth of the postwar generation were given scope and space to express a new youthful identity and to assert their independence from the parent culture, punk symbolized the collapse of that dream, emerging as it did against a backdrop of de-industrialization, youth unemployment, and a new era of hopelessness and uncertainty (Hebdige, 1979).

The most notorious punk artists of the late 1970s were the Sex Pistols, a four-piece band fronted by Johnny Rotten (a.k.a. John Lydon) and managed by former art school student Malcolm McLaren (Savage, 1992). A signature moment in the short-lived career of the Sex Pistols was when they were goaded into swearing on live prime-time TV by presenter Bill Grundy, a moment that ensured the emergence of a nationwide moral panic in Britain (Laing, 1985). Although punk's anti-authoritarian message for youth was clear, it is fair to say that for much of the time punk's impact was felt more through its delivery of aural and visual shock tactics than in its documenting the lives and life opportunities of young followers of punk per se. Indeed, as Frith (1997) observes, contrary to popular representations of punk as a working class type of music, many punk musicians emerged from middle class backgrounds and gravitated to punk from art school environments.

There were, however, exceptions, notably New York punk band the Ramones. Proclaiming themselves as a group of misfits and outcasts—the embodiment of the school geek who was too uncool to be with the in-crowd, ineffective at sports, and unable to find a girlfriend—the Ramones explored the world of such characters (i.e., themselves) in songs like "Sheena Is a Punk Rocker," "Rockaway Beach," "I Wanna Be Your Boyfriend," and "I Just Want to Have Something To Do." Undoubtedly, key to the appeal of the Ramones was the fact that the group attracted a high degree of self-identification on the part of the audience. For the fans of the Ramones their image and music bespoke a reality of youth missing from film and media representations, which tended to restrict the portrayal of youth to the more stereotypical images of physical attractiveness and athleticism.

In the UK, a similar, if rather more male-centric, example of artist–audience bonding was achieved by post-punk trio The Jam. Still in their late teens at the time of their first television appearance on the BBC popular music chart program *Top of the Pops*, The Jam epitomized the angry, desperate face of youth as this had emerged during the punk explosion of 1976. Songs like "Going Underground" bespoke a litany of frustration and disenchantment with the parent culture and the broader institutions of society, and promoted a need to escape—the imagery of the underground also suggestive at some level of the threat (still very real during the late 1970s) of nuclear holocaust, itself the unsavory byproduct of an adult world that had become embroiled in the paranoia of cold war politics. A subsequent single, "Eaton Rifles," mocked the upper middle class ritual of the public school system and its conditioning of youth to reproduce the bigotry and hypocrisy of its parent culture. The Jam's cover version of "David Watts," originally a Ray Davies song, reaffirmed the band's working class roots while simultaneously giving Davies's social commentary on the inequalities of the school system a new lease of life against a backdrop of socioeconomic dislocation in late-1970s Britain. The envy and jealousy directed at the character of David Watts mirrors the decreasing opportunities for working class, underachieving youth in the new era of postindustrialization.

During the 1980s, punk became an increasingly underground movement. Indeed, by the mid-1980s many observers suggested that the direction of popular music—by then dominated by soft metal acts such as Bon Jovi and a new generation of stadium acts such as Simple Minds—was such that it appeared as if punk had never happened (see, for example, Rimmer, 1985). By the end of the 1980s, however, it was clear that the legacy of punk was very much still in the frame as a new, punk-influenced style loosely termed *grunge* rose to prominence to be greeted by a youth audience who, as with the punks in the late 1970s, felt that popular music had distanced itself from its audience and had nothing of value to say. A key icon of grunge was Kurt Cobain, singer and guitarist with the Seattle-based trio Nirvana. Cobain connected with his audience at a variety of levels. Very much the anti–rock star, he presented as an ordinary, dispossessed, disenchanted youth, something with which his young audience could easily identify. Similarly, the simple construction of Nirvana's songs and the subject matter of Cobain's lyrics—although often cryptic—engaged a series of images that seemed to get to the very heart of the risk and uncertainty (Beck, 1992) encroaching on the everyday terrains of postindustrial cities. By this time, drugs, alcohol, partying, and risk taking (see Le Breton, 2004) had become integral aspects of youth cultural territory; the apparent nonchalance of Cobain's lyrics and their carnivalesque depiction of such ingrained and accepted practices and sensibilities of postindustrial Generation X youth goes a significant way toward explaining the artist's rapidly acquired iconic status. Cobain's suicide, in April 1994 at the age of 27, crystallized his status as a youth icon, and his music as youth music. In this respect, Cobain's metaphorical significance for an era of youth can be likened to a succession of previous rock causalities who had also died young and thus similarly retain an eternal aura of youth—among them Buddy Holly, Eddie Cochran, Jimi Hendrix, Janis Joplin, Jim Morrison, and Sid Vicious.

A further facet of the socioeconomic dislocation that accompanied the onset of deindustrialization was an increasing incidence of youth homelessness. This has been put down to a variety of factors, including the increase of domestic violence and child abuse in the home, and also youth joblessness. In 1993, U.S. post-grunge combo Soul Asylum released "Runaway Train," a song that documented the issue of youth homelessness and the plight of those it affected. The accompanying video for "Runaway Train" (different versions were made for the U.S. and UK releases) featured actual footage of homeless youth, which graphically brought home the song's message for those who saw the video on MTV and similar media channels.

## STAND UP FOR YOUR RIGHTS

A further and highly significant aspect of popular music in a post-1950s context has been in its representation of youth ethnic identities. In truth, popular music had taken nourishment from non-Western influences for a considerable period of time prior to the emergence of rock and roll in the 1950s (Oliver, 1990). A clear example of this is jazz, which embodies a rhythmic and tonal aesthetic derived from African American blues which, in turn, is derived from slave songs and their roots in traditional African music and storytelling traditions (Lopes, 2002). Although rock and roll in its initial form may be said to have extended the reach of the African American music lineage in the United States, its co-optation by white artists and a white teenage audience produced a more mainstream aura around the genre.

In subsequent decades, however, styles of music emerged that were to remain more identifiably African American, an obvious case in point being soul, a style that forged rhythm and blues with gospel song. Throughout the late 1950s and 1960s a succession of soul singers emerged whose high-energy performances appeared at some level to articulate an increasing frustration among young African American audiences concerning the racial tensions and inequality that remained embedded in U.S. society. This came to a head in the 1960s with the launching of organized protests in the form of the civil rights movement, which was later succeeded by the more militant black power movement (Snowman, 1984). The end of the decade also witnessed a succession of inner-city race riots during which African Americans took to the streets in protest over the continuing racial inequalities and intolerance of white, mainstream society. The emergence of soul during this period played a pivotal role, with artists such as Aretha Franklin and James Brown lending their support to the cause of black and other ethnic minorities in the United States. James Brown's "Say It Loud, I'm Black and I'm Proud" becoming a signature anthem of the era (Bennett, 2001).

During the late 1960s and early 1970s, a number of artists also focused more specifically on the plight of African American children and youth in their music. Elvis Presley's "In the Ghetto" laments the illegitimate birth and untimely death of one particular ghetto child. Although the narrative of the song is fictional, its story is better understood as a composite of news stories and street knowledge regarding the life chances of children born into poverty, and coming to terms with the pressures and uncertainties of life in the contemporary urban ghetto of the late 1960s and early 1970s. Stevie Wonder's "Livin' for the City," released in 1974, paints a similar picture of the everyday struggles experienced by poor urban blacks, the extended album version of the song featuring a spoken vignette in which the main character in the song, having made the trip to New York in search of a new life, is falsely implicated in a robbery by the police and sent to prison. Poetically articulating the basic tenets of Becker's (1963) labeling theory, Wonder's lyrics graphically spell out the systematic stigmatization of African American youth rife in the U.S. media and judicial system of the 1970s.

In the mid-1970s, a new black musical style emerged that was also to have a highly significant impact on the youth of the global African diaspora. Referred to as *reggae*, this style emerged from the Caribbean island of Jamaica. The leading exponent of reggae was Bob Marley, whose international success during the 1970s helped transform reggae into what Gilroy refers to as "a pan-Caribbean culture" (1993, p. 82). Marley's role in the transformation of reggae in this way was to have a considerable impact on African diasporic youth. As Hebdige (1979) observes, reggae's message, which, in keeping with the doctrine of the Rastafarian religion, advocated a black exodus from former slave colonies back to Africa, was readily appropriated and reworked by black youth angry about their decreasing opportunities in the decaying cities of the postindustrial west. The image of Bob Marley and other reggae artists, notably Peter Tosh, was also highly inspirational for young black reggae audiences. Marley's visual style reflected his Rastafarian beliefs. The Rasta dress code was characterized by tightly plaited hair (dreadlocks) and clothing made from natural fibers, such as cotton and wool, designed to produce a more authentic African look. Marley's image was eagerly latched onto and emulated by his audience. According to Hebdige, if other black youth cultural styles had been easily emulated by white youth, the Rasta presented as the living embodiment of a black aesthetic that was inaccessible to white youth. As such, the Rasta image, often much more than the religion behind it, became an important symbol of black identity and a form of symbolic resistance for black ethnic minority youth of western nations. Thus, as Hebdige notes in relation to the impact of the Rasta image on black youth in Britain during the mid-1970s,

[This] was a Rastafarianism at more than one remove, stripped of nearly all its original religious meanings: a distillation, a highly selective appropriation of all those elements of Rastafarianism which stressed the importance of resistance and black identity....The difference around which the whole Rasta style revolved was literally inscribed on the skin of black people and it was through appearance that this difference was to be extended, elaborated upon, realized. (1979, p. 43)

The late 1970s also saw the first commercial stirrings of rap, a musical style that was to have a crucial impact on the identity politics of the youth of ethnic minorities on a global scale. Rap originated during the early 1970s in the Bronx borough of New York City as an element of a street culture—also embracing graffiti art and breakdancing—known as *hip hop* (Lipsitz, 1994). Much of rap's appeal for its youth audience centered around the music's accessibility. Featuring spoken, or "rapped," lyrics as its main focus, rap dispensed with many of the conventions associated with previous genres of popular music, including the emphasis on proficiency at a musical instrument. This characteristic of rap gave the music an instant grassroots appeal that it retains to this day. The more commercially successful rappers command markets on a par with corporate rock giants such as the Rolling Stones and the Eagles (see Bennett, 1998, 1999, 2000). From the outset, rap's strong associations with the street and the fixation of its lyrics on urban problems such as crime, drugs, and gang violence gave the music a crucial resonance with its youth audience. Songs such as Grandmaster Flash's "White Lines" (a powerful antidrug statement) and Ice-T's "The Hunted Child" (a critique of black-on-black violence) remain key examples of rap's engagement with such issues and their very real impacts on the lives of young people, particularly those from ethnic minority backgrounds already disadvantaged through media stereotyping and concomitant social stigmatization.

Although rap's roots are in the ghetto culture of New York and other U.S. cities, since the early 1990s it has become an increasingly global form. Significantly, rap's global mobility has seen the diversification of the genre as artists and audiences in different locations have reworked the rap text in ways that engage with their specific socioeconomic and local cultural contexts (Bennett, 2001). There are now vibrant rap scenes across the globe in a variety of different locations, including France (Huq, 1999), Italy (Mitchell, 1996), Germany (Bennett, 2000), Japan (Condry, 1999), and the Pacific Rim (Maxwell & Bambrick, 1994). In each of these locations, rap has entered into a dialogue with particular social and cultural issues affecting young people on a day-to-day basis. In Germany, for example, rappers use a variety of languages, including German, Turkish, Moroccan, and English to engage with issues of racism and citizenship—these being key topics in one of the first commercially available German-language rap songs, Advanced Chemistry's "Fremd im Eigenen Land" ("A Foreigner in My Own Country").

A parallel, if less widely publicized, musical development that has also had a considerable impact on ethnic youth, particularly those of South Asian origin, is bhangra. Originally a Punjabi folk music, bhangra was fused with Western popular music styles by British Asian musicians during the early 1980s (Baumann, 1990). This new style of bhangra found an instant appeal among British Asian youth. Thus, as Banerji and Baumann observe, "The new style [of bhangra] was exactly what the new generation wanted. Young, fresh, lively and modern, it was as genuinely Indian as it was recognisably disco" (1990, p. 142). During the early 1990s, a new generation of what came to be referred to as post-bhangra musicians (Huq, 1996), among them Bali Sagoo and Apache Indian, fused the 1980s bhangra style with emergent urban dance music and rap genres to produce a bhangra-influenced style with a more contemporary feel that chimed well in the burgeoning club culture scene of the 1990s (Thornton, 1995). In the case of Apache Indian, the essence of his musical innovation marked a deliberate attempt to celebrate the multiethnic nature of his upbringing, the bhangra-muffin style for which he became well-known in the mid-1990s incorporating the bhangra and reggae styles that he had become accustomed to as a child growing up in the multiethnic district of Handsworth in the British city of Birmingham (see Back, 1996; Lipsitz, 1994).

## CONCLUSION

Although popular music in a post-1950 context has often been referred to as a youth music (Frith, 1983) or, more dramatically, as a soundtrack for youth, little attention has been paid to the actual representation of youth in and through popular music. However, as this chapter illustrates, since the early 1950s, issues pertaining to youth have often been saliently documented in popular music. In addition to themes of teen love and romance, which have become something of a perennial feature of several popular music genres, in many other cases representations of youth have been directly informed by particular socioeconomic and cultural circumstances pertaining to youth in specific eras. Indeed, it is fair to say that, since the advent of rock and roll, popular music has provided an important source of socialization for young people, serving as a key resource in the construction of individual as well as collective youth identities, and also providing the impetus for a range of alternative and resistant ideologies through which youth have been able to reject, or at least challenge, the dominant social institutions of the parent culture (see, for example, Chambers, 1985; Reich, 1971; Shumway, 1992). Moreover, as recent research illustrates, the impact of popular music in this way can no longer be regarded as an exclusively youth-centered phenomenon. Many individuals who came of age as punks, hippies, and so on have retained their musical tastes and attendant ideological sensibilities and practices into middle age and, increasingly, later life (see Bennett, 2008). My purpose in this chapter has been to examine, using illustrative examples, some of the ways in which the medium of popular music has engaged with and represented youth and youth culture over the last half-century. It is hoped that the basic themes and issues addressed in the chapter will form the basis for further research in this topic.

## REFERENCES

Back, L. (1996). *New ethnicities and urban culture: Racisms and multiculture in young lives.* London: LCL Press.

Banerji, S., & Baumann, G. (1990). Bhangra 1984–8: Fusion and professionalization in a genre of South Asian dance music. In P. Oliver (Ed.), *Black music in Britain: Essays on the Afro-Asian contribution to popular music* (pp. 137–152). Milton Keynes, UK: Open University Press.

Baumann, G. (1990). The re-invention of bhangra: Social change and aesthetic shifts in a Punjabi music in Britain. *Journal of the International Institute for Comparative Music Studies and Documentation, 32*(2), 81–95.

Beck, U. (1992). *The risk society.* London: Sage.

Becker, H. S. (1963). *Outsiders: Studies in the sociology of deviance.* New York: Free Press.

Bell, D. (Ed.). (1999). *Woodstock: An inside look at the movie that shook up the world and defined a generation.* Studio City, CA: Michael Wiese Productions.

Bennett, A. (1998). The Frankfurt rockmobil: A new insight into the significance of music-making for young people. *Youth and Policy, 60,* 16–29.

Bennett, A. (1999). Hip hop am Main: The localisation of rap music and hip hop culture. *Media, Culture and Society, 21*(1), 77–91.

Bennett, A. (2000). *Popular music and youth culture: Music, identity and place.* London: Macmillan.

Bennett, A. (2001) *Cultures of popular music.* Buckingham, UK: Open University Press.

Bennett, A. (2006). Punk's not dead: The significance of punk rock for an older generation of fans. *Sociology, 40,* 219–235.

Bennett, A. (2007). The forgotten decade: Rethinking the popular music of the 1970s. *Popular Music History, 2,* 5–24.

Bennett, A. (2008). *Growing old disgracefully? Popular music fandom and aging.* Unpublished manuscript.

Chambers, I. (1985). *Urban rhythms: Pop music and popular culture.* London: Macmillan.

Condry, I. (1999). The social production of difference: Imitation and authenticity in Japanese rap music. In H. Fehrenbach & U. Poiger (Eds.), *Transactions, transgressions, transformations: American culture in Western Europe and Japan* (pp. 166–184). Providence, RI: Berghan Books.

Frith, S. (1981). The magic that can set you free: The ideology of folk and the myth of rock. *Popular Music, 1*, 159–168.

Frith, S. (1983). *Sound effects: Youth, leisure and the politics of rock*. London: Constable.

Frith, S. (1997). Formalism, realism and leisure: The case of punk. In K. Gelder & S. Thornton (Eds.), *The subcultures reader* (pp. 163–174). London: Routledge.

Frith, S., & McRobbie, A. (1990). Rock and sexuality. In S. Frith & A. Goodwin (Eds.), *On record: Rock, pop and the written word* (pp. 371–389). London: Routledge.

Gillett, C. (1983). *The sound of the city: The rise of rock and roll* (2nd ed.). London: Souvenir Press.

Gilroy, P. (1993). *The Black Atlantic: Modernity and double consciousness*. London: Verso.

Hall, S., & Jefferson, T. (Eds.). (1976). *Resistance through rituals: Youth subcultures in post-war Britain*. London: Hutchinson.

Hebdige, D. (1979). *Subculture: The meaning of style*. London: Routledge.

Huq, R. (1996). Asian kool? Bhangra and beyond. In S. Sharma, J. Hutnyk, & A. Sharma (Eds.), *Dis-orienting rhythms: The politics of the new Asian dance music* (pp. 61–80). London: Zed Books.

Huq, R. (1999). Living in France: The parallel universe of hexagonal pop. In A. Blake (Ed.), *Living through pop* (pp. 130–165). London: Routledge.

Johnson, P. (1964, February 28). The menace of Beatlism. *The New Statesman*, 326–327.

Laing, D. (1985). *One chord wonders: Power and meaning in punk rock*. Milton Keynes, UK: Open University Press.

Le Breton, D. (2004). The anthropology of adolescent risk-taking behaviours. *Body & Society, 10*, 1–15.

Lewis, J. (1992). *The road to romance and ruin: Teen film and youth culture*. London: Routledge.

Lipsitz, G. (1994). *Dangerous crossroads: Popular music, postmodernism and the poetics of place*. London: Verso.

Lopes, P. (2002). *The rise of a jazz art world*. Cambridge, UK: Cambridge University Press.

Marcus, G. (1972). A new awakening. In R. S. Denisoff & R. A. Peterson (Eds.), *The sounds of social change* (pp. 127–137). Chicago: Rand McNally.

Maxwell, I., & Bambrick, N. (1994). Discourses of culture and nationalism in contemporary Sydney hip hop. *Perfect Beat, 2*, 1–19.

McRobbie, A., & Garber, J. (1976). Girls and subcultures: An exploration. In S. Hall & T. Jefferson (Eds.), *Resistance through rituals: Youth subcultures in post-war Britain* (pp. 209–222). London: Hutchinson.

Mitchell, T. (1996). *Popular music and local identity: Rock, pop and rap in Europe and Oceania*. London: Leicester University Press.

Mutsaers, L. (1990). Indorock: An early Eurorock style. *Popular Music, 9*, 307–320.

Oliver, P. (Ed.). (1990). *Black music in Britain: Essays on the Afro-Asian contribution to popular music*. Milton Keynes, UK: Open University Press.

Osgerby, B. (1998). *Youth in Britain since 1945*. Oxford, UK: Blackwell.

Palmer, T. (1976). *All you need is love: The story of popular music*. London: Futura.

Patrick, J. (1973). *The Glasgow gang observed.* London: Eyre Methuen.

Plasketes, G. M., & Plasketes, J. C. (1987). From Woodstock nation to Pepsi generation: Reflections on rock culture and the state of music, 1969–present. *Popular Music & Society, 2,* 225–252.

Reich, C. A. (1971) *The greening of America.* Middlesex, UK: Allen Lane.

Rimmer, D. (1985). *Like punk never happened: Culture Club and the new pop.* London: Faber and Faber.

Roszak, T. (1969). *The making of a counter culture: Reflections on the technocratic society and its youthful opposition.* London: Faber and Faber.

Savage, J. (1992). *England's dreaming: Sex Pistols and punk rock.* London: Faber and Faber.

Shuker, R. (2001). *Understanding popular music* (2nd ed.). London and New York: Routledge.

Shumway, D. (1992). Rock and roll as a cultural practice. In A. DeCurtis (Ed.), *Present tense: Rock and roll and culture* (pp. 117–134). Durham, NC: Duke University Press.

Snowman, D. (1984). *America since 1920.* London: Heineman.

Taylor, I., & Wall, D. (1976). Beyond the skinheads: Comments on the emergence and significance of the Glamrock cult. In G. Mungham & G. Pearson (Eds.), *Working class youth culture* (pp. 105–123). London: Routledge and Kegan Paul.

Thornton, S. (1995). *Club cultures: Music, media and subcultural capital.* Cambridge, UK: Polity Press.

Willis, P. (1978). *Profane culture.* London: Routledge and Kegan Paul.

Zak III, A. J. (2001). *The poetics of rock, cutting tracks, making records.* Berkeley and Los Angeles: University of California Press.

# 3

## Music Videos

### Media of the Youth, by the Youth, for the Youth

MICHAEL RICH

August 1981 started with a watershed event—the launching of a new broadcast medium and cultural phenomenon (MTV, 2001). At 12:01 A.M., with the portentous words, "Ladies and gentlemen, rock and roll!," images of a nighttime broadcast from twelve summers earlier, the first man walking on the moon, were aired to half a million American homes. In this case, the flag planted by the astronaut read "MTV Music Television"[1] (superscript numbers refer to endnotes that contain links to the video on YouTube, adding much to the understanding of the text). Having asserted its self-proclaimed position in contemporary history, the new network broadcast "Video Killed the Radio Star,"[2] an audiovisual rendition of a Buggles song popular in Great Britain and Australia two years earlier. Although the inaugural viewing audience was not huge and the importance of the event was self-generated by MTV, the music video rapidly vaulted to prominence during the 1980s as the sentinel entertainment medium of youth. Despite self-promoting claims of innovation and youth's rapid embrace of music videos as something new, this was not a new medium, but the latest incarnation of a long-established creative form that melded music and image.

# MUSIC VIDEO AS A DISTINCT MEDIUM

In their most common format, music videos couple a single piece of music with images to create a short audiovisual production intended to promote sales of recorded music (Frith, Goodwin, & Grossberg, 1993). Music video as a distinct form was codified, but hardly invented, by MTV when they launched their twenty-four-hour broadcast of music videos in a Top-40 radio format, complete with "VJs" and countdowns of the top-selling recordings.

## Historical Predecessors

From the time that motion pictures were first presented as entertainment, music accompanied animated, live action, and abstract images. At the turn of the twentieth century, silent films were accompanied by a pianist, organist, or, in showcase first-run theaters, a live orchestra (Parkinson, 1995). (Even these early combinations of images, story, and music had precursors; live images and music had already been combined to create opera for three and ballet for four centuries.) In the 1920s, Oskar Fischinger composed "visual music," animated films with dedicated orchestral scores, and created what may have been the first music videos, cartoons promoting Electrola Records's latest releases (Moritz, 2004). *Song Car-Tunes* was a mid-1920s version of video karaoke that encouraged audiences to sing along to popular melodies by "following the bouncing ball" (Fleischer, 2005). Most of the perennial animated cartoon series used music as a central component, a feature acknowledged in their titles: *Silly Symphonies*, *Merrie Melodies*, and the ever-popular *Looney Tunes*.[3] A 1929 Russian documentary film, *Man With a Movie Camera*,[4] synchronized rapidly edited documentary footage with a tightly synchronized live orchestral score (Hicks, 2007) and Eisenstein choreographed live-action battle scenes to an original score by Prokofiev in 1938's *Alexander Nevsky*[5] (Bordwell, 1994). Thousands of "soundies," single-song movies of jazz musicians, cabaret singers, and dancers performing their latest work, played in visual jukeboxes during the early 1940s, but disappeared during World War II (Bewley, n.d.).

## Media of Youth

Each of these historical predecessors has been proposed as a key ancestor to the contemporary music video, but it took the emergence of the teenager as a social phenomenon during the affluent postwar years to create the environment in which the music video would evolve. During World War II, the United States had rapidly transformed into a high-powered industrial economy. After the war, millions of veterans returned to the workforce. For the first time, a majority of adolescents completed high school, which became a massive, communal "coming of age" experience. Youth saw themselves as different from their parents—fresh, free, and exciting. They flocked to *The Wild One* and *Rebel Without a Cause*, movie portrayals that reflected teenagers' independent identities. White youth rejected mainstream popular music, reaching across racial barriers to mine the rich traditions of rhythm and blues (R & B) for a music of their own, rock and roll. Since its emergence in the 1950s, rock and roll has been about exuberance, desire, questioning authority, and brooding discontent. It is embraced by youth and, even better, rejected by their parents.

Fueled by rock and roll, youth culture exploded, with music and movies portraying adolescence as a time of devil-may-care fun, romance, and rebellion, reflecting and fueling adolescents' quests for autonomy. It was only a matter of time before music and moving pictures were joined. Elvis Presley rode the wave of his recording successes into motion pictures. In 1956, he co-starred in *Love Me Tender*,[6] a film in which he performed the title song and three others, promoted with the tagline, "It's Mr. Rock 'n' Roll...in the story he was born to play!" (*Love Me Tender*, 1956) This would be the first of thirty-one feature films in which, with one exception, Elvis would perform his current hit songs (Szatmary, 1996).

In 1959, "The Big Bopper," J. P. Richardson, first used the term "music video" in a magazine article (Anonymous, n.d.), but in 1961, Ozzie Nelson, who had been creating regular music slots for his son on *The Adventures of Ozzie and Harriet*, directed and edited what many believe to be the first contemporary music video of Ricky's song, "Travelin' Man"[7] (Frith et al., 1993). Three years later, Richard Lester established the vocabulary and structure of the music video genre in the feature film, *A Hard Day's Night*,[8] combining Beatles songs with visual sequences that intercut both concert footage and narrative visuals that illustrated or counterpointed the lyrics (Yule, 1994). Using a similar audiovisual vocabulary to make *Help!*[9] shortly thereafter, the Beatles started creating short films of individual songs, a promotional strategy for which, by 1966, they abandoned concert tours.

Hollywood knew a winning formula. The Monkees[10] were originally a fictional rock group cast from open acting auditions for "four insane boys" to create a television series that sought to emulate the style and success of *A Hard Day's Night* and *Help!* (Sandoval, 2005). The program featured the goofy antics of the attractive cast, jumpy editing, and fantasy sequences, centering on a self-contained music video–like vignette based on a single song (Reilly, McManus, & Chadwick, 1993). Ironically, the unexpected success of the television show, for which the performers sang but did not play their assigned instruments, forced them into crash lessons and rehearsals so that they could perform live as a real rock group (Lefcowitz, 1989). In spite of their fictional beginnings, the Monkees went on to become one of the most commercially successful acts of the 1960s.

The evolving music video form encouraged visual experimentation that could not be attempted in mainstream television or movies. Kenneth Anger used popular songs of the 1950s and 1960s instead of dialogue to tell the controversial homoerotic biker story of his 1964 experimental film *Scorpio Rising*.[11] In the 1966 *Subterranean Homesick Blues*,[12] Bob Dylan, instead of playing and singing the song, stood in front of the camera, flashing cue cards of the lyrics. These attempts to break out of straight documentation of musical performances gave rise to "concept videos," which used narrative or abstract imagery to portray the ideas and feelings of the song. Incorporating the aesthetics of contemporary art and avant garde cinema, concept videos firmly established themselves during the psychedelic era. The Beatles, joined by the Doors and the Rolling Stones and later David Bowie and Pink Floyd, experimented with the integration of music and feature films. Cinema classics of this period like *Easy Rider*[13] and *Rocky Horror Picture Show*[14] are remembered more for the music than for the film. Alan Parker's (1982) motion picture of *Pink Floyd The Wall*[15] brought music and image together on an equal footing, ushering in the contemporary era of the music video.

The advent of MTV was a result, rather than the cause of the golden age of music video during the 1980s. Broadcast quality electronic technology had finally become inexpensive enough that even start-up music groups could produce videos with minimal investment and small, often inexperienced crews. Video editing and electronic techniques such as bluescreen, animated transitions, and morphing allowed low-cost experimentation. Music videos became the way to break into the motion picture industry. Tyros fresh out of film school flocked to outdo each other, youth making video for youth about the experience of youth. Broadcast television allowed bands to present their work to audiences exponentially larger than any they could reach with a concert tour. MTV arose from this fertile turmoil as an inevitability rather than an innovation.

From its modest beginnings, MTV grew rapidly, reaching over twenty-seven million American households by 1986 and over fifty-two million by 1990 (Pember, 1992). The success of MTV and its 24/7 music video format provided lucrative opportunities for networks broadcasting different musical genres, including Country Music Television (CMT), Black Entertainment Television (BET), and Video Hits-1 (VH-1). Music video was at its height, artistically and commercially, and the majority of research and commentary on this media form was produced during the two decades after

MTV's birth. Music videos became the rock and roll of the 1980s, with youth watching many hours each week and their parents remaining clueless (Bleich, Zillmann, & Weaver, 1991).

## METHODS OF FINDING THE CONTENT AND INFLUENCES OF MUSIC VIDEOS

Research on the influence of media on youth has been conducted around the world by scientists in least thirteen different disciplines, whose literature is scattered across more than twenty databases. Data on music videos, what they portray about and for youth, and how they might affect young people have been accessed through the Database of Research at the Center on Media and Child Health (CMCH) based at Children's Hospital Boston, Harvard Medical School. Seeking to establish a single reliable source of rigorous scientific information on how media affect human health and development, CMCH has built and continues to develop a comprehensive database of the research literature on how media affect the physical, mental, and social health of young people. Posted at www.cmch.tv, searchable by keywords, and with a natural-language search engine, by September 2007 the CMCH Database of Research had collected 9,146 discrete papers, articles, and books on the subject, of which 3,979 were original research. Of these, 135 papers addressed the content and effects of music videos on youth.

### Who Is Watching, and Why?

In the mid-1980s, a study of 600 high school students showed that 80% reported that they watched MTV for an average of more than two hours each day; nearly 75% had watched it in the last several days (Sun & Lull, 1986). A survey in the late 1990s from the Annenberg Public Policy Center indicated that 53% of 10- to 17-year-olds watched MTV at that time (Annenberg Public Policy Center, 1997). A 2003 survey found that three-quarters of 16- to 24-year-olds watched MTV, with 58% watching weekly or more often and 20% watching for at least an hour every day (Rideout, 2003).

When youth were surveyed on why they watched MTV, most stated they wanted to be entertained, to watch particular groups, singers, and concerts, to learn how to play musical instruments, and to figure out how to dance, dress, or relate to others (Sun & Lull, 1986). Youth acknowledge that they learn from music videos, using them as socializing agents, tools with which they try to understand the world and develop an individual identity in it.

## The Effects of Music Videos on Youth

Ever since the rapid penetration of television into American homes in the early 1950s, there has been public concern about what television showed and how it affected young people (Smith, 1952). Between 1952 and 1955, the United States Senate conducted a series of hearings to determine whether television contributed to juvenile delinquency (Hoerrner, 1999). Over the ensuing fifty years, experimental and epidemiological studies have investigated the effects of entertainment media, especially television, on the development of attitudes, beliefs, and behaviors among youth users (Ashby & Rich, 2005; Austin & Meili, 1994; Brown, Walsh-Childers, & Steele, 2002; Bushman & Huesmann, 2006; Connolly, Casswell, Zhang, & Silva, 1994; Hearold, 1986; Klein et al., 1993; Rich, 2003; Sargent et al., 2005; Villani, 2001).

The accumulated evidence suggests that media content does influence adolescents, but there are several theories as to how this occurs. Social learning theory proposes that observing a behavior portrayed in media establishes it as normative, resulting in decreased inhibitions and a more positive attitude toward it, making the viewer more likely to engage in the behavior (Bandura, 1977). Cultivation theory suggests that heavy users of media develop perspectives, beliefs, and attitudes more consistent with media portrayals than with reality, so viewers of violent television develop the "mean world syndrome," seeing the world as a dangerous place (Gerbner, Gross, Morgan, & Signorielli, 1994). Cognitive priming theory proposes that behaviors portrayed and reinforced on television are encoded in the viewer's memory and readily accessible, potentially altering the individual's perceptions of and responses to real-life situations (Hansen, 1988). The media practice model establishes that the influence of media varies with age, gender, race, and other individual characteristics. This is because viewers choose, view, attend to, and interpret media through many aspects of their individual identities, and they eventually incorporate what they learn from media into their identities (Brown & Steele, 1995). Music videos can influence young people's perceptions, choices, and behaviors, but the age, race, gender, and life experiences of each viewer strongly influence how youth synthesize music video content.

## Youth as Music Video Viewers

How music videos are perceived and understood varies with the viewer's age (Greenfield, Bruzzone, Koyamatsu, & Satuloff, 1987). Among 9- to 12-year-olds, younger children were found to interpret music videos concretely, while preadolescents grasped abstract concepts presented by the video (Christenson, 1992; Christenson & Roberts, 1998). In a study assessing the influence of the viewer's gender and gender role self-perceptions on affective responses to soft ("tender"), neutral, or hard ("rebellious") music videos (Toney & Weaver, 1994), females preferred soft videos, but underestimated how much males liked them and how disturbed males were by all three types of videos. Males preferred hard music videos, but underestimated how much females liked them and overestimated how much females were disturbed by them. Viewer gender influences the effects of music videos on sexual risk behaviors—the correlation between video viewing and permissive sexual behavior has been found to be stronger for adolescent females than for males (Strouse, Buerkel-Rothfuss, & Long, 1995).

Gender and race combine to modify viewers' perceptions of music videos, whether the videos depict characters of different races or not. For one study, white and African American males and females 18 to 34 years old viewed the Madonna video *Papa Don't Preach*,[16] which features only white characters. African American youth predominantly interpreted the "baby" mentioned in the lyrics to mean a romantic partner, rather than the unborn child. Focusing on the relationships between individuals in the song, 50% of African American females and 43% of African American males interpreted the music video as being about the father–daughter relationship, as opposed to only 25% of white females and 22% of white males who saw it that way. White viewers (63% of the females and 56% of the males) perceived the *Papa Don't Preach* video to be about pregnancy, but only 40% of African American females and 21% of African American males understood it the same way (Brown & Schulze, 1990).

*Open Your Heart*,[17] a video about female sexuality that featured only white actors, also elicited responses that diverged on gender–race lines. White viewers, 50% of female and 43% of males, perceived the video to be about pornography, sexual perversion, or women as sexual objects, but only 22% of African American females and 21% of African American males agreed. Some white males (16%) were "turned on" by the video, but only 3 to 4% of the other race–gender categories responded similarly. African American females were more likely to think the video was about platonic love, and African American males and females were much more likely to think there was no clear theme to the video (Brown & Schulze, 1990).

## Do Music Videos Have a Unique Influence on Youth?

The synergy of music and television, two youth media, may have additive effects on the knowledge, attitudes, and behavior of youth (Greenfield & Beagles-Roos, 1988; Zillman & Mundorf, 1987). Music's powerful emotional effect on young people can alter viewers' receptivity and potentiate their responses to visual or narrative content (Rosenfeld, 1985). Images accompanied by music, especially music with which youth identify, can have a stronger effect than either the music or the images alone (Abt, 1987; Larson & Kubey, 1983). The addition of the visual component has been found to increase appreciation of the music (Zillman & Mundorf, 1987). College students described liking music videos better than music alone, because the combination of music and visuals was more "potent" (Rubin et al., 1986) and other research demonstrated that most music video viewers "always" or "frequently" visualized images from the music video when listening to an audio-only version of the song (Abt, 1987). These findings appear to indicate that youth would rather accept a prepackaged visualization of the music over their own imaginative response. Vision is our most effective sense for learning about the world, but music has a powerful influence on our emotions, coloring our understanding of and feelings about the images we view. The potent synergy between images and music can influence the attitudes and behaviors of youth who use them as socializing agents more powerfully than music or television alone.

## MUSIC VIDEO CONTENT

Content analyses of music videos and related effects research indicate, not surprisingly, that music videos strongly reflect key issues of the developmental challenges faced by youth: human relationships and how to manage them, how they feel about themselves, and how they are to achieve autonomy and establish themselves in the world. The themes of music videos—relationships with other genders, races, and romantic partners; the use of tobacco, alcohol, and other drugs; threats and violence toward others and themselves—correlate strongly with the health risks and behaviors of this age group (Ashby & Rich, 2005).

### Violence, Weapon-Carrying, and Suicide

Music videos are a creative amalgamation of popular music, movies, and television, media where many adolescents find role models. Protagonists in music videos are frequently portrayed as the perpetrators of interpersonal violence, which may serve to normalize these behaviors and socialize adolescents to accept them (Rehman & Reilly, 1985). Media violence and its influence on viewers is the most investigated area of media effects, generating more than 2,000 research reports on its prevalence, nature, and effects on viewers.

Two separate content analyses of music videos in the mid-1980s found that more than half of the videos broadcast portrayed violent behavior, often with exciting music and rapid editing that reinforced conceptual connections between violence and pleasure. In the first study (Baxter, De Rimer, Landini, Leslie, & Singletary, 1985), 26% of the videos studied portrayed interpersonal violence, 11% showed weapons being used, 8% depicted self-harming, and 3% contained murders. In the second, unrelated study (Sherman & Dominick, 1986), children were twice as likely as adults to be victims, while middle-aged adult males, often authority figures, were the perpetrators of violence in nearly 75% of the music videos.

In a study by this author of music videos in the mid-1990s, violence and weapon-carrying portrayals were more prevalent on MTV than on any of the other major music video networks, with 25% of videos demonstrating weapon carrying and 22% depicting violence (DuRant, Rich, et al., 1997). CMT and BET each broadcast 12% violent videos, closely followed by VH-1 at 11%. BET was a distant second in weapon-carrying portrayals (12%), followed by VH-1 at 8% and CMT at 7%. Across music genres, rap showed 22% overt violence, rock was second with nearly 20%, and country and western music had least at 11%. Violent characters tended to be young or middle-aged adults, but 11% of the videos portrayed children being violent and 15% showed children carrying weapons. An unrelated content analysis examining videos by music genre found that rap had significantly more talk of weapons and illegal substances, alcohol use, profanity, and gambling than any other genre, but there were no differences between genres in the prevalence of shootings, beatings, and stabbings (Jones, 1997). More recent research (Smith & Boyson, 2002) has demonstrated that rap videos continue to portray significantly more violence (29%) than rock (12%), R & B (9%), or adult contemporary (7%) music.

Youth viewers often admire and identify with the lead singer or characters in a music video. In further studies by this author, the protagonist of the music video was the perpetrator of over 80% and the victim of only 18% of the violence portrayed (Rich, Woods, Goodman, Emans, & DuRant, 1998). There were striking differences in the race and gender of aggressors and victims. African Americans were portrayed perpetrating violence twice as frequently as expected based on a representative population and were much more likely to be victims of violence than their white counterparts. Among African Americans, a male was the aggressor in 91% and the victim in 97% of the portrayals, while among whites, a male was violent 72% and a woman victimized 78% of the time.

Research examining whether music video viewing can directly influence violent attitudes or behaviors among youth has yielded varied results. Tenth grade students who watched violent music videos were more likely than other tenth graders to believe that a violent response to an attack is justified (Greeson & Williams, 1986). In a study testing whether the effects of music video viewing supported the cultivation theory, there was an only weak association between watching music videos and beliefs about the prevalence of violence in society among seventh and eleventh graders (Walker, 1987). The frequency and severity of aggressive behavior among youth patients of a maximum-security forensic psychiatric hospital was studied before and after removal of MTV from the hospital television system. Controlling for potential confounders, a 37% decrease in the overall frequency of verbal abuse and physical aggression against others and objects was observed following cessation of music video broadcasts (Waite, Hillbrand, & Foster, 1992).

Since content analyses have found rap and hip-hop music videos to portray more violence than those of other musical genres (DuRant, Rich, et al., 1997; Jones, 1997), several studies have examined the effects of this genre on viewers. Randomized into groups that viewed no music videos, nonviolent rap videos, and rap videos with violent images, acts, or lyrics condoning violence, 11- to 16-year-old African American males who watched the violent videos demonstrated greater acceptance of the use of violence and of violence against women, and reported a higher likelihood of committing the violent acts portrayed in the videos (Johnson, Jackson, & Gatto, 1995b). Compared to infrequent rap video viewers, African American female youth who reported frequently watching rap videos were three times more likely to have hit a teacher and 2.5 times more likely to have been arrested at twelve-month follow-up (Wingood et al., 2003).

In his classic social learning experiments Bandura showed that viewers who saw violence rewarded or condoned were more likely to imitate the behavior (Bandura, Ross, & Ross, 1963). With no punishment or pain resulting from violence and no empathy expressed, there is little to dissuade viewers from learning violence as an appropriate and effective means of conflict resolution. To estimate the risk of violence being learned, researchers assessed the context in which music video violence occurred, as well as the way in which aggressors and victims were portrayed (Smith & Boyson, 2002). There were no repercussions or punishment for nearly 80% of the violent perpetrators, with 74% showing them "getting away with it." Victims of violence showed no evidence of pain or suffering from 72% of the violent acts and no harm from 56%; only 11% showed significant negative outcomes. Comparing the context of music video violence across networks, 27% of the violence on BET, 21% on MTV, and 5% on VH-1 was portrayed as justified.

Although suicidal imagery and themes are relatively rare in music videos, self-loathing, rage, and risk-taking portrayals are much more common, particularly in heavy metal music (Arnett, 1991; Roberts, Dimsdale, East, & Friedman, 1998). Most youth who preferred heavy metal acknowledged that their favorite music contained messages of drugs, violence, suicide, death, war, and satanism, but only 33% felt that they connected with the messages (Martin, Clarke, & Pearce, 1993). Nevertheless, heavy metal listeners held lower survival and coping beliefs and reported weaker reasons for living than nonfans. Male listeners had lower moral objections to suicide, while the self-reported suicide risk of female heavy metal fans was higher than that of females who preferred other types of music (Scheel & Westefeld, 1999). A randomized control experiment found that youth who watched music videos depicting suicide had significantly higher negative affect and wrote more stories with suicidal or hostile themes than controls who watched music videos without suicide depictions; youth who listened to and read suicidal song lyrics wrote more suicidal themed stories but experienced no change in affect (Rustad, Small, Jobes, Safer, & Peterson, 2003). The suicidal content was communicated both by the lyrics alone and by the music videos, but the combination of music and images more powerfully engaged viewers' emotions and influenced their feelings.

### Tobacco, Alcohol, and Other Drug Use

Exposure to musicians and other stars using tobacco, alcohol, and other drugs in music videos may warp youths' perceptions of how many people use substances, how well they "handle" them, and how desirable substance use might be. As public health efforts have successfully banned televised advertising for tobacco and limited it for alcohol, portrayal of their use by attractive role models has become more prevalent in program material aimed at youth, such as teen-oriented television shows, movies, and music videos. Even when legally prohibited from paying for product placement, the tobacco industry has managed to get their products into the hands and mouths of popular stars under the condition that the production not associate smoking with negative behaviors or health effects (Mekemson & Glantz, 2002).

Content analyses of music videos have found tobacco and alcohol portrayals to be more prevalent than they actually are in real life. The Cultural Indicators Project at the University of Pennsylvania found that half of all music videos in 1998 portrayed the use of tobacco, alcohol, or other drugs as normative and often attractive behaviors (Gerbner, 2001).

As with violence, the prevalence and nature of substance use portrayals in music videos varies across broadcasters and music genres. In a content analysis from this author that assessed music videos shown during peak adolescent viewing hours in 1994 (DuRant, Rome, et al., 1997), MTV broadcast the highest proportion of music videos portraying smoking (26%), followed by VH-1 (23%), BET (17%), and CMT (12%). Smokeless tobacco use was much less common, with CMT leading at 1.9%, followed by MTV (1.3%), and BET (0.6%), with no portrayals on VH-1. Rap videos were more likely than other music video genres to portray smoking (30%), followed by adult contemporary (23%), rock (22%), country and western (12%), and R & B (11%). Smokeless tobacco was shown in 2% of country and western, 1% of R & B, rap, and rock, and 0% of adult contemporary music videos. Cigarette advertising appeared in 3% of MTV music videos, followed by 2% of VH-1, and 1% of CMT and BET videos. Rock videos had the highest prevalence of cigarette advertising (3%), followed by rap (2%), R & B and country and western (1%), with no advertising appearing in adult contemporary videos.

Alcohol use portrayals were most prevalent in MTV music videos (27%), followed by VH-1 (25%), CMT (21%), and BET (19%), while alcohol advertising was most common in CMT videos (7%), followed by VH-1 (5%), MTV (4%), and BET (3%). By music video genre, alcohol use was depicted in 27% of rap, 25% of rock, 21% of country and western, 19% of adult contemporary, and 17% of R & B. Advertising for alcohol was shown in 6% of country and western, 4% of rap and rock, 3% of adult contemporary, and 2% of R & B.

In music videos where tobacco or alcohol use occurred, the lead singer and actors were more likely to be using than other performers. The proportions of youth portrayed smoking (76%) or drinking alcohol (68%) were high. In all, 6 to 10% of the music videos portrayed illegal use of tobacco or alcohol based on apparent age of the performer. There was a positive emotional tone in 74% of the smoking scenes and 77% of the drinking scenes, and alcohol use was significantly associated with attractiveness and sexual activity (DuRant, Rome, et al., 1997). Portraying substance use as risk free and attractive increases the likelihood that adolescents will initiate substance use themselves (Bauman, Botvin, Botvin, & Baker, 1992).

A 2005 content analysis of MTV and BET found portrayals of tobacco, alcohol, or other drugs in 43% of network music videos (Gruber, Thau, Hill, Fisher, & Grube, 2005). Alcohol appeared in 35% of the videos, with 10% showing consumption, and 9% alcohol branding. Tobacco was shown in 10%, consumed in 8%, and product logos were prominent in 2%. Illicit drug paraphernalia was shown in 13% and drugs were used in 1%. Substance use in rap videos was nearly twice that appearing in other genres. Humor was 2.5 times as likely to be present in videos portraying substances as in those without substances.

Several studies have demonstrated an association between music video viewing and an increased risk of initiating alcohol use during adolescence (Connolly et al., 1994; Klein et al., 1993). Among 2,546 first- and fourth-year students in Belgium, the 68% who reported watching music videos several times a week or more often was 196% more likely to drink "alcopops" at home. Sweetened, malt liquor alcopops, which are often labeled as known hard liquor brands but taste like soft drinks, are frequently the entry drink for those initiating alcohol use. For each additional hour of TV watched by youth in the study, they were 17% more likely to be alcopop drinkers. Those who viewed music videos several times a week or more were 239% more likely to drink alcopops when going out; while each additional hour of TV watched was predictive of a 19% increase in drinking alcopops when going out (Van den Bulck, Beullens, & Mulder, 2006). Both music video viewing and television watching increased the risk of drinking alcopops, either at home or when going out, but the effects of music video viewing were dramatically more potent. Research with 1,533 ninth graders in the United States found that, among nondrinkers, music video viewers had a 131% increased risk of starting to drink in the ensuing eighteen months. In another Belgian study, both music video and television viewing at time 1 were significantly predictive of alcohol consumption one year later, even when controlling for gender, pubertal, tobacco, and previous alcohol use status (Van den Bulck & Beullens, 2005). In the United States, African American females who watched rap videos were 1.5 times more likely to use alcohol and illicit drugs within the subsequent twelve months (Wingood et al., 2003).

## Body Image, Gender Roles, and Sexual Violence

For youth who are establishing themselves as autonomous individuals and learning how to be "cool," music videos portray ideals of how males and females are expected to look, act, and relate to each other. Music videos provide very specific socializing messages about the roles, responsibilities, and behavior of their gender in society (Gow, 1993; Seidman, 1992, 1999).

Because of their visual "shorthand" and the potent synergy of images and songs, music videos powerfully communicate sociocultural ideals and can strongly influence young women's dissatisfaction with their bodies (Thompson, Pingree, Hawkins, & Draves, 1991). Perfect bodies, often anatomically or technically altered, proliferate in music videos and other youth-oriented media. Physical objectification and perspectives that value looks over substance may influence the expectations that youth of both genders have for their own appearance. Exposure to body ideals of impossibly thin women and unrealistically muscular men can contribute to negative self-images and viewers' attempts to alter their bodies through restrictive eating, exercise, or appearance-enhancing drugs or surgery.

Although neither overall media use nor any other media type were associated with specific attitudes toward personal weight or appearance among more than 800 ninth grade females, music video viewing has been significantly correlated with personal concern about weight and appearance (Borzekowski, Robinson, & Killen, 2000). In Australia, similar results were found among female youth. Even though overall television viewing was not associated with increased body image concerns, watching music videos, soap operas, and movies was associated (Tiggeman & Pickering, 1996). In a randomized control study where female college students viewed seven music videos featuring thin or normal weight females, those who viewed the "thin ideal" videos felt fatter, less attractive, and less satisfied than those who watched the "normal weight" videos (Tiggeman & Slater, 2004).

A pair of content analyses were conducted on MTV videos broadcast five years apart to assess the nature of gender role portrayals and determine what changes occurred over time. At time 1, males outnumbered females two to one, with a skewed distribution of occupations by gender (Seidman, 1992). Males played all of the scientists, politicians, and business executives and more than 90% of the soldiers, security officers, police, photographers, and athletes. All of the fashion models and telephone operators and over 80% of the hair stylists and dancers were females. Male characters were portrayed as more aggressive, violent, and dominating than females. The follow-up study found little change in the stereotyped portrayals of which genders pursued which occupations, but less gender stereotyped behavior was found (Seidman, 1999). Another study found that the advertising as well as the music videos on MTV consistently followed specific gender stereotypes. Commercials for cosmetics, clothes, and other products to enhance personal attractiveness targeted women and featured predominantly female characters; ads for entertainment and action-oriented fun focused on and featured males (Signorielli, McLeod, & Healy, 1994).

A content analysis of music videos broadcast on MTV during 1985 found that 55% condescendingly portrayed females as sex objects and targets of aggressive sexual behavior; only 16% treated women as equals (Vincent, Davis, & Boruszkowski, 1987). A second study of videos broadcast about one year later found a modest improvement—42% of the videos objectified females and 39% of videos portrayed women as equal to men (Vincent, 1989).

College students who have viewed music videos portraying female and male stereotypes have been shown to judge the behavior of male and female characters more stereotypically than students who had not seen the videos (Hansen, 1988). A more recent study compared youth who had viewed a music video with traditional gender stereotyping to those who viewed a video without gender stereotyping. After viewing the stereotype videos, male youth were more likely to endorse adversarial sexual beliefs, gender role stereotyping, and rape myths, and females were more accepting of interpersonal violence between males and females (Kalof, 1999). Experimental studies have shown that portrayals of women being demeaned or injured by men in music videos can change the attitudes of both males and females toward interpersonal relationships, making both genders more accepting of violence as part of a sexual relationship (Malamuth & Briere, 1986; Malamuth & Check, 1981; Peterson & Pfost, 1989; Ward & Hansbrough, 2005).

Research examining the relationships between music video viewing and attitudes toward gender roles among African American youth found that those who watched videos more frequently held more traditional gender role attitudes and attached greater importance to personal appearance than to substance. After viewing four music videos with stereotypical gender role portrayals, both males and females endorsed more sexual stereotypes and males attributed greater importance to appearance (Ward & Hansbrough, 2005). In this author's research, males were the perpetrators of violence over three times as frequently as females, and white females were the race–gender group most likely to be portrayed as victims (Rich et al., 1998). Female youth who watched nonviolent rap videos with women in sexually subordinate roles showed an increased acceptance of violence against women (Johnson, Jackson, & Gatto, 1995a).

## Sex

Coming into their own as sexual beings is one of the major tasks of adolescents. Understanding how to behave as a sexual being is a critical goal. A national survey of adolescents found that they ranked TV and movies after only school sex education and parents as their leading source of information about pregnancy and birth control (Farrar et al., 2003). Four out of five youth report that their peers learn "some or a lot" about sex from media (Kunkel, Cope, & Biely, 1999). Since music videos are aimed at a youth audience, sexual themes and concerns figure predominantly.

Of the top twenty singles for each year of music videos' peak popularity in the 1980s, 85% of the songs referred to sex and 72% had sexuality as the dominant theme (Edwards, 1994). Although sexual content has been found to enhance viewers' enjoyment of music videos, the combination of sex and violence decreases it (Hansen & Hansen, 1990). A content analysis of music videos in the mid-1980s found that nearly 50% communicated sexual themes through lyrics or imagery (Greeson & Williams, 1986), while another study showed that 60% portrayed sexual feelings or impulses primarily using innuendo, clothing, suggestive movements, and light physical contact (Baxter et al., 1985). Another found sexual images in over 75% of the music videos analyzed, that half of the women portrayed were provocatively dressed, and that sexual intimacy occurred an average of four times per video. Of the videos that portrayed violence, 81% contained sexual imagery (Sherman & Dominick, 1986). A more recent analysis found a lower percentage of videos with sexuality or eroticism, but portrayals of more explicit behavior in those with sexual themes (DuRant, Rome, et al., 1997).

As with violence and substance use, sexual content in music videos has been shown to vary by musical genre and network. The highest levels of sexual content, including scanty dress, fondling, sexualized dancing, and simulated intercourse, have been found in hip-hop and R & B videos (Jones, 1997), and rap, soul, and pop music videos have been shown to communicate sexual innuendo, symbolism, or explicit sexual references more frequently than country, heavy metal, alternative, and classic rock (Tapper, Thorson, & Black, 1994). African Americans engage in sexual behavior more than twice as frequently as white characters in music videos (Brown & Campbell, 1986). Although committed relationships and marriage were portrayed as positive less than 30% of the time, dating and sex were portrayed as positive nearly 60% of the time (Brown & Campbell, 1986).

The effect of music videos on sexual attitudes, beliefs, and behaviors has not been thoroughly studied (Escobar-Chaves et al., 2005; Rich, 2005). Seventh and tenth grade students who viewed MTV prior to completing a survey about sexual attitudes were much more likely to approve of premarital sex than students who did not view music videos beforehand (Greeson & Williams, 1986). High school students 14 to 18 years old who watched more music videos were found to have a higher level of sexual experience than their peers (D. S. Ward & Friedman, 2006). College students who viewed an erotic music video were more likely to demonstrate "liberal sexual attitudes" than those who viewed a nonerotic or no-music video (Calfin, Carroll, & Shmidt, 1993). Among female undergraduates, music video viewing was the only media exposure positively associated with a permissive sexual attitude (Strouse & Buerkel-Rothfuss, 1987). In one of the few studies to use biological outcomes to examine the relationship between exposure to music videos and sexual behavior, Wingood et al. found that greater exposure to rap music videos among African American females was associated with twice the likelihood of having multiple sexual partners and 1.5 times the risk of having a laboratory-documented infection with chlamydia, gonorrhea, or trichomonas within the next year (Wingood et al., 2003).

## THE SHORT, HAPPY LIFE OF MUSIC VIDEOS

Music videos enjoyed a meteoric rise in popularity and importance through the 1980s. From their underground and avant garde beginnings, music videos responded to their success with increasingly large budgets and complex productions. In 1983, music videos began airing on TBS and then NBC, allowing them to be seen by a much broader audience. *Thriller*,[18] Michael Jackson's fourteen-minute all-singing, all-dancing horror mini-movie dramatically transformed the gritty music video into big-budget Hollywood extravaganza in 1984. That same year, the Grammys gave their first awards for Best Short- and Long-Form Music Videos and the MTV Video Music Awards were launched. In the 1990s, MTV began to give on-screen credits to directors, and music videos became an auteur's medium rather than just a springboard to more prestigious productions. At least seventy-one television networks around the world specialized in music videos. In 1995, Michael Jackson's *Scream*,[19] at $7 million the most expensive music video to date, was released to an already waning audience that responded with indifference. By then, MTV had largely replaced music videos with more traditional television content, a mix of reality TV (a genre they spawned with *The Real World*), animation, comedies, novelty shows like *Jackass*, and music videos. The network launched MTV2 in 1996 and MTV Hits in 2002 as attempts to re-establish a successful twenty-four-hour music video channel. Today, six hours or less of MTV's broadcast day are dedicated to music videos, and those are from 4 A.M. to 10 A.M., low youth viewership periods. In February 2000, MTV broadcast its millionth music video, a reprise of *Video Killed the Radio Star*, as part of a rare afternoon–evening music video marathon to celebrate the self-proclaimed historic milestone. The marathon served to celebrate music videos, but also to demonstrate how far they have fallen from their heyday. The rate at which music videos were broadcast had dramatically slowed; two-thirds of the total was accounted for in the first nine years. It took another nine years, at an average rate of only 4.25 videos per hour, to broadcast the rest. The "classic videos" shown in the marathon were almost always interrupted by running commentary and many were cut short so they would not overtax the attention of a contemporary viewer. Except for the broadcasts in the early morning hours, MTV now seldom shows complete videos, offering excerpts of music videos along with text and overdub to provide a denser sensory experience for a shorter period of time. Music videos, originally created as marketing teasers for recorded music, are being distributed through different channels, such as video podcasts, Internet-based video streaming, and music video "albums" on DVD. Today's overdubbed excerpts are marketing teasers for full music videos.

## The Internet (and Radio) Killed the Video Star

Music videos were an ideal vehicle for promoting music and energizing the youth culture during a fertile period of time when the trajectories of technology and society coincided. Music was liberated from the home-bound stereo by the Walkman. Its quality was exponentially improved by digital recording and distribution on compact disc. Inexpensive, easy-to-use video equipment allowed risk taking and innovation. At music television's zenith, guerrilla video and postpunk, independent grunge music challenged the self-absorbed complacency and ennui of the Reagan era. The *Sesame Street*–nurtured generation simply kept watching television. The rapid cuts and irreverent concepts that they had learned from Bert and Ernie translated directly into the MTV environment. But technology and society continued onward, and the success of music videos drew money and a corporate sensibility to the medium. As "garage productions" gave way to increasingly expensive, "high production value" videos, the music video genre rapidly found its limitations and the audience grew bored. Music could no longer be sold with a flashy video—its success relied on the quality of the music.

The very technologies that rocketed the music video to success were, ironically, the harbingers of its collapse. The Walkman was the beginning of personal media, allowing people to select their own music mix and isolate themselves within an individualized media environment. Electronic and computer equipment continued to evolve so that everyone could make and distribute videos. The explosion of the Internet gave rise to music file sharing, which both panicked the music industry and dramatically altered the way in which new music was learned about and distributed.

Broadcast music videos were first recorded off the air, digitized, and shared over the Internet through Internet relay chat (IRC). With the advent and proliferation of broadband Internet connections, music videos began being legally distributed and illegally shared. MTV and America Online (AOL), among others, streamed music videos. Limelight, Kazaa, and other file sharing sites offered video content in much the same format and with many of the same problems and legal ramifications as Napster had offered music. Apple Computer's iTunes store offered music videos for download to video iPods.

Attitudes and strategies of the music industry in relation to the shift of recorded material to the Internet varied. Considering recorded music and videos to be protected by copyright, most music labels cut back on video production and redirected their attention and resources to fighting Internet distribution of recordings. The Recording Industry Association of America (RIAA) issued cease-and-desist letters and prosecuted file sharers to protect their copyrights. In a contrarian move, numerous musical groups and videomakers grabbed hold of the opportunity the Internet provided to promote their own work, forgoing record labels to introduce and distribute their work through MySpace pages and YouTube performances. Google's acquisition of YouTube promised to bring the medium-defining startup to which many individuals uploaded copyrighted videos into legal compliance. The interpretation and implementation of copyright law will continue to evolve, as some music labels produce music videos to be provided online as free promotional material to support sales of their recordings, some online providers develop bulk royalty agreements for the videos on their servers, and the RIAA continues to fight what they see as piracy that, if unchecked, will ultimately bring the music industry to its knees.

On the Internet, songs spread virally though technology amplified "word of mouth," resulting in a rapid and broad diversification of music. As film and video had obviated the need for large concerts a generation before, the personalization of music dispersed the large "virtual gathering" necessary for broadcast music. More than ever before, youth could define themselves as individuals, rather than as a homogeneous group of "anti-adults," with their personal mixes of eclectic music collections on digital players. Following the trend, radio reinvented itself by going digital, transmitting worldwide from satellites, developing a pocket-sized receiver, and charging a subscription fee. The satellite radio receiver, alone or combined with a cellular telephone or digital music player, aimed at becoming to contemporary youth what the transistor radio was to youth of the 1960s. The music business paradigm had been turned on its head. Where once music was played for free on the radio in an effort to get consumers to buy recordings, now audio and video recordings are provided for free online in hopes that customers will subscribe to satellite radio and buy high-definition video and audio downloads for their MP3 players. The creative ferment, technological evolution, and economic flux in which the industry finds itself will, as before, settle down and a clearer business strategy will emerge. When it does so, it is likely that big money and slick production will again seek to capitalize on the opportunity, elbowing aside the intensity, honesty, and creativity of music videos made of youth by youth for youth.

### The Music Video Is Dead! Long Live the Music Video!

Music videos have come and gone, even though they were always here and they have not left. Just as music videos existed in other forms before the advent of MTV, they exist now. Some are still produced by recording companies and shown in the wee hours on MTV, but they are also being created, inexpensively and quickly, by young, creative sound- and image-makers who share them on the information superhighway. Music videos are a rapid-cycling example of the evolution of all media, building on long-established traditions into "the next new thing," then subsiding slowly under the weight of their own success, and ultimately morphing into a new form.

## NOTES

1. http://www.youtube.com/watch?v=WpcAn_pwcng
2. http://www.youtube.com/watch?v=6LB6Q_oycfQ
3. http://www.youtube.com/watch?v=KQ3efT1kqXs
4. http://www.youtube.com/watch?v=PZAVMaXdR0k&feature=related
5. http://www.youtube.com/watch?v=IkwDxaDBqTw&feature=related
6. http://www.youtube.com/watch?v=HZBUb0ElnNY
7. http://www.youtube.com/watch?v=z7kmre-RxBE&feature=related
8. http://www.youtube.com/watch?v=fNf046Uo2gI
9. http://www.youtube.com/watch?v=YGakPl8a0eA
10. http://www.youtube.com/watch?v=nXjMr2-C1pM
11. http://www.youtube.com/watch?v=tjBJ0AZ3Jc4
12. http://www.youtube.com/watch?v=MAbtg9dz5P0
13. http://www.youtube.com/watch?v=tDKAQ2AkIZk
14. http://www.youtube.com/watch?v=zdu7xoHU9DA&feature=related
15. http://www.youtube.com/watch?v=M_bvT-DGcWw&mode=related&search=
16. http://www.youtube.com/watch?v=wp0oJL1dKlQ
17. http://www.youtube.com/watch?v=xd6vTJePVuY
18. http://www.youtube.com/watch?v=AtyJbIOZjS8
19. http://www.youtube.com/watch?v=vNl2Pm9-7Vk

## REFERENCES

Abt, D. (1987). Music video: Impact of the visual dimension. In J. Lull (Ed.), *Popular music and communication* (pp. 96–111). Newbury Park, CA: Sage.

Annenberg Public Policy Center. (1997). *Television in the home: The 1997 survey of parents and children*. Philadephia: University of Pennsylvania Press.

Anonymous. (n.d.). *J. P. "The Big Bopper" Richardson*. Retrieved from http://www.accuracyproject.org/cbe-Richardson,J.P.TheBigBopper.html

Arnett, J. J. (1991). Heavy metal music and reckless behavior among adolescents. *Journal of Youth & Adolescence, 20,* 573–592.

Ashby, S. L., & Rich, M. (2005). Video killed the radio star: The effects of music videos on adolescent health. *Adolescent Medicine Clinics, 16,* 371–393.

Austin, E., & Meili, H. (1994). Effects of interpretations of televised alcohol portrayals on children's alcohol beliefs. *Journal of Broadcasting & Electronic Media, 38,* 417–435.

Bandura, A. (1977). *Social learning theory*. Englewood Cliffs, NJ: Prentice Hall.

Bandura, A., Ross, D., & Ross, S. A. (1963). Imitation of film-mediated aggressive models. *Journal of Abnormal & Social Psychology, 66,* 3–11.

Bauman, K. E., Botvin, G. J., Botvin, E. M., & Baker, E. (1992). Normative expectations and the behavior of significant others: An integration of traditions of research on adolescents' cigarette smoking. *Psychological Reports, 71,* 568–570.

Baxter, R. L., De Rimer, C., Landini, A., Leslie, L., & Singletary, M. W. (1985). A content analysis of music videos. *Journal of Broadcasting & Electronic Media, 29*, 333–340.

Bewley, N. (n.d.). *Soundies—A new form of entertainment.* Retrieved from http://www.1940.co.uk/history/article/soundie/soundie.htm

Bleich, S., Zillmann, D., & Weaver, J. B. (1991). Enjoyment and consumption of defiant rock music as a function of adolescent rebelliousness. *Journal of Broadcasting & Electronic Media, 35*, 351–366.

Bordwell, D. (1994). *The cinema of Eisenstein.* Cambridge, MA: Harvard University Press.

Borzekowski, D. L., Robinson, T. N., & Killen, J. D. (2000). Does the camera add 10 pounds? Media use, perceived importance of appearance, and weight concerns among teenage girls. *Journal of Adolescent Health, 26*, 36–41.

Brown, J. D., & Campbell, K. (1986). Race and gender in music videos: The same beat but a different drummer. *Journal of Communication, 36*, 94–106.

Brown, J. D., & Schulze, L. (1990). The effects of race, gender, and fandom on audience interpretations of Madonna's music videos. *Journal of Communication, 40*, 88–102.

Brown, J. D., & Steele, J. (1995). *Sex and the mass media.* Menlo Park, CA: Henry J. Kaiser Family Foundation.

Brown, J. D., Walsh-Childers, K., & Steele, J. R. (2002). *Sexual teens, sexual media: Investigating media's influence on adolescent sexuality.* Mahwah, NJ: Erlbaum.

Bushman, B. J., & Huesmann, L. R. (2006). Short-term and long-term effects of violent media on aggression in children and adults. *Archives of Pediatrics & Adolescent Medicine, 160*, 346–352.

Calfin, M. S., Carroll, J. L., & Shmidt, J. (1993). Viewing music-videotapes before taking a test of premarital sexual attitudes. *Psychological Reports, 72*, 475–481.

Christenson, P. (1992). The effects of parental advisory labels on adolescent music preferences. *Journal of Communication, 42*, 106–113.

Christenson, P. G., & Roberts, D. F. (1998). *It's not only rock & roll: Popular music in the lives of adolescents.* Cresskill, NJ: Hampton Press.

Connolly, G. M., Casswell, S., Zhang, J.-F., & Silva, P. A. (1994). Alcohol in the mass media and drinking by adolescents: A longitudinal study. *Addiction, 89*, 1255–1263.

DuRant, R. H., Rich, M., Emans, S. J., Rome, E. S., Allred, E., & Woods, E. R. (1997). Violence and weapon carrying in music videos: A content analysis. *Archives of Pediatrics & Adolescent Medicine, 151*, 443–448.

DuRant, R. H., Rome, E. S., Rich, M., Allred, E., Emans, S. J., & Woods, E. R. (1997). Tobacco and alcohol use behaviors portrayed in music videos: A content analysis. *American Journal of Public Health, 87*, 1131–1135.

Edwards, E. (1994). The "mean world" of love and sex in popular music of the 1980s. In J. S. Epstein (Ed.), *Adolescents and their music: If it's too loud, you're too old* (pp. 225–249). New York: Garland.

Escobar-Chaves, S. L., Tortolero, S. R., Markham, C. M., Low, B. J., Eitel, P., & Thickstun, P. (2005). Impact of media on adolescent sexual attitudes and behaviors. *Pediatrics, 116*, 303–326.

Farrar, K., Kunkel, D., Biely, E., Eyal, K., Fandrich, R., & Donnerstein, E. (2003). Sexual messages during prime-time programming. *Sexuality and Culture, 7*(3), 7–37.

Fleischer, R. (2005). *Out of the inkwell: Max Fleischer and the animation revolution.* Lexington: University Press of Kentucky.

Frith, S., Goodwin, A., & Grossberg, L. (1993). *Sound & vision: The music video reader.* London: Routledge.

Gerbner, G. (2001). Drugs in television, movies, and music videos. In Y. R. Kamalipour & K. R. Rampal (Eds.), *Media, sex, violence, and drugs in the global village* (pp. 69–75). Lanham, MD: Rowman & Littlefield.

Gerbner, G., Gross, L., Morgan, M., & Signorielli, N. (1994). Growing up with television: The cultivation perspective. In J. Bryant & D. Zillmann (Eds.), *Media effects: Advances in theory and research* (pp. 17–41). Hillsdale, NJ: Erlbaum.

Gow, J. (1993, April). *Gender roles in popular music videos: MTV "top 100 of all time."* Paper presented at the Popular Culture Association/American Culture Association Convention, New Orleans.

Greenfield, P. M., & Beagles-Roos, J. (1988). Radio vs. television: Their cognitive impact on children of different socioeconomic and ethnic groups. *Journal of Communication, 38,* 71–92.

Greenfield, P. M., Bruzzone, L., Koyamatsu, K., & Satuloff, W. (1987). What is rock music doing to the minds of our youth? A first experimental look at the effects of rock music lyrics and music videos. *Journal of Early Adolescence, 7,* 315–329.

Greeson, L. E., & Williams, R. A. (1986). Social implications of music videos for youth: An analysis of the content and effects of MTV. *Youth & Society, 18,* 177–189.

Gruber, E. L., Thau, H. M., Hill, D. L., Fisher, D. A., & Grube, J. W. (2005). Alcohol, tobacco and illicit substances in music videos: A content analysis of prevalence and genre. *Journal of Adolescent Health, 37,* 81–83.

Hansen, C. H. (1988). *The impact of rock music video priming on appraisal of a stereotyped male–female interaction.* Unpublished doctoral dissertation, Michigan State University.

Hansen, C. H., & Hansen, R. D. (1990). The influence of sex and violence on the appeal of rock music videos. *Communication Research, 17,* 212–234.

Hearold, S. (1986). A synthesis of 1043 effects of television on social behavior. *Public Communication and Behavior, 1,* 65–133.

Hicks, J. (2007). *Dziga Vertov: Defining documentary film.* London: I. B. Tauris & Co.

Hoerrner, K. L. (1999). The forgotten battles: Congressional hearings on television violence in the 1950s. *Web Journal of Mass Communication Research, 2,* 3.

Johnson, J. D., Jackson, L. A., & Gatto, L. (1995a). Differential gender effects of exposure to rap music on African American adolescents' acceptance. *Sex Roles, 33,* 597–605.

Johnson, J. D., Jackson, L. A., & Gatto, L. (1995b). Violent attitudes and deferred academic aspirations: Deleterious effects of exposure to rap music. *Basic & Applied Social Psychology, 16,* 27–41.

Jones, K. (1997). Are rap videos more violent? Style differences and the prevalence of sex and violence in the age of MTV. *Howard Journal of Communications, 8,* 343–356.

Kalof, L. (1999). The effects of gender and music video imagery on sexual attitudes. *Journal of Social Psychology, 139,* 378–386.

Klein, J. D., Brown, J. D., Childers, K. W., Oliveri, J., Porter, C., & Dykers, C. (1993). Adolescents' risky behavior and mass media use. *Pediatrics, 92,* 24–31.

Kunkel, D., Cope, K. M., & Biely, E. (1999). Sexual messages on television: Comparing findings from three studies. *Journal of Sex Research, 36,* 230–236.

Larson, R., & Kubey, R. (1983). Television and music: Contrasting media in adolescent life. *Youth & Society, 15,* 13–31.

Lefcowitz, E. (1989). *The Monkees tale.* San Francisco: Last Gasp.

*Love Me Tender.* (1956). Retrieved September 2, 2007, from http://www.imdb.com/title/tt0049452/taglines

Malamuth, N. M., & Briere, J. (1986). Sexual violence in the media: Indirect effects on aggression against women. *Journal of Social Issues, 42*(3 [Special issue on media violence and antisocial behavior]), 75–92.

Malamuth, N. M., & Check, J. V. (1981). The effects of mass media exposure on acceptance of violence against women: A field experiment. *Journal of Research in Personality, 15,* 436–446.

Martin, G., Clarke, M., & Pearce, C. (1993). Adolescent suicide: Music preference as an indicator of vulnerability. *Journal of the American Academy of Child & Adolescent Psychiatry, 32,* 530–535.

Mekemson, C., & Glantz, S. A. (2002). How the tobacco industry built its relationship with Hollywood. *Tobacco Control, 11*(Suppl. 1), 1–20.

Moritz, W. (2004). *Optical poetry: The life and work of Oskar Fischinger.* Bloomington: Indiana University Press.

MTV. (2001). *MTV Uncensored.* New York: Pocket Books.

Parkinson, D. (1995). *History of film.* New York: Thames & Hudson.

Pember, D. (1992). *Mass media in America.* New York: Macmillan.

Peterson, D. L., & Pfost, K. S. (1989). Influence of rock videos on attitudes of violence against women. *Psychological Reports, 64*(1), 319–322.

Rehman, S., & Reilly, S. (1985). Music videos: A dimension of televised violence. *The Pennsylvania Speech Comunication Annual, 41,* 61–64.

Reilly, E., McManus, M., & Chadwick, W. (1993). *The Monkees: A manufactured image. The ultimate reference guide to Monkee memories and memorabilia.* Ann Arbor, MI: Popular Culture Ink.

Rich, M. (2003). Boy, mediated: The effects of entertainment media on the male adolescent health. In D. S. Rosen & M. Rich (Eds.), *Adolescent medicine: State of the art reviews—The adolescent male* (pp. 619–715). Philadelphia: Hanley & Belfus.

Rich, M. (2005). Sex screen: The dilemma of media exposure and sexual behavior. *Pediatrics, 116,* 329–331.

Rich, M., Woods, E. R., Goodman, E., Emans, S. J., & DuRant, R. H. (1998). Aggressors or victims: Gender and race in music video violence. *Pediatrics, 101,* 669–674.

Rideout, V. J. (2003). *Reaching the MTV generation: Recent research on the impact of the Kaiser Family Foundation/MTV public eduation campaign on sexual health.* Menlo Park, CA: Henry J. Kaiser Family Foundation.

Roberts, K. R., Dimsdale, J., East, P., & Friedman, L. (1998). Adolescent emotional response to music and its relationship to risk-taking behaviors. *Journal of Adolescent Health, 23,* 49–54.

Rosenfeld, A. H. (1985). Music, the beautiful disturber. *Psychology Today, 19,* 48–55.

Rubin, R. B., Rubin, A. M., Perse, E. M., Armstrong, C., McHugh, M., & Faix, N. (1986). Media use and meaning of music video. *Journalism Quarterly, 63,* 353–359.

Rustad, R. A., Small, J. E., Jobes, D. A., Safer, M. A., & Peterson, R. J. (2003). The impact of rock videos and music with suicidal content on thoughts and attitudes about suicide. *Suicide and Life-Threatening Behavior, 33,* 120–131.

Sandoval, A. (2005). *The Monkees: The day-by-day story of the 60s TV pop sensation.* Berkeley, CA: Thunder Bay Press.

Sargent, J. D., Beach, M. L., Adachi-Mejia, A. M., Gibson, J. J., Titus-Ernstoff, L. T., Carusi, C. P., et al. (2005). Exposure to movie smoking: Its relation to smoking initiation among US adolescents. *Pediatrics, 116,* 1183–1191.

Scheel, K. R., & Westefeld, J. S. (1999). Heavy metal music and adolescent suicidality: An empirical investigation. *Adolescence, 34,* 253–273.

Seidman, S. A. (1992). An investigation of sex-role stereotyping in music videos. *Journal of Broadcasting & Electronic Media, 36,* 209–216.

Seidman, S. A. (1999). Revisiting sex-role stereotyping in MTV videos. *International Journal of Instructional Media, 26,* 11–22.

Sherman, B. L., & Dominick, J. R. (1986). Violence and sex in music videos: TV and rock 'n' roll. *Journal of Communication, 36,* 79–93.

Signorielli, N., McLeod, D., & Healy, E. (1994). Gender stereotypes in MTV commercials: The beat goes on. *Journal of Broadcasting & Electronic Media, 38,* 91–101.

Smith, A. (1952). Influence of TV crime programs on children's health. *JAMA, 150,* 37.

Smith, S. L., & Boyson, A. R. (2002). Violence in music videos: examining the prevalence and context of physical aggression. *Journal of Communication, 52,* 61–83.

Strouse, J. S., & Buerkel-Rothfuss, N. (1987). Media exposure and the sexual attitudes and behaviors of college students. *Journal of Sex Education and Therapy, 13,* 43–51.

Strouse, J. S., Buerkel-Rothfuss, N. L., & Long, E. C. J. (1995). Gender and family as moderators of the relationship between music video exposure and adolescent sexual permissiveness. *Adolescence, 30,* 505–521.

Sun, S. W., & Lull, J. (1986). The adolescent audience for music videos and why they watch. *Journal of Communication, 36,* 115–125.

Szatmary, D. (1996). *A time to rock. A social history of rock 'n' roll.* Upper Saddle River, NJ: Prentice-Hall.

Tapper, J., Thorson, E., & Black, D. (1994). Variations in music videos as a function of their musical genre. *Journal of Broadcasting & Electronic Media, 38,* 103–113.

Thompson, M., Pingree, S., Hawkins, R. P., & Draves, C. (1991). Long-term norms and cognitive structures as shapers of television viewer activity. *Journal of Broadcasting & Electronic Media, 35,* 319–334.

Tiggeman, M., & Pickering, A. S. (1996). Role of television in adolescent women's body dissatisfaction and drive for thinness. *International Journal of Eating Disorders, 20,* 199–203.

Tiggeman, M., & Slater, A. (2004). Thin ideals in music television: a source of social comparison and body dissatisfaction. *International Journal of Eating Disorders, 35,* 48–58.

Toney, G. T., & Weaver, J. B. (1994). Effects of gender and gender role self-perceptions on affective reactions to rock music videos. *Sex Roles, 30,* 567–583.

Van den Bulck, J., & Beullens, K. (2005). Television and music video exposure and adolescent alcohol use while going out. *Alcohol and Alcoholism, 40,* 249–253.

Van den Bulck, J., Beullens, K., & Mulder, J. (2006). Television and music video exposure and adolescent "alcopop" use. *International Journal of Adolescent Medicine and Health, 18,* 107–114.

Villani, S. (2001). Impact of media on children and adolescents: a 10-year review of the research. *Journal of the American Academy of Child & Adolescent Psychiatry, 40,* 392–401.

Vincent, R. C. (1989). Clio's consciousness raised? Portrayal of women in rock videos, re-examined. *Journalism Quarterly, 66,* 155–160.

Vincent, R. C., Davis, D. K., & Boruszkowski, L. A. (1987). Sexism on MTV: The portrayal of women in rock videos. *Journalism Quarterly, 64,* 750–755.

Waite, B. M., Hillbrand, M., & Foster, H. G. (1992). Reduction of aggressive behavior after removal of Music Television. *Hospital & Community Psychiatry, 43,* 173–175.

Walker, J. R. (1987, May). *Mediated violence: The contribution of MTV.* Paper presented at the 78th Annual Meeting of the Eastern Communication Association, Syracuse, NY.

Ward, D. S., & Friedman, K. (2006). Using TV as a guide: Associations between television viewing and adolescents' sexual attitudes and behavior. *Journal of Research on Adolescence, 16,* 133–156.

Ward, L. M., & Hansbrough, E. (2005). Contributions of music video exposure to black adolescents' gender and sexual schemas. *Journal of Research on Adolescence, 20,* 143–166.

Wingood, G. M., DiClemente, R. J., Bernhardt, J. M., Harrington, K., Davies, S. L., Robillard, A., et al. (2003). A prospective study of exposure to rap music videos and African American female adolescents' health. *American Journal of Public Health, 93,* 437–439.

Yule, A. (1994). *The man who framed the Beatles: A biography of Richard Lester.* London: Dutton Adult.

Zillman, D., & Mundorf, N. (1987). Image effects in the appreciation of video rock. *Communication Research, 14,* 316–334.

# Part II

# Portrayal of Adolescents and Influential Behaviors

# 4

## It Matters What Young People Watch

### Health Risk Behaviors Portrayed in

### Top-Grossing Movies Since 1950

PATRICK E. JAMIESON, EIAN MORE, SUSAN S. LEE, PETER BUSSE, AND DANIEL ROMER

Did the suicides of adolescent females in the film *Virgin Suicides* typify a trend in movies or was that portrayal an aberration? Has portrayal of suicide in films become more or less explicit over time? Does the fact that most top-thirty movies now picture smoking represent an increase or decrease in portrayal of this deadly vice? How much health risk behavior is portrayed in films? If one believes that media portrayals affect behavior, particularly of the young, then the answers to such questions are important not only to health advocates but to parents and policy makers as well.

Attempts to answer such questions have been plagued by methodological problems. Reliance on convenience samples has limited the ability of scholars to generalize findings. Portrayals usually have been coded over short periods of time. Different scholars have employed different measures making it difficult to track change across time. As a result, there is not a clear answer to such basic questions as, How prevalent are risk behaviors in films and has prevalence changed across time? Earlier research using small samples, covering fewer years, and in some cases using less rigorous methodological standards, has identified inconsistent trends in the portrayal of tobacco and alcohol. Although trends have been observed in other behaviors, the findings are limited to G-rated films (violence) or convenience samples (suicide).

The Annenberg-Robert Wood Johnson Coding of Health and Media Project (CHAMP) was designed to address the problems that have characterized the research in this area by using consistent measures with high intercoder reliability to compare multiple health risk behaviors in a carefully drawn sample of films across time. It sampled more densely (825 films), more comprehensively (top-thirty grossing films), from a longer period (1950–2004), and met a higher reliability standard (intercoder reliability greater than .70) than earlier work. And unlike that work, the CHAMP applied similar coding strategies across many of the health risk behaviors that have been the focus of scattered studies in the past and thereby provides a uniform record of the trends in these behaviors over time. In this chapter, we examine the results of this analysis for tobacco use, alcohol consumption, sexual activity, violence, and suicide.

The presupposition of work examining media portrayals is that the media can elicit modeling in a significant segment of audience members. A number of theories and the research testing them posit that relationship. For example, Bandura's (2002) social cognitive theory of mass communication proposes that media portrayals, whether fictional or not, can influence real-world behaviors in the viewing audience. As noted by Bandura (2002, p. 126), "in observational learning, a single model can transmit new ways of thinking and behaving simultaneously to countless people in widely dispersed locales."

Bandura (2002, p. 129) argues that learning of new behavior occurs when an audience member observes an act, codes it symbolically, enters it into memory, reconstructs the memory in the form of recall, and translates symbolic conceptions into action. Once novel acts are learned, media portrayals can also serve to elicit those behaviors by prompting their enactment. For example, much of the influence of advertising serves not to teach new forms of behavior but merely to remind the audience to use a product. Furthermore, a meta-analysis by Mares and Woodard (2005) shows that portrayal of socially positive behaviors can elicit modeling just as well as depictions of negative behaviors.

Gerbner's cultivation theory (Gerbner, Gross, Morgan, & Signorielli, 1986) and Phillips's contagion theory (Phillips, 1980; Phillips, Lesnya, & Paight, 1992) also explain why violence and suicide portrayals could affect real world behavior. Cultivation theory holds that exposure to television over time can influence the audience's beliefs about the world. Consistent with that view, Gerbner et al. found that "heavy viewers in one or more subgroups are more likely to reflect in their responses what they have seen on television than are light viewers in the same subgroups" (1986, p. 37). Gerbner and colleagues found that those exposed to high levels of violence on television were more likely to believe that the world was a mean place than those with lower exposure. Romer, Jamieson, and Aday (2003) confirmed that this finding holds for high consumers of violence-laden local news.

In Phillips's contagion theory, the portrayal of suicide in the media can also influence real-world behavior (Phillips et al., 1992). According to this theory, suicide portrayals in the media can serve to disinhibit the same behavior in those already considering the act. In a carefully controlled study of television news, newspapers, movies, and movie rentals, Romer, Jamieson, and Jamieson (2006) found that local television news is responsible for a significant number of the suicides in those under age 25. Earlier research had confirmed that both news reporting (Bollen & Phillips, 1982) and fictional portrayals of suicide affected suicide rates. For example, Hawton et al. (1999) documented in adult hospital patients a 17% increase in self-poisoning after audience exposure to a fictional television drama featuring that method. In emergency rooms, 20% of those who had attempted suicide indicated that the media portrayal had influenced their decision to overdose, and 17% indicated that it had influenced their choice of method.

According to Bandura, explicit and detailed portrayal is more likely to produce learning and imitation. The CHAMP measured not only trends in the absolute levels of portrayal but also the explicitness of the portrayal. The explicitness measures in the study used a graded scale to assess in how much detail and completeness the behavior was shown. This enabled us to identify trends in the explicitness of the portrayal as well as the overall frequency with which behaviors have appeared in films. Finally, we also coded the identities of the characters who engaged in the recorded behavior. This enabled us to observe time trends in both age and gender of filmic portrayal of various risky behaviors.

We also compared trends in the portrayed behaviors with national records of the societal prevalence of the behaviors in both U.S. adults and adolescents. This enabled us to determine how closely portrayal in films coincided with societal trends. A theory of strong media influence would suggest that trends in film portrayal would precede real-world behavior trends. A theory of weaker influence would merely predict that films tracked trends in societal behavior, reflecting what some adults and adolescents already do and disseminating that information to the wider audience. This form of influence would still be important because it could reinforce ongoing trends and help to transmit them to the teen audience. A third possibility is that film trends follow societal trends. That is, films merely echo what is already happening in the culture and have no influence of their own on those trends. We will not be able to determine causal direction in these analyses; however, to the degree trends in film portrayal coincide with or precede societal trends, we would have evidence that films do more than merely follow those trends without any potential to influence them.

## CODING PROCEDURE

The CHAMP investigated movie content over a fifty-five-year period (1950–2004) by selecting a representative half of the top thirty top-grossing films for each year (15 × 55 = 825). Behaviors were coded for all human, nonhuman, and animated characters for the 825 films. We focus on five health risk behaviors: tobacco, alcohol, sex, violence, and suicide. In some cases, films were analyzed by rank, a measure determined by *Variety* magazine from rentals to theaters based on box office gross sales. At the writing of this chapter, suicide was only coded in half of the top fifteen films for every year during the study period, for a total of 414 films. Undergraduate coders, most of whom were communications majors, were recruited and trained to implement the extensive coding system.[1] The coding was performed in five-minute segments that were averaged within each movie to control for differences in movie length that might occur over the time period of the study. Hence, the unit of analysis was the movie. The project achieved high reliability on all coded outcomes reported in this chapter, Krippendorff's (2004) alpha greater than .70 among twenty-two coders.

## TRENDS IN THE REPRESENTATION OF AGE AND GENDER

We first examined trends in the representation of both adolescents and children as well as gender in films since 1950. We expected that with the increasing focus on youth in American culture, the representation of children and adolescents (under age 21) would increase in films. As seen in Figure 4.1a, this expectation was verified. The linear trend in the proportion of films with a character under age 21 increased over the period of the study. This finding also corroborates the analysis of television roles in the Introduction to this book, where we also found a strong increase in the number of youthful characters over time. Hence, we have strong support that the appearance of young people has increased over time in both films and television.

We were surprised, however, to learn that the representation of women has not increased in top-grossing films. Indeed, if anything, the trend has been the opposite. As seen in Figure 4.1b, the proportion of main characters that were male declined early in the study period (late 1950s) but then steadily increased and later leveled off. This trend suggests that about 70% of major characters in films are male and that this proportion has

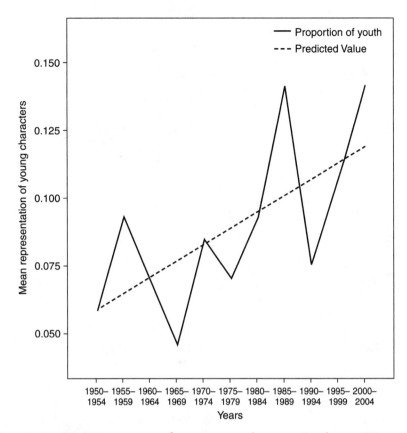

Figure 4.1a.  Mean proportions of young major characters (under age 21) in films with fitted trend from 1950 to 2004.

increased over the years. The best fitting linear trend in the figure is statistically significant.

## RISK BEHAVIORS IN FILM

### Tobacco in Film

Exposure to smoking in movies has been found to predict the initiation of smoking in adolescents (Sargent et al., 2005). Furthermore, Stern (2005) found that one-sixth of teen characters in teen-centered films from 1999 to 2001 smoked cigarettes. Does the literature reveal whether smoking is becoming less or more common in cinematic portrayals? Unfortunately, research on portrayal of tobacco in films only provides a confusing and contradictory picture.

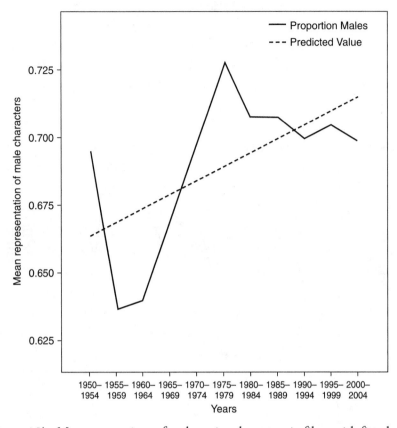

Figure 4.1b. Mean proportions of male major characters in films with fitted trend from 1950 to 2004.

It is possible to find studies that support any conclusion. McIntosh, Bazzini, Smith, and Wayne (1998) randomly selected twenty of the top-twenty grossing films from each decade between 1940 and 1989 and found a decline in percentage of main characters who smoked since the 1950s. They also found that smokers were portrayed slightly more positively than nonsmokers and that Hollywood's portrayals of smoking ignored its negative consequences. Hazan and Glantz (1995) found that the rate of tobacco portrayal in a random sample of sixty-two top-twenty films from 1960 to 1990 did not change. On the other hand, in comparing filmic portrayal in the 1950s with 2000 and 2001, Glantz, Kacirk, and McCulloch (2004, p. 261) reported that "smoking in movies has returned to the [high] level observed in 1950." The Glantz study randomly sampled twenty of the top-grossing films from 1950 to 1959 and five of the top-grossing films from 2001 and 2002 and estimated trends for the years in between with results from previous research. In view of the different definitions and sampling criteria of these studies, it is difficult to draw conclusions about actual trends in tobacco portrayal.

### Tobacco in Top-Thirty Grossing Films

Our research found that 712 out of the 825 (86.9%) films coded by CHAMP had tobacco-related content. About 91% of the tobacco films involved a male and 42% a female smoker. Featuring male smokers increased in the 1970s until the mid-1980s and then declined. Our analysis found that the average number of five-minute segments with tobacco content (any display of tobacco or use of the product) per movie from 1950 to 2004 has been steadily decreasing from a high of 38.5% in 1950–1954 to a low of 12.6% of five-minute segments in 2000–2004 (Figure 4.2). The explicitness

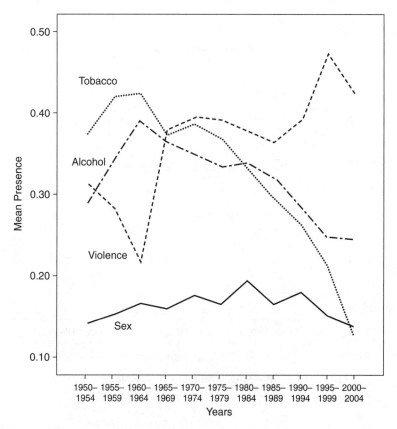

Figure 4.2. Mean proportions of segments containing violence, sex, and use of alcohol and tobacco in films from 1950 to 2004.

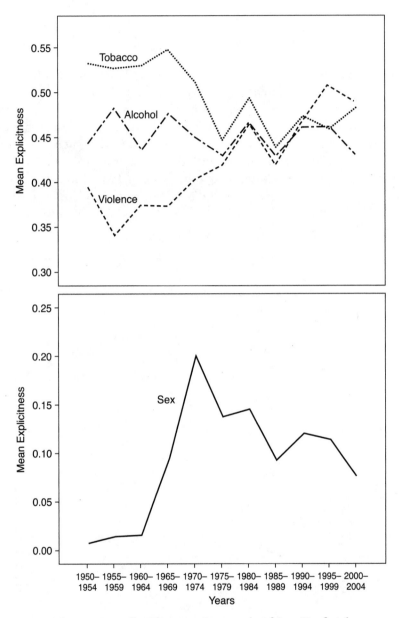

Figure 4.3. Mean ratings of explicitness (on a scale of 0 to 1) of violence, sex, and use of alcohol and tobacco in films from 1950 to 2004.

of portrayal within those films decreased over time as well (Figure 4.3). The decline in tobacco use portrayed in films closely matches the decline in adult consumption of tobacco in the United States (Figure 4.4). This pattern suggests that films provide a good barometer of tobacco use in society and that they reflect the growing concern about tobacco's health effects on both smokers and those exposed to their smoke.

Among films with tobacco content, only about 8% portrayed tobacco use by a main character under age 21, while 73% of the movies showed a character aged 21 to 40, 57% showed a character aged 41 to 64; representation of anyone over age 64 was minimal, at about 9%. These portrayal patterns undoubtedly reflect the fact that the dominant characters in films tend to be adults between the ages of 21 and 64.

Across tobacco films, the percentage of five-minute segments with any youth under age 21 tobacco use has not changed over time. But in tobacco film grossing ranks (16 through 30), there has been a significant increase over time (see Figure 4.5). An analysis testing for differences in trends by rank

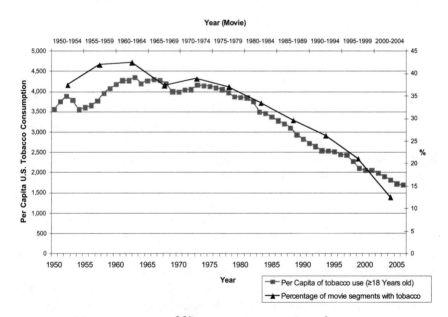

Figure 4.4. Mean percentage of film segments containing tobacco use in top-thirty U.S. films (right axis) and U.S. per-capita consumption of tobacco for ages 18 and older (left axis) from 1950 to 2004. (*Sources*: For 1950–1995, adapted from *Tobacco Situation and Outlook Report*, USDA, April 1996 and September 1987; R. Miller, U.S. cigarette consumption, 1900 to date. In W. Harr (Ed.), *Tobacco Yearbook, 1981* (p. 53). For 1996–2004, adapted from Alcohol and Tobacco Tax and Trade Bureau, *Monthly Statistical Release—Tobacco Products*, Washington, DC: U.S. Bureau of the Census, Population Estimates.)

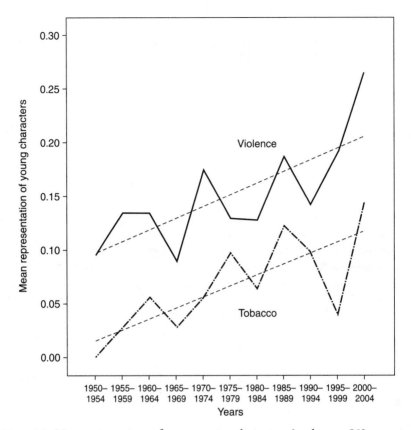

Figure 4.5. Mean proportions of young major characters (under age 21) engaging in violence in films with violent content (ranks 1 to 30) and purchasing, handling, or smoking tobacco in films with tobacco content (ranks 16 to 30) from 1950 to 2004 (along with fitted trends).

showed that youth portrayal in ranks 16 through 30 increased more strongly than in the higher-ranked films. Furthermore, the trend in the lower ranking films was significant on its own. Hence, our analysis indicates that although the rate of adult tobacco consumption per capita has been declining along with the overall frequency of smoking in films, the trend is more complicated and nuanced because there has been an increase in films ranked 16 through 30 with youth tobacco portrayals.

The increase in youth portrayal over time may actually contribute to the decline in U.S. youth smoking rates. As seen in Figure 4.6, trends in smoking among high school twelfth graders as tracked by the Monitoring the Future study (Johnston, O'Malley, Bachman, & Schulenberg, 2006) indicate that smoking has been on the downturn. However, the trend is often interrupted by cycles of heavy increases in smoking rates; the downward

Figure 4.6. Mean percentage of segments with tobacco use in top-thirty films from 1950 to 2004 (right axis) and percentage of twelfth grade students in the United States who smoked cigarettes in the previous thirty days from 1975 to 2006 (left axis). (*Source*: Adapted with permission from the Monitoring the Future Study, the University of Michigan; see Johnston et al., 2006.)

slope of the trend is not as steep as the overall portrayal rate in films or the trend in adult consumption. Hence, despite the overall decline of smoking in films, the rising representation of youth smoking may buck the overall trend and serve to inhibit reductions in youth smoking.

## Alcohol in Film

Research on alcohol portrayal trends in films has not been as plentiful. Nor has there been as much attention to the socializing influence of filmic portrayals of alcohol on youth as with tobacco. However, what evidence we have suggests that alcohol portrayal has declined in films since 1950. In addition, just as with tobacco, films tend to show youthful alcohol drinkers as more socially desirable than nonusers and fail to show the adverse effects of alcohol. Thompson and Yokota found a "significant decrease in both tobacco and alcohol use over time" (1937–2000) in G-rated animated feature films and concluded that these films "did not convey the long term consequences of this use" (2001, p. 1). Stern (2005) conducted a content analysis of top-rated films from 1999 to 2001, including forty-three teen-centered films that included at least one teenager within the ages 12 to 19 who was a main character. Stern found that 40% of main teen characters drank alcohol. Stern's study also concluded that teen drinkers were unlikely to show negative consequences from drinking. McIntosh, Smith, Bazzini, and Mills found that drinkers were portrayed as more "attractive, more romantically/sexually active, more aggressive, and having a higher socioeconomic status than non drinkers." Their data also suggested that "No systematic changes were found across decades (in top-twenty films) that might reflect the growing knowledge base regarding the adverse effects of alcohol use" (1999, p. 1).

Everett, Schnuth, and Tribble studied the top-ten grossing films from each year between 1985 and 1995 and found that "98% had references supporting tobacco use, and 96% had references supporting alcohol use" but that "only 38% had a reference that discouraged tobacco use and only 37% had one that discouraged alcohol" (1998, p. 317). They concluded that because of plentiful content and a lack of anti-substance messages, "The hazards of smoking and drinking are not reflected in the behaviors of film characters who are potential role models for youth facing the decision to smoke or drink" (p. 317).

## Alcohol in Top-Thirty Films

Of the sampled films, 93.6% had some alcohol-related content, with about 96.9% of the portrayals involving a male character and 62.5% involving a female character. There was no change in gender portrayal of alcohol over time. As seen in Figure 4.2, the frequency of alcohol use in top-thirty films has been steadily decreasing. However, our measure of alcohol explicitness showed no significant change over time (Figure 4.3).

As seen in Figure 4.7, the frequency of alcohol use portrayed in films has declined in advance of the drop in U.S. per-capita consumption of alcohol. National per-capita consumption of alcohol did not decline until around 1980, whereas portrayal in films began to drop in the early 1960s, perhaps foreshadowing the national trend. The portrayal of alcohol by youth (under age 21) did not change between 1950 and 2004, neither across all films nor by rank. About 8% of films with alcohol content showed a young person (under age 21) consuming or under the influence of alcohol. Nearly all of the portrayals (81.5%) involved a person between the ages of 21 and 40.

The rate of alcohol portrayal in films and prevalence of alcohol consumption by twelfth graders have both declined since the early 1980s (Figure 4.8). This pattern suggests that youth are following the same time trends as adults in their use of alcohol.

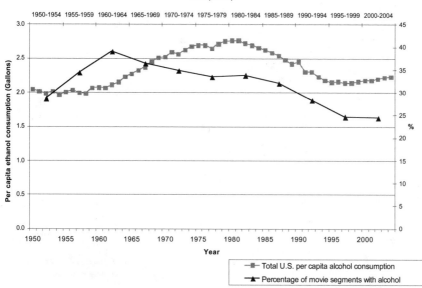

Figure 4.7. Mean percentage of film segments with drinking of alcohol in top-thirty films (right axis) and U.S. per-capita alcohol consumption of ages 15 and up prior to 1970; 14 and up thereafter (left axis) from 1950 to 2004. (*Source*: Adapted with permission from Alcohol Epidemiologic Data System, T. M. Nephew, H. Yi, G. D. Williams, F. S. Stinson, and M. C. Dufour, *U.S. Alcohol Epidemiologic Data Reference Manual*, Vol. 1, 4th ed. U.S. Apparent Consumption of Alcoholic Beverages Based on State Sales, Taxation, or Receipt Data. Washington, DC: NIAAA. NIH Publication No. 04-5563 [June 2004].)

## Sex in Film

Has sex in film changed over the years? We would expect increased sexual explicitness in the 1960s as the movie industry transitioned away from use of the Production Code (Brisbin, 2002). Previous research confirms this prediction. Abramson and Mechanic (1983), although using a small sample of five films from each of the years 1959, 1969, and 1979 (fifteen films) found that sexual explicitness increased over time.

It matters how sexual content in popular films is portrayed because such depictions can either foster healthy socialization (Ashcraft, 2003; Ward & Friedman, 2006) or emulation of problematic activities, such as not using contraception or appropriate protection from sexually transmitted infections (Greenberg et al., 1993). Exposure to media portrayals of sex can also lead to early sexual initiation. Pardun, L'Engle, and Brown (2005) found significant correlations between seventh and eighth graders' (mostly

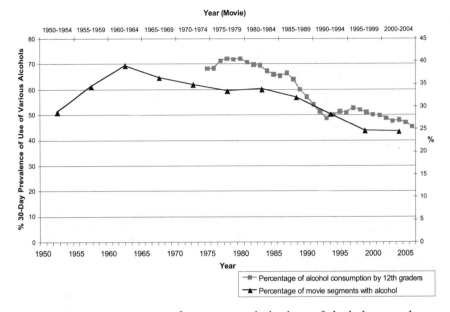

Figure 4.8. Mean percentage of segments with drinking of alcohol in top-thirty films from 1950 to 2004 (right axis) and percentage of twelfth grade students who drank alcohol in the past thirty days from 1975 to 2006 (left axis). (*Source*: Adapted with permission from the Monitoring the Future Study, the University of Michigan; see Johnston et al., 2006.)

12- through 14-year-olds') sexual media diets (including movies) and subsequent sexual activity. L'Engle, Brown, and Kenneavy (2006) also found support for the prediction that filmic exposure to sex can lead to increased intentions to have sex and sexual activity. The authors also noted that media depictions of sex rarely portrayed the use of condoms or contraception. This pattern of portrayal would be less problematic if sexual partners were in stable relationships. However, Dempsey and Reichert (2000) analyzed the top-twenty-five movie video rentals of 1998 and found that 15% of the sex was between married partners while 85% was between those who were not married. These studies suggest that films tend to portray sex in a way that will not only encourage the behavior but also fail to portray preventive measures that can avert potentially negative consequences. Furthermore, the explicitness of the portrayals has increased from the 1950s to the late 1970s.

## Sex in Top-Thirty Films

We found that about 85% of coded movies had sexual content. Although the amount of sex in popular films has not significantly changed over time

(Figure 4.2), the explicitness of the portrayal has indeed increased (Figure 4.3). The increase in sexual explicitness rose in the 1960s as the Production Code lost its influence. To illustrate the change across time, compare the 1953 sexual contact in *Kim*, where the kissing is a brief glancing of lips with the 1990 portrayal in *Presumed Innocent*. In that film, Harrison Ford's character drops his pants and positions himself to mount his sex partner as she lays back on an office desk and he fondles her bare breast.

Sexual explicitness in top-thirty movies parallels an important change in adolescent (ages 15 to 19) and adult sexual behavior since the 1960s, namely, the increase in the rate of births to unmarried women (Luker, 1996) (Figure 4.9). However, while sexual explicitness in films has leveled off in the 1990s, the birthrate in unmarried teens has continued to rise. Among films with any sexual content, 14.8% had an adolescent character age 0–20 engaged in sexual behavior, 88.4% had a character age 21 through 40, 37.3% had a character age 41 through 64, and 2.4% had a character over age 64. In popular movies, sex is a young person's game. Based on the numbers, much of the sexual content involved a character under the age of 40.

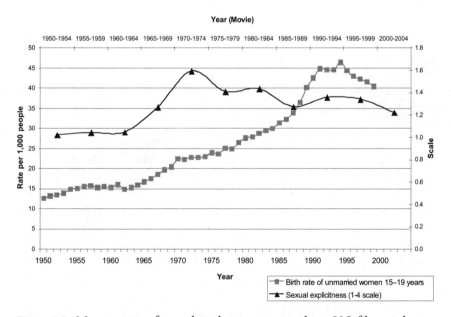

Figure 4.9. Mean ratings of sexual explicitness in top-thirty U.S. films and annual birthrates to unwed adolescents ages 15 to 19 from 1950 to 2004. (*Source*: Adapted from Table 1, Selected measures of teenage childbearing: United States, 1940–2000. NVSR, V. 49. N. 10, September 25, 2001, Centers for Disease Control and Prevention, National Center for Health Statistics, Department of Health and Human Services.)

Violence in Film

Considerable research reviewed in the Introduction to this book and Chapter 8 finds that media portrayals of violence can encourage similar behavior in adolescents. As noted by Anderson et al. (2003), research on media, including violent television and films, indicates that media exposure "increases the likelihood of aggressive and violent behavior in both immediate and long term contexts" (p. 81). At the same time, there is evidence of increasing violence in popular films. Yokota and Thompson (2000) analyzed all English-speaking G-rated films from 1937 to 1999 available in the United States. They found that nearly all of the films contained at least some violence, and that amount increased significantly over time. Monk-Turner et al. (2004) found that American war films after 1990 had more violence than earlier American war films and that recently released movies had more gore. Sargent et al. analyzed survey results from 10- to 14-year-olds and found that 28% had seen extremely violent movies and 20% had seen the R-rated *Natural Born Killers*, which had "extreme violence and graphic carnage, shocking images, language, and sexuality" (2002, p. 449). The authors pointed out the widespread exposure of these early adolescents to "movies with brutal, and often sexualized, violence" (2002, p. 1).

Violence in the Top-Thirty Films

The frequency of portrayed violence (Figure 4.2) was high. In all, 85% of films contained a main character initiating violence, with 91.4% involving male characters and 54.5% involving female characters. The amount of violent content (Figure 4.2), the level of explicit violence (Figure 4.3), and youth violence (Figure 4.5) has increased from 1950 to 2004. This overall rise is also consistent with the dropping of Hollywood's Production Code (see Introduction) in the mid-1960s. Under the code "ultraviolent" movies such as Penn's *Bonnie and Clyde* (1967) and Peckinpah's *The Wild Bunch* (1969) could not have been produced. The tradition of violent films continues unabated with recent examples such as Oliver Stone's *Natural Born Killers* in 1994 and Snyder's *300*, a 2006 retelling of the legend of 300 Spartans defending their homeland from thousands of invading Persians.

As seen in Figure 4.10, the upward trend in portrayal of violence in films since 1960 has paralleled the overall increase in youth violence as indexed by homicide rates in persons ages 15 to 24. We found that youth violence portrayals were more likely in higher grossing ranks (1–15)—16.7%—compared to 11% in the lower grossing ranks (16–30). Youth engaging in violence over time in lower rank films with violence increased as well (Figure 4.11). The increasing trend in youth film violence also appears to parallel youth (ages

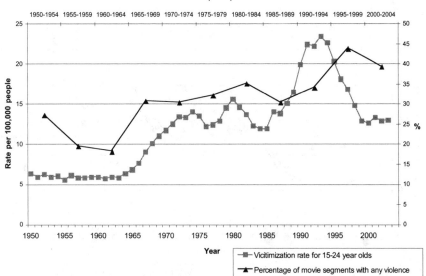

Figure 4.10.  Mean percentage of segments with violence in top-thirty films (right axis) and homicide rates for young people ages 15 to 24 (left axis) from 1950 to 2004. (*Source*: Adapted from unpublished trend table and Vital Statistics of the United States for 1950–59; Mortality, unpublished trend table 290A for 1960–67; Mortality, unpublished trend table 290 for 1968–78 and 1979–98; and Mortality, Worktable 12, for 1999–2003, Centers for Disease Control and Prevention, National Center for Health Statistics, National Vital Statistics System.)

15 to 24) homicide rates since 1950. Even though the increase over time we observe in youth portrayal of violence was only significant in lower ranked films, it is important because they still have a very large audience.

## Suicide in Film

Suicide content in movies is a concern for several reasons. First of all, the rate of adolescent suicide in the United States tripled between the 1960s and 1980s. Among the factors that could have contributed to this increase is contagion from media depictions in films. Gould, Jamieson, and Romer (2003) noted that "vulnerable youth are susceptible to the influence of reports and portrayals of suicide in the mass media" and that there is a "substantial opportunity for exposure to suicide" in newspapers and top-rated films (p. 1). Jamieson, Romer, and Jamieson (2006) found that suicidal youth who watch more movies that depict ineffective treatment for mental illness (with suicide often the result) are more likely to believe an individual

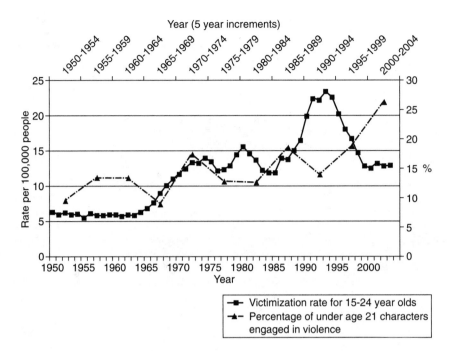

Figure 4.11. Mean percentages of young characters engaging in violence in films with violence ranks 1 to 30 (right axis) and homicide rates for young people ages 15 to 24 (left axis) from 1950 to 2004. (*Source*: Adapted from unpublished trend table and Vital Statistics of the United States for 1950–59; Mortality, unpublished trend table 290A for 1960–67; Mortality, unpublished trend table 290 for 1968–78 and 1979–98; and Mortality, Worktable 12, for 1999–2003, Centers for Disease Control and Prevention, National Center for Health Statistics, National Vital Statistics System.)

would not be helped by medical treatment. In a convenience sample of top-thirty rated movies, Jamieson (2003) found that approximately 10% of top-thirty movies contained suicidal content and that there was an increase in the number of movies with suicide and a significant increase in the modeling of suicide over time.

## Suicide in the Top-Fifteen Films

We found that approximately 11% of the top-fifteen films contained some suicidal content (*N* = 46). Most of these enactments were by male actors (67%), and this proportion did not change over time. Neither was there any change in the number of movies with any suicide content, nor in the number of suicide segments from 1950 to 2004. However, within films containing suicide portrayals, explicitness increased over time (see Figure 4.12). About 9% of the suicides occurred to persons under age 21. Hence, over time, the nature, not the amount of suicidal content, has increased. The finding that explicitness of portrayal has increased since 1950 is consistent with findings from Jamieson's (2003) study of popular films from 1950 to 2000, which used a viewer-generated sample of suicide films.

As seen in Figure 4.12, suicide explicitness in films increased in concert with the U.S. youth suicide rate (ages 15 to 24), which tripled between the

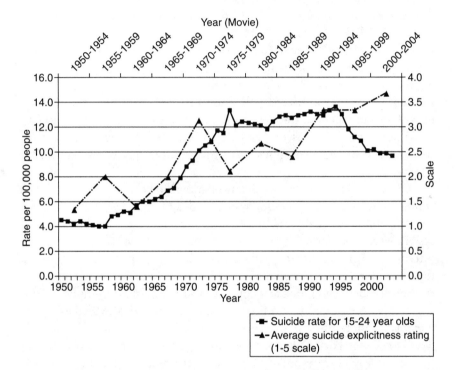

Figure 4.12. Mean suicide explicitness among films ranked 1 to 15 (right axis) and U.S. youth suicide rates for ages 15 to 24 (left axis) from 1950 to 2004. (*Source:* Adapted from Death rates for selected causes by 10-year age groups, race, and sex: United States, 1950–98, Centers for Disease Control and Prevention, National Center for Health Statistics, National Vital Statistics System; Grove, R. D., & Hetzel, A. M. Vital statistics rates in the United States, 1940–1960, Washington, DC: U.S. Government Printing Office, 1968; Mortality tables: Worktable 12, Death rates for 358 selected causes, by 10-year age groups, race, and sex: United States, 1999–2003, Centers for Diseases Control and Prevention, National Center for Health Statistics; Hoyert, D. L., Heron, M., Murphy, S. L., Kung, H. C. Deaths: Final data for 2003, National Vital Statistics Reports, Vol. 54, no. 13. Hyattsville, MD: National Center for Health Statistics, 2006.)

early 1960s and the late 1980s. This suggests that films served either as a good measure of the changes that were occurring in society or that they influenced these trends through media contagion.

## THE RELATIONSHIP BETWEEN CONTENT AND SALES RANK

Both the amount and explicitness of violence and the explicitness of sex have strongly increased in top-thirty movies since the 1950s. It is often argued that filmmakers rely on violence and sex to attract audiences (Emmers-Sommer, Paley, Hanzel, & Triplett, 2006; Hamilton, 1998). Although we found that violence was strongly related to rank ($p < .001$), sexual explicitness was not. Indeed, the strongest predictor of rank in our sample using content coding for tobacco, alcohol, sex, or violence was any violence per five-minute segment ($p = .001$). Tobacco explicitness predicts lower selling movie rank ($p = .018$) and alcohol frequency predicts better selling movie rank ($p = .045$) but not nearly as strongly as violence. Violent content appears to be the strongest predictor of movie sales. Surprisingly, sexual content is unrelated to sales.

One reason for the absence of any relationship between sales and sexual content may be the MPAA rating system. This system is designed to give parents the ability to shield children from objectionable content. If the rating system were more sensitive to sexual content than to violence, then it might filter films with ever-greater sexual content into more restrictive ratings and thereby reduce access to such films. To test this hypothesis, we examined the relationship between rating and content of the films in our sample.

The MPAA rating system first came into existence in 1968. However, a major addition to the system occurred around 1985, the first full year of the new PG-13 category. This category was designed to distinguish films that had previously been regarded as PG but that often contained content that parents felt was inappropriate for children under the age of 13. Since its introduction, PG-13 movies have been very popular. There are more PG-13 (36%) than R-rated (32%) movies in our sample starting in 1985. The next most popular rating, PG, comprised about 27% of the sample, with the remaining films in the G category (5%). It should also be noted that it is easier for unaccompanied adolescents to see PG-13 movies in the theater than it is R-rated films, and more than two-thirds of the movies in our sample were easily accessible to adolescents because they had a G, PG, or PG-13 rating.

Does the ratings system do a better job of screening sexual than violent content? Our coding system permits five main measures of violence and sex, including the proportion of five-minute segments with any violence or sex per movie, the explicitness of the violence or sex that was shown, and an

Table 4.1. Measures of Violence and Sex in Top-Thirty Grossing Movies by MPAA Rating, 1985–2004

| Rating | Violent Segments (%) | Violent Sequences (0–100 scale) | Violence Explicitness (0–100 scale) | Sexual Segments (%) | Sexual Explicitness (0–100 scale) |
|---|---|---|---|---|---|
| G | 35 | 28 | 48 | 10 | 2 |
| PG | 29 | 23 | 45 | 13 | 5 |
| PG-13 | 42 | 32 | 45 | 16 | 8 |
| R | 53 | 38 | 51 | 18 | 17 |
| Difference G vs. R | 18 | 10 | 3 | 8 | 15 |
| % Increase G to R | 51 | 36 | 6 | 80 | 750 |

additional measure of the number of violent sequences involving multiple acts of violence within a segment per film (for definition of sequence see the Appendix).

As seen in Table 4.1, the rating system systematically screens sexual content going from G to R. At each increase in restrictiveness, there is an increase in sexual content. The increase is especially noteworthy in regard to sexual explicitness, where the change from G to R is over eight times the amount shown in the G category.

The relationship between violence and ratings is much weaker. Although there are 36% more segments with violence in R than G films, the difference in violence explicitness is small. Even comparing R to PG-13 films, a similar pattern emerges. Sexual content is more severely restricted to R-rated compared to PG-13 films than violence. These patterns support the hypothesis that violence can be used across the rating system to attract audiences while explicit sexual content is more likely to be in the most restrictive R category.

## CONCLUSIONS

Our results reveal several interesting trends in portrayal of risky behavior since 1950. Tobacco and alcohol portrayals have trended downward and both trends show no signs of changing course. On the other hand, portrayal of violence and explicit sex has increased significantly since the 1950s. Moreover, the explicitness of suicide portrayals increased. The downward trends in tobacco portrayal coincide with decades of advocacy focused on reducing teen cigarette and tobacco consumption (see Chapter 9). The trend in alcohol also coincides with increased recognition of the hazards of drinking, especially in regard to driving while under the influence of alcohol (see Chapter 10).

While tobacco and alcohol portrayals have declined, the representation of young people in those portrayals has not; in the use of tobacco and involvement with violence, it has actually increased. These trends are not surprising given the increase in youthful characters in films since 1950. However, they do support the concern that the media portrayal of young people has served to increase risks to their socialization by increasingly showing them engaging in more risky behavior. These trends also suggest that advocacy efforts to reduce the portrayal of these behaviors, especially in youthful actors, have not been as effective as hoped.

It can be said that the U.S. market gets the sex and violence it wants. In *Channeling Violence,* Hamilton argues that "The portrayal of violence is used as a competitive tool in both entertainment and news shows to attract particular viewing audiences" (1998, p. 3). He also notes that the highest consumption of television violence is among males ages 18 to 34, followed by females of the same ages (p. 3). Additionally, Emmers-Sommer et al. note that, "men prefer films with sex and violence significantly more than women do" (2006, p. 1). Furthermore, the appeal of sex to both men and women can explain its use by the entertainment and advertising industries (Emmers-Sommer et al., 2006). The pattern that emerges from our CHAMP trends is that the U.S. movie industry is increasingly turning to content that will appeal to its disproportionately young audience. Although tobacco and alcohol portrayals are declining in general, depictions of youth smoking and violence are on the increase, youthful depictions of alcohol use have not changed, and explicit depictions of sex remain high while suicide is on the rise.

Do these popular movie portrayals influence the socialization of youth? The theoretical basis for relationships between portrayal and real-world behavior has been extensively elaborated, and considerable research in experimental contexts supports the relationship. When paired with real-world trends, the CHAMP data argue that movie portrayals influence those trends. Movie smoking rates paralleled declining societal trends in U.S. per-capita tobacco consumption by adults since the 1960s (Figure 4.4) and tobacco use by twelfth graders since the mid-1970s (see data for twelfth graders in Figure 4.6). The increase in youth smoking portrayal in films (Figure 4.6) could actually have contributed to a slowing of the overall downward trend in adolescent tobacco consumption. Movie alcohol portrayal (Figure 4.7) declined well before the drop in per-capita consumption of alcohol in the 1980s. However, robust advertising for beer (and, more recently, alcopops) on TV and in magazines (see Chapter 10) could well have helped maintain this behavior despite the early drop in film portrayals. Tobacco advertising was removed from TV by the early 1970s (see Chapter 9), making its media portrayal more dependent on films and magazines.

With regard to the other behaviors we have examined, film trends also appear to parallel societal trends. Sexual explicitness in films paralleled the increase in U.S. births to unwed youth aged 15 through 19 during the 1960s and 1970s (Figure 4.9). The U.S. youth homicide rate (ages 15–24) rose in concert with the increase in portrayed violent content (Figure 4.10), and increases in suicide explicitness paralleled the rise in U.S. youth suicide rate in persons ages 15 to 24 (Figure 4.12). If one considers that films require several years of production before release to the public, it is unlikely that they merely follow societal behavior. It is possible that the relationships we observe are all the result of other forces that affect both societal trends and the film industry, but the available evidence points to popular movie portrayals having some influence on real-world trends rather than merely following them.

While heartening, drops in the amount of popular movie portrayal of tobacco and alcohol use do not signal an end for the need for advocacy. Of particular concern are increases in portrayal of risk behaviors among those under 21. Even though the level of tobacco portrayal has declined overall, youth portrayals show the opposite trend for tobacco; portrayal of youth violence has increased as well. These trends are problematic because youth are more susceptible to the disinhibiting effects of the media, especially for behaviors that are otherwise socially unacceptable (see the Introduction). It is also a matter of concern because the increase in portrayal of smoking and violence among those under 21 is occurring for behaviors that are a particular vulnerability for that age. Most initiate smoking at an early age, and violence tends to peak during late adolescence and early adulthood. Indeed, the increased movie portrayal of youth violence occurs in a culture in which, according to the Centers for Disease Control (National Center for Health Statistics, 2004), homicide and suicide are leading killers of youth.

The audience for mass-market films is heavily both male and young (Motion Picture Association of America, 2007), a group at high risk for fatalistic expectations about the future (Jamieson & Romer, 2008), violence (National Center for Health Statistics, 2004), and suicide (Brent, Baugher, Bridge, Chen, & Chiappetta, 1999). As a result, these increases over time in popular movie portrayals may reinforce such dysfunctional real-world behaviors, encouraging aggression, violence, and suicide as solutions to the problems facing its youth audience.

It is also disappointing to see so much attention given to male actors in top-grossing films. With the increased entry of women into the workforce and the societal drive for gender equality, it is surprising to see a trend toward greater male representation in films. We do not know the effects of this pattern on young women's socialization (see Chapter 5), but it is clearly a lost opportunity that there are increasingly fewer female role models for adolescents in such a powerful and persuasive medium.

## ACKNOWLEDGMENTS

The authors would like to thank our funders for making this project possible. The Annenberg/Robert Wood Johnson Foundation Coding Health and Media Project is a joint initiative of the Adolescent Risk Communication Institute of the Annenberg Public Policy Center and the Robert Wood Johnson Foundation.

## APPENDIX: THE ANNENBERG/ROBERT WOOD JOHNSON FOUNDATION CODING HEALTH AND MEDIA PROJECT DEFINITIONS OF RISK BEHAVIORS

### ALCOHOL

The appearance of anything alcohol-related in the scene, ranging from signs, billboards, and logos to the direct (or implied) depiction of a character consuming alcohol.

### TOBACCO

The appearance of anything tobacco-related, including smoking ads, logos, or paraphernalia as well as implied or direct tobacco consumption.

### SEX

Any type of sexual contact, including kissing (on lips), nudity, sexual behavior, or sexual intercourse, implicitly or explicitly shown. If a segment contains multiple depictions of sexual content, we only code the highest degree of portrayal. Thus, if a couple is kissing in the first minute of the segment, but later at the fourth minute intercourse takes place, we code only the intercourse and the characters involved. We do not code for background depictions of sexual content (e.g., posters or magazines depicting nudity). However, we do code for sexual content if it is presented as the focus of the shot. For example, if the characters are watching pornography and the scene cuts to a full screen portrayal of the show.

### AGGRESSION AND VIOLENCE

Code for occurrences of violence, bullying, or the presence of guns. We follow Thompson and Yokota's (2000) definition of violence: "Physical acts where the aggressor makes or attempts to make some physical contact with the intention of causing injury or death" and "intentional acts where the aggressor makes or attempts to make some physical contact that has potential to inflict injury or harm," excluding natural disasters, accidents, objects not attributed to a character, and expected physical acts by sport games that are not intended to seriously injure (tackling, checking, boxing, stunts).

We do code for aggressive behavior by or against non-human characters. Like sexual content, we do not code background portrayals. We only code this if the focus of the shot shows aggressive behavior. For example, a full screen depiction of a TV broadcast with violent content.

A "sequence" of violence is defined as an uninterrupted display of a character or a group of characters engaged in violence. For example, a battle scene in which many persons are harmed in succession would constitute multiple acts of violence. We counted the number of such acts per segment as an index of violent sequences.

## SUICIDE

Suicides are defined as situations where a person has the option of living and chooses to take his or her own life. If a character is going to be killed but preempts the outcome, it is not coded as a suicide.

## NOTE

1. See http://www.youthmediarisk.org and the Appendix for more details.

## REFERENCES

Abramson, P. R., & Mechanic, M. B. (1983). Sex and the media: Three decades of best-selling books and major motion pictures. *Archives of Sexual Behavior, 12,* 185–206.

Anderson, C. A., Berkowitz, L., Donnerstein, E., Huesmann, L. R., Johnson, J. D., Linz, D., et al. (2003). The influence of media violence on youth. *Psychological Science in the Public Interest, 4,* 81–110.

Ashcraft, C. (2003). Adolescent ambiguities in American Pie: Popular culture as a resource for sex education. *Youth and Society, 35,* 37–70.

Bandura, A. (2002). Social cognitive theory of mass communication. In J. Bryant & D. Zillman (Eds.), *Media effects: Advances in theory and research* (pp. 121–153). Mahwah, NJ: Erlbaum.

Bollen, K. A., & Phillips, D. P. (1982). Imitative suicides: A national study of the effects of television news stories. *American Sociological Review, 47,* 802–809.

Brent, D. A., Baugher, M., Bridge, J., Chen, T., & Chiappetta, L. (1999). Age and sex related risk factors for adolescent suicide. *Journal of the American Academy of Child and Adolescent Psychiatry, 38,* 1497–1505.

Brisbin, R. A. (2002). Censorship, ratings, and rights: Political order and sexual portrayals in American movies. *Studies in American Political Development, 16*, 1–27.

Dempsey, J. M., & Reichert, T. (2000). Portrayal of married sex in the movies. *Journal of Sexuality and Culture, 4*, 31–36.

Emmers-Sommer, T. M., Paley, P., Hanzel, A. H., & Triplett, L. (2006). Love, suspense, sex, and violence: Men's and women's film predilections, exposure to sexually violent media, and their relationship to rape myth acceptance. *Sex Roles, 55*, 311–320.

Everett, S., Schnuth, R., & Tribble, J. (1998). Tobacco and alcohol use in top-grossing American films. *Journal of Community Health, 23*, 317–324.

Gerbner, G., Gross, L., Morgan, M., & Signorielli, N. (1986). Living with television: The dynamics of the cultivation process. In J. Bryant & D. Zillman (Eds.), *Perspectives on media effects* (pp. 17–40). Mahwah, NJ: Erlbaum.

Glantz, S. A., Kacirk, K. W., & McCulloch, C. (2004). Back to the future: Smoking in movies in 2002 compared with 1950 levels. *American Journal of Public Health, 94*, 261–263.

Gould, M., Jamieson, P., & Romer, D. (2003). Media contagion and suicide among the young. *American Behavioral Scientist, 46*, 1269–1284.

Greenberg, B. S., Siemicki, M., Dorfman, S., Heeter, C., Stanley, C., Soderman, A., et al. (1993). Sex content in R-rated films viewed by adolescents. In B. Greenberg & J. Brown (Eds.), *Media, sex, and the adolescent* (pp. 45–58). Cresskill, NJ: Hampton Press.

Hamilton, J. T. (1998). *Channeling violence: The economic market for violent television programming.* Princeton, NJ: Princeton University Press.

Hawton, K., Simkin, S., Deeks, J., O'Connor, S., Keen, A., Altman, D. G., et al. (1999). Effects of a drug overdose in a television drama on presentations to hospital for self poisoning: Time series and questionnaire study. *British Medical Journal, 318*, 972–977.

Hazan, A. R., & Glantz, S. A. (1995). Current trends in tobacco use on prime-time fictional television. *American Journal of Public Health, 85*, 116–117.

Jamieson, P. E. (2003). *Changes in United States popular culture portrayal of youth suicide: 1950–2000.* Unpublished doctoral dissertation, University of Pennsylvania.

Jamieson, P. E., & Romer, D. (2008). Unrealistic fatalism in U.S. youth ages 14–22: Prevalence and characteristics. *Journal of Adolescent Health, 42*, 154–160.

Jamieson, P. E., Romer, D., & Jamieson, K. H. (2006). Do films about mentally disturbed characters promote ineffective coping in vulnerable youth? *Journal of Adolescence, 29*, 749–760.

Johnston, L. D., O'Malley, P. M., Bachman, J. G., & Schulenberg, J. E. (2006, December 21). Decline in daily smoking by younger teens has ended. *Monitoring the future.* Retrieved from http://www.monitoringthefuture.org

Krippendorff, K. (2004). *Content analysis: An introduction to its methodology.* Thousand Oaks, CA: Sage.

L'Engle, K. L., Brown, J. D., & Kenneavy, K. (2006). The mass media are an important context for adolescents' sexual behavior. *Journal of Adolescent Health, 38*, 186–192.

Luker, K. (1996). *Dubious conceptions: The politics of teenage pregnancy*. Cambridge, MA: Harvard University Press.

Mares, M. L., & Woodard, E. (2005). Positive effects of television on children's social interactions: A meta-analysis. *Media Psychology, 7*, 301–322.

McIntosh, W. D., Bazzini, D. G., Smith, S. M., & Wayne, S. M. (1998). Who smokes in Hollywood? Characteristics of smokers in popular films from 1940 to 1989. *Addictive Behaviors, 23*, 395–398.

McIntosh, W. D., Smith, S. M., Bazzini, D. G., & Mills, P. S. (1999). Alcohol in movies: Characteristics of drinkers and nondrinkers in films from 1940 to 1989. *Journal of Applied Social Psychology, 29*, 1191–1199.

Monk-Turner, E., Ciba, P., Cunningham, M., McIntire, P. G., Pollard, M., & Turner, R. (2004). A content analysis of violence in American war movies. *Analyses of Social Issues and Public Policy, 4*, 1–11.

Motion Picture Association of America. (2007). *2007 U.S. movie attendance study*. Available at http://www.mpaa.org/moviattendancestudy.pdf

National Center for Health Statistics. (2004). *10 Leading causes of death, United States 2001, all races, both sexes*. Washington, DC: Centers for Disease Control, National Center for Health Statistics.

Pardun, C. J., L'Engle, K. L., & Brown, J. D. (2005). Linking exposure to outcomes: Early adolescents' consumption of sexual content in six media. *Mass Communication & Society, 8*, 75–91.

Phillips, D. P. (1980). Airplane accidents, murder, and the mass meida: Towards a theory of imitation and suggestion. *Social Forces, 58*, 1001–1024.

Phillips, D. P., Lesnya, K., & Paight, D. J. (1992). Suicide and the media: Assessment and prediction of suicide. In R. Maris, A. Berman, J. Maltsberger, & R. Yufit (Eds.), *Assessment and prediction of suicide* (pp. 499–519). New York: Guilford.

Romer, D., Jamieson K. H., & Aday, S. (2003). Television news and the cultivation of fear of crime. *Journal of Communication, 53*, 88–104.

Romer, D., Jamieson, P. E., & Jamieson, K. H. (2006). Are news reports of suicide contagious? A stringent test in six U.S. cities. *Journal of Communication, 2*, 253–270.

Sargent, J. D., Beach, M. L., Adachi-Mejia, A. M., Titus-Ernstoff, L. T., Gibson, J. J., Heatherton, T. F., et al. (2005). Exposure to movie smoking and smoking initiation among U.S. adolescents. *Pediatric Research, 58*, 410.

Sargent, J. D., Heatherton, T. F., Ahrens, B., Dalton, M. A., Tickle, J. J., & Beach, M. L. (2002). Adolescent exposure to extremely violent movies. *Journal of Adolescent Health, 31*, 449–454.

Stern, S. R. (2005). Messages from teens on the big screen: Smoking, drinking, and drug use in teen-centered films. *Journal of Health Communication, 10*, 331–346.

Thompson, K. M., & Yokota, F. (2001). Depiction of alcohol, tobacco, and other substances in G-rated animated feature films. *Pediatrics, 107*, 1369–1374.

Ward, L. M., & Friedman, K. (2006). Using tv as a guide: Associations between television viewing and adolescents' sexual attitudes and behavior. *Journal of Research on Adolescence, 16*, 133–156.

Yokota, F., & Thompson, K. M. (2000). Violence in G-rated animated films. *Journal of the American Medical Association, 283*, 2716–2720.

# 5

# Adolescent Gender Role Portrayals in the Media

## 1950 to the Present

JENNIFER L. WALSH AND L. MONIQUE WARD

Through the process of gender socialization, children and adolescents learn the norms and expectations for females and males in their culture (Golombok & Fivush, 1994). This process involves the development of gender schemas, which help individuals organize information about various aspects of gender, such as the typical behaviors, attributes, and appearance of women and men (Bem, 1981; Liben & Signorella, 1987; Martin & Halverson, 1981; Ruble & Martin, 1998; Ward, Hansbrough, & Walker, 2005). These schemas also affect how new information about gender is perceived and processed. Information obtained often takes the form of gender stereotypes, which are individuals' beliefs about characteristics associated with females and males in a general sense. While not necessarily harmful in and of themselves, these stereotypes can have negative effects when individuals perceive a discrepancy between the way they think, feel, and behave and the way they should act, according to gender stereotypes—an experience known as gender role conflict or stress (Eisler & Skidmore, 1987; O'Neil, Helms, Gable, David, & Wrightsman, 1986). Gender role conflict has been associated with poor mental health, physical health, and interpersonal outcomes (Arrindell, Kolk, Martin, Kwee, & Booms, 2003; Eisler, Skidmore, & Ward, 1988; Jakupcak, Lisak, & Roemer, 2002; Martz, Handley, & Eisler, 1995).

Gender socialization comes from many sources, including parents, peers, school, religion, and—of interest here—the media. The media may play a powerful role in socializing adolescents, making their portrayals important to understand. Whereas extensive research has been done on the media's gendered representations, little research has attended to adolescent portrayals specifically, and the work that exists has not been synthesized. After briefly discussing gender development in adolescence, we review adolescent gender role portrayals in various forms of media over the last half-century. Following this review, we discuss potential effects of these portrayals on adolescents and make suggestions for future research.

## GENDER DEVELOPMENT IN ADOLESCENCE

Adolescence is a time of biological, cognitive, social, and emotional changes, making it "a primary transition point during which gendered behaviors may be enacted, questioned, changed, or solidified" (Galambos, 2004, p. 240). Researchers have identified adolescence as a period during which there is extreme pressure to conform to traditional gender roles (Kahn, 1984; Lott, 1995; White, Donat, & Bondurant, 2001). Some have argued that gender awareness may even intensify during adolescence (Hill & Lynch, 1983; Huston & Alvarez, 1990). After a temporary increase in the flexibility of gender stereotypes immediately following the transition to junior high school, that flexibility has been found to decrease through adolescence (Alfieri, Ruble, & Higgins, 1996). The gender intensification hypothesis (Hill & Lynch, 1983) suggests that differences between adolescent girls and boys (in terms of behaviors, attitudes, and attributes) increase with age due to increased socialization pressures to conform to traditional feminine and masculine gender roles. This hypothesis also proposes that puberty serves as the signal to socialization sources (such as parents and peers) that the adolescent is becoming an adult and should begin to act in line with stereotypical female and male roles. Research has supported an increase in some gender differences, including levels of masculinity and gender role attitudes, in adolescence (Galambos, Almeida, & Petersen, 1990), although the hypothesis as a whole has mixed support and may not apply to all aspects of gender identity or to all gender-related constructs (Galambos, 2004).

What remains clear is that adolescents continue to learn about gender by observing those around them, and by drawing from models, both real and fictional, to help construct their norms and beliefs (Bandura, 1986, 1994). Young people may learn gender norms from watching their parents and peers, but they are also socialized by media models (Bandura, 1986, 1994; Ward, 2003). The question then becomes, what might adolescents be learning from media portrayals, and have there been any changes in these portrayals in recent years?

## CHANGES IN ADOLESCENT GENDER ROLE PORTRAYALS IN THE MEDIA

Believing adolescent gender role portrayals in the media to be both significant and understudied, we attempt to synthesize the existing literature on adolescent gender role portrayals in the media during the second half of the twentieth century. To do so, we review literature on six formats of media: television programs, television commercials, music videos, movies, magazine content, and magazine advertisements. Overall, few systematic, empirical analyses of adolescent gender portrayals across time exist. Although the media effects literature would suggest that adolescents would be most influenced by models their own age, and that media consumers of all ages might form ideas about adolescents based on portrayals of them, very few content analyses have focused on portrayals of adolescents at all (Strange, 2007).

In order to reach some preliminary conclusions about adolescent gender roles in the media without any existing systematic, empirical analyses across time, we drew from the following four sources: general content analyses that included some data about the age of characters and models, content analyses that covered media primarily consumed by young people, short-term longitudinal analyses of specific genres, and essays about the nature of media content featuring adolescents (when limited empirical work was available). Using these sources, we looked at both representation of the sexes—how many women versus men appeared in the various media—and roles played by men and women. We summarize the findings for each format of media.

### Television Programming

Television is perhaps the most researched media format, in addition to being the medium that accounts for a large portion of adolescents' media use. Adolescents are estimated to spend approximately three hours per day watching television, resulting in their spending more time per year watching television than in school (Rideout, Roberts, & Foehr, 2005). Content analyses of gender representation and roles on television in general have found consistent underrepresentation of women and pervasive gender typing over time (Calvert & Huston, 1987; Davis, 1990; Elasmar, Hasegawa, & Brain,

1999; McNeil, 1975; Signorielli, 1989). Here, we focus on the representation and roles of young people.

REPRESENTATION

In general, television programs feature a higher percentage of male youth than female youth, in line with the underrepresentation of females seen in research on adult television characters. Although no research has systematically traced the representation of adolescents across time, we can draw on a variety of studies that have included some data related to young people. We note that this trend of asymmetric gender representation seems to be consistent across time, although it may have improved slightly in the 1990s. Figure 5.1 depicts data from a variety of studies from the early 1970s to the late 1990s. In data aggregated for the years 1969 through 1985, Signorielli (1987) found that male teenagers outnumbered female teenagers three to

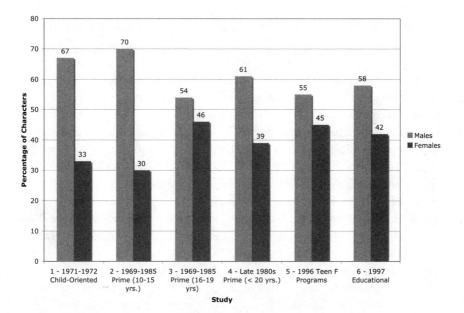

Figure 5.1.  Gender representation in various genres of youth-oriented and youth-containing television programming across time. (*Note*: 1 = Sternglanz and Serbin [1974], characters in popular child-oriented programming; 2 and 3 = Signorielli [1987], network prime-time major characters in two age groups; 4 = Peirce [1989], network prime-time characters up to age 20; 5 = Signorielli [1997], characters in the top twenty-five programs among female teens; 6 = Barner [1999], characters in network educational/ informational programming.)

two. Males outnumbered females in both prime time and weekend daytime programming, and early adolescent females (ages 10–15) were more outnumbered than later adolescent females (ages 16–19). However, some studies have found that the older adolescent to young adult age group is the age group where women are *least* underrepresented, with women making up 45% of this group (Signorielli, 1987). Robinson and Skill (2001) looked at network programming featuring families from the 1950s to the 1990s and found that male children outnumbered female children in the 1950s (when 56% of all children were male) and 1960s (55%), but the gender distribution became more equitable in the 1970s (52%) and 1980s (50%). However, boys outnumbered girls once again in the 1990s, when 55% of children in family-oriented series were male.

ROLES

To demonstrate how young people have been represented over time, we summarize several key empirical studies that examined gender roles on television in the 1970s, 1980s, and 1990s.

Sternglanz and Serbin (1974) examined three episodes each of ten popular child-oriented programs from the 1971–1972 television season (e.g., *Josie and the Pussycats*, *Bewitched*, and *Scooby-Doo*), comparing the behaviors of male and female characters in twelve categories. Although the authors did not focus on characters of any specific age, their choice of child-oriented programs makes it likely that young characters were included, and five of the ten programs had teenage casts. The authors found behavior differences in line with traditional gender stereotypes. They found that males were depicted as more aggressive (25% of males versus 13% of females), constructive/achieving (38% of males versus 24% of females), and succorant (6% of males versus 3% of females), while females were shown as more deferent (37% of females versus 25% of males), as well as punished more for high levels of activity. However, males and females did not significantly differ in general activity, dominance, autonomy, harm avoidance, recognition of others, self-recognition, or use of magic.

Peirce (1989) looked at the characteristics of television youth up to age 20 from a week of prime-time network programming during the late 1980s. She rated thirteen traits and described the activities of twenty male and thirteen female characters from the thirteen programs containing youth characters (e.g., *Family Ties*, *Who's the Boss*, and *Growing Pains*). Peirce found that child and adolescent male characters were more associated with the character traits active, aggressive, rational, and unhappy, while female and male characters did not differ on the other nine traits. She also identified "female" and "male" activities. The majority of characters (89%) participating in "female" activities (including doll play, helping in the kitchen, talking on the phone, and watching television) were girls, whereas *all* of the people doing "male" activities (including participating in sports, mischievous activities, and outdoor activities) were boys.

Signorielli (1997) examined eleven dimensions of gender roles in a two-week sample of the top twenty-five Nielsen programs for girls ages 12 to 17 in fall 1996. By our count, ten of these twenty-five programs had prominent teen characters (e.g., *Clueless, Sabrina the Teenage Witch,* and *Boy Meets World*). Overall, Signorielli found the sexes were more alike than different, significantly differing on only three of fifteen activities, one of six motivations, and three of thirteen behaviors. Males were more likely to be shown on the job (41% of males versus 28% of females), whereas females were more likely to be shown engaging in gender-stereotyped chores (27% of females versus 1% of males) and grooming (10% of women versus 3% of men). Females were also more likely to be shown talking about dating and romance (63% of females versus 49% of males). However, males and females did not differ in their rates of participation in activities such as sports, dating, or talking on the telephone. Females were more likely to be shown crying or whining (34% of females versus 20% of males), making threats (19% of females versus 11% of males), and promising sex (9% of females versus 3% of males), but the sexes did not differ in terms of intelligent behavior, flirting, joking or teasing, or risk taking. Consistent gender differences did exist in levels of dress, with female characters shown more often in sleepwear and lingerie (15% of females versus 5% of males) and less often in business clothing or uniforms (23% of females versus 35% of males) than males.

Barner (1999) coded ten categories of behaviors in thirty-three episodes of eleven programs with narrative storylines that were listed as educational/informational on broadcast networks in summer 1997. Many of these programs had teen casts (e.g., *Saved by the Bell—The New Class, California Dreams,* and *Sweet Valley High*). Overall, males and females differed in eight of the ten categories of behavior. He found that males were more likely than females to engage in activity, construction, dominance, aggression, and attention-seeking behaviors, while females were more likely to demonstrate deference, dependence, and nurturance. Males and females did not differ in autonomy or harm avoidance. Barner coded many of the same behaviors as Sternglanz and Serbin (1974) and found more gender differences (in line with traditional stereotypes), suggesting differences across time or genre (child-oriented versus educational/informational).

## SUMMARY OF FINDINGS

In general, across time, youth were often shown doing stereotypical activities. For example, females groomed, whined, shopped, and did chores, while males rebelled, worked, constructed, and fought. Young characters also generally exhibited stereotypical attributes, with females being nurturant, domestic, passive, and dependent, while males were active, aggressive, dominant, and rational. Although there may have been a reduction in gender differentiation since the 1970s, because we lack a systematic study of the portrayal of adolescent television characters, it is difficult to tell, and some studies (e.g., Barner, 1999) seem to suggest large stereotypical gender differences still exist and may even have intensified again in the 1990s.

## Television Commercials

Over 20% of the typical hour of broadcast television is comprised of commercials, and the average American views approximately 30,000 to 37,000 television commercials per year (Allan & Coltrane, 1996; Bretl & Cantor, 1988). Some studies have suggested that female representation may have increased and roles expanded in recent years, but findings are mixed (Bretl & Cantor, 1988; Lovdal, 1989; Signorielli, 1991). Here, we review the representation and roles of young women and men in television commercials.

### REPRESENTATION

In general, television commercials, like television programming, feature more male than female characters. Although the greatest female representation is seen in recent years, no general systematic trends in representation seem to exist over time. Figure 5.2 shows the percentage of male and female characters in relevant studies from 1987 to 2001 (focusing on characters in ads during children's or teen programming, programming popular with adolescents, or adolescent characters, specifically). Between 29% and 55% of characters were female, with the highest female representation in 2001 prime-time advertisements featuring 13- to 20-year-olds, and the lowest in 1995 commercials during children's programming.

### ROLES

Overall, conventional gender images have been found to be even more common in commercials than in television programming. Indeed, commercials may present "condensed typifications of gender relations," showing men as dominant, active, and knowledgeable and women as dependent, passive, and preoccupied with their physical appearance (Allan & Coltrane, 1996, p. 187). Little early research focused on young people in commercials, but we review three empirical studies from more recent years to demonstrate how youth have been represented in commercials.

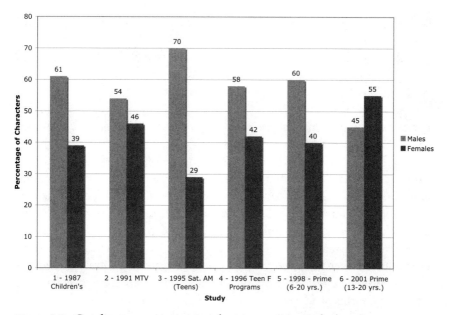

Figure 5.2.  Gender representation in television commercials during various genres of youth-oriented programming and among child and adolescent characters across time. (*Note*: 1 = Riffe, Goldson, Saxton, and Yu [1989], human characters in commercials during network children's Saturday morning programming; 2 = Signorielli, McLeod, and Healy [1994], characters in MTV commercials; 3 = Browne [1998], characters in Saturday morning commercials containing teens in the United States and Sydney, Australia; 4 = Signorielli [1997], characters in commercials during prime-time programs most popular with teen females ages 12 to 17; 5 = Ganahl, Prinsen, and Netzley [2003], characters 6 to 20 years old in prime-time network commercials; 6 = Stern and Mastro [2004], characters 13 to 20 years old in prime-time network commercials.)

Signorielli, McLeod, and Healy (1994) examined 550 commercials (110 unique) from six hours of MTV programming in November 1991. They coded commercials for gender composition and product, and major human characters (*N* = 522) for four appearance-related variables. Although the authors coded characters of all ages, 48.5% of those coded were young adults (ages 18 to 25), and 11.1% were teens. Among all characters, males were overrepresented (54.4% versus 45.6%), and the authors noted that the commercials were male-oriented overall. Whereas 23.7% of ads featured only males, only 9.6% featured exclusively females. Additionally, males were product users in 40% of the commercials, whereas females were product users in only half as many (20%). Male characters were much more likely to have average bodies (73.2%) than females (34.6%), whereas females were more likely than males to have very fit bodies (55.7% versus 14.2%), to be physically attractive (76.9% versus 36.6%), to wear sexy and skimpy clothing (53.8% versus 6.5%), and to be the object of others' gazes (60.5% versus 19%). Finally, product types oriented toward the two genders differed, with products related to looking good being advertised in commercials with only female characters and products reflecting action and fun being advertised in those commercials with only males.

Maher and Childs (2003) looked at gender roles in ninety child-oriented commercials drawn from after-school and Saturday-morning programming on five networks in March 2000. They coded the ad orientation (the gender most people would think of as being most appropriate for the advertised product), the gender of the voice-over, the gender of dominant product user, and the gender of the main character, and compared their results to similar analyses conducted over the twenty-seven previous years. In contrast to Signorielli et al. (1994), they found that gender dynamics were quite evenhanded, with three-fourths of ads (67%) being neutral, 17% female oriented, and 16% male oriented. However, this evenhandedness did not extend to voice-overs or characters—62% of voice-overs were by males, and 62% of main characters were male (versus 19% who were female). Notably, however, in making comparisons to previous studies (Browne, 1998; Macklin & Kolbe, 1984; Verna, 1975), the authors found slight (but consistent) decreases over time in the percentages of male-oriented commercials, male voice-overs, and male main characters. For example, 58% of commercials in 1975 were male-oriented (Verna, 1975) compared to the 16% Maher and Childs found.

Finally, Stern and Mastro (2004) examined 2,880 national commercials from a composite week of prime-time programming on the six major networks in February 2001, coding commercials and prominent human characters ($N = 2,315$) for age and gender as well as nine dimensions. They found that among teens (ages 13 to 20), males and females were equally represented (45% versus 55%), and differed significantly on only two of nine dimensions: primary behaviors and settings. In terms of primary behaviors, male adolescents were more likely to be shown working (17% of males versus 0% of females), whereas females were more likely to be shown doing home chores (5% of females versus 0% of males). With regard to setting, 37.5% of females, versus only 15.2% of males, were depicted in the home, whereas more male adolescents were depicted in the employment setting (8.7% of males versus 0% of females). Males and females did not differ in terms of the other seven dimensions, including attractiveness, degree of dress, body type, degree of physical activity, and product type. Thus, Stern and Mastro also found fewer gender differences than Signorielli et al. (1994) did ten years earlier, possibly due to changes over time, differences between advertising on MTV and other networks, or their focus on teenagers rather than women and men in general.

## SUMMARY OF FINDINGS

Drawing from these studies and other recent findings (Browne, 1998; Larson, 2001; Signorielli, 1997; Smith, 1994), the equitable presentation of male and female youth seems to be improving with time, but commercials still remain somewhat male-oriented in terms of both characters and voice-overs. Adolescent girls and boys are often portrayed in different settings (with females in home settings and males away from home, at work, and in fantasy settings), and are shown participating in different, gender-typed activities, which are more diverse for male characters. A primary gendered message from television commercials is that appearance matters for women—female characters are more likely to be thin, partially clothed, and to have their appearances commented on. Beauty appeals are also more often directed at women. Finally, there are sex differences in attributes displayed by characters, with female characters exhibiting more deference and shyness and male characters engaged in more domination and instrumental and executive behaviors.

## Music Videos

Nearly 40% of MTV's audience is between 12 and 18 years old (Nielsen Media Research, 2000), and surveys have suggested that three-fourths of 16- to 24-year-olds watch MTV (Kaiser Family Foundation, 2003). Additionally, Signorielli (1997) found that 79% of the women and 64% of the men in the top-twenty music videos shown on MTV in November 1996 appeared to be young adults. Therefore, even though specific studies reviewed rarely included information on model age, it is assumed that music videos often offer gender portrayals of young people and that young people are exposed to these portrayals.

## REPRESENTATION

Like television programming in general, music videos underrepresent women. In fact, underrepresentation of women in music videos may exceed that in other television programming. Looking at a variety of studies that collected data on gender representation in music videos between 1984 and 1997 (Figure 5.3), we see no systematic changes in gender ratios. Between 59% and 86% of artists and lead characters have been men, while the representation of women has ranged from 14% to 37%.

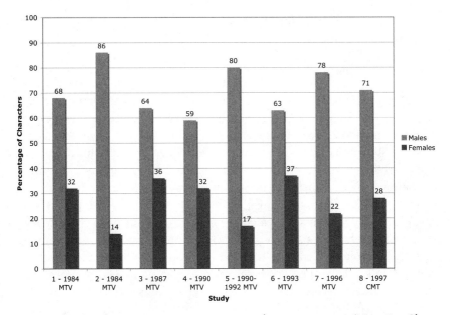

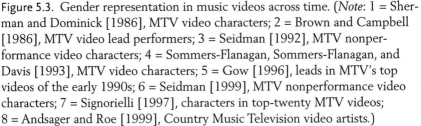

Figure 5.3. Gender representation in music videos across time. (*Note*: 1 = Sherman and Dominick [1986], MTV video characters; 2 = Brown and Campbell [1986], MTV video lead performers; 3 = Seidman [1992], MTV nonperformance video characters; 4 = Sommers-Flanagan, Sommers-Flanagan, and Davis [1993], MTV video characters; 5 = Gow [1996], leads in MTV's top videos of the early 1990s; 6 = Seidman [1999], MTV nonperformance video characters; 7 = Signorielli [1997], characters in top-twenty MTV videos; 8 = Andsager and Roe [1999], Country Music Television video artists.)

ROLES

To demonstrate how gender portrayals in music videos have changed over time, we summarize several key empirical studies looking at gender roles in music videos in the 1980s and 1990s.

Both Sherman and Dominick (1986) and Brown and Campbell (1986) conducted studies of MTV music videos in 1984, setting a baseline for future studies. Sherman and Dominick examined 166 videos, whereas Brown and Campbell looked at 75 videos. Both found a male-dominated world, in which the majority of solo performers (76% to 86%), groups (82%), and characters (68%) were male. Additionally, they found stereo-typical sex differences in terms of behaviors and activities. For example, females were more likely than males to be provocatively dressed (50% of females versus 10% of males; Sherman & Dominick) and less likely than males to be portrayed in professional work (5% of females versus 14% of males; Brown & Campbell). Additionally, 73% of aggressors and 77% of victims were male (Sherman & Dominick). However, there were also a variety of gender similarities—for example, the sexes were noted to participate equally in social activities and solitary actions (Brown & Campbell).

Another way in which videos, as a whole, have been analyzed is via a coding of their general level of sexism. Vincent (1989) and Andsager and Roe (1999) both looked at the level of sexism in music videos. Vincent examined 110 music videos in summer 1985 and 122 in winter 1986–1987, all from MTV, whereras Andsager and Roe looked at 285 videos on Country Music Television (CMT) in January 1997. Both coded what they identified as "consciousness level," the nature in which women were portrayed (Vincent, 1989, as adapted from Pingree, 1976). Female portrayals could be coded as condescending (depicting women as sex objects and as victims), keeping her place (depicting women in traditional feminine roles), contradictory, or fully equal. Andsager and Roe split the videos they coded based on whether the artists were male or female. In 1985, Vincent found that 54.6% of MTV portrayals could be labeled as condescending, 17.3% as keeping her place, 12.7% as contradictory, and 15.5% as fully equal. In 1986–1987, condescending portrayals had dropped to 41.8%, while fully equal portrayals had risen to 38.5%, possibly indicating progress. Looking at a different genre of music in 1997, Andsager and Roe found that 35.1% of CMT portrayals in videos by male artists were coded as condescending, 32.4% as keeping her place, 23.4% as contradictory, and 9% as fully equal—representing fewer condescending and fully equal portrayals and many more keeping her place and contradictory portrayals than Vincent found. However, findings for videos by female artists differed dramatically, with only 12.9% of portrayals being condescending and nearly half (49.5%) of portrayals being fully equal.

Seidman (1992) coded 182 MTV nonperformance videos from 1987 and their characters for the presence of fourteen behaviors. There were sex differences for twelve of these fourteen behaviors. Seidman found that the most prevalent male behaviors were aggression, violence, and victimization, while the most prevalent female behaviors were affection and being pursued sexually. Female characters and artists also wore more revealing clothing. Six years later, Seidman (1999) conducted a similar study to look for changes, coding ninety-one nonperformance music videos from 1993 for fourteen behaviors. This time, he found sex differences for less than half (six) out of the fourteen attributes. The most prevalent male behaviors were anger and aggression, whereas the most prevalent female behaviors were anger and affection, possibly suggesting an increase in the portrayal of women as angry over time. Although male characters and artists were still more adventuresome and violent than female characters and artists, they were no longer more domineering, victimized, or aggressive than the women. Women were no longer more fearful, dependent, or in sexual pursuit than men, although they still frequently wore revealing clothing. The percentage of male and female characters in the two years did not dramatically differ—in 1987, 36.7% of characters were male and 4.2% female, while in 1993, 33.4% of characters were male and 7% female.

In summary, music videos have been found to be consistently male dominated and highly stereotyped. The medium often features women as sexual objects in terms both of the roles they play and the clothing they wear. Whereas male artists and characters are shown as aggressive, dominant, and violent, female artists and characters are more frequently shown as affectionate and sexual. Although the level of sexism and some specific sex differences may have diminished since the 1980s, the prominence of stereotypical depictions of men and women has not changed.

## Movies

Very few empirical studies have attended to teen gender roles in movies, although adolescents are major consumers of movies, comprising the largest demographic segment of moviegoers (Strasburger, 1995). We discuss one empirical study focusing on portrayals of adolescents, then turn to observations on gender roles from the field of film criticism.

Stern (2005) examined movies with central teen characters (ages 12 to 19) in the top 125 movies from 1999, 2000, and 2001, a total of 43 movies. She coded the gender, behaviors, and motivations of 146 characters in these movies. A large number of behaviors were coded, while motivations coded included motivations to obtain or succeed at a job or school, to be prosocial, to do well financially, to be popular or maintain current popularity, to have a romantic relationship, and to improve appearance. Stern found that adolescent men and women were nearly equally represented (48.6% females versus 51.4% males). The percentage of men and women performing most behaviors did not differ—for example, male and female teens had equal rates of participation in hanging out, socializing at school, and making out, the three most common behaviors overall. However, men and women did significantly differ in rates of grooming, committing violence, completing chores, practicing religion, and caring for family. As would be expected from traditional gender norms, women were more likely to groom (72.0% of women versus 39.4% of men), complete chores (17.3% of women versus 4.2% of men), and care for family members (8.0% of women versus 0.0% of men), as well as practice religion (14.7% of women versus 4.2% of men), while men were more likely to commit violence (52.9% of men versus 28.4% of women). Finally, the most popular motivation for both male and female teens was to be in a romantic relationship, expressed by half ($N = 73$) of the characters. All other motivations were much less popular, and none differed based on gender.

Another body of research addressing adolescent gender roles specifically comes from film criticism. Several recent books, such as *Sugar, Spice, and Everything Nice: Cinemas of Girlhood* (Gateward & Pomerance, 2002), *Where the Boys Are: Cinemas of Masculinity and Youth* (Pomerance & Gateward, 2005), and *Generation Multiplex: The Image of Youth in Contemporary American Cinema* (Shary, 2002a), have focused specifically on film portrayals of adolescents. However, although this body of research does address the target population of adolescents, it is generally not systematic. Instead, themes are often extracted from a small number of films, and these critics look for both generalities and exceptions. As a result, the character types they identify that adhere to or violate traditional gender norms may or may not be representative.

Critics have identified several character types appearing in teen-oriented films that are in line with traditional gender roles. Shary (2005) discusses delinquent boys and reforming girls who appear in movies from the 1950s to the 1990s. He claims that, until recently, films have portrayed deviant boys in ever more threatening ways, and that delinquent boys in the 1980s became more inexplicably evil. In most films with delinquents prior to the 1990s, girls played the role of reformer for the delinquent boy, and female domesticity was both salvation for men's problems and a threat to masculine progress. Although this pattern started to change during the 1970s, Shary argues these gendered norms remained to some extent until the 1990s. In the 1990s, girl delinquents became more popular. Also in line with traditional gender norms, De Vaney (2002) discusses "Daddy's girls" in John Hughes's 1980s movies, such as *Sixteen Candles* and *The Breakfast Club*, arguing that Hughes depicts stereotyped gender roles and reinforces a domestic ideal for women of remaining within the family and continuing to be "Daddy's girl." Shary (2002b) also discusses "nerdly" and beautiful, smart girls in movies of the 1980s and 1990s. Although smart girls might seem to counter stereotypes, Shary notes that these girls appear infrequently and are either tormented and ostracized if they are "nerdly" (e.g., *Welcome to the Dollhouse*) or transformed by minimizing their intellect if they are beautiful smart girls (e.g., *She's All That*).

Film critics have also discussed adolescent portrayals that counter traditional gender roles. For example, Clover (1992) discusses the "Final Girls" of horror films beginning in the late 1970s. These girls' "smartness, gravity, competence in mechanical and other practical matters, and sexual reluctance" (p. 40) sets them apart from other girls and makes them the last to survive in horror movies. "Final Girls" are eventually saved by their skills, but also endure sustained torture. "Angry Girls" and "Tough Girls" (Shary, 2002a) became popular in the 1990s. Roberts (2002) discusses how these teenage girls use (justifiable) anger as a "weapon against gender crimes" (p. 217), often behaving violently. These tough, angry girls obviously counter traditional gender norms of women as passive. Finally, Kearney (2002) identifies a trend of independent films in the mid-1990s that privilege friendship (often same-sex) relationships over heterosexual romance, showing girls gaining confidence and assertiveness through their friendships. In these films, girls are sometimes masculinized, engaging in activities typically associated with boys, wearing traditionally masculine clothing, and inhabiting male-dominated spaces, but they also engage in caretaking and emotional intimacy.

Film criticism has focused specifically on adolescent roles and attended to gender to some extent. However, there are both stereotypical and counterstereotypical characters across time, and some commentary has suggested that gender roles in teen movies did not dramatically change during the second half of the twentieth century (Franklin, 1991). Additionally, the character types these critics discuss are not necessarily the most frequently appearing characters and may not come from the most popular films.

SUMMARY OF FINDINGS

There is little we can conclude on portrayals of adolescent gender roles in film from the existing body of literature. Both gender stereotypical and gender counterstereotypical adolescent character types have appeared in films across time, with film critics providing examples of each from the 1970s, 1980s, and 1990s. Empirical evidence suggests some stereotypical gender differences remained in teen movies at the turn of the century, but there were also many similarities between male and female adolescents in terms of both behaviors and motivations, and the sexes were nearly equally represented.

## Magazines

Teen magazines are regularly read by 50% to 70% of teenage girls in the United States (Strange, 2007). Although research has rarely examined general portrayals of adolescents in these magazines, their content might be viewed as highlighting adolescent gender role expectations, especially for young women. Unfortunately, research has primarily focused on gender roles for adolescent girls as portrayed by magazines while neglecting adolescent boys.

However, one advantage of this research, in contrast to that on other media formats, is that some of it has been done in a fairly systematic way over time. We review several key studies focusing on the nature of gender roles in teen magazines.

### REPRESENTATION

Because research has focused only on magazines targeted at adolescent girls (and, indeed, there are not equivalent publications aimed at adolescent boys), we would not expect the same underrepresentation of females as is found in other forms of media. In line with this, looking at issues of the four leading teen magazines (*Sassy, Teen, YM,* and *Seventeen*) in fall 1996, Signorielli (1997) found that 70% of the models in article photos were women.

### ROLES

Both Peirce (1990) and Schlenker, Caron, and Halteman (1998) looked at the percentage of editorial pages devoted to traditional versus feminist content in *Seventeen* magazine over time. Peirce examined issues from the years 1961 (before the feminist movement in the 1970s), 1972 (in the midst of the movement), and 1985 (following the feminist movement of the 1970s). Schlenker et al. replicated this study over an extended time period, looking at all issues of the magazine in 1945, 1955, 1965, 1975, 1985, and 1995. In this case, feminist movements were predicted to affect content in 1945 (post–World War II), 1975 (during the second-wave feminist movement), and 1995 (during "third-wave" feminism), whereas more traditional content was hypothesized in the other years.

The authors concluded that teen magazines primarily enforce traditional gender roles in their editorial content across time. Both studies found that the majority of the editorial content of *Seventeen* magazine (between just under 50% and 75%) in all years was devoted to traditional content concerning beauty, fashion, cooking, and decorating. Peirce found that approximately 50% of content in 1961, 1972, and 1985 focused on appearance alone. Despite the centrality of traditional content in *Seventeen* magazine, Peirce found that coverage of self-development (more feminist topics including education, vocations, avocations, and physical and mental health) increased in 1972 (to 16.6% of content from 7.5% in 1961), and that the coverage of male–female relations decreased (to 2.7% from 7% in 1961), in line with the feminist movement. However, she suggested that this effect was not long term, as coverage of both topics returned to 1960s levels in 1985. Schlenker et al. found that more articles on self-development, career development, and political/world issues appeared in *Seventeen* magazine during 1945, 1975, and 1995 as compared to 1955, 1965, and 1985, presumably in response to important periods in the women's movement. The wave of feminism in the 1970s may even have had lasting effects, as feminist content in the conservative 1980s was still much higher than in the 1950s and 1960s.

What do these studies tell us about adolescent gender roles? Much of the content presented in *Seventeen* is in line with traditional female gender roles, focusing on appearance, domesticity, and sexual relationships, and might be seen to encourage adherence to these gender roles for young women. Feminist content, with its focus on self- and career development, expands these traditional gender roles. Traditional gender role portrayals in *Seventeen* have seemed to vary somewhat in line with important periods in the women's movement, but have not shifted substantially and consistently in one direction over time.

In addition to these longitudinal studies, Peirce (1993) conducted an analysis of all fiction (104 stories) in *Seventeen* and *Teen* magazines between 1987 and 1991. She looked at dependence in the protagonists, categories of conflicts experienced by the protagonists, and occupations of all characters in the stories. She found that fictional stories in teen magazines presented traditional feminine gender roles. In 62% of the stories, the main characters depended on someone else to solve their problems, with 43% of these problems related to boys (compared to 27% for the next most common source of conflict, family). Additionally, these stories depicted primarily stereotypical occupations, with male characters as doctors, lawyers, judges, and bankers and female characters as nurses, clerical workers, social workers, and secretaries. These traditional gender portrayals are in line with findings about the stereotypical nature of fiction in adult women's magazines and nonfiction in teen magazines.

The trend of presenting primarily traditional gender roles in teen magazines aimed at young women continued in the late 1980s and 1990s, with most content of teen magazines *Sassy*, *Seventeen*, and *YM* in 1988 and 1989 focusing on fashion, physical beautification, and female–male relationships (Evans, Rutberg, Sather, & Turner, 1991). Prominent messages identified by Evans et al. included the importance of attracting males through physical beautification and an emphasis on slimness. Few females were presented in progressive roles, and even career articles focused primarily on modeling. In 1993, Duffy and Gotcher (1996) concluded from a case study–style analysis that teen magazine *YM* depicted a world where girls must aspire to a nearly impossible physical beauty ideal to attract men, who are almost the sole focus of life. Additionally, young women were shown few educational or occupational opportunities.

Signorielli (1997) also found appearance, dating, and fashion to be the most common topics addressed in teen magazines directed at girls, in line with traditional gender roles. Fewer articles addressed topics such as self-confidence (16%), family (15%), career (12%), school (12%), and becoming independent (5%). However, in contrast to Peirce's (1993) earlier findings on the depiction of dependence in magazines, Signorielli (1997) found that teen magazine articles (from *Sassy, Teen, YM*, and *Seventeen*) in 1996 stressed relying on oneself to solve problems—28% of articles implied readers should solve problems themselves, compared to 6% for the next most likely source of help (mothers). Additionally, few articles suggested readers seek out help from romantic partners.

SUMMARY OF FINDINGS

Overall, teen magazine content aimed at young women has been found to be stereotypical from the 1950s through the present, focusing primarily on appearance and dating. However, studies have suggested that how traditionally stereotypical the content is in a given year may be related to the state of the feminist movement (Peirce, 1990; Schlenker et al., 1998). More recent research has found some positive trends—for example, teen magazine readers are encouraged to be self-reliant (Signorielli, 1997)—but little else of significance seems to have changed.

## Magazine Advertising

Magazine advertisements are one of the genres very frequently examined in research on gender role portrayals in the media. According to Courtney and Whipple (1983), even by the early 1980s, there were over 300 published sources addressing sex stereotyping in advertising in the United States, Canada, the United Kingdom, and other countries. In general, this body of research has found that in the 1960s and early 1970s, images of women in magazine ads were overwhelmingly traditional, emphasizing that a woman's place is in the home rather than the workforce, that women are dependent on men for protection, and that women are sex objects or beautiful decorations (Butler & Paisley, 1980; Courtney & Lockeretz, 1971; Kang, 1997; Thomas & Treiber, 2000; Venkatesan & Losco, 1975). Some studies have reported improvements in these overall representations over the last twenty-five years, with more women depicted as employed outside the home or in professional positions, and fewer women depicted solely as homemakers, but these changes have been minor at best (Busby & Leichty, 1993). Despite this large body of research, very little is directly relevant to adolescents. Here, we present two studies that focus on print advertisements in publications frequently read by teens.

Signorielli (1997) examined magazine ads ($N = 602$) and models in these ads ($N = 352$) from issues of the top four teen magazines directed at girls (*Seventeen, Sassy, Teen,* and *YM*) from September to December 1996. She coded these ads for demographics of the models and product appeals of the ads themselves. As expected, Signorielli found that the majority of ad models in these teen magazines (82%) were women. Of these, the majority were adolescents or young adults, with these two groups comprising 74% of all female ad models. Signorielli also found that the main product appeals in these ads were beauty (50% of ads) and youthfulness (37% of ads), in line with traditional gender roles. Other appeals less in line with traditional gender roles, such as independence, were less common (17% of ads).

Cuneen and Sidwell (1998) conducted a content analysis of gender portrayals in advertisements in *Sports Illustrated for Kids* (*SIFK*) from 1989 to 1994. They looked at the gender of prominent and supporting models as well as the types of activities and types of products models were engaged in and advertising. Although the authors did not note model age, *SIFK* has 2.5 million readers between 13 and 17, and the median reader age is 11 or 12, indicating that these advertisements are directed to early adolescent boys and girls. Cuneen and Sidwell found that boys and men were depicted dramatically more often than girls and women in both prominent and supporting roles (with a 12:1 male-to-female ratio for prominent roles and a 6:1 ratio for supporting roles). Additionally, girls and women were primarily depicted in supporting roles in ads featuring combined sport and recreational activities or individual sports (like tennis) rather than team sports. They were also frequently posed, not active, and provocative, regardless of model age. The most equal male-to-female ratio was seen in the individual sports category (2:1), and the largest disparity was seen in the team sports category (31:1). The authors suggest these findings indicate the persistence of gendered norms, with females infrequently portrayed in this sports context and shown in traditional ways—inactive, provocative—when they are.

## SUMMARY OF FINDINGS

It is difficult to draw conclusions about adolescent gender roles as portrayed in magazine advertising from the limited findings about advertising in two very different genres of magazines—those directed to teenage girls and *Sports Illustrated for Kids*. Additionally, because the relevant research has all been conducted in the past twenty years, it is difficult to comment on trends over time. However, gender portrayals in both types of magazine seem to be in line with traditional stereotypes. Ads directed at young women stress beauty and youthfulness, and women are dramatically underrepresented in most sports contexts.

## EFFECTS OF GENDER PORTRAYALS ON ADOLESCENTS

From this review of six forms of media—television programming, television advertising, music videos, movies, magazine content, and magazine advertising—we see there has been only limited, if any, change in adolescent gender roles as portrayed in the media over the past thirty to fifty years. What are the effects on adolescent girls and boys of exposure to the gender stereotypical media content that continues to exist?

As noted throughout, adolescents are major media consumers, devoting over seven hours a day to media use throughout adolescence (Roberts & Foehr, 2003; Roberts, Foehr, Rideout, & Brodie, 1999). Adolescents may be attracted to media for many reasons—for entertainment, tension relief, escape, information, or to help with personal identity formation (Arnett, 1995; Christenson & Roberts, 1998; Dominick, 1996; Dorr, 1986; Rosengren, Wenner, & Palmgreen, 1985; Rubin, 2002). The media's prominence in young people's lives has raised concerns about the messages young people might take away. Additionally, whereas adolescents have many sources of gender information—for example, parents, peers, schools, and religion—the messages from media may be especially consistent, ubiquitous, and frequent (Morgan, 1982). Media exposure may affect young people's gender schemas both by defining what is normative and what is ideal for women and men (Ward et al., 2005). Because adolescent gender portrayals in the media are constrained, young media consumers might come to limit their own aspirations and self-conceptions based on gender (Rivadeneyra & Ward, 2005).

Although empirical effects found are generally small, the media's potential influence on gender conceptions remains a concern because of the broad-reaching impact of gender role norms in our lives (Signorielli, 2001). Research finds that adolescents' thoughts about appropriate gender roles may influence their career planning, intimate relationships, sexual decision making, and attitudes toward parenthood (Ward et al., 2005). Additionally, attempting to adhere to stereotypical gender roles has been associated with mental health problems such as substance abuse, sexual risk taking, and poor body image for both girls and boys (Monk & Ricciardelli, 2003; Pleck, Sonenstein, & Ku, 1993; Stice, Schupak-Neuberg, Shaw, & Stein, 1994; Tolman,

1999). Such mental health problems may result from gender role stress, an individual's assessment of the degree to which she or he adheres (or fails to adhere) to the stereotypical male or female role (Cohn & Zeichner, 2006).

In the existing literature, media exposure has been found to be associated with multiple aspects of adolescents' gender roles. One domain affected is adolescents' beliefs about gender and their perceptions of gendered reality. Here, data indicate that frequent television viewing is associated with holding more stereotypical beliefs about masculine and feminine traits, activities, chores, and occupations for children and adolescents (Beuf, 1974; Freuh & McGhee, 1975; Morgan, 1987; Rothschild, 1979; Signorielli, 2001; Signorielli & Lears, 1992). Additionally, increased exposure to some genres is related to viewers' beliefs about the distribution of real-world roles and occupations (Carveth & Alexander, 1985; Potter & Chang, 1990). Related to this, exposure to programs with nontraditional characters or educational television has been found to be associated with less stereotypical sex role beliefs (Rosenwasser, Lingenfelter, & Harrington, 1989). Similar effects have been found in samples of children, pre-adolescents, middle schoolers, high schoolers, and undergraduate students.

A second domain of adolescent gender roles affected by media exposure is gender ideology, or attitudes and stereotypes about gender roles. Television viewing has been associated with viewers' sexism through both correlational and experimental research (Gross & Jeffries-Fox, 1978; Kimball, 1986; Morgan & Rothschild, 1983; Potter & Chang, 1990; Signorielli, 2001; Ward & Rivadeneyra, 1999). A meta-analysis of nineteen nonexperimental and eleven experimental studies found a moderately significant association (effect size = .101) between total television viewing and endorsement of gender stereotypes (Herrett-Skjellum & Allen, 1996). This meta-analysis found no patterns associated with age of participants—effects occurred for children, adolescents, and adults. In one specific study, Morgan (1982) examined the relation over two years between television viewing and sixth through tenth graders' sex-role stereotypes. He found that girls' (but not boys') amount of television viewing was significantly associated with their sexism scores a year later. Rivadeneyra and Ward (2005) found that girls who watched more total hours of television and more hours of specific genres of English- and Spanish-language programming (particularly English-language talk shows) exhibited more traditional gender role attitudes. Notably, some studies have failed to find a correlation between television exposure and endorsement of traditional gender roles (e.g., Ex, Janssens, & Korzilius, 2002; Kalof, 1999; McCauley, Thangavelu, & Rozin, 1988; Meyer, 1980), showing that such correlations may depend on the genres of television programming watched or viewer characteristics.

Exposure to music videos has also consistently been associated with gender attitudes. For example, Strouse and colleagues (Strouse & Buerkel-Rothfuss, 1987; Strouse, Buerkel-Rothfuss, & Long, 1995; Strouse, Goodwin, & Roscoe, 1994) reported that frequent viewing of music videos was associated with stronger support of traditional sex roles, while involvement with both popular music and music videos was related to more accepting attitudes toward sexual harassment. Consistent with this, Ward (2002) found that frequent music video exposure predicted more traditional gender role attitudes and stronger support of dating as a game among undergraduate men and greater acceptance of women as sexual objects among undergraduate women. Adding to these correlational findings, Ward et al. (2005) looked at the impact of experimental as well as regular music video exposure on African American high school students' conceptions about gender. They found that more frequent music video viewing was related to more traditional gender role attitudes and to assigning more importance to stereotypical attributes (such as physical appearance and sexiness). Additionally, adolescents exposed to videos heavy in gender stereotypes expressed more traditional views of gender than did members of a control group. Researchers have also found that laboratory exposure to stereotypical music videos leads neutral behavior to seem more sexualized and actions fitting stereotypical gender schemas to appear more favorable (Hansen, 1989; Hansen & Hansen, 1988; Hansen & Krygowski, 1994).

In addition to affecting young peoples' gender beliefs and attitudes, the media's gendered portrayals may affect actual behaviors. Experimentally, researchers have found effects of television commercials on women's behaviors. Jennings-Walstedt, Geis, and Brown (1980) found that undergraduate women exposed to four commercials with nontraditional gender roles showed more independence of judgment in a conformity task and greater self-confidence when delivering a speech than those exposed to traditional commercials. They suggested that the commercials acted as social cues, triggering and reinforcing sex-role stereotypes. In three experiments, Davies, Spencer, and Quinn (2002) found that women who viewed gender-stereotypic television commercials underperformed on a math test, avoided math in favor of verbal items on an aptitude test, and expressed less interest in pursuing educational and vocational options in quantitative domains. They attributed these findings to the activation of self-relevant stereotypes, which led to stereotype threat (the awareness that one may be judged by negative stereotypes about one's group). Thus, experimental findings indicate that exposure to both stereotypic and nontraditional gender role portrayals can cause changes in multiple domains of behavior.

It must be noted, however, that connections between media consumption and gender outcomes are not uniform, and instead depend on factors of the individual as well as the type of media. One of the most significant factors affecting media-gender associations is gender—girls' ideas about gender are consistently found to be more tied to their media use than are boys' (e.g., Morgan, 1982; Rivadeneyra & Ward, 2005; Ward & Rivadeneyra, 1999). Researchers have suggested that this might be due to boys generally holding more traditional ideas about gender, which are already in place by adolescence (Galambos et al., 1990). Other factors, such as socioeconomic status (SES), may also moderate the association between media consumption and gender attitudes.

Some researchers have suggested that media exposure (more specifically, television viewing) may be most likely to affect the gender attitudes of those who are otherwise least likely to hold traditional views through "mainstreaming" (Gerbner, Gross, Morgan, & Signorielli, 1994; Morgan, 1982). For example, Morgan (1982) found that the longitudinal relation between television viewing and girls' sexism scores was strongest for girls of medium and high SES and IQ, indicating that heavy television viewing may have a mainstreaming effect on those least likely to hold traditional gender attitudes when they are light television viewers. Viewers' perceptions of media content as realistic (Rivadeneyra & Ward, 2005), as well as their involvement and identification with media portrayals, have also been found to be important moderators of the association between media consumption and gender attitudes and behaviors. Additionally, adolescents might extract different messages from the media based on the developmental issues that are most prominent in their lives (Brown, 2000a; Brown, White, & Nikopoulou, 1993; Roberts, Henriksen, & Foehr, 2004).

Although all media forms send gendered messages, as discussed earlier, some media may address certain aspects of gender roles and gender relations more explicitly than others, and type of programming is important when looking at media effects (Potter & Chang, 1990). For example, music videos may be even more dominated than other media forms by the themes of love and sex (Andsager & Roe, 1999; Brown & Campbell, 1986; Greeson & Williams, 1986), and their limited length may cause them to rely even more on gender stereotypes (Andsager & Roe, 1999; Aufderheide, 1986). Magazines very explicitly address gendered audiences and may also be more prescriptive in their gender messages. R-rated movies are able to portray more violence and sexual behavior than television, and thus may differ in their gendered messages as well. In conclusion, it seems that the media plays a role in the gender socialization of adolescents, affecting beliefs, attitudes, and behaviors.

## WHERE TO GO FROM HERE: DIRECTIONS
## FOR FUTURE RESEARCH AND POLICY

A review of adolescent gender portrayals in the media demonstrates that it is difficult to determine change in these portrayals over time. This difficulty exists for a variety of reasons. First, most content analyses to this point have analyzed men versus women across all ages, including only adults or all males and females from children to the elderly. Next, there have been few longitudinal studies, and different methods have been used across individual cross-sectional studies of the same media types. Although there are certainly exceptions, it is generally difficult to track changes across time because of these factors. Finally, there have been relatively few analyses of media from the 1950s, 1960s, and 1970s. Although this makes sense for some genres, such as music videos, early media in other genres, like television and film, have been neglected.

With these shortcomings in mind, we call for more full-scale analyses focused on adolescent gender role portrayals in the media. Adolescents are heavy media consumers, and research has demonstrated the effects of media exposure on their gender-related beliefs, attitudes, and behaviors. Therefore, we need to increase our awareness of media content in order to educate adolescents and their parents about the nature, extent, and impact of gender stereotypes in the media. We also need to expand the genres studied to include music lyrics, teen fiction, male-oriented teen magazines, and cable television beyond MTV. More systematic empirical study of films and teen advertising would also enhance our knowledge of adolescent gender role portrayals. Future research should assess multiple domains of gender, including physical appearance, personality attributes, responses, body language, and gender scripts, not just behaviors and occupations. Finally, we should examine the consequences depicted of gender conformity and nonconformity, since these consequences likely affect adolescents' own responses to viewing gendered content.

The existing research suggests that adolescent gender portrayals across media are stereotypical and that heavy exposure to this content is related to adolescents' gender attitudes, including sexism. The connections between media exposure and gender attitudes are stronger and more consistent for girls, but have also been found for boys, and seem to exist for both younger and older adolescents. Although further research is needed to understand both the portrayals and the effects, this literature does suggest that changes in the media themselves might be beneficial to adolescents. Such changes could include the portrayal of more diverse gender-role options for adolescents, including flexible gender roles for women and men (Remafedi, 1990).

Research also suggests that counterstereotyping—portraying characters who oppose traditional stereotypes—may be an effective way to expand the gender role options perceived by adolescents (Johnston & Ettema, 1982; Money & Ehrhardt, 1972). Notably, having women involved in television production may affect the stereotypicality of the content (Signorielli, 2001). However, because these portrayals seem resistant to change across time, more effective strategies for lessening negative effects of stereotypical content might involve teaching media literacy to adolescents (Brown, 2000b; Schwarz, 2005) or encouraging adolescents and their families to carefully select and evaluate the gender-related media content they expose themselves to (Nathanson, Wilson, & McGee, 2002; Remafedi, 1990). With these efforts, researchers, educators, and media producers can help adolescent girls and boys successfully negotiate the gender socialization process.

## REFERENCES

Alfieri, T., Ruble, D. N., & Higgins, E. T. (1996). Gender stereotypes during adolescence: Developmental changes and the transition to junior high school. *Developmental Psychology, 32*, 1129–1137.

Allan, K., & Coltrane, S. (1996). Gender displaying television commercials: A comparative study of television commercials in the 1950s and the 1980s. *Sex Roles, 35*, 185–203.

Andsager, J. L., & Roe, K. (1999). Country music video in country's year of the woman. *Journal of Communication, 49*, 69–82.

Arnett, J. J. (1995). Adolescents' uses of media for self-socialization. *Journal of Youth and Adolescence, 24*, 519–533.

Arrindell, W. A., Kolk, A. M., Martin, K., Kwee, M. G. T., & Booms, E. O. H. (2003). Masculine gender role stress: A potential predictor of phobic and obsessive-compulsive behaviour. *Journal of Behavior Therapy and Experimental Psychiatry, 34*, 251–267.

Aufderheide, P. (1986). Music videos: The look of the sound. *Journal of Communication, 36*, 57–78.

Bandura, A. (1986). *Social foundations of thought and action: A social cognitive theory.* Upper Saddle River, NJ: Prentice-Hall.

Bandura, A. (1994). Social cognitive theory of mass communication. In J. Bryant & D. Zillman (Eds.), *Media effects: Advances in theory and research* (pp. 61–90). Hillsdale, NJ: Erlbaum.

Barner, M. R. (1999). Sex-role stereotyping in FCC-mandated children's educational television. *Journal of Broadcasting & Electronic Media, 43*, 551–564.

Bem, S. L. (1981). Gender schema theory: A cognitive account of sex typing. *Psychological Review, 88*, 354–364.

Beuf, A. (1974). Doctor, lawyer, household drudge. *Journal of Communication, 24*, 142–145.

Bretl, D. J., & Cantor, J. (1988). The portrayal of men and women in U. S. television commercials: A recent content analysis and trends over 15 years. *Sex Roles, 18,* 595–609.

Brown, J. D. (2000a). Adolescents' sexual media diets. *Journal of Adolescent Health,* supplement to *24*(2), 25–40.

Brown, J. D. (2000b). Media literacy has potential to improve adolescents' health. *Journal of Adolescent Health, 39,* 459–460.

Brown, J. D., & Campbell, K. (1986). Race and gender in music videos: The same beat but a different drummer. *Journal of Communication, 36,* 94–106.

Brown, J. D., White, A. B., & Nikopoulou, L. (1993). Disinterest, intrigue, resistance: Early adolescent girls' use of sexual media content. In B. S. Greenberg, J. D. Brown, & N. L. Buerkel-Rothfuss (Eds.), *Media, sex and the adolescent* (pp. 177–195). Creskill, NJ: Hampton Press.

Browne, B. A. (1998). Gender stereotypes in advertising on children's television in the 1990s: A cross-national analysis. *Journal of Advertising, 27,* 83–96.

Busby, L. J., & Leichty, G. (1993). Feminism and advertising in tradition and nontraditional women's magazines, 1950s–1980s. *Journalism Quarterly, 70,* 247–265.

Butler, M., & Paisley, W. (1980). *Women and the mass media.* New York: Human Sciences Press.

Calvert, S, L., & Huston, A. C. (1987). Television and children's gender schemata. In L. S. Liben & M. L. Signorella (Eds.), *New directions for child development, No. 38: Children's gender schemata* (pp. 75–88). San Francisco: Jossey-Bass.

Carveth, R., & Alexander, A. (1985). Soap opera viewing motivation and the cultivation process. *Journal of Broadcasting & Electronic Media, 29,* 259–273.

Christenson, P. G., & Roberts, D. F. (1998). *It's not only rock and roll: Popular music in the lives of adolescents.* Cresskill, NJ: Hampton Press.

Clover, C. J. (1992). *Men, women, and chain saws: Gender in the modern horror film.* London: BFI.

Cohn, A., & Zeichner, A. (2006). Effects of masculine identity and gender role stress on aggression in men. *Psychology of Men and Masculinity, 7,* 179–190.

Courtney, A. E., & Lockeretz, S. (1971). A woman's place: An analysis of the roles portrayed by women in magazine advertisements. *Journal of Marketing Research, 8,* 92–95.

Courtney, A. E., & Whipple, T. (1983). *Sex stereotyping in advertising.* Lexington, MA: D. C. Heath.

Cuneen, J., & Sidwell, M. J. (1998). Gender portrayals in *Sports Illustrated for Kids* advertisements: A content analysis of prominent and supporting models. *Journal of Sport Management, 12,* 39–50.

Davies, P. G., Spencer, S. J., & Quinn, D. M. (2002). Consuming images: How television commercials that elicit stereotype threat can restrain women academically and professionally. *Personality and Social Psychology Bulletin, 28,* 1615–1628.

Davis, D. M. (1990). Portrayals of women in prime-time network television: Some demographic characteristics. *Sex Roles, 23,* 325–332.

De Vaney, A. (2002). Pretty in pink? John Hughes reinscribes daddy's girl in homes and schools. In F. Gateward & M. Pomerance (Eds.), *Sugar, spice, and everything nice: Cinemas of girlhood* (pp. 201–215). Detroit: Wayne State University Press.

Dominick, J. (1996). *The dynamics of mass communication* (5th ed.). New York: McGraw-Hill.

Dorr, A. (1986). *Television and children: A special medium for a special audience.* Beverly Hills, CA: Sage.

Duffy, M., & Gotcher, J. M. (1996). Crucial advice on how to get the guy: The rhetorical vision of power and seduction in the teen magazine YM. *Journal of Communication Inquiry, 20,* 32–48.

Eisler, R. M., & Skidmore, J. R. (1987). Masculine gender role stress: Scale development and component factors in the appraisal of stressful situations. *Behavior Modification, 11,* 123–136.

Eisler, R. M., Skidmore, J. R., & Ward, C. H. (1988). Masculine gender-role stress: Predictor of anger, anxiety, and health-risk behaviors. *Journal of Personality Assessment, 52,* 133–141.

Elasmar, M., Hasegawa, K., & Brain, M. (1999). The portrayal of women in U.S. prime-time television. *Journal of Broadcasting and Electronic Media, 43,* 20–34.

Evans, E. D., Rutberg, J., Sather, C., & Turner, C. (1991). Content analysis of contemporary teen magazines for adolescent females. *Youth and Society, 23,* 99–120.

Ex, T. G. M., Janssens, J. M. A. M., & Korzilius, H. P. L. M. (2002). Young females' images of motherhood in relation to television viewing. *Journal of Communication, 52*(4), 955–971.

Franklin, P. (1991). Teen flicks since 50s: Girls still chicks and boys must get laid. *New Directions for Women, 20.*

Frueh, T., & McGhee, P. E. (1975). Traditional sex-role development and amount of time spent watching television. *Developmental Psychology, 11,* 109.

Galambos, N. L. (2004). Gender and gender role development in adolescence. In R. M. Lerner & L. Steinberg (Eds.), *Handbook of adolescent psychology* (2nd ed., pp. 233–262). Hoboken, NJ: Wiley.

Galambos, N. L., Almeida, D. M., & Petersen, A. C. (1990). Masculinity, femininity, and sex role attitudes in early adolescence: Exploring gender intensification. *Child Development, 61,* 1905–1914.

Ganahl, D. J., Prinsen, T. J., & Netzley, S. B. (2003). A content analysis of prime time commercials: A contextual framework of gender representation. *Sex Roles, 49,* 545–551.

Gateward, F., & Pomerance, M. (2002). *Sugar, spice, and everything nice: Cinemas of girlhood.* Detroit: Wayne State University Press.

Gerbner, G., Gross, L., Morgan, M., & Signorielli, N. (1994). Growing up with television: The cultivation perspective. In J. Bryant & D. Zillmann (Eds.), *Perspectives on media effects* (pp. 17–41). Hillsdale, NJ: Erlbaum.

Golombok, S., & Fivush, R. (1994). *Gender development.* Cambridge: Cambridge University Press.

Gow, J. (1996). Reconsidering gender roles on MTV: Depictions in the most popular music videos on the early 1990s. *Communication Reports, 9,* 151–161.

Greeson, L. E., & Williams, R. A. (1986). Social implications of music videos for youth: An analysis of the content and effects of MTV. *Youth and Society, 18,* 177–189.

Gross, L., & Jeffries-Fox, S. (1978). What do you want to be when you grow up, little girl? In G. Tuchman, A. K. Daniels, & J. Benet (Eds.), *Hearth and home: Images of women in the mass media* (pp. 240–265). New York: Oxford University Press.

Hansen, C. H. (1989). Priming sex role stereotypic event schemas with rock music videos: Effects on impression favorability, trait inferences, and recall of a subsequent male-female interaction. *Basic and Applied Social Psychology, 10,* 371–391.

Hansen, C. H., & Hansen, R. D. (1988). How rock music videos can change what is seen when boy meets girl: Priming stereotypic appraisal of social interactions. *Sex Roles, 19,* 287–316.

Hansen, C. H., & Krygowski, W. (1994). Arousal-augmented priming effects: Rock music videos and sex object schemas. *Communication Research, 21,* 24–47.

Herrett-Skjellum, J., & Allen, M. (1996). Television programming and sex stereotyping: A meta-analysis. In B. R. Burleson (Ed.), *Communication yearbook* (Vol. 19, pp. 157–185). Thousand Oaks, CA: Sage.

Hill, J. P., & Lynch, M. E. (1983). The intensification of gender-related role expectations during early adolescence. In J. Brooks-Gunn & A. C. Petersen (Eds.), *Girls at puberty: Biological and psychosocial perspectives* (pp. 201–228). New York: Plenum.

Huston, A. C., & Alvarez, M. M. (1990). The socialization context of gender role development in early adolescence. In R. Montemayor, G. R. Adams, & T. P. Gullota (Eds.), *From childhood to adolescence: A transitional period?* New York: Russell Sage.

Jakupcak, M., Lisak, D., & Roemer, L. (2002). The role of masculine ideology and masculine gender role stress in men's perpetration of relationship violence. *Psychology of Men and Masculinity, 3,* 97–106.

Jennings-Walstedt, J., Geis, F. L., & Brown, V. (1980). Influence of television commercials on women's self-confidence and independent judgment. *Journal of Personality and Social Psychology, 38,* 203–210.

Johnston, J., & Ettema, J. S. (1982). *Positive images: Breaking stereotypes with children's television.* Beverly Hills, CA: Sage.

Kahn, A. (1984). The power war: Male response to power loss under equality. *Psychology of Women Quarterly, 8,* 234–247.

Kaiser Family Foundation (2003). *Reaching the MTV generation: Recent research on the impact of the Kaiser Family Foundation/MTV public education campaign on sexual health.* Menlo Park, CA: Henry J. Kaiser Family Foundation.

Kalof, L. (1999). The effects of gender and music video imagery on sexual attitudes. *Journal of Social Psychology, 139,* 378–385.

Kang, M. E. (1997). The portrayal of women's images in magazine advertisements: Goffman's gender analysis revisited. *Sex Roles, 37,* 979–996.

Kearney, M. C. (2002). Girlfriends and girl power: Female adolescence in contemporary U.S. cinema. In F. Gateward & M. Pomerance (Eds.), *Sugar, spice, and everything nice: Cinemas of girlhood* (pp. 125–142). Detroit: Wayne State University Press.

Kimball, M. M. (1986). Television and sex-role attitudes. In T. M. Williams (Ed.), *The impact of television: A natural experiment in three communities* (pp. 265–301). New York: Academic Press.

Larson, M. S. (2001). Interactions, activities, and gender in children's television commercials: A content analysis. *Journal of Broadcasting & Electronic Media, 45,* 41–56.

Liben, L. S., & Signorella, M. L. (1987). *Children's gender schemata. New directions for child development.* San Francisco: Jossey-Bass.

Lott, B. (1995). Distancing from women: Interpersonal sexist discrimination. In B. Lott & D. Maluso (Eds.), *The social psychology of interpersonal discrimination* (pp. 12–49). New York: Guilford Press.

Lovdal, L. (1989). Sex role messages in TV commercials: An update. *Sex Roles, 21,* 715–724.

Macklin, M. C., & Kolbe, R. H. (1984). Sex role stereotyping in children's advertising: Current and past trends. *Journal of Advertising, 13,* 34–42.

Maher, J. K., & Childs, N. (2003). A longitudinal content analysis of gender roles in children's television advertisements: A 27-year review. *Journal of Current Issues and Research in Advertising, 25,* 71–81.

Martin, C. L., & Halverson, C. F. (1981). A schematic processing model of sex typing and stereotyping in children. *Child Development, 52,* 1119–1132.

Martz, D. M., Handley, K. B., & Eisler, R. M. (1995). The relationship between feminine gender role stress, body image, and eating disorders. *Psychology of Women Quarterly, 19,* 493–508.

McCauley, C., Thangavelu, K., & Rozin, P. (1988). Sex stereotyping of occupations in relation to television representations and census facts. *Basic and Applied Social Psychology, 9,* 197–212.

McNeil, J. C. (1975). Feminism, femininity and the television series: A content analysis. *Journal of Broadcasting, 19,* 259–271.

Meyer, B. (1980). The development of girls' sex-role attitudes. *Child Development, 51,* 508–514.

Money, J., & Ehrhardt, A. (1972). *Man and woman, boy and girl: The differentiation and dysmorphism of gender identity from conception to maturity.* Baltimore, MD: Johns Hopkins University Press.

Monk, D., & Ricciardelli, L. A. (2003). Three dimensions of the male gender role as correlates of alcohol and cannabis involvement in young Australian men. *Psychology of Men and Masculinity, 4,* 57–69.

Morgan, M. (1982). Television and adolescents' sex-role stereotypes: A longitudinal study. *Journal of Personality and Social Psychology, 43,* 947–955.

Morgan, M. (1987). Television, sex-role attitudes, and sex-role behavior. *Journal of Early Adolescence, 7,* 269–282.

Morgan, M., & Rothschild, N. (1983). Impact of the new television technology: Cable TV, peers, and sex-role cultivation in the electronic environment. *Youth and Society, 15,* 33–50.

Nathanson, A., Wilson, B. J., & McGee, J. (2002). Counteracting the effects of female stereotypes on television via active mediation. *Journal of Communication, 52,* 922–937.

Nielsen Media Research. (2000). *2000 report on television.* New York: Author.

O'Neil, J. M., Helms, B. J., Gable, R. K., David, L., & Wrightsman, L. S. (1986). Gender role conflict scale: College men's fear of femininity. *Sex Roles, 14,* 335–350.

Peirce, K. (1989). Sex-role stereotyping of children on television: A content analysis of the roles and attributes of child characters. *Sociological Spectrum, 9,* 321–328.

Peirce, K. (1990). A feminist theoretical perspective on the socialization of teenage girls through *Seventeen* magazine. *Sex Roles, 23,* 491–500.

Peirce, K. (1993). Socialization of teenage girls through teen-magazine fiction: The making of a new woman or an old lady? *Sex Roles, 29,* 59–68.

Pingree, S. (1976). A scale for sexism. *Journal of Communication, 26,* 193–200.

Pleck, J. H., Sonenstein, F. L., & Ku, L. C. (1993). Masculinity ideology: Its impact on adolescent males' heterosexual relationships. *Journal of Social Issues, 49,* 11–29.

Pomerance, M., & Gateward, F. (2005). *Where the boys are: Cinemas of masculinity and youth.* Detroit: Wayne State University Press.

Potter, W. J., & Chang, I. C. (1990). Television exposure measures and the cultivation hypothesis. *Journal of Broadcasting and Electronic Media, 34,* 313–333.

Remafedi, G. (1990). Study group report on the impact of television portrayals of gender roles on youth. *Journal of Adolescent Health Care, 11,* 59–61.

Rideout, V. J., Roberts, D. F., & Foehr, U. G. (2005). *Generation M: Media in the Lives of 8–18 year-olds.* Menlo Park, CA: Henry J. Kaiser Family Foundation.

Riffe, D., Goldson, H., Saxton, K., & Yu, Y. C. (1989). Females and minorities in TV ads in 1987 Saturday children's programs. *Journalism Quarterly, 66,* 129–136.

Rivadeneyra, R., & Ward, L. M. (2005). Ally McBeal to Sabado Gigante: Contributions of television viewing to the gender role attitudes of Latino adolescents. *Journal of Adolescent Research, 20,* 453–475.

Roberts, D. F., & Foehr, U. G. (2003). *Kids and media in America: Patterns of use at the millennium.* New York: Cambridge University Press.

Roberts, D., Foehr, U., Rideout, V., & Brodie, M. (1999). *Kids and media at the new millennium.* Palo Alto, CA: Henry J. Kaiser Foundation.

Roberts, D. F., Henriksen, L., & Foehr, U. G. (2004). Adolescents and media. In R. M. Lerner & L. Steinberg (Eds.), *Handbook of adolescent psychology* (2nd ed., pp. 487–521). Hoboken, NJ: Wiley.

Roberts, K. (2002). Pleasures and problems of the "angry girl." In F. Gateward & M. Pomerance (Eds.), *Sugar, spice, and everything nice: Cinemas of girlhood* (pp. 217–233). Detroit: Wayne State University Press.

Robinson, J. D., & Skill, T. (2001). Five decades of families on television: From the 1950s through the 1990s. In J. Bryant & J. A. Bryant (Eds.), *Television and the American family* (2nd ed., pp. 139–162). Mahwah, NJ: Erlbaum.

Rosengren, K. E., Wenner, L. A., & Palmgreen, P. (Eds.). (1985). *Media gratifications research: Current perspectives.* Beverly Hills, CA: Sage.

Rosenwasser, S. M., Lingenfelter, M., & Harrington, A. F. (1989). Nontraditional gender role portrayals on television and children's gender role perceptions. *Journal of Applied Developmental Psychology, 10,* 97–105.

Rothschild, N. (1979). *Group as a mediating factor in the cultivation process among young children.* Unpublished master's thesis, Annenberg School of Communications, University of Pennsylvania.

Rubin, A. M. (2002). The uses-and-gratifications perspective of media effects. In J. Bryant & D. Zillmann (Eds.), *Media effects: Advances in the theory and research* (2nd ed., pp. 525–548). Mahwah, NJ: Erlbaum.

Ruble, D. N., & Martin, C. L. (1998). Gender development. In W. Damon & N. Eisenberg (Eds.), *Handbook of child psychology: Vol. 3, Social, emotional and personality development* (5th ed., pp. 933–1016). New York: Wiley.

Schlenker, J. A., Caron, S. L., & Halteman, W. A. (1998). A feminist analysis of *Seventeen* magazine: Content analysis from 1945 to 1995. *Sex Roles, 38,* 135–149.

Schwarz, G. (2005). Overview: What is media literacy, who cares, and why? In G. Schwarz & P. U. Brown (Eds.), *Media literacy: Transforming curriculum and teaching* (pp. 5–17). Malden, MA: Blackwell.

Seidman, S. A. (1992). An investigation of sex-role stereotyping in music videos. *Journal of Broadcasting & Electronic Media, 36,* 209–216.

Seidman, S. A. (1999). Revisiting sex-role stereotyping in MTV videos. *International Journal of Instructional Media, 26,* 11–22.

Shary, T. (2002a). *Generation multiplex: The image of youth in contemporary American cinema.* Austin: University of Texas Press.

Shary, T. (2002b). The nerdly girl and her beautiful sister. In F. Gateward & M. Pomerance (Eds.), *Sugar, spice, and everything nice: Cinemas of girlhood* (pp. 235–250). Detroit: Wayne State University Press.

Shary, T. (2005). Bad boys and Hollywood hype: Gendered conflict in juvenile delinquency films. In M. Pomerance & F. Gateward (Eds.), *Where the boys are: Cinemas of masculinity and youth* (pp. 21–39). Detroit: Wayne State University Press.

Sherman, B. L., & Dominick, J. R. (1986). Violence and sex in music videos: TV and rock n' roll. *Journal of Communication, 36,* 79–93.

Signorielli, N. (1987). Drinking, sex, and violence on television: The cultural indicators perspective. *Journal of Drug Education, 17,* 245–260.

Signorielli, N. (1989). Television and conceptions about sex roles: Maintaining conventionality and the status quo. *Sex Roles, 21,* 341–360.

Signorielli, N. (1991). Adolescents and ambivalence toward marriage: A cultivation analysis. *Youth and Society, 23,* 121–149.

Signorielli, N. (1997). *Teens and the media: Images in six media.* Research report prepared for Children Now, Oakland, CA.

Signorielli, N. (2001). Television's gender role images and contribution to stereotyping. In D. G. Singer & J. L. Singer (Eds.), *Handbook of children and the media* (pp. 341–358). Thousand Oaks, CA: Sage.

Signorielli, N., & Lears, M. (1992). Children, television, and conceptions about chores: Attitudes and behaviors. *Sex Roles, 27,* 157–170.

Signorielli, N., McLeod, D., & Healy, E. (1994). Gender stereotypes in MTV commercials: The beat goes on. *Journal of Broadcasting & Electronic Media, 38*, 91–101.

Smith, L. J. (1994). A content analysis of gender differences in children's advertising. *Journal of Broadcasting and Electronic Media, 38*(3), 323–337.

Sommers-Flanagan, R., Sommers-Flanagan, J., & Davis, B. (1993). What's happening on music television? A gender role content analysis. *Sex Roles, 28*, 745–753.

Stern, S. R. (2005). Self-absorbed, dangerous, and disengaged: What popular films tell us about teenagers. *Mass Communication and Society, 8*, 23–38.

Stern, S. R., & Mastro, D. E. (2004). Gender portrayals across the lifespan: A content analytic look at broadcast commercials. *Mass Communication and Society, 7*, 215–236.

Sternglanz, S., & Serbin, L. (1974). Sex-role stereotyping in children's television programs. *Developmental Psychology, 10*, 710–715.

Stice, E., Schupak-Neuberg, E., Shaw, H. E., & Stein, R. I. (1994). Relation of media exposure to eating disorder symptomatology: An examination of mediating mechanisms. *Journal of Abnormal Psychology, 103*, 836–840.

Strange, J. J. (2007). Adolescents, media portrayals of. In J. J. Arnett (Ed.), *Encyclopedia of children, adolescents, and the media* (pp. 5–11). Thousand Oaks, CA: Sage.

Strasburger, V. C. (1995). *Adolescents and the media: Medical and psychological impact.* Thousand Oaks, CA: Sage.

Strouse, J. S., & Buerkel-Rothfuss, N. L. (1987). Media exposure and the sexual attitudes and behaviors of college students. *Journal of Sex Education and Therapy, 13*, 43–51.

Strouse, J. S., Buerkel-Rothfuss, N. L., & Long, E. C. (1995). Gender and family as moderators of the relationship between music video exposure and adolescent sexual permissiveness. *Adolescence, 30*, 505–521.

Strouse, J. S., Goodwin, M. P., & Roscoe, B. (1994). Correlates of attitudes toward sexual harassment among early adolescents. *Sex Roles, 31*, 559–577.

Thomas, M. E., & Treiber, L. A. (2000). Race, gender, and status: A content analysis of print advertisements in four popular magazines. *Sociological Spectrum, 20*, 357–371.

Tolman, D. L. (1999). Female adolescent sexuality in relational context: Beyond sexual decision-making. In N. G. Johnson, M. C. Roberts, & J. Worell (Eds.), *Beyond appearance: A new look at adolescent girls* (pp. 227–246). Washington, DC: American Psychological Association.

Venkatesan, M., & Losco, J. (1975). Women in magazine advertisements, 1959–1971. *Journal of Advertising Research, 15*(5), 49–54.

Verna, M. E. (1975). The female image in children's television commercials. *Journal of Broadcasting, 19*, 301–319.

Vincent, R. C. (1989). Clio's consciousness raised? Portrayal of women in rock videos, re-examined. *Journalism Quarterly, 66*, 155–160.

Ward, L. M. (2002). Does television exposure affect emerging adults' attitudes and assumptions about sexual relationships? Correlational and experimental confirmation. *Journal of Youth and Adolescence, 31*, 1–15.

Ward, L. M. (2003). Understanding the role of entertainment media in the sexual socialization of American youth: A review of empirical research. *Developmental Review, 23,* 347–388.

Ward, L. M., Hansbrough, E., & Walker, E. (2005). Contributions of music video exposure to black adolescents' gender and sexual schemas. *Journal of Adolescent Research, 20*(2), 143–166.

Ward, L. M., & Rivadeneyra, R. (1999). Contributions of entertainment television to adolescents' sexual attitudes and expectations: The role of viewing amount versus viewer involvement. *Journal of Sex Research, 36,* 237–249.

White, J. W., Donat, P. L. N., & Bondurant, B. (2001). A developmental examination of violence against girls and women. In R. K. Unger (Ed.), *Handbook of the psychology of women and gender* (pp. 343–357). Hoboken, NJ: Wiley.

# 6

# Adolescent Body Image and Eating in the Media

## Trends and Implications for Adolescent Health

KRISTEN HARRISON

To parents, teachers, physicians, and other adults interested in adolescent health, it may seem more urgent to study high-risk behaviors such as drug use, sexual activity, and violence than more mundane, quotidian concerns such as body image and eating behavior. In 2004, 36.4% of all deaths in America were attributable to cardiovascular disease, which is linked to imbalanced eating (American Heart Association, 2007). Just like overeating, undereating is a form of imbalance; moreover, research shows that unhealthful dieting behavior in youth increases the risk for the development of anorexia nervosa and bulimia nervosa as well as obesity in adolescence and beyond, even for individuals who were thin when they started dieting (Neumark-Sztainer, Wall, et al., 2006; Stice, Cameron, Killen, Hayward, & Taylor, 1999). Although body- and food-related behaviors take time to affect health, these influences can be grave; therefore, there is just as great a need to study body- and food-related behaviors among adolescents as there is to study health behaviors, such as sex and drug use, that are associated with more immediate health risks.

## DEFINITIONS, PREVALENCE, AND RATIONALE

### Definitions and Prevalence

Far more young people—32.9%, according to the Centers for Disease Control and Prevention (2007)—are afflicted by obesity than by eating disorders. Prevalence estimates range from 0.5% to 3.7% for anorexia (American Psychiatric Association, 2000); 1.1% to 4.2% for bulimia (American Psychiatric Association, 2000); and, according to at least one study, 4.4% for "eating disorders not otherwise specified" (Lewinsohn, 2001). Even so, eating disorders are an important health issue for adolescent media users due to their intimate connection with body image. Anorexia nervosa and bulimia nervosa are both associated with a strong drive for thinness and intense fear of fatness (American Psychiatric Association, 2000). Further, anorexia has the highest mortality rate of any psychiatric disorder, with one study reporting a death rate of 15.6% over twenty-one years (Zipfel, Lowe, Deter, & Herzog, 2000). Even if they stop short of death, the medical complications of disordered eating are serious and include depression, anxiety disorders, attempted suicide, chronic pain, infectious diseases, insomnia, cardiovascular and neurological problems (Johnson, Cohen, Kasen, & Brook, 2002), strained interpersonal relationships (Holt & Espelage, 2002), and depleted bone density and delayed menarche among prepubescent youth (Nicholls, 2004).

It is now widely known that more adolescent girls than boys have eating disorders. Anorexia and bulimia are about ten times more common among girls and women than boys and men (Thompson & Kinder, 2003), but anabolic steroid use with the intention of building a lean, muscular body is much more common among males; one study involving a sample of almost 5,000 middle and high school students reported a usage rate of 5.4% for boys compared to 2.9% for girls (Irving, Wall, Neumark-Sztainer, & Story, 2002). Furthermore, the drive for muscularity is a robust predictor of anabolic steroid use in young men (Brower, Blow, & Hill, 1994). Just as the conviction that one's body is too fat can lead to dieting among girls (and boys), the conviction that one's body is not muscular enough can lead to steroid use among boys (and girls).

The conviction that one's body's appearance is inadequate in its natural state is termed *body image disturbance*. Body image is generally defined as a person's evaluative perceptions of his or her body, particularly its appearance. Following this, a disturbance in body image (that is, poor body image) is conceptualized as either demonstrably inaccurate perceptions of the body's size or proportions, or discontent with one or more of the body's observable features, such as adiposity (i.e., amount of body fat) or musculature (Botta, 2000). The body image disturbance most frequently identified in research is body dissatisfaction. Research suggests that 40% to 60% of adolescent girls and women are dissatisfied with some aspect of their bodies (Thompson, 2004), and that boys and men are becoming increasingly dissatisfied with theirs (Cafri, Strauss, & Thompson, 2002).

## Rationale

The conviction that one's body is insufferably flawed can erode quality of life, prevent optimal functioning, disrupt relationships, and may lead to disordered eating as well as vanity driven overspending among young people for products and services, both legal and illegal, to fix perceived flaws (Morris, McDaniel, Worst, & Timm, 1995). Therefore, among adolescent girls and boys alike, poor body image is of concern in its own right, not just as a predictor of disordered eating, obesity, and steroid use. Understanding those factors within the sociocultural context surrounding adolescents that serve to bolster or damage their body image is central to understanding how these factors increase their risk for problematic health outcomes like eating disorders, obesity, and steroid use.

The surrounding context that concerns us for the purposes of this volume is the mass media, in particular media content depicting human bodies and eating behaviors. Of particular importance are *ideal-body media*, which display and idealize a body shape that is lean and low in fat, whether small and willowy (in the case of female fashion models) or powerful and bulky (in the case of male athletes). In this chapter I summarize media portrayals of adolescent bodies and, to a lesser extent because the research is far less plentiful, adolescent eating behaviors. I also present original research findings on eating behavior among adolescent characters in television food commercials. I conclude by specifying potential effects that should be of concern to media and health researchers and offering strategies for minimizing such effects.

Media portrayals are certainly not the only causal factor, or even the most important causal factor, in the development of body image problems and poor eating habits in adolescence and beyond. Still, portrayals of bodies and eating speak volumes to young viewers about what is "good" and "normal" vis-à-vis their emerging adult bodies. Exposure to these media messages can encourage poor body image, activate cognitions and emotions associated with these images, and bring eating imbalances into expression (Groesz, Levine, & Murnen, 2002). The basic argument undergirding the claims presented in this chapter is that the media's chief role in affecting body image is to help create and reinforce a social environment that normalizes dieting and extreme thinness in females and muscularity in males, and to encourage young people to repeatedly evaluate their bodies and find them inadequate in comparison to media-depicted ideals (Botta, 2003).

## TRENDS IN PORTRAYALS OF THE IDEAL BODY

A truly comprehensive media content analysis reports not only the presence of some phenomenon (e.g., the proportion of teenage television characters who appear to be thinner than normal), but also features of the context in which the phenomenon appears (e.g., whether thin characters are more likely than fat characters to be portrayed as socially popular or involved in romantic relationships). Ample presence and a positive context both speak to the "ideal" aspect of thin-ideal media. If thinness is so prevalent in the media that it becomes the norm, its very regularity underscores its "ideal" status. The opposite condition, deemed "symbolic annihilation" (Tuchman, 1978), describes the situation in which the absence of a certain group (e.g., fat people) from mass media depictions implies that members of the group are so lacking in value as to be unworthy of representation. Likewise, if thin characters are portrayed more positively than other characters and receive more social rewards in the form of romantic relationships, happy endings, and the like, regardless of their degree of presence, their glowing portrayal speaks to their status as "ideal."

Content analyses of the thin body ideal in the mass media are a relatively recent phenomenon. Very few published studies date back to the middle of the twentieth century, when television first became popular, and adolescents have been the specific focus of only a few such analyses. Moreover, not all analyses explore the independent contributions of both presence and context to the idealistic nature of the portrayals, nor do all studies employ the same units of analysis. Nonetheless, the studies summarized below are key contributors to our knowledge of adolescent body image in the media because they were the only studies exploring adolescent and young adult body ideals in the media at the time of their publication.

### Trends for Adolescent Girls and Young Women

#### THE THIN IDEAL IN PRINT MEDIA

The earliest analyses of the body sizes of women in the media reported the weights and "vital statistics" (i.e., bust, waist, and hip circumferences) of *Playboy* magazine centerfold subjects, also known as Playmates. Playmates must be over 18 to pose nude, but very few are older than their early 20s; therefore, we may regard them as late-adolescent role models. The likely reason that early content analyses focused on Playmates is that their weights and measurements are printed within the centerfold of the magazine, rendering data collection and analysis a simple matter. Research concerning Playmates' body sizes tends to focus more on the presence of the thin ideal than on its context, although the fact that Playmates represent sexual ideals suggests a consistently positive context. The first analysis of Playmates, from the 1950s through the 1970s, showed that their body sizes declined significantly over time (Garner, Garfinkel, Schwartz, & Thompson, 1980), and a replication (Wiseman, Gray, Mosimann, & Ahrens, 1992) revealed a continuing decline through the 1980s. In the Wiseman et al. analysis, by the 1980s, 69% of Playmates weighed at least 15% less than expected for their height and age, a reduction considered symptomatic of anorexia nervosa (American Psychiatric Association, 2000).

A similar analysis from 1977 to 1996 (Spitzer, Henderson, & Zivian, 1999) converted Playmates' heights and weights to their body mass index (BMI), a score representing the ratio of weight to height. The Centers for Disease Control and Prevention (2006) maintain that a BMI of 18.5–25 is optimal for health. People with BMIs below 18.5 are considered to be underweight, with an elevated anorexia risk. Spitzer et al. (1999) showed that the average BMIs of Playmates, which ranged from 17.91 to 18.40, did not decline over the period studied. The reason for the absence of a significant decline is unclear, but one possibility is that the Playmates' BMIs were already as low as they could be for models who need to appear somewhat voluptuous. Interestingly, a recent replication of this research by Sypeck et al. (2006) showed that the measurements of Playmates have *increased* slightly since the 1980s, although their body mass has still not exceeded 90% of that expected for their height (see Figure 6.1). The authors argued that perhaps this increase represents a response to the public's increasing awareness of the perils of disordered eating. It is also possible that the slight increase represents an important change in the editorial leadership of *Playboy* magazine in 1988, when Hugh Hefner's daughter Christie Hefner took over as CEO of Playboy Enterprises (Gupte, 2005).

Additional research on portrayals of young women in magazines shows a similarly increasingly slim ideal during the same years analyzed in the early *Playboy* studies. For instance, a multimedia content analysis by Silverstein, Perdue, Peterson, and Kelly (1986) revealed that women's magazines featured more messages to become slim than did men's magazines, and that the bust-to-waist ratio of popular movie actresses decreased significantly—from 1.34 to 1.22—during the twenty years preceding the study's publication, representing a move toward a slimmer, less curvaceous figure. Unfortunately, this research did not distinguish adolescent models and actresses from adult models and actresses, although it is likely that most of the individuals

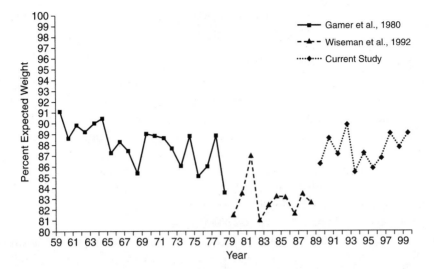

Figure 6.1. Percent normative weight of *Playboy* Playmates from 1959 to 1999. (*Source*: From "Cultural Representations of Thinness in Women, Redux: *Playboy* Magazine's Depiction of Beauty From 1979 to 1999," by M. F. Sypeck, J. J. Gray, S. F. Etu, A. H. Ahrens, J. E. Mosimann, & C. V. Wiseman, 2006, *Body Image*, 3, pp. 229–235. Reprinted with permission.)

analyzed were adults because women's magazines were the sampling unit. Adolescent girls are arguably more likely to spend their time with magazines directed toward teen girls than with *Playboy* or with the titles, such as *Ladies Home Journal*, that Silverstein et al. (1986) studied. Accordingly, Ballentine and Ogle (2005) conducted a rhetorical analysis of the way "body problems" from 1992 to 2003 were represented within articles in *Seventeen*, a magazine popular with female adolescents. In general, body problems such as excess weight and flabbiness tended to be framed as fixable with consumer products and services such as surgery, laser treatment, well-chosen swimsuits, concealers, and the like. However, over time, *Seventeen* articles were also more likely to include messages about resisting a narrowly defined view of the body and making the most of what you have (e.g., "superskinny girls aren't typical…bear in mind that to some extent, what your body looks like is determined by your genes" [p. 299]). The authors argued that such conflicting messages are likely to be confusing to adolescent readers.

THE THIN IDEAL IN ELECTRONIC MEDIA

Content analyses of female body ideals have also employed television characters as units of analysis. Several of the studies analyzing *Playboy* Playmates also analyzed the measurements of Miss America Pageant contestants and winners, during the years when the pageant's ownership made that information available to the public. Like *Playboy* Playmates, Miss America Pageant contestants tend to be late adolescents within a few years of their eighteenth birthday. Spitzer et al. (1999) reported that pageant winners' BMIs declined significantly from an average of 19.35 for the years 1953 to 1958, to an average of 18.06 for the years 1983 to 1988. Like *Playboy* Playmates, Miss America Pageant winners had become increasingly underweight over time. What is particularly interesting about the study by Spitzer et al. (1999) is that, when the authors compared Playmates' and pageant winners' BMIs with those of American and Canadian women as accessed through national health databases, they found that as real women (especially Americans) have grown heavier, the ideal women embodied by pageant winners and centerfold subjects have grown lighter. Thus, the discrepancy between the real women adolescent girls see on a daily basis and the ideal women they see in publications like *Playboy* and programs like the Miss America Pageant has grown wider over time.

Although many regard Miss America Pageant winners as important role models for girls and young women, the potential impact of exposure to a once-a-year pageant is limited. Content analyses of television genres to which young people are routinely exposed may offer a better view of the media body ideals children and adolescents witness on a regular basis. Silverstein et al. (1986) reported that in a sample of television programs from the 1960s and 1970s, 69.1% of female characters and only 17.5% of male characters were rated by coders as conspicuously thin. More recently, Greenberg, Eastin, Hofschire, Lachlan, and Brownell (2003) coded and reported the body sizes of 1,018 major characters in a sample comprising 275 episodes of 56 different prime-time fictional television programs during the 1999–2000 season. Analyses showed that, whereas about 5% of U.S. women are underweight, over 30% of female television characters were judged to be underweight. Greenberg et al. (2003) also coded male characters and reported that, whereas 2% of U.S. men are underweight, 12% of male television characters were judged to be underweight. The status quo today seems to be that the underweight are overrepresented on prime-time television.

## PORTRAYALS OF FATNESS, THE ANTI-IDEAL

There are two ways to communicate the lean body ideal. One is to cast thinness in a positive light via both overrepresentation (i.e., excessive presence) and associations with beauty and success (i.e., a positive context); the other is to portray fatness as abnormal (through underrepresentation or lack of presence) and bad (through association with a negative context). This latter frame has been explored in several content analyses of television characters. In the content analysis cited above, Greenberg et al. (2003) found that fatness, which has become normative in the general population, is a rarity on prime-time television; compared to 51% of U.S. women and 59% of U.S. men, only 13% of female characters and 24% of male characters were overweight or obese. In terms of context, overweight female and male characters had fewer positive interactions and fewer romantic interactions than did thinner characters, and overweight male characters had fewer interactions with friends. Further, overweight characters of both sexes were judged by coders to be less attractive and to have more negative personality and social attributes than thinner characters.

Gregory Fouts and his colleagues have studied portrayals of body weight within a social context by analyzing how thin and fat female characters are talked about on television situation comedies. Based on analyses of a 1997 sample, Fouts and Burggraf (1999) reported that thin female characters were more likely than fat female characters to receive praise from male characters, whereas fat female characters were more likely than thin female characters to be insulted by male characters (Fouts & Burggraf, 2000). Observing that insults were almost always followed by audience laughter, Fouts and Burggraf (2000) argued that audience laughter serves to reinforce the acceptability of insulting fat women. In a follow-up study analyzing male sitcom characters, Fouts and Vaughan (2002) found that fat male characters were more likely than thin male characters to make fun of themselves, with similar audience reinforcement. The resulting implication, that fatness is both nonnormative and worthy of ridicule, reinforces the thin ideal.

## Trends for Adolescent Boys and Young Men

### THE LEAN BODY IDEAL

A few of the studies cited above analyzed male characters along with female characters, and reported largely similar findings for both genders. Much of the research on positive portrayals of thinness and negative portrayals of fatness among males in electronic media can be found in analyses of media aimed specifically at child audiences. Although these media depict children more frequently than adolescents, they are consumed by children prior to adolescence and thus may influence their perceptions of their own bodies in a way that remains durable through adolescence. An analysis of animated cartoons by Klein and Shiffman (2005) showed that thin characters were more likely than fat characters to display positive characteristics such as intelligence, physical attractiveness, prosocial behavior, and positive affect. A similar analysis of popular children's videos and books by Herbozo,

Tantleff-Dunn, Gokee-Larose, and Thompson (2004) showed that body-related messages were conveyed an average of 8.7 times per video and 2.8 times per book. Thinness was portrayed as a positive female trait in 60% of videos, and muscularity was depicted as a positive male trait in 32% of videos. In 64% of the videos and 20% of the books, obesity was associated with negative traits such as evil, unattractiveness, and cruelty. Even prepubescent children are receiving messages about body ideals that may influence their perceptions in a subtle but pervasive way, extending into adolescence.

## THE MUSCULAR BODY IDEAL

Depictions of male body ideals through history have tended toward leanness; like the female ideal, the male body ideal possesses little body fat. Research through time suggests that this has not changed, but what has changed, and remarkably so, is the musculature of the male ideal. One location for studying this change is in the evolution of the bodies of popular action figures, toy dolls that are marketed to boys through mass media such as television advertising. Pope, Olivardia, Gruber, and Borowiecki (1999) recorded the body measurements of various action figures (e.g., G.I. Joe, *Star Wars*, *Star Trek*, and superhero figures) sold to boys from 1964 through 1998, and translated these measurements into adult male body measurements to see just how much the dolls changed over time and how similar they were to an average (5'10") man's body. Overall, the authors found that the dolls' bodies became markedly larger over time, through the addition of muscle bulk and definition (see Figure 6.2). For instance, if G.I. Joe Extreme, Batman, and Wolverine (all introduced in 1998) were 5'10" tall, their measurements would be as follows: G.I. Joe Extreme (waist 36.5", chest 54.8", biceps 26.8"); Batman (waist 30.3", chest 57.2", biceps 26.8"); Wolverine (waist 33.0", chest 62.0", biceps 32.0"). Comparing these modern measurements with the 1973 G.I. Joe Land Adventurer (waist 31.7", chest 44.4", biceps 12.2") illustrates how much muscle bulk action figures have acquired over time.

Like female bodies in magazines, male bodies in magazines have evolved, although there are far fewer analyses of males and they do not go as far back in history as those of females. In a notable exception, Spitzer et al. (1999) analyzed the BMIs of male *Playgirl* magazine centerfold subjects from 1986 to 1997 and found that their BMIs increased significantly over time. Unlike the increase in BMI resulting from higher rates of obesity in the general public, this increase in BMI, according to the authors, was almost certainly due to hypermuscularity. Some of the centerfold subjects had BMIs above 32, which would translate to more than 235 pounds of muscle on a 6-foot frame. Other content analyses of advertisements in male audience magazines like

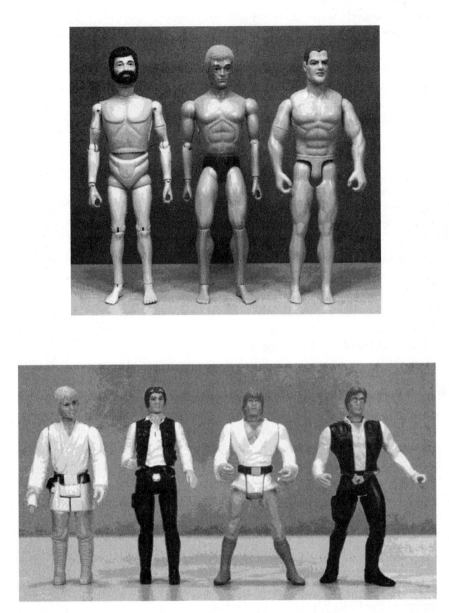

Figure 6.2. Changes in the muscularity of G.I. Joe and *Star Wars* figures, from 1975 to 1998. (*Source*: From "Evolving Ideals of the Male Body as Seen Through Action Toys," by H. G. Pope, R. Olivardia, A. Gruber, & J. Borowiecki, 1998, *International Journal of Eating Disorders*, 26, 65–72. Reprinted with permission.)

*Business Week, Rolling Stone,* and *Sports Illustrated*—the latter two of which are very popular among male adolescents (Kolbe & Albanese, 1996)—show that the mesomorphic, or V-tapered, muscular body was depicted into the 1990s as the male ideal, achieving representation much more frequently than the ectomorphic (thin and lightly muscled) or endomorphic (thicker and overweight) body types.

In summary, within both print media and television, depictions of male and female body ideals have increasingly favored a lean, delicate frame for young women and a lean yet bulky and muscular frame for young men. As the female body ideal has grown smaller and the male ideal bulkier, the discrepancy between the ideal female and the ideal male has grown, illustrating an extreme sexual dimorphism that does not exist among real human beings.

## IDEAL BODY PORTRAYALS ON THE INTERNET

The preceding discussion focuses on print media and television because those media have been studied most vis-à-vis body ideals. The Internet is worth mentioning, though, as another electronic medium whose portrayal of different body types merits analysis. Compared to studies of television, content analyses of body types on the Internet are practically nonexistent, and none investigates adolescents specifically. In a rare content analysis on this topic, Owen and Laurel-Seller (2000) compared the bodies of female models in Internet advertisements with those of *Playboy* centerfold subjects and reported that a curvaceously thin body ideal (large breasts atop a thin body) was the norm for both Internet models and centerfold subjects.

Although studies of body ideals on the Internet at large are scarce, scholars have studied the phenomenon known as the pro-ana (pro-anorexia) Web site. Pro-ana (and pro-mia, or pro-bulimia) sites offer information, resources, and opportunities for connection for individuals with eating disorders who seek support from others who view disordered eating as a lifestyle choice and wish to maintain rather than overcome their disorders. A content analysis of twelve pro-ana sites by Norris, Boydell, Pinhas, and Katzman (2006) revealed that themes such as control, success, sacrifice, transformation, and coping were communicated visually through elements like religious icons and "thinspirational" photographs of extremely thin girls and women, intended to motivate viewers to redouble their commitment to lose weight. Such sites offer adolescent Internet users "trigger pictures" that they can print and post in their bedrooms, lockers, cars, or wherever else they want to be reminded that, to quote the oft-used weight-loss phrase, "nothing tastes as good as being thin feels." Clearly, continued efforts to analyze male and female body ideals on the Internet should be encouraged, given the popularity of the Internet among children and adolescents and its increasing importance in their lives (Rideout, Roberts, & Foehr, 2005).

In conclusion, both general audience and child audience electronic and print media convey messages in favor of a lean body. In the case of pro-ana Web sites, this content can be extreme in its promotion of dietary restraint. This observation raises a question that is particularly important to those interested in how social learning (Bandura, 2002) occurs from media exposure: Exactly what sort of dietary habits are portrayed in the media? What and how much are adolescents eating? Furthermore, how is body size linked with eating behaviors among adolescent characters? The following section summarizes the small body of research on this topic and presents new data from recent research linking character body size with eating behavior in commercials.

## PORTRAYALS OF EATING BEHAVIOR

### Existing Research on Eating Behavior Among Adolescents in the Media

Unfortunately, research on trends in portrayals of eating behavior in the media is sorely lacking. The available research is fairly recent; still, it offers a valuable glimpse of the media world to which adolescents are exposed today. According to a study of health-related content in a sample of 792 minutes of broadcast prime-time programming, a total of 133.9 minutes (17.0% of programming time) contained references to food and nutrition (Byrd-Bredbenner, Finckenor, & Grasso, 2003), more than any other health-related topic. (Alcohol was next, at 49.8 minutes or 6.3% of programming time.) Tellingly, only 15% of the characters involved in scenes about food and nutrition were overweight. Of all scenes containing food/nutrition content 79% featured adult characters. Unfortunately, Byrd-Bredbenner and colleagues did not distinguish between adolescent and child characters, so it is unknown how many of the remaining 21% were adolescents; still, the results speak to the prominence of food and eating within prime-time television narratives.

Aside from modern content analyses like those of Byrd-Bredbenner and her associates (2003), there are few analyses, even recently published ones, that code eating behavior in the media in connection with the body types of characters. This issue is important because the body types of characters provide a context for evaluation of the eating behavior. For instance, if overweight characters are portrayed as eating more frequently, and eating more snack and "junk" foods than thinner characters, their weight status is linked to the foods they are eating, and vice versa. Stereotypes such as "all fat people eat junk food and everyone who eats junk food will get fat" are supported by such portrayals. On the other hand, if thinner characters are portrayed eating as much as or more than heavier characters, the implication is that one may eat all kinds of foods, even fattening ones, without consequence.

The previously cited study by Greenberg et al. (2003) showed that overweight males were portrayed eating more frequently than average-weight males, who were shown eating more frequently than thin males. There were no significant differences for females. Although the Greenberg et al. (2003) study coded age, their youngest age category was "teens to 30s"; therefore, there was no way to examine teen eating and body size specifically. Likewise, Byrd-Bredbenner et al. (2003) did not distinguish adolescents from children (although she did distinguish adults from nonadults as a group), so it is impossible to use her findings to compare food and eating portrayals involving adolescent characters with those involving nonadolescent characters.

Fortunately, in an effort to fill this void, I was able to make use of original data to explore the intersection of adolescent status, eating behavior, and body size in a sample of television food advertisements. The data set is the same used by Harrison and Marske (2005) and Harrison (2006a) for analyses of the nutritional breakdown of foods marketed during the television programs children ages 6 to 11 watch most. However, neither of these articles presented differences in portrayals by age group, nor did they analyze body size and eating within age groups. Thus, the statistics presented here constitute a new analysis of these data, one that, it is hoped, will offer a useful view of adolescents, body image, and eating behavior in the context of food advertising.

## New Findings on Adolescent Eating Behavior and Body Size in Advertisements

### SUMMARY OF METHOD

A sample of food advertisements was assembled from forty hours of television programming taped in north-central Illinois over a five-week period during spring 2003. The selected programs had been rated by Nielsen Media Research as most popular nationwide in fall 2002 and spring 2003 among viewers in the preadolescent age bracket. The sample consisted of the ten most-viewed hours from each of four sources: network Saturday, network prime time, syndication, and cable. About half of the programs were aimed at children; the other half were adult oriented or general audience shows.

The programming sample yielded 426 advertisements for food products, 380 of which featured human characters. There were 78 advertisements with adolescent characters.

In each advertisement the first four food products (e.g., Big Mac, fries, and a Coke) and four characters appearing onscreen were coded, yielding 1,194 characters and 644 foods in total (including repeat advertisements); there were 275 unique foods across all of the advertisements, and 155 teenage characters. Characters were coded for apparent gender, age, body size, and eating behavior. Apparent age was coded as baby/toddler (0 to 3 years old), young child (4 to 8), preteen (9 to 12), teenager (13 to 19), young adult (20 to 29), or adult (30 and over). The apparent body size of each character was coded using a validated figure drawing scale (Stunkard, 2000) ranging from very underweight to very overweight. Finally, the eating behavior of each character was coded as either *never shown eating* or *shown eating at least once*. When characters were shown eating, the primary eating occasion was coded as breakfast, lunch, dinner, snack, or nondiscernible. Advertised foods were also classified by type as breads/cereals, fruits/vegetables, dairy products, meats/poultry/fish, candy/sweets/soft drinks, alcohol, or convenience/fast foods (e.g., Burger King, pizza, Lunchables). Lastly, the nutritional breakdown of the advertised foods was obtained using Nutrition Facts labels, which appear on most commercial food packaging. (More detailed information on coding and reliability estimation can be found in Harrison & Marske, 2005.)

BODY SIZE AND EATING BEHAVIORS BY AGE GROUP

Table 6.1 presents a summary of comparisons by age group. Body size increased with age, such that babies and toddlers (0 to 3) were judged smallest and adults age 30 and over were judged largest. Adolescents fell in between, with few significant differences between groups. Most characters were judged "average" in body size. However, adolescents as a group were portrayed as eating more frequently than all other groups. When adolescent characters appeared, they were shown eating almost half the time. The only group who approached adolescents in terms of frequency of eating was preteens, the 9- to 12-year-old group, who were shown eating almost a third of the time.

The fact that adolescents eat a lot in real life is not news; in this regard, the commercials were painting an accurate picture of human development. But what adolescents are eating has great import for their health and weight. Fully 77% of adolescent characters appeared in ads for snack foods, more than any other age group. Since snacking is associated with excess weight (Forslund, Torgerson, Sjostrom, & Lindroos, 2005), this finding, coupled with

Table 6.1. Mean Body Size Scores and Percentages of Eating Behaviors for Key Variables by Age Group

| Variable | Age Group | | | | | |
| --- | --- | --- | --- | --- | --- | --- |
|  | 0–3 | 4–8 | 9–12 | 13–19 | 20–29 | 30 and over |
| Body size | $3.52_a$ | $3.94_{ab}$ | $4.01_{ab}$ | $3.94_{ab}$ | $3.79_{ab}$ | $4.29_b$ |
|  | 23 | 100 | 371 | 155 | 192 | 353 |
| Portrayed eating in ad | $9_a$ | $23_a$ | $32_{bc}$ | $49_c$ | $29_{ab}$ | $21_{ab}$ |
|  | 22 | 100 | 367 | 154 | 190 | 352 |
| Appearing in ads for snack foods | $0_a$ | $41_b$ | $59_{bc}$ | $77_c$ | $53_{bc}$ | $47_{bc}$ |
|  | 9 | 32 | 149 | 90 | 70 | 111 |
| Appearing in ads for fast foods | $0_a$ | $31_{ab}$ | $52_b$ | $36_{ab}$ | $53_b$ | $47_{ab}$ |
|  | 3 | 42 | 194 | 78 | 101 | 176 |

Note. The body size scale ranged from 1 (thinnest) to 7 (heaviest), with coders instructed to designate 4 "average," or neither conspicuously thin nor conspicuously fat. Scores for the remaining three variables are percentages. Numbers appearing below means and percentages are $N$s for each age group. Means with different subscripts in the same row are significantly different at $p < .05$.

the fact that adolescent characters were actually shown eating the advertised foods more than any other age group, points to a tendency for food ads to depict adolescents engaging in unhealthful eating behaviors. Interestingly, as Table 6.1 shows, adolescent characters did not lead the group in terms of appearances in fast/convenience food ads; preteens, young adults, and older adults appeared more frequently. However, depictions of preteens should be of concern as well, because preteen viewers are a few short years away from being adolescent viewers.

BODY SIZE AND EATING BEHAVIORS BY GENDER

Further analyses were conducted to explore body size and eating behaviors within the adolescent (13 to 19) group. Using the $p < .05$ criterion, there was no difference in body size for teen girls ($M = 3.98$) and teen boys ($M = 3.93$) overall, but when the 7-point body size scale was broken into categories for underweight (1–3), average (4), and overweight (5–7), deviations from the norm revealed interesting patterns by gender, $\chi^2(2, N = 155) = 9.49, p < .01$. Essentially, there was more variation in the male body type than in the female body type. Whereas all but one of the 46 female characters were coded as average (the one deviation was coded as underweight), 17 (15.6%) of the 109 male characters were coded as underweight and 7 (6.4%) were coded as overweight. While it is encouraging that most teen characters are portrayed as average or normal rather than excessively thin, it is disconcerting that not a single female teen character was overweight. There were also gender differences in eating behavior, such that boys were shown eating more frequently than girls (56% versus 31%) and appearing more often in ads for snack foods (89% versus 28%).

The intersection of eating behavior and body size is also of interest for this analysis. Are characters of different body sizes more or less likely to be shown eating? Correlational analyses tabulating the relationship between body size (using the 1–7 scale) and eating behavior, conducted separately for each gender, yielded a negative correlation for the 45 female teen characters ($r = -.23$, n.s.), and a positive correlation for the 109 male teen characters ($r = .37$, $p < .001$). In other words, the heavier they were, the less likely female characters were to be shown eating (although this coefficient is non-significant due to the small sample size). In contrast, the heavier they were, the more likely male characters were to be shown eating. Thus, the landscape of food advertising presents a picture in which teen girls do not eat much, especially if they are not skinny, and not a single teen girl character is fat. In contrast, teen boys eat lots of snacks, have a range of body shapes, and are more likely to be shown eating the heavier they are.

NUTRITIONAL BREAKDOWN OF FOODS ASSOCIATED WITH TEEN CHARACTERS

A final question concerns the nutritional breakdown of the foods marketed in advertisements in which teen characters appear: Are teens associated with nutritious foods? To answer this question, the Nutrition Facts data were used to calculate the average amounts of nutrients in the foods appearing in ads with teen characters. These amounts were then translated to percentages of USDA recommended daily values (%RDVs; United States Food and Drug Administration, n.d.) for each nutrient, given a 2,000-calorie daily diet. The goal of this transformation was to answer the following question: If an adolescent viewer ate a 2,000-calorie diet of the advertised foods, would he get his recommended daily allotment of necessary nutrients? Percentages that fall short of 100 may reflect deficiencies, whereas those that exceed 100 may reflect excesses.

The resulting data are reported in Table 6.2. A scan of the %RDV column reveals that in terms of total fat, foods in ads with teen characters are nutritionally acceptable. Although the amount of saturated fat exceeds the %RDV for that nutrient, the excess is negligible. The %RDV for cholesterol is excellent, at less than half that recommended for a whole day's intake. The amount of carbohydrates is close to the %RDV without exceeding it, and there appears to be more than enough vitamin C. On the other hand, the foods in ads featuring teen characters have too much sodium, far too little fiber, and inadequate amounts of vitamin A, calcium, and iron. With 160.33 grams of sugar, this diet consists of 641 empty calories (32% of the total 2,000), so an adolescent eating such a diet would need to obtain all of her necessary micro- and macronutrients from the remaining two-thirds of her diet; in effect, she would be forced to overeat (in terms of calories) to obtain 100% of her RDVs of vitamins, minerals, and fiber. A quick frequency analysis revealed the reason why the advertised foods were so high in sugar and salt and so low in fiber: of the seventy-eight ads with teen characters, 61.5% were for candy, sweets, and/or soft drinks, and 35.9% were for fast/convenience foods. There was only one advertisement for breads/cereals and one for fruits/vegetables.

These data, while admittedly limited by a small sample size and by the fact that they only represent one genre (food advertisements), still offer a useful glimpse into the world of food and body portrayals involving adolescent characters. The foods with which adolescents are associated on television are not healthful. Candy, sweets, soft drinks, fast foods, and prepackaged, premade, preservative-filled convenience foods have been implicated as major villains in the "toxic environment" (Horgen, Choate, & Brownell, 2001)

Table 6.2. Average Amounts and Percent Recommended Daily Values of Nutrients in a 2,000-Calorie Diet of Foods in Advertisements Featuring Adolescent Characters ($N = 73$)

| Nutrient | Amount | % RDV |
|---|---|---|
| Fat (g) | 56.35 | 86.69 |
| Saturated fat (g) | 20.19 | 100.95 |
| Cholesterol (mg) | 130.57 | 45.52 |
| Sodium (mg) | 3059.91 | 127.50 |
| Carbohydrates (g) | 266.72 | 88.91 |
| Fiber (g) | 8.26 | 33.04 |
| Sugar (g) | 160.33 | — |
| Protein (g) | 57.85 | — |
| Vitamin A | — | 66.85 |
| Vitamin C | — | 116.01 |
| Calcium | — | 63.15 |
| Iron | — | 45.14 |

*Note.* Vitamin A, Vitamin C, Calcium, and Iron are listed on the Nutrition Facts label as %RDV rather than as amounts. %RDVs are not provided on the Nutrition Facts label for sugars and protein. According to the label, for a 2,000-calorie diet, total fat should amount to no more than 65 g, saturated fat to no more than 20 g, cholesterol to no more than 300 mg, sodium to no more than 2,400 g. Total carbohydrate should not exceed 300 g and total fiber should be at least 25 g. Values for %RDV in the table were calculated using these reference values.

contributing to obesity in America. What is more, in spite of the fattening nature of the advertised foods, few teen characters were overweight, and those who were, were all male. Females were shown eating only a fraction of the time. Ads with teen characters present a world in which boys subsist on snack foods and still remain average in weight, and girls associate themselves with fattening foods but avoid eating them and thus avoid becoming fat. The contradiction apparent in these ads, especially for girls, is disturbing. In this one medium, fattening foods are promoted in a format that simultaneously reinforces avoidance of eating and maintenance of a thin-to-normal body ideal. It is hard for an adult to make sense of such a contradictory set of messages, let alone an adolescent.

## EFFECTS OF CONCERN FOR ADOLESCENTS

The primary focus of this chapter is on content rather than effects. However, there is a strong body of research demonstrating that ideal body portrayals and portrayals of food and eating do indeed affect the health behaviors of adolescents. Those who work with adolescents should be aware of these effects. Given the trends reported in the first section of this chapter, that the thin female body ideal and the muscular male body ideal in the media have reached an extreme, and that the quality of marketed foods and adolescents' eating behaviors portrayed in television commercials are both unhealthful, the potential effects of exposure to such media on adolescents' body image should be of great concern. There are two broad categories of potential effects of primary interest in this section: (1) body image, eating disorders, and unhealthful body change strategies; and (2) misguided perceptions of the link between body size and eating behavior.

### Body Image, Eating Disorders, and Unhealthful Body Change Strategies

BODY IMAGE

The majority of studies on ideal body portrayals show that exposure to these portrayals is associated with decreased body satisfaction. A meta-analysis of twenty-five experiments with female samples yielded forty-three $d$ values (i.e., effect sizes) representing the standardized difference between control and experimental conditions on subsequently measured body satisfaction (Groesz et al., 2002). The average $d$ value was $-0.31$, $z = -7.37$, $p < .0001$, indicating a modest but significant drop in body satisfaction after exposure to thin-ideal images compared to controls. Importantly, the average effect size was greater for participants who were not yet in college ($d = -.36$), suggesting some degree of heightened sensitivity to thin-ideal images during adolescence. Research involving boys as well as girls tends to reveal smaller effects for boys (Hargreaves & Tiggemann, 2004). However, research with older adolescent boys and young men (ages 17 to 27) reports increases in depression and muscle dissatisfaction following exposure to television advertisements featuring the muscular male body ideal (Agliata & Tantleff-Dunn, 2004).

EATING DISORDERS

Since eating disorders are not singular behaviors but patterns of behavior that unfold over time (American Psychiatric Association, 2000), experimental research generally does not measure disordered eating as an outcome variable. One exception is a longitudinal experiment performed by Stice, Spangler, and Agras (2001), who assigned some adolescent girls to receive a subscription to *Seventeen* magazine while others received no subscription. The girls were then tracked over fifteen months. There was no overall effect of the subscription on body image or disordered eating, but for girls who initially reported low levels of social support from parents and peers, receiving the subscription was associated with a modest but significant increase in bulimic symptoms. Other studies, mostly cross-sectional and longitudinal surveys, document a positive correlation between thin-ideal print and electronic media exposure, as well as overall television exposure, and measures of body dissatisfaction, the drive for thinness, restrained eating, and bulimic symptomatology (Becker, Burwell, Gilman, Herzog, & Hamburg, 2002; Botta, 2003; Harrison, 2001). Again, these relationships tend to be stronger for girls than for boys (Harrison, 2001).

The cognitive and developmental processes behind these potential effects are illuminated by the research program of Anne Becker, whose work on the Polynesian island of Fiji documents the effects of television on the body perceptions and dieting habits of its young adolescent citizens. The citizens of Fiji have historically embraced a robust female body ideal; by the mid-1990s there was only one reported case of anorexia (Becker et al., 2002). Television was introduced to the island in 1995, with broadcast content consisting chiefly of Western commercial programming. Becker and her colleagues compared secondary school girls' levels of disordered eating one month after the introduction of television, when household television ownership was 26%, with the scores of a similar sample of girls three years later, by which time household television ownership had risen to 46%. Girls' disordered eating scores were significantly greater three years after television's introduction (19% versus 8%), and vomiting as a means of controlling weight had increased from an incidence of zero to 7%. Qualitative interviews with participants revealed that 77% felt pressure to lose weight from television, with a primary motivation being to emulate a Western television personality. This motivation is revealed in the following statements by girls in the study:

> I just want to be slim because (the television characters) are slim. Like it's influencing me so much that I have to be slim. (Becker et al., 2002, p. 513)

It's good to watch (TV) because…it's encouraged me that what I'm doing is right: when I see the sexy ladies on television, well, I want to be like them, too. (Becker et al., 2002, p. 513)

UNHEALTHFUL BODY CHANGE STRATEGIES

When body image is linked to health issues in the media-effects literature, anorexia and bulimia are usually the only ones mentioned. Yet body image is relevant to other adolescent health issues. Idealization of a thin body has been linked to smoking, with adolescent girls reporting fear of gaining weight as a major deterrent to quitting (Forman & Morello, 2003). Body dissatisfaction also prospectively predicts adolescent boys' likelihood of taking up smoking (Neumark-Sztainer, Paxton, Hannan, Haines, & Story, 2006). A heightened drive for muscularity increases young men's likelihood of using anabolic steroids (Brower et al., 1994), and research on college women shows that television exposure predicts not only the idealization of a busty-yet-skinny body, but approval of the surgical methods necessary to acquire such a body, including liposuction and breast augmentation or reduction (Harrison, 2003). Lastly, although no published research describing this phenomenon could be located, my conversations with students have uncovered a disturbing pattern of behavior involving the deliberate ingestion of small amounts of benzodiazepines such as Rohypnol (a.k.a. "the date rape drug") prior to socializing, with the intent of allowing the effects of two bottles of beer to resemble the intoxicating effects of ten bottles of beer. The goal is to become inebriated but avoid excess calories and thus stay thin. Since mixing benzodiazepines and alcohol increases the risk of behaving violently (Daderman & Lidberg, 1999), this kind of drug mixing is risky to both self and others. Smoking, steroid use, surgery, and drug mixing are only four of many potentially risky health behaviors associated with internalization of the thin and/or muscular body ideal. Researchers wishing to understand the impact of thin-ideal media more completely would do well to expand their notion of the kinds of health behaviors associated with the decision to embrace this ideal.

## Misguided Perceptions of the Link Between Body Size and Eating Behaviors

Harrison and Marske (2005) reported no significant correlation between the body size of characters in television food advertisements and their likelihood of being shown eating. Greenberg et al. (2003), on the other hand, reported that for male characters, having a larger body was positively associated with eating in prime-time television. Like Greenberg and associates' data, the original data presented here on adolescent characters in food advertisements showed that an increase in body size was positively correlated with a tendency to be shown eating for male characters only. In one respect, then, these portrayals should be lauded for their realism, in that more frequent eating is associated with a larger body. This is how it works in the real world. While it would be extremely unwise to advocate stereotypical portrayals of jolly fat people constantly eating, the opposite portrayal—that body weight is unresponsive to eating behavior, or, even more inaccurately, that the thinnest characters eat the most (as was revealed here in a moderate but nonsignificant correlation for female characters)—is arguably more damaging to adolescent viewers inasmuch as it flies in the face of basic nutritional principles. Such a portrayal, especially in the context of advertisements for snack foods and fast/convenient foods, both of which have been implicated in the obesity "epidemic" (Horgen et al., 2001), sends a very confusing message to young viewers, especially girls: *buy this tempting product, but do not eat much of it and do not get fat.*

Should adolescent viewers buy (and eat) the products advertised, Table 6.2 offers a snapshot of the nutritional value of their diet, which would consist almost exclusively of candy, sweets, soft drinks, fast foods, and convenience foods, all eaten primarily as snacks: too much sodium, not enough fiber, inadequate amounts of vitamin A, calcium, and iron, and 160.33 grams of sugar, which is equivalent to forty teaspoons or more than four-fifths of a cup. Obviously adolescents do not eat only what they see advertised, but since many of them have discretionary money and the freedom to spend it (Kraak & Pelletier, 1998), not to mention access to vending machines in school and convenience stores, grocery stores, and fast food outlets around school (Austin et al., 2005), they have many opportunities to buy and consume the foods they see advertised.

## RESEARCH AND POLICY SUGGESTIONS

### Outstanding Questions and Problems

Since 1990 when the late Lori Irving conducted one of the first experiments testing the effects of exposure to thin-ideal imagery (Irving, 1990), we have learned a great deal about how media ideals exert their influence and how this influence differs for girls and boys. However, many of these processes and characteristics remain poorly understood within a developmental context. Research on prepubescent children (e.g., Harrison & Hefner, 2006) points to potentially different processes from those operating among older adolescents. With an eye toward solving these developmental mysteries, we now turn to a discussion of three outstanding theoretical questions or problems that remain pertaining to health issues, social issues, and maturational issues.

#### HEALTH ISSUES

As previously explained, much of the research on body image treats the construct as an end in itself or as a precursor to disordered eating, and not part of a broader health context that may involve multiple health behaviors. Internalization of the lean or muscular body ideal has been linked to smoking (Forman & Morello, 2003; Neumark-Sztainer, Paxton, et al., 2006); anabolic steroid use (Brower et al., 1994); and approval of cosmetic surgery (Harrison, 2003). Moreover, as described earlier in this chapter, the desire to become or remain thin may also be linked to hazardous drug use and mixing of drugs to achieve the "high" of alcohol without consuming the calories. Future research on the health outcomes of ideal-body media exposure should measure these behaviors along with disordered eating. In addition, because the literature review in the first section of this chapter revealed so little research linking portrayals of adolescent bodies to food and eating portrayals, a great deal more research is needed to paint an accurate picture of what adolescent media audiences are learning about food, eating, their bodies, and the meaning of health in this context.

#### SOCIAL ISSUES

The drug-mixing scenario described above illustrates the importance of considering media effects within a social context. Virtually all of the research on media effects on body image and eating disorders relies upon the assumption of direct effects. Yet peer relationships may play an important mediating role, as illuminated by this quotation from the Becker et al. (2002) study in Fiji:

I think all those actors and actresses that they show on TV, they have a good figure and so I, I would like to be like them...since the characters (on *Beverly Hills 90210*) are slimbuilt, (my friends) come and tell me that they would also like to look like that. So they, they change their mood, their hairstyles, so that they can be like those characters...so in order to be like them, I have to work on myself, exercising and my eating habits should change. (Becker et al., 2002, p. 513)

Adolescent girls interviewed by Milkie (1999) reported that they personally resisted emulating the media portrayed thin ideal but felt pressured to lose weight anyway because they believed their friends "bought into" that ideal. This finding describes a model of media effects wherein adolescents' presumptions about the media's influence on their peers exerts its own influence (Gunther & Storey, 2003). A teenage boy, for instance, might view action-adventure media in which the male leads all have hypermuscular bodies. Knowing that his peers are also exposed to these media, he assumes that they are impressed by such a body shape, and hence he feels pressured to gain the respect and admiration of his peers by gaining muscle. Recent research on the effects of this presumed media influence on the desire to be thin suggests that it may play as important a role as exposure itself in the development of body dissatisfaction and disordered eating among adolescent girls and young women (David & Johnson, 1998; Gentles & Harrison, 2006; Park, 2005).

MATURATIONAL ISSUES

Research on mass media and body ideals almost always considers youngsters' desire for a different current or child body to be the most important indicator of body dissatisfaction and a drive for thinness, yet prepubescent and pubescent children actually have two body ideals: their current (preadolescent or early-adolescent) body and their future (late-adolescent or postpubescent) body. Harrison and Hefner (2006) reported that, among a sample of preadolescent girls studied over the course of a year, television viewing predicted the subsequent idealization of a thin postpubescent body but not a thin prepubescent body. Since television viewing also predicted subsequent increases in disordered eating, Harrison and Hefner argued that media induced dieting may be done in the service of the body type a girl wishes to have as a sexually mature teenager or adult even if it does not influence the type of body she idealizes as a prepubescent child. This research speaks to the importance of using developmentally sensitive methods and measures to study the way media exposure may influence adolescents' body perceptions before, during, and after sexual maturation.

## Recommendations for Policy Makers and Caregivers

The idea that encouraging teens to dismiss ideal-body media and problematic food and eating portrayals as unrealistic and unhealthy will protect them from adverse effects holds great appeal, but unfortunately a viable solution will be more complicated. Multiple protective strategies are needed. In the final section of this chapter I address what the media, family and peers, educators, and adolescent viewers themselves can do to minimize negative effects of ideal-body media and unhealthy eating portrayals.

### MEDIA STRATEGIES

Attractive models sell products (Dickson, Hargie, & Hargie, 1995) by fostering more favorable consumer evaluations of those products (Arnett, 2005; Reichert & Lambiase, 2003), and consumer insecurity is the stuff of profits—hence the enduring tendency for a magazine like *Seventeen* to use its editorial pages to construct "body problems" that can then be "solved" using products and services that are, not surprisingly, similar to those advertised in its pages (Ballentine & Ogle, 2005), along with the tendency, revealed in the data presented here, for food advertisers to cast thin and normal-weight adolescent actors in ads for foods that are known to be fattening. Thus, although it is tempting to recommend that producers, editors, and advertisers cut back on the number of thin, attractive models and actors featured in their offerings, a much more feasible approach may be to offer adolescents media that encourage the viewer to focus more on the body as an instrument (e.g., sports—see Bissell & Zhou, 2004, and Harrison & Fredrickson, 2003) than as an ornament.

Advertisers who choose to use attractive models with normal-weight bodies to sell their products should also be supported. The Dove "Campaign for Real Beauty," for instance, features photographs of curvy, underwear-clad, regular women, not models. The company's decision to feature women who are not model thin generated a great deal of publicity and more recognition for the product than a body cream would ordinarily receive (Petrecca, 2006). Thus, it can be lucrative for advertisers to break the too-thin mold and feature healthier body ideals. Likewise, the conscientious decision of Fashion Week organizers in Spain in fall 2006 to ban models with BMIs in the anorexic range from participating was followed by organizers in several other countries (CNN.com, 2006). It is hoped that the organizers' beauty standards make their way to the United States.

Research also suggests that the Internet might be of value in combating the negative effects of other media. In particular, it could be used to provide psychological interventions designed to prevent, treat, and help guard against relapses associated with body dissatisfaction and disordered eating (Luce, Winzelberg, Zabinski, & Osborne, 2003). One longitudinal experiment measured the effectiveness of such a program. Its authors reported that Web-delivered psychoeducational interventions designed to reduce body dissatisfaction and disordered eating symptoms significantly reduced those attitudes and behaviors over the course of four months (Celio et al., 2000). The Internet might also be a useful medium to deliver nutrition education to help adolescents interpret what they see in commercial media as realistic or unrealistic within the context of their own lives and bodies.

## FAMILY/PEER STRATEGIES

Adolescents' perceptions of what their family members and peers think about them play a crucial role in their adherence or resistance to media messages extolling the virtues of thinness. The *Seventeen* magazine experiment by Stice et al. (2001) suggests that the perception that one is accepted and supported *as one is* may serve a protective function. On the other hand, research on the influence of presumed influence on peers (Milkie, 1999; Park, 2005) suggests that the perception that others are influenced by thin-ideal media can itself pressure young people to diet in an attempt to meet that ideal. Associating with supportive others who openly reject commercial body ideals, and who have a clear idea of which foods and eating behaviors are healthful, therefore seems essential to minimizing negative effects. However, if the source is parents, too strong a condemnation of the thin ideal could backfire. A retrospective study by Nathanson and Botta (2003) showed that college women whose mothers openly commented on the media's idealized depiction of extreme thinness—even if their commentary was critical—reported more body image disturbance than women whose mothers did not offer overt commentary. Given the study's retrospective method, it is unknown whether the mothers who openly commented on the thin ideal did so because they were more likely to have body issues themselves, which they passed to their daughters independent of their parental mediation style. If active mediation is indeed risky, family members and friends might do best to encourage young people to avoid thin-ideal media altogether, so issues pertaining to body composition and appearance are not a topic for discussion.

## CAREGIVER AND EDUCATOR STRATEGIES

Too much critical evaluation of the media's idealization of thinness may backfire for parents, but in some arenas, like school, a little criticism has undisputed value. Research on media literacy programs shows that teachers, principals, mentors, and other educators can enhance young people's ability to resist the adverse effects of exposure to thin-ideal media through media literacy programs encouraging healthy eating behaviors and body attitudes (Levine & Harrison, 2003). Plenty of research has substantiated the value of media literacy programs that encourage a healthy skepticism of excessively thin portrayals (e.g., Irving, DuPen, & Berel, 1998; Posavac, Posavac, & Weigel, 2001). In one study, high school sophomores enrolled in a media literacy program designed to help teen girls think critically about media and body satisfaction reported lower perceived realism of thin-ideal media images and less internalization of the thin beauty standard than girls who did not participate (Irving et al., 1998). In another study, media literacy curricula with an externally oriented, feminist sociocultural approach were compared to curricula with an internally oriented cognitive approach, and both approaches were shown to be effective at increasing participants' skepticism of the realism and desirability of media images of the thin ideal (Irving & Berel, 2001). Thus, media literacy programs may be effective regardless of whether they adopt a "reject them" or "accept yourself" frame.

AUDIENCE STRATEGIES

What can adolescent audience members themselves do to minimize the effects of exposure to depictions of an excessively lean body ideal? They can start by choosing to view "healthy body" media such as sports (Bissell & Zhou, 2004; Harrison & Fredrickson, 2003), or media that take the focus off the body entirely. Harrison (2000) found that having favorite television characters who were average in weight—neither conspicuously thin nor conspicuously fat—predicted the greatest body acceptance in preadolescent children. This finding suggests that identifying with characters who are not defined visually or textually by their body weight may be protective. The final option is to cut back on media exposure altogether. Harrison (2006b) reported a pattern that emerged in several studies with adolescents such that teens who viewed more television defined themselves and their bodies more unidimensionally. It seems that television's messages may encourage a narrow-minded view of self, while the time demands of a heavy television diet limit teens' opportunities to take part in the real-world experiences that would otherwise broaden and add complexity to their definition of who they are.

## CONCLUSION

The goals of this chapter were to (a) review research demonstrating the increasing prevalence of a thin adolescent body ideal in electronic and print media; (b) present original data linking unhealthful eating behaviors with body size among adolescent characters; (c) specify the effects of primary concern, given these trends in portrayals; and (d) offer suggestions for continued research and strategies for improving the situation.

With respect to the first two goals, we may conclude that demonstrations of the thin female adolescent body ideal and the male muscular body ideal have become increasingly ubiquitous in American media. The idealization of thinness is communicated through depictions of thinness as good and fatness as bad. The idea that fatness is aberrant among teenagers was reflected in the analyzed food advertisements, where fewer than 7% of teen male characters and zero teen female characters were overweight. Female characters were also shown eating only about a third as frequently as male characters. These thinness-promoting messages were embedded in advertisements for unhealthful sweets and fast foods that, if consumed regularly in real life, would increase the risk of being overweight. This mixed message offers a baffling view of the world of bodies, food, and eating to teens who may not be receiving adequate education vis-à-vis nutrition, body image, and health from other sources of information, such as parents and school.

With respect to the second two goals, effects research shows that exposure to ideal body portrayals, and even overall television exposure, predict body image disturbance, disordered eating, and a drive for muscularity among adolescents. Thus these and other risky health behaviors intended to alter the body or maintain an unhealthful state of underweight remain of great concern among those studying this issue. Regarding sources of effects, it is still unknown how much additional variance in body image disturbance, disordered eating, and other risky health behaviors can be explained by indirect media exposure, such as the acquisition of body ideals and eating behaviors from peers who learned them directly from television and magazines. Researchers attempting to find a way to estimate this indirect influence so they can add it to that of direct exposure and estimate a cumulative effect should be heartily encouraged in their efforts. Furthermore, attempts to solve the problem by persuading producers and advertisers to use only average-looking actors and models, or feature only overweight characters when advertising unhealthful foods, are likely to be met with derision. Beautiful media personalities sell movie tickets and products. The industry is not being asked to abandon beauty, merely to redefine it, as the architects of the Dove "Campaign for Real Beauty" and the organizers of Fashion Week in Spain have done.

Increased industry culpability is merely a start. The trends reviewed in this chapter offer three additional guidelines for addressing the adverse effects of the media's thin body ideal. First, it is important to recognize that disordered eating and obesity are not opposing conditions. The fact that adolescent obesity is on the rise does nothing to negate the fact that excessive dieting and disordered eating are critical health problems affecting an increasing proportion of America's youth. Indeed, since excessive dieting in childhood actually increases the risk of obesity in adolescence and adulthood, those who profess concern about obesity should be just as concerned about overzealous adherence to the thin body ideal. We will not be able to effectively solve the obesity problem until we are willing to acknowledge its linkages to all types of eating pathology, whether they lead to underweight or overweight. Second, media professionals, parents, teachers, and other caregivers need to acknowledge that consistent exposure to the thin ideal may raise the risk for a multitude of health conditions beyond body dissatisfaction and disordered eating. Obesity, smoking, steroid use, surgery, and drug mixing are five identified in this chapter, but there are likely many others. The health effects of an excessively thin or muscled thin body ideal are numerous and far-reaching, and we have only begun to identify and understand them. Third, we need to better understand the role played by media messages about bodies, food, and eating in the way children and adolescents think about health. Longitudinal research on elementary school girls and boys has shown that television viewing predicts decrements in nutritional knowledge and reasoning, particularly for diet foods, such that heavier viewers are more likely to think that foods like fat-free ice cream and diet soda are better for helping them grow up strong and healthy than nondiet but more nutritious foods like cottage cheese and orange juice (Harrison, 2005). Parents and educators need to take special care to teach children about the foods their bodies need to grow soundly into adulthood, and about the real-world effects of a diet heavy in sweets, fast foods, and snack foods.

To conclude on a positive note, research summarized earlier demonstrates that adolescents who feel socially supported by parents and peers are more resistant to the influence of thin-ideal media, and youngsters whose favorite television characters are average weight (not conspicuously thin or fat) have the healthiest, most balanced body ideals. Since critical parental mediation may backfire, the most effective strategy for helping adolescents may be minimizing their exposure to appearance oriented media by encouraging them to watch, read, and listen to alternatives (e.g., historical documentaries, music, live performances, and books) that inspire the viewer to ponder what the human body and mind can do. In this way, parent–child discussions of media content are freed up to focus less on appearance and more on character attributes like personality, values, deeds, interests, talents, and aspirations.

## REFERENCES

Agliata, D., & Tantleff-Dunn (2004). The impact of media exposure on males' body image. *Journal of Social and Clinical Psychology, 23*, 7–22.

American Heart Association (2007). *Cardiovascular disease statistics*. Retrieved July 30, 2007, from http://www.americanheart.org/presenter.jhtml?identifier=4478

American Psychiatric Association (2000). *Diagnostic and statistical manual of mental disorders* (4th ed., text revision). Washington, DC: Author.

Arnett, J. J. (2005). Talk is cheap: The tobacco companies' violations of their own cigarette advertising code. *Journal of Health Communication, 10,* 419–431.

Austin, S. B., Melly, S. J., Sanchez, B. N., Patel, A., Buka, S., & Gortmaker, S. L. (2005). Clustering of fast-food restaurants around schools: A novel application of spatial statistics to the study of food environments. *American Journal of Public Health, 95,* 1575–1581.

Ballentine, L.W., & Ogle, J. P. (2005). The making and unmaking of body problems in *Seventeen* magazine, 1992–2003. *Family and Consumer Sciences Research Journal, 33,* 281–307.

Bandura, A. (2002). Social cognitive theory of mass communication. In J. Bryant & D. Zillmann (Eds.), *Media effects: Advances in theory and research* (2nd ed., pp. 121–154). Mahwah, NJ: Erlbaum.

Becker, A. E., Burwell, R. A., Gilman, S. E., Herzog, D. B., & Hamburg, P. (2002). Eating behaviors and attitudes following prolonged exposure to television among ethnic Fijian adolescent girls. *British Journal of Psychiatry, 180,* 509–514.

Bissell, K., & Zhou, P. (2004). Must-See TV or ESPN: Entertainment and sports media exposure and body-image distortion in college women. *Journal of Communication, 54,* 5–21.

Botta, R. A. (2000). The mirror of television: A comparison of black and white adolescents' body image. *Journal of Communication, 50,* 144–159.

Botta, R. (2003). For your health? The relationship between magazine reading and adolescents' body image and eating disturbances. *Sex Roles, 48,* 389–399.

Brower, K. J., Blow, F. C., & Hill, E. M. (1994). Risk factors for anabolic-androgenic steroid use in men. *Journal of Psychiatric Research, 28,* 369–380.

Byrd-Bredbenner, C., Finckenor, M., & Grasso, D. (2003). Health related content in prime-time television programming. *Journal of Health Communication, 8,* 329–341.

Cafri, G., Strauss, J., & Thompson, J. K. (2002). Male body image: Satisfaction and its relationship to psychological functioning using the somatomorphic matrix. *International Journal of Men's Health, 1,* 215–231.

Celio, A. A., Winzelberg, A. J., Wilfley, D. E., Eppstein-Herald, D., Springer, E. A., Dev, P., et al. (2000). Reducing risk factors for eating disorders: Comparison of an Internet- and a classroom-delivered psychoeducational program. *Journal of Consulting & Clinical Psychology, 68,* 650–657.

Centers for Disease Control and Prevention (2006). *BMI—Body mass index: About BMI for adults.* Retrieved October 16, 2006, from http://www.cdc.gov/nccdphp/dnpa/bmi/adult_BMI/about_adult_BMI.htm

Centers for Disease Control and Prevention (2007). Overweight and obesity: Introduction. Retrieved July 30, 2007, from http://www.cdc.gov/nccdphp/dnpa/obesity/

CNN.com. (2006, September 13). Skinny models banned from catwalk. Retrieved April 14, 2008, from http://www.cnn.com/2006/WORLD/europe/09/13/spain.models/index.html

Daderman, A. M., & Lidberg, L. (1999). Flunitrazepam (Rohypnol) abuse in combination with alcohol causes premeditated grievous violence in male juvenile offenders. *Journal of the American Academy of Psychiatry and the Law, 27,* 83–99.

David, P., & Johnson, M. A. (1998). The role of self in third-person effects about body image. *Journal of Communication, 48*, 37–58.

Dickson, D. A., Hargie, O., & Hargie, C. (1995). Interpersonal attraction and the influence of video-mediated advertising presentations on young people. *International Journal of Adolescence and Youth, 5*, 287–301.

Forman, V. L., & Morello, P. (2003). Weight concerns, postexperimental smoking, and perceived difficulty in quitting in Argentinean adolescents. *Eating Behaviors, 4*, 41–52.

Forslund, H. B., Torgerson, J. S., Sjostrom, L., & Lindroos, A. K. (2005). Snacking frequency in relation to energy intake and food choices in obese men and women compared to a reference population. *International Journal of Obesity, 29*, 711–719.

Fouts, G., & Burggraf, K. (1999). Television situation comedies: Female body images and verbal reinforcements. *Sex Roles, 40*, 473–481.

Fouts, G., & Burggraf, K. (2000). Television situation comedies: Female weight, male negative comments, and audience reactions. *Sex Roles, 42*, 925–932.

Fouts, G., & Vaughan, K. (2002). Television situation comedies: Male weight, negative references, and audience reactions. *Sex Roles, 46*, 439–442.

Garner, D. M., Garfinkel, P. E., Schwartz, D., & Thompson, M. (1980). Cultural expectations of thinness in women. *Psychological Reports, 47*, 483–491.

Gentles, K. A., & Harrison, K. (2006). Television and perceived peer expectations of body size among African American adolescent girls. *Howard Journal of Communications, 17*, 39–55.

Greenberg, B. S., Eastin, M., Hofschire, L., Lachlan, K., Brownell, K. D. (2003). Portrayals of overweight and obese individuals on commercial television. *American Journal of Public Health, 93*, 1342–1348.

Groesz, L. M., Levine, M. P., & Murnen, S. K. (2002). The effect of experimental presentation of thin media images on body satisfaction: A meta-analytic review. *International Journal of Eating Disorders, 31*, 1–16.

Gunther, A. C., & Storey, J. D. (2003). The influence of presumed influence. *Journal of Communication, 53*, 199–215.

Gupte, P. (2005, May 9). Hugh Hefner's daughter has *Playboy* hopping again. *The New York Sun*. Retrieved July 31, 2007, from http://www.nysun.com/article/13515

Hargreaves, D., & Tiggemann, M. (2004). Idealized media images and adolescent body image: "Comparing" boys and girls. *Body Image, 1*, 351–361.

Harrison, K. (2000). Television viewing, fat stereotyping, body shape standards, and eating disorder symptomatology in grade school children. *Communication Research, 27*, 617–640.

Harrison, K. (2001). Ourselves, our bodies: Thin-ideal media, self-discrepancies, and eating disorder symptomatology in adolescents. *Journal of Social and Clinical Psychology, 20*, 289–323.

Harrison, K. (2003). Television viewers' ideal body proportions: The case of the curvaceously thin woman. *Sex Roles, 48*, 255–264.

Harrison, K. (2005). Is "fat-free" good for me? A panel study of television viewing and children's nutritional knowledge and reasoning. *Health Communication, 17*, 17–132.

Harrison, K. (2006a). Fast and sweet: Nutritional attributes of television food advertisements with and without Black characters. *Howard Journal of Communications, 17*, 249–264.

Harrison, K. (2006b). Scope of self: Toward a model of television's effects on
self-complexity in adolescence. *Communication Theory, 16*, 251–279.

Harrison, K., & Fredrickson, B. L. (2003). Women's sports media, self-objectification,
and mental health in Black and White adolescent females. *Journal of Communication, 53*, 216–232.

Harrison, K., & Hefner, V. (2006). Media exposure, current and future body ideals,
and disordered eating among preadolescent girls: A longitudinal panel study.
*Journal of Youth and Adolescence, 35*, 146–156.

Harrison, K., & Marske, A. L. (2005). Nutritional content of foods advertised during
the television programs children watch most. *American Journal of Public Health,
95*, 1568–1574.

Herbozo, S., Tantleff-Dunn, S., Gokee-Larose, J., & Thompson, J. K. (2004). Beauty
and thinness messages in children's media: A content analysis. *Eating Disorders:
The Journal of Treatment and Prevention, 12*, 21–34.

Holt, M. K., & Espelage, D. L. (2002). Problem-solving skills and relationship attributes among women with eating disorders. *Journal of Counseling and Development, 80*, 346–354.

Horgen, K. B., Choate, M., & Brownell, K. D. (2001). Television food advertis-
ing: Targeting children in a toxic environment. In D. G. Singer & J. L. Singer
(Eds.), *Handbook of children and the media* (pp. 447–461). Thousand Oaks,
CA: Sage.

Irving, L. M. (1990). Mirror images: Effects of the standard beauty on the self- and
body esteem of women exhibiting varying levels of bulimic symptoms. *Journal
of Social and Clinical Psychology, 9*, 230–242.

Irving, L. M., & Berel, S. R. (2001). Comparison of media-literacy programs to
strengthen college women's resistance to media images. *Psychology of Women
Quarterly, 25*, 103–122.

Irving, L. M., DuPen, J., & Berel, S. (1998). A media literacy program for high school
females. *Eating Disorders: Journal of Treatment and Prevention, 6*, 119–131.

Irving, L. M., Wall, M., Neumark-Sztainer, D., & Story, M. (2002). Steroid use
among adolescents: Findings from Project EAT. *Journal of Adolescent Health,
30*, 243–252.

Johnson, J. G., Cohen, P., Kasen, S., & Brook, J. S. (2002). Eating disorders during
adolescence and the risk for physical and mental disorders during early adulthood. *Archives of General Psychiatry, 59*, 545–552.

Klein, H., & Shiffman, K. S. (2005). Thin is "in" and stout is "out": What animated
cartoons tell viewers about body weight. *Eating and Weight Disorders, 10*, 107–
116.

Kolbe, R. H., & Albanese, P. J. (1996). Man to man: A content analysis of sole-male
images in male-audience magazines. *Journal of Advertising, 25*, 1–20.

Kraak, V., & Pelletier, D. L. (1998). The influence of commercialism on the food purchasing behavior of children and teenage youth. *Family Economics and Nutrition
Review, 11*, 15–24.

Levine, M. P., & Harrison, K. (2003). Media's role in the perpetuation and prevention of negative body image and disordered eating. In J. K. Thompson (Ed.), *Handbook of eating disorders and obesity* (pp. 695–717). New York: Wiley.

Lewinsohn, P. M. (2001, December). *The role of epidemiology in prevention science.* Paper presented at the annual meeting of the Eating Disorders Research Society, Bernalillo, NM.

Luce, K. H., Winzelberg, A. J., Zabinski, M. F., Osborne, M. I. (2003). Internet-delivered psychological interventions for body image dissatisfaction and disordered eating. *Psychotherapy: Theory, Research, Practice, Training, 40,* 148–154.

Milkie, M. (1999). Social comparisons, reflected appraisals, and mass media: The impact of pervasive beauty images on Black and White girls' self-concepts. *Social Psychology Quarterly, 62,* 190–210.

Morris, S. B., McDaniel, M. A., Worst, G. J., & Timm, H. (1995). Vanity-motivated overspending: Personnel screening for positions of trust. *Educational and Psychological Measurement, 55,* 95–104.

Nathanson, A. I., & Botta, R. A. (2003). Shaping the effects of television on adolescents' body image disturbance. *Communication Research, 30*(3), 304–331.

Neumark-Sztainer, D., Paxton, S. J., Hannan, P. J., Haines, J., & Story, M. (2006). Does body satisfaction matter? Five-year longitudinal associations between body satisfaction and health behaviors in adolescent females and males. *Journal of Adolescent Health, 39,* 244–251.

Neumark-Sztainer, D., Wall, M., Guo, J., Story, M., Haines, J., & Eisenberg, M. (2006). Obesity, disordered eating, and eating disorders in a longitudinal study of adolescents: How do dieters fare 5 years later? *Journal of the American Dietetic Association, 106,* 568.

Nicholls, D. (2004). Eating problems in childhood and adolescence. In J. K. Thompson (Ed.), *Handbook of eating disorders and obesity* (pp. 635–655). Hoboken, NJ: Wiley.

Norris, M. L., Boydell, K. M., Pinhas, L., & Katzman, D. K. (2006). Ana and the Internet: A review of pro-anorexia websites. *International Journal of Eating Disorders, 39,* 443–447.

Owen, P. R., & Laurel-Seller, E. (2000). Weight and shape ideals: Thin is dangerously in. *Journal of Applied Social Psychology, 30,* 979–990.

Park, S. Y. (2005). The influence of presumed media influence on women's desire to be thin. *Communication Research, 32,* 594–614.

Petrecca, L. (2006, April 3). More ads star regular people. Retrieved April 14, 2008, from http://www.usatoday.com/money/advertising/2006-04-02-mcdonalds -usat_x.htm

Pope, H. G., Olivardia, R., Gruber, A., & Borowiecki, J. (1999). Evolving ideals of male body image as seen through action toys. *International Journal of Eating Disorders, 26,* 65–72.

Posavac, H. D., Posavac, S. S., & Weigel, R. G. (2001). Reducing the impact of media images on women at risk for body image disturbance: Three targeted interventions. *Journal of Social and Clinical Psychology, 20,* 324–340.

Reichert, T., & Lambiase, J. (2003). How to get "kissably close": Examining how advertisers appeal to consumers' sexual needs and desires. *Sexuality & Culture, 7*, 120–136.

Rideout, V. J., Roberts, D. F., & Foehr, U. G. (2005). *Generation M: Media in the lives of 8–18 year-olds.* Menlo Park, CA: Henry J. Kaiser Family Foundation.

Silverstein, B., Perdue, L., Peterson, B., & Kelly, E. (1986). The role of the mass media in promoting a thin standard of attractiveness for women. *Sex Roles, 14*, 519–532.

Spitzer, B. L., Henderson, K. A., & Zivian, M. T. (1999). Gender differences in population versus media body sizes: A comparison over four decades. *Sex Roles, 40*, 545–565.

Stice, E., Cameron, R. P., Killen, J. D., Hayward, C., & Taylor, C. B. (1999). Naturalistic weight-reduction efforts prospectively predict growth in relative weight and onset of obesity among female adolescents. *Journal of Consulting and Clinical Psychology, 67*, 967–974.

Stice, E., Spangler, D., & Agras, W. S., (2001). Exposure to media-portrayed thin-ideal images adversely affects vulnerable girls: A longitudinal experiment. *Journal of Social and Clinical Psychology, 20*, 270–288.

Stunkard, A. (2000). Old and new scales for the assessment of body image. *Perceptual and Motor Skills, 90*, 930.

Sypeck, M. F., Gray, J. J., Etu, S. F., Ahrens, A. H., Mosimann, J. E., & Wiseman, C. V. (2006). Cultural representations of thinness in women, redux: Playboy magazine's depiction of beauty from 1979 to 1999. *Body Image, 3*, 229–235.

Thompson, J. K. (2004). Eating disorders and obesity: Definitions, prevalence, and associated features. In J. K. Thompson (Ed.), *Handbook of eating disorders and obesity* (pp. xiii–xix). Hoboken, NJ: Wiley.

Thompson, J. K., & Kinder, B. (2003). Eating disorders. In M. Hersen & S. Turner (Eds.), *Handbook of adult psychopathology* (4th ed., pp. 555–582). New York: Plenum.

Tuchman, G. (1978). The symbolic annihilation of women by the mass media. In G. Tuchman, A. Daniels, & J. Benet (Eds.), *Hearth and home: Images of women in the mass media* (pp. 3–38). New York: Oxford University Press.

United States Food and Drug Administration. (n.d.). *Food labeling and nutrition.* Retrieved October 31, 2003, from http://www.cfsan.fda.gov/label.html

Wiseman, C. V., Gray, J. J., Mosimann, J. E., & Ahrens, A. H. (1992). Cultural expectations of thinness in women: An update. *International Journal of Eating Disorders, 11*, 85–89.

Zipfel, S., Lowe, B., Deter, H. C., & Herzog, W. (2000). Long-term prognosis in anorexia nervosa: Lessons from a 21-year follow-up study. *Lancet, 355*, 721–722.

# 7

# African Americans, Latinos, Asians, and Native Americans in the Media

## Implications for Adolescents

CAROLYN A. STROMAN AND JANNETTE L. DATES

Adolescence, as other pivotal points in the life cycle, is a time of great transitions. The family, schools, and peers assume monumental importance during the transition from childhood to adulthood. Since engagement in media-related activities comprises substantial portions of many adolescents' daily lives, the media must be added to the list of entities that influence adolescent development and health.

One way in which the media can affect adolescent development and identity formation is the through portrayals of various cultural groups. This chapter charts changes in the portrayals of African Americans, Latinos, Asians, and Native Americans (ALANAs) in the media during the past fifty years. We explore how media representations are related to the development of beliefs and attitudes about race and ethnicity. We then explore the changing portrayals of ALANAs and the implications of such portrayals for adolescent development, focusing on both the potentially positive and negative effects of exposure. Finally, we provide a research agenda that suggests issues and questions warranting consideration in future research.

## MEDIA AND ADOLESCENT SOCIALIZATION

The media environment for adolescents is ever expanding as personal computers, the Internet, video games, cell phones, and MP3 players are added to the traditional media such as television and radio. With access to such an array of media channels, numerous choices are available that might influence adolescent health and development. Historically, adolescents have devoted a great amount of time to television viewing. Though television viewing decreases and use of music and music videos increases from childhood to adolescence, television remains the most heavily used medium, especially for African American and Latino adolescents (Roberts, Foehr, & Rideout 2005; Ward, 2004; Warren, 2007).

For adolescents, average daily media use exceeds six hours or more (Roberts et al., 2005). This repeated, prolonged exposure has continually sparked parent and educator concern about its effects on children's and adolescents' knowledge, attitudes, and behavior. Over two decades ago, Berry (1980) suggested that adolescents use televised information, messages, and portrayals as a way of validating and reinforcing their beliefs and, in the process, grant television a role comparable to traditional socializing agents. African American adolescents may also be more susceptible to television's socializing effects because they report using television as a source of guidance (Anderson & Williams, 1983; Dates, 1980; Gerson, 1968).

This concern is not without substance as a number of theories offer explanations of the importance that media portrayals may have for adolescent development. Two theories are instructive in this regard: social learning/social cognitive theory (Bandura, 2002) and cultivation theory (Gerbner, Gross, Morgan, & Signorielli, 1994). The former proposes that adolescents may model the antisocial behavior featured in such media products as music videos. The latter posits that adolescents who are heavy viewers may come to believe that the images and messages presented about African Americans in situation comedies are realistic reflections of African American life and culture. Both theories suggest that media exposure may encourage the development of norms and expectations based on media content, assuming the media serve as role models for adolescents.

These theoretical propositions are especially important in helping to assess the role of the media in ethnic socialization. Aware that media representations may exert an influence on adolescents' behavior, attitudes, values, and beliefs, African American parents and professionals have repeatedly expressed the view that television might (1) influence African American children's attitudes toward their own racial group; (2) facilitate African American children's development of low self-concepts because of its nonrecognition or negative, stereotyped treatment of blacks, and (3) compete with black family socialization by teaching attitudes and behaviors that are not taught in the home. Ward (2004) captures the important role media representations may play in what Erikson (1968) labels as an important developmental life task during adolescence—the formation of a healthy identity:

During this critical time of self-definition, what happens, then, when members of one's group are not represented in the media, or when they do appear, are portrayed negatively or one-dimensionally? Might minority youth come to feel badly about themselves as a consequence of exposure to material that seldom includes them and relies heavily on stereotypes? (p. 284)

Concern has also been expressed about the potential of the media to influence European American and non–European American audiences' beliefs and perceptions about ethnic groups. As has been noted, many adolescents lack regular contact with adolescents from other ethnic groups, and much of what they know about other adolescents derives from media content (Greenberg, Mastro, & Brand, 2002; Ward, 2005). Furthermore, research has shown the potential for media depictions of race to influence policy decisions related to race, such as affirmative action, crime, and welfare (Bodenhausen, Schwarz, Bless, & Wanke, 1995; Mastro & Kopacz, 2006; Fujioka, Tan, & Tan, 2000).

In short, the significance of media portrayals of racial and ethnic groups derives from the body of research that suggests media images and messages about ALANAs affect the perceptions of those inside and outside of specific cultural, racial, and ethnic groups. Media messages may influence identity formation in ALANAs and attitudes about race and ethnicity in both Europeans and non-Europeans. Thus, it is important to understand the media messages, both explicit and implicit, presented in the media about ALANAs.

In the next section, we review what is known about trends in portrayals of African, Latino, Asian, and Native Americans in the media. A great deal of the focus is on television since the newer media have a shorter history, and thus, it is difficult to establish trends. Also, since they were the first and most studied group, we focus on African Americans, inserting what is known about Latino, Asian, and Native Americans to the extent possible.

## PRIME-TIME TELEVISION

Trends in the portrayals of adult ALANAs are captured in research syntheses (Comstock & Cobbey, 1979; Dates & Stroman, 2001; Greenberg et al., 2002; Poindexter & Stroman, 1981). Poindexter and Stroman summarized the portrayals of African Americans in television from the 1950s to the end of the 1970s in three propositions. Although these statements were derived from analyses of research that focused solely on African Americans and were published prior to the 1980s, revised versions of these propositions can serve as a framework for charting changes in televised representations of African Americans and other ethnic groups.

## Historically, African Americans, Latinos, Asian Americans, and Native Americans Have Been Underrepresented in Television Portrayals

In the 1950s, African Americans and other ethnic minority groups were almost nonexistent on television, comprising 1% to 2% of the characters (U.S. Commission on Civil Rights, 1977). Mostly as a result of the civil rights movement, the 1960s witnessed a slight increase in the portrayal of African Americans. Dominick and Greenberg (1970) analyzed the representation of African Americans in television commercials in the 1960s and found that the percentage of commercials with African American models increased from 5% to 11% between 1967 and 1969. However, research conducted in the 1970s indicated that the number of portrayals of ALANAs fell short of their proportion in the national population (Gerbner & Signorielli, 1979; Seggar, 1977; Seggar & Wheeler, 1973). For example, in an examination of shows from NBC, ABC, and CBS over a twenty-eight-day period in 1973, O'Kelly and Bloomquist (1976) found that out of 2,309 characters, ALANAs comprised only 4.9%, compared to their comprising more than 20% of the population in the 1970s.

This underrepresentation continued throughout the 1970s and beyond. However, a trend toward increased visibility of African Americans on television began to surface in the mid-1980s (Greenberg & Collette, 1997). Wilkes and Valencia (1989), for example, reported that African Americans appeared in 26% of all television commercials.

Continuing into the 1990s, studies found that African Americans were no longer underrepresented (Glascock, 2003; Mastro & Greenberg 2000). For example, in an examination of the portrayal of African American families from 1950 to 1995, Robinson and Skill (2001) found that African Americans comprised 14% of family portrayals in the 1970s and from 1990 to 1995, and Glascock (2003) reported that African Americans made up 15.3% of the characters appearing on Fox, the WB, and UPN during the fall 2001 season, compared to their 13% representation in the U.S. population.

Seemingly, the trend toward increased African American participation on television has been sustained as the proportion of televised portrayals of African Americans exceed their numbers in the population. In fact, an examination of the 2003–2004 season revealed that African Americans comprised 16% of the prime-time characters (Children Now, 2004).

The representation of Latinos differs from that of African Americans. Initially, Latinos were underrepresented to the point where they were almost nonexistent in television shows (U.S. Commission on Civil Rights, 1977; 1979). From the 1950s up to 1980, Latinos comprised between 1.5% and 2.5% of television characters (Gerbner & Signorielli, 1979; Greenberg & Bapista-Fernandez, 1980). This status continued beyond the 1980s as the proportion of Latino characters fluctuated between 2% and 4% (Greenberg et al., 2002; Mastro & Behm-Morawitz, 2005; Mastro & Greenberg, 2000). Latinos fared a little better in commercials, as the percentage of Latinos increased from 1.5% to 6% of television commercials (Greenberg & Baptista-Fernandez, 1980; Wilkes & Valencia, 1989).

Although the percentage of Latino characters on prime-time television has increased since the 1990s, they continue to be underrepresented. There is evidence of increased visibility. The Children Now studies (2001, 2004) charted an increase in Latino characters from 4% in 2001 to 6.5% in 2003 and noted that at least one Latino character appeared in 52% of all prime-time programs during the 2003 season (Children Now, 2004). Also, during this time period a milestone was reached: For the first time, a show featured a program comprised exclusively of Latino characters.

Prior to the 1960s, Asians were nonexistent on television (Greenberg et al., 2002). Although there was an increase beginning in the late 1960s, as late as the mid-1990s, Asian Americans comprised 1% of the characters on television (Mastro & Greenberg, 2000). By the 2000–2001 season, Asian American increased to 3% of all characters and this percentage appears to have been sustained, as Children Now (2004) reported that Asian Americans comprised 3% of the characters in the 2003–2004 season compared to their more than 5% in the U.S. population.

Native Americans have remained almost nonexistent on television. Robinson and Skill (2001) found that the percentage of Native American families on television never exceeded 1% of the programs aired from 1950 to 1995, and no Native Americans were featured during the 1960s and 1970s. Similarly, Children Now (2004) found no Native American characters represented in shows appearing in the 2003 season. Thus, Native Americans continue to be nonexistent in media representations.

## African Americans and Latinos Are Generally Presented on Television in Minor Roles and Low-Status Occupational Roles

In an examination of prime-time shows appearing during 1973, Hinton, Seggar, Northcott, & Fontes (1974) found that African Americans generally appeared in minor and insignificant roles.[1] This continued throughout the

1980s (Cummings, 1988). The most recent research suggests that changes have occurred; for example, in the 2003–2004 season, the percentage of characters playing a role that was central to the storyline was about equal for African Americans (33%), Latinos (33%), and whites (34%). Only for Asian characters was the percentage lower—14% (Children Now, 2004).

Historical research critically documents the roles initially assigned to African Americans on television. During the 1950s, African Americans were frequently portrayed on television as servants, overweight mammies, or unemployed (Dates, 1993; Fearn-Banks, 2006; MacDonald, 1992). Other studies have also found that African Americans were more likely to be concentrated in personal service occupations and low-status occupational roles during the ensuing decades (Northcott, Seggar, & Hinton, 1975; Seggar & Wheeler, 1973). Changes in the occupational portrayal of African Americans began appearing with the highly rated *The Cosby Show*, which featured two of the main characters portrayed as an attorney and a medical doctor. This trend continued through the 1980s and 1990s (Cummings,1988; Matabane & Merritt, 1996; Stroman, Merritt, & Matabane, 1989–1990; Wilson & Gutierrez, 1995), and figures from the 2003 season indicated that one-fourth of African American characters were employed in high-status professional occupations such as physician, attorney, judge, journalist, or elected official (Children Now, 2004).

## Stereotyping and Negative Connotations of African Americans, Latinos, Asians, and Native Americans Continue to Be Presented in Television Programs

Research conducted during the 1970s examined the behavior as well as the frequency of appearance of African Americans on television. Analyses of the portrayals of African Americans revealed that although they were portrayed in major roles, the roles still conveyed stereotypical messages (Donager, Poulos, Liebert, & Davidson, 1975; Seegar & Wheeler, 1973; U.S. Commission on Civil Rights (1977, 1979). For example, Reid (1979) found that African American females were shown as especially low on achievement but high on dominance and nurturance. Banks (1977) added an interesting twist: African American characters appearing in all-black programs were more likely to display stereotypical characteristics than were those in integrated casts.

Previous research has identified program attributes that contribute to stereotyping. For example, it has been noted that concomitant with the increase in African American representation came the tendency for African Americans to appear in situation comedies featuring all-black casts (Graves, 1993; Stroman et al., 1989–1990). Also, Glascock (2003) found that African

Americans (76.5%) were represented more frequently in comedies than European Americans (58.2%), and three-fourths of all African Americans appeared in nine (23%) of the shows aired during fall 2001. The fact that African Americans were included in comedic, not dramatic offerings, and were cast in stories designed to make people laugh, not to think seriously about issues, helps to reinforce stereotypes of African Americans (Dates & Stroman, 2001). The stereotype of black people being brought out for the entertainment of whites, not having serious concerns about their own lives, and not being taken seriously by others has been a prevalent theme from the minstrel era to the present day.

Also, research on news programming aired during the 1990s suggests that another stereotype (the savage brute) is reinforced by the tendency of television news to portray African Americans males as criminals and more physically threatening than European Americans (Dixon & Azocar, 2006; Dixon & Linz, 2000a, 2000b; Entman, 1992, 1994).

Research has found a somewhat more positive portrayal of African Americans on television during the 1990s. Dates (1993) and Stroman et al. (1989–1990) found that African American characters were likely to appear in a situation comedy as generally competent members of a middle-class, two-parent family. Yet, it can be argued that stereotyping of racial and ethnic groups continues.

Elaborating on the nature of stereotyping of African Americans, Dates concluded that "what evolved were mass media that favored black stereotypes created by whites over the more authentic and positive black characters by black image makers" (1993, p. 16). It has been argued that, over time, many creative African Americans became discouraged because their positive characterizations of their people were routinely rejected by those in power. In order to continue to be a part of the craft, many of them began to deliver what was wanted, and rewarded: stereotypical images of African Americans that replicated what had been created by white image makers over the years. In other instances, creative artists from the black community who had grown up in the same world as the white artists and were caught up in the stereotypical ideas about black people as were their white counterparts, rarely understood that their ideas were stereotypical, but merely saw them as "keeping it real." For them, real meant stereotypical because that is what they had learned about their people through the lens of others.

When Latinos have been portrayed, they, too, have appeared in unflattering or stereotypical roles. As an example, in an examination of the 1995 through 1997 seasons, Dixon and Linz (2000a) reported that Latinos were more likely than European Americans to be portrayed as criminals.

Greenberg and Baptista-Fernandez (1980, p. 11) provided the following qualitative analysis of Hispanic Americans based on their analysis of dramas aired during the 1970s:

- They are gregarious and pleasant, with strong family ties.
- Half work hard, half are lazy, and very few show much concern for their futures.
- Most have very little education, and their jobs reflect that fact.

In a brief review of studies focusing on portrayals of ethnic groups, Signorielli (2007) argues that although Latinos continue to be underrepresented, they are presented with more diversity than African Americans. As an example, Latinos were more likely to have appeared in shows aired during the 2003–2004 season with integrated casts on the major networks (ABC, CBS, and NBC), rather than UPN, which often featured programs with all-black casts (Children Now, 2004).

Tan, Fujiola, and Lucht (1997) suggest that televised portrayals of Native Americans share characteristics with those of African Americans and Latinos. In addition to being shown infrequently, Native Americans are often portrayed as alcoholics and poor. Also, the portrayals give the impression that although Native Americans are family-oriented, their families are dysfunctional. Other portrayals include the image of Native Americans as lazy and tied to ancient, mystical religions (Greenberg et al., 2002).

In the 1980s, the invisibility of Asian Americans on television was summarized thusly: "Asian Americans are seldom seem, seldom heard, seldom felt on American television" (Iiyama & Kitano, 1982, p. 151). When Asians were portrayed, it was in an unflattering manner. For example, in one of the few studies of its kind, Shu (1979) analyzed the portrayal of Chinese Americans on television and found that in comparison to white characters, Chinese were more likely to be poor, teenage, and criminals.

Descriptions of portrayals of Asian Americans are mixed. While Greenberg et al. (2002) maintain that the portrayal of Asian American women as the peasant or prostitute has not disappeared from television, present-day portrayals may cast them in a different light. For example, Ramasubramanian described the portrayal of Asians from the 1990s into the 2000s as depictions of seemingly positive stereotypes of the "model minorities" who are noncontroversial, polite, hard-working people who do not raise their voices against the existing system (2007, p. 249). Yet, Lee and Joo (2005) concluded that Asian Americans are still limited to narrowly defined stereotypical roles, including the commonly held stereotypes of Asian Americans as being technically competent, hardworking, serious, and well-assimilated.

## PORTRAYAL OF ADOLESCENCE AND ADOLESCENTS IN THE MEDIA

### Television

Little research has explored the nature of the portrayal of adolescent characters or of program content aimed specifically at adolescents. This may be partially due to the fact that adolescents are generally underrepresented in prime-time television programming (Children Now, 2004; Signorielli, 2001). What is known about the portrayal of African Americans and adolescents from other ethnic groups has been gleaned from research on adults.

Beginning in the 1970s, a number of shows, including *Good Times*, *The Fresh Prince of Bel-Air*, *Family Matters*, *The Cosby Show*, and *That's My Mama* featured African American adolescents as main characters. This continued through the 1980s and 1990s with such shows as *What's Happening Now!*, *227*, and *Family Matters*. Many of these shows are now in reruns.

In the 2006–2007 and 2007–2008 seasons, adolescents served in roles that were central to the plot of several shows, including Raven-Symoné Pearman as Raven Baxter in the Disney Channel's *That's So Raven* and *Cory in the House*, and as Monique in *Kim Possible*; Giovonnie Samuels as Nia in Disney's *The Suite Life of Zack and Cody*, as well as *That's So Raven*; Little JJ as Jordan Lewis in Nickelodeon's *Just Jordan*; Camille Winbush as Vanessa Thomkins in Fox's *The Bernie Mac Show*; Jeremy Suarez as Jordan Thomkins in *The Bernie Mac Show*; China Anne McClain as Jasmine in CW's *House of Payne*; Julito McCullum as Namond Brice, Nathan Corbett as Donut, Tristan Wilds as Michael Lee, Jermaine Crawford as Dukie Weems, and Maestro Harrell as Randy Wagstaff in HBO's *The Wire*; and Tyler James Williams as Chris Rock, Tequan Richmond as Drew Rock, and Imani Hakim as Tanya Rock in CW's *Everybody Hates Chris*.

As in the past, most of the adolescent characters appear in programs with all-black casts and in shows that fail to provide much opportunity for interactions with whites. In addition, except for the comedies, most often the plots and storylines revolved around decadence and despair in African American communities.

The Disney Channel offered adolescents silly escape stories that did little harm and entertained across racial groups. The Raven Baxter character, played by Raven-Symoné Pearman, former child star on *The Cosby Show*, was pleasantly funny on *That's So Raven* and *Cory in the House*, as well as *Kim Possible*, teaching small life lessons within the storylines of some shows. By contrast, the adolescents on *The Wire* were developed by the writers as troubled youngsters, who clearly were not going to make their way through life as contributing members of society because the systems (educational, political, judicial) had failed them and their communities.

During the period 2005 to 2007, the Disney Channel and the Fox Network offered African American adolescents more programs that addressed their interests than did other networks. The standout series that seemed to capture the interests of viewers across the racial, gender, and age divides was CW's *Everybody Hates Chris*. Apparently, executive producers Chris Rock and Ali Leroy managed to strike a chord with audiences that made them want to return to see the latest events in the life of this young African American male that had a ring of authenticity while it amused and entertained. Viewers seemed to like *Everybody Hates Chris* because of the universal lessons about life and living that are evoked by the stories and characters. Similar to the 1980s *The Cosby Show*, this series shows a strong African American father who requires the best of his children and a supportive mother who is rougher around the edges than was Clair Huxtable of *The Cosby Show*, but just as demanding and loving.

African American adolescents, in particular, report a tendency to identify with popular African American TV characters (Ward, 2004). Among the characters identified with during the 1970s and 1980s were Theo (*The Cosby Show*), Will (*The Fresh Prince of Bel-Air*), and Steve Urkel (*Family Matters*). In later years, Moesha and Jamie (*The Jamie Foxx Show*), Kim (*The Parkers*), and Tia (*Sister, Sister*) were among those identified with by adolescents.

This is just a snapshot of how African American adolescents are portrayed in the genre. We realize that these images are constantly changing, and we are mindful of Strange's (2007) observation that "the explosion of teen-centric expression makes it increasingly difficult to generalize about the portrayal of adolescents in the media as these portrayals become even more varied."

## Music Videos

Music videos are a favorite among children and adolescents. Ward, Hansbrough, & Walker (2005) reported that African American adolescents spent about three hours per day watching music videos. However, there has been little empirical research documenting how racial and ethnic groups are portrayed in music videos—despite the heated discussions about the stereotypical images of black women portrayed in music videos (Milloy, 2007; Nelson, 2004).

Initially, the characters in music videos were mostly European American males. As soul, hip-hop, and rap music videos appeared increasingly on Black Entertainment Television (BET), African American performers, both men and women, appeared more frequently. Signorielli (2007, p. 70) noted that hip-hop and rap videos "show more scenes with sex, alcohol, smoking, violence, guns, and profanity than rock videos and typically show black males exhibiting these behaviors." Other research supports this assertion with findings that African American males appearing in music videos are more likely to both perpetuate violence and to be the victims of violence than are European American males (Rich, Woods, Goodman, Emans, & Durant, 1998).

Many of the depictions of African Americans in popular music are associated with romantic relationships and frequently are sexual in content (Martino et al., 2006; Squires, Kohn-Wood, Chavous, & Carter, 2006). Depictions of African Americans in romantically themed music videos vary but often feed the negative stereotype of the sex-driven black male and the black woman as a sex object (Martino et al., 2006). In spite of the lack of availability of content analysis data, we know that African American culture is grossly misrepresented in music videos (Squires et al., 2006).

## Movies

Historical research has documented the early portrayals of African Americans in film (Berry & Berry, 2007; Bogle, 1989; Cripps, 1977, 1993), however, there have been few quantitative content analyses of the depiction of African Americans and other ethnic groups in film. In the 1950s, a cadre of talented African American actors and actresses began performing in film, including Ethel Waters, Sidney Poitier, and Dorothy Dandridge. Throughout the 1960s, a number of actors such as Sidney Poitier, who starred in *A Raisin in the Sun* (1961), *In the Heat of the Night* (1967); and *Guess Who's Coming to Dinner* (1967), performed major roles in film. However, African Americans were underrepresented as actors and actresses and strong, dignified roles for black actors were limited (Berry & Berry, 2007).

Melvin Van Peebles's independent film *Sweet Sweetback's Baadasssss Song* (1971) ushered in the blaxploitation era. Films produced in this era could be characterized as dramatically increasing blacks in the film industry's sense of agency and power (Berry & Berry, 2007). However, the tendency of the movies to glorify pimps, hookers, and drug dealers was seen as perpetuating stereotypes. In the mid-1970s, the number of African American films began to decline, as did African American representation in film. Berry and Berry attribute this decline to "black people being tired of seeing themselves portrayed as pimps, pushers, and prostitutes" (p. xxxvii).

During the late 1980s and 1990s, several movies were produced that explicitly dealt with race and racism. Examples included Spike Lee's *Do the Right Thing* (1989) and *Bamboozled* (2000), which were reportedly made to motivate people to think and converse about race relations, racial identity, and media images of racial groups (Brooks & Daniels, 2004).

In recent years, HBO has produced stories about black communities that show many dimensions. In addition to producing *The Wire* and *The Corner*, they also produced, promoted, and offered on DVDs such in-depth stories as *Something the Lord Made*, *Introducing Dorothy Dandridge*, *Lackawanna Blues*, *Unchained Memories: Readings from the Slave Narrative*, and the outstanding production of the story of Martin Luther King Jr. during the civil rights era, *Boycott*.

Historical analyses of the inclusion of African Americans in film reveal that the pattern has been similar to that of the television in that there have been increases in the number of African Americans appearing in movies, and the roles run the gamut from being highly stereotypical to those seeking to reflect African American life and culture accurately (Berry & Berry, 2007; Bogle, 1989). Furthermore, our analysis points to the conclusion that the media offer content regarding race and ethnicity that are likely to influence adolescent health and development, and attitudes about race and ethnicity in the general population.

## EFFECTS OF MEDIA EXPOSURE ON ADOLESCENT DEVELOPMENT

As noted earlier, the majority of the portrayals of ALANAs are on television, most often about African Americans; Latinos, Asian Americans, and Native Americans are represented more infrequently. Over the years, the representation of African Americans has increased, and currently, African American characters are highly visible. Also, the types of roles assigned to African American characters have run the gamut and changed from decade to decade. Today, the majority of African American characters with recurring roles appear in all-black situation comedies that are found on WB and BET—networks that target African Americans and youth, and are frequently watched by African Americans. How do these changes influence adolescent development?

Persons from various institutions—families, schools, governmental agencies, churches—have all expressed concerns about the effects of media portrayals on children and adolescents. In this section, we consider the question, "What are the effects of media exposure to messages and images of ALANAs on adolescent development?" and we present evidence of the media's potential to influence adolescents, both negatively and positively.

Previous research has provided evidence that indicates there is a link between media use/content and adolescent health and development. A great deal of the literature in this area has focused on the self-concept of ALANA children and adolescents (Harrison, 2006; Stroman, 1986; Ward, 2004). The emerging view is that the expected negative influence of television on African American adolescents is not constant, and the association varies according to the content and self-complexity (i.e., variability within the self-concept) of the content (Harrison, 2006; Ward, 2004). Among Latino high school and college students, frequent exposure to mainstream programming is associated with lower self-esteem (Rivadeneyra, Ward, & Gordon (2007).

Researchers have also examined media effects on physical health. For example, Klein et al. (1993) analyzed data collected in 1987 of over 2,500 adolescents; their analysis revealed a positive relationship between exposure to radio, music videos, and movies on television and participation in risky behaviors (e.g., consumption of alcoholic beverages and marijuana use), regardless of race or gender. Also, in an examination of the impact of exposure to rap music videos among African American females, Wingood et al. (2003) found that exposure to rap music was positively associated with the likelihood of engaging in health risk behaviors, such as having multiple sex partners and of contacting a sexually transmitted disease among African American adolescent females. Similarly, a survey of over 500 African American adolescent females revealed an association between perceptions of sexual stereotypes in rap music videos and participating in risky behaviors, and having a negative body image (Peterson, Wingood, DiClemente, Harrington, & Davies, 2007). Other studies have found that African American males exposed to violent rap music were more likely than those exposed to nonviolent rap music to report that they would engage in violence and expressed greater acceptance of the use of violence against women (Johnson & Adams, 1995; Johnson, Jackson, & Gatto, 1995).

## Potential Negative Effects

As early as 1950, when television was first introduced into American society, critics began to discuss the medium's negative influence. Among the potentially negative effects of television is the cultivation of stereotypes about racial and ethnic groups. For example, the depiction of African Americans as criminals may lead European American viewers to cognitively associate criminal behavior with all African Americans.

Of greater concern has been television's potential to negatively affect the self-concept of members of ethnic groups, especially children and adolescents. Many years ago, Powell (1982) argued that the exclusion of blacks from television was destructive to black children's self-concept because it minimizes the importance of their existence. Others have suggested that the television roles in which blacks are cast communicate to black children the negative value society places on them (Barnes, 1980). Pouissant (1974) maintained that because African Americans were frequently portrayed in a menial and stereotypical manner, African American children and adolescents might acquire the impression that they do not count in this society, and they should not aspire to professional and leadership positions.

More recently, Berry and Asamen (2001) theorized that the mass media play a role in the negative perceptions of the social contributions made by ethnic groups. In their view, "these inaccurate representations can become a part of the individual's schema about others, prejudiced thinking, and subtle and not so subtle stereotypes" (p. C3). Activists have also been involved, waging campaigns against "demeaning and offensive portrayals of African Americans" (Milloy, 2007; Newhall, 2007). Criticism has been leveled against music videos that some believe perpetuate negative stereotypes of African Americans.

What about other ethnic groups? Noting that different ethnic groups may acquire different sets of messages from commercials, Mastro and Stern (2003) discussed the possible impact of advertisements on Latinos' self-perceptions:

> Latinos exposed to ads in which the characters were suggestively dressed and engaging in sexual gazing and alluring behaviors may learn to identify physical appearances and sexuality rather than intellect as the most important components of self. Ads featuring young, passive adults at work in technology ads may serve to reinforce perceptions of Asian Americans as dedicated to work only, ultimately tying self-worth to submissiveness and superior achievement. (p. 645)

Focusing specifically on the portrayals of Asian Americans in magazine ads, Lee and Joo (2005) noted that when stereotypes are reflected and reinforced through advertising, biased expectations may ensue, resulting in negative consequences for the group members. Mastro and Kopacz (2006) point to one such consequence with their caution that media representation of race and ethnicity may ultimately affect how policy decisions related to race and ethnicity are made.

## Potential Positive Effects

Just as televised and other portrayals have been linked with negative behavior, other research has related them to positive behavior. As noted earlier, the media have tremendous potential to impart new information. Television influences social behavior not only by teaching new behavior but also by contributing to children's definition of what constitutes appropriate and inappropriate behavior (Liefer & Roberts, 1972). A good example of this is found in a study by Anderson and Williams (1983) in which African American children were shown an episode of *Good Times* in which one of the main characters, Michael, the youngest son, became involved with a gang. The children reported that they learned from the episode that street gangs were bad and one should not join them. They also said that they learned that one should confide in family members and that family members should help one another when in trouble. The authors interpreted their findings as suggesting that African American children "are conscious that the lessons and modeling presented on TV are more than mere entertainment" (p. 41).

Currently, the media have the potential to provide much needed health information. There have been and continue to be attempts to use entertainment education to disseminate HIV/AIDS prevention information specifically targeted to African American and Latino adolescents. BET's Rap-It-Up campaign is an example of what can be done to use the media to improve the health and well-being of adolescents. Research suggests that the combined efforts of the Kaiser Family Foundation and BET have resulted in increased knowledge about HIV/AIDS prevention in African American adolescents and college students (Keys, Morant, & Stroman, in press; Stroman, 2005).

Just as adolescent media use has changed with the introduction of new media and thus the media portrayals to which adolescents are exposed to, so have the effects of the media. During the time periods when African Americans were underrepresented in television, scholars noted the potential negative effect of television. Recent research has suggested more positive effects. For example, Ward's (2004, 2005) research has shown that African American adolescents identify with characters in programs featuring all-black casts and this identification has been associated with higher self-esteem. Related to this, Schooler, Ward, Merriwether, and Caruthers (2004) found that African American undergraduate females exposed to white casts had no effect on their body images, whereas greater exposure to programs with predominantly black casts was associated with a more positive body image. Thus, when African Americans adolescents identify with African American characters they seem to benefit from seeing characters who share their ethnic heritage. Also, portrayal of ALANAs in nonstereotypical roles may send the message to both adolescents and the larger society that "people of all races are valuable and integral to the society" (Children Now, 2004). Such messages could contribute to decreases in stereotyping.

An observation made almost thirty years ago is still highly relevant: media impact is greatest when children encounter phenomena and situations about which direct experience, interpersonal communication, or other sources have not provided information (Comstock, Chaffe, Katzman, Mc-Combs, & Roberts, 1978). This observation points to the complexity involved in studying media effects; moreover, it holds significance for and is pertinent to the research agenda which follows.

## DIRECTIONS FOR FUTURE RESEARCH

The notion that media representations influence knowledge, attitudes, and behavior is pivotal to effects research. However, little empirical research exists that clearly demonstrates the process by which the outcome occurs. As noted earlier, the effects of the media are complex and often it is difficult to isolate the media's effects. However, recent research offers guidance for future research on the effects of media representation of racial and ethnic groups.

Three examples are instructive in that they go beyond portrayals and attempt to theoretically link media portrayals with potential effects on adolescents. Ward's research (2004) has examined the impact of exposure to both black-oriented programming (e.g., all-black situation comedies appearing on BET) and mainstream programming on the self-concept of African American high school students. Her work suggests that exposure to black-oriented media may have a positive influence on self-concept, whereas exposure to mainstream media may have a negative impact on self-concept.

Harrison (2006) explicates a new model of media effects—the scope of self model. Comprised of two key constructs, the model attempts to broaden our understanding of the impact of media on adolescents by explaining the effects of television exposure on self-complexity, that is, the number of unique aspects within the self-concept. This is a developing model and other researchers should be involved in its development because of its potential to uncover the implications of media reduced self-complexity vis-à-vis adolescents' mental, emotional, and physical health.

Recent research holds out the possibility that stereotypes activated by media presentations may be reduced by providing audiences with relevant information. Ramasubramanian (2007) conducted an experiment testing the effects of two strategies to reduce stereotypes primed by race-related new stories. Results of the study indicated that the combined effects of both explicitly instructing participants to be critical media consumers and exposing them to counterstereotypical news stories are likely to reduce stereotype activation.

All of the lines of research described above hold great promise and should be pursued. Future research should involve Asian American and

Native American adolescents and continue to consider how portrayals of ALANAs contribute to perceptions and stereotyping.

A critical need in future research is to understand how adolescents process media portrayals. We know very little about adolescents' interpretation of their portrayal in general or of their interpretations of portrayals of ALANAs. Especially useful would be studies in which participants describe how they process portrayals of each cultural group.

A revised version of a question posed years ago by Greenberg and Brand (1994) may serve as a guide for future research: Do ALANA adolescents alter or shape their behavior toward European Americans on the basis of anything they see on television and vice versa? We have little research that provides the voices of adolescents; such research is sorely needed to address these and other questions.

Health communication research offers an ideal path through which to examine media's impact on adolescent health. Continuous research is needed to determine the relative efficacy of the different channels for each cultural group. For example, African Americans are increasingly identifying the Internet as a vehicle for obtaining health information. Additional research is needed to further examine the potential of interactive media for disseminating health information to ALANA adolescents through entertainment education.

Researchers will need to employ new methods in order to increase our understanding of (1) the consequences for ALANAs as a result of repeated exposure to mainstream media content and (2) perceptions of ALANAs that are fostered in the minds of both ALANAs and European Americans as a result of inclusion of ALANAs in the media. The ultimate goal for research in this area is the identification of factors that increase the likelihood of the media making a positive contribution to the healthy development of all adolescents. This nation is growing increasingly diverse and adolescents are our future; to the extent that we help ALANA and non-ALANA adolescents reach their potential, we will help make a more productive nation.

## SUMMARY AND CONCLUSION

In making the transition from childhood to adulthood, adolescents experiment with different identities, including gender, racial, and sexual ones. In this chapter, we have been concerned with how media images of African Americans, Latinos, Asian Americans, and Native Americans fit into adolescents' identity schema. Our analyses reveal that the most prominent images available for consumption by adolescents emerge from television and most of the images are about African Americans.

The data suggest that, on television, African Americans have reached and sustained a level representative of their numbers in the population, while other ethnic groups have remained underrepresented. Yet, while we have more images, they are not necessarily more accurate images. Thus, we must continue to ask questions about the significance of media portrayals of racial and ethnic groups for adolescent health and development, and researchers must use complex designs to address these questions.

## NOTE

1. Because Asian and Native Americans have been portrayed so infrequently, we are unable to document changes for these groups.

## REFERENCES

Anderson Jr., W. H., & Williams, B. M. (1983). TV and the black child: What black children say about the shows they watch. *The Journal of Black Psychology, 9*(2), 27–42.

Bandura, A. (2002). Social cognitive theory of mass communication. In J. Bryant & D. Zillmann (Eds.), *Media effects: Advances in theory and research* (2nd ed., pp. 121–154). Mahwah, NJ: Erlbaum.

Banks, C. A. M. (1977). A content analysis of the treatment of Black Americans on television. *Social Education, 41,* 336–339.

Barnes, E. J. (1980). The Black community as the source of positive self-concept for Black children: A theoretical perspective. In R. L. Jones (Ed.), *Black psychology* (pp. 106–130). New York: Harper & Row.

Berry, G. L. (1980). Television and Afro-Americans: Past legacy and present portrayals. In S. B. Withey & R. P. Abeles (Eds.), *Television and social behavior: Beyond violence and children* (pp. 231–248). Hillsdale, NJ: Erlbaum.

Berry, G. L., & Asamen, J. K. (2001). Television, children, and multicultural awareness: Comprehending the medium in a complex multimedia society. In D. G. Singer & J. C. Singer (Eds.), *Handbook of children and adolescence* (pp. 359–373). Thousand Oaks, CA: Sage.

Berry, S. T., & Berry, V. T. (2007). *Historical dictionary of African American cinema.* Lanham, MD: Scarecrow Press.

Bodenhausen, G., Schwarz, N., Bless, H., & Wanke, M. (1995). Effects of atypical exemplars on racial beliefs: Enlightened racism or generalized appraisals? *Journal of Experimental Social Psychology, 31,* 48–63.

Bogle, D. (1989). *Tom, coons, mulattoes, mammies & bucks: An interpretive history of Blacks in American films.* New York: Bantam.

Brooks, D. E., & Daniels, G. L. (2004). BAMBOOZLED? Audience reactions to a Spike Lee Film. In R. Lind (Ed.), *Race/gender media: Considering diversity across audiences, content, and producers* (pp. 92–98). Boston: Pearson.

Children Now. (2001). Fall colors: Prime time diversity report, 2001. Retrieved October 27, 2007, from http://publications.childrennow.org

Children Now. (2004). Fall colors: 2003–04: Prime time diversity report. Retrieved October 23, 2007, from http://publications.childrennow.org

Comstock, G., & Cobbey, R. E. (1979). Television and the children of ethnic minorities. *Journal of Communication, 29,* 104–115.

Comstock, G., Chaffe, S., Katzman, N., McCombs, M., & Roberts, D. (1978). *Television and human behavior.* New York: Columbia University Press.

Cripps, T. (1977). *Slow fade to Black: The Negro in American film 1900–1942.* New York: Oxford University Press.

Cripps, T. (1993). Film. In J. L. Dates & W. Barlow (Eds.), *Split image: African Americans in the mass media* (pp. 131–185). Washington, DC: Howard University Press.

Cummings, M. (1988). The changing image of the Black family on television. *Journal of Popular Culture, 22,* 75–85.

Dates, J. (1980). Race, racial attitudes, and adolescents' perceptions of Black characters. *Journal of Broadcasting, 24,* 549–560.

Dates, J. L. (1993). Commercial television. In J. L. Dates & W. Barlow (Eds.), *Split image: African-Americans in the mass media* (pp. 267–329). Washington, DC: Howard University Press.

Dates, J. L., & Stroman, C. A. (2001). Portrayals of families of color on television. In J. Bryant & J. A. Bryant (Eds.), *Television and the American family* (pp. 207–228). Mahwah, NJ: Erlbaum.

Dixon, T. L., & Azocar, C. L. (2006). The representation of juvenile offenders by race on Los Angeles area television news. *Howard Journal of Communications, 17,* 143–161.

Dixon, T. L., & Linz, D. (2000a). Overrepresentation and underrepresentation of African Americans and Latinos as lawbreakers on television news. *Journal of Communication, 50,* 131–154.

Dixon, T. L., & Linz, D. (2000b). Race and the misrepresentation of victimization on local television news. *Communication Research, 27,* 547–573.

Dominick, J., & Greenberg, B. (1970). Three seasons of Black on television. *Journal of Advertising Research, 10,* 21–27.

Donagher, P. C., Poulos, R. W., Liebert, R. M., & Davidson, E. S. (1975). Race, sex, and social example: An analysis of character portrayals on inter-racial television entertainment. *Psychological Reports, 37,* 1023–1034.

Entman, R. (1992). Blacks in the news: Television, modern racism, and cultural change. *Journalism Quarterly, 69,* 341–361.

Entman, R. (1994). Representation and reality in the portrayal of Blacks on network television news. *Journalism Quarterly, 71,* 509–520.

Erikson, E. (1968). *Identity: Youth and crisis.* New York: Norton.

Fearn-Banks, K. (2006). *Historical dictionary of African-American television.* Lanham, MD: Scarecrow Press.

Fujioka, Y., Tan, A. S., & Tan, G. K. (2000). Television use, stereotypes of African Americans and opinions on affirmative action: An affective model of policy reasoning. *Communication Monograph, 67,* 362–371.

Gerbner, G., & Signorielli, N. (1979). *Women and minorities in television drama*. Philadelphia: Annenberg School of Communication, University of Pennsylvania.

Gerbner, G., Gross, L., Morgan, M., & Signorielli, N. (1994). Growing up with television: The cultivation perspective. In J. Bryant & D. Zillman (Eds.), *Media effects: Advances in theory and research* (pp. 17–41). Hillsdale, NJ: Erlbaum.

Gerson, W. M. (1968). Mass media socialization behavior: Negro–white differences. *Social Forces, 45,* 40–50.

Glascock, J. (2003). Gender, race and aggression in newer TV networks' primetime programming. *Communication Quarterly, 51*(1), 90–100.

Graves, S. B. (1993). Television, the portrayal of African Americans, and the development of children's attitudes. In G. L. Berry & J. K. Asamen (Eds.), *Children and television: Images in a changing sociocultural world* (pp. 179–190). Newbury Park, CA: Sage.

Greenberg, B. S., & Baptista-Fernandez, P. (1980). Hispanic-Americans: The new minority on television. In B. S. Greenberg (Ed.), *Life on television: Content analysis of U.S. TV drama* (pp. 3–12). Norwood, NJ: Ablex.

Greenberg, B. S., & Brand, J. (1994). Minorities and the mass media: 1970s to 1990s. In J. Bryant & D. Zillmann (Eds.), *Media effects: Advances in theory and research* (pp. 273–314). Hillsdale, NJ: Erlbaum.

Greenberg, B. S., & Collette, L. (1997). The changing faces of TV: A demographic analysis of network television's new seasons, 1966–1992. *Journal of Broadcasting and Electronic Media, 41,* 1–13.

Greenberg, B. S., Mastro, D., & Brand, J. E. (2002). Minorities and the mass media: Television into the 21st century. In J. Bryant & D. Zillman (Eds.), *Media effects: Advances in theory and research* (pp. 331–351). Mahwah, NJ: Erlbaum.

Harrison, K. (2006). Scope of self: Toward a model of television's effects on self-complexity in adolescence. *Communication Theory, 16,* 251–279.

Hinton, J. L., Seggar, J. F., Northcott, H. C., & Fontes, B. (1974). Tokenism and improving imagery of Blacks in TV drama and comedy: 1973. *Journal of Broadcasting, 18,* 423–437.

Iiyama, P., & Kitano, H. H. L. (1982). Asian Americans and the media. In G. Berry & C. Mitchell-Kernan (Eds.), *Television and the socialization of the minority child* (pp. 151–186). New York: Academic Press.

Johnson, J., & Adams, M. S. (1995). Differential gender effects of exposure to rap music on African American adolescents' acceptance of teen dating violence. *Sex Roles, 33,* 597–605.

Johnson, J. D., Jackson, L. A., & Gatto, L. (1995). Violent attitudes and deferred academic aspirations: Deleterious effects of exposure to rap music. *Basic and Applied Social Psychology, 16*(1–2), 27–41.

Keys, T. R., Morant, K., & Stroman, C. A. (in press). Black youth's personal involvement in the HIV/AIDS issue: Does the Public Service Announcement still work? *Journal of Health Communication.*

Klein, J., Brown, J. D., Walsh-Childers, K., Oliveri, J., Porter, C., & Dykers, C. (1993). Adolescents' risky behavior and mass media use. *Pediatrics, 92,* 24–31.

Lee, K., & Joo, S. (2005). The portrayal of Asian Americans in mainstream magazines ads; An update. *Journalism and Mass Communication Quarterly, 82,* 654–671.

Liefer, A. D., & Roberts, D. F. (1972). Children's responses to television violence. In J. P. Murrary, E. A. Rubinstein, & G. A. Comstock (Eds.), *Television and social behavior* (Vol. 2: *Television and social learning*) (pp. 43–80). Washington, DC: U.S. Government Printing Office.

MacDonald, J. F. (1992). *Black and white TV: Afro-American in television since 1948* (2nd ed.). Chicago: Nelson-Hall.

Martino, S. C., Collins, R. L., Elliot, M. N., Strachman, A., Kanouse, D. E., & Berry, S. H. (2006). Exposure to degrading versus nondegrading music lyrics and sexual behavior among youth. *Pediatrics, 118*, 430–441.

Mastro, D. E., & Behm-Morawitz, E. (2005). Latino representation on primetime television. *Journalism and Mass Communication Quarterly, 82*, 110–130.

Mastro, D. E., & Greenberg, B. S. (2000). The portrayal of racial minorities on prime time television. *Journal of Broadcasting & Electronic Media, 44*, 690–703.

Mastro, D. E., & Kopacz, M. A. (2006). Media representations of race, prototypicality, and policy reasoning: An application of self-categorization theory. *Journal of Broadcasting & Electronic Media, 50*(2), 305–322.

Mastro, D. E., & Stern, S. R. (2003). Representations of race in television commercials: A content analysis of prime-time advertising. *Journal of Broadcasting & Electronic Media, 47*, 638–647.

Matabane, P. M., & Merritt, B. (1996). African Americans on television: Twenty-five years after Kerner. *Howard Journal of Communications, 7*, 329–337.

Milloy, C. (2007, September 19). Gangsta rap, dying in the street. *The Washington Post*, pp. B1, 6.

Nelson, J. (2004, May 7). Raw rap videos fuel disrespect of women. *USA Today*, p. 15a.

Newhall, M. (2007, September 16). Channeling their discontent: 500 gather at Executive's D.C. home to protest stereotypes. *Washington Post*, p. C3.

Northcott, H. C., Seggar, J. F., & Hinton, J. L. (1975). Trends in TV portrayal of Blacks and women. *Journalism Quarterly, 52*, 741–744.

O'Kelly, C. G., & Bloomquist, L. E. (1976). Women and Blacks on TV. *Journal of Communication, 26*, 179–192.

Peterson, S. H., Wingood, G. M., DiClemente, R. J., Harrington, K., & Davies, S. (2007). Images of sexual stereotypes in rap videos and the health of African American female adolescents. *Journal of Women's Health, 16*, 1157–1164.

Poindexter, P. M., & Stroman, C. A. (1981). Blacks and television: A review of the research literature. *Journal of Broadcasting, 25*, 103–122.

Poussaint, A. F. (August, 1974). Building a strong self-image in the black child. *Ebony*, 138–143.

Powell, G. (1982). The impact of television on the self-concept development of minority group children. In G. L. Berry & C. Mitchell-Kernan (Eds.), *Television and the socialization of the minority child* (pp. 105–131). New York: Academic Press.

Ramasubramanian, S. (2007). Media-based strategies to reduce racial stereotypes activated by news stories. *Journalism & Mass Communication Quarterly, 84*, 249–264.

Reid, P. M. (1979). Racial stereotyping on TV: A comparison of the behavior of both Black and White television characters. *Journal of Applied Psychology, 64,* 465–471.

Rich, M., Woods, E. R., Goodman, E., Emans, S. J., & DuRant, R. H. (1998). Aggressors or victims: Gender and race in music video violence. *Pediatrics, 101*(4), 669–674.

Rideout, V., Roberts, D. F., & Foehr, U. G. (2005). *Generation M: Media in the lives of 8–18 year-olds.* Menlo Park, CA: Kaiser Family Foundation.

Rivadeneyra, R., Ward, L. M., & Gordon, M. (2007). Distorted reflections: Media exposure and Latino adolescents conception of self. *Media Psychology, 9,* 261–290.

Robinson, J. D., & Skill, T. (2001). Five decades of families on television: From the 1950s through the 1990s. In J. Bryant & J. A. Bryant (Eds.), *Television and the American family* (pp. 139–162). Mahwah, NJ: Erlbuam.

Schooler, D., Ward, L. M., Merriwether, A., & Caruthers, A. (2004). Who's that girl: Television's role in the body image development of young white and black women. *Psychology of Women Quarterly, 28,* 38–47.

Seggar, J. L. (1977). Television's portrayal of minorities and women. *Journal of Broadcasting, 21,* 435–446.

Seggar, J. L., & Wheeler, P. (1973). World of work on TV: Ethnic and sex representation in TV drama. *Journal of Broadcasting, 17,* 201–214.

Shu, J. I. (1979). *The portrayal of Chinese on network television as observed by Chinese and White raters.* Unpublished doctoral dissertation, State University of New York at Stony Brook, New York.

Signorielli, N. (2001). Aging on television: The picture in the nineties. *Generations, 25,* 34–39.

Signorielli, N. (2007). Media images of African Americans. In J. J. Arnett (Ed.), *Encyclopedia of children, adolescents, and the media* (pp. 67–70). Thousand Oaks, CA: Sage.

Squires, C., Kohn-Wood, L. P., Chavous, T., & Carter, P. (2006). Evaluating agency and responsibility in gendered violence: African American youth talk about violence and hip hop. *Sex Roles, 55,* 725–737.

Strange, J. J. (2007). Media portrayals of adolescents. In J. J. Arnett (Ed.), *Encyclopedia of children, adolescents, and the media* (pp. 5–11). Thousand Oaks, CA: Sage.

Stroman, C. A. (1986). Television and self-concept among Black children. *Journal of Broadcasting and Electronic Media, 30,* 87–93.

Stroman, C. A. (2005). Disseminating HIV/AIDS information to African Americans. *Journal of the Poor and Underserved, 16* (4) Supplement B, 24–37.

Stroman, C. A., Merritt, B. D., & Matabane, P. W. (1989–1990). Twenty years after Kerner: The portrayal of African Americans on prime-time television. *Howard Journal of Communications, 2,* 44–56.

Tan, A., Fujioka, Y., & Lucht, N. (1997). Native American stereotypes, TV portrayals, and personal contact. *Journalism and Mass Communication Quarterly, 74,* 265–284.

U.S. Commission on Civil Rights. (1979). *Window dressing on the set: An update.* Washington, DC: Author.

U.S. Commission on Civil Rights. (1977). *Window dressing on the set: Women and minorities in television.* Washington, DC: Author.

Ward, L. M. (2004). Wading through the stereotypes: Positive and negative associations between media use and Black adolescents' conception of self. *Developmental Psychology, 40,* 284–294.

Ward, L. M. (2005). Children, adolescents, and the media: The molding of minds, bodies, and deeds. *New Directions for Child and Adolescent Development, 109,* 63–71.

Ward, L. M., Hansbrough, E., & Walker, E. (2005). Contributions of music video exposure to Black adolescents' gender and sexual schema. *Journal of Adolescent Research, 20,* 143–166.

Warren, R. (2007). Children's use of electronic media. In J. Arnett (Ed.), *Encyclopedia of children, adolescents, and the media* (pp. 286–288). Thousand Oaks, CA: Sage.

Wilkes, R., & Valencia, H. (1989). Hispanics and Blacks in television commercials. *Journal of Advertising, 18,* 19–25.

Wilson, C. C., & Gutierrez, F. (1995). *Race, multiculturalism, and the media: From mass to class communication* (2nd ed.). Thousand Oaks, CA: Sage.

Wingood, G., DiClemente, R., Bernhardt, J., Harrington, K. Davies, S., Robillard, A., et al. (2003). A prospective study of exposure to rap music videos and African American female adolescents health. *American Journal of Public Health, 93,* 437–439.

# 8

# Adolescents and Television Violence

W. JAMES POTTER

The purpose of this chapter is to address the focal question: Since the early days of television, what has changed and what has stayed the same with the portrayals of adolescents in television violence? This is a very important question, because its answer could help assess the changing risks for negative effects compared to past generations that adolescents are now experiencing. As I show, the content analysis literature suggests there have been few noteworthy changes either in the amount of violence presented in television shows or in the way that violence is portrayed that would cue viewers about its meaning. Also, it should be noted that there are many gaps in this research literature; while there have been over sixty content analyses of violence in fictional television programming, only a handful profile characters involved in violence by age.

This chapter is structured in three sections. First, I examine the content analysis literature to identify findings that can be used to construct an answer to the focal question. Second, I discuss the implications for risks of negative effects on adolescents, given the patterns identified in the first section. Then I examine the broader issue of what constitutes a negative effect in the context of adolescents and their media exposures. This third section is important, because the examination of content patterns becomes especially useful when we link them to potential effects on viewers. As the effects literature has grown and scholars learn more about content factors that change risks for all kinds of effects, it becomes increasingly important to examine in more depth the issue of what is a negative effect.

## THE CONTENT ANALYSIS LITERATURE

In this section I analyze the media violence content literature and identify indicators of three issues: frequency, seriousness, and context of portrayals. For each of these issues, I present general findings and trends, then focus on adolescents.

Before presenting findings from the content analysis research, I need to acknowledge that there are many definitions of violence used across these studies (for a more complete analysis of this variety, see Potter, 1999). However, there are some commonalities across those definitions. The studies reported here typically use definitions for violence that focus on acts of physical aggression of one fictional character against another fictional character. Characters are typically human, but can also be animals and anthropomorphized objects. Most of these definitions also count accidents and acts of nature as violence, because these acts are conscious constructions of the writers and producers of television shows. Most of these definitions also count acts of physical aggression in humorous and fantasy contexts; thus the violent action on "children's" Saturday morning programming is counted. Also, most definitions do not require the victim to show harm from the physical aggression in order for it to count as violence. If one character fires a gun at another character but misses, this is usually counted as an act of violence. This "nonharm" condition also allows for verbal threats to be counted even when the threats are not carried out. However, other acts of verbal aggression are almost never counted; these other acts would include things such as hate speech as well as comments meant to embarrass or maliciously harm another character. For example, if a Nazi SS officer says to a Jewish prisoner, "I am going to kill you," this would be counted as violence, but if the Nazi SS officer says, "I am going to kill all Jews," this would not be counted as violence, given the definitions used in almost all of these content analyses.

### Adolescents in Violent Actions on Television

The literature of studies that have analyzed media messages for violence is relatively large. When writing my book *On Media Violence* (Potter, 1999), I found sixty-one published content analyses of violence on television. These were primarily of U.S. television, but also included analyses of television in other countries, especially the United Kingdom and Japan. Since that time there have been a handful of studies added to that literature.

The earliest content analyses (Head, 1954; Smythe, 1953) were conducted in the first decade of television in the United States. Neither of these studies provided a breakdown by age grouping. For example, Smythe and his team analyzed the content of the seven New York City television stations, and published a book that presented twelve chapters, each focusing on a different topic of content. In his chapter on violence, he reported that there were 6.8 acts per hour in 1952 and 7.1 acts per hour in 1953. He provided no breakdowns by age groupings in his chapter on TV violence. But in a later chapter dealing with profiles of TV characters in general, he provided some age breakdowns. He found that teens made up 4.8% of all characters on TV while teens made up 14.4% of the U.S. population. He also found that children made up 3.8% of all TV characters while children made up 19.5% of the U.S. population. In sum, characters who were either children or teens were underrepresented on TV (8.6% of all characters) compared to the U.S. population (33.9% of all people). He also reported that children or teens were never the villains, but about 8% of all heroes were children or teens.

Then, in the decade of the 1960s, there were a few more content analyses of violence published (Lyle & Wilcox, 1963; Schramm, Lyle, & Parker, 1961). Again, these studies did not include breakdowns for age groupings, although the Schramm et al. book included a listing of all violent acts in one hundred hours of television that was purportedly aimed at children. They found more than one act of violence per hour, but they reported no profiling of perpetrators or victims of these acts by age.

In the 1970s, the number of content analyses of television violence increased, and figures of adolescents began to appear. As part of the Surgeon General's Report, Gerbner (1972) presented a chapter on violence in television drama that included 113 tables of findings. A few of those tables presented breakdowns by age but children and adolescents were lumped together. He reported that from 1967 to 1969 children and adolescents made up 7.3% of leading characters on television drama and they accounted for 7.3% of the victims. However, adolescents made up only 5.7% of characters committing violence. Likewise, Dominick (1973) coded for age categories but did not distinguish among children and adolescents, lumping them all together in an "under 20" group. In his analysis of crime shows, he found that 18% of the victims were characters under 20. Gerbner, Gross, Jackson-Beeck, Jeffries-Fox, and Signorielli (1978) reported some age breakouts but again their figures were confounded by children and adolescents being treated the same. They report that among male children/adolescent characters, 65.5% were found to be involved in some violence while 49.5% of female children/adolescents were. The profiles of victims and perpetrators are fairly similar.

Not until the 1990s, did we see a content analysis of television violence provide frequency figures by age grouping. The National Television Violence Study (NTVS) reported that about 5% of all violent interactions had a teen as a perpetrator and 7% had a teen as a victim (Smith et al., 1998). These figures varied little over the three years of their analysis from the 1994–1995 season to the 1996–1997 season for either perpetrator (5%, 6%, and 5%) or victim (7%, 8%, and 7%). In a major two-year study of violence on British television, Gunter and his colleagues found that teenagers (15 to 19) were aggressors in about 4.5% of all violent acts and were victims in about 4.3% of all violent acts (Gunter, Harrison, & Wykes, 2003).

OVERALL TRENDS IN AMOUNT OF TV VIOLENCE

There appears to be no discernable increase or decrease in the amount of violence on U.S. television. The earliest trend analysis of violence on television was conducted by Clark and Blankenburg (1972) who reported that, in 1953, 19.2% of prime-time network television shows contained violence; this percentage climbed to 41.3% in 1959, then dropped to a low of 17.7% in 1965, then shot up to 37.7% in 1967. However, we must be careful about giving too much credence to these results, because these percentages were not computed from an analysis of the actual television shows; instead, the authors inferred whether each show was violent or not from reading its synopsis in *TV Guide*. It is likely that many shows containing some violence were not counted in the violent percentage; therefore, these percentages are underreporting of the actual proportion of TV shows that contained violence. Much better data were generated by the Cultural Indicators Project at the University of Pennsylvania, which coded network prime-time and children's Saturday morning television programs for violent acts from 1967 to 1985 (for a summary, see Signorielli, 1990). This project found that while the overall frequency of violence on television fluctuates from year to year, there is no general downward or upward trend. They show that the percentage of prime-time television programs that present violence each year fluctuates from a low of 64% to a high of 79%, and that the hourly rates during that time fluctuated from a low of 3.9% to a high of 6.9%. Then in the mid-1990s, the NTVS conducted a three-year study of violence appearing in programs on twenty-three television broadcast and cable networks for a composite week of seven days from 6 A.M. until 10:59 P.M. (see Smith et al., 1998, for their three-year report). They reported "striking evidence that there is no increase or decrease in the overall prevalence of violence on television across the three-year course of this study" (p. 114). They found about 60% of all programs contained at least one violent act. This percentage is slightly lower than what was reported by the Cultural Indicators Project, but this difference is likely to be explained by the NTVS sample including many channels and dayparts that were not analyzed by the Cultural Indicators Project. The Cultural Indicators Project analyzed dramatic shows broadcast on three TV networks (ABC, CBS, and NBC) during prime time (8 P.M. to 11 P.M.) and children's dramatic programs shown on weekend mornings (8 A.M. to 2 P.M.) for a composite week each year. NTVS analyzed all fictional programs on five broadcast networks (ABC, CBS, NBC, Fox, and PBS), three independent local TV stations, twelve basic cable channels, and three premium cable channels; also, NTVS analyzed programs in all dayparts from 6 A.M. to 11 P.M. for all seven days of the week.

## CONCLUSIONS ABOUT ADOLESCENTS AND TV VIOLENCE

Given the limitations in the television violence content analysis literature, it is hazardous to draw conclusions about trends in the appearance of adolescents in violent scenes. There are widely differing types of samples, unitizing procedures, and definitions across the studies in this literature. Many of these studies do not code for age, and among the several that do provide age groupings, figures are aggregated for children and adolescents. With this caveat in mind, I hazard two conclusions.

First, violence has appeared in the majority of television shows since the beginning of TV broadcasting in the United States. We have very good trend data from the mid-1960s to the late 1990s that show yearly fluctuations that stay above a floor of 60% of all TV shows. Content analyses conducted before the mid-1960s also reveal a good deal of violence across the television landscape, and there is no reason to conclude that violence was any lower during the earliest two decades of television broadcasting.

Second, it appears that children and adolescents are rarely depicted in violent acts on television and that these depictions may be getting even rarer. Dominick (1973) reported that 18% of victims were children/adolescents, while NTVS (1997) found that 11% of all victims were either children or adolescents. However, the conclusion that youth portrayals of violence are diminishing may be inaccurate when we consider some broader patterns. Since the 1950s, the percentage of the U.S. population from birth to 19 shrank from 39% to 29%, while the percentage of characters under 20 years of age across all kinds of television shows has stayed around 10%. Youth have consistently been underrepresented in the television landscape. However, when children and adolescents are shown in a television story, there is a fairly high probability they will be involved in violence—65.5% of boys were and 49.5% of girls were (Gerbner et al., 1978).

## Patterns of Seriousness of Violence

Some acts of violence are very serious, such as murder and rape; others are a bit less serious, such as assaults; and still others may be relatively minor in their consequences, such as verbal violence. In general, studies that include counts of verbal types of violence in addition to physical types of violence typically find many more verbal acts than physical acts. Williams, Zabrack, and Joy (1982) found a ratio of 1.1 acts of verbal aggression to every act of physical aggression in their analysis of American and Canadian prime-time television in 1980. Potter and Ware (1987) reported a ratio of 1.4 to 1 in 1985 prime-time television. Greenberg, Edison, Korzenny, Fernandez-Collado, & Atkin (1980) reported a ratio of about 1.8 to 1. Potter and Vaughan (1997) found a ratio of 2.4 to 1. Of course, there are differences of definition and sample across these studies, but even so, the findings are so robust that they continue to emerge: Verbal aggression (such as hate speech and malicious remarks intended to harm another character) is at least as prevalent as physical aggression on television.

Has there been a change in the prevalence of different types of violence over the years? The answer to this question appears to be yes. A decade ago, we replicated the study of Greenberg et al. (1980) to see if rates of different types of violence have changed from the mid-1970s to the mid-1990s (Potter & Vaughan, 1997). We found that overall rates of physical violence stayed the same (from 12.7 to 12.3 acts per hour), but rates of verbal violence had climbed (from 22.8 to 27.0) when comparing Greenberg et al.'s findings from the mid-1970s to our findings in the early 1990s. This change is even clearer with two genres. With situation comedies, physical violence has stayed the same at 7.2 acts per hour, but verbal violence went up from 33.5 to 41.9 acts per hour. With action/adventure programs, physical violence was about the same (12.7 to 12.3), but verbal violence was up (22.8 to 27.0). Our categories of verbal violence included intimidation (threatening physical harm without actually committing physical harm), hostile remarks (words directed to another character with the intention of harming that character emotionally or psychologically), and social harm (disparaging a group of people in general, an institution, or society).

What is the pattern with adolescents? That is, when adolescents are portrayed as being involved in violent actions, are those actions typically different in nature from the violent portrayals of older characters? The answer to this question appears to be yes, given the findings of a study we conducted almost fifteen years ago (Potter et al., 1995), where we provided a cross tabulation of age with different categories of aggressive acts, which were largely violent acts. Table 8.1 shows that adolescents (13 to 18) were more likely to be perpetrators of verbal aggression (such as deception and hostile remarks) than physical aggression (such as assaults, property harm, or physical intimidation). The same pattern generally holds when adolescents are portrayed as victims.

Table 8.1. Types of Violent Acts Across Age Groupings on Television

| | Physical Violence | | | | Verbal Violence | |
|---|---|---|---|---|---|---|
| | Serious Assault | Minor Assault | Property Harm | Intimidation | Hostile Remarks | Social Harm |
| *Perpetrators* | | | | | | |
| Birth to 5 | 0.4 | 1.9 | 4.9 | 0.2 | 0.2 | — |
| 6 to 12 | 0.8 | 2.1 | — | 1.8 | 2.7 | — |
| 13 to 18 | 1.5 | 6.5 | 6.8 | 3.2 | 10.2 | 4.7 |
| 19 to 30 | 17.2 | 12.1 | 8.7 | 13.2 | 11.6 | 31.3 |
| 31 to 60 | 42.5 | 55.2 | 50.5 | 67.3 | 67.3 | 46.9 |
| 61 and over | 1.5 | 2.7 | 1.0 | 6.2 | 6.0 | 1.6 |
| Multiple | 3.1 | 3.4 | 4.9 | 2.3 | 1.1 | 3.1 |
| Unknown | 33.0 | 16.1 | 23.3 | 5.9 | 1.0 | 12.5 |
| *Victims* | | | | | | |
| Birth to 5 | 0.4 | 1.7 | 5.8 | — | 0.2 | — |
| 6 to 12 | — | 5.4 | 2.9 | 3.6 | 2.4 | — |
| 13 to 18 | 4.2 | 7.7 | 3.9 | 10.0 | 11.9 | — |
| 19 to 30 | 17.2 | 15.3 | 2.9 | 18.9 | 14.0 | — |
| 31 to 60 | 37.5 | 51.5 | 23.3 | 54.9 | 56.5 | 20.3 |
| 61 and over | 3.8 | 2.1 | 6.8 | 3.9 | 6.4 | — |
| Multiple | 6.9 | 4.8 | 5.8 | 5.7 | 5.2 | 37.5 |
| Unknown[a] | 29.9 | 11.5 | 48.5 | 3.0 | 3.5 | 42.2 |

*Note.* Numbers are column percentages for perpetrators and for victims. Adapted with permission from Potter et al (1995).
[a]The high percentages for unknown characters is due to characters either not being shown on screen (i.e., we hear the violent act and see the aftermath) or the characters are cartoon figures, such as animals or supernatural beings.

We can conclude that within the category of physical violence, there has been a shift away from more serious forms (such as murders and rapes) to less serious forms (such as assaults). Also, there has been an increase in the frequency of verbal violence, so that by the 1990s, there were about 2.4 acts of verbal violence for every act of physical violence. This increase in verbal violence occurred most dramatically in situation comedies, and adolescents are more likely to be characters in situation comedies than in other genres.

## Patterns of Consequences and Characteristics of Violence

It was not until the early 1970s that a content analysis of television violence was reported examining those characteristics of the portrayals that might lead viewers to construct different meanings of the actions. These "contextual" variables include whether the violence was rewarded or punished; whether the perpetrators of the violence were the villains or heroes; whether the victims were depicted as suffering harm; and whether the violence act was portrayed as being justified. Dominick (1973) looked at type of perpetrator (hero/villain) and punishment of perpetrators (arrest of criminal), but limited his analysis to crime and law enforcement on prime-time television. Several other studies reported on context over the next twenty-five years (Estep & Macdonald, 1983; Potter & Ware, 1987; Sherman & Dominick, 1986; Williams et al., 1982), then in the mid-1990s, NTVS conducted a major analysis of the full television landscape and coded for many contextual variables. As a result of all this work, we have a good picture of how violence is presented on television in addition to how much violence is presented (see Table 8.2). Despite differences in definitions and samples across studies, the findings are remarkably robust and do not seem to change much over time (Center for Media and Public Affairs, 1994; Dominick, 1973; NTVS, 1996, 1997; Potter et al., 1995; Sherman & Dominick, 1986; Williams et al., 1982). Thus it is possible to conclude that there is a standard formula for presenting violence on television.

What is this standard formula? It can be summarized in three words— glamorized, sanitized, and trivialized—as depicted in the conclusions of the NTVS (Smith et al., 1998). As for glamorizing violence, the perpetrators of much of the violence are the good guys—the story's heroes—and their actions are presented as not only justified but also as necessary. For example, the good guys are shown using violence to subdue the bad guys; thus, the lesson being taught is that if you are a good guy (which is likely the way all viewers regard themselves), it is not only okay to use violence but that it is often necessary to use it. Nearly 40% of all violent actions are perpetrated by "good" characters and with 82% of those violent actions, those good characters are either rewarded or get away with committing the violence. With clearly "bad" characters, only 55% are punished for their actions somewhere in the program; thus, almost half of bad characters are depicted as getting away with their violent actions. This ratio has remained relatively constant over time. Violence is sanitized so as not to offend viewers; 55% of victims show no pain or suffering and 36% of victims experienced unrealistically low levels of harm. In only 15% of violent programs was the long-term harm of violent acts portrayed. And violence is trivialized, with 40% being presented in a humorous context. The pattern of these characteristics may serve to teach viewers that violence is often justified and solves problems successfully; it does not really harm victims; and it is not a big deal worthy of punishment or even remorse. If this contextual pattern were the opposite and exhibited an antiviolence theme—that is, violence shown in a negative

Table 8.2. Profiles of Characters Involved With Violence on Television

*A high proportion of the violence is committed by "good" characters.* The Center for Media and Public Affairs (1994) reported that "violence on television is typically not a tool of evil...most violence in network shows is committed by positive characters" (p. 12). This conclusion was based on their finding that much of the violence (42%) is committed primarily by "positive" characters, while negative or criminal characters account for 20% and neutral characters account for 17%. "Good characters" are sometimes operationalized as heroes, and when they are, heroes are found to commit as many antisocial acts as villains (Potter & Ware, 1987).

*Most of the violence is intentional and most often the motives are not prosocial* (Dominick, 1973; Larsen, Gray, & Fortis, 1968; NTVS, 1996, 1997; Potter et al., 1995, 1997; Smith et al., 1999; Williams, Zabrac, & Joy, 1982). As for motives in fictional shows, Williams et al., (1982) report that in 97% of violent acts on television the perpetrators intended harm. Potter et al. (1995) found that 58% of the acts were malicious and 33% were inconsiderate. Also, in half the acts, the motive was to hurt the victim either physically or emotionally. Dominick (1973) reported that the most popular motives for crime were greed (32%) and to avoid detection (31%). NTVS found that most of the violent interactions were intentionally motivated, either for personal gain (30%), protection of life (26%), or anger (24%) (NTVS, 1997; Smith et al., 1999). As for motives in nonfiction, Potter et al. (1997) found that 60% was motivated by maliciousness.

*Much of the violence is justified.* The amount of justification changes depending on the perspective from which it is judged. Potter and Ware (1987) found 93% were justified from the perspective of the perpetrator—not society. That is, if the perpetrator was portrayed as regarding the violent act as warranted, the coder recorded it as being justified. But if the perpetrator displayed a negative feeling, such as remorse, the act was coded as being unjustified from the character's point of view. But the results would be different if the judgment of justification were made from the point of view of what society would condone. NTVS defined justification primarily in terms of motives where violence used to protect oneself or family or to retaliate against an attack were regarded as justified. With this perspective on justification, NTVS found that 32% of all violent interactions were judged to be justified by the coders (Smith et al., 1999).

*With much of the violence, the perpetrators are not punished* (Dominick, 1973; NTVS, 1996, 1997; Potter et al., 1997; Potter & Ware, 1987). For example, Potter and Ware (1987) found that only 12% of violent acts were portrayed as being punished. NTVS (1997) reported that 19% of violent interactions in fictional programming were shown as punished, and another 8% were shown with both reward and punishment immediately after the action. When looking at the entire show, the rates of punishment were higher as another 40% of perpetrators were punished at the end of the show (NTVS, 1997; Smith et al., 1999). Still, this leaves about 37% of the perpetrators as not being punished anywhere in the program for committing a violent act. Much of the violence on television is portrayed as being successful, except for criminals (Estep & Macdonald, 1983; Oliver, 1994; Williams et al., 1982). For example, Williams et al. (1982) found that the most common response to aggression was for victims to respond unconditionally (29.1%) or to withdraw from the encounter (15.8%).

Table 8.2. (*continued*)

---

*Consequences to the victims are rarely shown* (Center for Media and Public Affairs, 1994; Dominick, 1973; NTVS, 1996, 1997; Potter et al., 1995; Sherman & Dominick, 1986; Williams et al., 1982). In fictional programming, Williams et al. (1982) report that over 81% of violent acts depicted no impairment to the victims. In 76% of violent scenes, there was no physical outcome shown to the violence, and 90% of the scenes showed no emotional impact on characters (Center for Media and Public Affairs, 1994). NTVS reported that in 47% of all violent interactions, there was absolutely no harm shown and in 58% of violent scenes, there was no pain to the target. Also, in only 16% of all programs with violence is there a portrayal of long-term negative consequences such as psychological, financial, or emotional harm (NTVS, 1997; Smith et al., 1999). The same pattern was found in music videos. Sherman and Dominick (1986) reported that in almost 80% of all violence in performance music videos, no outcome of the violence was shown.

*Weapons are often found in violent acts.* NTVS says that in fictional programming guns were used in one quarter of all violent interactions, and that other kinds of weapons were used in another one-third of all violent interactions. However, the most prevalent form of violence was natural means, which is the use of nothing more than the perpetrator's body (NTVS, 1997; Smith et al., 1999).

*The presentation style is rarely graphic and explicit.* NTVS (Smith et al., 1999) found that within fictional programming, rarely (10%) is violence shown graphically—that is, where the violence is shown closer than a long shot. Less than 3% of all violent scenes featured a close up of the violence. Also, in 85% of all acts there was no blood or gore shown, and in only 15% of violent scenes was there any blood or gore.

*Much of the violence is portrayed in a humorous context* (NTVS, 1996, 1997; Potter et al., 1995; Signorielli, 1990; Smythe, 1954; Williams et al., 1982). For example, Smythe (1953) found that about one quarter of all acts and threats of violence were committed in a humorous context, and that the humorous context was more common in programs for children than those for a general audience. In Gerbner's analyses from 1967 to 1985, children's (weekend daytime) programming was found to have the highest rates of violence, but 73% of that programming presented violence in at least a partly comic context, compared to only 20% of prime-time violent programming using a comic context (Signorielli, 1990). More recently, NTVS found that there was a humorous context to 39% of violent interactions in fictional programming, but only 3% of acts in reality programs are coupled with humor (Wartella et al., 1998).

*Violence is often shown in a fantasy context or in an unrealistic pattern.* NTVS reports that about half of the violent acts were shown in a fantasy context, such as with anthropomorphized animals and puppets (NTVS, 1997; Smith et al., 1999). But the concept of realism is more complex than simply determining if there are puppets or not.

---

context of being punished, very harmful to victims and perpetrators alike, and very serious—then viewers would learn an opposite lesson, that is, that committing violence is not a good way to solve problems. NTVS found that only 3% of all violent programs in their 8,000 program sample portrayed an antiviolence theme.

In a subsequent analysis of one year of the NTVS data, Wilson, Colvin, and Smith (2002) conducted an age-based analysis of perpetrators of violent acts and how they were portrayed. They found that on some characteristics, teen perpetrators were portrayed very similarly to child perpetrators and very different from adult perpetrators. For example, about 80% of children and teen perpetrators were portrayed as committing behavioral acts of violence (compared to credible threats), while 69% of adult perpetrators were portrayed committing behavioral acts. Also, children and teens were less likely to engage in lethal violence (35%) and to use guns (5%) than were adult perpetrators (52% of actions were lethal and they used guns in 28% of their violent portrayals). On other characteristics, teenage perpetrators were portrayed much more like adult perpetrators. For example, teen and adult perpetrators were rarely nonhuman (19%) compared to children (41% nonhuman); were rarely in animated (30%), fantasy (35%), or humorous (4%) contexts compared to children (58% animated, 61% fantasy, and 69% humorous); experienced much more frequent portrayals of being punished for their violent actions somewhere in the program (53%) compared to children (30%); were more likely to have their victims portrayed with long-term negative consequences (26%) compared to the violence from child perpetrators (10%); and were more likely to engage in repeated acts of aggression (60%) compared to children (48%).

## Summary of Content Analyses

While there are many content analyses of violence on television, few of these studies report their results by age groupings, and among the few studies that do, adolescents are usually grouped with children in an "under-20" category (see Table 8.1 for an exception). The one study that does provide a profile of violent acts and their context by age grouping reports that teens are sometimes portrayed in a similar manner to children but on other characteristics, teens are portrayed with patterns similar to adults (Wilson et al., 2002).

While it is not possible to use the existing literature to draw confident conclusions about how violent adolescent portrayals have changed over time, I attempt a reasoned speculation here constructed from (a) general patterns reported across the studies in the media violence literatures and (b) indicators of adolescent characters and influences where they are provided. Those patterns of findings (presented in Table 8.3) lead to the overriding conclusion that the quantitative frequency as well as the qualitative context of the portrayals of violence on American television have not changed in any appreciable way over the past five decades. In contrast, there is evidence

## Table 8.3. Factors Influencing a Disinhibition Effect

*Characteristics of Viewer*

Demographics
  *Gender*: Boys more affected
  *Age*: Younger children more affected, if they can follow meaning of the story
  *SES status*: Lower class more affected because they watch more TV
  *Ethnicity*: Minority and immigrant groups more vulnerable because they watch more TV
Traits
  *Cognitive processing skills*: Lower skills, greater risk
  *Personality type*: Higher trait aggressiveness, higher risk
  *Socialization against aggression*: Lower socialization, higher risk
  *Intelligence*: Lower IQ, greater risk
States
  *Aroused state*: Higher arousal, greater risk
  *Emotional state*: More anger and frustration, greater risk
  *Degree of identity*: Higher degree of identity, greater risk
    Heroes—greater identity
    Attractive characters—greater identity
    POV characters—greater identity

*Portrayal of Characters*

  *Rewards/punishments*: Violent actions that are not punished and especially those that are rewarded increase risk
  *Consequences to victims*: The fewer negative consequences (pain, blood, suffering) depicted by the victim, the greater the risk
  *Justification*: The greater the justification for the violent action, the greater the risk; justification is also keyed to appropriateness of the violent action

*Production Techniques*

  *Realism*: The greater the realism, the greater the risk
  *Graphicness and explicitness*: These increase the dramatic nature of the narrative, increase arousal, and thereby increase risk
  *Degree of action*: The more action on the screen, the higher the attention and the greater the risk
  *Suspense*: The greater the outcome uncertainty for the hero, the greater the risk if the hero is successful
  *Presence of weapons*: The results here are mixed
  *Eroticism*: The results are mixed

*Situational Cues*

  *Cues*: When there is the presence of cues in real life that remind viewer of media portrayal, risk is increased

For more detail and citations, see Potter (1999).

of a shift away from the most serious forms of physical violence to less serious forms of physical violence. Furthermore there has been a growth in the number of acts of verbal violence.

## IMPLICATIONS FOR RISKS OF NEGATIVE EFFECTS ON ADOLESCENTS

Given the speculative nature of my conclusions, there are some important implications for risks to adolescents. In this section, I discuss those risks in terms of the three most research-based negative effects from exposure to media violence: stimulating aggressive behavior, fear, and desensitization (Potter, 1999).

### TV Violence Effects on Aggressive Behavior

There has been a good deal of research using experiments that have found that participants who are in treatment groups where they view violent portrayals are more likely to behave aggressively immediately after those exposures. With children, aggressive behavior is usually measured in play situations where their choice of toys (hammers and swords versus dolls and building blocks) as well as their interactions with other children are monitored. With adolescents and adults, aggressive behavior is usually measured as their actions in shocking a confederate in a learning task or retaliation against someone who frustrated or angered them during the experiment.

Narrative reviews as well as meta-analyses of this literature (Anderson et al., 2003; Bushman & Anderson, 2001; Hearold, 1986; Paik & Comstock, 1994; Wood, Wong, & Chachere, 1991) have concluded that exposure to violence in the media is associated with higher levels of antisocial behavior. For example, Wood et al. concluded, "media violence enhances children's and adolescents' aggression in interactions with strangers, classmates, and friends" (1991, p. 380). This effect works through a process of social learning that results in disinhibition so that after the violent exposure adolescents who are presented with certain cues and opportunities in real life are more likely to behave in an aggressive manner. This disinhibition effect has been examined predominately in the short term (within a few hours or days), but there is also evidence that the effect can persist over the course of a person's life. Bushman and Huesmann (2001) point out that longitudinal research has found that males who watch a lot of violence on television as young children are more likely to behave aggressively as children and this appetite for violent messages as well as violent behavior continues throughout adolescence and well into adulthood.

In their meta-analysis, Paik and Comstock (1994) reported that the overall effect size of the relationship between exposure to television violence and aggressive behavior was relatively strong ($d = .69$). Breaking their analysis down by age grouping, they found that the overall effect size with adolescents was relatively low ($d = .46$) but still a moderate effect compared to children ($d = .65$), young adults 18 to 21 years of age ($d = .79$), and pre-schoolers ($d = 1.02$). The only age group with a lower effect size was adults ($d = .37$). While some of these effect sizes are stronger than others, it should be noted that all are strong relative to social science standards.

More recent scholarship continues to find these effects on adolescents (Coyne, 2004; Funk & Buchman, 1996; Slater, Henry, Swaim, & Anderson, 2003). Furthermore, this aggression effect is not limited to physical aggression but extends to other forms of aggression such as psychological and emotional forms. For example, Coyne (2004) conducted a study with 347 British adolescents to examine what was called "indirect aggression," which is characterized by attempts to harm and manipulate others via plotting and scheming behind their backs; it includes bullying, gossiping, spreading rumors, and excluding others from the social group. The Coyne study found that indirectly aggressive girls viewed more indirect aggression on television than nonaggressive girls did. He explained that after viewing rewarded gossiping, backbiting, and rumor spreading, these girls are particularly likely to use this form of aggression in their own lives.

Why do adolescents who are exposed to media violence tend to behave aggressively afterward? Effects studies have found four types of characteristics that influence the probability of such an effect occurring (see Table 8.4). Notice that most of these characteristics are traceable to the way characters are portrayed or to the production techniques used when presenting violence on television. However, characteristics about the viewer are also important. Perhaps the most powerful and consistent predictor of this effect is trait aggressiveness. That is, adolescents who are already highly aggressive and expose themselves to violence in the media run a high risk of behaving aggressively subsequent to the exposure, even with controls for IQ and gender (Kronenberger, Mathews, Dunn, Wang, Wood, & Larsen, et al., 2005). Also, when highly aggressive adolescents experience high exposure to media violence, they are less likely to control their behavior. In one recent study (Kronenberger, Mathews, Dunn, Wang, Wood, & Giauque, et al., 2005), moderate to strong relationships were found between higher amounts of media violence exposure and deficits in self-report, parent-report, and laboratory-based measures of executive functioning, which they defined as the "ability of the individual to inhibit, regulate, plan, direct and execute behavior...failure or deficit in executive function is likely to underlie impulsive, poorly planned, aggressive behavior" (p. 726).

Table 8.4. Factors Influencing a Fear Effect

*Characteristics of Viewer*

> *Identification*: The greater the degree of identification with the target, the greater the fear
>
> *Prior experience*: More experience with fearful events in real life leads viewers, especially children, to identify more strongly with the characters and events and thereby involve them more emotionally
>
> *Beliefs*: Higher the belief that the violent action depicted could happen to the viewer, the greater the fear
>
> *Ability to perceive the reality of the portrayals*: Lower the ability, the greater the fear because of lower ability to cope
>
> *Level of arousal*: Higher the level, greater the fear
>
> *Ability to use coping strategies*: More ability, less the fear
>
> *Developmental differences*: Lower the developmental maturity, the greater the fear because of lower ability to cope

*Characteristics About the Portrayal*

> *Justification*: The more the violence is unjustified, the greater the fear
>
> *Graphicness*: Higher explicitness and graphicness, greater the fear
>
> *Rewards*: Less punishment for perpetrators, greater the fear
>
> *Realism*: Live action violence provokes more intense fear than cartoon violence
>
> *Type of stimuli*: Cantor (1994) says that the fright effect is triggered by three categories of stimuli that usually are found in combination with many portrayals of violence in the media:
>
> 1. Dangers and injuries, which are stimuli that depict events that threaten great harm; includes natural disasters, attacks by vicious animals, large scale accidents, and violent encounters that can be interpersonal or range in scale to the intergalactic.
> 2. Distortions of natural forms; includes familiar organisms that are shown as being deformed or unnatural through mutilation, accidents of birth, or conditioning.
> 3. Experience of endangerment and fear by others. This type of stimuli evokes empathy for particular characters, and the viewer then feels the fear that the characters in the narrative are portraying.

FEAR EFFECT

A media-induced fear effect is typically regarded as an emotional reaction "involving components of anxiety, distress, and increased physiological arousal that are frequently engendered in viewers as a result of exposure to specific types of media productions" (Cantor, 2002, p. 288). It occurs during exposure and can be of short duration or last for hours or even the rest of one's life. It is typically measured by self-report with adolescents and adults; with children, measures are usually gathered from parents.

In a major review of the literature on fright reactions to media messages, Cantor (2001) clearly shows that exposure to violence in the media can produce fear. However, she says that "one might expect that, as children get older, they become less and less susceptible to all media-produced emotional disturbances, but this is not the case. As children mature cognitively, some things become less likely to disturb them, whereas other things become potentially more upsetting" (p. 211). She says that one change is that the effects of perceptual characteristics of frightening messages decrease with age and that the conceptual aspects of the stimuli become more important. Thus there is a shift away from being frightened by something that looks scary (especially when it is really harmless) to something that is harmful even if it looks attractive. Also, as children age, they become more attuned to the realistic dangers and less influenced by fantasy dangers. Also, with age children become more concerned with the danger in abstract dangers, such as a growing fear over the potential of harm from nuclear devices delivered by terrorists.

Several studies have asked people in late adolescence and early adulthood to recall film and TV exposures that greatly frightened them at the time (Harrison & Cantor, 1999; Hoekstra, Harris, & Helmick, 1999). All of the respondents in the Hoekstra study and 90% of the respondents in the Harrison and Cantor study reported at least one intense fear reaction to a media exposure during childhood or adolescence. Also, vivid images in certain media stories can have a lasting impact. Fremont, Pataki, and Beresin (2005) found that terrorist attacks and their aftermath have had a powerful fear impact on children and adolescents. Factors that predict a fear effect are summarized in Table 8.4.

DESENSITIZATION EFFECT

A desensitization media effect is the reduction of people's natural levels of sympathy and empathy for victims of harm. It has been found to occur immediately during exposure to certain portrayals and it can last a short time or persist over the course of a person's life with repeated exposures to these portrayals.

Adolescents who are exposed to larger amounts of television violence are usually found to be more susceptible to this immediate effect (Cline, Croft, & Courier, 1973; Thomas, 1982). This effect has been found to be influenced by several factors, especially graphicness of violent portrayals (Cline et al., 1973; Lazarus & Alfert, 1964; Speisman, Lazarus, Mordkoff, & Davison, 1964) and humor in those portrayals (Gunter, 1985; Sander, 1995).

## WHAT CONSTITUTES A NEGATIVE EFFECT?

In this section, I focus on three issues that need to be considered in order to understand the complex nature of media effects. These issues concern the frequency of exposures, context of portrayals, and the shift from major acts of physical violence to more minor forms of physical violence along with the increase in the frequency of verbal violence.

## Frequency of Exposure to Violence

The patterns in content analyses reveal that the frequency of violence on television has remained high. This is a negative thing; it is what the public typically criticizes. But let's look at this more closely. If violence were shown as a morality play, then the high frequency would not be seen as a problem. That is, if violence were shown as being perpetrated by unattractive characters who were punished for their bad deeds while victims were shown in great harm and suffering, then viewers would learn that violence is very harmful to both perpetrators and victims. Increasing the number of this type of portrayal would teach pro-social lessons, so an increase of this type of portrayal would be a good thing. Thus the value of the effect is traceable less to the frequency and more to the meaning conveyed in the portrayal. Some scholars argue for the elimination of violence, but this is neither realistic nor helpful. It is unrealistic to expect storytellers to eliminate violence altogether from their tales, especially when the public has grown so accustomed to it. Nor is the elimination of violence helpful to viewers. People should realize that violence has been a part of all societies throughout time. We should not ignore this fact. But neither should we sanitize it. Storytellers need to use violence but they should show that it is something that always harms its victims and usually harms the perpetrators as well.

Now let's focus on the frequency of adolescents appearing in portrayals of violence. Are adolescent characters more likely than other age characters to be involved in violence, given their numbers in the television world? Gerbner et al. (1978) found that among male children/adolescent characters, 65.5% were found to be involved in some violence while 49.5% of girl children/adolescents were. This means that when a child or adolescent character appears on TV, she (and especially he) is likely to be involved in violence. That is a high percentage; however, we must remember that characters under the age of 20 are much rarer than adult characters on television. So the important finding is this: The likelihood of a young character (under age of 20) being involved in violence is about the same as adult characters, but viewers are less likely to see a young character involved in violence because these characters are more rare than are adult characters.

Is it good that only a small percentage of perpetrators and victims were youth? On the surface, it might appear to be a good thing. But let's analyze this. The reason that youth are rarely portrayed in violent scenes is because youth are rarely portrayed at all in television stories compared to adults. Greenberg and his colleagues (1980), who content analyzed all speaking characters appearing on prime-time and Saturday morning network programming from 1975 to 1978, found that while children and adolescents made up 29% of all people in the United States, they comprised only 15% of all speaking characters on television and they committed only 11.9% of all antisocial acts on television. Thus, if youth were being portrayed on television proportional to their size in the U.S. population, they should make up about 29% of all TV characters, so their low numbers of antisocial activity (physical violence, verbal aggression, theft, and deceit) can be traced largely not to prosocial portrayals but to a low number of characters.

Let's take this analysis one step further and address the question of whether or not youth should be shown more often in violent scenes. One context that we can use to answer this question is to look at real-world figures for violent crime. Dominick (1973) reported that in 1970, 35% of all arrests in the United States were of people under 20 years of age, yet on TV there were no arrests of people under 20; as for victims, 14% of real-world victims were under 20 and on TV 18% of victims were under 20. More recent real-world figures are still fairly close to what Dominick found thirty-five years ago. In the United States in 2005, about 41% of all violent crimes were committed by people 12 to 20 years of age, and 20% of victims of violent crimes were between the ages of 12 and 17 (U.S. Department of Justice, 2005, Tables 39 and 45). Given these figures, it appears that the television world is unrealistic in its portrayals of adolescents involved in violence by greatly under-portraying their involvement in violence.

Given these contexts for comparison, it is safe to conclude that adolescents are very much underrepresented in violent portrayals in fictional television stories. But is this a good thing or a bad thing? It is good in the sense that TV programmers are "protecting" adolescents by underrepresenting them in violent actions. However, it can be viewed as a bad thing, because TV programmers are giving viewers—of all ages—a highly unrealistic picture of violence. Also, this underdepiction of adolescents in violent scenes can be regarded as a good thing if we believe that adolescents focus on other adolescents as role models; thus underdepicting their involvement in violence compared to real-world figures might gradually shift adolescents in general away from involvement in violence in the real world. However, adolescents are preparing for adulthood and they look to adults as role models in that preparation (Brown, 2000). When adults are overrepresented in violent scenes in media portrayals and at the same time adolescents are underrepresented in violent action in media portrayals, adolescent viewers are likely to perceive a big gap in behavior and this could lead to dissonance.

Television producers, of course, are under no obligation to create a TV world that accurately represents the real world. Their goal is to attract audiences with entertaining messages. In the pursuit of this goal, producers have created a TV world that deviates from the real world in many significant ways. These deviations have been found to be influential in shifting viewers' perceptions of the real world in some negative ways (see tests of cultivation theory, such as Gerbner et al., 1977). The way violence is portrayed in the TV world is highly unrealistic in terms of seriousness of violent acts and profiles of perpetrators as well as victims (Dominick, 1973; Oliver, 1994; Potter et al., 1995). For example, Oliver (1994) found that on reality-based police shows, demographics deviated from the real world significantly. Among television police officers, only 9% were African American, but in the real world 17% of all police officers are African American. Among criminal suspects, the demographics were very similar to real-world demographics. Also, white characters were more likely to be portrayed as police officers than criminal suspects, whereas African American and Hispanic characters were more likely to be portrayed as criminal suspects than as police officers.

Perhaps the under-portrayal of adolescents in violent acts is an attempt by story producers to "protect" adolescents. That by itself is a noble motive. However, it is not likely to result in any positive outcome unless adolescents are most influenced by role models who were their own age. However, we know that this is not the case. Adolescence is a time of seeking social lessons, learning how the social world works, and finding their place in that world (Brown, 2000). While peers are an extremely important group (Harris, 1998), adolescents are also attracted to stories with older characters to show them how to behave in the next phase of their lives. And adult characters are portrayed in a highly dangerous, highly unrealistic manner. Thus the guidance provided by this type of character is not likely to lead to positive outcomes.

## Pattern of Portrayal

Scholars claim that the way violence is portrayed on television is likely to increase the risk for a negative effect. For example, the National Television Violence Study (1996) criticized the contextual patterns that dominate the portrayal of television violence for being likely to increase the risk to viewers of condoning or engaging in aggression. This argument is based on the proposition in social learning theory (Bandura, 1978) that people, especially children, watch people perform in social situations and vicariously learn from the consequences of their behavior. Specifically when role models are attractive and are rewarded (or at least not punished) for a behavior, observers will learn that this behavior is a good one to try in their own lives. The effects literature clearly shows that when violent portrayals are justified, rewarded, and committed by attractive characters, they are more likely to disinhibit viewers and this would make it more likely those viewers would behave aggressively when given the opportunity in real life. Furthermore this effect is enhanced when the violence is portrayed in a realistic context, with more action, with more suspense, and when the victims are not shown in pain (see Table 8.3). As reviews of the effects literature continually show, each of these factors increases risk of a disinhibition effect (Bushman & Huesmann, 2001; Hearold, 1986; Paik & Comstock, 1994; Potter, 1999). The NTVS study (1997) as well as other content analyses of television violence (Dominick, 1973; Potter & Ware, 1987; Potter et al., 1995; Williams et al., 1982) clearly show that these factors are prevalent in the way violence is continually portrayed on television. Therefore, there is good reason to believe that the way violence is portrayed on television leads to a heightening of risk for an aggressive behavioral effect in viewers. That would clearly be a negative effect.

Now let's examine this conclusion from a slightly different perspective. Let's say we were more concerned about a fear effect than a disinhibition effect. Notice that some of the factors that increase the probability of a disinhibition effect also contribute to the probability of a fear effect—but in an opposite direction. To illustrate, let's say we wanted to reduce the risk of a fear effect, especially in children. We would want television producers to have the violence perpetrated by the attractive heroes rather than by the ugly villains. Also, we would want the violence to be justified; we would want it to be sanitized so as not to show much harm to the victims. It would also help to make the violence fantasy and it would especially help to make the violence humorous. This contextual pattern that would serve to reduce a fear effect is the same pattern that increases the disinhibition effect. There is almost a direct trade-off. So to achieve lower risk of a fear effect we ratchet up the risk level for a disinhibition effect.

Let's go one step further in this analysis. If we are stuck considering a trade-off of risk, we must ask ourselves which is the less desirable effect. That is, is it better to move to a higher risk for disinhibition if we achieve a lower risk for fear? Or should we err on the side of trying to avoid a disinhibition effect? At this point we need to access a moral code to guide our decisions. For example, those who hold a moral code that says it is always wrong to harm another person will want to do everything that can be done to reduce the risk of aggressive behavioral effects. However, there are others who strongly believe that people should self-actualize, avoid depression, and try to achieve happiness. For these people, a persistent, general fear effect is especially damaging to the human psyche. There is also a third position; that is, calling for the elimination of all violence in television stories. By eliminating violence in all stories, we don't have to worry about portrayals increasing risk either on a disinhibition or a fear effect. However, there are many people in this country who abhor censorship, so this would be the worst of all three alternatives.

Yet another way to look at this trade-off is to consider which negative effects are people more able to handle. The literature on coping strategies indicates that most children and adolescents have developed strategies to help them handle a fear effect. For example, Hoffner (1995) conducted a survey of 228 ninth and tenth graders (mean age 15.1 years) asking them about their perceptions of the effectiveness of various strategies (distraction, unreality, momentary avoidance, interpersonal comfort) for coping with scary films. She found two general coping styles, blunting and monitoring. Blunting is characterized by distraction or reinterpretation of scary events, whereas monitoring is characterized by attention to threat cues. She found that when adolescents use an effective coping strategy, their enjoyment of scary films increases. Cantor (2001) makes a distinction between cognitive and noncognitive strategies in dealing with fear reactions. Noncognitive strategies are those that are relatively automatic and avoid the need to engage thinking processes. An example would be physically interrupting the exposure by walking away, getting something to eat or drink. In contrast, cognitive strategies require the processing of verbal information, such as casting the threat in a different light. An example would be the thinking through the fantasy elements in the depiction and thus reminding oneself of the unreality of the threat.

Considering the trade-offs among countervailing effects is a complex issue, even when we consider the trade-offs with only two negative effects. This issue becomes even more complex when we realize that there may be as many as nineteen potentially negative effects from television violence (see Potter, 1999). There are many trade-offs to be debated. At bottom, these debates reveal what we value most in our society and the risks we are willing to take to protect ourselves.

## Shift from Serious to Minor Acts

There is the seemingly positive conclusion that the shift away from portraying serious acts of violence toward portraying less serious acts of violence serves to reduce the risk of a negative effect. Notice that I have characterized these as "seemingly" negative or positive. In this section I analyze each of these conclusions to show that what seems to be the case on the surface might not hold as we analyze the conclusion in more depth. These analyses, or "peeling the onion," force us to consider the issue of what makes an effect negative. The documented shift away from portraying the more serious acts toward portraying the less serious acts of violence appears to be a positive trend. Continual portrayals of murders and rapes are more likely to make us fearful of crime in society and at the same time teach people how to commit these serious crimes as well as making those people feel more willing to commit them. This clearly is not desirable, so a shift toward portraying less serious acts would appear to be a good thing.

However, when we examine this more closely, it might appear to be a negative trend. When the frequencies of murders, rapes, and serious assaults are high, the TV world is teaching viewers that the world is a mean and violent place, in general. By using the phrase "in general" I mean that viewers are given a macro picture that exists outside their own personal experience. Fortunately, few people have committed, been a victim of, or even witnessed a real-life murder, rape, or serious assault. So the implication is that shifting the high frequency of violent acts away from murders, rapes, and serious assaults and into minor assaults and verbal forms such as hate speech and harsh insults would tend to reduce the probability that viewers would construct the belief that the world is a mean and violent place. However, there is no research evidence to back up this speculation. Cultivation coefficients are typically small (in the .07 to .12 range of $r$) and there is no consistent trend of these coefficients being reduced over time as television shifts to depictions of less serious violence (Potter, 1999). However, most viewers are likely to see many examples of minor assaults, hate speech, and harsh insults in their everyday lives. When the occurrence of these acts is reinforced and amplified by television stories, it is likely to increase viewers' sense of personal vulnerability, which is a form of belief that their world is mean and violent. This would seem to be a negative trend.

Also, this shift from more serious to less serious forms of violence suggests a trend toward another negative effect—imitation. The inhibitions preventing the average person from committing a murder, rape, or major assault are much higher than inhibitions preventing people from delivering harsh insults. So the shift to more minor forms of violence may serve to work to reduce already low inhibitions. This, too, is a negative trend.

## CONCLUSIONS

The overriding conclusion in this chapter is that while violent television content leads to all sorts of effects on viewers, it is not a simple matter to determine which of those effects are negative and which are not. To make such determinations it takes some careful analysis along with an awareness of the values we hold about society and about how to treat other people. For most people, protecting adolescents is important. This means helping adolescents to internalize values that will, on the one hand, make them secure members of society while on the other hand give them adequate freedom to express themselves and live happy lives. Being a secure member of society means fitting in by respecting the rights of others as well as accepting boundaries on behavior that prevent each of us from aggressing into the space of others. This insures that we all live peacefully and in harmony. Being able to live a productive and happy life means protecting adolescents from unreasonable fears and unrealistic expectations about the world.

The persistent patterns of television violence limit society's ability to help adolescents in any of these ways. Television violence teaches the next generation the belief that violence is a useful tool in achieving personal gain and protecting society. Then, by consistently presenting this message, television reinforces this belief from adolescence onward throughout life. Stories are told in a way that makes adolescents and all of us believe that when we are the good guy—which is the role each of us plays in our own lives—violence is often a justified tool to use to get what we want. It makes us powerful and successful. And it rarely results in serious harm to our victims, who really deserved such treatment anyway. However, there is an irony that while we teach this lesson of increasing one's success and power, we are also teaching that the world is a violent place where everyone else is aggressively taking what they want. We are teaching fear and a loss of natural sensitivity to the suffering of others. Adolescents learn these norms while watching the standard portrayals of television.

Furthermore, producers who sanitize their violence by avoiding graphic depictions are also likely doing more harm than good. While sanitized portrayals of violence help producers avoid criticism from viewers who are offended by graphicness, this type of portrayal also serves to lower inhibitions and reduce sensitivity. Violence is ugly and frequently graphic in the real world. When people are exposed to these types of realistic portrayals of violence, they are taught that violence is harmful and therefore viewing inhibitions increase and their sensitivity for victims also is likely to increase. These are positive effects, so producers who sanitize violence reduce the chance of these positive effects occurring.

Given the complexity of the issue, the path toward ameliorating the problem does not lie with censorship. This path is likely to lead to many negative effects of its own. Instead, the path of education leads toward building a population that can make more informed choice of media exposures and achieving more control over the effects process in their own lives.

## RECOMMENDATIONS

This chapter ends with two sets of recommendations. One set is for scholars and the other is for the general public.

### Recommendations for Scholars

The scholarly literature about violence in fictional television is strong in many ways, but it has three limitations that have been revealed in the analysis conducted in this chapter. First, content analysts need to be more focused on coding age of characters portrayed in violent stories on television. The existing content analysis of violence literature contains too few studies that provide a clear profiling of perpetrators and victims by age. This is a troubling limitation when we try to develop a clear picture about how adolescents have been treated in violent portrayals over time.

Second, content analysts need to account for verbal forms of violence in addition to physical forms. There are few analyses of verbal forms of violence in the existing literature. This is a troubling limitation, because there is evidence that the amount of verbal violence increased substantially from the mid-1970s to the early 1990s. Scholars who are concerned about the modeling effects of physical violence on adolescents should be even more concerned about the modeling effects of verbal forms of violence. The social norms against verbal attacks are less strong than the social norms against physical attacks, so it is likely that the depiction of verbal violence repeatedly in television stories would have a more widespread behavioral effect on adolescents than depictions of physical violence.

Third, content analysts need to continue examining the television landscape for violence. It appears from the published literature that interest in this topic is cyclical and that there has been little interest in it for almost a decade. Given the stability in the amount of violence found in television programming from the 1950s to the 1990s, it is not surprising that content analysts may be assuming that the patterns are continuing to remain stable and therefore there is a need to shift their efforts into other areas. However, given the major impact of the NTVS studies in the mid-1990s, along with the mandating of the v-chip and program ratings, it is reasonable to be curious about how these factors might have altered the amount of violence on television or the way it is portrayed.

### Recommendations for the Public

How can we best deal with the problem of a high frequency of sanitized violence across the television landscape and its persistent power to increase the probability of all kinds of negative effects to adolescents and other viewers? There would seem to be three strategies available. In ascending order of cost as well as effectiveness, the three strategies are censorship, health/economic strategy, and education.

Censorship usually comes to mind first when the public criticizes media violence. Many people think the problem can be reduced by simply eliminating portrayals of violence on television. (For a more complete examination of this, see my 2003 book *The 11 Myths of Media Violence.*) While this might have a small positive effect in the short term, it is deeply flawed and does not warrant the high price our society would have to pay for allowing the government to regulate television content and thereby significantly reducing our freedom of speech. It places the responsibility with the government instead of with the active players in the problem—television and viewers.

The health/economic strategy is better than censorship because it recognizes that the media are businesses that aggressively construct audiences with content that they believe will be the most successful in attracting those audiences. If the market exists for a particular kind of content, the media will provide and profit from it. If the market is small or nonexistent, the media will offer other kinds of content. This is not to say that media companies should not be held accountable for providing content that has been found to bring about serious widespread negative effects; they should be held accountable. There are health risks associated with violent content. In manufacturing industries, companies that produce products that are unhealthy are taxed to raise funds to help treat those harmed. With the media, companies who want to use sanitized violence to attract audiences and thereby benefit economically should be taxed to raise money to subsidize the institutions that have to deal with the downstream negative effects of this cultural pollution (see Hamilton, 1998, for a more detailed argument).

The education strategy is the best, I believe, because it is the viewers who are ultimately harmed by exposures and viewers who have the power to reduce or eliminate that harm—if they know what to do. We need to educate people about what the harmful effects are and how those can be controlled. The more people understand about media content and their effects, the more likely it is that they will create markets for different kinds of programming. Furthermore, when people do decide to consume violent portrayals, they will better understand how to prevent risks from increasing across the range of potentially negative effects. This strategy preserves freedom of speech as well as an individual's health. However, this strategy comes with a high cost beginning with individuals accepting personal responsibility for the problem and not expecting the government or some taxing agency to bail them out when they make bad decisions. It also requires a commitment to learning. Enough information already exists to make this educational strategy viable. What is lacking is the willingness of individuals to do the required work in their own lives.

## REFERENCES

Anderson, C. A., Berkowitz, L., Donnerstein, E., Huesmann, L. R., Johnson, J. D., Linz, D., et al., (2003). The influence of media on youth. *Psychological Science in the Public Interest, 4*, 81–110.

Bandura, A. (1978). A social learning theory of aggression. *Journal of Communication, 28*(3), 12–29.

Brown, J. D. (2000). Adolescents' sexual media diets. *Journal of Adolescent Health, 27S*, 35–40.

Bushman, B. J., & Anderson, C. A. (2001). Media violence and the American public: Scientific facts versus media misinformation. *American Psychologist, 56*, 477–489.

Bushman, B. J., & Huesmann, L. R. (2001). Effects of televised violence on aggression. In D. G. Singer & J. L. Singer (Eds.), *Handbook of children and the media* (pp. 223–254). Thousand Oaks, CA: Sage.

Cantor, J. (2001). The media and children's fears, anxieties, and perceptions of danger. In D. G. Singer & J. L. Singer (Eds.), *Handbook of children and the media* (pp. 207–221). Thousand Oaks, CA: Sage.

Cantor, J. (2002). Fright reactions to mass media. In J. Bryant & D. Zillmann (Eds.), *Media effects: Advances in their and research* (2nd ed., pp. 287–306). Mahwah, NJ: Erlbaum.

Center for Media and Public Affairs. (1994). *Violence in prime time television*. Washington, DC: Center for Media and Public Affairs.

Clark, D. G., & Blankenburg, W. B. (1972). Trends in violent content in selected mass media. In G. Comstock & E. Rubinstein (Eds.), *Television and social behavior: Vol. 1. Media content and control* (pp. 188–243). Washington, DC: U.S. Government Printing Office.

Cline, V. B., Croft, R. G., & Courier, S. (1973). Desensitization of children to television violence. *Journal of Personality and Social Psychology, 27*, 260–265.

Coyne, S. M. (2004). Indirect aggression on screen: A hidden problem? *The Psychologist, 17*(12), 688–691.

Dominick, J. (1973). Crime and law enforcement on prime-time television. *Public Opinion Quarterly, 37*, 241–250.

Estep, R., & Macdonald, P. T. (1983). How prime time crime evolved on TV, 1976–1981. *Journalism Quarterly, 60*, 293–300.

Fremont, W. P., Pataki, C., & Beresin, E. V. (2005). The impact of terrorism on children and adolescents: Terror in the skies, terror on television. *Child and Adolescent Psychiatric Clinics of North America, 14*, 429–451.

Funk, J. B., & Buchman, D. D. (1996). Playing violent video and computer games and adolescent self-concept. *Journal of Communication, 46*(2), 19–32. Retrieved February 1, 2007, from PsycINFO database.

Gerbner, G. (1972). Violence in television drama: Trends and symbolic functions. In G. Comstock & E. Rubinstein (Eds.), *Television and social behavior: Volume 1. Media content and control* (pp. 28–187). Washington, DC: U.S. Government Printing Office.

Gerbner, G., Gross, L., Eleey, M. F., Jackson-Beeck, M., Jeffries-Fox, S., & Signorielli, N. (1977). Television violence profile no. 8: The highlights. *Journal of Communication, 27,* 171–180.

Gerbner, G., Gross, L., Jackson-Beeck, M., Jeffries-Fox, S., & Signorielli, N. (1978). Cultural indicators: Violence profile no. 9. *Journal of Communication, 28,* 176–207.

Greenberg, B. S., Edison, N., Korzenny, F., Fernandez-Collado, C., & Atkin, C. K. (1980). In B. S. Greenberg (Ed.), *Life on television: Content analysis of U. S. TV drama* (pp. 99–128). Norwood, NJ: Ablex.

Gunter, B. (1985). *Dimensions of television violence.* Aldershot, UK: Gower.

Gunter, B., Harrison, J., & Wykes, M. (2003). *Violence on television: Distribution, form, context, and themes.* Mahwah, NJ: Erlbaum.

Hamilton, J. T. (1998). *Channeling violence: The economic market for violent television programming.* Princeton, NJ: Princeton University Press.

Harris, J. R. (1998). *The nurture assumption: Why children turn out the way they do.* New York: Free Press.

Harrison, K., & Cantor, J. (1999). Tales from the screen: Enduring fright reactions to scary media. *Media Psychology, 1,* 97–116.

Head, S. W. (1954). Content analysis of television drama programs. *Quarterly of Film, Radio and Television, 9,* 175–194.

Hearold, S. (1986). A synthesis of 1043 effects of television on social behavior. In G. Comstock (Ed.), *Public communication and behavior* (Vol. 1, pp. 65–133). San Diego, CA: Academic Press.

Hoekstra, S. J., Harris, R. J., & Helmick, A. L. (1999). Autobiographical memories about the experience of seeing frightening movies in childhood. *Media Psychology, 1,* 117–140.

Hoffner, C. (1995). Adolescents' coping with frightening mass media. *Communication Research, 22,* 325–346. Retrieved February 1, 2007, from PsycINFO database.

Kronenberger, W. G., Mathews, V. P., Dunn, D. W., Wang, Y., Wood, E. A., Giauque, A. L., et al. (2005). Media violence exposure and executive functioning in aggressive and control adolescents. *Journal of Clinical Psychology, 61,* 725–737.

Kronenberger, W. G., Mathews, V. P., Dunn, D. W., Wang, Y., Wood, E. A., Larsen, J. J., et al. (2005). Media violence exposure in aggressive and control adolescents: Differences in self- and parent-reported exposure to violence on television and in video games. *Aggressive Behavior, 31,* 201–216.

Larsen, O. N., Gray, L. N., & Fortis, J. G. (1968). Achieving goals through violence on television. In O. N. Larsen (Ed.), *Violence and the mass media* (pp. 97–111). New York: Harper & Row.

Lazarus, R. S., & Alfert, E. (1964). Short-circuiting of threat by experimentally altering cognitive appraisal. *Journal of Abnormal and Social Psychology, 69,* 195–205.

Lyle, J., & Wilcox, W. (1963). Television news—an interim report. *Journal of Broadcasting, 7*, 157–166.

National Television Violence Study. (1996). *Technical report, volume 1*. Thousand Oaks, CA: Sage.

National Television Violence Study. (1997). *Technical report, volume 2*. Thousand Oaks, CA: Sage.

Oliver, M. B. (1994). Portrayals of crime, race, and aggression in "reality based" police shows: A content analysis. *Journal of Broadcasting & Electronic Media, 38*, 179–192.

Paik, H., & Comstock, G. (1994). The effects of television violence on antisocial behavior: A meta-analysis. *Communication Research, 21*, 516–546.

Potter, W. J. (1999). *On media violence*. Thousand Oaks, CA: Sage.

Potter, W. J. (2003). *The 11 myths of media violence*. Thousand Oaks, CA: Sage.

Potter, W. J., & Vaughan, M. (1997). Antisocial behaviors in television entertainment: Profiles and trends. *Communication Research Reports, 14*, 116–124.

Potter, W. J., Vaughan, M., Warren, R., Howley, K., Land, A., & Hagemeyer, J. (1995). How real is the portrayal of aggression in television entertainment programming? *Journal of Broadcasting & Electronic Media, 39*, 496–516.

Potter, W. J., & Ware, W. (1987). An analysis of the contexts of antisocial acts on prime-time television. *Communication Research, 14*, 664–686.

Sander, I. (1995). *How violent is TV-violence? An empirical investigation of factors influencing viewers' perceptions of TV-violence*. Paper presented at the annual conference of the International Communication Association, Albuquerque, NM.

Schramm, W., Lyle, J., & Parker, E. P. (1961). *Television in the lives of our children*. Stanford, CA: Stanford University Press.

Sherman, B. L., & Dominick, J. R. (1986). Violence and sex in music videos: TV and rock 'n' roll. *Journal of Communication, 36*, 79–93.

Signorielli, N. (1990). Television's mean and dangerous world: A continuation of the cultural indicators perspective. In N. Signorielli & M. Morgan (Eds.), *Cultivation analysis: New directions in media effects research* (pp. 85–106). Newbury Park, CA: Sage.

Slater, M. D., Henry, K. L., Swaim, R. C., & Anderson, L. L. (2003). Violent media content and aggressiveness in adolescents: A downward spiral model. *Communication Research, 30*, 713–736.

Smith, S. L., Wilson, B. J., Kunkel. D., Linz, D., Potter, W. J., Colvin, C. M., et al. (1999). *National television violence study 3*. Thousand Oaks, CA: Sage.

Smythe, D. W. (1953, July). *Three years of New York television 1951–1953, January 4–10*. Urbana, IL: National Association of Educational Broadcasters.

Speisman, J. C., Lazarus, R. S., Mordkoff, A., & Davison, L. (1964). Experimental reduction of stress based on ego-defense theory. *Journal of Abnormal and Social Psychology, 68*, 367–380.

Thomas, M. H. (1982). Physiological arousal, exposure to a relatively lengthy aggressive film, and aggressive behavior. *Journal of Research in Personality, 16*, 72–81.

U.S. Department of Justice. (2005). Criminal victimization in the United States, 2005 statistical tables. Retrieved February 6, 2007, from http://www.ojp.usdoj .gov/bjs/pub/pdf/cvus0502.pdf

Williams, T. M., Zabrack, M. L., & Joy, L. A. (1982). The portrayal of aggression on North American television. *Journal of Applied Social Psychology, 12,* 360–380.

Wilson, B. J., Colvin, C. M., & Smith, S. L. (2002). Engaging in violence on American television: A comparison of child, teen, and adult perpetrators. *Journal of Communication, 52,* 36–60.

Wood, W., Wong, F. Y., & Chachere, J. G. (1991). Effects of media violence on viewers' aggression in unconstrained social interaction. *Psychological Bulletin, 109,* 371–383.

# 9

# Tobacco Portrayals in U.S. Advertising and Entertainment Media

TIMOTHY DEWHIRST

U.S. media representations of tobacco use is an important subject given that the pivotal period for smoking initiation is early adolescence and that cigarette smoking represents the single most important cause of preventable illness and premature death in the United States. Roughly 440,000 Americans die prematurely each year as a result of smoking; tobacco use is responsible for a greater number of deaths among Americans than the total caused by motor vehicle crashes, suicides, murders, AIDS, and illicit drug use combined (U.S. Department of Health and Human Services, 2004). Many tobacco control groups, health practitioners, and policy makers are concerned about the continued frequency of tobacco depictions in the media, given the impact that positive smoking portrayals might have on youth initiation. Reviews of internal tobacco industry documents, obtained through whistleblowers and litigation, reveal that cigarette brands are successfully marketed to youth, including consumers who are classified as "starters" or "new smokers" (Cohen, 2000; Cummings, Morley, Horan, Steger, & Leavell, 2002; Dewhirst & Sparks, 2003; Glantz, Slade, Bero, Hanauer, & Barnes, 1996; Goldberg, Davis, & O'Keefe, 2006; Perry, 1999). The U.S. Centers for Disease Control and Prevention (2002, 2004) have named tobacco portrayals in the movies a major factor in adolescent smoking. Considerable research has suggested that youth are influenced to smoke by both positive smoking portrayals in the movies and celebrities serving as role models (Dal Cin, Gibson, Zanna, Shumate, & Fong, 2007; Dalton et al., 2003; Distefan, Gilpin, Sargent, & Pierce, 1999; Distefan, Pierce, & Gilpin, 2004; Gibson &

Maurer, 2000; Hines, Saris, & Throckmorton-Belzer, 2000; Jetté, Wilson, & Sparks, 2007; McCool, Cameron, & Petrie, 2003; Pechmann & Shih, 1999; Sargent et al., 2001, 2005, 2007; Song, Ling, Neilands, & Glantz, 2007).

This chapter is meant to serve several purposes. With the post–World War II era serving as the historical period of analysis, the chapter broadly illustrates how tobacco has been represented in both U.S. advertising and the entertainment media. First, the chapter clarifies the importance of the youth market to tobacco marketers, and internal corporate documents make known that cigarette brands have historically been successfully marketed to this demographic. Studying the marketing and promotion strategies of to-bacco firms is unique from most industries, in view of numerous internal corporate documents, which would ordinarily be considered proprietary, being available to the public as a result of litigation. Second, the chapter provides an overview of content analysis studies pertaining to U.S. cigarette advertising. The studies regarding cigarette magazine advertising content have commonly assessed the impact of health/smoking controversy events and the broadcast advertising ban. Third, the chapter identifies how tobacco is commonly portrayed in the U.S. entertainment media by outlining the role of product placement practices, and then providing a review of content analysis studies concerning tobacco use portrayals in television program-ming and film. Finally, the chapter identifies prevailing trends in U.S. to-bacco marketing practices, emerging issues in tobacco media representation, suggests areas for future research, provides a summary of main findings, and offers implications for policy.

## TOBACCO USE AND THE RELEVANCE OF YOUTH CONSUMERS

For corporations, including U.S. tobacco companies, a promotional strategy typically starts with a clear target market in mind, and *market segmentation* is a commonly used approach in which specific audiences are identified for a product by dividing a mass market into well-defined consumer groups on the basis of variables such as demographics (e.g., gender), geography (e.g., place of residence), psychographics (e.g., lifestyles, interests, and values), and behavioral components (e.g., user status, usage situation, extent of use, and product benefits sought) (Kotler, Armstrong, & Cunningham, 2005). Age is a key demographic dimension for marketing strategists when utilizing a segmentation approach.

The tobacco industry's use of age segmentation has been well docu-mented. Based on a review of internal corporate documents, Pollay (2000) concluded that two key typologies of cigarette consumers traditionally used by tobacco firms are "new users" (young starters) and "latent quitters" (concerned smokers who need reassurance). The rationale for why tobacco companies would direct their promotions toward youth is that the pivotal period for smoking initiation in the United States has historically been early adolescence (U.S. Department of Health and Human Services, 1994). Smokers are also known to be extremely brand loyal, so the brand choice of consumers during the early stages of their smoking "careers" becomes crucial. If someone begins smoking Marlboro as an adolescent, it is highly likely that he or she will be smoking Marlboro if still a smoker twenty years later; changes in product selection are commonly within the same brand family (e.g., from Marlboro Medium to Marlboro Light). In the United States, brand switching among smokers is less than 10% annually, with less than 8% switching companies (Cummings, Hyland, Lewit, & Shopland, 1997).

Internal documentation from each of the major U.S. cigarette firms has revealed that youth are an important target of tobacco promotional activities. A Philip Morris report from the early 1980s, for example, monitored smokers as young as 12 years old and states that,

> It is important to know as much as possible about teenage smoking patterns and attitudes. Today's teenager is tomorrow's potential regular customer, and the overwhelming majority of smokers first begin to smoke while still in their teens....The smoking patterns of teenagers are particularly important to Philip Morris. (Johnston, 1981)

During the late 1970s, market research for Lorillard Tobacco acknowledged, "The success of Newport has been fantastic during the past few years. Our profile locally shows this brand being purchased by black people (all ages), young adults (usually college age), but the base of our business is the high school student" (Achey, 1978). For Kool, a menthol cigarette brand directly competing with Newport, Brown and Williamson's market research from the mid-1980s stated that the "Kool media target audience principle remains the same. Most valuable prospect is young adult male and female new smoker and switcher....Promotion philosophy of trial generation and meeting competition approved" (Brown & Williamson, 1984). According to an advertising agency advising the R.J. Reynolds marketing department, "Many manufacturers have 'studied' the 14–20 market in hopes of uncovering the 'secret' of the instant popularity some brands enjoy to the almost complete exclusion of others....Creating a 'fad' in this market can be a great bonanza" (McCain, 1973).

U.S. cigarette firms have undergone considerable scrutiny for placing promotions during media programming that includes youthful audiences, utilizing youthful-appearing models in their advertising, and for developing particular creatives in advertising campaigns such as the use of cartoon characters. Pollay (1994) assessed the efficacy of the U.S. cigarette industry's self-regulation of broadcast advertising from 1963, in which each of the major firms (with the exception of Brown and Williamson) agreed to Tobacco Institute guidelines specifying that programs directed at youthful audiences should not be sponsored. Despite the tobacco industry's voluntary course of action, American Research Bureau data (accessible from a Federal Trade Commission [FTC] report on cigarette advertising) combined with census information and trade data on spot television advertising revealed that children and adolescents still represented 26% of the audiences for purchased network television programming. Winston, for example, was the sponsor of *The Beverly Hillbillies* and *The Flintstones* programs on television.

According to the U.S. tobacco industry's self-regulatory 1964 Cigarette Advertising Code, "Natural persons depicted as smokers in cigarette advertising shall be at least twenty-five years of age and shall not be dressed or otherwise made to appear to be less than twenty-five years of age." Nevertheless, Mazis, Ringold, Perry, & Denman (1992) examined how 561 respondents perceived the ages of models in a representative sample of fifty cigarette advertisements, which were accessed from an extensive and diverse set of October 1987 magazine issues. The percentage of respondents who perceived the models to be younger than 25 years old reached as high as 76% for a Kool Milds model, 89% for a Lucky Strike Lights model, 79% for a Virginia Slims Ultra Lights model, and 91% for a Winston Lights model. More than 80% of the models perceived to be less than 25 years old were women. Moreover, the cigarette advertisements with younger-appearing models were more likely to be seen in magazines with younger readerships and for menthol brands such as Newport and Kool.

Based on the content of magazine advertising from 1996 to 1997, research has also found that a disproportionate number of cigarette advertisements featuring cartoon characters were placed in magazines with younger readerships (Kelly, Slater, Karan, & Hunn, 2000). Additionally, there is evidence that some tobacco advertising was able to appeal to children as young as age 3. During the late 1980s and much of the 1990s, R.J. Reynolds's Camel advertising campaign depicted a cartoon camel (Old Joe) as the central figure, with the theme "Smooth character" (Figure 9.1). A study by Fischer, Schwartz, Richards, Goldstein, & Rojas (1991) assessed recognition levels of twenty-two brand logos by having preschool children aged 3 to 6 years old match logo cards to one of twelve products pictured on a game board; they found that 91% of the 6-year-old children in their sample matched the Old Joe Camel character with a cigarette. Logo recognition was highly associated with age for each of the assessed product categories (i.e., recognition rates were higher among the older study participants). Moreover, several internal corporate documents pertaining to the origins and aims of the "Joe

Figure 9.1. A wide-format magazine advertisement from 1990 that de-picts a cartoon camel (Joe Camel). Joe Camel is wearing sunglasses, a black leather jacket, and a helmet; smoking Camel cigarettes; riding a (moving) motorcycle; and holding out the cigarette package. (*Source*: From The Richard W. Pollay 20th Century Tobacco Advertisement Collection, Roswell Park Cancer Institute. Reprinted with permission. Available online at: http://tobaccodocuments.org/pollay_ads/Came35.15.html)

Camel" campaign, and its effects on youth, were disclosed publicly as a re-sult of the *Mangini v. R.J. Reynolds Tobacco Company* court case.

## CONTENT ANALYSIS STUDIES ASSESSING TOBACCO ADVERTISING

There have been at least two major challenges to the marketing and por-trayal of smoking in the media since 1950. One concerns the increasing public awareness of the hazards of smoking to health. Perhaps the strongest initial statement of this recognition was the Surgeon General's report of 1964 (U.S. Department of Health, Education, and Welfare [USDHEW], 1964). However, beginning in the early 1950s, scientific and popular articles began to associate smoking with lung cancer, leading smokers to become increasingly "health concerned." The second challenge was the increasing restriction on the ability of the tobacco industry to advertise its products in the media. In particular, the Public Health Cigarette Smoking Act banned cigarette advertising in the U.S. broadcast media starting January 2, 1971. Because conventional cigarette advertising on television was effectively ended by 1971, there has been little research on the content of this material. Only two studies have analyzed the content of U.S. tobacco billboard advertising (Altman, Schooler, & Basil, 1991; Taylor & Taylor, 1994), but cigarette billboard advertising has also been banned (the ban was effective April 1999 in accordance with the 1998 U.S. Master Settlement Agreement). Rather, most studies have focused on magazine advertising, which has a long history of cigarette ads (content analysis studies examine advertisements from as early as 1926), thus enabling us to observe trends in the portrayal of smoking over a considerable period. Content analysis studies have typically assessed the impact of "health/smoking controversy events," such as the various reports of smoking hazards and restrictions on advertising in the media.

## The Impact of Health/Smoking Controversy Events and the Broadcast Advertising Ban

The first known study to use content analysis specific to cigarette magazine advertising was done by Weinberger, Campbell, and DuGrenier (1981). They utilized content analysis, as well as media spending and market share data, to assess possible shifts in U.S. tobacco industry advertising tactics resulting from various regulatory measures. Several dimensions were examined, including advertising volume, physical aspects, major appeals, models employed, product attributes, and brand extensions. Using *Newsweek*, *Sports Illustrated*, and *Ladies Home Journal* as sources for cigarette advertisements, three separate sampling years were selected (1957, 1967, and 1977) to determine the possible impact of various influential events and surrounding circumstances. For example, in 1964, the first U.S. Surgeon General's report specific to smoking was released and greatly influenced public perceptions about the potential health consequences of smoking (USDHEW, 1964). Additionally, cigarette advertising was removed from the broadcast media in 1971. The authors were particularly interested in changes that might be apparent in magazine advertising as a result of the broadcast ban.

Weinberger et al.'s three-year sample included a total of 251 cigarette advertisements. The authors observed that, taken as a percentage of the total advertising spending by the six major U.S. tobacco manufacturers, the amount of cigarette advertising found in magazines dramatically increased from

1967 to 1977. Tobacco companies also responded to the broadcast media ban by placing more resources toward print media advertising, evident by more frequent use of special positioning, color, and full-page or double-page advertisements. Advertisements were typically placed on right-hand pages and during the observed period (1957 to 1977) were increasingly located on the back covers of magazines. They noted, however, that some of the observed changes, such as the increased use of color, might be reflective of innovations being utilized by magazine advertisers in general.

Weinberger et al. observed several changes in the use of product attributes and appeals during the 1957 to 1977 period. Claims related to low tar, implied health benefits, and cigarette length became more frequent in magazine advertising, whereas social appeals were uncommon in the 1967 sample. In the 1977 sample, brand comparisons were much more common and most of these comparative advertisements were for low tar brands. Additionally, brand extensions became more consistently used over the observed twenty-year period.

Warner (1985) also used content analysis to assess how the U.S. cigarette industry had responded to various significant events publicizing the association between smoking and various health consequences. He sought to identify whether tobacco advertisers' approaches had changed over time with respect to addressing the health concerns of consumers. Several significant periods related to the publicity of health concerns were identified within the study. First, the American Cancer Society released a major study linking smoking with lung cancer in 1951. Second, popular press articles, most notably in *Reader's Digest*, emerged in 1953 discussing the relationship of smoking with cancer. The first U.S. Surgeon General's report on smoking and health was published in 1964 (USDHEW, 1964), and Fairness Doctrine antismoking messages were prominently shown on television and radio from 1968 to 1970. In 1978, USDHEW secretary Joseph Califano announced a new antismoking campaign. Moreover, the U.S. Surgeon General released a report in 1979, which was given special attention because it marked the fifteenth anniversary of the 1964 report (USDHEW, 1979).

Warner used selected issues of *Time* magazine from 1929 to 1984 to generate a total sample of 716 cigarette advertisements. Data was provided for the number of cigarette advertisements found per issue, as well as the percentage of advertisements containing filter-tipped cigarettes, low tar cigarettes, a predominant or exclusively health-related theme, mostly or all words, visible smoke, no models, and modern design.

Like Weinberger et al. (1981), Warner discovered that the number of cigarette advertisements found in each magazine issue dramatically increased during the 1970s, largely the result of the broadcast ban. Warner also found that, during periods of elevated health concerns, cigarette firms responded by increasingly utilizing advertisements that included health themes and "technological fixes." Filter-tipped cigarettes were introduced in the 1951 sample and became prominent. By 1968 and thereafter, all sampled advertisements were for filtered cigarettes. Meanwhile, low tar cigarettes first appeared in the 1967 sample and became more and more commonplace over time. The 1970s marked the launch of several cigarette brands that were promoted with lower (machine-measured) tar deliveries, which commonly made use of the "Light" product descriptor (Pollay & Dewhirst, 2002). Some of the product launches were line extensions of familiar trademarks (e.g., Marlboro Lights was introduced by Philip Morris in 1971), whereas others were new, stand-alone trademarks (e.g., Merit was introduced by Philip Morris in 1976). Warner (1985) found that low tar cigarette advertising was often positively correlated with the use of health-related claims. Interestingly, visible smoke became less frequently observed in advertisements (with no observations after 1975), even in cases in which a cigarette was clearly lit. This trend was likely prompted by scientific research findings relating to the health consequences of exposure to secondhand smoke and an increasing number of proposed bylaws that prohibited smoking in indoor, public settings. With the possible exception of the 1964 Surgeon General's report (USDHEW, 1964), cigarette firms engaged in "responsive" advertising for each smoking and health controversy event by more frequently using health-related claims (most notably during the 1953 sample). "Responsive" advertisements were less likely to feature models and employed more verbal content. Advertisements conveying a health message relied more heavily on words as opposed to visual images. It also held true that advertisements placing greater emphasis on pictorial aspects typically had deemphasized health themes. Warner concluded that through advertising "cigarette companies 'talk' with consumers about the health issue, but only when 'necessary' (i.e., to counter visible adverse publicity)" (1985, pp. 124, 125).

Altman, Slater, Albright, and Maccoby (1987) used content analysis to examine cigarette magazine advertising specifically with the intention of determining whether tobacco industry tactics differed among magazines with a youth- or women-oriented readership. The sample comprised advertisements from eight magazines with varied readership demographics: *Rolling Stone, Cycle World, Mademoiselle, Ladies Home Journal, Time, Popular Science, TV Guide,* and *Ebony*. One issue of each magazine was randomly selected for the years 1960 through 1985. The sample analyses were largely limited to image-based advertisements with settings or models present (advertisements for low tar and low nicotine cigarettes were exempted from this requirement and represented 22% of the advertisements in the data set). In total, 778 advertisements were coded. Data were collected for seven variables that fell under three broad categories: act of smoking, presence of low tar and low nicotine, and vitality of smoking. More specifically, coding was done for the presence of visible smoke, cigarettes being held or consumed, cigarettes within the ad photo, explicit low tar or low nicotine appeals, and appeals pertaining to adventure/risk, recreation, and romance/eroticism.

They found that, beginning in the late 1960s, visible smoke became more and more infrequent among advertisements from all eight sampled magazines. In fact, the 1984 and 1985 samples contained no advertisements with visible cigarette smoke. Although advertisements with people smoking or holding a cigarette also declined over time, it remained a feature for 68% of the advertisements in the 1985 sample. Until 1979, low tar and low nicotine cigarettes were increasingly emphasized. Beginning in 1980, some advertisements started to highlight additional brand extensions, such as those that were of differing lengths or mentholated. Health and vitality were increasingly associated with cigarette smoking. While risk/adventure, recreation, and erotic images were more frequently depicted over time in both youth- and women-oriented magazines, recreation and adventure/risk-taking images were particularly emphasized in youth readership magazines, and erotic images were particularly emphasized in women's magazines. The findings supported all three hypotheses: during the observed 1960 to 1985 period, the act of smoking was featured less frequently, low tar and low nicotine cigarettes were increasingly emphasized, and vitality became a theme more prominent in advertising content. The authors alleged that through advertising the tobacco industry differentially targeted women and youth and portrayed misleading images to reassure "health concerned" smokers.

Using the same eight magazines and similar methodology, Albright, Altman, Slater, and Maccoby (1988) also determined that the average number of cigarette advertisements per magazine issue increased substantially from 1960 to 1985 (most notably following the broadcast ban in 1971). Initiating in the late 1960s and early 1970s, a greater proportion of cigarette advertisements were placed in magazines with a female- and youth-oriented readership. The study accounted for the frequency of cigarette advertisements found in magazines with varied readerships, but coding was not reported for the information or lifestyle content of the sampled advertisements.

King, Reid, Moon, and Ringold (1991) analyzed visual aspects of cigarette magazine advertising during the period 1954 to 1986. The magazines sampled included *Time, Ladies Home Journal, Vogue, Sports Illustrated, Popular Mechanics, Redbook, Esquire,* and *Playboy.* The selected magazines represented diverse readerships with regard to age, gender, and hobbies/interests; the resulting sample for analysis included 1,100 cigarette advertisements. The thirty-three-year period being studied was divided into three distinct "event eras": the pre–broadcast ban era (1954 to 1970), the post–broadcast ban era (1971 to 1983), and the antismoking ideology era (1984 to 1986). They anticipated that important changes in visual content would be observed as tobacco firms shifted their advertising resources from broadcast to print media.

King et al. (1991) found that the number of cigarette magazine advertisements increased following the broadcast ban (as did other previous studies) and over the three event eras the advertisements became larger in size and were more often printed in color. Meanwhile, artwork was used less frequently and photos became the preferred ad illustration class. Pictures, as opposed to words, became the predominant means of communicating to consumers. The presence of human models did not steadily increase over the three event eras (models were present for 82% of pre–broadcast ban advertisements, 65% of post–broadcast ban advertisements, and 84% of antismoking ideology advertisements). Male models were more frequently depicted than female models during each event era, with male models typically appearing in advertisements placed in men's magazines and female models usually appearing in advertisements placed in women's magazines. Models were increasingly engaged in activities over the three event eras (reaching nearly 83% during the "antismoking ideology" era), although the typical type of activity portrayed differed among eras. During the three event eras, portrayals of adventure and work steadily increased, while portrayals of eroticism or romance declined. Overall, individualistic/solitary and recreation themes were depicted most frequently. Accounting for magazines with diverse readerships, King et al. (1991) concluded that youth-oriented magazines did not contain a greater number of cigarette advertisements or "targeted" attention with respect to the common themes portrayed.

Pollay (1991) examined both the verbal and visual content of cigarette advertisements, measuring the frequency of claims made for twelve different attributes (i.e., well made, good deal [value], enjoyable, feminine, masculine, bold/lively, glamorous/luxurious, healthy/safe, relaxing, official certification [seals of approval and assertions regarding product performance from named experts, groups, or external agencies], popular, and purity). An additional variable called *healthiness* was established to integrate the health/safety, lively/bold, and pure scene claims. Definitions were provided for each of the coding categories. The categories monitored the cost–benefit reasons for purchase, sex-role modeling, lifestyle portrayals, the consequences of consumption, the nature of social support for smoking, and associated physical environments. The sample was generated from 108 available back copies of *Life* (from 1938 to 1983) and 26 back copies of *Look* (from 1962 to 1971), yielding an overall sample of 567 advertisements. While the total sample included the representation of fifty-seven different brands, fourteen of these brands (Camel, Chesterfield, Kent, Kool, L&M, Lucky Strike, Marlboro, Old Gold, Pall Mall, Philip Morris, Salem, Herbert Tareyton, Viceroy, and Winston) accounted for 75% of the advertisements studied.

Pollay found that throughout the forty-six-year period studied, healthiness was a manifest theme in the vast majority of American cigarette magazine advertisements. During the late 1950s and early 1960s, however, the typical means of communicating healthiness shifted from verbal to visual. The frequency of health/safety claims notably increased during the 1973 to 1983 period. Overall, claims about being well made and enjoyable were also featured in the majority of advertisements. Moreover, data were generated for the joint appearance of two attributes, with statistical tests being run to indicate which pairs were highly improbable by chance alone. It was revealed that official certification or endorsement and healthy/safe assertions appeared hand-in-hand ("well made" was also commonly associated with both of these assertions). Lively/bold and pure scene assertions were often associated, suggesting that such advertisements often displayed people engaged in lively and robust activities in outdoor, nature settings (Figure 9.2).

## Tobacco Advertising Content Appealing to Youth and Women

In the United States, cigarettes that are lengthier and have a reduced circumference and a supposed low tar delivery are commonly identified by smokers as "feminine," and brands with such product characteristics are typically advertised in mediums with notable female audiences (Carpenter, Wayne, & Connolly, 2005; Pollay & Dewhirst, 2002; U.S. Department of Health and Human Services [USDHHS], 2001). The revelations of internal corporate documents are corroborated by the findings of content analysis studies that have examined American tobacco advertising. For example, Weinberger et al. (1981) assessed U.S. cigarette advertising from 1957 to 1977 and determined that as ad appeals became increasingly directed toward a female readership, there was an emergence of slimness claims (the Virginia Slims brand was launched in 1968), a greater use of female models, and a heavy upswing of low tar claims. Similarly, Altman et al. (1987) discovered that cigarette ads placed in U.S. magazines with a predominantly female readership were more likely to have low tar or low nicotine themes. Moreover, Pollay (1991) found that female-oriented advertisements were more likely to feature claims pertaining to enjoyment, glamour/luxury, and popularity, whereas male-oriented advertisements were commonly associated with bold/lively lifestyle portrayals.

Brands with cross-gender positioning often use promotional appeals about upward status and being upscale. Meanwhile, American advertisements for ultra-feminine cigarette brands tend to highlight themes related to relaxation, calmness, and stress relief, whereas their ultra-masculine

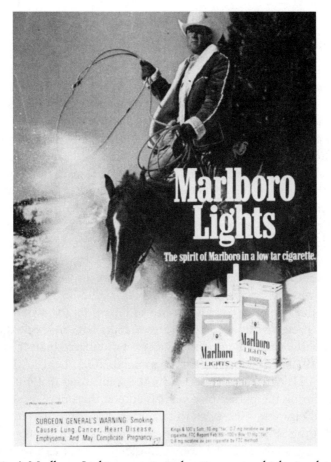

Figure 9.2. A Marlboro Lights magazine advertisement, which circulated in 1988. The ad depicts a cowboy on horseback, riding through the snow, with lariat in hand. The ad copy claims, "The spirit of Marlboro in a low tar cigarette. Also available in Flip-Top box." (*Source*: From The Richard W. Pollay 20th Century Tobacco Advertisement Collection, Roswell Park Cancer Institute. Reprinted with permission. Available online at: http://tobaccodocuments .org/pollay_ads/Marl26.03.html)

counterparts are often linked with risk taking and action-oriented activities (Dewhirst & Sparks, 2003). In the U.S. market, Marlboro is well recognized for being flavorful and for its rugged, masculine, independent, and heroic positioning; the brand is a long-time sponsor of Formula One and Indy Car auto racing. Virginia Slims, meanwhile, has historically conveyed women's liberation, femininity, and glamour; the brand was a longstanding sponsor of women's professional tennis and fashion events. Mentholated brands, such as

Newport, Kool, and Salem, are commonly depicted in cigarette advertising that is targeted toward African Americans. Advertising for menthol brands frequently uses lifestyle appeals relating to fantasy and escapism, expensive objects, nightlife, silliness, youthfulness, and fun, as well as messages conveying the refreshing and medicinal aspects of menthol (Balbach, Gasior, & Barbeau, 2003; Gardiner, 2004; Sutton & Robinson, 2004). Such cigarette brands have traditionally been invested with these cultural meanings through the use of symbols and appropriately themed product advertising. In brief, tobacco brands are commonly associated with status, sophistication and social acceptance, athleticism and healthfulness, glamour and fashion, rewarded risk taking and adventure, and masculinity or femininity. The enhancement or reinforcement of brand imagery is a primary objective of tobacco promotion, with cigarette advertising layouts often characterized by visual lifestyle elements (Dewhirst, 2004; Dewhirst & Davis, 2005; Kelly et al., 2000; Pollay, 2004).

Academic research has shown that U.S. youth disproportionately smoke heavily advertised brands (Pollay et al., 1996). Although it has been demonstrated that the tobacco industry has an interest in the attitudes and behaviors of preteens and adolescents, researchers have also called attention to the importance of young adults as a target of tobacco industry marketing strategies (Biener & Albers, 2004; Hammond, 2005; Lantz, 2003; Ling & Glantz, 2002). Whereas adolescents are the main group that initiates smoking, it is during the period of young adulthood that more established and committed cigarette use begins to take place. Cigarette advertising that is targeted at the 18- to 24-year-old age segment can often simultaneously appeal to young adults and adolescents, considering that many teenagers start smoking as a way to propel themselves into maturity (i.e., smoking serves as a tool for attempts to look older and act independent) (Dewhirst & Sparks, 2003). Furthermore, as advertising restrictions become increasingly stringent, licensed (age-of-majority) venues become a key setting for tobacco promotion (Gilpin, White, & Pierce, 2005; Katz & Lavack, 2002; Rigotti, Moran, & Wechsler, 2005; Sepe, Ling, & Glantz, 2002).

## Shifts in U.S. Tobacco Industry Promotional Spending

More recently, several tobacco firms, such as Philip Morris, have demonstrated a strong commitment to integrated forms of communication such as sponsorship, direct marketing, and sales promotion, consequently moving away from traditional mass media promotion. According to Federal Trade Commission (FTC) (2003) data, by the early 2000s merely 2% of U.S. tobacco advertising budgets were dedicated toward magazines, newspapers, and outdoor locations, while 85% of promotional dollars were directed to retailers (i.e., concentrated on point-of-purchase). The shift in promotional spending toward nontraditional media has been further prompted by regulated restrictions on access to different media (e.g., U.S. cigarette advertising is banned from radio, television, and billboards) and the desire to make use of emerging technologies and new media.

Sponsorship became an increasingly important form of promotion for U.S. tobacco companies during the early 1970s. Virginia Slims, for example, began sponsoring women's professional tennis in 1970, whereas Winston Cup auto racing and Marlboro Cup horse racing started in 1971 and 1973, respectively (Crompton, 1993). Tobacco firms were strategically aware that cigarette brand exposure could persist on radio and television if broadcast sporting events were sponsored. Blum (1991), Madden and Grube (1994), Siegel (2001), and Morrison, Haygood, and Krugman (2006) have illustrated that by sponsoring sports such as auto racing, U.S. tobacco companies continue to receive millions of dollars worth of low-cost national television exposure, despite the cigarette broadcast advertising ban being in effect. A videotaped recording of the Marlboro Grand Prix, on July 16, 1989, revealed that Marlboro was seen or mentioned 5,933 times. Tobacco companies have used sponsorship as a means of circumventing various advertising regulations or restrictions (Cornwell, 1997; Dewhirst, 2004).

Sponsored events, Web sites, contests, and retail initiatives have provided tobacco companies with opportunities to collect personal information from consumers as part of a direct marketing and database marketing strategy. FTC (2003) data reveals that the largest percentage increase in promotional spending from 1997 to 2001 among U.S. cigarette firms was for direct mail; expenditures for this promotional category increased 259% during this period, with expenditures reaching more than $133 million (Lewis, Yulis, Delnevo, & Hrywna, 2004). Several tobacco companies have launched lifestyle magazines that are specifically designed to improve the profile of particular brands. The magazines are distributed by direct mail to those on a particular tobacco company's database. Philip Morris's magazines *Unlimited* and *All Woman*, for example, contain content that closely matches the psychographic dimensions of the target market for their Marlboro and Virginia Slims brands, respectively, while *CML* is a publication by R.J. Reynolds with content matching the brand imagery of the Camel brand. The readership of these custom magazines is difficult to ascertain, but during the early 2000s, in the state of New Jersey, it was estimated that roughly 15% of those aged 18 to 24 had received direct mail within the previous six months from the tobacco industry; overall, smoking status was an important determinant, evident by "current smokers" being 4.5 times more likely than "never/former smokers" to receive direct mail (Lewis, Delnevo, & Slade, 2004).

Overall, FTC data reveals that point-of-purchase retail settings are now the principal site of paid promotion for U.S. tobacco companies. According to U.S. advertising trade press, retail merchandising contracts currently represent the most potent part of a tobacco company's marketing arsenal, and "the contracts are cigarette marketers' primary marketing tool since the 1998 Master Settlement Agreement prohibited most tobacco advertising" (Beirne, 2002). U.S. tobacco firms typically provide incentives to retailers in exchange for their brands having at least 40% of shelf space (Philip Morris and R.J. Reynolds purportedly negotiate for as much as 55%), obtaining desirable shelf placement, displaying promotional items and signage, meeting minimum sales volume standards, providing "buydowns" (retailers pass along reduced prices to consumers), and maintaining one of their brands as the cheapest available (Beirne, 2001, 2002; Bloom, 2001; Feighery, Ribisl, Clark, & Haladjian, 2003). Internal corporate documentation from the tobacco industry reveals that key objectives of point-of-purchase promotion include attracting attention and arousing consumer interest, communicating brand image, enhancing brand recognition, and conveying product and brand "presence," which in effect contributes to the perceived popularity of both smoking and particular brands (Pollay, 2007). Concern has been expressed about children and youth being exposed to cigarette promotions at point-of-purchase environments (e.g., convenience stores); retailers with in-store tobacco promotions are often located in close proximity to primary and secondary schools (Schooler, Feighery, & Flora, 1996; Slater, Chaloupka, & Wakefield, 2001). Moreover, in-store promotions and cigarette products are often displayed at low eye levels and near candy (Cummings, Sciandra, & Lawrence, 1991; Feighery, Ribisl, Schleicher, Lee, & Halvorson, 2001; Terry-McElrath et al., 2002).

## TOBACCO USE REPRESENTATION IN THE ENTERTAINMENT MEDIA

As tobacco promotion activities have become ever more restricted, attention has increasingly been directed toward monitoring tobacco use portrayals in popular culture and the entertainment media. Until at least the early 1990s, U.S. tobacco companies strategically utilized paid product placement, particularly in movies, for promoting their cigarette brands. Cigarette product placement payments are now prohibited according to the 1998 U.S. Master Settlement Agreement, but tobacco use is still frequently portrayed in the entertainment media, seemingly at the discretion of directors, producers, and actors.

## Product Placement: Origins, Objectives, and Effectiveness

Historically, tobacco companies garnered considerable publicity for various cigarette brands through *product placement*, which is defined as "the purposeful incorporation of a brand into an entertainment vehicle" (Russell & Belch, 2005, p. 74). The practice of product placement involves contractual agreements that stipulate on-screen exposures of brand-name goods and services in exchange for fees or services being provided (Russell, 2002). For movies, the use of Reese's Pieces in *E.T.*—released in 1982—is commonly pointed to as the inaugural event in product placement, yet formal product placement agreements were apparent during the 1930s for major brands such as Bell telephones, Buick, Coca-Cola, De Beers diamonds, as well as Chesterfield cigarettes and White Owl cigars, with major studios like Columbia, MGM, and Warner Brothers (Elliott, 2005).

Product placement practices evolved in the 1980s purportedly to make sets look more realistic (i.e., a creative scene is likely to be more credible and believable if a familiar brand name, such as Coke or Marlboro, is represented rather than a no-name, generic product) and simultaneously served as a source of offset revenue (Russell & Belch, 2005; Solomon & Englis, 1994). The fees or services often provided to producers through product placement now play an increasingly important role with the high operating and promotional budgets of many Hollywood films. *Minority Report*, for example, had a $102 million budget, yet with the "placement" of more than fifteen major brands, generated roughly $25 million in offset revenue (according to *Daily Variety*).

Key objectives for product placement include reaching desirable target markets with a product or promotional representation, developing brand recognition, helping ensure that the "placed" products are portrayed in a favorable manner, being cost effective relative to buying commercial time or obtaining celebrity endorsements, and being synergistic with other promotion and communication pertaining to the given brand (Karrh, McKee, & Pardun, 2003; Russell & Belch, 2005).

Studies generally reveal that product placement is likely to be most effective when the placed product seems naturalistic, the placement is made during the latter parts of the movie or program, the placed brand is previously well-known among viewers, the placed brand has a particularly recognizable package or design, there is congruency between the brand and the movie or show's plot, the product is shown in use, and the placement is prominent with both an audio and visual component (Auty & Lewis, 2004; Babin & Carder, 1996; Brennan & Babin, 2004; DeLorme & Reid, 1999; Gupta & Lord, 1998; Karrh, et al. 2003; Law & Braun, 2000; Russell, 2002; Van Reijmersdal, Neijens, & Smit, 2007).

Product placement can be particularly useful to directors and producers in movies or shows with a historical setting or context. Product category leaders often change over time, thus depicted brands can add authenticity to movies or shows in establishing the historical setting (much like fashion, hairstyle, and technology portrayals) (DeLorme & Reid, 1999). For tobacco use portrayals, Chesterfield and Old Gold exemplify cigarette brands that have moved from positions of dominance to near extinction in the U.S. market; these brands might be featured in films with U.S. settings during the 1950s, whereas Marlboro would be a more likely depiction for a movie with a contemporary setting. For market and product category leaders, brand representation in the entertainment media can help reinforce an image of popularity and serve to normalize smoking.

### Product Placement for Tobacco Products

Internal tobacco industry documents, made available to the public from whistleblowers and litigation, give many examples of product placement initiatives by the U.S. tobacco industry. Brown and Williamson, for example, paid Associated Film Promotion nearly $1 million over roughly a four-year period from 1979 to 1983 to generate product placement arrangements for the company's brands in movies and television programs. In 1983, obligations were made to pay actor Sylvester Stallone $500,000 in exchange for him smoking the company's brands in a minimum of five feature films (the contract listed the initial schedule of films as *Rhinestone, The Godfather: Part III, Rambo, 50/50,* and *Rocky IV*) (Ripslinger, 1983). Brown and Williamson also had a product placement deal in place for the television program *The A-Team* (Glantz, et al., 1996).

Philip Morris had product placement arrangements for the 1980 movie, *Superman II*, paying $42,500 to have the Lois Lane character smoke Marlboro cigarettes, despite the fact that the character did not smoke in the comic book series. The company also allegedly spent a notable $200,000 to have actor Martin Sheen smoke Marlboro in the 1979 movie *Apocalypse Now*. Moreover, Philip Morris spent $350,000 during the late 1980s to have the Lark cigarette brand depicted in the movie *Licence to Kill*, which featured actor Timothy Dalton playing the role of James Bond (Glantz et al., 1996). Smoking featured heavily in the movie, and following the movie's release, Timothy Dalton endorsed Lark cigarettes in advertising that ran in Japan. Pierce Brosnan, the subsequent actor playing the role of James Bond, was also featured in a series of commercials for Lark cigarettes in Japan.

Tobacco company Liggett & Myers spent $30,000 in product placement fees to have Eve cigarettes appear in the 1984 movie *Supergirl*. Alta Marea

Productions, the production company of *Supergirl*, actively solicited product placement arrangements with multiple tobacco companies. Additionally, American Tobacco provided cash and props to have their Lucky Strike brand depicted in the 1984 movie *Beverly Hills Cop* (Glantz et al., 1996).

U.S. tobacco firms amended the self-regulatory Cigarette Advertising and Promotion Code in 1990 and agreed to no longer "place" their products in movies. A review of internal tobacco industry documents by Mekemson and Glantz (2002), however, revealed that product placement initiatives remained active at least three years after the code was amended. Payments toward promoting tobacco products in television shows and movies are now prohibited in accordance with the 1998 U.S. Master Settlement Agreement, but many public health groups remain concerned about the continued frequency of tobacco depictions and how tobacco use is commonly portrayed.

## Content Analysis Studies Assessing Tobacco Use Representation

Content analysis is a commonly used research method for examining tobacco use frequency and portrayals in television shows and movies. For studies pertaining to television shows, prime-time programming has been the typical sampling frame, although some studies account for music videos, programming during Saturday morning hours, fictional series, soap operas with the highest ratings, and programming shown on a public television network. For studies that assess tobacco use portrayals in film, top-grossing movies are usually selected to generate a sampling frame, but a few studies have focused on children's animated films.

## Tobacco Use Portrayals and Frequency in Television Shows

The frequency and nature of tobacco use portrayals has often been compared to alcohol use portrayals. Study findings reveal that tobacco is infrequently depicted relative to alcohol in television programming. McEwen and Hanneman (1974), for example, utilized content analysis to measure the depiction of drug use in prime-time television programming. Coding was done for television programs and commercials shown by the three major networks (NBC, CBS, and ABC) and public television during the week of March 12 to 18, 1973, from 7 P.M. to 11 P.M. For each assessed program, the program name, date, channel, drug involved, and the type of drug incident (i.e., use, refusal to use, reference, and/or visual presentation) was recorded. Moreover, various contingent descriptions (i.e., characters using drugs, number of drug users depicted during each incident, extent of drug use, and type of physical and social consequences depicted) and the tone of drug incidents were examined. Eight descriptors were developed for assessing the tone of drug incidents: humorous, exciting, warm, informative, sexy, aggressive, favorable to drug use, and unfavorable to drug use. Drug-related incidents were defined as any verbal or nonverbal use, mention, or depiction persisting for at least a few seconds of program time.

McEwen and Hanneman found that commercial appeals promoting licit drug use far outweighed public service advertisements with respect to total time, typical duration, frequency, and optimal viewing times. While public interest advertisements promoting anti- or responsible drug use messages occupied 0.3% of available commercially sponsored time, 1.24% of time was comprised of advertisements promoting drug use. Despite the broadcast ban of cigarette advertising in 1971, 13 of the 127 drug-relevant commercials were for tobacco (mainly little cigars and pipe tobacco). All tobacco advertisements utilized appeals that associated use of the product with positive social or psychological consequences.

For television programming, alcohol by far represented the most frequently depicted drug. Tobacco incidents occurred on twenty-one occasions: twelve times during drama programming, five times during comedy programming, and four times during news/talk shows/documentary features. Although tobacco use was not common among major characters, the way in which it was portrayed was noteworthy. Two-thirds of tobacco depictions included actual use of the product by a character, the highest proportion among all drug types. According to McEwen and Hanneman, "tobacco is simply used rather than talked about" (1974, p. 290). No characters were observed to refuse tobacco and the consequences of usage were rarely emphasized. The most frequently classified tone of tobacco incidents was humorous.

Greenberg, Fernandez-Collado, Graef, Korzenny, and Atkin (1979) analyzed the use of alcohol, tobacco, and illicit drugs during the prime-time and Saturday morning hours of the 1976–1977 and 1977–1978 television seasons. One episode of each prime-time and Saturday morning fictional series was videotaped, resulting in approximately sixty hours of television programming and eighty different programs being analyzed per season. Programming from three commercial television networks (ABC, CBS, and NBC) was represented. Instances of tobacco use (i.e., consumption, attempts to consume, inducement to consume, and laudatory remarks about consumption) were recorded, and for each character engaged in such behavior, demographic information was collected. Greenberg and colleagues found that for both seasons, alcohol accounted for greater than two-thirds of all coded substance depictions. Tobacco use incidents occurred on average 0.7 times per hour during the 1976–1977 season, whereas tobacco was depicted 0.48 times per hour during the 1977–1978 season, thus indicating that viewers typically watched two hours of television programming before observing a character smoke a cigarette, cigar, or pipe.

Greenberg (1981) analyzed the ten highest rated prime-time fictional television series and the two top-rated soap operas for the 1979–1980 season. Four episodes of each top-rated prime-time fictional television series and eight episodes of each soap opera were videotaped, resulting in a total of fifty-six episodes and forty hours of television programming being examined (eight of the top-rated series were half-hour programs, two of the top-rated series were one-hour programs, and both soap operas were one-hour programs). A coding form was developed in which all instances of speaking characters smoking, drinking, or using illicit drugs were itemized. Overall, only eleven tobacco incidents were identified, indicating that viewers were required to watch nearly four hours of television programming on average before observing a character smoke a cigarette, pipe, or cigar. Five of the ten top-rated prime-time fictional television series featured absolutely no tobacco incidents and total tobacco use for the sixteen soap opera episodes amounted to a single cigar. By contrast, alcohol consumption rates on top-rated television series ranged from 3.0 to 16.5 incidents per program hour.

Breed and De Foe (1984) assessed the portrayal of drinking and smoking for situation comedies and dramatic prime-time programming from 1950 to 1982. The thirty-three-year time span was categorized into four separate periods (1950 to 1963, 1964 to 1970, 1971 to 1977, and 1981 to 1982) to determine changes that might have resulted from the release of the 1964 Surgeon General's report (USDHEW, 1964) and the cigarette advertising broadcast ban in 1971. Each time period and type of entertainment show (i.e., dramas and situation comedies) were represented by a minimum of ten series, twenty hours, and thirty episodes of programming and a ceiling was set to ensure that no series was represented by more than five episodes. To be included in the data set, television programs were required to have an historical setting since 1940 and be located in the United States. In total, 418 episodes, 101 series, and 274.5 hours of television programming were analyzed.

Breed and De Foe found that cigarette use steadily dropped in television programming from 1950 to 1982 (by a factor of six in situation comedies and by greater than twelve in dramas). Cigarette acts were more frequently depicted within dramatic programming for all time periods. Interestingly, cigarettes were lit for 94% of the acts, whereas the remaining cigarette acts were classified as "prepared" to smoke. During the 1950 to 1963 time frame, several types of adult characters (including heroes, heroines, and villains) were depicted smoking. From 1964 to 1970, some primary characters and "stars" were still seen smoking, but during the 1971 to 1977 time period smokers were typically villains or insecure characters. Scenes parodying cigarettes became apparent during the 1981 to 1982 timeframe. Smoking depictions among doctors dramatically declined over the thirty-three-year span.

Cruz and Wallack (1986) analyzed the frequency of smoking acts in regularly scheduled prime-time television programming during the 1984 fall season. Smoking acts included preparing to smoke or actively smoking a cigarette, cigarillo, cigar, or pipe. Randomly drawing from a seven-week period, a composite two-week sample was videotaped for analysis purposes. Coding was based on a total of 116 episodes and 115.5 hours of fictional programming.

Cruz and Wallack observed 107 smoking acts, thus 0.93 smoking acts occurred during each hour of television programming. The rate of smoking acts was highest for feature films shown on television and drama programs, and lowest for situation comedies. Male smokers outnumbered females by a three-to-one ratio. For observed smoking acts, nearly two-thirds of smokers were lead characters and 70% were cast in strong and enduring roles. Only one incident was observed in which it was evident that a smoker may desire to quit.

Diener (1993), during the autumns of 1986 and 1991, conducted a content analysis of daytime soap operas to determine the frequency and context of tobacco and alcohol portrayals, and to discover whether there were observable changes during this five-year period. General coding categories were established such as the number of overall scenes, who was present, the location of the scene, the activity in the scene, the topic of discussion, whether conflict was present, and the type of conflict. For tobacco portrayals, coding categories established whether it was present, the type being used, and whether it was being consumed. The content analysis included eight different one-hour long soap opera programs (e.g., *General Hospital*, *The Young and the Restless*, *All My Children*) shown on three different U.S. television networks. All eight programs were aired both in 1986 and 1991, although their relative rank, rating, and share had obviously shifted over this time period. Forty hours of soap opera programming were recorded from August to October during both 1986 and 1991. Each soap opera program was evenly represented in the sample and, in total, eighty hours of programming were analyzed.

Diener found that alcohol cues dramatically exceeded tobacco cues for both 1986 and 1991 soap opera programming. Alcohol and tobacco cues occurred more frequently during scenes in 1991 compared to 1986, but this finding was not statistically significant for tobacco cues due to their overall infrequency during both 1986 and 1991. For 1986, viewers would on average watch ten hours of programming before observing a tobacco/smoking cue, whereas for the 1991 data set viewers would eye nearly four hours before observing such cues.

Despite decades of declining tobacco frequency rates, more recent studies suggest a slight upswing in tobacco representations for television shows from the 1990s. Hazan and Glantz (1995) examined tobacco use by randomly selecting three composite weeks of fictional prime-time television programming during fall 1992. The ABC, CBS, and NBC networks were each represented and a total of 157 programs, spanning 111 hours, were analyzed. Hazan and Glantz found that 24% of episodes included at least one tobacco event. Overall, 0.99 tobacco events were apparent during each hour of television programming. In drama programs, 1.13 tobacco events occurred per hour and comedies included 0.86 events per hour. Smokers were predominately male (outnumbering females by more than a three-to-one ratio), white (78%), and middle class (42%). The researchers classified 92% of tobacco events as "pro-tobacco," and "good-guy" smokers (55%) outnumbered "bad-guy" smokers (45%). Statistically significant differences were not apparent among the various networks.

With the advent of music videos, there was an opportunity to showcase more youthful actors and to reach a largely youth audience. Hence, any portrayals on these specialty networks (MTV in particular) would be expected to have a strong impact on youthful audiences. DuRant and colleagues (1997) utilized content analysis to study both the frequency and the portrayal of tobacco and alcohol use within music videos shown on television. From May 26 to June 23, 1994, music videos were recorded during times in which adolescents were likely viewers. Music videos from MTV, Video Hits One, Country Music Television, and Black Entertainment Television were studied and included five genres of music (adult contemporary, country, rock, rap, and rhythm and blues). In total, 518 unduplicated music videos were recorded. Positive portrayals of tobacco and alcohol use were assessed with particular attention directed toward when such behavior corresponded with frequent displays of sexuality or eroticism.

DuRant and colleagues found that, among the five music genres, rap videos had the highest proportion (30%) of smoking-related behaviors. Meanwhile, despite playing primarily rock videos, MTV represented the television network with the highest proportion (27%) of videos featuring tobacco use. Several videos had multiple exposures of smoking-related behavior and the lead singer or performer was nearly twice as likely to smoke as a background singer or musician. Similar observations were noted for videos that featured acting sequences rather than music performance coverage. For 76% of the videos featuring smoking-related behavior, young adults were said to be engaging in such behavior. Smokers were male 90% of the time and typically white. Finally, 74% of smoking portrayal scenes had a positive emotional tone. Unlike alcohol, tobacco use was not associated with depictions of sexuality or eroticism.

## Tobacco Use Portrayals and Frequency in Movies

Charlesworth and Glantz (2005) provide a comprehensive overview of the literature pertaining to tobacco use portrayals in the movies. Hazan, Lipton, and Glantz (1994), for example, assessed feature-length, top-grossing U.S. films from 1960 through 1990. The films were randomly selected from a listing of the twenty top-grossing U.S. films for each year. The researchers recorded the title, year of release, rating (G, PG, PG-13, R, or X), genre, target audience, and historical era for each of the sixty-two films studied. Data were also collected for the presence of "tobacco events" (defined as implied or actual tobacco consumption, paraphernalia, talking about tobacco, "no smoking" signs, and tobacco product logos). For each "tobacco event," coding was done for a further twenty-five variables that included smoker characteristics (i.e., age, sex, role), tobacco characteristics (i.e., product, brand names, presence of paraphernalia such as ashtrays and matches), and scene characteristics (i.e., number of smokers, health messages).

The key findings by Hazan et al. were (1) the overall rate of tobacco use remained virtually unchanged (despite a significant decline in smoking rates among the general U.S. population), (2) smoking groups became larger and smoking alone declined, (3) smoking involving relatively young people (aged 18 to 29) increased, (4) business activities were customarily the most popular smoking context, (5) smoking by minor characters became more common, whereas smoking by major characters became less frequent, and (6) smoking was increasingly associated with hostility and stress reduction. Furthermore, a gradual, consistent drop in the presence of ashtrays was noted. They found that, overall, films typically depicted smokers as middle class, successful, attractive, white, and male.

Stockwell and Glantz (1997) extended this research by adding a random sample of top-grossing films that were released between 1990 and 1996. Referring to the Hazan et al. (1994) data, the rate of tobacco use per minute of film had reached a minimum during the 1980s, but once again increased during the 1990s, reaching levels comparable to the 1960s. Stockwell and Glantz went on to state:

> The view that the films are merely reflecting society is not supported by the evidence; tobacco use in films, 1990–1996, is increasing at a

time that it is still falling—or at least is not on the rise—in society at large. In addition, the presentation of smoking in the movies continues to be pro-tobacco, with only 14% of screen time dealing with tobacco presenting adverse social or health effects. (1997, p. 284)

Accounting for comparable socioeconomic status, smoking prevalence among major film characters was more than three times greater than found among the U.S. population at large. Glantz, Kacirk, and McCulloch (2004) then further extended this research by adding a random sample of films released during the 1950s and up to 2002. Again, they found the rate of tobacco use per minute of film had reached a minimum during the 1980s, but increased during the 1990s and early 2000s, eventually reaching levels comparable to the 1950s.

Rather than looking at the raw number of smoking depictions, McIntosh, Bazzini, Smith, and Wayne (1998) argued that it is more useful to consider who is smoking in films and how they are depicted. They analyzed 100 popular movies spanning five decades (1940 to 1989) and all film characters appearing in a significant number of scenes were rated according to nine different dimensions: smoking, outcome at film's end, physical attractiveness, aggressiveness, friendliness, goodness, intelligence, romantic activity, and socioeconomic status. McIntosh and colleagues found that 21% of characters smoked at least once during the observed films, and that smoking frequency among characters reached a high during the 1950s and reached a low during the 1980s. Characters that smoked were depicted as more sexually active and romantic than nonsmoking characters. Furthermore, smokers were represented as scarcely more intelligent than nonsmokers. Differences were not observed among smokers and nonsmokers in terms of attractiveness, goodness, socioeconomic status, aggression, friendliness, or outcome at film's end. Overall, smokers were depicted in slightly more positive terms than nonsmokers and the negative consequences of smoking were largely ignored.

Finally, Goldstein, Sobel, and Newman (1999) examined the prevalence of tobacco and alcohol use in children's animated films that were released between 1937 and 1997. Coders viewed each of the films (in videotape form) and assessed content for variables such as presence of tobacco use, type of tobacco being used, duration that tobacco use was visible, number of characters using tobacco, overall character quality of user (i.e., good, bad, or neutral), and presence of any implied or explicit health message. They found that 56% of the films portrayed tobacco use, including all seven animated movies released during 1996 and 1997. Cigars were the most commonly depicted type of tobacco, followed by cigarettes and pipes, in that order. A diverse number of characters were associated with cigars, whereas cigarettes were often reserved for independent, sexy characters, and pipes typically denoted wise, sweet, or older characters. Since 1992, a trend has emerged that characters using tobacco were more commonly classified as good. While more than two-thirds of animated films featured tobacco or alcohol use, none of them contained verbal messages about the negative, long-term health consequences of tobacco use or alcohol abuse. The films used in the study were by five major production companies: Walt Disney, MGM/United Artists, Warner Brothers Studios, Universal Studios, and 20th Century Fox. The portrayal of tobacco use was not limited to a particular production company.

## DISCUSSION AND CONCLUSIONS

Despite contrasting sample frames, sample sizes, time frames, data coding instruments, and coding category definitions, several robust findings are apparent from the content analysis studies reviewed in this chapter. Several studies confirm that the number of cigarette advertisements found in American magazines dramatically increased during the 1970s, largely the result of the U.S. broadcast ban in 1971. Also evident were more frequent use of special positioning, color, and full-page or double-page advertisements. Healthfulness has been a consistent theme in magazine advertising content, reflecting attempts by the tobacco industry to reassure smokers concerned about potential health risks. Low-yield products have become more commonly promoted over time and health-related themes are increasingly communicated through visual imagery. When cigarettes are depicted (even in cases where cigarettes are obviously lit), current advertisements are less likely to feature visible smoke.

Content analysis studies have also assessed the frequency of smoking depictions in television shows and movies, as well as examined who is likely to smoke and how they are portrayed. Directors and producers may use cigarette smoke to enhance atmosphere, depth, distance, or to focus attention toward a character's face. The cigarette is a classic floating signifier, indicating that cigarettes may be used to express a wide variety of meanings (both positive and negative), depending on the context of the situation and the character being developed or depicted (Chapman & Davis, 1997). If attempting to accurately reflect actual tobacco consumption rates, an ongoing television series or current-release movie set in the 1950s would be expected to portray greater tobacco usage than a program or movie set in the 2000s. Studies have commonly found that when tobacco use is portrayed, negative consequences (i.e., the adverse social or health effects) rarely seem to be emphasized. With respect to the frequency of tobacco depictions, some recent studies suggest that, after decades of declining rates, there has been an upswing in tobacco representations for television shows and movies from the 1990s and early 2000s, which contradicts smoking prevalence rates being observed in society at large. Chapter 4, however, examines content from a representative half of the thirty top-grossing movies from 1950 to 2004 and their findings were not in agreement; they found that overall tobacco use steadily declined over the observed period and reached a low during the early 2000s. Nevertheless, they did find an escalating representation of tobacco use among youth characters (those under age 21).

Given the impact that positive smoking portrayals in both tobacco advertising and the entertainment media might have on youth initiation, several policy initiatives have been put forward. The 1998 U.S. Master Settlement Agreement contains several marketing stipulations, including bans on cigarette broadcast advertising, billboard advertising, and product placement. Considerable debate now exists with the U.S. Food and Drug Administration potentially serving as a governing body for a new set of tobacco regulations. Thus far, a piecemeal approach in which regulatory attention is focused on one communication vehicle after another has led to some undesirable results. The FTC (2003) data show that, in the United States, $11.22 billion was spent on tobacco promotion during 2001, which was a record-setting level of U.S. tobacco industry promotional spending. As particular types of advertising become banned, tobacco companies have simply shifted their promotional spending toward permissible mediums and consequently found media "substitutes."

A global treaty has recently taken effect that deals with transnational and transborder dimensions of tobacco promotion. The World Health Organization's Framework Convention on Tobacco Control is legally binding for those countries that ratify the treaty and stipulates a comprehensive ban of all tobacco promotion directed toward consumers, in accordance with each country's respective constitution. The United States, however, has not yet ratified the treaty and this represents a significant omission with the global pervasiveness of U.S. media.

Efforts are also underway with the objective of limiting the longstanding practice of promoting smoking through movies. Smoke Free Movies, for example, is a science-based education and advocacy campaign based at the University of California, San Francisco,[1] that proposes the implementation of four policy stipulations: (1) certifying in the closing credits that payoffs were not made by the tobacco industry, (2) showing antismoking ads before films with smoking scenes, (3) prohibiting tobacco brand identification, and (4) rating any film that shows or implies tobacco use as R. The only exceptions, it is argued, should be when the presentation of tobacco clearly and unambiguously reflects the dangers and consequences of tobacco use, or is necessary to represent the smoking of a real historical figure. Each of these four policy recommendations were made during recent U.S. Congress hearings on smoking in the movies.

The social acceptability of smoking has considerably declined during the past sixty years. Prompted by a complaint from British media regulator, Ofcom, Turner Broadcasting is removing scenes that glamorize smoking from more than 1,700 classic Hanna-Barbera cartoons. The complaint stemmed from the recent airing of two episodes of *Tom and Jerry* (first made in 1949 and 1950) on the Turner-owned Boomerang channel (the channel has a majority audience aged 4 to 14 years old) (Frith, 2006). Moreover, the United States Postal Service has issued stamps in which cigarettes have been digitally removed from images honoring various American artists (e.g., stamps showing legendary painter Jackson Pollock and blues guitarist Robert Johnson). Similarly, in a revised edition of the children's classic book, *Goodnight Moon*, publisher HarperCollins has digitally removed a cigarette from the photograph of illustrator Clement Hurd (Wyatt, 2005). Such decisions have prompted considerable ethical debate about the social and health consequences stemming from gratuitous media representations of smoking, while simultaneously being respectful to the accuracy of the historical representation.

An additional emerging issue in tobacco media representation includes celebrity interviews in which journalists name particular cigarette brands. This is exemplified by the feature article of the May 2001 issue of *Vanity Fair* that pertains to Jennifer Aniston; the interview takes place at Aniston's home, while she was still married to Brad Pitt, and the article states that Aniston "lights a Merit cigarette…and is sipping a Diet Mountain Dew, which appears to be the house drink" (p. 166). Although the naming of brands might be largely seen by journalists as a way of giving authenticity to their narrative, the association of celebrities with the consumption of particular brands can be recognized as an unconventional form of celebrity endorsement that serves an important promotional effect. Moreover, the significance of tobacco portrayals on user-generated media, such as blogs, online bulletin boards, and podcasts, has recently been recognized as an emerging area of concern; although YouTube, MySpace, and Wikipedia exemplify Internet sites that are primarily consumer generated, there is an opportunity for undisclosed use by tobacco firms and other corporations (Freeman & Chapman, 2007). Given the persistence of tobacco promotion and entertainment media smoking portrayals, as well as continuing public health concerns, additional research and further debate concerning ethical and freedom of speech issues, and the need for public policy interventions is inevitable.

## NOTE

1. See http://www.smokefreemovies.ucsf.edu

## REFERENCES

Achey, T. L. (1978, August 30). Product information. Letter from T. L. Achey to C. Judge, Lorillard Tobacco Company. Trial Exhibit 10,195, *State of Minnesota and Blue Cross and Blue Shield of Minnesota v. Philip Morris, Inc., et al.* Bates No. 03537131 [TINY 0003062]. Retrieved from http://www.tobaccoinstitute.com

Albright, C. L., Altman, D. G., Slater, M. D., & Maccoby, N. (1988). Cigarette advertisements in magazines: Evidence for a differential focus on women's and youth magazines. *Health Education Quarterly, 15,* 225–233.

Altman, D. G., Schooler, C., & Basil, M. D. (1991). Alcohol and cigarette advertising on billboards. *Health Education Research, 6,* 487–490.

Altman, D. G., Slater, M. D., Albright, C. L., & Maccoby, N. (1987). How an unhealthy product is sold: Cigarette advertising in magazines, 1960–1985. *Journal of Communication, 37,* 95–106.

Auty, S., & Lewis, C. (2004). Exploring children's choice: The reminder effect of product placement. *Psychology and Marketing, 21,* 697–713.

Babin, L. A., & Carder, S. T. (1996). Advertising via the box office: Is product placement effective? *Journal of Promotion Management, 3,* 31–51.

Balbach, E. D., Gasior, R. J., & Barbeau, E. M. (2003). R.J. Reynolds' targeting of African Americans: 1988–2000. *American Journal of Public Health, 93,* 822–827.

Beirne, M. (2001, May 14). Big tobacco gets tough. *Brandweek,* pp. 29–34.

Beirne, M. (2002, December 2). Tobacco row: Cigarette makers step up retail war. *Brandweek,* p. 3.

Biener, L., & Albers, A. B. (2004). Young adults: Vulnerable new targets of tobacco marketing. *American Journal of Public Health, 94,* 326–330.

Bloom, P. N. (2001). Role of slotting fees and trade promotions in shaping how tobacco is marketed in retail stores. *Tobacco Control, 10,* 340–344.

Blum, A. (1991). The Marlboro Grand Prix: Circumvention of the television ban on tobacco advertising. *New England Journal of Medicine, 324,* 913–917.

Breed, W., & De Foe, J. R. (1984). Drinking and smoking on television, 1950–1982. *Journal of Public Health Policy, 5,* 257–270.

Brennan, I., & Babin, L. A. (2004). Brand placement recognition: The influence of presentation mode and brand familiarity. *Journal of Promotion Management, 10,* 185–202.

Brown and Williamson. (1984). *1984 Kool operational plan.* Bates No. 670249922–670250102. Retrieved from http://www.tobaccodocuments.org/bw/227219.html

Carpenter, C. M., Wayne, G. F., & Connolly, G. N. (2005). Designing cigarettes for women: New findings from the tobacco industry documents. *Addiction, 100,* 837–851.

Chapman, S., & Davis, R. M. (1997). Smoking in movies: Is it a problem? *Tobacco Control, 6*(4), 269–271.

Charlesworth, A., & Glantz, S. A. (2005). Smoking in the movies increases adolescent smoking: A review. *Pediatrics, 116,* 1516–1528.

Cohen, J. B. (2000). Playing to win: Marketing and public policy at odds over Joe Camel. *Journal of Public Policy and Marketing, 19,* 155–167.

Cornwell, T. B. (1997). The use of sponsorship-linked marketing by tobacco firms: International public policy issues. *Journal of Consumer Affairs, 31,* 238–254.

Crompton, J. L. (1993). Sponsorship of sport by tobacco and alcohol companies: A review of the issues. *Journal of Sport and Social Issues, 17,* 148–167.

Cruz, J., & Wallack, L. (1986). Trends in tobacco use on television. *American Journal of Public Health, 76,* 698–699.

Cummings, K. M., Hyland, A., Lewit, E., & Shopland, D. (1997). Discrepancies in cigarette brand sales and adult market share: Are new teen smokers filling the gap? *Tobacco Control, 6*(Suppl. II), S38-S43.

Cummings, K. M., Morley, C. P., Horan, J. K., Steger, C., & Leavell, N.-R. (2002). Marketing to America's youth: Evidence from corporate documents. *Tobacco Control, 11*(Supplement I), i5-i17.

Cummings, K. M., Sciandra, R., & Lawrence, J. (1991). Tobacco advertising in retail stores. *Public Health Reports, 106,* 570–575.

Dal Cin, S., Gibson, B., Zanna, M. P., Shumate, R., & Fong, G. T. (2007). Smoking in movies, implicit associations of smoking with the self, and intentions to smoke. *Psychological Science, 18,* 559–563.

Dalton, M. A., Sargent, J. D., Beach, M. L., Titus-Ernstoff, L., Gibson, J. J., Ahrens, M. B., et al. (2003). Effect of viewing smoking in movies on adolescent smoking initiation: A cohort study. *The Lancet, 362,* 281–285.

DeLorme, D. E., & Reid, L. N. (1999). Moviegoers' experiences and interpretations of brands in films revisited. *Journal of Advertising, 28,* 71–95.

Dewhirst, T. (2004). Smoke and ashes: Tobacco sponsorship of sports and regulatory issues in Canada. In L. R. Kahle & C. Riley (Eds.), *Sports marketing and the psychology of marketing communication* (pp. 327–352). Mahwah, NJ: Erlbaum.

Dewhirst, T., & Davis, B. (2005). Brand strategy and integrated marketing communication (IMC): A case study of Player's cigarette brand marketing. *Journal of Advertising, 34*(4), 81–92.

Dewhirst, T., & Sparks, R. (2003). Intertextuality, tobacco sponsorship of sports, and adolescent male smoking culture: A selective review of tobacco industry documents. *Journal of Sport and Social Issues, 27,* 372–398.

Diener, B. J. (1993). The frequency and context of alcohol and tobacco cues in daytime soap opera programs: Fall 1986 and fall 1991. *Journal of Public Policy and Marketing, 12,* 252–257.

Distefan, J. M., Gilpin, E. A., Sargent, J. D., & Pierce, J. P. (1999). Do movie stars encourage adolescents to start smoking? Evidence from California. *Preventive Medicine, 28,* 1–11.

Distefan, J. M., Pierce, J. P., & Gilpin, E. A. (2004). Do favorite movie stars influence adolescent smoking initiation? *American Journal of Public Health, 94,* 1239–1244.

DuRant, R. H., Rome, E. S., Rich, M., Allred, E., Emans, S. J., & Woods, E. R. (1997). Tobacco and alcohol use behaviors portrayed in music videos: A content analysis. *American Journal of Public Health, 87,* 1131–1135.

Elliott, S. (2005, February 28). Greatest hits of product placement. *New York Times.* Retrieved from http://www.nytimes.com/2005/02/28/business/media/28adcol.html

Federal Trade Commission. (2003). *Federal Trade Commission cigarette report for 2001.* Washington, DC: Author.

Feighery, E. C., Ribisl, K. M., Clark, P. I., & Haladjian, H. H. (2003). How tobacco companies ensure prime placement of their advertising and products in stores: Interviews with retailers about tobacco company incentive programs. *Tobacco Control, 12,* 184–188.

Feighery, E. C., Ribisl, K. M., Schleicher, N. C., Lee, R. E., & Halvorson, S. (2001). Cigarette advertising and promotional strategies in retail outlets: Results of a statewide survey in California. *Tobacco Control, 10,* 184–188.

Fischer, P. M., Schwartz, M. P., Richards, Jr., J. W., Goldstein, A. O., & Rojas, T. H. (1991). Brand logo recognition by children aged 3 to 6 years: Mickey Mouse and Old Joe the Camel. *JAMA, 266,* 3145–3148.

Freeman, B., & Chapman, S. (2007). Is "YouTube" telling or selling you something? Tobacco content on the YouTube video-sharing website. *Tobacco Control, 16,* 207–210.

Frith, M. (2006, August 22). Broadcast watchdog bares its teeth at Tom and Jerry over smoking scenes. *The Independent* [online edition]. Retrieved from http://news.independent.co.uk/mdia/article1220835.ece

Gardiner, P. S. (2004). The African Americanization of menthol cigarette use in the United States. *Nicotine and Tobacco Research,* 6(Supplement I), S55–S65.

Gibson, B., & Maurer, J. (2000). Cigarette smoking in the movies: The influence of product placement on attitudes toward smoking and smokers. *Journal of Applied Social Psychology, 30,* 1457–1473.

Gilpin, E. A., White, V. M., & Pierce, J. P. (2005). How effective are tobacco industry bar and club marketing efforts in reaching young adults? *Tobacco Control, 14,* 186–192.

Glantz, S. A., Kacirk, K., & McCulloch, C. (2004). Back to the future: Smoking in movies in 2002 compared with 1950 levels. *American Journal of Public Health, 94,* 261–263.

Glantz, S. A., Slade, J., Bero, L. A., Hanauer, P., & Barnes, D. E. (1996). *The cigarette papers.* Berkeley: University of California Press.

Goldberg, M. E., Davis, R. M., & O'Keefe, A. M. (2006). The role of tobacco advertising and promotion: Themes employed in litigation by tobacco industry witnesses. *Tobacco Control* 15(Supplement IV), iv54–iv67.

Goldstein, A. O., Sobel, R. A., & Newman, G. R. (1999). Tobacco and alcohol use in G-rated children's animated films. *JAMA, 281,* 1131–1136.

Greenberg, B. S. (1981). Smoking, drugging and drinking in top rated TV series. *Journal of Drug Education, 11,* 227–233.

Greenberg, B. S., Fernandez-Collado, C., Graef, D., Korzenny, F., & Atkin, C. K. (1979). Trends in use of alcohol and other substances on television. *Journal of Drug Education, 9,* 243–253.

Gupta, P. B., & Lord, K. R. (1998). Product placement in movies: The effect of prominence and mode on audience recall. *Journal of Current Issues and Research in Advertising, 20,* 47–59.

Hammond, D. (2005). Smoking behaviour among young adults: Beyond youth prevention. *Tobacco Control, 14,* 181–185.

Hazan, A. R., & Glantz, S. A. (1995). Current trends in tobacco use on prime-time fictional television. *American Journal of Public Health, 85,* 116–117.

Hazan, A. R., Lipton, H. L., & Glantz, S. A. (1994). Popular films do not reflect current tobacco use. *American Journal of Public Health, 84,* 998–1000.

Hines, D., Saris, R. N., & Throckmorton-Belzer, L. (2000). Cigarette smoking in popular films: Does it increase viewers' likelihood to smoke? *Journal of Applied Social Psychology, 30,* 2246–2269.

Jetté, S., Wilson, B., & Sparks, R. (2007). Female youths' perceptions of smoking in popular films. *Qualitative Health Research, 17,* 323–339.

Johnston, M. E. (1981, March 31). *Young smokers: Prevalence, trends, implications, and related demographic trends.* Philip Morris U.S.A. Research Center. Bates No. 1000390808. Retrieved from http://www.pmdocs.com

Karrh, J. A., McKee, K. B., & Pardun, C. J. (2003). Practitioners' evolving views on product placement effectiveness. *Journal of Advertising Research, 43,* 138–149.

Katz, S. K., & Lavack, A. M. (2002). Tobacco related bar promotions: Insights from tobacco industry documents. *Tobacco Control 11*(Supplement I), i92-i101.

Kelly, K. J., Slater, M. D., Karan, D., & Hunn, L. (2000). The use of human models and cartoon characters in magazine advertisements for cigarettes, beer, and non-alcoholic beverages. *Journal of Public Policy and Marketing, 19,* 189–200.

King, K. W., Reid, L. N., Moon, Y. S., & Ringold, D. J. (1991). Changes in the visual imagery of cigarette ads, 1954–1986. *Journal of Public Policy and Marketing, 10,* 63–80.

Kotler, P., Armstrong, G., & Cunningham, P. H. (2005). *Principles of marketing* (6th Canadian edition). Toronto, ON: Pearson Prentice Hall.

Lantz, P. M. (2003). Smoking on the rise among young adults: Implications for research and policy. *Tobacco Control, 12*(Supplement I), i60–i70.

Law, S., & Braun, K. A. (2000). I'll have what she's having: Gauging the impact of product placements on viewers. *Psychology and Marketing, 17,* 1059–1075.

Lewis, M. J., Delnevo, C. D., & Slade, J. (2004). Tobacco industry direct mail marketing and participation by New Jersey adults. *American Journal of Public Health, 94,* 257–259.

Lewis, M. J., Yulis, S. G., Delnevo, C., & Hrywna, M. (2004). Tobacco industry direct marketing after the Master Settlement Agreement. *Health Promotion Practice, 5,* 75S–83S.

Ling, P. M., & Glantz, S. A. (2002). Why and how the tobacco industry sells cigarettes to young adults: Evidence from industry documents. *American Journal of Public Health, 92,* 908–916.

Madden, P. A., & Grube, J. W. (1994). The frequency and nature of alcohol and tobacco advertising in televised sports, 1990 through 1992. *American Journal of
Public Health, 84,* 297–299.

Mazis, M. B., Ringold, D. J., Perry, E. S., & Denman, D. W. (1992). Perceived age and
attractiveness of models in cigarette advertisements. *Journal of Marketing, 56,*
22–37.

McCain, J. H. (1973, March 8). Re: NFO preference share data: "Youth" market. Letter from J. H. McCain, William Esty Company, to J. O. Watson, R.J. Reynolds
Marketing Department. Bates No. 50116 7050. Retrieved from http://www
.rjrtdocs.com

McCool, J. P., Cameron, L. D., & Petrie, K. J. (2003). Interpretations of smoking in
film by older teenagers. *Social Science and Medicine, 56,* 1023–1032.

McEwen, W. J., & Hanneman, G. J. (1974). The depiction of drug use in television
programming. *Journal of Drug Education, 4,* 281–293.

McIntosh, W. D., Bazzini, D. G., Smith, S. M., & Wayne, S. M. (1998). Who smokes
in Hollywood? Characteristics of smokers in popular films from 1940 to 1989.
*Addictive Behaviors, 23,* 395–398.

Mekemson, C., & Glantz, S. A. (2002). How the tobacco industry built its relationship with Hollywood. *Tobacco Control, 11*(Supplement I), i81-i91.

Morrison, M., Haygood, D. M., & Krugman, D. M. (2006). Inhaling and accelerating:
Tobacco motor sports sponsorship in televised automobile races, 2000–2002.
*Sport Marketing Quarterly, 15,* 207–216.

Pechmann, C., & Shih, C. F. (1999). Smoking scenes in movies and antismoking
advertisements before movies: Effects on youth. *Journal of Marketing, 63,*
1–13.

Perry, C. L. (1999). The tobacco industry and underage youth smoking. *Archives of
Pediatrics and Adolescent Medicine, 153,* 935–941.

Pollay, R. W. (1991). Signs and symbols in American cigarette advertising: A historical analysis of the use of "pictures of health." In H. H. Larsen, D. G. Mick, &
C. Alsted (Eds.), *Marketing and semiotics: Selected papers from the Copenhagen
symposium* (pp. 160–176). Copenhagen: Handelshojskolens Forlag.

Pollay, R. W. (1994). Exposure of US youth to cigarette television advertising in the
1960s. *Tobacco Control, 3,* 130–133.

Pollay, R. W. (2000). Targeting youth and concerned smokers: Evidence from Canadian tobacco industry documents. *Tobacco Control, 9,* 136–147.

Pollay, R. W. (2004). Considering the evidence, no wonder the Court endorses Canada's restrictions on cigarette advertising. *Journal of Public Policy and Marketing,
23,* 80–88.

Pollay, R. W. (2007). More than meets the eye: On the importance of retail cigarette
merchandising. *Tobacco Control, 16,* 270–274.

Pollay, R. W., & Dewhirst, T. (2002). The dark side of marketing seemingly "light"
cigarettes: Successful images and failed fact. *Tobacco Control, 11,* i18-i31.

Pollay, R. W., Siddarth, S., Siegel, M., Haddix, A., Merritt, R. K., Giovino, G. A., et al.
(1996). The last straw? Cigarette advertising and realized market shares among
youths and adults, 1979–1993. *Journal of Marketing, 60,* 1–16.

Rigotti, N. A., Moran, S. E., & Wechsler, H. (2005). US college students' exposure to tobacco promotions: Prevalence and association with tobacco use. *American Journal of Public Health, 95,* 138–144.

Ripslinger, J. F. (1983, June 14). Letter from James F. Ripslinger, Senior Vice President of Associated Film Productions, Inc. (Century City, CA) to Mr. Sylvester Stallone. Bates No. 2404.01. Retrieved from http://legacy.library.ucsf.edu/tid/slb72d00/pdf

Russell, C. A. (2002). Investigating the effectiveness of product placements in television shows: The role of modality and plot connection congruence on brand memory and attitude. *Journal of Consumer Research, 29,* 306–318.

Russell, C. A., & Belch, M. (2005). A managerial investigation into the product placement industry. *Journal of Advertising Research, 45,* 73–92.

Sargent, J. D., Beach, M. L., Adachi-Mejia, A. M., Gibson, J. J., Titus-Ernstoff, L. T., Carusi, C. P., et al. (2005). Exposure to movie smoking: Its relation to smoking initiation among US adolescents. *Pediatrics, 116,* 1183–1191.

Sargent, J. D., Beach, M. L., Dalton, M. A., Mott, L. A., Tickle, J. J., Ahrens, M. B., et al. (2001). Effect of seeing tobacco use in films on trying smoking among adolescents: Cross sectional study. *British Medical Journal, 323,* 1–6.

Sargent, J. D., Stoolmiller, M., Worth, K. A., Dal Cin, S., Wills, T. A., Gibbons, F. X., et al. (2007). Exposure to smoking depictions in movies: Its association with established adolescent smoking. *Archives of Pediatrics and Adolescent Medicine, 161,* 849–856.

Schooler, C., Feighery, E. C., & Flora, J. A. (1996). Seventh graders' self-reported exposure to cigarette marketing and its relationship to their smoking behavior. *American Journal of Public Health, 86,* 1216–1221.

Sepe, E., Ling, P. M., & Glantz, S. A. (2002). Smooth moves: Bar and nightclub tobacco promotions that target young adults. *American Journal of Public Health, 92,* 414–419.

Siegel, M. (2001). Counteracting tobacco motor sports sponsorship as a promotional tool: Is the tobacco settlement enough? *American Journal of Public Health, 91,* 1100–1106.

Slater, S., Chaloupka, F. J., & Wakefield, M. (2001). State variation in retail promotions and advertising for Marlboro cigarettes. *Tobacco Control, 10,* 337–339.

Solomon, M. R., & Englis, B. G. (1994). The big picture: Product complementarity and integrated communications. *Journal of Advertising Research, 34,* 57–64.

Song, A. V., Ling, P. M., Neilands, T. B., & Glantz, S. A. (2007). Smoking in movies and increased smoking among young adults. *American Journal of Preventive Medicine, 33,* 396–403.

Stockwell, T. F., & Glantz, S. A. (1997). Tobacco use is increasing in popular films. *Tobacco Control, 6,* 282–284.

Sutton, C. D., & Robinson, R. G. (2004). The marketing of menthol cigarettes in the United States: Populations, messages, and channels. *Nicotine and Tobacco Research, 6* (Supplement I), S83-S91.

Taylor, C. R., & Taylor, J. C. (1994). Regulatory issues in outdoor advertising: A content analysis of billboards. *Journal of Public Policy and Marketing, 13,* 97–107.

Terry-McElrath, Y., Wakefield, M., Giovino, G., Hyland, A., Barker, D., Chaloupka, F., et al. (2002). Point-of-purchase tobacco environments and variation by store type—United States, 1999. *Morbidity and Mortality Weekly Report, 51*, 184–187.

U.S. Centers for Disease Control and Prevention. (2002). Trends in cigarette smoking among high school students: United States, 1991–2001. *Morbidity and Mortality Weekly Report, 51*, 409–412.

U.S. Centers for Disease Control and Prevention. (2004). Cigarette use among high school students: United States, 1991–2003. *Morbidity and Mortality Weekly Report, 53*, 499–502.

U.S. Department of Health, Education, and Welfare, Public Health Service. Office of the Surgeon General. (1964). *Smoking and health: Report of the Advisory Committee to the Surgeon General of the Public Health Service* (Public Health Service Publication No. 1103). Washington, DC: Author. Also available at http://www.cdc.gov/tobacco/data_statistics/sgr/previous_sgr.htm

U.S. Department of Health, Education, and Welfare, Public Health Service, Office on Smoking and Health. (1979). *Smoking and health: A report of the Surgeon General* (DHEW Publication No. (PHS) 79-50066). Washington, DC: Author. Also available at http://profiles.nlm.nih.gov/NN/B/C/M/D/_/nnbcmd.pdf

U.S. Department of Health and Human Services. (1994). *Preventing tobacco use among young people: A report of the Surgeon General*. Atlanta, GA: U.S. Department of Health and Human Services, Public Health Service, Centers for Disease Control and Prevention, National Center for Chronic Disease Prevention and Health Promotion, Office on Smoking and Health.

U.S. Department of Health and Human Services. (2001). *Women and smoking: A report of the Surgeon General*. Washington, DC: U.S. Government Printing Office.

U.S. Department of Health and Human Services. (2004). *The health consequences of smoking: A report of the Surgeon General*. Atlanta, GA: U.S. Department of Health and Human Services, Centers for Disease Control and Prevention, National Center for Chronic Disease Prevention and Health Promotion, Office on Smoking and Health.

Van Reijmersdal, E. A., Neijens, P. C., & Smit, E. G. (2007). Effects of television brand placement on brand image. *Psychology and Marketing, 24*, 403–420.

Warner, K. E. (1985). Tobacco industry response to public health concern: A content analysis of cigarette ads. *Health Education Quarterly, 12*, 115–127.

Weinberger, M. G., Campbell, L., & DuGrenier, F. D. (1981). Cigarette advertising: Tactical changes in the pre and post broadcast era. In H. K. Hunt (Ed.), *Advertising in a new age, Proceedings of the Annual Conference of the American Academy of Advertising, 1981* (pp. 136–141). Provo, UT: American Academy of Advertising.

Wyatt, E. (2005, November 17). 'Goodnight moon,' smokeless version. *New York Times*. Retrieved from http://www.nytimes.com/2005/11/17/books/17moon.html

# 10

# The Changing Portrayal of Alcohol
# Use in Television Advertising

JENNIFER HORNER, PATRICK E. JAMIESON, AND DANIEL ROMER

In this chapter we examine changes since 1950 in the content of television advertising for beer, the most heavily promoted alcohol product (Bonnie & O'Connell, 2004). Advertising plays an important role in socialization and identity formation in adolescents (La Ferle, Li, & Edwards, 2001; Ritson & Elliott, 1999), and beer advertisements are recognized and enjoyed by youth (Chen, Grube, Bersamin, Waiters, & Keefe, 2005; Collins, Ellickson, McCaffrey, & Hambarsoomians, 2005). Compared to other demographic groups, adolescents are disproportionately exposed to alcohol advertising (Federal Trade Commission, 2003; Ringel, Collins, & Ellickson, 2006). Research into problem drinking among young people has focused on issues of alcohol expectancies, peer socialization, and identity development (Demant & Jarveinen, 2006; Lewis & Goker, 2007). Exposure to advertising predicts favorable alcohol beliefs and expectancies in youth (Austin & Knaus, 2000; Dunn & Yniquez, 1999; Grube & Wallack, 1994; Wallack, Cassady, & Grube, 1990a, 1990b) as well as alcohol consumption (Collins, Ellickson, McCaffrey, & Hambarsoomians, 2007; Snyder, Milici, Slater, Sun, & Strizhakova, 2006; Stacy, Zogg, Unger, & Dent, 2004). Ownership of alcohol-branded merchandise has also been linked to teen drinking (Hurz, Henriksen, Wang, Feighery, & Fortmann, 2007; McClure, Cin, Gibson, & Sargent, 2006) and the initiation of binge drinking (Fisher, Miles, Austin, Camargo, & Colditz, 2007).

The societal costs of adolescent drinking are considerable. Consumption of alcohol by youth under the age of 21 (the legal age for purchase of the product in the United States) accounts for about 16% of alcohol sales and results in an estimated $62 billion in medical expenses and loss of productivity in 2005 (Miller, Levy, Spicer, & Taylor, 2006). These costs result primarily from the many side effects of alcohol use, including motor vehicle crashes, homicides, suicides, and other unintentional injuries, all of which are leading causes of morbidity and mortality in young people. Furthermore, people who drink at an early age are at increased risk for dependence and abuse of alcohol throughout life (Grant & Dawson, 1997), especially if they consume heavy amounts of alcohol during adolescence (Bonomo, Bowes, Coffey, Carlin, & Patton, 2004; Hill, White, Chung, Hawkins, & Catalano, 2000). Hence, media portrayal of alcohol consumption is of great concern.

There is little doubt that the industry spends heavily on beer advertising. In the most recent year for which data are available,[1] the beer industry was reported to have spent over a billion dollars in advertising, the majority of it (nearly $900 million) on television ads. Figure 10.1 shows the trend in overall beer advertising based on data available from 1975 to 2005. The trend in spending clearly peaked in the 1980s only to return to new high levels early in the twenty-first century.

In light of evidence that advertising plays an important role in adolescent use of alcohol, the American Medical Association supports a ban on broadcast alcohol advertising (American Medical Association, 2007); however, the

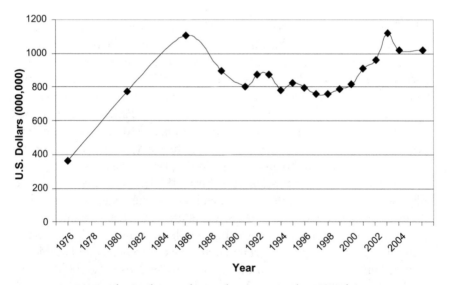

Figure 10.1. Annual spending on beer advertising in the United States in constant 2000 dollars. (*Sources:* From "Beer Advertising and Marketing Update: Structure, Conduct, and Social Costs," by Jon P. Nelson, 2005, *Review of Industrial Organization, 26,* 269–306; *Beer Handbook, 1991–2006.* San Francisco: Bev-Al Publications.)

Federal Trade Commission (2003) has recommended ongoing self-regulation by the industry. The Beer Institute's (2006) guidelines for advertisers advise against advertising to youth audiences. What constitutes youth-oriented advertising is very much subject to debate, and while advertisers maintain that their work is targeted to an adult audience, researchers have noted that certain elements of beer advertising appeal strongly to children. Animals (Lieber, 1996; Wallack et al., 1990b), youthful role models (Austin & Meili, 1994), and celebrities (Atkin & Block, 1984) have all been identified as attractive to young viewers. Studies have also found that children and adolescents enjoy alcohol commercials using humor (Aitken, 1989; Aitken, Leathar, & C., 1988) and are attracted to advertising that focuses on an image or lifestyle rather than the characteristics of the product itself (Austin & Hurst, 2005; Kelly & Edwards, 1998; Zwarun & Farrar, 2005). Our historical analysis examines changes in the way beer has been portrayed with particular emphasis on its relevance to adolescents. Despite the intentions of the industry to adhere to its guidelines against appealing to youth, the storylines and narratives that have evolved since 1950 reflect a clear tendency to express the concerns and anxieties that accompany the transition to adulthood in our culture, especially as this transition affects young men.

## A FOCUS ON NARRATIVE

Although manifest features of ads lend themselves well to quantitative analysis, adolescents' liking of beer advertisements has been more closely linked to their appreciation of the story and humor of the ad than to the presence of particular images or individuals (Chen et al., 2005). Accordingly, qualitative studies have assessed television commercials in terms of their themes, stories, or mythologies (Gronbeck, 1983; Stern, 1998). Parker (1998) defined the "mythologies" underlying alcohol advertising as "strong, commonly-held beliefs that are unconscious and resistant to change" (p. 98). An ad resonates because of its "narrative fidelity"—in plain language, it "rings true" with what the audience already knows (Bush & Bush, 1994). From this perspective, advertising "works" by improvising on and reinforcing wider cultural beliefs about the product and the contexts for its use. Advertising resonates with what the audience already knows, but emphasizes and highlights certain beliefs for certain people, in certain circumstances, to depict a plausible, attractive fantasy context for consumption (Messner & de Oca, 2005).

Previous qualitative studies have used a narrative analysis to assess advertising media during narrowly defined time periods. For example, Postman, Nystrom, Strate, and Weingartner (1987), in their study *Myths, Men and Beer*, analyzed forty beer commercials broadcast during February and March of 1987 with respect to their portrayal of "cultural myths," or "patterns of beliefs, associations, values, and meanings." The study, funded by the American Automobile Association's Foundation for Traffic Safety, focused on the depiction of masculinity in the context of drinking and driving. One primary narrative identified by the researchers was initiation into masculine culture, with beer serving as proof of maturity as well as reward for accomplishment. Work and leisure provide opportunities for male bonding, with a strong emphasis on speed, risk, conquest of nature, and indifference to social pressures as markers of masculinity. These themes were spoofed in ads for "light" beer products; for example, initiation into drinking culture is treated humorously in ads for Bud Light, and the erosion of boundaries between boys and men provide comic narratives for Miller Lite. Postman and colleagues term this latter theme "the boys will be boys approach," and suggest the narrative plays on the notion that beer dissolves the boundaries between men and boys, either because mastery of the drinking environment proves manhood, or because inebriation frees men from their adult roles and allows them to act childish. Aside from an ad featuring film star Madeline Kahn, women were for the most part either absent or used tangentially as proof of male prowess and desirability.

Other studies have echoed or developed the basic ideas and premises of *Myths, Men, and Beer* (e.g., Domzal & Kernan, 1992) or explored audience reactions to beer advertising themes in interview-based studies (Parker, 1998). More recently, Messner and Montez de Oca (2005) reinterpreted the advertising themes of the 1970s and 1980s as evidence of anxieties around masculinity brought by incursions of the women's liberation movement into traditionally male-dominated work and leisure. The authors argue that unlike the ads described by Postman and colleagues, ads in the early twenty-first century "are less about drinking and leisure as a reward for hard work and more about leisure as a lifestyle in and of itself." (p. 1886). Instead of depicting drinking as a reward for masculine achievement, ads of the early twenty-first century offer drinking as a means for escape from the inevitable failures of life. Masculine anxieties are satirized in attempts to control, punish, or escape the female "hotties" and "bitches" who provoke these anxieties. Release from these pressures and anxieties is found in the "safe haven" of buddies and beer. Each study set out to explore themes and elements of alcohol advertising that resonate with the cultural articulation of masculinity in the context of alcohol use. Postman and colleagues concluded that drinking provides a context for proving and affirming achievement, because drinking enhances the risks and rewards of male performance. Fifteen years later, Messner and Montez de Oca argued that beer commercials enact revenge fantasies against females who stand in the way of masculine success. Aside from some suggestive remarks about the blurring of the boundary between boys and men, neither directly addresses the question of whether appeals to underage audiences (male or female) have increased or changed over time.

## BEER ADVERTISING AND THE CHANGING LEGAL DRINKING ENVIRONMENT

A narrative perspective focuses on the stories television ads tell about the social aspects of drinking. In keeping with the principle of narrative fidelity, commercials should reflect the norms and expectations for alcohol use that resonate with the audience advertisers are trying to reach. One implication of the narrative perspective is that changes in the cultural contexts for drinking over time would be reflected in marketing approaches used by brewers. Historically, what we might consider a "youth" market for alcoholic beverages has undergone several shifts in the past fifty years. In the wake of the 1971 constitutional amendment to lower the voting age to 18, many states lowered the minimum legal drinking age; therefore, a legitimate market for beer among youth aged 18 to 20 emerged in many parts of the country during the 1970s. However, in the next decade, federal legislation reduced highway funding for any state with a minimum drinking age below age 21; by 1989, every state had complied with the new law, and many stepped up their efforts to curtail underage drinking. To assess the relationship between alcohol advertising and youth audiences, we might ask how advertising narratives reflected or accommodated the legislative and social movements to restrict adolescent alcohol use since the early 1980s. If advertising narratives are intended to resonate with the anxieties, concerns, and lived realities of targeted consumers, we would expect that beer advertising would in some ways reflect the changing regulatory environment of alcohol use. Hence, our analysis focuses on how changes in advertising narratives reflect changes in the conception of a "youth" market for beer. In a review of fifty years' worth of television beer commercials, we expected changes in the types of individuals pictured in television advertising as well as the appropriate methods and contexts for obtaining, serving, and enjoying beer.

### Analysis Materials: 1950s and 1960s

To obtain samples of television advertising dating back to the 1950s, we relied on several particularly rich online sources. From YouTube, the popular video-sharing site,[2] we used keyword searches such as "beer commercials" to view 137 advertisements posted by users. These included many of the comedic commercials from the early- and mid-2000s, as well as "classic" commercials gleaned by site users from recorded television programming. At a subscription-only site for advertising professionals,[3] we viewed 243 U.S. advertisements including Super Bowl commercials dating back to 1969. The Center on Alcohol Marketing to Youth maintains an online advertising gallery,[4] at which we viewed sixty-one beer ads. Additional ads were found at television nostalgia sites[5] (eighteen ads). Only a few television commercials from the 1960s and early 1970s were found in these searches. Therefore, 175 examples of television commercials from the 1950s and 1960s were drawn from two compilation DVDs: *Vintage TV Beer Commercials* (2003) and *Beer Commercial Mania* (2006). Table 10.1 lists ads viewed by decade.

National prohibition officially ended in 1933, but state and local governments reserved the right to control or prohibit the sale of alcoholic beverages. In 1946, 19.1% of the American population lived in "dry" areas, a figure that dropped to 12.7% by 1960 (Pennock, 2007). Beer advertising of the 1950s and 1960s embraced a strategy of "normalization" in order to combat lingering moral objections to drinking (Packard, 1957; Pennock, 2007). Beginning in the 1940s, the Brewers' Federation launched the "Beer Belongs" ad campaign. Print ads celebrated beer as "America's beverage of moderation," as white couples, young and old, enjoyed beer in domestic settings. Some brands sustained the "beer belongs" theme in television advertising; ads for Budweiser and Miller High Life ("the champagne of bottled beer") depicted beer served to white couples at suburban house parties and with meals at restaurants. The market was not yet dominated by a handful of national brands, and a proliferation of regional brewers, including Hamms in Minnesota, Piels in New York, and Stag in Cincinnati, produced commercials for airing on local stations. The technical standards and motifs of beer ads of the 1950s and 1960s varied widely, relying on a mix of animation and live action.

Today, the Beer Institute guidelines warn that cartoon characters in advertising campaigns have "special attractiveness" to children. In the 1950s and 1960s, beer ads were filled with cartoon characters: Mr. Magoo, the Hamm's Bear, Bert and Harry Piel, animated beer mugs for Oertels, and a variety of animated characters for Genessee, Falstaff, Carling, Blatz, and others. At the time, twenty-six states produced alcohol advertising guidelines limiting

Table 10.1. Ads Viewed by Decade

| Decade | Number of Ads |
|---|---|
| 1950s/1960s | 108 |
| 1970s | 38 |
| 1980s | 116 |
| 1990s | 99 |
| 2000s | 222 |
| *Total* | 583 |

"appeals to children" (Trussell, 1958). However, animation was not as firmly linked to children's entertainment as it would later become. *The Flintstones* was created in 1960 as a prime-time "adult cartoon" and was originally sponsored by Winston cigarettes. Animated ads for all sorts of products became a popular trend in 1961 ("TV cartoonists found in demand," 1960). Perhaps the most pervasive theme of early beer advertising is that beer does, in fact, belong in the home. A 1958 ad for Stag depicts nearsighted Mr. Magoo watching what he thinks is a television (in fact, it is a fish tank). He exclaims, "Another commercial! Time to get myself a Stag Beer!" Similarly, a Blatz ad depicts cartoon animals watching a movie; an intermission title appears, and the camera reveals that a group of adults are watching the scene on television. A voiceover announces, "You have just enough time to go to the kitchen and get Blatz beer for your guests." Miller High Life is included on the buffet table at a suburban house party, advertising for Budweiser's "new" plastic ring six-pack holders places the product in a shopping cart, and couples "make friends with Valley Forge" at a backyard barbecue.

In advertising of the period, a common narrative centered on a "gifting" moment. Hosts give beer to guests, bartenders give beer to customers, women give beer to men, men give beer to each other, and, less frequently, husbands give beer to wives. Bottles of beer (with glasses for pouring in, of course) are constantly changing hands in these ads, reinforcing the link between drinking and sociability. Some ads depicted the exchange of beer in mildly comic situations. A Busch Bavarian ad features a man in pajamas sneaking into the kitchen at night to get beer from the fridge; his wife intercepts him and winkingly pours the beer for herself. In a Schmidt's ad, a man has brought his television outside to watch the game; he speaks into a walkie-talkie and his wife sends him beer in a bucket on a pulley-line. Another features a St. Bernard dog with bottles of Schmidt's in a bucket around his neck bringing sustenance to a man mowing the lawn. Beer is freely given and never in short supply. "Mabel" of the Carling Black Label ads cheerfully serves her many customers, and several ads of the era made reference to drinking multiple beers at a sitting. The taste of Shaefer "doesn't fade after one or two. Even after your thirst is gone, your last beer is as rewarding as your first." Well before the "tastes great/less filling" ads of the early 1970s, Falstaff was touted as "light enough to leave room for more." The Piels jingle urged, "Have a good meal with it. Drink a good deal of it." Budweiser ads encouraged the viewer to "stock up."

An enduring theme established during the 1950s and 1960s was that beer is a reward for accomplishment in leisure time activities. As a Pabst jingle put it, "Well done! Now, have a beer." In a few ads, drinking marks the transition from paid work to leisure, but most of the "reward" ads focused on recreation or unpaid work. A number of ads broadcast during this period depicted beer drinking after (not during) sporting activities requiring a high level of skill and precision, such as golf, archery, or hunting. Red Cap ads of the early 1960s claimed its beer was "as satisfying as a good duck shoot." Beer was offered as a reward for household chores, but it also accompanied temporary breaks. In a Hudepohl ad, a man becomes frustrated while fixing a table; he takes a break with a beer and the jingle explains, "when you've finished the job, or the job's finished you, you deserve a glass of that golden brew." An ad from the late 1960s depicts a young woman rewarding her two male friends with Olympia beer after they help move her things to a top-floor apartment; the camera pulls away to reveal that the sofa on which they are seated remains on a landing halfway up. Although beer is a reward, it is also treated as an incentive.

With respect to their ages, the men in beer commercials of the 1950s and early 1960s were generally middle aged. The "Ale Man" of the Ballantine ads was consistently craggy, as were the men depicted drinking beer alone with sandwiches, in front of televisions, with their wives in taverns or restaurants, or after sports. In an ad for Drewry's, beer is explicitly linked with adult status. Over a scene of two men and two women talking, eating, smoking, and drinking, the narrator states, "These are the people we make Drewry's beer for. Adults. With a taste that's about a million miles away from soda pop....Kind of nice to be an adult, isn't it?" In the world depicted in beer commercials of the era, children and senior citizens do not exist. Parties, barbecues, and restaurants are populated entirely by obviously adult couples, and beer is enjoyed in the context of food and meals as well as by itself. The late-1960s Olympia ad, however, gestured toward a younger market. The men are described as "friends," and it is clear that the young woman is moving into her own apartment. Although the characters are younger, the narrative remains consistent with other ads of the period. Effort expended during leisure time activities is followed by relaxation as beer is handed from friend to friend.

## The 1970s: Miller Time

In July 1971, the 26th Amendment established national suffrage at age 18. Forty-five states lowered their voting age, and twenty-nine states lowered their minimum legal drinking age as well (Wechsler & Sands, 1980). By 1979, less than a third of the United States population lived in states with a legal drinking age of 21 for all alcoholic beverages; almost half of the U.S. population lived in states where teens legally purchased beer at age 18 (Wechsler & Sands, 1980). Although the early 1970s saw the expansion of a legal adolescent market for beer, the commercials broadcast during that decade do not suggest that advertisers focused heavily on youth. While some ads were populated by apparently younger people, and social groups were no longer tightly organized as sets of heterosexual couples, the narratives of the ads did not diverge from earlier decades, nor did ads featuring young people use different narratives from ads featuring seemingly older people.

Men were often the focus of beer ads of the 1960s, but women were also depicted as beer drinkers, albeit with the suggestion that beer was ultimately a man's drink. For example, the Piels "Honest Beer—Brewed for Men" ads included a woman stating that she, too, liked a beer that was "brewed for men." On the face of it, the 1970s hypermasculine "Miller Time" commercials (and Anheuser-Busch's similar "This Bud's for You" campaign) demonstrate a shift of focus away from leisure and onto the male world of paid work. An archetypal "Miller Time" ad from 1976 features construction workers enduring a long and dangerous day on a skyscraper "with nothing to hold on to but the wind and a cold steel beam." After work, they bond and socialize in a warmly lit tavern. Blue collar men working together and drinking together represented a variation on the "beer as reward" theme of prior decades. During this period, the Lite Beer from Miller ads gently lampooned the masculine world of work by featuring retired sports heroes spending their time arguing about beer and, in one 1976 ad featuring football star Rosey Grier, learning needlepoint.

Two industry factors may have contributed to the shift toward themes of masculinity and work. First, the Philip Morris Company, producer of Marlboro cigarettes, purchased Miller Beer in 1970. The ban on broadcast cigarette advertising in 1971 resulted in the Marlboro Man's retirement from television advertising (although cigarette brand exposure continued on TV through sponsored events such as Formula One and Indy Car auto racing; see Chapter 9). However, his image lived on in Western-themed print ads for Miller products and copycat ads for other brands. For example, a Lone Star Beer advertisement aired during the Super Bowl of 1972 looked exactly like a Marlboro commercial: it featured hardworking ranchers rewarded with cold beer after rounding up wild horses. (Schlitz ran a practically identical ad featuring a bison round-up during the 1975 Super Bowl.) Second, disputes between Anheuser-Busch and the Teamsters union caused a highly publicized ninety-day strike in the spring of 1976; Miller's tributes to the working man might have capitalized on its rival's problems with organized labor. The Miller ad campaigns of the 1970s established a pattern successfully copied by Anheuser-Busch in the next decade and beyond: advertising for the flagship brand gestured toward traditional values while advertising for the light brand provided irreverent comedy (Dawson, 2001; Van Munching, 1997).

The ads of the 1950s and early 1960s depicted the sociable transfer of beer from one individual to another. Through the 1970s, beer also served as an emblem of inclusion of an individual into a larger group. A 1975 Schlitz ad featured off-duty firemen playing competitive games at a sunny outdoor picnic; a narrator explains that firemen fight fires at work, but at play they fight each other. However, the "fight" is clearly in fun and after the contest a keg is tapped and pitchers of beer are passed through the crowd. At one point, the camera focuses on a young woman spectator holding a toddler on her hip. The inclusion of the woman and her child normalizes beer drinking as part of wholesome family fun, and the passing of beer from hand to hand symbolizes group togetherness.

Some ads continued to emphasize individual accomplishment at sports (skiing for Budweiser in 1975, hang-gliding for Genessee in 1979), but ads of the 1970s also focused on competition in team sports. In a Schlitz ad with the "You Know It!" tagline, beer represents reconciliation as well as reward after leisure time competition. A young man makes a touchdown in a casual game of football but continues to run, chased by his friends. They eventually reach a bar and order beer, and the competition is over. In a 1976 Hamm's ad, Grizzly Adams, a character from a popular 1974 wilderness film, happens across a pickup basketball game played by three young men at a lodge in the woods. He takes the ball and misses the shot, but stays to share a beer. Aside from Adams himself, the characters in these ads appear to be in their late teens or early twenties. The notion that sharing a beer resolves the tensions of competition also characterizes ads of the period featuring older groups. For example, adult men play touch football in a Schlitz ad from 1979 ("Beer Makes it Good") and reward their balding running back with a friendly rub on the head and a mug of beer.

Not all of the ads from this period depict groups in work and sports. For example, Löwenbräu ads aimed at a more upscale market ("Here's to good friends, tonight is kinda special") echoed the 1960s theme of adult couples enjoying leisure time together. Two commercials in the series depict several couples in a vacation setting—one takes place on the ski slopes (1979), the other on a beach (1981). In each, the group realizes that one of their friends is missing. They worry briefly, but are relieved and pleasantly surprised when the friend reappears, offering Löwenbräu. They are happy to have the beer, but they are more relieved to have found their friend; in the 1979 ad, as they sit by the fire enjoying beer, one man confesses, "For a minute there, you really had us worried." His friend replies sincerely, "I know. Thanks." The commercial goes out of its way to avoid implying that the beer is the reason the couples are happy to see their friend. Sharing a beer means group membership, but beer is not the price of admission to the group.

During the 1970s, brewing was an increasingly successful and lucrative industry. As the demographic bulge of the baby boom came of age and the minimum legal drinking age dropped, each year of the 1970s saw an increase in per-capita beer consumption (see Figure 10.2). From today's perspective, we might expect to see advertisers change their advertising techniques in order to appeal to an emerging teen market for beer in the 1970s. However, aside from the fact that animation was no longer used, the characters and themes depicted in television commercials of the 1970s did not represent a distinct departure from the ads of the 1950s and 1960s. Two possible factors explain the relative stasis in beer advertising themes: first, in the 1970s, television broadcasting was dominated by the "big three" television networks: ABC, CBS, and NBC. Advertising appealed to a general audience of all ages, for whom youth culture was recognizable but not necessarily relevant. Until the proliferation of cable stations and the increased sensitivity of ratings measures, a narrow focus on certain demographic groups did not typify advertising (Turow, 1997). A second explanation for the lack of distinctly youth-oriented narratives in advertising of the 1970s is the fact that the industry was doing well, with production and sales increasing yearly. Although this statement is certainly debatable, we would suggest that heavy advertising was not a priority: beer was a product that sold itself. In the next decade, the regulatory environment for alcoholic beverages tightened significantly, and the brewing industry's boom years came to an end (Figure 10.2).

## The 1980s: Beer as Achievement

The 1980s witnessed a series of transitions in the advertising and marketing of alcoholic beverages. The decade began with beer consumption at an all-time high (National Institute on Alcohol Abuse and Alcoholism, 2007), but by 1987 beer sales had fallen 7%, wine sales fell 14%, and sales of distilled spirits dropped 23%. One advertising executive blamed the new temperance on "tougher laws, public advertising campaigns, and peer pressure" (Pennock, 2007, p. 194). The legitimate teen market for beer evaporated. By 1984, the organization Mothers Against Drunk Driving (MADD) had risen to national prominence and helped push through a federal law mandating a uniform minimum drinking age of 21 for all states. Finally, the baby boom was beginning to age out of the primary drinking demographic. The era was marked by consolidation of the market, with a few powerful brewers (Anheuser-Busch and Miller) buying up smaller regional brewers and competing directly with one another for a shrinking national market. Beer consumption fell between 1981 and 1989, but alcohol advertising increased by more than 40% (Egan, 1990). Rather than viewing drinking as an outcome of advertising, we would reverse the causal arrow and note that weak sales prompted more vigorous attempts by brewers to increase and secure their brands' share of a dwindling market. In tracking advertising strategies of the

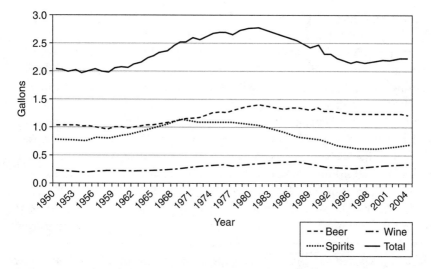

Figure 10.2. Annual per-capita consumption of beer, wine, and spirits from 1950 to 2004. Estimates based on ages 15+ prior to 1970; 14+ thereafter. (*Source*: Adapted with permission from "Alcohol Epidemiologic Data System," by T. M. Nephew, H. Yi, G. D. Williams, F. S. Stinson, and M. C. Dufour, U.S. *Alcohol Epidemiologic Data Reference Manual*, Vol. 1, 4th ed., *U.S. Apparent Consumption of Alcoholic Beverages Based on State Sales, Taxation, or Receipt Data*. Washington, DC: NIAAA. NIH Publication No. 04-5563 [June 2004]).

1980s, what can we learn about the new cultural contexts for drinking in television beer advertising?

Advertising during the first half of the decade looked much like advertising of the 1970s. Miller continued to run "Miller Time" and "Tastes Great / Less Filling" ads featuring blue collar workers and retired sports celebrities, while Anheuser-Busch ran "This Bud's for You" and tried various approaches for Bud Light. Blatz and Schlitz both mimicked the "Pepsi Challenge" approach during the 1981 Super Bowl, asking blind taste testers to choose a product over its rival (industry advertising standards prohibited the literal depiction of drinking, so the subjects tasted the product off screen). Ads played on tensions between upscale striving (Heineken's 1981 "Someday soon you may have the best of everything") and the back-to-basics lifestyle (Genessee's 1982 ads emphasized nature and a simple approach to work and leisure). Screen star Mark Harmon appeared in product-centered ads for Coors, explaining the unique qualities of the Coors brewing process. However, over the second half of the decade, the messages changed. In 1989 the Surgeon General accused alcohol advertisers of deliberately targeting underage drinkers and supported congressional attempts to ban beer advertising (Hilts, 1991; Koop, 1989; Van Munching, 1997). On one hand, the changes reflected a more general shift in advertising techniques from a focus on product characteristics to the depiction of user lifestyles. However, beer advertising of the late 1980s also employed narratives about alcohol use and alcohol users that departed from earlier approaches and came to dominate beer advertising through the 1990s and into the present day.

During the 1960s and 1970s, beer marked the boundary between work and leisure. During the mid-1980s, as part of their "This Bud's for You" campaign, Budweiser ads began to address the boundary between inexperience and adulthood. Postman et al. (1987) analyzed an ad in which a young construction worker struggles to prove himself on the job; at the end of the day he is validated as a peer of the more experienced workers when the foreman gives him a beer. Several other Budweiser ads employed this narrative during the mid-1980s: in one, a young man takes over his father's silk-screening business; the customers are skeptical but the young man does well, and his success is affirmed when his father gives him a beer. In another, a young saxophone player goes from audition to audition. He finally lands a gig at a nightclub, and the bar owner rewards him with a mug of beer. These ads resonate with the "job-well-done" theme of the "Miller Time" approach but with the additional narrative element of beer symbolizing the initiation of a novice into the adult world of work.

In the 1970s, beer functioned as a reward, but it also served to reaffirm friendship by resolving the tensions of friendly competition. Over the course of the 1980s, we see a subtle change in the framing of beer as a reward. In a 1981 ad, men play touch football, having established that the winners get Michelob Light. Over a montage of energetic play, a narrator asks, "Would a bunch of guys go at it this hard just for a beer? Well, consider it's Michelob Light." In the end, one man remarks, "You never played like that before," and the other replies, "We never played for a Michelob Light before." The ad depicts all the elements of earlier beer-as-reward scenarios, but with a key difference: the ad implies (albeit unrealistically) that the losers will not get Michelob Light. In contrast to the ads of the 1950s and 1960s, in which beer is bountiful and freely given, beer in this ad from the 1980s is explicitly framed as something that must be earned. An emphasis on winning in individual sports also informs Stroh's ads from 1983 and 1984; in one, "Steady Eddie" Barnes becomes "the best darts player in the county"; in another, Eddie Hatcher wins at poker with four queens. Each ends with the jingle, "Looks like a Stroh Light night!" Unlike the Michelob campaign, the Stroh's ads do not suggest that beer is the reason for competition; however, the ads emphasize the link between success and beer while downplaying the prior decade's emphasis on reconciliation.

This shift in the presentation of beer as a reward is significant in light of another development in beer commercial narratives. During the latter half of the 1980s, satirical ads began suggesting that obtaining beer was not just a reward, it was an accomplishment in itself. In 1985, Anheuser-Busch launched the "Gimme a Light" series. Bar patrons requested "a Light," were handed something flammable, then specified "*Bud* Light" in order to get a beer. Postman et al. (1987) characterized Bud Light's general approach as "upscale initiation," and noted the emphasis on bar etiquette—one must know how to order properly. A 1987 Super Bowl spot for Bud Light, "Thomas Edison," continues the "Gimme a Light" narrative while echoing the initiation theme of "This Bud's for You." Edison presents his new invention, the electric lamp, to an older man and seeks his approval. The older man sighs, "That's very nice, Thomas, but I wanted a *Bud* Light." Thomas had apparently misinterpreted the old man's request for "a Light," as in earlier "Gimme a Light" ads, but the ad also parodies the themes of accomplishment, reward, and initiation of the "This Bud's for You" series. In short, the premier American inventor is told that beer is more desirable than the electric light. Behind the humorous exaggeration of Thomas's failure is an exaggeration of the importance of beer. For adolescent drinkers in the late 1980s, providing beer had become an achievement that peers would appreciate. This theme would inform several ad campaigns over the next two decades.

Another idea that would prove highly fertile to advertisers in the 1990s found its roots in ads of the 1980s. A 1986 Super Bowl ad starred sportscasters and former athletes Bob Uecker and Tommy Heinsohn as "famous comet watchers." Bob, sitting on a hillside at night, is joined by Tommy, who remarks, "You've been up here three weeks waiting for Haley's comet!" Bob says he's already celebrating with Miller Lite, because he doesn't want to get "filled up" and miss it. Tommy requests a beer, but when Bob leans down to get it out of the cooler, the comet suddenly flashes by. Tommy makes a hasty exit, and Bob continues to eagerly watch the skies. The ad fits neatly into the Lite beer advertising tradition, with retired athletes poking fun at themselves. However, it adds a twist: Bob misses the comet because he is engaged in the act of getting beer. One interpretation suggests a negative view of beer consumption: reaching for beer causes you to miss out. However, in the 1990s, this notion would evolve into the idea that obtaining beer requires certain sacrifices. Bob and Tommy are clearly adult characters; however, we would argue that the narrative of the ad resonates with the new social constraints on underage drinking. Getting beer had become riskier and more difficult. The point was made mildly in "Comet Watchers" but became more pronounced as the next decade came to a close.

## Beer, Animals, and the MTV Lifestyle

In early 1987, Anheuser-Busch introduced Spuds MacKenzie, a beer-loving, high-living bull terrier, to promote Bud Light. Spuds was credited with increasing Bud Light sales by 20% ("Media business: Ads in which animals speak better than humans," 1989). Critics have catalogued the youth-oriented facets of the campaign, particularly product tie-ins including toys, T-shirts, and posters. Spuds's extravagant lifestyle, his bevy of young female groupies, and his music-video milieu all suggested a deliberate bid for the attention of the young. Surgeon General C. Everett Koop argued that the ads "tell youth that alcohol consumption leads to athletic, social, and sexual success" (Koop, 1989), and Senator Strom Thurmond displayed a Spuds doll on the Senate floor to garner support for a bill banning alcohol advertising (Hilts, 1991; Van Munching, 1997). Spuds eventually retired, but the use of animal mascots for beer advertising, as well as many other products, continued in the following decades. From a narrative perspective, we focus not only on the presence of the animals, but on the role they play within the story of the ad. Just as adult characters can populate narratives that resonate with adolescent experience, beginning in the late 1980s animal characters increasingly articulated the plight of the underage drinker. A new advertising theme emerged: the notion that an animal, a creature whose access to alcohol is blocked by a number of significant barriers, would be motivated to obtain beer. This shift is illustrated in a 1988 ad for Stroh's Light. "Alex," a golden retriever owned by a regular guy living in a suburban house, buries beer (plus an entire beer truck) in the neighbor's yard. It is possible that Alex, as man's best friend, is hoarding the beer for his master; nevertheless, Alex's ability to recognize the importance of the product is the point of the ad. Over the course of the 1990s, beer advertising made liberal use of the comic fiction of animals getting beer.

## 1990s: Risk, Achievement, and Parody

In the 1990s, satirical treatments of earlier beer advertising themes became a common advertising trope. Mid-1980s ads for Old Milwaukee depicted groups of middle-aged male friends on wilderness trips together. Each ad ended with friends sharing a beer after a day of strenuous activity and concluding, "It doesn't get any better than this." A 1991 Old Milwaukee commercial begins in the traditional manner: a group of male friends are fly fishing. One announces, "It doesn't get any better than this." Suddenly, the Swedish Bikini Team arrives, and the ensuing party demonstrates that it does, indeed, get better, if you're surrounded by hot blondes and beer. The ad plays on the viewer's memories of the earlier ads while employing two common themes of the 1990s. First, beer not only enhances leisure, it prompts a fantasy transformation of the environment itself. Second, sexually stereotyped young women are an essential part of that new environment. Coors Extra ran a similar ad during the 1990 Super Bowl. A man celebrates his birthday in a bar with male friends; before blowing out the candles he announces "Special birthday tips from Extra Gold." The first is to have plenty of Coors on hand. As for the second tip: "When you make a wish, make it a *wish!*" He blows out the candles and four bikini-clad women magically appear, cooing "Happy Birthday, Tom!" The ad ends as Tom flees the advances of one of his male friends, also stripped to his briefs as a result of the "wish." In the Old Milwaukee ad and, more blatantly, in the Coors ad, the narrative of male bonding is invoked only to be satirically overridden by the notion that the real goal of socializing is fantasy-fueled partying. In keeping with this approach, a Budweiser campaign of the mid-1990s spoofed the father–son bonding of the "initiation" ads of the 1980s; a schlub in his thirties "bonds" with various older men (including, in 1996, Charlton Heston). The older men see through his sentimental act and shrewdly reply, "You're not getting my Bud Light." Echoing the new emphasis on the rarity of beer, the series suggested that instead of viewing drinking as a means for facilitating friendship among men, male bonding is just a pretext for obtaining beer.

A satirical notion that beer is more important than other basic needs played itself out in a variety of contexts through the late 1990s. The point subtly made in the 1986 comet watchers ad is brought more clearly into focus in the 1990s: obtaining beer is difficult, but is worth the sacrifices one might make to get it. A 1998 Coors ad features two young men driving in a hot dusty desert. At the gas station they face a dilemma; they have only a few dollars and must choose between gas and beer. The ad ends with the two pushing their jeep through the desert, carrying a six-pack of Coors. In 1999 ads, young men at the grocer's checkout choose Bud Light over toilet paper, a coach trades his star player for a case of Michelob Light, and an elderly man chooses Miller Lite over romance with an elderly woman. A certain amount of physical risk may be necessary to obtain beer. In a 1997 ad, the McKenzie Brothers, a pair of Canadian comics, leap from a plane in pursuit of a falling bottle of Molson Ice. In another 1997 ad, a caveman is struck by falling Budweiser beer bottles; excited by his discovery, he continues to eagerly watch the sky and is knocked unconscious by a falling keg.

Getting beer may also require ingenuity: For example, a young man trains a mouse to scare a pretty girl (and her six-pack of Bud Light) into the safety of his apartment in 1999. Once obtained, beer is protected and cherished. In a 1998 Heineken ad, a man patiently waits for the very last drop of beer to fall from bottle to glass as romantic lyrics profess, "My devotion is deep as the ocean." Another Heineken ad, "Mood Swing," turns a sports fan's elation at a touchdown to abject sorrow when he accidentally spills his beer. Because of its value, beer must be protected: in a 1998 ad, a young man installs a false front in his fridge in order to hide Bud Light from his roommate. A 1999 Rolling Rock ad features a man explaining why he will not share his beer. Finally, because beer is so precious, other people's desire for beer can be used to one's advantage. A salesman sells a client a fake photocopier because it seems to turn one beer into many (an assistant is revealed pushing Bud Light through the slot). A lobster escapes a pot by holding a bottle of beer hostage against attacks by kitchen staff ("He's got a Budweiser!"). A scrappy dog wins Best in Show when the judge sees a twelve-pack in his kennel.

In the 1990s, humans were not the only creatures willing to go to great lengths to obtain beer. In ads for a number of Anheuser-Busch products, animals conspire to steal it from humans. In a 1995 ad, a couple drives through a safari game preserve. Chimps jump on the vehicle; the people are distracted by their antics while a second team of chimps steals Bud Light from the back of the jeep. In 1996, a series of horror movie spoofs featured penguins attempting to frighten people away from their Bud Ice. In another 1996 ad, vultures snatch the last Bud Light from a man lost in the desert. The man mumbles, "They'll never get it open," but the final shot reveals the bird's beak holding the bottle cap. Humans take risks and make sacrifices to get beer, and so do animals. In 1997, a chicken "crosses the road" to get to a bar, and an absurdist ad set in a power plant reveals that the entire city's power is generated from a hamster running on an exercise wheel, lured by the sight of a bottle of Budweiser. Miller employed beer-seeking animals in two ads from the 1998 "Dick" series. One features an "Evil Beaver" terrorizing settlers and stealing their beer. The other depicts a steer informing a rancher of an upcoming stampede in exchange for payment in cases of Miller Lite. Aliens from outer space also enjoy beer: In a 1997 ad, a spaceship beams up an entire Budweiser delivery truck. Several years later, aliens would use bottles of beer as "bait" for catching humans.

Computer-generated animation enhanced the visual sophistication of animal-themed commercials during the 1990s and the Budweiser Frogs series, which was launched in 1995, exemplified technical as well as social changes in beer advertising. Like Spuds MacKenzie, the frogs were criticized for their appeal to children (Collins et al., 2005; Hays, 1999). Viewed in its entirety, the series of ads illustrates more than an instance of advertisers using animals to catch children's attention. The first ad featured three frogs in a nighttime swamp, randomly croaking syllables until all three come together to say "Budweiser." As an amusing vignette, it functioned more like a sponsored piece of entertainment than an attempt to sell product. In 1996, a new Super Bowl ad features the frogs in winter. The frogs have trouble croaking out "Budweiser" because their tongues are frozen to a can of beer. Presumably, like the animals described above, the frogs were attracted to beer and tried to obtain it. The next year, Anheuser-Busch introduced two lizard characters (Louie and Frank) and ran ads serializing the story of one lizard's failed attempts to usurp the frogs' role as Budweiser mascot. The popularity of the series, and Anheuser-Busch's own enthusiasm for it, helps explain an ad campaign of the next decade featuring various animals aspiring to be part of the Clydesdale wagon team. For example, a 2006 Super Bowl ad depicted a young Clydesdale colt attempting to pull the Budweiser wagon and succeeding with the help of the older horses. The ads promote the brand, but the product itself is rarely if ever shown. In a study of reception of television advertising by children aged 9 to 15, Waiters, Treno, and Grube (2001) found that younger children disliked beer ads that focused on the product itself. In arguing that they do not "sell" to children, brewers tell the truth, albeit disingenuously. These ads do not urge the viewer to get a beer right now; rather, they invest in brand loyalty, with the expectation that children, like the young colt, will aspire to someday identify themselves with the prestige of the Budweiser label.

## 2000s: Kill Your Good Friends

In a review of the 2007 Super Bowl ads, a *New York Times* columnist joked that "here's to good friends" had morphed into "kill your good friends" in the new black comedy of beer advertising (Salkin, 2007). In fact, the 2007 ads embodied an advertising trend begun in ads of the 1950s and accelerated and intensified through the late 1990s to the present. We see its basis in early television ads representing beer as a reward for accomplishment and a catalyst for friendship. However, the tone and implications of beer advertising changed in two distinct ways. First, advertising reflected a growing sense that beer was not a given, natural part of everyday life. Stiffened constraints on legal purchase made beer rare and difficult to get for the underage drinking population. When the men in the 1979 "Schlitz makes it great" ads enjoy a beer after touch football, they are reaffirming friendship after tough competition. On the other hand, when the men in 1980s Michelob commercials compete for a beer, the ad implies that the men "go at it this hard" because the beer itself is valuable. Getting the beer, not preserving the friendship, is the primary goal in these ads. Second, as the "I love you, man" series illustrates, a view of beer as a precious, hard-to-get substance lends itself to a variety of satirical narratives in which individuals will sacrifice any number of goods, including their dignity, to get it.

In the years following the World Trade Center attack of September 11, 2001, Anheuser-Busch had come to dominate Super Bowl advertising and sponsorship, and Bud Light ads broadcast during the game most clearly exemplified the "beer as precious" approach with advertising depicting human, animal, and alien creatures overcoming barriers to getting or keeping beer. However, during the same period, ads for the flagship Budweiser brand became increasingly serious, patriotic, and elegiac. During the 2002 Super Bowl, roughly four months after 9/11, the Clydesdales took a sober journey through the snow to kneel before the ruins of the Twin Towers, and an ad playing tribute to the "Five Generations" of the Busch family pledged to sustain their tradition of quality. In 2005, a sentimental "Tribute to the Troops" depicted the arrival home of weary soldiers whose walk through the airport generates grateful applause. A small number of ads on the topics of underage drinking, moderation, and drunk driving also appeared (Center on Alcohol Marketing and Youth, 2007a). The branding approach typified by the "frogs," "horse football," and "Clydesdales" series also continued to characterize the Anheuser-Busch approach. Nevertheless, the dominant theme in advertising has been the "beer is precious" narrative featured during the first half of this decade.

A 2004 Heineken ad demonstrates the importance of having lots of beer on hand; a young man asks for salsa and his roommate tells him it's "behind the Heineken." We see the entire fridge and every cabinet loaded with the product. The humor comes from exaggeration; however, the image suggests that beer is not just being stocked; it is being hoarded at the expense of food. The hoarding theme is expanded in a number of satirical ads in which young men guard against theft of their beer. In a 2004 ad, a young woman asks her date whether he feels comfortable leaving Rusty at home alone. A shot of the apartment reveals that Rusty is a young man wearing an electric shock collar to dissuade him from stealing his roommate's Bud Light from the fridge. Regardless, his desire for Bud Light overrides the pain of being shocked. A 2005 ad depicts an office worker installing a beer cam so he can keep an eye on his refrigerator during work; his roommates rig the cam and throw a party anyway. Beer might also be guarded by animals. An ad from 2000 features a young woman whose "cat" gets jealous when other people drink her Bud Light; her beer-filching date discovers, to his dismay, that the cat is actually a tiger. In 2005 a young man a trains a Brazilian fighting cockatoo to protect his Bud Light; in 2007 another uses Walter the attack squirrel. Outside of theft, beer is at risk of loss in other ways. In a 2006 ad, a young man installs rubber floors to protect falling bottles from breaking. Hiding beer, as with the false front refrigerator ad from the 1990s, is also an option. The tactic backfires in a 2006 ad in which young men install a fridge that rolls into the wall to hide itself and the beer. Ironically, the fridge appears in the next apartment, where other young men hail the "magic fridge" and raid it.

Another set of ads from the first half of this decade features individuals making extra efforts and sacrifices to get access to beer. In a 2005 Heineken ad, superheroes mock a regular-guy aspirant. He then demonstrates his "special power," and his ability to transform everyday objects into bottles of beer wins him instant acceptance in the group. People will go to particular lengths to get Bud Light: in one ad, men use tools to cut a hole through their own apartment wall to gain access to the Bud Light in a neighbor's refrigerator. In another, a man thrusts his hand holding a six-pack into a closing elevator door to hold it; the people in the elevator keep him trapped and mercilessly take his beer. A worker hides bottles of beer around the workplace to "raise morale"; employees ransack and destroy their offices to find it. Men climb on top of their houses, on the pretense of fixing the roof, in order to drink beer. In a 2006 Miller ad, a man rigs his television with an extremely long extension cord so that he can walk all the way to the store for more beer without missing any of the game. Animals can also help procure beer. In a 2002 Bud Light ad, a falcon swoops down from his master's high-rise apartment to snatch beers from tables in sidewalk cafes. In 2004 a scruffy dog bites his owner's rival, forcing him to give up his beer.

The sacrifices made for the sake of beer characterize a number of advertising narratives. A person might sacrifice safety to get access to beer. A 2007 ad depicts a young man stopping his car to pick up a hitchhiker. "But he has an axe!" protests his horrified girlfriend. "But he has Bud Light!" argues the young man. Beer lovers will sacrifice their dignity; dressed in ridiculous disco outfits, two young men attend "70s Night" because of the free beer; on arrival they learn that it's actually a night for people in their seventies, but they stay anyway, because of the beer. In a 2006 ad, a young man kneeling to retrieve his fallen beer from under the sofa is mounted by his dog just as his mother-in-law walks into the room. In 2004, Cedric the Entertainer accidentally strays into the bikini wax room when he is distracted by a fridge full of Bud Light at a spa. Finally, in the quest for beer, one might also sacrifice friends: In a 2007 ad for Bud Light, two young men agree to compete for the last beer using the childhood game "rock, paper, scissors;" one throws a real rock at his rival's head and steps over the fallen body to take the last beer.

Within the "beer is precious" narrative, jokes about the relative importance of beer and women are common. A 2006 Coors ad introducing the new cooler box depicts young men at a wedding who bring their own beer; they need ice, so they chop the head off an ice sculpture of the bride. A 2004 Sam Adams ad depicts a young man at a house party invited into a bedroom by a pretty young woman; partygoers raise eyebrows at the excited whooping that ensues, but the real source of the young man's ecstasy is a Sam Adams Light. In a 2006 Bud Light ad, a young man brings a date on a romantic sleigh ride at night; he leans down to get beer from the cooler and the horse's attack of gas turns a candle into a blowtorch and scorches the woman. In contrast to the narrative of the comet watchers, in which retrieving a beer caused hardship, getting the beer saves the young man from a fiery fart. In another Bud Light ad, a man is not interested in his female partner in her black teddy, but when she offers him a Bud Light, he lunges into the bedroom and slips on the satin sheets. He loses his dignity and compromises his safety but at least he gets the beer. According to Messner and de Oca (2005), these ads play on the notion that women may bring disappointment, but beer always satisfies.

From these descriptions, it would seem that ads following the "beer is precious" narrative would violate the Beer Institute's code of advertising standards, with its admonitions against portraying illegal and risky activities. However, the code allows "strategic ambiguity" (Zwarun & Farrar, 2005), creating opportunities for suggestion rather than assertion. Item 2(d) in the Beer Institute's list of guidelines states, "Beer advertising and marketing materials should not portray or imply illegal activity of any kind by an individual prior to, during, or after the individual consumes, purchases, or is served beer, *unless the portrayal or implication of illegal activity is a basic element or feature of a parody or spoof and is readily identifiable as such*" (2006, p. 2, emphasis added). Depicting hoarding also violates the code, but the presence of parody redeems it. Comedy and the use of animals as protagonists allow advertisers to push the envelope on the question of what constitutes the portrayal or implication of risky or illegal activity. Everyone knows that vultures and monkeys don't *really* drink beer, and that young men's efforts to "protect" their beer in TV commercials are ridiculously over the top. Our point is not necessarily that the beer industry is promoting theft. Rather, we would argue that all of the ads discussed in this section resonate with the notion that beer is a valuable and limited substance, and that one must be willing to take risks and, sometimes, break the law to get it. Getting (or keeping) the beer is the dominant plotline of these ads, just as overcoming legal barriers to beer is a typical challenge for teenage drinkers.

## CONCLUSION: OVERCOMING BARRIERS TO BEER

Looking back fifty years, the most noteworthy change in the content of alcohol advertising is the depiction of beer as a precious, valuable, and rare substance for which one should be willing to commit any number of outrageous acts. Although this theme appears in comic or farcical contexts, the fact that it is almost completely absent from advertising prior to 1985 links the trend with attempts to curb teen risk behaviors over the course of the 1980s. The movement to limit the social costs of alcohol abuse began with organized anti–drunk driving campaigns of the late 1970s and culminated with the 1984 federal highway funding legislation. Coupled with increased enforcement of minimum purchase age laws through sting operations and the institution of civil liability suits (dram shop laws), these efforts were successful in creating a substantial set of barriers to underage drinking. Setting aside the question of whether these events measurably affected the societal costs of adolescent and problem drinking, the fact remains that, generally speaking, in the mid-1970s adolescents experienced far fewer legal and social barriers to obtaining beer than those of the same age group would come to know by 1990. The culture of drinking changed, and the cultural narratives of alcohol advertising changed as well.

The industry insists that marketing efforts are not directed at underage drinkers. This statement is hard to falsify. However, there is ample evidence that market dominance of a few established national brands coupled with a yearly decrease in new nonloyal drinkers resulted in fiercer competition for the attention and loyalties of the young. The advertising resulting from this competition demonstrates the following paradox. Research has shown that underage drinking is common, with binge drinking constituting a serious public health problem. The trends in Figure 10.3, taken from the Monitoring the Future surveys, indicate that use of all kinds of alcohol is common by at least the tenth grade (ages 15 and 16). Clearly, adolescents have access to alcohol. However, the "beer is precious" narrative of so many recent beer advertisements suggests that the notion of needing to overcome barriers to obtain the product must be deeply resonant not only for the individuals who develop the ads, but for the audience groups with whom they pretest prior to airing. In fact, these themes would probably appeal to adults of drinking age, for they reflect the reality that many individuals experience illegal use of alcohol long before reaching age 21. For those of us who came of age after 1984, the drama of the underage quest for beer is a memorable aspect of adolescence. The notion that beer is precious, hard to get, worth defending, and constantly in threat of being taken away is an artifact of adolescent drinking culture, just as "rock, paper, scissors" resonates with early adolescent game culture. The frequent use of animal characters, some with cartoonlike qualities, also suggests that beer advertising aims to reach viewers below the legal drinking age (Kilbourne, 1999). By using narratives and themes that speak to adolescent drinking experiences, alcohol marketing co-opts, subverts, and ultimately benefits from efforts to reduce the harmful impact of underage alcohol use.

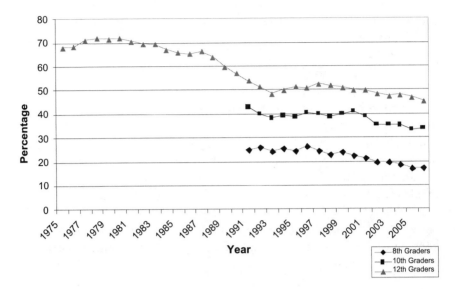

Figure 10.3. Trends in past thirty-day use of alcohol from 1975 to 2006 among eighth, tenth, and twelfth grade students. (*Source*: Monitoring the Future Survey, the University of Michigan, available at http://www.monitoringthefuture.org) Data not collected for eighth and tenth graders until 1991.

## Other Advertising for Alcohol

We have focused entirely on television beer advertising to permit an historical analysis. However, there is considerable advertising on radio for beer products. Indeed, a recent analysis by the Center on Alcohol Marketing and Youth (2007b) found that a large proportion of radio ads (36%) for alcohol (mostly beer) were placed during periods when youth under the legal drinking age were more likely to be listening than adults. A new form of alcoholic beverage, flavored alcoholic drinks (also known as alcopops), have also been introduced in recent years. These products use sweeteners to virtually hide the taste of alcohol and are often branded with distilled-spirits labels (e.g., Smirnoff Ice). A survey by the Center for Science in the Public Interest (2001) found that 51% of adolescents ages 17 to 18 (and 35% of 14- to 16-year-olds) had tried these drinks while only 24% of adults had done so. Adolescents were much more likely to recall alcopop brands than adults, and girls were more likely to express a preference for these products than boys. Subsequent surveys of magazine advertising for alcoholic beverages found that female adolescents were exposed to over twice as much advertising for alcopops in 2002 as in 2001. This amounted to as much advertising as for the claimed target of these ads, women between the ages of 21 and 34 (Jernigan, Ostroff, Ross, & O'Hara, 2004). A survey sponsored by the

American Medical Association (2004) found that adolescents were exposed to advertising for alcopops to a greater degree on television than on radio or magazines. All of these findings support to the conclusion that this new form of beverage is being marketed to entice female adolescents into the alcohol habit (Kilbourne, 1999). The findings also suggest that advertising for alcoholic drinks is reaching youth at a high rate.

Policy Implications

Does alcohol advertising influence underage drinking? Although research suggests a relationship between exposure to advertising and underage drinking, the difficulty of proving causality in a complex media environment hampers the ability of researchers to reach definitive conclusions (Hastings, Anderson, Cooke, & Gordon, 2005). However, given the heavy exposure to alcohol advertising in the media, it is likely that youth are at least prompted to try alcoholic beverages, and the rapid rise in popularity of alcopops, especially in adolescent girls, strongly suggests that awareness of these products has been aided by advertising. Aside from these direct effects on youth, advertising practices play a role in shaping the larger cultural context for alcohol use and abuse (Gerbner, 1995), and further research into the relationship between advertising and problem drinking is needed to assess the potentially harmful effects of youth overexposure to alcohol advertising.

In response to accusations that they target youth, the alcohol industry argues that it would make bad business sense to pitch product to audiences who can't legally purchase it (Rich, 1997; "TV beer ads defended," 1956). In turn, media scholars and advertising practitioners argue that youth are valuable targets for building brand loyalty for many products (La Ferle, et al., 2001; Wright-Isak, Faber, & Horner, 1997; Zollo, 1999). Although Beer Institute marketing guidelines prohibit advertising on programs for whom young viewers exceed 30% of the total viewing audience, research has shown that, compared to viewers over age 21, youth are disproportionately exposed (that is, overexposed) to television (Center on Alcohol Marketing and Youth, 2006) and radio alcohol advertising (Center on Alcohol Marketing and Youth, 2007b). Research has suggested that a limit of 15% would more accurately reflect the proportion of children aged 12 to 20 in the population (Jernigan, Ostroff, & Ross, 2006).

Our analysis suggests that beer advertising relies on narratives that resonate with adolescent drinking culture. Hence, it is not surprising that such advertising would find a receptive audience among youth under the age of 21. One application of our findings toward understanding the link between media effects and underage drinking would be in the area of alcohol expectancies. Adolescents' beliefs about their own eventual alcohol use have been assessed as mediating factors between advertising exposure and alcohol use (Christiansen, Smith, Roehling, & Goldman, 1989; Fleming, Thorson, & Atkin, 2004; Smith, Goldman, Greenbaum, & Christiansen, 1995). If researchers have a clearer sense of how advertisers depict the process of getting and keeping beer, the links between beliefs about the role of alcohol in adolescent culture and the thematic portrayals of alcohol use in television advertising can be more subtly drawn, and a more persuasive case for the reduction of youth overexposure to alcohol advertising might be made.

## NOTES

1. See http://www.beersoaksamerica.org/ads.htm
2. See http://www.youtube.com
3. See http://commercial-archive.com
4. See http://camy.org
5. See, for example, http://advertisementave.com and http://tvparty.com

## REFERENCES

Aitken, P. P. (1989). Television alcohol commercials and under-age drinking. *International Journal of Advertising, 8,* 133–150.

Aitken, P. P., Leathar, D. S., & C., S. A. (1988). Ten- to sixteen-year-olds' perceptions of advertisements for alcoholic drinks. *Alcohol and Alcoholism, 23,* 491–500.

American Medical Association. (2004). *Girlie drinks: Women's diseases.* Retrieved from http://www.alcoholpolicyMD.com

American Medical Association. (2007). *Policy position on alcohol availability, promotion, taxation, and labeling.* Retrieved June 14, 2007, from http://www.ama-assn.org/ama/pub/category/3342.html

Atkin, C. K., & Block, M. (1984). The effects of alcohol advertising. *Advances in Consumer Research, 11,* 688–693.

Austin, E. W., & Hurst, S. J. T. (2005). Targeting adolescents? The content and frequency of alcoholic and nonalcoholic beverage ads in magazine and video formats November 1999–April 2000. *Journal of Health Communication, 10,* 769–785.

Austin, E. W., & Knaus, C. (2000). Predicting the potential for risky behavior among those "too young" to drink as a result of appealing advertising. *Journal of Health Communication, 5,* 13–27.

Austin, E. W., & Meili, H. K. (1994). Effects of interpretations of televised alcohol portrayals on children's alcohol beliefs. *Journal of Broadcasting & Electronic Media, 38,* 417–435.

*Beer Commercial Mania.* (2006). [DVD]. Retro Video Festival.

Beer Institute. (2006). *Advertising and marketing code.* Washington, DC: Beer Institute.

Bonnie, R. J., & O'Connell, M. E. (2004). *Reducing underage drinking: A collective responsibility.* Washington, DC: National Academies Press.

Bonomo, Y. A., Bowes, G., Coffey, C., Carlin, J. B., & Patton, G. C. (2004). Teenage drinking and the onset of alcohol dependence: A cohort study over seven years. *Addiction, 99,* 1520–1528.

Bush, A. J., & Bush, V. D. (1994). The narrative paradigm as a perspective for improving ethical evaluations of advertisements. *Journal of Advertising, 23,* 31–41.

Center for Science in the Public Interest. (2001). *Alcopops: Summary of findings. What teens and adults are saying about alcopops.* Retrieved from http://www .cspinet.org

Center on Alcohol Marketing and Youth. (2006). *Still growing after all these years: Youth exposure to alcohol advertising on television, 2001–2005.* Retrieved July 31, 2007, from http://www.camy.org

Center on Alcohol Marketing and Youth. (2007a). *Drowned out: alcohol industry "responsibility" advertising on television, 2001–2005.* Retrieved June 20, 2007, from http://www.camy.org

Center on Alcohol Marketing and Youth. (2007b). *Youth exposure to alcohol advertising on radio, 2006.* Retrieved September 17, 2007, from http://www.camy .org

Chen, M., Grube, J. W., Bersamin, M., Waiters, E., & Keefe, D. B. (2005). Alcohol advertising: What makes it attractive to youth? *Journal of Health Communication, 10,* 553–565.

Christiansen, B. A., Smith, G. T., Roehling, P. V., & Goldman, M. S. (1989). Using alcohol expectancies to predict adolescent drinking behavior after one year. *Journal of Clinical and Consulting Psychology, 7,* 93–99.

Collins, R. L., Ellickson, P. L., McCaffrey, D. F., & Hambarsoomians, M. S. (2005). Saturated in Beer: Awareness of beer advertising in late childhood and adolescence. *Journal of Adolescent Health, 37,* 29–36.

Collins, R. L., Ellickson, P. L., McCaffrey, D. F., & Hambarsoomians, M. S. (2007). Early adolescent exposure to alcohol advertising and its relationship to underage drinking. *Journal of Adolescent Health, 40,* 527–534.

Dawson, H. (2001). 125 Years Young. *Beverage World, 120,* 26–31.

Demant, J., & Jarveinen, M. (2006). Constructing maturity through alcohol experience: focus group interviews with teenagers. *Addiction Research & Theory, 14,* 589–602.

Domzal, T. J., & Kernan, J. B. (1992). Reading advertising: The what and how of product meaning. *The Journal of Consumer Marketing, 9,* 48–64.

Dunn, M. E., & Yniquez, R. M. (1999). Experimental demonstration of the influence of alcohol advertising on the activation of alcohol expectancies in memory among fourth- and fifth-grade children. *Experimental and Clinical Psychopharmacology, 7,* 473–483.

Egan, T. (1990, December 31). Washington State may curb liquor ads aimed at youths. *New York Times,* p. 8.

Federal Trade Commission. (2003). *Alcohol advertising and marketing: A report to Congress*. Washington, DC: Author.

Fisher, L. B., Miles, I. W., Austin, B., Camargo, C. A., & Colditz, G. A. (2007). Predictors of initiation of alcohol use among US adolescents. *Archives of Pediatric and Adolescent Medicine, 161*, 959–966.

Fleming, K., Thorson, E., & Atkin, C. K. (2004). Alcohol advertising exposure and perceptions: Links with alcohol expectancies and intentions to drink or drinking in underaged youth and young adults. *Journal of Health Communication, 9*, 3–29.

Gerbner, G. (1995). Alcohol in American culture. In S. E. Martin (Ed.), *The effects of the mass media on the use and abuse of alcohol* (Research monograph ed., Vol. 28, pp. 3–29). Bethhesda, MD: NIH Publication No. 95-3743. U.S. Department of Health and Human Services.

Grant, B. F., & Dawson, D. A. (1997). Age at onset of alcohol use and its association with DSM-IV alcohol abuse and dependence: Results from the National Longitudinal Alcohol Epidemiologic Survey. *Journal of Substance Abuse, 9*, 103–110.

Gronbeck, B. (1983). Narrative, enactment, and television programming. *Southern Speech Communication Journal, 48*, 229–243.

Grube, J., & Wallack, L. (1994). Television beer advertising and drinking knowledge, beliefs, and intentions among school children. *American Journal of Public Health, 84*, 254–259.

Hastings, G., Anderson, S., Cooke, E., & Gordon, R. (2005). Alcohol marketing and young people's drinking: A review of the research. *Journal of Public Health Policy, 26*, 296–311.

Hays, C. (1999, September 10). Report addresses standards in marketing of alcohol. *New York Times*, p. C2.

Hill, K. G., White, H. R., Chung, I.-J., Hawkins, J. D., & Catalano, R. F. (2000). Early adult outcomes of adolescent binge drinking: Person- and variable-centered analyses of binge drinking trajectories. *Alcoholism: Clinical and Experimental Research, 24*, 892–901.

Hilts, P. J. (1991, November 5). Alcohol ads criticized as appealing to children. *New York Times*, p. A16.

Hurz, S. Q., Henriksen, L., Wang, Y., Feighery, E. C., & Fortmann, S. P. (2007). The relationship between exposure to alcohol advertising in stores, owning alcohol promotional items, and adolescent alcohol use. *Alcohol and Alcoholism, 42*, 143–149.

Jernigan, D. H., Ostroff, J., & Ross, C. (2006). Alcohol advertising and youth: A measured approach. *Journal of Public Health Policy, 26*, 312–325.

Jernigan, D. H., Ostroff, J., Ross, C., & O'Hara, J. A. (2004). Sex differences in adolescent exposure to alcohol advertising in magazines. *Archives of Pediatric and Adolescent Medicine, 158*, 629–634.

Kelly, K. J., & Edwards, R. W. (1998). Image advertisements for alcohol products: Is their appeal associated with adolescents' intention to consume alcohol? *Adolescence, 33*, 47–60.

Kilbourne, J. (1999). *Deadly persuasion: Why women and girls must fight the addictive power of advertising*. New York: Free Press.

Koop, C. E. (1989). *Press conference statement on the Surgeon General's Workshop on Drunk Driving: Proceedings.* Retrieved July 23, 2007, from http://profiles.nlm. nih.gov/

La Ferle, C., Li, H., & Edwards, S. M. (2001). An overview of teenagers and television advertising in the United States. *International Communication Gazette, 63,* 7–24.

Lewis, T. F., & Goker, J. E. (2007). Ideological maturity and drinking behaviors among college students. *Journal of Alcohol & Drug Education, 51,* 17–34.

Lieber, L. (1996). *Commercial and character slogan recall by children aged 9–11 years: Budweiser frogs versus Bugs Bunny.* Berkeley, CA: Center on Alcohol Advertising.

McClure, A. C., Cin, S. D., Gibson, J., & Sargent, J. D. (2006). Ownership of alcohol-branded merchandise and initiation of teen drinking. *American Journal of Preventive Medicine, 30,* 277–283.

Media business: Ads in which animals speak better than humans. (1989, April 17). *New York Times,* p. D11.

Messner, M. A., & de Oca, J. M. (2005). The male consumer as loser: Beer and liquor ads in mega sports media events. *Signs: Journal of Women in Culture and Society, 30,* 1879–1909.

Miller, T. R., Levy, D. T., Spicer, R. S., & Taylor, D. M. (2006). Societal costs of under-age drinking. *Journal of Studies on Alcohol, 67,* 519–528.

National Institute on Alcohol Abuse and Alcoholism. (2007). *Apparent per capita ethanol consumption, United States, 1977–2004.* Retrieved May 10, 2007, from http://www.niaaa.nih.gov

Packard, V. (1957). *The hidden persuaders.* New York: D. McKay Co.

Parker, B. J. (1998). Exploring life themes and myths in alcohol advertisements through a meaning-based model of advertising experiences. *Journal of Advertising, 1,* 98–112.

Pennock, P. E. (2007). *Advertising sin and sickness: The politics of alcohol and tobacco marketing, 1950–1990.* De Kalb: Northern Illinois University Press.

Postman, N., Nystrom, C., Strate, L., & Weingartner, C. (1987). *Myths, men, and beer: An analysis of beer commercials on broadcast television.* Washington, DC: AAA Foundation for Traffic Safety.

Rich, F. (1997, April 24). The liars' club. *New York Times,* p. A29.

Ringel, J. S., Collins, R. L., & Ellickson, P. L. (2006). Time trends and demographic differences in youth exposure to alcohol advertising on television. *Journal of Adolescent Health, 39,* 476–480.

Ritson, M., & Elliott, R. (1999). The social uses of advertising: An ethnographic study of adolescent advertising audiences. *Journal of Consumer Research, 26,* 260–277.

Salkin, A. (2007, February 11). Noir lite: Beer's good-time humor turns black. *New York Times,* p. 3.

Smith, G. T., Goldman, M. S., Greenbaum, P. E., & Christiansen, B. A. (1995). Expec-tancy for social facilitation from drinking: The divergent paths of high-expectancy and low-expectancy adolescents. *Journal of Abnormal Psychiatry, 104,* 32–40.

Snyder, L. B., Milici, F. F., Slater, M., Sun, H., & Strizhakova, Y. (2006). Effects of alcohol advertising exposure on drinking among youth. *Archives of Pediatrics & Adolescent Medicine, 160,* 18–24.

Stacy, A. W., Zogg, J. B., Unger, J. B., & Dent, C. W. (2004). Exposure to televised alcohol ads and subsequent adolescent alcohol use. *American Journal of Health Behavior, 28,* 498–509.

Stern, B. (1998). Medieval allegory: roots of advertising strategy for the mass market. *Journal of Marketing, 52,* 84–94.

Trussell, C. P. (1958, April 2). Liquor ad fight widens in scope. *New York Times,* p. 84.

Turow, J. (1997). *Breaking up America: Advertisers and the new media world.* Chicago: University of Chicago Press.

TV beer ads defended. (1956, February 18). *New York Times,* p. 37.

TV cartoonists found in demand. (1960, August 3), p. 59.

Van Munching, P. (1997). *Beer blast: The inside story of the brewing industry's bizarre battles for your money.* New York: Times Business / Random House.

*Vintage TV Beer Commercials.* (2003). [DVD]. Cleveland, OH: Schnitzelbank Press.

Waiters, E. D., Treno, A. J., & Grube, J. W. (2001). Alcohol advertising and youth: A focus-group analysis of what young people find appealing in alcohol advertising. *Contemporary Drug Problems, 28,* 695–718.

Wallack, L., Cassady, D., & Grube, J. (1990a). Television entertainment programming and socio-political attitudes. *Journalism Quarterly, 57,* 150–155.

Wallack, L., Cassady, D., & Grube, J. W. (1990b). *TV beer commercials and children: Exposure, attention, beliefs, and expectations about drinking as an adult.* Falls Church, VA: AAA Foundation for Traffic Safety.

Wechsler, H., & Sands, E. S. (1980). *Minimum drinking age laws: An evaluation.* Lexington, MA: Lexington Books.

Wright-Isak, C., Faber, R. J., & Horner, L. R. (1997). Comprehensive measurement of advertising effectiveness notes from the marketplace. In W. D. Wells (Ed.), *Measuring advertising effectiveness* (pp. 3–12). Mahwah, NJ: Erlbaum.

Zollo, P. (1999). *Wise up to teens: Insights into advertising and marketing to teenagers.* Ithaca, NY: New Strategist Publications.

Zwarun, L., & Farrar, K. M. (2005). Doing what they say, saying what they mean: Self-regulatory compliance and depictions of drinking in alcohol commercials in televised sports. *Mass Communication and Society, 8,* 347–371.

# 11

## From Twin Beds to Sex at Your Fingertips

### Teen Sexuality in Movies, Music, Television, and the Internet, 1950 to 2005

SUSANNAH STERN AND JANE D. BROWN

Adolescents in the United States today have unprecedented access to an array of media, including television, movies, music, and the Internet. Most spend much more time with the media than they spend with their parents or in school (Roberts & Foehr, 2004). Much of the content they attend to includes messages and images about sexual attraction, romantic relationships, and sexual behavior. Very little of this content includes any information about sexual health. Other potential agents of sexual socialization in the culture, including parents, schools, and religious institutions, are remarkably reticent or punitive about teens' sexual behavior. In this context, the media are important sources of sexual information and norms for their attentive teen audiences (Brown, 2000).

In this chapter we provide a historical overview of the portrayal of adolescent sexuality since the 1950s based on existing analyses of content. Using a chronological framework, we discuss media popular with young people (movies, music, television, and Internet), attempting to draw a portrait of dominant sexual themes and characterizations of teens' sexuality in each medium over time. Because young people have frequently attended to media portrayals of sexuality involving adult characters, we also discuss such portrayals when they attracted large youth audiences. We highlight the types of content that might be most influential in the developing sexual lives of young people, and conclude with suggestions for what should be taken into account in future analyses of the sexual portrayal of teens in the media.

Parents, educators, and scholars have long been concerned about the possible effects of the media on teens' sexual knowledge, attitudes, and behavior. One of the first steps in understanding the effects of media exposure on teens is to consider the media content to which young people commonly attend. Knowing the range and frequency of portrayals helps establish the parameters of what kinds of effects might occur.

Some of the earliest social scientific media research focused on what teens were learning about sex from the movies in the late 1920s (Dale, 1935). For the next seventy years, concern waxed and waned as newer media, such as radio soap operas, rock and roll, music videos, teen-oriented television shows, and most recently the Internet, were introduced. Each time a new medium came on the scene and content was directed at teen audiences, critics complained that the media were corrupting youth with inappropriately sexual fare, such as music videos in the 1980s (Gore, 1987) and pornography on the Internet in the 2000s (Pecora, Murray, & Wartella, 2006).

Adolescents frequently cite the media as sources of sexual information. Since friends and even parents may also be influenced by what they see, hear, and read in the media about sex, the cumulative effects of the media may actually outweigh other influences. In a 2004 national survey of 519 teens (15 to 19 years old) the media far outranked parents or schools as a source of information about birth control (Kaiser Family Foundation/ *Seventeen* Magazine, 2004). Systematic research on the content or the effects of sexual portrayals has been relatively sparse, however, until recently. As we see in this chapter, content analyses have shown a trend toward increasing frequency and explicitness of sexual portrayals across media directed toward young audiences, a lack of sexual health information, and stereotypical gender roles in sexual relationships.

A growing body of studies has also documented the media's ability to transmit information about sex, shape attitudes and perceptions of sexual norms, and encourage sexual activity (for comprehensive reviews, see Escobar-Chaves et al., 2005; Huston, Wartella, & Donnerstein, 1998; Strasburger, 2005; Ward, 2003). Most of the research has focused on the effects of television as an especially powerful medium because it combines visual and audio components and is watched for three to four hours every day by most young Americans (Roberts & Foehr, 2004). Television and other media influence viewers' perceptions of social behavior and social reality (Bandura, 1993), contribute to the development of cultural norms (Gerbner, Gross, Morgan, Signorielli, & Shanahan, 2002), and offer teenagers "scripts" for sexual behavior that they might not be able to observe elsewhere (Gagnon & Simon, 1987).

In the late 1990s, with encouragement from Congress, the U.S. National Institutes of Health (NIH) issued a call for proposals for further investigation of the effects of the media on adolescents' sexual behavior. NIH-funded longitudinal studies have concluded that early exposure to sexual content on television and other teen-oriented media such as music, movies, and magazines "hastens" initiation of sexual intercourse (Ashby, Arcari, & Edmonson, 2006; Brown et al., 2006; Collins et al., 2004; Martino et al., 2006). Such studies take us closer to establishing the causal sequence of media's effects because they measure adolescents' media use and sexual behavior over time and in teens' natural media-use settings.

One outcome of this most recent round of concern and studies is the realization that no standard for what is meant by "sex in the media" has been established. Previous studies have sometimes built on existing content analysis protocols and definitions, but rarely has more than one study used the same coding scheme. Some media and genres, such as music, music videos, and movies, do not lend themselves readily to quantitative content analysis, so have rarely been included in studies of effects. The Internet poses a new set of challenges for definitions and categories as whole new genres, such as social networking sites, are developed and the consumer is provided more control over and even authorship of content (e.g., YouTube). In this chapter, we identify themes, continuities, and changes that have emerged over the past six decades in sexual content in movies, prime-time television, soap operas, popular music and music videos, and on the Internet, with an eye also toward what should be included in future studies.

## MOVIES

For almost a century, movies have endeared themselves to audiences with larger-than-life narratives about reality, fantasy, and the blurry area in between. Teenagers, in particular, have relished the cinema as a place to vicariously experience the excitement of adventure, the thrills of horror, and the risks and pleasures of romance. Sexual content has been featured in many of the films viewed by teens over the years, ranging from subtle innuendo to frank dialogue to overt imagery. Social scientific examinations of sexual content in movies are surprisingly scarce, especially in comparison to other media such as television and magazines, and quantitative examinations of teen sexuality are virtually absent. Several film scholars, however, have examined the stories that films tell about teen sexuality from a more qualitative and critical perspective. The insights they have gleaned, while not quantifiable, are valuable in shaping an understanding of how teen sexuality in film has been portrayed.

Through the 1950s and first half of the 1960s, the Hollywood Production Code played a large role in the portrayal—or, more accurately, nonportrayal—of sex in films. Concerned that audiences might "infer that low forms of sex relationship are the accepted or common thing," the Code forbade "scenes of passion" that might "stimulate the lower and baser element." The list of prohibited content included such elements as "sex perversion," "scenes of childbirth," "seduction or rape," "venereal diseases," as well as "complete nudity," references to genital sexuality, and "indecent or undue exposure" (cited in Williams, 2006, p. 298). Williams argued that the lengthy inventory of barred material left kissing as the only potentially sexual act in films during this era (and even the kiss was forbidden to be "excessive and lustful").

Despite these restrictions, films in the 1950s and early 1960s did portray teenage sexuality, albeit nonexplicitly. For instance, sexuality was at times alluded to by the depiction of teen characters who pronounced themselves pregnant, although the sexual acts leading to pregnancy and births were never included in the films. Common to films of this time period, Considine (1985) noted, was that teen characters' parents seemed not to understand their teens and tried to stifle their sexual feelings. Young female characters, in particular, were urged to resist sexual intimacy at all costs. Such portrayals worked to convey the impression that teens were "victims of social attitudes toward sex" (p. 231) (e.g., *Splendor in the Grass*, 1961). At the same time, however, when experienced by teen characters, sex typically resulted in pregnancy, marriage, and uncomplicated parenthood. This sequence of events did little to convey the reality of what Considine referred to as the "post-coital situation" (p. 226), such as the difficulties a baby places on a relationship, the financial pressures involved with raising a child, and other such likely outcomes of teen pregnancy (e.g., *A Summer Place*, 1959).

In the 1960s, several changes made way for somewhat more honest and frank depictions of adolescent sexuality in films. For example, the newly formed MPAA ratings replaced the Movie Production Code, and, in consequence, both adult and teen cinema became more liberal in their portrayals of sex and sexuality. Also, as other media, especially music, began to address sexuality more explicitly and provocatively, the film industry appeared to gradually follow suit. Female teen characters in dramas were increasingly depicted as more sexual and less passive than in previous years, and they were also more commonly shown to take pleasure in sexual activity without desire for love or marriage. Alternatively, male teen characters were depicted as more sexually vulnerable and uncertain than they had been in the past (e.g., *Last Summer*, 1969) (Considine, 1985).

Beach party films, a new breed of teen cinema, were popular among adolescents throughout the 1960s. Interestingly, although these films dealt specifically with teens coming of age, they generally did not address sexuality head on. In fact, the key to films like *Gidget* (1959), *Beach Party* (1963), and *Beach Blanket Bingo* (1965), as a *New York Times* article noted at the time, "is lots of flesh but no sex. No hearts are broken and virginity prevails" (cited in Lisante, 2005, p. 13). Sandra Dee, Annette Funicello, Frankie Avalon, and other youthful icons of virtue and good looks were catapulted to fame in this teen film genre. And parents were comfortable with their teens watching the films because, as McCrohan proposed, they showed "it's possible to spend the whole summer on the sand in practically no clothes, fall in love with another terrific nearly-naked person and still not 'go all the way'" (cited in Lisanti, 2005, p. 13). The nostalgic view of teen life that these films propagated was compelling because it showed "good clean fun," although the films were often critiqued for their unrealism.

The 1970s introduced images of teenagers that better reflected the highs and lows of real teens' actual sexual experiences. Stories about the fears, doubts, and failures that commonly accompany sexual awakening and practice were now situated among stories about youthful optimism and romance (e.g., *American Graffiti*, 1973; *Grease*, 1978). Considine (1985), the only scholar who appears to have specifically attended to teen sexuality in film during the 1970s, contended that films in this decade began to suggest that the reality of sex often failed to live up to the fantasy. As he put it, several films in the 1970s showed "eager but gauche youngsters stumbl[ing] through their initial sexual encounters" (p. 258).

Teen sexuality in 1980s' films received more attention than any other decade—and with good reason. The early 1980s saw a surge of what have been labeled teen "sex romp" movies, including those whose titles explicitly highlighted a preoccupation with sex, such as *Porky's* (1982), *Losin' It* (1983), *Goin' All the Way* (1982), *The Last American Virgin* (1982), *Risky Business* (1983), and *The Sure Thing* (1985). In fact, Shary (2002) identified twenty-five "teen sexploitation" films made between 1980 and 1987. In one of the only social scientific studies to examine film sex content, Greenberg, Siemicki, et al. (1993) analyzed sixteen R-rated films from 1982 to 1984, finding that sex most often took place between unmarried partners and that discussions or images of contraception were virtually absent. The average age of the characters engaging in sex in these films was 22 years old.

A common plot line in nearly all of the "sex romp" films was the loss of teen characters' virginity. Indeed, in many cases, losing virginity (and, by transitive property, the stigma attached with being a virgin), rather than the act of sexual intercourse itself, appeared to be the primary goal of many of the protagonists, and thereby constituted the "ultimate resolution" of the film (Shary, 2002, p. 228). Shary argued that by the late 1980s, when fear of AIDS became widespread, such crude and coarse depictions of teen sexuality decreased drastically. In their place, period films highlighting more innocent youthful times became popular (e.g., *Peggy Sue Got Married*, 1986; *Dirty Dancing*, 1987).

Also in the mid-1980s, director John Hughes and others promoted an alternative view of teen sexuality that attended more to youths' emotions and relationships than had the sex romp films. Shary categorized two types of 1980s youth narratives: teen love stories and teen sex stories. He wrote, "In most youth love stories, sex is either not an issue or is experienced as a natural result of romantic achievement, whereas in most youth sex stories, love is either not an issue or is experienced as a natural result of sexual achievement" (p. 212). Commonly, in youth love stories, such as John Hughes's *Sixteen Candles* (1984), *The Breakfast Club* (1985), and *Pretty in Pink* (1986), teens "struggle to confirm their romantic feelings and secure a union in the face of an oppressive obstacle that must be overcome for the couple to either live happily ever after or realize that their union was not meant to be" (p. 213). Alternatively, Whatley (1991) suggested that Hughes's films constructed virginity as an "abnormality," especially for males. In fact, in Whatley's estimation, "nailing a woman" was a primary way for characters (especially nerds) to acquire status in Hughes's "brat pack" films.

Bulman (2005), who examined more than 185 films about high school from 1981 to 2001, argued that sexuality in films about suburban, middle-class teens (e.g., *Fast Times at Ridgemont High*, 1982; *Pump up the Volume*, 1990) was treated substantially differently from sexuality in films about poor, urban youth (*Stand and Deliver*, 1988; *Dangerous Minds*, 1995). He wrote, "While the students in the suburban school films race to lose their virginity and are celebrated by audiences when they do so, casual sex often results in pregnancy and dropping out for the girls in the urban school films" (p. 110). Poor, urban youth are constructed as deviant and depraved when they engage in sex, yet "when the students of middle- and upper-middle class status act deviantly…their actions are excused, ignored, or treated as normal expressions of adolescence" (p. 111).

Bulman's critique is valuable in its recognition that teen sexuality has rarely been consistently portrayed on the big screen, with important differences often hinging on characters' race and class, as well as their gender. Indeed, scholars across the past half-century have illuminated the double standard for sexual behavior that exists for women but not for men. Whereas sexual desire and activity are generally accepted as normal for male teen characters, female teen characters must walk a narrow line between pro-miscuity and prudishness (Hentges, 2006). This double standard is actually incorporated into the plot lines of many films (e.g., *Grease*, 1978; *The Break-fast Club*, 1985), and teen girls are often condemned within the films and in the eyes of viewers for transgressing sexual boundaries.

In the 1990s, films about youth sexuality became more pessimistic and cynical, and sex itself was generally shown as more problematic than in the 1980s. Teens' "first" sexual experiences were less commonly portrayed as teen characters were increasingly assumed to be sexually experienced before the start of the film or remained virgins throughout the film. Shary (2002, p. 235) observed, "Even the films that did continue to feature deflower-ing scenes (e.g., *Titanic* [1997], *Virgin Suicides* [1999])...featured the fated moment as solemn and sincere, quite a remove from the silly and lascivious nature of teen sex scenes in the more immature early 80s." *Kids* (1995), a film directed by Larry Clark, shot in a documentary style and featuring early teens engaging in unsafe and violent sex, provided an especially grim view of teen sexuality, and one which many critics and scholars agreed served to demonize youth (e.g., Giroux, 1996).

Pardun (2002) evaluated fifteen movies that teens viewed in large num-bers in 1995 (according to the Simons Market Research Bureau) to con-clude that romance and sexual intercourse were often portrayed as separate phenomena. The couples shown to engage in sex in the films studied were typically unmarried and did not know each other well. Very little overt sexual imagery was evident in these films, however. Pardun did not interpret this finding as particularly positive, because, she suggested, the absence of sexual imagery preempted depictions of negative consequences of sexual activity or the benefits of appropriate behavior.

By the end of the 1990s and into the new millennium, sex romp–type films made a comeback in the form of such movies as *American Pie* (1999), although some critics (e.g., Shary, 2002) praised the film for more honest portrayals of the emotions and fears surrounding teen sexuality, for empha-sizing female desire, and for depicting contraception (features that were virtually absent in the early 1980s). More serious films dealing with teen sexuality (e.g., *Boys Don't Cry*, 1999) as well as lighter fare (e.g., *10 Things I Hate About You*, 1999; *Saved!*, 2004) offered a variety of messages about the social ramifications of teen sexual activity. Movies for teens often sug-gested that being in a romantic relationship should be a priority, especially for teen girls (e.g., *Win a Date with Tad Hamilton!*, 2004; *She's All That*, 1999), and that sexual activity could turn teen boys and girls from nerds into cool kids (e.g., *Can't Hardly Wait*, 1998; *The Girl Next Door*, 2004).

In one of the only social scientific studies specifically addressing teen characters in films, Stern (2005) found that among the top box-office sellers from 1999 to 2001 featuring teen characters, "making out" was the third most commonly coded behavior teens engaged in, preceded only by "hanging out in school" and "socializing outside of school." The same content analysis showed that more than a quarter of the youth characters studied in the films had engaged in sexual intercourse. In the short term, negative consequences were more common than positive consequences, although overall, no consequences typically in either the short or long term were portrayed. Only four of the forty characters who engaged in sexual activity were shown to use a condom, and no other forms of contraception were portrayed. No films showed a character who contracted a sexually transmitted disease, and parents who gave positive messages about sexuality or sexual health were rare in the movies studied.

Applying a more qualitative lens to the same box office hits from 1999 to 2001 featuring teen characters, Stern and Levkoff (2006) explored the reasons why teen characters engaged in sexual activity. Surprisingly, teens were rarely shown to behave sexually purely because it felt good. Although popular assumptions are that movies glamorize sex as a fun-filled activity, in the films studied, sexual pleasure was generally presented as either incidental or absent (*American Pie* was a notable exception). More typically, teens were motivated to have sex as a way to connect with other teen characters emotionally. For example, in films such as *Here on Earth* (2000), sex was shown as a symbol of commitment between two characters, a shared experience, and as a way to express love and nurture a relationship. Across the films, sex was also frequently shown as a way to gain or maintain social status (e.g., *Election*, 1999), as well as a technique to exploit others. For instance, characters would persuade others to engage in sex to hurt, humiliate, or intimidate them, such as in *Cruel Intentions* (1999), where the two lead characters make a game out of deflowering virgins. Notably, such behavior was not glorified in the films. Finally, teen characters sometimes behaved sexually as a way to achieve a new lifestyle (e.g., *Varsity Blues*, 1999) or to acquire something more concrete, such as drugs (e.g., *Traffic*, 2000). In this way, sex was portrayed as a commodity that could help teens achieve specific ends.

Altogether, the history of teen sexuality in films suggests a trend toward increasing realism, cynicism, and explicitness in both dialogue and imagery. Given the diversity of films, however, such generalizations are crude, and dozens of exceptions can be identified. The lack of systematic, longitudinal examinations of sexual portrayals makes it impossible to specify precisely how teen sexuality has changed over the years, and difficult to contrast the specific motivations, behaviors, and consequences that characterize individual films. A few general conclusions seem appropriate, nonetheless.

First, taken as an aggregate, films featuring teen sexuality, especially in the past few decades, do not celebrate or promote teen sexual behavior. Indeed, many scholars (e.g., Lewis, 1992; Shary, 2002) concur that the more common message films send is that sex is rarely as pleasurable as one might expect. As Shary puts it, "Youth are frequently reminded through films how disheartening and deflating the experiences (of sex and love) can be, far more so than adult-oriented films about the same issues, as if young people need to develop a healthy cynicism about romance in order to prevent them from expecting too much of it" (p. 254). Second, the appropriateness of sexual behavior is not dealt with evenhandedly for all teen characters, with important differences often depending on gender, race, and class. Finally, images of safe sex (e.g., contraception, planning for sex, etc.) have received very little screen time over the years, and the consequences of sexual behavior have been underrepresented when compared with reality. Sexually transmitted diseases, in particular, are nearly invisible in films featuring teen sexuality despite an ongoing epidemic among adolescents (Weinstock, Berman, & Cates, 2004).

## POPULAR MUSIC

Popular music has always focused on love and sex and is the medium most clearly intended for the young of heart. And, as such, popular music has always generated criticism for the sexual connotations of both the music and lyrics. As rock and roll entered the scene in the early 1950s, criticism and outrage was levied primarily at the "throbbing sexual implications of rock's rough, primitive, musical structure and the provocative physical gyrations these 'jungle rhythms' produced in performers and audience alike" (Christenson & Roberts, 1998, p. 116).

Even though the music itself continues to evoke a visceral response and objections primarily from adults, most criticism and research has focused on the lyrics of the songs and the visual images now associated with the music through music videos. Debate continues about whether young listeners actually know the words to songs and/or interpret lyrics as sexual, but lyrics are much more accessible now than ever before. Most CDs include a full transcript of the words, and various Web sites feature lyrics to most of the songs ever recorded.

Early studies of music lyrics developed unique coding schemes that focused on the love and courtship themes that dominated early popular music. In one of the first systematic studies, sociologist Donald Horton (1957, p. 570) identified five distinct "acts in a drama of courtship" played out in a sample of the lyrics of popular songs from 1955:

1. *Prologue* (wishing and dreaming about love in general—"Here I wait with open arms for a girl to love");
2. *Active courtship* (seeking a specific person—"You've been teasing long enough, now I'm gonna call your bluff");
3. *Honeymoon* (finding the perfect person—"I found out since we've been kissin,' all the things I've been missin'");
4. *Downward course of love* (outside forces threaten a relationship—"Mama he treats me badly");
5. *All alone* (sad about a lost love—"There goes the one I love").

Of 235 songs analyzed, 83.4% were what Horton called "conversational songs about love" that could be coded into one of the five categories. Over time, love and romance themes have remained the focus of the largest proportion of popular songs, although in the 1960s and 1970s, more politically oriented songs temporarily reduced the proportion of love/romance oriented songs (Carey, 1969; Hyden & McCandless, 1983; Rice, 1980). But by the 1980s, more than 70% of the top-forty songs were again "built around a love relationship theme" (Christenson & Roberts, 1998). Another analysis of songs for seven decades (1930–1999) found a remarkably consistent pattern that about three-fourths of popular songs focused on some aspect of love, sex, or romance (Scheff, 2001).

What has changed since the early days of popular music is a greater emphasis on the physical aspects of love and sex and less on the emotional, nonphysical aspects (Cole, 1971). Carey (1969) noted much less focus on courtship or the honeymoon stage in the songs of the 1960s and more interest in satisfying sexual need (e.g., the Mamas and the Papas singing, "Oh, please, please believe me, I need someone to relieve me," in "Somebody Groovy").

Music has gotten even more graphic since then, both in terms of the lyrics and the visual imagery of the accompanying music videos that often leaves little to the imagination. The move to more explicit lyrics appears to have paralleled the introduction of MTV, rap, and alternative music in the 1980s. By 1990, explicit references to sex had increased to 15% from 4% a decade earlier. More than one-third of the songs included explicit and sometimes raunchy lyrics (e.g., "Evil dick likes warm wet places") ("Evil Dick" by Body Count, 1992) or implicit references to sex (e.g., "Let's go all the way") (Christenson & Roberts, 1998).

An analysis of the lyrics on albums most frequently listened to by early adolescents (12- to 14-year-olds) in 2002 found that 40% of the lines made some reference to bodies as sexual objects, relationships, and/or intercourse (Pardun, L'Engle, & Brown, 2005). Only about 6% of the lyric lines included any mention of what might be construed as sexually healthy messages (e.g., physical/sexual development, refusal of advance/abstinence, masturbation, STDs, negative emotional consequences, condoms, and contraception).

Another analysis of the content of songs produced by adolescents' favorite musicians in 2002 found that all but three of the sixteen artists studied had one or more songs on their most recent albums that made reference to sexual behavior (Martino et al., 2006). The highest concentration of "degrading sexual lyrics," which treat women as sex objects and men as sexually insatiable, was found on the songs of rap and rap metal artists. The lyrics to Ja Rule's "Livin it Up," are an example: "Half the ho's hate me, half them love me/ The ones that hate me/ Only hate me 'cause they ain't f__ked me." A three-wave longitudinal study found that the adolescents who listened to songs containing such lyrics were those most likely to have had sexual intercourse a year later, even after controlling for a number of other factors that are predictive of early sexual behavior.

## MUSIC VIDEOS

Within a couple of years of the launch of Music Television Network (MTV) in August 1981, music videos had changed young people's viewing and listening habits. Nielsen surveys in the mid-1980s found that more than 40% of cable subscribers had watched MTV in the preceding week for up to two hours a day. MTV quickly supplanted radio stations as the place to learn about which musicians were hot and which were not (Sherman & Dominick, 1986).

A spate of studies set out to see if music videos were as sexual (and violent) as critics claimed. One of the first of these studies lamented that developing a coding scheme for music videos "stretches the content analysis model to its limits." Specifically, Sherman and Dominick (1986, p. 82) wrote, "The rapid shot changes, transformations, and anthropomorphisms common to music video present unique difficulties in identifying and describing manifest content."

One way to reduce the difficulty was to code manifest visual content without worrying about the sound or lyrics and to code presence or absence of actions/behaviors for the whole video as the unit of analysis. Using that approach, Baxter, DeRiemer, Landini, Leslie, and Singletary (1985, p. 336) found in a sample of sixty-two videos from 1984 that "music video sexual content may have a decidedly adolescent orientation, suited to its audience; fantasy exceeds experience and sexual expression centers primarily on attracting the opposite sex." About 60% of the videos included some "portrayal of sexual feelings or impulses" but most of that was due to women in provocative clothing, embraces, and sexually suggestive dancing. Fewer than one in five of the videos included depictions of courtship or kissing.

Sherman and Dominick (1986) adapted the physical/sexual intimacy continuum and the "scale of sexuality" code that had been developed earlier for prime-time television (Silverman, Sprafkin, & Rubinstein, 1979). Ignoring the music and lyrics, they applied the code to 166 "concept" videos. They characterized the world of popular music as a young white male domain in which younger teens, children, and senior citizens were rarely shown. Women were much more likely to be provocatively dressed than men, yet sex was seldom more overt than flirting and nonintimate touching. In fact, the sexual portrayals were rather traditional and ultimately quite similar to other kinds of media depictions of sexual behavior, with almost no exhibitionism, voyeurism, or bondage. The sexiest videos in 1984 included "Legs" by ZZ Top and "Let's Get Physical" by Olivia Newton-John. However, more than three-fourths of coded videos that contained violence also included some sexual behavior, and more than one-fourth of the sexual episodes were coded as occurring between same-sex partners. Sherman and Dominick (1986, p. 89) quoted Frith's (1978) description of "the chauvinism of rock culture" where the music means "having a good time—physically, irresponsibly, spontaneously. It means drinking and laughing and doing nothing and (having) sex and trying anything once before you have to do something forever."

Subsequent analyses showed that sexual references and portrayals varied by musical genre. In a study of 161 videos from four different music video sites (Black Entertainment Television [BET], The Nashville Network, MTV, and Video Hits-1), sexual appeals were most common in soul, rap, and pop music videos. The rap and soul videos that appeared on BET contained the most sexual content (46% and 50%, respectively); heavy metal videos were surprisingly low in sexual content (8%); 14% of the country music videos included sexual innuendo, symbolism, or explicit sexual reference (Tapper, Thorson, & Black, 1994).

In sum, music and music videos have frequently portrayed adolescents as preoccupied with love, romance, and sex. Some genres have been more likely to include this kind of content than others. Over the years, sexual references in popular music have become more explicit, and, when combined with images in music videos, it would be difficult for a listener/viewer to not interpret the messages as sexual. Rarely does any genre include safe-sex messages or portrayals.

## PRIME-TIME TELEVISION

In the early days of American network television, programming was designed for families to watch together and, except for the occasional bawdy joke, sex was not family fare (Spigel, 1992). Dour Ed Sullivan's variety show ran from 1948 to 1971, and the Lennon Sisters's harmonizing the occasional love song was about the closest the show came to suggesting that young people might enjoy something more than waltzing to muted trumpets and clarinets (Barnouw, 1990). The lower part of Elvis (the Pelvis) Presley was shielded from public view when he appeared on the *The Ed Sullivan Show* in 1956, ostensibly for fear of unleashing adolescents' repressed lust (Garner, 2002).

Somehow Lucille Ball, the star of the immensely popular *I Love Lucy* show, got pregnant even though she and husband Desi Arnaz always slept in twin beds and weren't allowed to say the word "pregnant" on network TV. More than two-thirds of the 20 million television sets in America on January 19, 1953, were tuned in to see the arrival of their baby (Andrews, 1976). Dick Clark's *American Bandstand* brought rock and roll music to national television in 1957, but the dancing was strictly monitored so as not to offend (Shore & Clark, 1985). Teen heartthrob Ricky Nelson sang his first song on the television show that featured his real parents (*The Adventures of Ozzie & Harriet* [1952–1966]) the same year. Annette Funicello, the prettiest of Disney's Mouseketeers, and Miss Kitty, the only woman in the long-running western *Gunsmoke* (1955–1975), were models of female beauty and goodness. *Bonanza* (1959–1973) was a favorite of teen girls as well as boys, not only because it was one of the first Westerns broadcast in color, but because the youngest son "Little Joe" was so cute. Big brother Wally on *Leave It to Beaver* (1957–1963) had similar appeal. Both were the kind of guys the white, middle-class parents on early television shows would have been happy to have as a future son-in-law (Spigel, 1992). Eva Gabor's glamour and seductive ways on *Green Acres* (1965–1971), and the perky genie's bare midriff on *I Dream of Jeannie* (1965–1970), were about as sexy as it got visually on 1960s TV (Garner, 2002). In short, the early years of network television only hinted at the possibility of sexual behavior, instead cherishing "family values in an all-White trouble-free suburbia" (Hetsroni, 2007, p. 339).

The Puritan world of network television continued into the early 1970s with the introduction of other happy families such as on *The Partridge Family* (1970–1974) and *The Waltons* (1972–1981). Only a few shows, such as *All in the Family* (1971–1979) and *M\*A\*S\*H* (1972–1983), suggested that all was not well in the larger culture, even as the women's liberation, civil rights, and anti-war movements questioned fundamental notions of gender roles, female sexuality, race relations, and America's role in the world (Garner, 2002; Spigel, 1992).

The first systematic content analyses of American entertainment television documented the shift toward more sexual content in the mid-1970s, as more shows were created for younger audiences and as the short-lived (1975–1977) Family Viewing Hour (8–9 P.M.) provided the networks some cover for producing more realistic and sexual fare in other time slots (Lowry, Love, & Kirby, 1981). The world of television was also getting much more competitive as cable and satellite television were introduced and viewers learned they no longer had to rely only on the three networks (Barnouw, 1990).

So, there was a charming "bad boy," the Fonz, on *Happy Days* (1974–1984), (rated number two with women 18 to 24 in 1976), and a powerful *Wonder Woman* (1976–1979) in a bathing suit uniform. *Charlie's Angels* (1976–1981) were sexy and powerful, although sex was still primarily fantasy on the part of viewers rather than depicted on the screen (Levine, 2003). Silverman et al. (1979, p. 33) summed up the 1977–1978 prime-time season, in comparison to prime-time content analyses of the preceding two years: "low on sex but high on suggestion…big increase in TV's use of flirtatious behaviors and verbal innuendos." They found that implied or verbal sexual references occurred 2 to 3.5 times per hour.

Based on a comprehensive meta-analysis of twenty-five studies, Hetsroni (2007), in fact, found that the frequency of all kinds of sexual content, except depictions of homosexuality, actually diminished on American prime-time network programming between 1975 and 2004. He argued that the major networks are inherently conservative because the "larger bulk of loyal viewers are older conservative people who reside in rural states, describe themselves as more religious than the average, show concern about the potential harmful effects of sex, and support the censorship of such content" (p. 338). Thus, much of the increase in sexual content has occurred in non-network programming, some of it especially targeting the lucrative adolescent and young adult audience (Bodroghkozy, 2003).

Things heated up a bit even on the networks as the soap opera format moved to prime time in 1978, and *Dallas* began a thirteen-year run of narratives about sexual infidelity. The *Dukes of Hazzard* (1979–1985), featuring a couple of wild young men and a young woman in cut-off shorts, was number two in the ratings and *Dallas* number one in 1980 when televangelist Jerry Falwell's "Moral Majority," a conservative Christian coalition of political action committees, threatened to boycott "sex and violence" on network TV (Barnouw, 1990). The networks backed off such fare, while the new channels picked up the slack.

The launch of the upstart network Fox's show *Married with Children* in 1987 spawned an advertiser boycott because of its sexual humor and raunchy dialogue, which often featured the exploits of Kelly Bundy, the promiscuous adolescent daughter (Perren, 2003). The boycott, however, apparently did little more than attract young viewers to the show (Bodroghkozy,

2003). The same year, *Baywatch* (1989–2001) upped the ante on what could happen when muscle men and girls in bathing suits spend summers together, quickly becoming one of the most popular television shows in the world (Parks, 2003) despite being dropped by a nervous NBC after its first season. By 1992, the sexual norms promoted by such shows as *Murphy Brown* (1988–1998), in which the unmarried star has a baby, were prime fodder for the political debate about "family values." Then–Vice President Dan Quayle criticized the lead character as an example of the decline of the American family. In 1992, conservative media critic Michael Medved in his book *Hollywood vs. America* (1992) declared "the dream factory has become the poison factory."

Content analyses of television favored by young audiences since the 1980s have documented an increasingly sexual world, commonly occupied by young, unmarried, attractive characters who frequently engage in sexual talk and behavior. The Kaiser Family Foundation biennial studies begun in 1997 are the most comprehensive ongoing monitor of trends in sex on television. Those studies have documented an increase in sexual content over the past decade, with more frequent reference to and depiction of sexual behavior, including (implied) intercourse. The proportion of prime-time shows with sexual content increased from 65% in the 1997–1998 season to 76% in 2004–2005. Programs that portrayed sexual behavior rather than just talk about sex increased from 24% to 38% (Kunkel et al., 2007). An analysis of only the top-twenty shows watched by teens in 2004–2005 showed a decline in the average number of scenes of sexual behavior per show as compared to the 2001–2002 season, however (Kunkel, Eyal, Finnerty, Biely, & Donnerstein, 2005). Although portrayals of intercourse have become more common across the television landscape over time, it became more likely (between the 1997–1998 and 2001–2002 seasons) that the characters were age 25 or older rather than younger (Kunkel et al., 2007).

In a comprehensive review of forty-one published studies that conducted statistical analyses of television's sexual content through the 1990s, Ward (2003) identified several recurring trends. First, although the frequency of sexual content increased, the content still was rarely visually graphic and most typically was verbal or depictions of "precursor" sexual behaviors (e.g., flirting, kissing, hugging) rather than sexual intercourse. An analysis of twelve television programs children and adolescents watched most in the 1992–1993 season (which typically included at least one adolescent character, such as Will Smith as *The Fresh Prince of Bel-Air*, *Roseanne*'s teen-age daughters, and the wealthy adolescents on *Beverly Hills 90210*), Ward (1995) found that between 29% and 50% of the interactions between characters contained references to sexual issues. She also identified consistent gender differences in the depiction of sexuality. Specifically, Ward suggested, in the "game" of dating and romance, men frequently commented on women's physical appearance, sexual activity was considered a defining feature of masculinity, and women discussed men's attributes as potential sexual partners. These trends are clearly seen in reality shows such as *The Bachelor* (2002) and *The Bachelorette* (2003) in which twenty-five women or men competed to see who the target single person ultimately chose.

Second, in keeping with the game metaphor, most sexual talk and behavior on television occurred outside marital relationships (Ward, 2003). For example, in the fifteen programs most popular with 12- to 17-year-olds in 1996, including *The Simpsons, Friends, Boy Meets World, Married with Children,* and *Seinfeld,* Cope-Farrar and Kunkel (2002) found that more than three-fourths (79%) of the sexual behavior occurred between people not married to each other. Ten years earlier, Greenberg, Stanley, et al. (1993) had come to similar conclusions with a similar sample of top-ten shows. Some analyses have found, however, what might be called a "norm of exclusivity" in which most of the sexual behavior occurs between partners who are at least in committed relationships. In a year-long analysis of *All My Children,* a soap opera popular with teens, Larson (1991) found that the vast majority (83%) of the kisses occurred between people who were either married or in a committed relationship. Kunkel et al. (2007) found that in the 2001–2002 television season, the majority of all scenes with intercourse involved characters who had an established relationship with each other.

Third, despite an increase in sexual content on television and the advent of virulent and deadly sexually transmitted diseases such as HIV/AIDS in the late 1980s, television has rarely included any discussion or depiction of disease prevention or health consequences. In the Kaiser Foundation analysis of the top-twenty TV programs watched by teens, the depiction of "risks and responsibilities" occurred in 12% of the shows with sexual content in 2002 and 10% in 2004 (Kunkel et al., 2005). Discussion and/or portrayal of potential risks, the need for precaution, and the possibility of patience were more likely on shows that implied sexual intercourse (about 8% of teen programs), but in 2005 depictions of such sexual health practices occurred only one-fourth of the time even in those shows (see Table 11.1).

Television and the context of use have changed dramatically since the introduction of television as a mass medium for entertainment in the early 1950s. Early on, most homes had only one television set, so industry executives programmed for the families they assumed would be watching together. Content reflected a presumed audience of all ages and sexuality was camouflaged with jokes inside married relationships (Spigel, 1992; Taylor,

Table 11.1. Sexual Content on Top-Twenty Teen TV Programs (2002–2005)

|  | 2002 (N = 59) | 2005 (N = 60) |
|---|---|---|
| Any *sex* | 83% | 70% |
| Scenes per hour | 6.7 | 6.7 |
| Percent with mention of risk/responsibility | 12% | 10% |
| Any *talk* about sex | 80% | 68% |
| Scenes per hour | 6.0 | 6.4 |
| Any sexual *behavior* | 49% | 45% |
| Scenes per hour | 3.1 | 2.1* |
| Any sexual *intercourse* | 20% | 8% |
| Scenes per hour | 2.1 | 1.8 |
| Percent with mention of risk/responsibility | 45% | 25% |

*Note*: Adapted from Kunkel et al. (2005). Scenes per hour and percentage of shows with risk/responsibility talk or depictions were calculated for only those shows that included any of a particular kind of sexual content (e.g., talk about sex, sexual behavior).
*Statistically significant difference between the sample years at $p < .05$.

1989). As the medium matured, so did the content, as teen characters became more prominent and eventually whole channels, such as BET and the WB (which merged with UPN in 2006 to become the CW Network), were developed for adolescent audiences who often had access to television sets in their own rooms, out of sight of their parents (Roberts & Foehr, 2004). Interestingly, about the same time, a number of teen-oriented shows that featured adolescents, such as *Beverly Hills 90210*, and later *Dawson's Creek* and *One Tree Hill*, rarely included any depiction of parents. It was as if the kids were fending for themselves.

Over the past five decades of television, governmental and citizen pressure for "cleaner" and more "family friendly" content has waxed and waned. The networks have remained relatively conservative compared to the newer cable channels, which have not had the same pressures or legal imperatives to adhere to government standards or more demographically diverse and larger audiences (Hetsroni, 2007). The networks were put on notice again in 2004 when the Federal Communications Commission (FCC) applied their seldom-used indecency rules to the Janet Jackson–Justin Timberlake "wardrobe malfunction" at the Super Bowl halftime show. After receiving more than 200,000 complaints, the FCC levied a $550,000 fine against Viacom, the parent corporation at the time, and the twenty CBS-owned television stations that aired the broadcast. Congress passed the Broadcast

Decency Enforcement Act of 2005, which raised the maximum FCC fine penalty to $325,000 per violation. The fine apparently had a ripple effect throughout the broadcast industry, as subsequent live broadcasts went on tape delay, and partial nude scenes were cut from daytime soap operas as well as prime-time dramas (Aherns, 2006). It remains to be seen if the FCC will continue to flex its regulatory muscle in regard to sexual content, and to what extent the threat of fines will inhibit content producers.

In sum, since the mid-1990s, sexual behavior on television has increased in frequency and explicitness outside of marital relationships, although in teen-oriented shows sex is still more talk than action. Sex is often depicted as a kind of game in which males and females are objectified as sexually attractive or not. Discussion and/or portrayal of sexual risks and responsibilities are rarely portrayed, although they are more likely in episodes that depict sexual intercourse.

## SOAP OPERAS

Soap operas moved quickly from radio to television in the late 1940s, and during the 1950s and 1960s were geared toward stay-at-home mothers and housewives. In the mid-1970s, as more women entered the work force, younger characters were introduced and soaps were aired as late as 4:30 and 5:00 in the afternoon to appeal to younger audiences. Teenagers and college students were a significant portion of the soap audience by the early 1980s. Some 50 million people "followed" one or more soap operas, including two-thirds of all women living in homes with televisions (Allen, 1985).

Critics began to wonder if the soaps were fueling the fires of the sexual revolution that had been spawned by the women's liberation and peace movements of the preceding decade. In 1980, for example, *People* magazine (October 27) ran a cover story "Torrid Teens on the Soaps: With sugar and spice and lots of vice, they're luring a younger audience," picturing three young women from the top-rated afternoon soaps. In 1981, *Us* magazine (November 24) featured *General Hospital*'s famous young couple, Luke and Laura, in an embrace, and an inset of three other "sexiest soapers" from *The Young and the Restless*, *The Edge of Night*, and *Ryan's Hope*.

The first systematic study of televised soap operas resulted in what the authors themselves called a "curious document" that was based on the viewing of fourteen soap operas for a week in 1970 (Katzman, 1972). "Romantic and marital affairs" were identified as one of the four main "strands" of problems and events ($N = 85$) in the soaps (the other three were "social problems," "medical developments," and "criminal activity"). In that week of soap operas, coders reported three romances and four marriages in trouble, three new romances, eight clear and two potential cases of marital infidelity, three divorces or annulments, a reconciliation of a married couple, and seven impending marriages. By the mid-1980s, in three soaps watched frequently by teens (*General Hospital, All My Children,* and *One Life to Live*), unmarried intercourse occurred more frequently (1.56 times per hour) than any other sexual behavior, and twice as often as married intercourse. Most of the intercourse was talked about rather than visually depicted, however. Talk about intercourse and "long kisses" accounted for 88% of all the sexual activity (Greenberg, Stanley, et al., 1993).

As on prime time, little of the sexual content in soap operas included depiction or discussion of sexually transmitted disease, safe sex, or contraception. A study of afternoon soap operas in 1987 identified a "norm of promiscuous sex with few attendant consequences" (Lowry & Towles, 1989, p. 76). Some observers argued, however, that the soaps were more likely than other genres to depict the emotional consequences (i.e., betrayal, pain, embarrassment) of sexual acts and thus might be viewed as cautionary tales by at least some viewers (Greenberg & Busselle, 1996; Greenberg & D'Alessio, 1985).

Few systematic analyses of televised soap operas have been conducted since the 1980s, however, apparently because concern about sexual content shifted to other genres, such as music videos, and more recently the Internet. In the Kunkel et al. (2007) overview of sex on television (2001–2002 season), however, soap operas and situation comedies were found to have the highest average number of sexual scenes per hour (5.1 and 7.8, respectively) of any of the seven genres studied.

## INTERNET

When the World Wide Web (WWW) became publicly available in the early 1990s, it seemed that almost overnight thousands (and by some estimations hundreds of thousands) of Web sites featuring sexually explicit content materialized. Although many adults were clearly delighted that pornography was now easily and anonymously available (as suggested by the popularity of the sites), parents and other youth advocates were alarmed by the possibility that teenagers could have unlimited access to such a wide and varied range of sexually explicit material. Adults worried that teens who intentionally sought pornography online would easily find an abundance of visual and textual content that could be unhealthy or even dangerous. Teens' unintentional encounters with pornography also troubled many adults, because of the chance that young people could be caught off guard at ages and times when they might be ill-equipped to understand or handle what they had seen.

Simultaneously reflecting and inflaming the public outcry, the popular press commonly characterized the WWW as a smut-filled danger zone for unsuspecting youth. With headlines like "'On a screen near you:' Cyberporn—It's Popular, Pervasive, and Surprisingly Perverse" (Elmer-DeWitt, 1995), "No Place for Kids?" (Levy, 1995), "Red Light District," (Chidley, 1995), "The Web's Dirty Secret" (Simons, 1996), and "The XXX-Files" (Segal, 1997), the media helped breed an atmosphere in which Congress felt obliged to take action. With the goal of protecting children and youth from disturbing and potentially harmful content, Congress passed two pieces of legislation (the Communications Decency Act in 1996 and the Children's Online Protection Act in 1998) that aimed to circumvent youth's access to or encounters with online sexual content. The courts subsequently declared both pieces of legislation unconstitutional, however, because they were overly broad and inhibited adults' rights to free speech.

Despite such concerns, very little empirical research has actually documented the extent or kinds of sexual material available online. The main obstacle, of course, is the vastness of the Internet. Simply put, there is no way to reliably account for all sexual content online, or even all pornography, even assuming it is possible to distinguish it from other sexual content.

As some researchers have reasoned, time might be better spent examining the extent to which young people actually encounter sexual content online. A 2002 Kaiser Family Foundation Study, for example, found that 70% of teens aged 15 to 17 said they had "accidentally come across pornography on the Internet." In a national survey published a year later, Mitchell, Finkelhor, and Wolak (2003) found that one-fourth of youth ages 10 to 17 had unwanted exposure to sexual pictures on the Internet in the preceding year. Most of the images they encountered were of naked people, but one-third reported seeing images of people having sex, and 7% involved violence in addition to nudity and sex. Older boys were most likely to report having had unwanted exposure. Two years after that, Ybarra and Mitchell (2005) concluded from a nationally representative Youth Internet Safety Survey of 1,500 youths ages 10 to 17 that nearly all (95%) teens who accessed porn online were male, and most were more than 14 years old, when sexual curiosity is developmentally appropriate. They concluded that concerns about large numbers of healthy, well-adjusted young children being exposed to online pornography were overstated.

Although concerns about youth access to online pornography have waned slightly, a new concern seems to have taken center stage in the new millennium: the creation of online sexual content *by* teens. With the growth of user-generated content in chat rooms and on bulletin boards, personal home pages, blogs, and most recently social networking sites, adolescents have had greater opportunity than ever before to present themselves publicly to a geographically disparate audience. Many young people choose to post pictures of themselves in poses and clothes that could be considered sensual and sexually suggestive. Some also write about their sexual identities, sexual behaviors, and sexual desires online. Stern (2004), for example, found among the 233 teen home pages she analyzed, nearly one-tenth of the authors mentioned sex, with girls three times as likely as boys to do so. We might expect that social networking sites such as MySpace.com and Facebook.com would yield even more sexual content, although no systematic study of these sites has been conducted.

Critics find teens' own sexual content problematic for a variety of reasons, some of which are rooted in a cultural discomfort with youths' (especially female youths') sexuality, and some of which are grounded in concerns for the health and well-being of youthful content creators. The possibility that youth's own sexual content might invite sexual predation by (usually male) adults has led to substantial apprehension. Concerns also surround the idea that the provocative and/or sexual imagery teens, especially girls, post online is a form of self-objectification, in which young people "learn to think of and treat their own bodies as objects of others' desires." In so doing, young people may "internalize an observer's perspective on their physical selves and learn to treat themselves as objects to be looked at and evaluated for their appearance" (American Psychological Association, 2007).

Alternately, some have suggested that sexual self-expression on the Internet can be functional for adolescents. Stern (2002), for example, argued that girls express their sexual selves on personal home pages as a way to define and distinguish their self-identities. Sexuality is an important part of development during adolescence, and the Internet provides a relatively safe space to explore how one views and presents oneself as a sexual person. Similarly, Grisso and Wise (2005) examined teen girls' discourse about romance and sex on the Web site gURL.com. Focusing on two bulletin boards, the authors noted how participants answered questions and provided support and reassurance for one another. The authors concluded that the site served as a place for girls to "explore and define themselves as sexual beings" (p. 36). Alexander (2004) looked at how queer youth used the WWW to communicate about their lives. Analyzing forty community building Web sites where youths could post thoughts, ideas, and insights, they concluded that queer youth used the Internet to discuss a variety of sexual identities, to address issues of bisexuality and transgenderism, to examine sociopolitical aspects of being queer, and to frankly discuss sexual practices, including safe sex.

Subrahmanyam, Greenfield, and Tynes (2004) analyzed conversations in a teen chat room to conclude that young people used the space to discuss their concerns about sexuality and share information with peers. These authors argued that the anonymous nature of the Internet allows teens to engage in candid discussion of sex, a potentially embarrassing topic.

Moreover, they noted, teens need not actually participate in the chat to get information; they can simply "lurk." The authors also suggested that teen chat rooms provided a relatively safe place for teens to practice dating and other kinds of new relationship behaviors that can seem more intimidating in the real world.

As a space for teens to address embarrassing topics, ask uncomfortable questions, and search for information about intimate body parts, conditions, and practices, the Internet, most youth advocates agree, holds considerable promise. For example, sexual health information Web sites can help adolescents determine if certain conditions are normal or if they warrant treatment from a doctor or other professional. They can also provide ideas about how to handle sexual situations, how to use birth control, and how to seek help when needed. In certain cases, access to emergency phone numbers and information about emergency contraception can be vital, too (Borzekowski & Rickert, 2001). Because the WWW can be navigated anonymously, the Internet may be particularly useful to teens who view discussions about sex and sexuality with doctors, parents, and peers with apprehension. The WWW is a useful alternative because teens can navigate in private while still receiving current information (Suzuki & Calzo, 2004).

Hundreds, if not thousands, of sexual health sites are maintained online by health organizations, nonprofits, government agencies, foundations, educational institutions, and companies. These sites offer an extensive array of information about the basic facts of sexual behavior, anatomy, sexually transmitted diseases, pregnancy, and sexuality. Such information has not gone unnoticed by youths. Borzekowski and Rikert (2001) found that among the 42% of those adolescents they studied who tried to get health information from the Internet, 27% specifically sought information about sex. The following year, the Kaiser Family Foundation (2002) reported that 24% of the online teens ages 15 to 17 said they had gone online to do research on sexually transmitted diseases, and 21% researched pregnancy or birth. A 2005 study found that nearly a third of teen Internet users went online for information about health, dieting, or fitness, and about a fifth of online teens looked for information online about a health topic that's "hard to talk about," such as drug use, sexual health, or depression (Lenhart, Madden, & Hitlin, 2005).

A few studies have assessed the quality and nature of sexual health information sites. Noar, Clark, Cole, and Lustria (2006), for example, content analyzed twenty-one interactive safer sex Web sites. Nearly nine out of ten sites were directed exclusively at adolescents or included areas targeted specifically at teens. The most prevalent messages about safe sex were to use condoms and be sexually abstinent, and the most common strategy used to motivate site visitors to engage in safe sex was to heighten their perceived threat of sexually transmitted diseases and HIV. Keller, Labelle, Karimi, and Gupta (2002) evaluated how the Internet promoted sexual health among adolescents, noting that carefully performed WWW searches could help teens to attain valuable educational information about sex that was specifically designed for them. These researchers, as well as Noar et al. (2006), concluded that existing sexual health sites could take greater advantage of Web technology to provide more usable and interactive experiences for youths seeking sexual health information.

## CONCLUSIONS

The stories our media have told about teen sexuality over the past half-century vary by medium, decade, and genre. Some are stories of pleasure, and others are stories of pain. Some narratives highlight sexual escapades, while others emphasize the relationships that contextualize sexual activity. Some accounts reinforce norms and stereotypes, while others boldly break new ground. The only overall conclusion that can be drawn is that each of these stories, in their own way, has contributed to the current ambiguity that generally characterizes Americans' sentiments about teen sexuality. For example, in 2008, we want teens to "wait" but often expect that they will, nevertheless, engage in sexual activity. Parents and educators promote abstinence, and yet teens' peer culture often suggests that only nerds and prudes abstain. On the other hand, teens, especially girls, learn quickly that having sex might hurt their reputations. Adults often approach the topic of sexuality with discomfort and alarm, and teens have come to expect that "sex talks" with adults will be awkward, if not intolerable. To make sense of it all, teens often turn to the media.

Yet, as this summary chapter suggests, the media do not now and have not ever sent consistent messages about sexuality. There is little question that sexual behaviors have become more frequent and explicit across all media with each passing decade. Images that would have been censored in the 1950s became increasingly common in the 1980s, and, by 2005, were mainstream. Romance and courtship—practices that used to only hint at sexuality—have received shorter and shorter shrift as media producers vie for the lucrative youth market, which is presumed to be sexually curious and easily bored. In consequence, content that might have shocked a 15-year-old in the 1960s might not even earn a second glance from a contemporary teenager, who encounters such imagery daily from an array of media sources.

Although sexual content has increased over the years, representations of safe sexual practices and sexually healthy behaviors have not kept pace.

In fact, such depictions in any of the media discussed here have been rare, if not absent altogether. Although we might have expected little sexual health content in the 1950 and 1960s because sexual content was relatively rare, it is hard to understand why portrayals of sexual health behaviors weren't included in the decades since. In one analysis across four media (movies, television, music, and magazines) used regularly by young teens (12 to 14 years old) in 2002, less than one percent of the content depicted any kind of sexual health message (Hust, Brown, & L'Engle, 2008). The sexual revolution, *Roe v. Wade*, the legalization of the pill, the spread of HIV and the AIDS epidemic, and high teen pregnancy and STD infection rates have put sexual health issues on the public's agenda for the last thirty years. Incorporating references to or images of healthy sexual practices in the media could easily occur, but typically does not. One promising development is that the Internet provides online resources that might provide the information left out of mainstream entertainment media.

Quantitative content analyses tell only one part of the picture of sexual content in the media, however. The overall message a song, TV program, or movie conveys about teen sexuality is more than just a sum of the number of times in which teens engage in sexy activities. Although studies suggest, for example, that films featuring teens often show teens having sex, it has been persuasively argued that many of these same films actually work to discourage sex, or at least to dispel the myth that sex is generally fun, pleasurable, and fulfilling. Music videos, on the other hand, may rarely show teens actually engaging in sexual activity, but their overall message suggests that sexual behavior is normal and recreational for strangers, as well as a good way to gain or signal status.

Future researchers who aim to analyze sexual content in the media have much to address. First, it will be valuable to establish measures that capture context and a sense of the whole. This may mean including more and/or larger units of analysis. It could be valuable, for example, to analyze an entire music video in addition to each scene that portrays sex to decipher the "message" of the video. Alternatively, because this approach might introduce an unacceptable amount of unreliability between coders, a study might be better served by including a qualitative component that could complement the quantitative findings. Perhaps James Lull put it best when he described the difficulties of identifying and describing the manifest content in music videos as a situation for which "not everything that can be counted counts, and not everything that counts can be counted" (as quoted in Sherman & Dominick, 1986, p. 82). It would be good if researchers focused not only on the sex acts themselves, but also on the scripts that serve to celebrate, demonize, or normalize teen sex. Researchers would be wise, too, to refrain from judging teen sexual behavior exclusively in a negative light; indeed, Buckingham (2004) and others have warned against the proclivity to label all teen sex as immoral or unscrupulous.

We have seen in this overview of sexual content in the media that adolescents rarely see what might be called the three Cs of sexual health: commitment, contraceptives, and consequences. As some have noted (e.g., Brown & Strasberger, in press), the media could be helpful in presenting a healthier picture of teen sexuality if they included the three Cs in teen-oriented content. Some organizations, such as the Kaiser Family Foundation and the National Campaign to Prevent Teen Pregnancy, have had some success in working with media directed at teen audiences to embed more depictions of sexual responsibility in entertainment programming and editorial content. Entertainment education has been used effectively to encourage family planning and other socially desirable behavior in other countries for many years (Singhal, Cody, Rogers, & Sabido, 2003).

In one of the few tests of the effectiveness of the approach in the United States, a survey showed that two-thirds of adolescent viewers of a *Friends* episode in which a pregnancy resulted from condom failure learned that condoms can fail, and another third learned about condoms' efficacy in preventing pregnancy (Collins, Elliott, Berry, Kanouse, & Hunter, 2003). An experiment with college students found that young women who saw episodes of popular television shows with depictions of condoms held more favorable attitudes toward condoms than women who saw shows that depicted sexual intercourse but no condoms (Farrar, 2006). Such studies suggest that putting condoms in sexual scripts could make a difference in attitudes, and perhaps even behavior, among young media consumers who are developing their own scripts about sexual behavior and sexual health.

Future content studies should also attend to the particulars of teen sexuality. For example, although studies have frequently assessed how male and female characters/performers are treated differently in terms of their sexuality, more attention should be paid to other demographic disparities as well, such as how characters of different race, ethnicity, and class are displayed as sexual beings and how their sexual behaviors are constructed within the texts. Greater emphasis might also be placed on examining the type of characters who engage or do not engage in sexual behaviors. Are cool, popular teens more likely to be shown as sexually active? Good-looking characters? Rebellious characters?

Accounting for the consequences of teen sexuality is also important, in both the short and long term, because we know from basic social learning theory (e.g., Bandura, 1993) that portraying any risky behavior as positive and/or without potential negative consequences increases the possibility of imitation. It would be also be valuable for future studies to account for the emotional consequences as well as the behavioral consequences of sexual activity, as some of the soap opera studies have. Are characters who engage in one night stands sexually satisfied? Do they suffer guilt or concern about their partner? Are the hardships and joys of young motherhood displayed?

Very little attention has been paid to sexual violence in the media content adolescents attend to. According to a couple of small studies, attitudes about rape and fighting among dating couples can be affected by exposure to sexual violence, even the pseudoviolence between men and women depicted in professional wrestling and on music videos (DuRant, Champion, & Wolfson, 2006; Kaestle, Halpern, & Brown, 2007). More attention should be paid to such depictions.

Finally, future researchers might usefully consider the differences between images of teen sexuality and images of adult sexuality that teens are likely to see. Teen characters/singers shown engaging in sex help construct norms about teen life, and may make it easy for teen viewers/listeners to identify with them. Most characters in American media are young adults, however, and thus, teens are more likely to encounter adult rather than teen sexual activity in the media. Because adult sexual content is even less frequently couched in terms of safe sex than media directed toward teens, and because it is generally more likely to be glamorized or at least to occur without penalty, depictions of young adults' sexual behavior should be included in analyses of content that might influence teens.

This chapter demonstrates that sexual content has enjoyed a long and varied history in the mass media popular with adolescent audiences, often reflecting the sexual contradictions of the larger culture. Across the different media adolescents use, sex has been used to attract and maintain audiences, not teach sexually responsible behavior. Although it would be nice to imagine that newer media technologies, such as the Internet, could contribute to a healthier approach to adolescent sexuality, that remains to be seen.

## REFERENCES

Aherns, F. (2006, June 8). The price for on-air indecency goes up. *Washington Post*, p. D01.

Alexander, J. (2004). *In their own words: LGBT youth writing the world wide web*. New York: GLAAD Center for the Study of Media & Society.

Allen, R. (1985). *Speaking of soap operas*. Chapel Hill: University of North Carolina Press.

American Psychological Association (2007). *Report of the APA task force on the sexualization of girls*. Retrieved February 19, 2007, from http://www.apa.org/pi/wpo/sexualizationsum.html

Andrews, B. (1976). *The "I Love Lucy" book*. New York: Doubleday.

Ashby, S. L., Arcari, C. M., & Edmonson, M. B. (2006). Television viewing and risk of sexual initiation by young adolescents. *Archives of Pediatric Adolescent Medicine, 160,* 375–380.

Bandura A. (1993). *Social learning theory.* Englewood Cliffs, NJ: Prentice Hall.

Barnouw, E. (1990). *Tube of plenty: The evolution of American television.* New York: Oxford University Press.

Baxter, R. L., DeRiemer, C., Landini, A., Leslie, L., & Singletary, M. W. (1985). A content analysis of music videos. *Journal of Broadcasting & Electronic Media, 29,* 333–340.

Bodroghkozy, A. (2003). The "youth revolution" and American television. In M. Hilmes (Ed.), *The television history book* (pp. 81–86). London: BFI Publishing.

Borzekowski, D. L. G., & Rikert, V. I. (2001). Adolescent cybersurfing for health information: A new resource that crosses barriers. *Archives of Pediatrics & Adolescent Medicine, 155,* 813.

Brown, J. D. (2000). Adolescents' sexual media diets. *Journal of Adolescent Health, 27*(2, Supplement), 35–40.

Brown, J. D., L'Engle, K. L., Pardun, C. J., Guo, G., Kenneavy, K., & Jackson, C. (2006). Sexy media matter: Exposure to sexual content in music, movies, television and magazines predicts Black and White adolescents' sexual behavior. *Pediatrics, 117,* 1018–1027.

Brown, J. D., & Strasburger, V. (in press). From Calvin Klein, to Paris Hilton and MySpace: Adolescents, sex & the media. In M. J. Blythe & S. L. Rosenthal (Eds.), *Adolescent sexuality* (Adolescent medicine: State of the art reviews). Washington, DC: American Pediatrics Association Press.

Buckingham, D. (2004). *Young people, sex, and the media.* Hampshire, UK: Palgrave Macmillan.

Bulman, R. C. (2005). *Hollywood goes to high school: Cinema, schools, and American culture.* New York: Worth.

Carey, J. (1969). Changing courtship patterns in the popular song. *American Journal of Sociology, 4,* 720–731.

Chidley, J. (1995, May 22). Red-light district: From S&M to bestiality; porn flourishes on the Internet. *Macleans,* p. 58.

Christenson, P. G., & Roberts, D. F. (1998). *It's not only rock & roll: Popular music in the lives of adolescents.* Creskill, NJ: Hampton Press.

Cole, R. (1971). Top songs in the sixties: A content analysis. *American Behavioral Scientist, 14,* 389–400.

Collins, R. L., Elliott, M. N., Berry, S. H., Kanouse, E., & Hunter, S. B. (2003). Entertainment television as a healthy sex educator: The impact of condom-efficacy information in an episode of *Friends. Pediatrics, 112,* 1115.

Collins, R. L., Elliott, M. N., Berry, S. H., Kanouse, D. E., Kunkel, D., Hunter, S. B., & Miu, A. (2004). Watching sex on television predicts adolescent initiation of sexual behavior. *Pediatrics, 114,* e280–e289.

Considine, D. (1985). *The cinema of adolescence.* Jefferson, NC: McFarland & Co.

Cope-Farrar, K. M., & Kunkel, D. (2002). Sexual messages in teens' favorite prime-time TV programs. In J. D. Brown, J. R. Steele, & K. Walsh-Childers (Eds.), *Sexual teens, sexual media* (pp. 59–78). Hillsdale, NJ: Erlbaum.

Dale, E. (1935). *The content of motion pictures*. New York: Macmillan.

DuRant, R. H., Champion, H., & Wolfson, M. (2006). The relationship between watching professional wrestling on television and engaging in date fighting among high school students. *Pediatrics, 118*, 265–272.

Elmer-DeWitt, P. (1995, July 3). On a screen near you. *Time Magazine*, 34–41.

Escobar-Chaves, S. L., Tortolero, S. R., Markham, C. M., Low, B.J., Eitel, P., & Thickstun, P. (2005). Impact of the media on adolescent sexual attitudes and behaviors. *Pediatrics, 116*, 303–326.

Farrar, K. M. (2006). Sexual intercourse on television: Do safe sex messages matter? *Journal of Broadcasting & Electronic Media, 50*, 635–650.

Frith, S. (1978). *The sociology of rock*. London: Constable.

Gagnon, J. H., & Simon, W. (1987). The sexual scripting of oral genital contacts. *Archives of Sexual Behavior, 16*, 1–25.

Garner, J. (2002). *Stay tuned: Television's unforgettable moments*. Kansas City, MO: Andrews McMeel Publishing.

Gerbner, G., Gross, L., Morgan, M., Signorielli, N., & Shanahan, J. (2002). Growing up with television: Cultivation processes. In J. Bryant & D. Zillmann (Eds.), *Media effects: Advances in theory and research* (2nd ed., pp. 43–68). Hillsdale, NJ: Erlbaum.

Giroux, H. (1996). Hollywood, race, and the demonization of youth: The "kids" are not "alright." *Educational Researcher, 25*, 31–35.

Gore, T. (1987). *Raising PG kids in an X-Rated society*. Nashville, TN: Parthenon Press.

Greenberg, B. S., & Busselle, R. W. (1996). Soap operas and sexual activity: A decade later. *Journal of Communication, 46*(4), 153–161.

Greenberg, B. S., & D'Alessio, D. (1985). Quantity and quality of sex in the soaps. *Journal of Broadcasting & Electronic Media, 29*, 309–321.

Greenberg, B. S., Siemicki, M., Dorfman, S., Heeter, C., Stanley, C., Soderman, A., & Linsangan, R. (1993). Sex content in R-rated films viewed by adolescents. In B. S. Greenberg, J. D. Brown, & N. L. Buerkel-Rothfuss (Eds.), *Media, sex and the adolescent* (pp. 45–58). Cresskill, NJ: Hampton Press.

Greenberg, B. S., Stanley, C., Siemicki, M., Heeter, C., Soderman, A., & Linsangan, R. (1993). Sex content on soaps and primetime television series most watched by adolescents. In B. S. Greenberg, J. D. Brown, & N. L. Buerkel-Rothfuss (Eds.), *Media, sex and the adolescent* (pp. 29–44). Cresskill, NJ: Hampton Press.

Grisso, A., & Wise, D. (2005). What are gURLS talking about? Adolescent girls' construction of sexual identity on gURL.com. In S. Mazzarella (Ed.), *Girl wide web: Girls, the internet, and the negotiation of identity* (pp. 31–50). New York: Peter Lang.

Hentges, S. (2006). *Pictures of girlhood: Modern female adolescence on film*. Jefferson, NC: McFarland.

Hetsroni, A. (2007). Three decades of sexual content on prime-time network programming: A longitudinal meta-analytic review. *Journal of Communication, 57*, 318–348.

Horton, D. (1957). The dialogue of courtship in popular songs. *The American Journal of Sociology, 62,* 569–578.

Hust, S., Brown, J. D., & L'Engle, K. L. (2008). Boys will be boys and girls better be prepared: An analysis of the rare sexual health messages in young adolescents' media. *Mass Communication & Society, 11,* 1–21.

Huston, A. C., Wartella, E., & Donnerstein, E. (1998). *Measuring the effects of sexual content in the media: A report to the Kaiser Family Foundation.* Menlo Park, CA: Kaiser Family Foundation.

Hyden, C., & McCandless, N. (1983). Men and women as portrayed in popular music lyrics. *Popular Music and Society, 9,* 19–26.

Kaestle, C. E., Halpern, C. T., & Brown, J. D. (2007). Music videos, pro wrestling, and acceptance of date rape among middle school males and females: An exploratory analysis. *Journal of Adolescent Health, 40,* 185–187.

Kaiser Family Foundation (2002). *Key facts: Teens online.* Menlo Park, CA: Kaiser Family Foundation.

Kaiser Family Foundation/*Seventeen Magazine* (2004). *Sex smarts: Birth control and protection.* Menlo Park, CA: Kaiser Family Foundation.

Katzman, N. (1972). Television soap operas: What's been going on anyway? *Public Opinion Quarterly, 36,* 200–212.

Keller, S., Labelle, H., Karimi, N., & Gupta, S. (2002). STD/HIV prevention for teenagers: A look at the Internet universe. *Journal of Health Communication, 7,* 341–353.

Kunkel, D., Eyal, K., Donnerstein, E., Farrar, K. M., Biely, E., & Rideout, V. (2007). Sexual socialization messages on entertainment television: Comparing content trends 1997–2002. *Media Psychology, 9,* 595–622.

Kunkel, D., Eyal, K., Finnerty, K., Biely, E., & Donnerstein, E. (2005). *Sex on TV 4: A biennial report to the Kaiser Family Foundation.* Menlo Park, CA: Kaiser Family Foundation.

Larson, S. G. (1991). Television's mixed messages: Sexual content on *All My Children. Communication Quarterly, 39,* 156–163.

Levine, E. (2003). U.S. networks in the 1970s and 80s. In M. Hilmes (Ed.), *The television history book* (pp. 89–94). London: BFI Publishing.

Levy, S. (1995, July 3). No place for kids? *Newsweek,* p. 47.

Lewis, J. (1992). *The road to romance and ruin.* New York: Routledge.

Lisante, T. (2005). *Hollywood surf and beach movies: The first wave 1959–1969.* Jefferson, NC: McFarland.

Lowry, D. T., Love, G., & Kirby, M. (1981). Sex on the soap operas: Patterns of intimacy. *Journal of Communication, 31*(3), 90–96.

Lowry, D. T., & Towles, D. E. (1989). Soap opera portrayals of sex, contraception, and sexually transmitted diseases. *Journal of Communication, 39*(2), 76–83.

Martino, S. C., Collins, R. L., Elliott, M. N., Strachman, A., Kanouse, D. E., & Berry, S. H. (2006). Exposure to degrading versus non-degrading music lyrics and sexual behavior among youth. *Pediatrics, 118,* e430-e431.

Medved, M. (1992). *Hollywood vs. America: Popular culture and the war on traditional values.* New York: HarperCollins Publishers/Zondervan.

Mitchell, K., Finkelhor, D., & Wolak, J. (2003). The exposure of youth to unwanted sexual material on the internet: A national survey of risk, impact, and prevention. *Youth & Society, 34,* 330–358.

Noar, S. M., Clark, A., Cole, C., & Lustria, M. L. (2006). Review of interactive safer sex web sites: Practice and potential. *Health Communication, 20,* 233–241.

Pardun, C. (2002). Romancing the script: Identifying the romantic agenda in top-grossing movies. In J. D. Brown, J. R. Steele, & K. Walsh-Childers (Eds.), *Sexual teens, sexual media* (pp. 211–226). Mahwah, NJ: Erlbaum.

Pardun, C., L'Engle, K. L., & Brown, J. D. (2005). Linking exposure to outcomes: Early adolescents' consumption of sexual content in six media. *Mass Communication & Society, 8*(2), 75–91.

Parks, L. (2003). U.S. television abroad: Exporting culture. In M. Hilmes (Ed.), *The television history book* (pp. 115–118). London: BFI Publishing.

Pecora, N., Murray, J. P., & Wartella, E. A. (2006). Children and television (TV): 50 years of research. Mahwah, NJ: Erlbaum.

Perren, A. (2003). New U.S. networks in the 1990s. In M. Hilmes (Ed.), *The television history book* (pp. 107–111). London: BFI Publishing.

Rice, R. (1980). The content of popular recordings. *Popular Music and Society, 7,* 140–158.

Roberts, D. F., & Foehr, U. G. (2004). *Kids and media in America.* Cambridge: Cambridge University Press.

Scheff, T. J. (2001). Individualism and alienation in popular love songs, 1930–1999. Retrieved June 6, 2007, from http://www.soc.ucsb.edu/faculty/scheff

Segal, D. (1997, Oct. 26). The XXX-Files. *The Washington Post,* p. W7.

Shary, T. (2002). *Generation multiplex: The image of youth in contemporary American cinema.* Austin: University of Texas.

Sherman, B. L., & Dominick, J. R. (1986). Violence and sex in music videos: TV and rock 'n' roll. *Journal of Communication, 36,* 79–93.

Shore, M., with Clark, D. (1985). *The history of* American Bandstand. New York: Ballantine.

Silverman, L. T., Sprafkin, J. T., & Rubinstein, E. A. (1979). Physical contact and sexual behavior on prime-time TV. *Journal of Communication, 29,* 33–43.

Simons, J. (1996, August 19). The Web's dirty secret. *U.S. News & World Report,* p. 51.

Singhal, A., Cody, M. J., Rogers, E. M., & Sabido, M. (Eds.) (2003). *Entertainment-education and social change: History, research and practice.* Mahwah, NJ: Erlbaum.

Spigel, L. (1992). *Make room for TV: Television and the family ideal in postwar America.* Chicago: University of Chicago Press.

Stern, S. (2002). Sexual selves on the World Wide Web: Adolescent girls' home pages as sites for sexual self expression. In J. D. Brown, J. R. Steele, & K. Walsh-Childers (Eds.), *Sexual teens, sexual media* (pp. 265–286). Mahwah, NJ: Erlbaum.

Stern, S. (2004). Expressions of identity online: Prominent features and gender differences in adolescents' World Wide Web home pages. *Journal of Broadcasting & Electronic Media, 48,* 218–243.

Stern, S. (2005). Self-absorbed, dangerous, and disengaged: What popular films tell us about teenagers. *Mass Communication & Society, 8,* 23–38.

Stern, S., & Levkoff, L. (2006) *Thematic analysis of teen sexuality in popular teen films*. Unpublished manuscript.

Strasburger, V. C. (2005). Adolescents, sex, and the media: oooo, baby, baby—a Q&A. *Adolescent Medicine Clinics, 16*, 269–288.

Subrahmanyam, K., Greenfield, P., & Tynes, B. (2004). Constructing sexuality and identity in an online teen chat room. *Journal of Applied Developmental Psychology, 25*, 651–666.

Suzuki, L., & Calzo, J. (2004). The search for peer advice in cyberspace: An examination of online teen bulletin boards about health and sexuality. *Journal of Applied Developmental Psychology, 25*(6), 685–698.

Tapper, J., Thorson, E., & Black, D. (1994). Variations in music videos as a function of their musical genre. *Journal of Broadcasting & Electronic Media, 38*, 103–114.

Taylor, E. (1989). *Prime-time families: Television culture in postwar America*. Berkeley: University of California Press.

Ward, L. M. (1995). Talking about sex: Common themes about sexuality in the prime-time television programs children and adolescents view most. *Journal of Youth and Adolescence, 24*, 595–615.

Ward, L. M. (2003). Understanding the role of entertainment media in the sexual socialization of American youth: A review of empirical research. *Developmental Review, 23*, 347–388.

Weinstock, H., Berman, S., & Cates, W., Jr. (2004). Sexually transmitted diseases among American youth: Incidence and prevalence estimates, 2000. *Perspectives on Sexual and Reproductive Health, 36*, 6–10.

Whatley, M. (1991). Raging hormones and powerful cars: The construction of men's sexuality in school sex education and popular adolescent films. In H. Giroux (Ed.), *Postmodernism, feminism, and cultural politics* (pp. 119–143). Albany: State University of New York Press.

Williams, L. (2006). Of kisses and ellipses: The long adolescence of American movies. *Critical Inquiry, 32*, 288–340.

Ybarra, M. L., & Mitchell, K. J. (2005). Exposure to Internet pornography among children and adolescents: A national survey. *CyberPsychology & Behavior, 8*, 473–486.

# Part III

# Evolving Forms of Media Influence

# 12

# The Games, They Are a-Changin'

## Technological Advancements in Video Games and Implications for Effects on Youth

JAMES D. IVORY

When William Higinbotham, a nuclear scientist at the U.S. Department of Nuclear Energy's Brookhaven National Laboratory in Upton, NY, created a simple game of tennis using an oscilloscope screen in 1958, he was merely looking to create a novelty to entertain visitors from the public during his lab's open house sessions (Consalvo, 2006; Lowood, 2006; Rockwell, 2002). When a group of students at the Massachusetts Institute of Technology pitted dueling rocket ships against each other in their *Spacewar!* game, their simple goal was to suitably demonstrate the processing and display technology of a newly acquired research computer (Kirriemuir, 2006; Lowood, 2006). It's unlikely that these innovators, now retrospectively recognized as video game pioneers, had any inkling of how much high-tech entertainment their gadgets' descendants would provide around the world in the years to come.[1]

Video games (using the term broadly here to include the wide range of electronic digital games played on computers, handheld devices, home consoles attached to television sets, and arcade machines) may have once been novelties on the computers of government and university labs, but now they drive a multibillion dollar entertainment media industry. During 2006, retail sales of video games and related equipment in the United States totaled $12.5 billion (Richtel, 2007). Although a substantial portion of the video game audience consists of adults (Scott, 2006), including seniors (Schiesel, 2007), children and adolescents nonetheless represent a major video game–playing demographic (Harris Interactive, 2007; Roberts, Foehr, & Rideout, 2005)—even though the vast majority of video game characters are adults, while children and adolescents are portrayed relatively rarely (Dill, Gentile, Richter, & Dill, 2005).

Considering this vast and often youthful audience, it is not surprising that a large body of research has adamantly pursued an understanding of video games' psychological, social, and physical effects (see Anderson, 2004; Anderson & Bushman, 2001; Bensley & van Eenwyk, 2001; Dill & Dill, 1998; Ferguson, 2007; Griffiths, 1999; Schott & Hodgetts, 2006; Sherry, 2001). Despite such extensive research, a consensus on the scope and nature of video games' effects remains elusive. Some researchers conclude with confidence that the existing research identifies violent video games as a clear culprit for negative effects (e.g., Anderson & Bushman, 2001; Gentile & Anderson, 2006), while others claim that a final determination on the issue cannot be made without further study (e.g., Ferguson, 2007; Griffiths, 1999) or argue that a focus on negative effects in research presents an incomplete picture of video games' influence by ignoring positive applications (e.g., Griffiths, 2004; Schott & Hodgetts, 2006).

Further complicating an assessment of video games' effects is the medium's extremely rapid evolution. There may be some discord regarding video games' effects, but there is broad agreement on another issue: they are changing extremely rapidly and becoming increasingly realistic in their presentation, and this advancement may change the way video games affect their players (e.g., Calvert & Tan, 1994; Carnagey & Anderson, 2004; Chory & Cicchirillo, 2007; Eastin, 2006; Eastin & Griffiths, 2006; Gentile & Anderson, 2003; Kirsh, 2003; Persky & Blascovich, 2006; Sherry, 2001; Tamborini, Eastin, Skalski, Lachlan, Fediuk, et al., 2004; Weber, Ritterfeld, & Mathiak, 2006).

In this chapter I focus on how these technological advancements in video games may influence the medium's effects, especially on youth. First, I provide a brief overview of the current state of the video game industry and audience. Then, I give a short review of research findings and theoretical frameworks dealing with the effects of video games and follow with a section summarizing major changes in video games over the history of the medium and how these changes may influence the medium's effects. Finally, I discuss implications for future research and policy.

## VIDEO GAMES' POPULARITY AMONG YOUTH

Although the video game industry endured what Williams (2003) calls "a spectacular crash" (p. 525) in the early 1980s after the medium's initial commercial emergence during the previous decade, there are no signs of another slowdown in the future. During some recent years, the video game industry's revenue has been larger than the Hollywood box office, both in the United States (Chmielewski, 2006; Hillis, 2006) and globally (Hutchins, 2006). While the 2004 film *Spider-Man 2* broke opening weekend records with $114 million in ticket receipts, the video game *Halo 2* hauled in $125 million in sales on its first day of release later that year (Clarke, 2006).

Video games enjoy a healthy audience across age ranges, with surveys indicating that 40% of U.S. adults play video games (Slagle, 2006), but the medium is an especially large presence in the lives of children and adolescents. A 2004 Kaiser Family Foundation survey of U.S. children ages 8 to 18 found that 83% lived in a home with a video game console; 63% of boys and 33% of girls had one in their rooms (Roberts et al., 2005). Respondents spent an average of an hour and eight minutes playing games daily, with 59% playing for at least some time daily and 30% playing more than an hour daily. According to a 2007 poll (Harris Interactive, 2007), eight in ten U.S. youth ages 8 to 18 play video games at least once a month, with the average 8- to 12-year-old playing for thirteen hours per week and the average 13- to 18-year-old playing for fourteen hours per week. Meanwhile, as the video game industry booms, new players are being groomed very early in life. In the last few years, specialized video game systems have been designed for target audiences as young as 3 years old (Garrison & Christakis, 2005).

Previous research confirms that the popularity of video games with youth has been long-standing. In surveys of fourth through eighth grade boys and girls conducted between 1992 and 1996, Buchman and Funk (1996) found that all sampled age and gender groups averaged more than two hours of video game play a week, although males and respondents from younger grades tended to report more video game play; weekly averages for males in fourth through eighth grades, in order, were 9.44, 8.23, 6.89, 6.15, and 4.97 hours, while averages for female respondent age groups, in the same order, were 5.67, 3.96, 3.18, 2.25, and 2.52 hours. Popularity of video games with youth has also been consistent outside of the United States, with surveys of UK adolescents finding that 31% of 12- to 16-year-old respondents played games daily (Griffiths & Hunt, 1995) and 25.8% of 11-year-olds played daily (Griffiths, 1997).

## VIDEO GAMES' POTENTIAL EFFECTS ON YOUTH

It is no surprise that so much video game playing, especially by youths, should prompt concern among researchers about the games' effects. Historically, the advent of a new entertainment medium that is popular with youth has been closely followed by a surge in research on the medium's potential for negative effects (Wartella & Reeves, 1985). The case of video games is no different. A large body of empirical research documents decades of efforts to assess the potential negative effects of video games on psychological, social, and physical outcomes such as aggression (e.g., Anderson & Dill, 2000; Bartholow, Sestir, & Davis, 2005; Scott, 1995; Williams & Skoric, 2005), addiction (e.g., Charlton & Danforth, 2007; Grüsser, Thalemann, & Griffiths, 2007; Wood & Griffiths, 2007), displacement of other activities (e.g., Griffiths, Davies, & Chappell, 2004), obesity (e.g., Burke et al., 2006; Vandewater, Shim, & Caplovitz, 2004), affected school performance (e.g., Anderson & Dill, 2000; Gentile, Lynch, Linder, & Walsh, 2004), changes in self-concept (e.g., Funk & Buchman, 1996; Roe & Muijs, 1998), altered perceptions of crime and violence in the real world (e.g., Van Mierlo & Van den Bulck, 2004; Williams, 2006a), and even injuries resulting from excessive game controller use (e.g., Macgregor, 2000; Rushing, Sheehan, & Davis, 2006). While a detailed overview of all video game effects research areas is far beyond the scope of this chapter, a short summary of empirical research, primarily involving experiments and surveys, in a number of the areas is presented below.

## Effects of Violent Content on Aggression and Antisocial Behavior

Content analyses have consistently found violence to be a common feature in popular video games. Dietz (1998) analyzed thirty-three popular games from 1995, finding that 79% "included some kind of aggression or violence" (p. 436). A content analysis of popular games from 1999 (Smith, Lachlan, & Tamborini, 2003) found that 68% contained at least one act of violence with 78% of observed acts of violence representing "lethal acts of aggression that would result in moderate or extreme harm in the real world" (p. 68). Dill et al. (2005) analyzed the top twenty computer games from 1999, finding that 60% included "violence as a major theme" (p. 122). A study of games rated "E" (for "everyone," suitable for all audiences) and available for sale in early 2001 found that 64% included intentional violence, with 60% rewarding violence or requiring it for advancement (Thompson & Haninger, 2001); a similar study of games rated "T" (for "teen,") from the same year found that 98% included intentional violence, with 90% requiring or rewarding injury of other characters and 69% requiring or rewarding killing (Haninger & Thompson, 2004).

Given that violence is so prevalent in video games, it is reasonable that there has been a corresponding research focus on aggressive behavior in video game players. For example, a pair of meta-analyses from 2001 (Anderson & Bushman, 2001; Sherry, 2001; see also Anderson, 2004) each identified more than thirty studies examining the effects of violent video games. There have been many more studies conducted in the area since then (e.g., Bartholow et al., 2005; Eastin, 2006; Eastin & Griffiths, 2006; Farrar, Krcmar, & Nowak, 2006; Ivory & Kalyanaraman, 2007; Kirsh, Olczak, & Mounts, 2005; Weber et al., 2006; Williams, 2006a; Williams & Skoric, 2005; see also Ferguson, 2007).

Research-based theoretical frameworks posit that media users, especially youth, are more likely to learn to emulate violence media when they are engaged, when violence is presented as justified, when the perpetrators are characters who are attractive or otherwise positively perceived by the viewer, when violence is rewarded, when violence is portrayed with graphical realism, and when the consequences of violence are not clearly presented (see Bandura 2002; Huesmann & Taylor, 2006; Wilson et al., 2002; see also Chapter 8 of this volume for a more detailed review of violent media effects). Because video game violence is often presented in ways that match a number of these characteristics (e.g., with a character controlled by the player who is rewarded for graphic killings), it has been argued that violence in video games is particularly conducive to player aggression, even more so than in other media such as television (see Carnagey & Anderson, 2004).

Proposed mechanisms explaining how violent video game content may influence aggression in players focus on three psychological effects as mediators in the process: aggressive thoughts, aggressive feelings, and arousal (see Anderson & Bushman, 2001; Bushman & Anderson, 2002). Theoretical models dealing with the concept of priming describe networks of associative pathways in the brain that link related thoughts, feelings, and behaviors (see Berkowitz & Rogers, 1986; Roskos-Ewoldsen, Roskos-Ewoldsen, & Carpentier, 2002). In the case of violent media, the implication is that exposure to violent media can lead to quicker activation of aggressive constructs by users (Bushman, 1998), as well as more hostile feelings (Anderson, 1997). According to the excitation transfer theory, arousal from exciting media can also influence aggressive behavior by intensifying reactions to unrelated situations because arousal from the media source is misattributed to the subsequent situation (see Zillmann, 1971). For example, a video game player who is very excited by a game, then later angered by an insult, may have an intensified anger reaction because the excitement from the earlier game is attributed to the unrelated provocation. Although many video games are exciting by nature, evidence that violent media are especially exciting (Bushman, 1995; Sparks & Sparks, 2002) draws special attention to the role of arousal in the effects of violent games. Because they are therefore singled out as links in the process by which aggressive behavior can stem from violent video game play, aggressive thoughts, aggressive feelings, and physiological arousal are often used as measures in research on violent video game effects in addition to more direct aggressive behavior measures (see Anderson & Bushman, 2001; Sherry, 2001).

Another often mentioned potential negative effect of video game violence is desensitization. Research with other media has shown that viewing violence can lead to increased habituation, with viewers of violence eventually becoming less responsive to violence (see Drabman & Thomas, 1974; Mullin & Linz, 1995; Wilson et al., 2002). Desensitization to violence could lead to increased aggressive behavior, but even if a violent media user does not become increasingly aggressive, desensitization could still result in negative social outcomes such as a decreased likelihood of helping a victim of violence. A number of studies have measured effects of violent video game play on desensitization, both in terms of diminished physiological response (e.g., Ballard, Hamby, Panee, & Nivens, 2006; Bartholow, Bushman, & Sestir, 2006) and diminished prosocial helping behavior (see Anderson & Bushman, 2001).

A meta-analysis (Anderson & Bushman, 2001) found that in the sizable body of research, violent video game play was positively linked to aggressive behavior for each of the indirect outcomes: aggressive thoughts, aggressive feelings, and physiological arousal. A negative relationship between violent video game play and prosocial behavior was also found. Such a preponderance of findings has led some to determine that violent video games are conclusively linked to player aggression and antisocial behavior (Anderson & Bushman, 2001; Carnegy & Anderson, 2004; Gentile & Anderson, 2006). Others are not as willing to make a conclusive judgment, especially with regard to effects on behavioral outcomes, citing objections ranging from appropriateness of specific measures to generalizability of research results to possible overrepresentation of significant results in the literature due to a general preference for statistically significant results (see Ferguson, 2007; Williams & Skoric, 2005). Another meta-analysis (Sherry, 2001), while finding an effect of violent video game play on aggression, noted that the effect may be smaller than similar effects observed with previous media such as television. Counterarguments have been presented in response to such doubts of a strong and conclusive causal link between violent games and aggression (e.g., Carnagey & Anderson, 2004; Gentile & Anderson, 2006), but suffice it to say that scholarly opinions about the extent to which video game violence presents a significant danger currently lack consensus.

This impasse is not a new problem in the field of media effects. Zillmann and Weaver sum up the near impossibility of presenting completely unequivocal and unchallengeable evidence for negative media effects, stating,

It seems that critics of media-violence research could only be satisfied with longitudinal experimental studies in which, within gender and a multitude of personality variables, random assignment is honored and exposure to violent fare is rigorously controlled—that is, with research that in a free society simply cannot be conducted. (Zillmann & Weaver, 1999, p. 147)

Given this well-put assessment, complete agreement in the research community with regard to video games' effects on real-life aggression and violence is not likely to be imminent, although use of novel methods ranging from longitudinal studies (e.g., Williams & Skoric, 2005) to functional magnetic imaging research informed by neuroscience (e.g., Weber et al., 2006) will continue to shed light on the difficult, but important, question. Meanwhile, the potential effects of video games on aggression and violence remain an issue worthy of concern even in the absence of a uniform consensus regarding their presence and magnitude, especially for adolescents, given suggestions that emotional and hormonal conditions during their developmental stage may exacerbate such effects.

## Effects of Violent and Sexual Content on Perceptions of Reality

In addition to research on whether violent video games affect players' behavior, some research has explored whether violent video game play affects how people see the world. Research in other entertainment media has found that heavy users are likely to perceive their world as more like the world represented in the media through a process of cultivation (see Gerbner, Gross, Morgan, & Signorielli, 1980). For example, heavy television users may estimate higher crime rates than those who watch less television because the heavy users' perceptions are affected by the unrealistically high number of violent acts depicted on television (see Romer, Jamieson, & Aday, 2003). As has been shown in the content analyses mentioned above, the world of video games is a very violent one, so the same effect with heavy video game players would result in perceptions of a more violent world. Given that a number of studies find that adolescents are susceptible to effects of television on perceptions of reality (see Gerbner, Gross, Morgan, Signorielli, & Shanahan, 2002), similar effects of video games on youthful users' perceptions are plausible. Anderson and Dill (2000) used a survey to examine the relationship between participants' violent video game play and their perceptions of personal safety and crime likelihood, but observed no significant effects of violent video game play after controlling for gender. Van Mierlo and Van den Bulck (2004) also measured the effects of video game play on perceptions of crime and violence, finding some limited evidence for effects on perceptions of reality using measures adapted from similar studies with television and concluding that future research with video games should develop new measures and take into account individual game preferences and content. Williams (2006a) explored altered perceptions of reality in a more specific context in a study using one online video game, finding that participants assigned to play a specific game estimated higher rates of violence than those who did not play the game. The effect was only seen, though, for the type of violence depicted in the game (violent assault with weapons), and not for other types of violence not depicted in the game, such as sexual assault.

Violence is not the only type of video game content that prompts concern about altered perceptions of social reality. While not as prevalent as violence, sexual content is also common in video games, especially sexualized depictions of female characters; even though female characters tend to be proportionally underrepresented in video games, they are much more likely than male characters to be portrayed in a sexually provocative and suggestive manner (e.g., Beasley & Standley, 2002; Dietz, 1998; Haninger & Thompson, 2004; Ivory, 2006). The potential effects of this sexual content on video game players' perceptions of social reality is often mentioned in content analyses (e.g., Beasley & Standley, 2002; Dietz, 1998; Ivory, 2006), but research directly examining such effects of sexual content in video games is lacking.

## Potential for Addiction and Displacement of Other Activities

While concerns about effects of specific content abound, much research is concerned more generally with the medium's popularity and allure. For decades, scholars have explored video games' potential for addiction and problematic usage, particularly among school-age youth (e.g., Keepers, 1990). Surveys of game players, often employing questionnaire items adapted from clinical measures for pathologies such as gambling addiction and substance abuse, indicate that a significant minority may exhibit problematic usage patterns that could be described as "dependency" or "addiction" (e.g., Griffiths, 2000; Griffiths et al., 2004; Griffiths & Hunt, 1998; Grüsser et al., 2007; Harris Interactive, 2007). There are also some indications that prevalence of such problematic usage is higher among adolescents than adults (see Griffiths et al., 2004; Grüsser et al., 2007), although such patterns are likely limited to players with extremely high usage (Griffiths, 2004). Interpretation of apparent evidence for addiction, though, is clouded by alternative explanations, such as suggestions that addiction-oriented measures may instead be merely capturing high involvement with the games (see Charlton, 2002; Charlton & Danforth, 2007). In addition to clinical addiction measures, a number of studies have linked video game play to relevant problematic outcomes such as losing track of time while playing (e.g., Wood & Griffiths, 2007) or neglecting other activities such as sleep and hobbies (e.g., Griffiths et al., 2004).

In 2007, the American Medical Association addressed troubling—if at times ambiguous—evidence for video game addiction and considered formally declaring video game addiction as a mental disorder (Gould & Lite, 2007). After some discussion, the organization backed away from the proposal, electing to shy away from formal addiction classification in favor of continued examination of "video game overuse" (Pham, 2007, p. C1).

## Effects on Self-Perception

There is some evidence that high levels of video game play are associated with lowered self-concept in adolescents. Dominick (1984) found that time spent in an arcade was negatively correlated with self-esteem in a survey of eleventh and twelfth grade students, and Roe and Muijs (1998) found a similar relationship between heavy game play and lower self-esteem in a survey of 10- to 11-year-olds. Funk and Buchman (1996) found a similar connection between amount of video game play and lowered self-concept, but only for girls, in a study of seventh and eighth graders. Other studies with adolescents, though, have failed to find a connection between video game play and self-esteem measures (e.g., Fling et al., 1992), while others have found positive associations between video game play and measures of self-concept and mental health (e.g., Durkin & Barber, 2002). As with many of the aforementioned effects areas, therefore, research on video games and adolescent players' self-concept presents mixed results, with negative effects evidence appearing primarily among those with very high video game use.

## Effects on Physical Fitness, Physical Skills, and Health

Along with the many studies on the psychological and social impact of video games on players, the physical drawbacks and benefits of video game play have also earned the attention of researchers. The repetitive motion involved in operating video game controllers has been named as a culprit for a number of injuries documented in the medical literature (e.g., Macgregor, 2000; Rushing et al., 2006), although such cases are identified as isolated incidences stemming from extreme overuse and typically remedied by cessation of play (Griffiths, 2004). Similarly rare, but documented, are seizures as a result of play, and various other ailments ranging from auditory hallucinations to loss of urinary control (see Griffiths, 2004, for a review).

A more common health complaint leveled at video games is the medium's role in obesity, especially among youth. Vandewater et al. (2004) found a relationship between video game play and obesity among 1-year-old to 12-year-old children, but not a corresponding relationship between television viewing and obesity, suggesting that obesity may be more strongly linked to video game play than to use of other media. Worldwide, results of similar studies are mixed; Stettler, Signer, and Suter (2004) found an association between video game play and obesity in a study of Swiss first, second, and third graders, but Burke et al. (2006) failed to link video game play to obesity in a study of Australian children.

In contradistinction to research linking obesity and other detrimental health effects, a number of studies indicate physical benefits of video game play. Research has observed links between video game play and quickened reaction time (Orosy-Fildes & Allan, 1989), enhanced anticipatory timing (Kuhlman & Beitel, 1991), hand–eye coordination and skills among surgeons (Miskry, Magos, & Magos, 2002; Rosser et al., 2004), and enhanced visual processing (Green & Bavelier, 2003, 2006, 2007). Video games have also successfully been used in clinical studies for reduction of nausea in pediatric cancer patients receiving chemotherapy (e.g., Kolko & Rickard-Figueroa, 1985; Redd et al., 1987; Vasterling, Jenkins, Tope, & Burish, 1993), and as tools in physical therapy, such as rehabilitation from physical and neurological illness or injury, and psychiatric therapy (see Griffiths, 2004, for a review).

## Educational and Learning Outcomes

A number of studies have also examined the effects of video game play on adolescents' school performance, with some results indicating that increased game play is associated with lower grades (e.g., Anderson & Dill, 2000; Gentile et al., 2004; Roe & Muijn, 1998) and others suggesting the reverse (e.g., Durkin & Barber, 2002). Other research stresses that if video games can be implicated for teaching violent behaviors (e.g., Gentile & Anderson, 2006), they can be effective tools for positive educational outcomes. Video games have been used effectively with youth in teaching health practices such as smoking prevention, management of diabetes and asthma, and healthful eating (e.g., Baranowski et al., 2003; Cullen, Watson, Baranowski, Baronowski, & Zakeri, 2005; Lieberman, 2001), as aids in teaching social and logical skills to children and adolescents with intellectual disabilities (see Griffiths, 2004, for a review), as well as in teaching traditional educational curricula such as mathematics (Lopez-Morteo & López, 2007) and science (Ketelhut, 2007; Neulight, Kafai, Kao, Foley, & Galas, 2007; Rosenbaum, Klopfer, & Perry, 2007; Squire & Jan, 2007).

## Summary

In general, the picture presented by results from research on video game effects can be described as complex and somewhat ambiguous in that there is no sweeping unidirectional "bad" or "good" influence that can be attributed to video games. There is evidence that video game play can lead to negative outcomes, such as increased aggression, desensitization to violence, reduced prosocial behavior, distorted perceptions of social reality, addiction and dependency, diminished self-esteem, obesity, injuries, and lowered academic performance. In particular, the evidence is mounting that violent video game content presents particularly strong potential for negative effects, although negative effects potential is not limited exclusively to violent video games (e.g., addiction to a nonviolent game seems as plausible as to a violent game). On the other hand, there is also evidence that video game players may enjoy positive effects on their self-esteem, social and mental health, perceptual and motor skills, ability to manage injury and illness, and learning. It seems likely that these positive effects would best be harnessed in nonviolent games given the evidence for negative effects of violent games, although the potential positive effects are not limited exclusively to nonviolent games (e.g., improved visual processing can result from playing a violent game as much as from a nonviolent game). Violence is likely just one of many video game characteristics that vary widely in video games, consequently producing variety in effects that prevents sweeping conclusions on whether video games in general are harmful or helpful.

Griffiths (1999) succinctly concludes that "there are many different types of video games which probably have different effects" (p. 211), summing up the difficulties in assessing the effects of video games in general even though evidence for certain effects of specific types of video games is more compelling (e.g., negative effects of violent games on aggression, positive effects of health campaign–oriented games on health knowledge and behavior). A broad conclusion as to whether video games' effects are generally helpful or harmful, if such a conclusion is possible, is therefore beyond the aims of this chapter. Also beyond the current discussion is a final judgment on debates surrounding the validity and practical importance of specific findings in the area, such as the scholarly conversation regarding the extent of violent video game content's effect on negative behavior in players (see Carnagey & Anderson 2004; Ferguson, 2007; Gentile & Anderson, 2003). Instead, the following section focuses on the role of changes in video games over the years in the effects picture, exploring a few ways in which video games are advancing and changing, and how these changes may affect the nature and magnitude of video games' various effects on youth.

## VIDEO GAMES' CHANGES OVER TIME AND IMPLICATIONS FOR EFFECTS ON YOUTH

Although there is some disagreement and varied evidence about the many potential effects both positive and negative of video game play, agreement is widespread that video games are changing rapidly and dramatically and that these changes may greatly influence the games' effects (e.g., Calvert & Tan, 1994; Carnagey & Anderson, 2004; Chory & Cicchirillo, 2007; Eastin, 2006; Eastin & Griffiths, 2006; Gentile & Anderson, 2003; Kirsh, 2003; Persky & Blascovich, 2006; Sherry, 2001; Tamborini et al., 2004; Weber et al., 2006). A general overview of a few trends in video game advancements—past, present, and possibly future—is presented below, with changes categorized along three general dimensions. For each dimension, implications for effects on the youthful player base are discussed, along with some relevant research findings.

### Technical Fidelity and Realism

CHANGES OVER TIME

Perhaps the most notable technological change in video games over time is the fidelity of their graphics, sound, and other presentation characteristics. These changes are engendered by exponential increases in computer processing power for both personal computers (Molebash & Fisher, 2003) and home video game consoles (Gallagher & Park, 2003). Consider, for example, processor changes in one popular video game company's consoles over time. The popular Nintendo Entertainment System home console, released in 1985, boasted a 1.79 MHz (megahertz) 8-bit processor, meaning that it could process two bits[2] (binary digits) of data per operation and (very roughly) that its processor performed its most basic operations 1.79 million times per second.[3] The same company's Super NES, released in 1991, had a 3.58 MHz 16-bit processor, and the Nintendo 64 came on the market in 1995 with a 93.75 MHz 64-bit processor. Nintendo's GameCube, released in 2001, had a 485 MHz 128-bit processor and CPU. Nintendo's latest entry, 2006's Wii, has a 729 MHz processor, which is dwarfed by the 3.2 GHz (3.2 gigahertz, with a gigahertz equal to 1,000 megahertz) processors of its closest competitors, 2005's Microsoft Xbox 360 and 2006's Sony PlayStation 3 (Nintendo, 2006).[4]

In addition to rapid increases in processing power, advances in other capabilities relevant to presentation such as memory and data storage have been similarly exponential. Add to that programming innovations such as use of polygons to represent three-dimensional shapes, and the result is a progression in video games' presentation from simple dots and beeps to represent characters and actions to photorealistic characters, lifelike movement, and high-fidelity voices and music. A single, silent pixel might represent a character or object from thirty years ago; now, video game development routinely includes practices such as developing animation by filming famous athletes in motion-capture suits, employing Hollywood stars as voice actors, and commissioning chart-topping artists to produce and record background music. In short, more processing power means games look and sound more real.

## IMPLICATIONS FOR EFFECTS

What does this enhanced realism mean for players? One feeling enhanced by more realistic media depiction is that of presence (a.k.a. telepresence), the feeling of "being there" when using media (see Lee, 2004; Lombard & Ditton, 1997; Steuer, 1992). Increased television image quality, for example, has been found to increase viewers' feelings of presence (Bracken, 2005). In a study comparing the experiences of college students assigned to play either new or old games of the same genre on a computer, Ivory and Kalyanaraman (2007) found that players of the newer games tended to report greater feelings of presence and also reported feeling more involved with the game.

Closely related to feelings of presence is physiological arousal, which has been identified as a potential effect of presence (Lombard & Ditton, 1997). Technological presentation advancements such as motion in film (Detenber, Simons, & Bennett, 1998) and animation in Web advertisements (Sundar & Kalyanaraman, 2004) have been found to increase physiological arousal. Similarly, Ivory and Kalyanaraman (2007) found that playing a newer game increased both physiological and self-reported arousal in college students compared to playing an otherwise similar older game.

These findings are promising in some ways, considering that the arousal and involvement elicited by video games have been cited as reasons they are a powerful potential tool for learning (Garris, Ahlers, & Driskell, 2002; Johnson, 2005). If newer video games increase these experiences, then their educational potential may also be increased, as well as their aforementioned potential for therapeutic and clinical purposes (Griffiths, 2004).

The implications, however, are not all rosy. More advanced video game presentation has been tagged as potentially more likely to increase player aggression, at least in the case of violent games (e.g., Bensley & van Eenwyk, 2001; Gentile et al., 2004). In fact, it has been suggested that mixed results concerning links between violent video game play and aggression may have been a result of inconsistent levels of realism in the games used in previous studies (Bensley & van Eenwyk, 2001; Persky & Blascovich, 2006). Arousal has previously been implicated as a component in violent video games' effects on aggression (see Anderson & Bushman, 2001), so the finding that newer video games are more arousing may suggest that newer video games elicit more aggression. Others have theorized that increasing presence in video game players may also increase aggressive outcomes (e. g., Persky & Blascovich, 2006; Tamborini et al., 2004), so the finding that newer games increase feelings of presence in video game players is also ominous. So far, though, research comparing the effects of newer and older versions of commercial video games has failed to find effects of advancement on measures of aggression, even while finding that advancement increases arousal and feelings of presence (Ivory & Kalyanaraman, 2007).

Given that research in television has found links between graphical realism and aggression in youthful viewers (Potter, 1999; Wilson et al., 2002), more research in the area is warranted (Gentile & Stone, 2005) to clear up the issue of whether more realistic game presentation increases effects on aggression.

## Interface and Play Control

### CHANGES OVER TIME

Just as changes in video game technology have engendered dramatic changes in the realism of video games' presentation, the way players interact with their games has also been influenced by technological advances. Although handheld controls and monitors have long been popular ways to interact with video games and remain so, virtual reality (VR) devices (a.k.a. immersive virtual environments) have eagerly been explored as alternative video game interfaces since the 1990s (see Persky & Blascovich, 2006). VR systems have been evaluated favorably by players (e.g., Heeter, 1995) but have not become the format of choice for video game play. However, console, computer, and arcade video games have adopted conventions of VR in their controls by using devices such as cameras, light guns, mock musical instruments, and pressure-sensitive floor pads as controls.

Although many of these devices are novelty controllers designed for and packaged with a single game or series of games, standard video game controllers have also added features similar to VR interfaces, such as motion-sensing devices and haptic feedback (e.g., a rumbling in a game controller when a tackle is made in a sports-themed game). Standard console controllers have also altered their traditional button and joystick controls to accommodate player movement that is more isomorphic to game tasks, such as adding trigger-style buttons or using paired joysticks to allow character movement and view to be controlled separately (e.g., allowing a character to run forward while looking to the side).

Perhaps the most notable use of VR-style technology in a console-style game is the Nintendo Wii, released in 2006. Although the Wii's controller, called a "remote," has buttons and a directional control like most video game controllers, its multiple motion-sensing devices rely heavily on player gestures to control games (Snider, 2006). For example, a player swings the remote to play a tennis or baseball game (Dudley, 2006). Despite being otherwise technically inferior to major competitors, the Wii enjoyed massive success upon its release and remained difficult to find in stores for months (Bulik, 2007).

## IMPLICATIONS FOR EFFECTS

As with advanced presentation, advances in interface technology raise concerns regarding effects on aggression. Other research on the effects of media violence suggests that identifying with an aggressor (e.g., Leyens & Picus, 1973; Perry & Perry, 1976) and physically reproducing the movements of a violent act (e.g., Bandura, 2002) can be conducive to aggressive outcomes. These aspects of video games have been noted as potential causes of increased player aggression (e.g., Carnagey & Anderson, 2004; Dill & Dill, 1998), and in the case of a VR game, negative effects may be magnified even more because VR games are designed to create high feelings of presence and rely on physical movement for input from the player (Persky & Blascovich, 2006; Tamborini et al., 2004).

Some research exploring the effects of violent VR games on aggression confirms suspicions that the advanced interface is especially conducive to aggression. Studies have observed that playing a violent game using a VR interface increases measures of aggressive thoughts, feelings, behavior, and physiological responses associated with aggression compared to playing the same game on a desktop computer (Eastin & Griffiths, 2006; Persky & Blascovich, 2006; Tamborini et al., 2004). Results have suggested, however, that feelings of presence may operate independently from feelings of aggression in players of VR games because effects on presence have not tended to correspond with effects on aggression (Eastin & Griffiths, 2006; Tamborini et al., 2004). In fact, studies have tended to find that playing violent VR games elicited fewer feelings of presence than playing the same games on a computer, possibly because of the VR interface's novelty to participants. Aside from VR, one study (Ballard & Hamby, 2003) looked at the effects of a smaller interface enhancement, the addition of a light gun to a violent game, on measures of aggressive feelings and behavior. There were no effects of the light gun, either when it was used or when it was present nearby as a visual cue, on any of the aggression measures, suggesting that effects of such a peripheral control interface dimension on aggression may not be as problematic as with more significant interface advancements like a VR simulator.

Although findings regarding VR and aggression are troubling, VR games have promise for positive outcomes as well. Just as increased quality of presentation in games may have increased learning potential vis-à-vis their ability to elicit more arousal and feelings of presence (Ivory & Kalyanaraman, 2007), virtual reality games can enhance learning by providing multiple modes of input and allowing realistic rehearsal of skills and practices. VR games and environments have been used effectively to teach youth, both in a scholastic setting (Di Blas & Poggi, 2007) and to those with intellectual disabilities (e.g., Padgett, Strickland, & Coles, 2006), and as a therapeutic pain management tool (e.g., Das, Grimmer, Sparnon, McRae, & Thomas, 2005). Like other advancements in video game technology, VR may have great educational potential, although a failure of VR games to elicit more feelings of presence than other game formats in some studies (Eastin & Griffiths, 2006; Tamborini et al., 2004) suggests that the format may not always be most effective.

Less dramatic interface advances also show potential for positive effects. Although video game play has generally been implicated as conducive to obesity among youth (e.g., Stettler et al., 2004; Vandewater et al., 2004), alternate controllers encouraging physical activity may have the opposite effect. Research has begun to explore the promise of the *Dance Dance Revolution* series, a game franchise whose players imitate on-screen dance moves on a floor pad while fast-paced popular songs play, as an anti-obesity tool for youth, with some studies finding promise (Epstein, Beecher, Graf, & Roemmich, 2007; see also Brown, 2006). There is also evidence, however, that the game might not generate enough use among overweight youth to be effective (Madsen, Yen, Wlasiuk, Newman, & Lustig, 2007). With the advent of the Nintendo Wii, even more buzz surrounds video games' newfound potential to encourage exercise and health. Anecdotal tales of gaming-induced weight loss appeared in news media within months of the game system's release (e.g., Cromley, 2007; Musgrove, 2007), accompanied by reports of strain and overuse injuries (e.g., Bray, 2006b; Chung, 2006).

## Social Interaction and Representation

### CHANGES OVER TIME

This history of video games is marked by a few ebbs and flows in the extent of association between the medium and social interaction. After a short boom and subsequent crash in home video game sales in the late 1970s and early 1980s, the video game sales market was dominated by arcade sales as players gathered at public arcades (Williams, 2006b). By the late 1980s, however, home video game sales again dominated the market as arcade activity waned. In the late 1990s, video game players again began to gather in public places in numbers to play—but this time, they could do so without leaving home, as the gathering was done in virtual worlds (a.k.a. massively multiplayer online role-playing games) via the Internet (Castronova, 2001, 2002). Although text-based online games have existed in some form since before 1980 (Rheingold, 1994), and a three-dimensional commercial virtual world was commercially released in 1996, Electronic Arts' 1997 release of *Ultima Online* is often credited as the first successful large-scale virtual world (Castronova, 2001).

Since then, the virtual world business has taken off. By mid-2007, the popular quasi-medieval themed *World of Warcraft* boasted more than eight million paying subscribers (Gerson, 2007), for example. Around the same time, in *Second Life*, another popular virtual world where people create an avatar to represent themselves as they navigate a landscape filled with property and objects created mostly by other users, hundreds of thousands of dollars in real transactions changed hands daily between users buying and selling virtual goods, services, and property (Moulds, 2007). The themes of virtual worlds may vary from science fiction to simulated everyday life, but all virtual worlds share a few characteristics (Castronova, 2001). They are all interactive in that a large number of players access the same game environment, and their actions therein influence the environment for others. A virtual world is also physical, meaning that it provides a simulated first-person environment that is governed by physical laws for the avatars that players use to experience it. Lastly, a virtual world must be persistent, continuing to function and maintain its traits whether a player is connected to it or not. These characteristics ensure that virtual worlds have an intrinsic social component because they provide a consistent and enduring environment to which players share access.

For video game players who are not keen to involve themselves in virtual worlds for the long haul, the trend of online play has extended to traditional video game formats as well. Video game players with Microsoft Xbox 360 or Sony PlayStation 3 consoles can turn on their favorite shoot-'em-up game, log in to a subscription online service via an Internet connection, and do "multiplayer mode" battle with and against a gang of automatically assigned friends and foes from all over the world—complete with real-time voice chat via headset (Bray, 2006a; Tilley, 2006). Unlike virtual worlds, these games end forever when players disconnect or start another game. Between these one-time contests and the more enduring virtual worlds, virtual social interaction is a hallmark of the video game experience for many today.

### IMPLICATIONS FOR EFFECTS

The question of how video games' effects are influenced by their move to the Internet is an extremely challenging one, as the virtual sociality of online games conflates the many issues of video game effects with the effects documented by an extremely large and complex body of effects research (see Chapter 13 of this volume for a more detailed review of Internet effects; see also Bargh & McKenna, 2004; McKenna & Bargh, 2000). The increased trend toward Internet connection in video games is extremely salient, however, to one area of video game effects that has been receiving special attention and causing consternation: video game addiction. Surveys of virtual worlds (Griffiths et al., 2004; Yee, 2006a, 2006b) indicate that the majority of users are adults, but that up to one-fourth are adolescents.

Griffiths et al. (2004) found evidence that adolescents played more frequently than adults, but adolescents did not significantly differ in time spent playing compared to young adults under 25 years old. Adolescents were significantly less likely to sacrifice other social activities than are adults, but more likely to sacrifice their education or work. Among both age groups, only about one in five denied sacrificing any other aspects of their lives to facilitate gameplay. Such findings, although not necessarily alarming regarding adolescents when compared to their adult counterparts, justify concerns that online video games can encourage problematic overuse and poor school performance. Griffiths et al. (2004) conclude that online video games may be more addictive than their console counterparts and that adolescents may be more prone to addiction (see also Grüsser et al., 2007), although they acknowledge alternative explanations such as that put forth by Charlton (2002), that findings suggesting addiction may actually represent only highly involved nonpathological use.

Along with concerns about addiction, however, are suggestions that online community participation may be beneficial. Schott and Hodgetts

(2006) emphasize the opportunities online games provide for healthy social interaction and beneficial community formation. Yee (2006a, 2006b) also shows evidence of meaningful online relationships in games and in indications of emotional and community involvement. There is some evidence that this relationship- and community-building is more prevalent among adolescents, such as their higher likelihood to have disclosed a personal issue or secret in an online game that had not been shared with "real-life" friends (Yee, 2006b).

Although a lengthy discussion of interpersonal effects and dynamics of online games is not possible here, another result particularly relevant to interaction and self-representation is worth noting, especially given that online video games of all types are increasingly likely to use player-selected avatars to represent a player in virtual space and that avatars in games may have little similarity to the represented player (e.g., in *World of Warcraft*, a player may choose from a number of imaginary humanoid creatures). In a pair of studies exploring the effect of avatar traits on users' behavior in a virtual environment, Yee and Bailenson (2007) found that players randomly assigned to an attractive avatar were more intimate during interactions with other virtual avatars than players assigned an unattractive avatar. Similarly, they also found that players assigned a tall avatar displayed more confident behavior than did players assigned a short-statured avatar. These results, dubbed "the Proteus effect" after a shape-changing deity from Greek mythology, present interesting possibilities for both healthy and problematic effects on self-concept, as well as addiction. There is some speculation that virtual worlds may be the template for the Internet interfaces of the future (i.e., in lieu of present applications like the World Wide Web) (Kirkpatrick, 2007), so effects of avatar traits on their users may grow increasingly salient in years to come.

## CONCLUSIONS AND RECOMMENDATIONS

In general, video game effects research often presents ambiguous results. The same aspects that may make video games teach young players to behave antisocially also inspire excitement over the medium's educational potential. Worries abound, justified by research, that video game play may result in poor physical and mental health, and diminished attention to other areas of life such as school, but other findings suggest that video game play might have a positive influence in all of these areas. Addiction to video games remains another point of attention, although classification and categorization—let alone a remedy—remain elusive. The upshot of the results is a mixed bag of pros and cons.

While video games have changed, and are changing, very much in terms of their presentation, interface with users, and social dimensions, the potential effects of these changes are also marked by a degree of ambiguity. Observed effects of increased technical presentation dimensions, namely increased feelings of presence and increased arousal, suggest a potential for both desirable entertainment and educational outcomes and undesirable negative effects on aggression. Both potential effects, however, need more investigation. The same is true in the case of interface and control dimensions, where some potential for negative effects via aggression increase has been observed, as well as potential for positive health effects (but not without some injury risk) via more physically active play. As video games increasingly make use of the Internet and real-time virtual interaction, the medium's potential for both addiction and healthy social relationships will need more monitoring, along with the effects of increasingly ubiquitous avatars on self-representation and self-concept.

Given so many ambiguous, preliminary, contested, or contradictory findings, what should be done next? From a research perspective, the answer to understanding technological factors' impact on video game effects may be to isolate them specifically and systematically in research to subsequently isolate their effects (see Nass & Mason, 1990). By clearly identifying effects of specific technological dimensions, researchers can not only understand the effects of current video games, but reconcile existing research with previous research and even extrapolate findings into the future. Much attention has been given to video game content characteristics, such as violence. Hopefully, attention to form dimensions (see Detenber, Simons, & Reiss, 2000), such as technological features, will receive comparable attention in the future.

As for individuals looking for guidance regarding their own video game play, or that of a family member or friend, there is no need to be overwhelmed by the swarm of questions and answers that effects research has presented thus far. Some helpful guidance comes from Griffiths (2004), who reminds us that most notable negative effects of video game play have occurred in cases of excessive use. Avoiding overuse, or taking appropriate measures to discourage overuse by adolescents, is therefore one healthy strategy. In other cases, suggestions in the literature can be heeded even when their merit is debated. For example, some may dispute the extent to which violent games elicit negative effects, but considering that there are no apparent negative repercussions from avoiding violent content, it seems that limiting violent video game content is a good practice regardless of how potent its negative effects may or may not be.

It is also useful to remember that very strong, very well-intentioned research in any area may be guided by assumptions that limit what may be found. If empirical research measured only the potential negative effects of eating and exercise, the resulting conclusion would be that one would do well to stay as hungry and idle as possible. Were the same methods employed to measure only the positive influences of wine and sunlight, the evidence might suggest that tipsy and sunburned is the safe bet. Similarly, we can look at the same body of video game effects literature and see clear evidence of a potential hazard to the public's well-being (Gentile & Anderson, 2003, p. 131), but we should probably also recall warnings that a balance of positive and negative outlooks will complete the picture of video game effects (Griffiths, 2004; Schott & Hodgetts, 2006). Although further study is in order, there is mounting evidence for both negative and positive video game effects, and that technological advancement may be exacerbating both. The proper course of action, then, may be the same one taken by a video game player navigating a challenging task: Proceed carefully. Look to pick up the good things and avoid the bad, and get ready for the next level, because it keeps getting trickier. And turn the game off now and again.

## NOTES

1. While these two games are two widely recognized examples of early innovations in video game history, they are not necessarily the first two video games. Depending on how the term *video game* is defined in terms of technological features, game play, audience, and other factors, a number of preceding and subsequent computer programs and devices may lay claim to the title of "first video game." The games described here are merely examples of early video game prototypes; a detailed examination of video games' many historical roots is beyond the scope of this chapter. For more thorough exploration of early video game devices and applications, see Kirriemuir (2006) and Lowood (2006).
2. To provide more meaning to descriptions of processing power here using the bit as a unit, the byte, a commonly seen information storage unit, typically refers to a binary digit number that is eight bits long. A byte is approximately the amount of data needed to represent one letter in a plain text document. An eight-bit byte can represent one of 256 values (all of the possible binary combinations in an eight-bit series).
3. Because different computing devices may require a different number of operations to accomplish the same task, this figure (clock rate) is not a pure measure of relative processing performance. (For a discussion, see Asaravala, 2004.) The measure is an effective enough indicator of processing power, however, to provide context here in comparing gross differences between video game machines over time.
4. The processors in all three of these consoles could be described as "128-bit," although the "bit" descriptor of processing power, once a key aspect of some consoles' marketing materials, has long-since diminished in importance due to changes in processing design and function.

## REFERENCES

Anderson, C. A. (1997). Effects of violent movies and trait hostility on hostile feelings and aggressive thoughts. *Aggressive Behavior, 23*, 161–178.

Anderson, C. A. (2004). An update on the effects of playing violent video games. *Journal of Adolescence, 27*, 113–122.

Anderson, C. A., & Bushman, B. J. (2001). Effects of violent video games on aggressive behavior, aggressive cognition, aggressive affect, physiological arousal, and prosocial behavior: A meta-analytic review of the scientific literature. *Psychological Science, 12*, 353–359.

Anderson, C. A., & Dill, K. E. (2000). Video games and aggressive thoughts, feelings, and behavior in the laboratory and in life. *Journal of Personality and Social Psychology, 78*, 772–790.

Asaravala, A. (2004, March 30). Good riddance, gigahertz. *Wired*. Retrieved July 22, 2007, from http://www.wired.com/techbiz/media/news/2004/03/62851

Ballard, M. E., & Hamby, R. H. (2003, April). *Weapons priming? The effects of video game peripherals*. Paper presented at the biennial meeting of the Society for Research in Child Development, Tampa, FL.

Ballard, M. E., Hamby, R. H., Panee, C. D., & Nivens, E. E. (2006). Repeated exposure to video game play results in decreased blood pressure responding. *Media Psychology, 8*, 323–341.

Bandura, A. (2002). Social cognitive theory of mass communication. In J. Bryant & D. Zillmann (Eds.), *Media effects: Advances in theory and research* (2nd ed., pp. 121–153). Mahwah, NJ: Erlbaum.

Baranowski, T., Baranowski, J., Cullen, K. W., Marsh, T., Islam, N., Zakeri, I., et al. (2003). Squire's Quest! Dietary outcome evaluation of a multimedia game. *American Journal of Preventative Medicine, 24*, 52–61.

Bargh, J. A., & McKenna, K. Y. A. (2004). The Internet and social life. *Annual Review of Psychology, 55*, 573–590.

Bartholow, B. D., Bushman, B. J., & Sestir, M. A. (2006). Chronic video game exposure and desensitization to violence: Behavioral and event-related brain potential data. *Journal of Experimental Social Psychology, 42*, 532–539.

Bartholow, B. D., Sestir, M. A., & Davis, E. B. (2005). Correlates and consequences of exposure to video game violence: Hostile personality, empathy, and aggressive behavior. *Personality and Social Psychology Bulletin, 31*, 1573–1586.

Beasley, B., & Standley, T. C. (2002). Shirts vs. skins: Clothing as an indicator of gender role stereotyping in video games. *Mass Communication and Society, 5*, 279–293.

Bensley, L., & van Eenwyk, J. (2001). Video games and real-life aggression: Review of the literature. *Journal of Adolescent Health, 29*, 244–257.

Berkowitz, L., & Rogers, K. H. (1986). A priming effect analysis of media influence. In J. Bryant & D. Zillmann (Eds.), *Perspectives on media effects* (pp. 57–81). Hillsdale, NJ: Erlbaum.

Bracken, C. C. (2005). Presence and image quality: The case of high-definition television. *Media Psychology, 7*, 191–205.

Bray, H. (2006a, December 16). Nintendo's Wii system proves a smashing success. *The Boston Globe*, p. D1.

Bray, H. (2006b, November 18). PS3 and Xbox are set to make killing with new battle games. *The Boston Globe*, p. D1

Brown, D. (2006). Playing to win: Video games and the fight against obesity. *Journal of the American Diatetic Association, 106*, 188–189.

Buchman, D. D., & Funk, J. B. (1996). Video and computer games in the '90s: Children's time commitment and game preference. *Children Today, 24*, 12–15, 31.

Bulik, B. S. (2007, July 16). PlayStation, Xbox regroup after being waxed by Wii. *Advertising Age*, p. 3.

Burke, V., Beilin, L. J., Durkin, K., Stritzke, W. G. K., Houghton, S., & Cameron, C. A. (2006). Television, computer use, physical activity, diet and fatness in Australian adolescents. *International Journal of Pediatric Obesity, 1*, 248–255.

Bushman, B. J. (1995). Moderating role of trait aggressiveness in the effects of violent media on aggression. *Journal of Personality and Social Psychology, 69*, 950–960.

Bushman, B. J. (1998). Priming effects of violent media on the accessibility of aggressive constructs in memory. *Personality and Social Psychology Bulletin, 24*, 537–545.

Bushman, B. J., & Anderson, C. A. (2002). Violent video games and hostile expectations: A test of the General Aggression Model. *Personality and Social Psychology Bulletin, 28*, 1679–1686.

Calvert, S. L., & Tan, S. (1994). Impact of virtual reality on young adults' physiological arousal and aggressive thoughts: Interaction versus observation. *Journal of Applied Developmental Psychology, 15*, 125–139.

Carnagey, N. L., & Anderson, C. A. (2004). Violent video game exposure and aggression: A literature review. *Minerva Psichiatrica, 45*, 1–18.

Castronova, E. (2001, December). *Virtual worlds: A first-hand account of market and society on the cyberian frontier* (CESifo Working Paper No. 618). Retrieved July 21, 2007, from http://ssrn.com/abstract=294828

Castronova, E. (2002, July). *On virtual economies* (CESifo Working Paper No. 752). Retrieved June 10, 2007, from http://ssrn.com/abstract=338500

Charlton, J. P. (2002). A factor analytic investigation of computer "addiction" and engagement. *British Journal of Psychology, 93*, 329–344.

Charlton, J. P., & Danforth, I. D. W. (2007). Distinguishing addiction and high engagement in the context of online game playing. *Computers in Human Behavior, 23*, 1531–1548.

Chmielewski, D. C. (2006, November 16). The state: Game is afoot for Sony's Playstation 3. *Los Angeles Times*, p. A1.

Chory, R. M., & Cicchirillo, V. (2007). The relationship between video game play and trait verbal aggressiveness: An application of the general aggression model. *Communication Research Reports, 24*, 113–119.

Chung, M. (2006, December 3). A bad case of Wii whack. *The Toronto Star*, p. C03.

Clarke, D. (2006, June 2). Big players square up for a fight. *The Irish Times*, p. 17.

Consalvo, M. (2006). Console video games and global corporations: Creating a hybrid culture. *New Media and Society, 8*, 117–137.

Cromley, J. (2007, March 5). Take that, body fat! Nintendo's Wii is getting video game players off the couch and into a mini-workout. *Los Angeles Times*, p. F12.

Cullen, K. W., Watson, K., Baranowski, T., Baranowski, J. H., & Zakeri, I. (2005). Squire's Quest: Intervention changes occurred at lunch and snack meals. *Appetite, 45*, 148–151.

Das, D. A., Grimmer, K. A., Sparnon, A. L., McRae, S., & Thomas, B. H. (2005). The efficacy of playing a virtual reality game in modulating pain for children with acute burn injuries: A randomized controlled trial. *BMC Pediatrics, 5*. Retrieved July 21, 2007, from http://www.biomedcentral.com/1471-2431/5/1

Detenber, B. H., Simons, R. F., & Bennett, G. G., Jr. (1998). Roll 'em: The effects of picture motion on emotional responses. *Journal of Broadcasting and Electronic Media, 42*, 113–127.

Detenber, B. H., Simons, R. F., & Reiss, J. F. (2000). The emotional significance of color in television presentations. *Media Psychology, 2*, 331–335.

Di Blas, N., & Poggi, C. (2007). European virtual classrooms: Building effective "virtual" educational experiences. *Virtual Reality, 11*, 129–143.

Dietz, T. L. (1998). An examination of violence and gender role portrayals in video games: Implications for gender socialization and aggressive behavior. *Sex Roles, 38*, 425–442.

Dill, K. E., & Dill, J. C. (1998). Video game violence: A review of the empirical literature. *Aggression & Violent Behavior, 3*, 407–428.

Dill, K. E., Gentile, D. A., Richter, W. A., & Dill, J. C. (2005). Violence, sex, race, and age in popular video games: A content analysis. In E. Cole & D. J. Henderson (Eds.), *Featuring females: Feminist analyses of the media* (pp. 115–130). Washington, DC: American Psychological Association.

Dominick, J. R. (1984). Videogames, television violence, and aggression in teenagers. *Journal of Communication, 34*, 136–147.

Drabman, R. S., & Thomas, M. H. (1974). Does media violence increase children's toleration of real-life aggression? *Developmental Psychology, 10*, 418–421.

Dudley, J. (2006, December 6). A game for all levels of players. *The Courier Mail*, p. T06.

Durkin, K., & Barber, B. (2002). Not so doomed: Computer game play and positive adolescent development. *Journal of Applied Developmental Psychology, 23*, 373–392.

Eastin, M. S., (2006). Video game violence and the female game player: Self- and opponent gender effects on presence and aggressive thoughts. *Human Communication Research, 32*, 351–372.

Eastin, M. S., & Griffiths, R. P. (2006). Beyond the shooter game: Examining presence and hostile outcomes among male players. *Communication Research, 33*, 448–466.

Epstein, L. H., Beecher, M. D., Graf, J. L., & Roemmich, J. N. (2007). Choice of interactive dance and bicycle games in overweight and nonoverweight youth. *Annals of Behavioral Medicine, 33*, 124–131.

Farrar, K. M., Krcmar, M., & Nowak, K. L. (2006). Contextual features of violent video games, mental models, and aggression. *Journal of Communication, 56*, 387–405.

Ferguson, C. J. (2007). Evidence for publication bias in video game violence effects literature: A meta-analytic review. *Aggression and Violent Behavior, 12,* 470–482.

Fling, S., Smith, L., Rodriguez, T., Thornton, D., Atkins, E., & Nixon, K. (1992). Videogames, aggression, and self-esteem: A survey. *Social Behavior and Personality, 20,* 39–45.

Funk, J. B., & Buchman, D. D. (1996). Playing violent video and computer games and adolescent self-concept. *Journal of Communication, 46,* 19–32.

Gallagher, S., & Park, S. H. (2003). Scoring video games' standard contributions. *IEEE Potentials, 22,* 4–14, 22–27.

Garris, R., Ahlers, R., & Driskell, J. E. (2002). Games, motivation, and learning: A research and practice model. *Simulation and Gaming, 33,* 441–467.

Garrison, M., & Christakis, D. (2005). *A teacher in the living room? Educational media for babies, toddlers, and preschoolers.* Menlo Park, CA: Kaiser Family Foundation.

Gentile, D. A., & Anderson, C. A. (2003). Violent video games: The newest media violence hazard. In D. Gentile (Ed.), *Media violence and children* (pp. 131–152). Westport, CT: Praeger.

Gentile, D. A., & Anderson, C. A. (2006). Violent video games: Effects on youth and public policy implications. In N. E. Dowd, D. G. Singer, & R. F. Wilson (Eds.), *Handbook of children, culture, and violence* (pp. 225–246). Thousand Oaks, CA: Sage.

Gentile, D. A., Lynch, P. J., Linder, J. R., & Walsh, D. A. (2004). The effects of violent video game habits on adolescent hostility, aggressive behaviors, and school performance. *Journal of Adolescence, 27,* 5–22.

Gentile, D. A., & Stone, W. (2005). Violent video game effects on children and adolescents: A review of the literature. *Minerva Pediatrica, 57,* 337–358.

Gerbner, G., Gross, L., Morgan, M., & Signorielli, N. (1980). The "mainstreaming" of America: Violence profile no. 11. *Journal of Communication, 30,* 10–29.

Gerbner, G., Gross, L., Morgan, M., Signorielli, N., & Shanahan, J. (2002). Growing up with television: Cultivation processes. In J. Bryant & D. Zillmann (Eds.), *Media effects: Advances in theory and research* (2nd ed., pp. 269–286). Mahwah, NJ: Erlbaum.

Gerson, M. (2007, July 6). Where the avatars roam. *Washington Post,* p. A15.

Gould, J., & Lite, J. (2007, June 22). Got game? Don't get addicted. *New York Daily News,* p. 26.

Green, C. S., & Bavelier, D. (2003). Action video game modifies visual selective attention. *Nature, 423,* 534–537.

Green, C. S., & Bavelier, D. (2006). Enumeration versus multiple object tracking: The case of action video game players. *Cognition, 101,* 217–245.

Green, C. S., & Bavelier, D. (2007). Action-video-game experience alters the spatial resolution of vision. *Psychological Science, 18,* 88–94.

Griffiths, M. D. (1997). Computer game playing in early adolescence. *Youth and Society, 29,* 223–237.

Griffiths, M. D. (1999). Violent video games and aggression: A review of the literature. *Aggression & Violent Behavior, 4,* 203–212.

Griffiths, M. D. (2000). Does Internet and computer "addiction" exist? Some case study evidence. *CyberPsychology and Behavior, 3,* 211–218.

Griffiths, M. D. (2004). Can videogames be good for your health? *Journal of Health Psychology, 9,* 339–344.

Griffiths, M. D., Davies, M. N. O., & Chappell, D. (2004). Online computer gaming: A comparison of adolescent and adult gamers. *Journal of Adolescence, 27,* 87–96.

Griffiths, M. D., & Hunt, N. (1995). Computer game playing in adolescence: Prevalence and demographic indicators. *Journal of Community and Applied Social Psychology, 5,* 189–193.

Griffiths, M. D., & Hunt, N. (1998). Dependence on computer games by adolescents. *Psychological Reports, 82,* 475–480.

Grüsser, S. M., Thalemann, R., & Griffiths, M. D. (2007). Excessive computer game playing: Evidence for addiction and aggression? *CyberPsychology and Behavior, 10,* 290–292.

Haninger, K., & Thompson, K. M. (2004). Content and ratings of teen-rated video games. *Journal of the American Medical Association, 291,* 856–865.

Harris Interactive (2007, April 2). *Video game addiction: Is it real?* Retrieved July 15, 2007, from http://www.harrisinteractive.com/news/allnewsbydate .asp?NewsID=1196

Heeter, C. (1995). Communication research on consumer VR. In F. Biocca & M. Levy (Eds.), *Communication in the age of virtual reality* (pp. 191–218). Hillsdale, NJ: Erlbaum.

Hillis, S. (2006, May 1). New chip adds detail, realism to video games. *The Toronto Star,* p. C05.

Huesmann, L. R., & Taylor, L. D. (2006). The role of media violence in violent behavior. *Annual Review of Public Health, 27,* 393–415.

Hutchins, B. (2006, June 24). Fun! (and games). *The Age.* Retrieved July 18, 2007, from http://www.theage.com.au/news/technology/fun-and-games/2006/06/21/ 1150845236873.html

Ivory, J. D. (2006). Still a man's game: Gender representation in online reviews of video games. *Mass Communication and Society, 9,* 103–114.

Ivory, J. D., & Kalyanaraman, S. (2007). The effects of technological advancement and violent content in video games on players' feelings of presence, involvement, physiological arousal, and aggression. *Journal of Communication, 57,* 531–554.

Johnson, S. (2005). *Everything bad is good for you: How today's popular culture is actually making us smarter.* New York: Riverhead Books.

Keepers, G. A. (1990). Pathological preoccupation with video games. *Journal of the American Academy of Child and Adolescent Psychiatry, 29,* 49–50.

Ketelhut, D. J. (2007). The impact of student self-efficacy on scientific inquiry skills: An exploratory investigation in *River City,* a multi-user virtual environment. *Journal of Science Education and Technology, 16,* 99–111.

Kirkpatrick, D. (2007, February 5). It's not a game. *Fortune,* 56.

Kirriemuir, J. (2006). A history of digital games. In J. Rutter & J. Bryce (Eds.), *Understanding digital games* (pp. 21–35). London: Sage.

Kirsh, S. J. (2003). The effects of violent video games on adolescents: The overlooked issue of development. *Aggression and Violent Behavior, 8,* 377–389.

Kirsh, S. J., Olczak, P. V., & Mounts, J. R. W. (2005). Violent video games induce an affect processing bias. *Media Psychology, 7,* 239–250.

Kolko, D. J., & Rickard-Figueroa, P. M. E. (1985). Effects of video games on the adverse corollaries of chemotherapy in pediatric oncology patients. *Journal of Consulting and Clinical Psychology, 53,* 223–228.

Kuhlman, J. S., & Beitel, P. A. (1991). Videogame experience: A possible explanation for differences in anticipation of coincidence. *Perceptual and Motor Skills, 72,* 483–488.

Lee, K. M. (2004). Presence, explicated. *Communication Theory, 14,* 27–50.

Leyens, J. P., & Picus, S. (1973). Identification with the winner of a fight and name mediation: Their differential effects upon subsequent aggressive behavior. *British Journal of Social and Clinical Psychology, 12,* 374–377.

Lieberman, D. A. (2001). Management of chronic pediatric diseases with interactive health games: Theory and research findings. *Journal of Ambulatory Care Management, 24,* 26–38.

Lombard, M., & Ditton, T. B. (1997). At the heart of it all: The concept of presence. *Journal of Computer-Mediated Communication, 3*(2). Retrieved June 5, 2006, from http://jcmc.indiana.edu/vol3/issue2/lombard.html

Lopez-Morteo, G., & López, G. (2007). Computer support for learning mathematics: A learning environment based on recreational learning objects. *Computers and Education, 48,* 618–641.

Lowood, H. E. (2006). A brief biography of computer games. In P. Vorderer & J. Bryant (Eds.), *Playing computer games: Motives, responses, and consequences* (pp. 25–41). Mahwah, NJ: Erlbaum.

Macgregor, D. M. (2000). Nintendonitis? A case report of repetitive strain injury in a child as a result of playing computer games. *Scottish Medical Journal, 45,* 150.

Madsen, K. A., Yen, S., Wlasiuk, L., Newman, T. B., & Lustig, R. (2007). Feasibility of a dance videogame to promote weight loss among overweight children and adolescents. *Archives of Pediatric and Adolescent Medicine, 161,* 105–107.

McKenna, K. Y. A., & Bargh, J. A. (2000). Plan 9 from cyberspace: The implications of the Internet for personality and social psychology. *Personality and Social Psychology Review, 4,* 57–75.

Miskry, T., Magos, T., & Magos, A. (2002). If you're no good at computer games, don't operate endoscopically! *Gynaecological Endoscopy, 11,* 345–347.

Molebash, P., & Fisher, D. (2003). Teaching and learning literacy with technology. *Reading Improvement, 40,* 63–70.

Moulds, J. (2007, May 21). Virtual worlds to get their own market. *The Daily Telegraph,* p. 8.

Mullin, C. R., & Linz, D. (1995). Desensitization and resensitization to violence against women: Effects of exposure to sexually violent films on judgments of domestic violence victims. *Journal of Personality and Social Psychology, 69,* 449–459.

Musgrove, M. (2007, February 4). Exercise that's all fun and games. *Washington Post,* p. F01.

Nass, C., & Mason, L. (1990). On the study of technology and task: A variable-based approach. In J. Fulk & C. Steinfeld (Eds.), *Organizations and communication technology* (pp. 46–67). Newbury Park, CA: Sage.

Neulight, N., Kafai, Y. B., Kao, L., Foley, B., & Galas, C. (2007). Children's participation in a virtual epidemic in the science classroom: Making connections to natural infectious diseases. *Journal of Science Education and Technology, 16,* 47–58.

Nintendo. (2006, August 15). Nintendo hopes Wii spells wiinner. *USA Today,* p. B3.

Orosy-Fildes, C., & Allan, R. W. (1989). Videogame play: Human reaction time to visual stimuli. *Perceptual and Motor Skills, 69,* 243–247.

Padgett, L. S., Strickland, D., & Coles, C. D. (2006). Case study: Using a virtual reality computer game to teach fire safety skills to children diagnosed with fetal alcohol syndrome. *Journal of Pediatric Psychology, 31,* 65–70.

Perry, D. G., & Perry, L. C. (1976). Identification with film characters, covert aggression verbalization, and reactions to film violence. *Journal of Research in Personality, 10,* 399–409.

Persky, S., & Blascovich, J. (2006). Consequences of playing violent video games in immersive virtual environments. In R. Schroeder & A. Axelsson (Eds.), *Avatars at work and play: Collaboration and interaction in shared virtual environments* (pp. 167–186). London: Springer.

Pham, A. (2007, June 28). Gaming junkies get no diagnosis. *Los Angeles Times,* p. C1.

Potter, W. J. (1999). *On media violence.* Thousand Oaks, CA: Sage.

Redd, W. H., Jacobsen, P. B., Die-Trill, M., Dermatis, H., McEvoy, M., & Holland, J. C. (1987). Cognitive/attentional distraction in the control of conditioned nausea in pediatric cancer patients receiving chemotherapy. *Journal of Consulting & Clinical Psychology, 55,* 391–395.

Rheingold, H. (1994). The virtual community: Homesteading on the electronic frontier. Retrieved July 22, 2007, from http://www.rheingold.com/vc/book

Richtel, M. (2007, January 12). Demand outpaced supply for new game consoles. *New York Times,* p. C4.

Roberts, D. F., Foehr, U. G., & Rideout, V. J. (2005). *Generation M: Media in the lives of 8–18 year-olds.* Menlo Park, CA: Kaiser Family Foundation.

Rockwell, G. (2002). Gore galore: Literary theory and computer games. *Computers and the Humanities, 36,* 345–358.

Roe, K., & Muijs, D. (1998). Children and computer games: A profile of the heavy user. *European Journal of Communication, 13,* 181–200.

Romer, D., Jamieson, K. H., & Aday, S. (2003). Television news and the cultivation of fear of crime. *Journal of Communication, 53,* 88–104.

Rosenbaum, E., Klopfer, E., & Perry, J. (2007). On location learning: Authentic applied science with networked augmented realities. *Journal of Science Education and Technology, 16,* 31–45.

Roskos-Ewoldsen, D. R., Roskos-Ewoldsen, B., & Carpentier, F. D. R. (2002). Media priming: A synthesis. In J. Bryant & D. Zillmann (Eds.), *Media effects: Advances in theory and research* (2nd ed., pp. 97–120). Mahwah, NJ: Erlbaum.

Rosser, J. C., Jr., Lynch, P. J., Haskamp, L. A., Yalif, A., Gentile, D. A., & Giammaria, L. (2004, January). *Are video game players better at laparoscopic surgery?* Paper presented at the Medicine Meets Virtual Reality Conference, Newport Beach, CA. Retrieved July 21, 2007, from http://www.psychology.iastate.edu/faculty/dgentile/publications.htm

Rushing, M. E., Sheehan, D. J., & Davis, L. S. (2006). Video game induced knuckle pad. *Pediatric Dermatology, 23*, 455–457.

Schiesel, S. (2007, March 30). Another world conquered by video games: Retirees. *New York Times*, p. A24.

Schott, G., & Hodgetts, D. (2006). Health and digital gaming: The benefits of a community of practice. *Journal of Health Psychology, 11*, 309–316.

Scott, D. (1995). The effect of video games on feelings of aggression. *Journal of Psychology, 129*, 121–132.

Scott, M. (2006, March 4). Parents who play: A generation raised on video games is passing the console on to their kids. *The Gazette*, p. I1.

Sherry, J. L. (2001). The effects of violent video games on aggression: A meta-analysis. *Human Communication Research, 27*, 409–431.

Slagle, M. (2006, May 8). Poll: 4 in 10 Americans play video games. *Washington Post*. Retrieved June 18, 2007, from http://www.washingtonpost.com/wpdyn/content/article/2006/05/07/AR2006050700172.html

Smith, S. L., Lachlan, K., & Tamborini, R. (2003). Popular video games: Quantifying the presentation of violence and its context. *Journal of Broadcasting and Electronic Media, 47*, 58–76.

Snider, M. (2006, July 12). Wii getting up and moving: Now, developers get in the game. *USA Today*, p. 5D.

Sparks, G. G., & Sparks, C. W. (2002). Effects of media violence. In J. Bryant & D. Zillmann (Eds.), *Media effects: Advances in theory and research* (2nd ed., pp. 269–286). Mahwah, NJ: Erlbaum.

Squire, K. D., & Jan, M. (2007). Mad City Mystery: Developing scientific argumentation skills with a place-based augmented reality game on handheld computers. *Journal of Science Education and Technology, 16*, 5–29.

Stettler, N., Signer, T. M., & Suter, P. M. (2004). Electronic games and environmental factors associated with childhood obesity in Switzerland. *Obesity Research, 12*, 896–903.

Steuer, J. (1992). Defining virtual reality: Dimensions determining telepresence. *Journal of Communication, 42*, 73–93.

Sundar, S. S., & Kalyanaraman, S. (2004). Arousal, memory, and impression-formation effects of animation speed in Web advertising. *Journal of Advertising, 33*, 7–17.

Tamborini, R., Eastin, M. S., Skalski, P., Lachlan, K., Fediuk, T. A., & Brady, R. (2004). Violent virtual video games and hostile thoughts. *Journal of Broadcasting & Electronic Media, 48*, 335–357.

Thompson, K. M., & Haninger, K. (2001). Violence in E-rated video games. *Journal of the American Medical Association, 286*, 591–598.

Tilley, S. (2006, November 26). No clear victor in battle with Gears of War. *The Toronto Sun*, p. S19.

Vandewater, E. A., Shim, M., & Caplovitz, A. G. (2004). Linking obesity and activity level with children's television and video game use. *Journal of Adolescence, 27,* 71–85.

Van Mierlo, J., & Van den Bulck, J. (2004). Benchmarking the cultivation approach to video game effects: A comparison of the correlates of TV viewing and game play. *Journal of Adolescence, 27,* 97–111.

Vasterling, J., Jenkins, R. A., Tope, D. M., & Burish, T. G. (1993). Cognitive distraction and relaxation training for the control of side effects due to cancer chemotherapy. *Journal of Behavioral Medicine, 16,* 65–80.

Wartella, E., & Reeves, B. (1985). Historical trends in research on children and the media: 1900–1960. *Journal of Communication, 35,* 118–133.

Weber, R., Ritterfeld, U., & Mathiak, K. (2006). Does playing violent video games induce aggression? Empirical evidence of a functional magnetic resonance imaging study. *Media Psychology, 8,* 39–60.

Williams, D. (2003). The video game lightning rod: Constructions of a new media technology, 1970–2000. *Information, Communication & Society, 6,* 523–550.

Williams, D. (2006a). Virtual cultivation: Online worlds, offline perceptions. *Journal of Communication, 56,* 69–87.

Williams, D. (2006b). A brief social history of game play. In P. Vorderer & J. Bryant (Eds.), *Playing video games: Motives, responses, and consequences* (pp. 197–212): Mahwah, NJ: Erlbaum.

Williams, D., & Skoric, M. (2005). Internet fantasy violence: A test of aggression in an online game. *Communication Monographs, 72,* 217–233.

Wilson, B. J., Smith, S. L., Potter, W. J., Kunkel, D., Linz, D., Colvin, C. M., et al. (2002). Violence in children's television programming: Assessing the risks. *Journal of Communication, 52,* 5–35.

Wood, R. T. A., & Griffiths, M. D. (2007). Time loss whilst playing video games: Is there a relationship to addictive behaviors? *International Journal of Mental Health and Addiction, 5,* 141–149.

Yee, N. (2006a). The demographics, motivations, and derived experiences of users of massively multi-user online graphical environments. *Presence: Teleoperators and Virtual Environments, 15,* 309–329.

Yee, N. (2006b). The psychology of massively multi-user online role-playing games: Motivations, emotional investment, relationships and problematic usage. In R. Schroeder & A. Axelsson (Eds.), *Avatars at work and play: Collaboration and interaction in shared virtual environments* (pp. 187–207). London: Springer.

Yee, N., & Bailenson, J. (2007). The Proteus effect: The effect of transformed self-representation on behavior. *Human Communication Research, 33,* 271–290.

Zillmann, D. (1971). Excitation transfer in communication-mediated aggressive behavior. *Journal of Experimental Social Psychology, 7,* 419–434.

Zillmann, Z., & Weaver, J. B. (1999). Effects of prolonged exposure to gratuitous media violence on provoked and unprovoked hostile behavior. *Journal of Applied Social Psychology, 29,* 145–165.

# 13

## Adolescents and the Internet

LINDA A. JACKSON

This chapter examines the impact of Internet use on adolescents. Two broad questions are addressed. First, what are the possible effects on adolescents of exposure to Internet content and activities? Second, what are the implications of differential access to the Internet? The chapter begins by examining the frequency and nature of adolescents' Internet use. Next, it examines a broad range of potential effects of Internet use on adolescents, in particular, social, cognitive, psychological and physical effects of using the Internet. After a brief consideration of the digital divide among adolescents, public policy implications of the findings are discussed.

Throughout the chapter the focus is on adolescents in the United States. Adolescents in other countries are considered to the extent that relevant data are available. Thus, there is a discussion of Internet use by youth in the United Kingdom (UK), where large-scale national surveys have been conducted (Livingstone & Bober, 2005). There is also discussion of the handful of findings about Internet use by Canadian and East Asian adolescents.

### FREQUENCY OF ADOLESCENTS' INTERNET USE

Findings from multiple large-scale national surveys in the United States and the UK, and from hundreds of small-scale studies in the United States and elsewhere, indicate that large numbers of adolescents are spending a significant portion of their everyday lives online. Moreover, the frequency and intensity of adolescents' Internet use have been increasing since the Internet first entered the public consciousness (circa, 1994; Annenberg Digital Future Project [ANN], 2004, 2006; Livingstone & Bober, 2005; Pew Internet & American

Family Life [PEW], 2000a, 2001, 2005a, 2005b, 2005c, 2006a: UCLA Internet Project, 2000, 2001, 2003). Table 13.1 summarizes the results.

In brief, 87% of adolescents (ages 12 to 17) in the United States use the Internet, more than half using it daily. Males and females are equally likely to use the Internet. Older adolescents (15 to 17 years old) are more likely to use it than younger adolescents. There is a small but significant difference in Internet use by region; urban and suburban adolescents are more likely to use it than are rural adolescents.

Sociodemographic characteristics distinguish between adolescents who use the Internet and those who do not. African American adolescents are less likely to use it than adolescents of other racial/ethnic groups. Adolescents whose family annual income is less than $30,000 are less likely to use the Internet than those whose family annual income is greater. Adolescents whose parents have a high school diploma or less are less likely to use the Internet than those whose parents have some college education or a college degree or more. Adolescents in single-parent homes are less likely to use the Internet than those in married, divorced/separated, or widowed parent homes. The vast majority of adolescent Internet users access the Internet mainly from home. Nearly half of these users now have broadband access, a huge increase over just five years ago.

The U.K. Children Go Online Project provides evidence of the frequency and intensity with which UK youth (ages 9 to 19) use the Internet (Livingstone & Bober, 2005). Key findings, summarized in Table 13.1, indicated that 75% of UK youth access the Internet from home, 24% with a broadband connection. Youth were about equally divided between those who use the Internet daily and those who use it weekly. Most youth are online less than one hour a day. Youth from middle class families are more likely to have home Internet access than those from working class families. There are dramatic regional differences in Internet access among UK youth. Youth residing in East Anglia are most likely to access the Internet whereas youth residing in Wales and Yorkshire are least likely to access it.

A large-scale national survey of Canadian youth provides evidence of the extent to which they use the Internet (Media Awareness Network, 2005). In 2005 nearly all (94%) Canadian youth said they had gone online from home, compared to 79% on 2001. Over one-third (37%) had their own Internet-connected computer.

## NATURE OF ADOLESCENTS' INTERNET USE

What do adolescents do when the go online? Large-scale national surveys provide a "big picture" of the nature of adolescents' Internet use. They indicate

Table 13.1. Frequency of Adolescents' Internet Use: United States and United Kingdom

|  | United States[a] | United Kingdom[b] |
|---|---|---|
| Internet use | 87%<br>12–14 years old: 82%<br>15–17 years old: 92%<br>Males: 87%<br>Females: 87% | 98%<br>9–11 years old: 96%<br>12–15 years old: 99%<br>16–17 years old: 98%<br>18–19 years old: 92% |
| Intensity of Internet use | Daily: 51%<br>At least once a week: 69% | Daily: 41%<br>At least once a week: 43% |
| Use by region | Urban: 87%<br>Suburban: 87%<br>Rural: 83% | East Anglia: 91%<br>South West: 80%<br>Wales: 63%<br>Yorkshire: 66% |
| Use by race/ethnicity | White Caucasian: 86%<br>Hispanic American: 89%<br>African American: 77% | No differences |
| Use by parent income/class | Less than $30K annual: 73%<br>$30K to $50K annual: 89%<br>Over $50K annual: 90% | Working class: 61%<br>Middle class: 88% |
| Use by parent education | High school or less: 81%<br>Some college: 91%<br>College degree or more: 93% |  |
| Use by parent marital status | Single: 63%<br>Married: 88%<br>Divorced: 82%<br>Widowed: 87% |  |
| Home Internet access | 87% of Internet users | 75% of all youth |
| Broadband access at home | 50% of Internet users | 24% of Internet users |
| Time online | Mean = 27 hours/week | 10 minutes: 19%<br>30 minutes to 1 hour: 48%<br>1 to 3 hours: 20%<br>More than 3 hours: 5% |

[a] U.S. data have been adapted with permission from Pew Internet & American Family Life Project (2005b). The sample consisted of 1,100 youth, ages 12 to 17 years old, who participated in a phone survey between October 26 and November 28, 2004.
[b] UK data have been adapted with permission from Livingstone & Bober (2005). The sample consisted of 1,511 youth, ages 9 to 19 years old, who completed in-home surveys in spring 2004.

that adolescents use the Internet for a variety of purposes, such as doing homework, playing games, shopping, and downloading music. But the most popular reason for going online is to communicate with their peers (Bargh & McKenna, 2004; Boneva, Quinn, Kraut, Kiesler, & Shklovski, 2006; Gross, 2004; PEW, 2001, 2005a, 2005b, 2005c, 2006a, 2007; Roberts, Foehr, & Rideout, 2005; Tapscot, 1998; Weiser, 2001; Wellman & Haythornthwaite, 2002). The ways in which adolescents communicate online have been changing as the technology itself is changing. Whereas e-mail was once the most popular way to communicate online, today interactive forms of communication, such as instant messaging, are becoming more popular.

Research by the Pew Internet and American Life Project has been examining how adolescents in the United States use the Internet (PEW, 2005a, 2000b, 2000c, 2006a). Findings are summarized in Table 13.2. In order of popularity, adolescents use the Internet to e-mail, visit entertainment Web sites (e.g., movies, TV, music, sports), play online games, visit news and current events Web sites, instant message, search for information about college or advanced education, search for information about politics or campaigns, make purchases, search for information about health, dieting, and physical fitness, look for job information, seek religious or spiritual information, and search for information about health topics that are difficult for them to talk about (e.g., drug- and sex-related health issues; see Table 13.2 for percentages of adolescents who engage in these activities). More details about the nature of how U.S. youth use the Internet are provided in Table 13.2.

The U.K. Children Go Online Project describes how UK youth (ages 9 to 17) use the Internet (Livingstone & Bober, 2005). Findings are summarized in Table 13.3. Most youth in the UK who use the Internet frequently (i.e., daily or weekly) use it for schoolwork or to get information about other things. UK youth, like their U.S. counterparts, use the Internet to communicate via e-mail, instant messaging, and chat. Other Internet activities of UK youth are visiting interactive Web sites, playing games, visiting civic Web sites, downloading music, window shopping, making a Web site, reading the news, getting personal advice, plagiarizing, and viewing pornography. More details about how UK youth use the Internet are provided in Table 13.3.

Other research supports the findings of large-scale national surveys that adolescents use the Internet for a variety of purposes that may be broadly categorized as communication, information, entertainment, self-expression, and escape (e.g., Gross, 2004; Gross, Juvonen, & Gable, 2002; Roberts et al., 2005; Seiter, 2005; Tapscot, 1998; Valkenburg & Soeters, 2001; Weiser, 2001; Wellman & Haythornthwaite, 2002). Adolescents spend more time online than do adults, and integrate their online activities, especially their communication activities, more strongly into their everyday lives than do adults (e.g., Gross et al., 2002; Hartman, Shim, Barber, & O'Brien, 2006;

Table 13.2. Nature of Adolescents' Internet Use: United States

| Activity | Percent |
| --- | --- |
| E-mail | 89 |
| Entertainment Web sites | 84 |
| Play games | 81 |
| News | 76 |
| Instant messaging | 75 |
| Daily | 50 |
| Created and posted a profile | 56 |
| Created content | 57 |
| Blog | 19 |
| Personal Web page | 19 |
| Other Web page | 32 |
| Shared original content (e.g., photos) | 33 |
| Remixed online content | 19 |
| Information: College/education | 57 |
| Chat room visit | 56 |
| Social networking Web sites | 55 |
| Older girls (15–17 years old) | 70 |
| Older boys | 54 |
| Daily or more | 48 |
| Once a day | 26 |
| Several times a day | 22 |
| Information: Politics | 55 |
| Download music | 51 |
| Purchase product | 43 |
| Read blogs | 38 |
| Download videos | 31 |
| Information: Health/diet/fitness | 31 |
| Information: Jobs | 30 |
| Information: Religious/spiritual | 26 |
| Information: Health-related (sex, drugs) | 22 |

*Note.* Data have been adapted with permission from Pew Internet & American Family Life Project (2005b). The sample consisted of 1,100 youth, ages 12 to 17 years old, who participated in a phone survey between October 26 and November 28, 2004.

PEW, 2001, 2002, 2005a, 2005b, 2005c, 2006a, 2007). Adolescents view virtual communication as a supplement to rather than a replacement for telephone and face-to-face interaction (Subrahmanyam, Kraut, Greenfield, & Gross, 2000). Adolescent girls spend more time in online communication than do adolescent boys, consistent with well-established gender differences in the importance of interpersonal communication (Jackson, Ervin, Gardner, & Schmitt, 2001a; Leung, 2001; Valkenburg & Soeters, 2001).

Table 13.3. Nature of Adolescents' Internet Use: United Kingdom

| Activity | Percent |
| --- | --- |
| School work | 90 |
| Information search | 94 |
| E-mail | 72 |
| Visit interactive Web sites | 70 |
| Play game | 70 |
| Instant messaging | 55 |
| Visit civic Web sites | 54 |
| Download music | 46 |
| Window shopping | 40 |
| Making a Web site | 34 |
| Reading the news | 25 |
| Getting personal advice | 25 |
| Chat | 21 |
| Plagiarizing | 21 |
| Intentionally viewing pornography | 10 |

*Note*. Data have been adapted with permission from Livingstone and Bober (2005). The sample consisted of 1,511 youth, ages 9 to 19 years old, who completed in-home surveys in spring 2004.

Supporting the findings of national surveys, small-scale studies indicate that friends are the primary targets of adolescents' online communication activities. Only about one-third of adolescents (39%) say they have communicated with strangers online. Only 14% have developed a relationship with a stranger they met online and only 2% have developed a romantic relationship with someone they met online (Wolak, Mitchell, & Finkelhor, 2002, 2003). However, more recent evidence suggests that adolescents' contact with strangers online may be increasing (Adolescent Risk Communication Institute [ARCI], 2006). A recent survey of over 900 adolescents indicated that almost two-thirds (60%) used social networking Web sites and over 80% used them daily, regardless of gender or sociodemographic characteristics. Almost half (40%) had been contacted by an unsolicited stranger, twice the rate (20%) of those who go online for other purposes than social networking. However, only about 3% reported meeting these strangers face to face.

Results of a study of Asian adolescents in Seoul, Singapore, and Taipei are consistent with U.S. and UK findings regarding the importance of the Internet for communicating with friends. In all three cities the breadth and intensity of adolescents' Internet use was related to the percentage of social network members online (Kim, Cheong, Lin, & Jung, 2004). Thus, the more friends an adolescent had online the more time he or she spent using the Internet.

## UTOPIA VERSUS DYSTOPIA: IS INTERNET USE
## HELPFUL OR HARMFUL TO ADOLESCENTS?

Public and academic discourse on the effects of Internet use on adolescent well-being—both general well-being and specific dimensions of well-being—has been fraught with controversy since the Internet first entered the public consciousness over a decade ago. On the one hand is the *utopian perspective*, which argues that the Internet provides adolescents with new opportunities for creativity and active learning while simultaneously facilitating the development of technology skills—skills that are increasingly important in contemporary society. The utopian perspective celebrates the emergence of the information age and the rise of the networked society. It views electronic media as tools to empowerment that ultimately liberate all people from real-world social inequalities.

On the other hand is the *dystopian perspective*, which argues that Internet use has negative effects on its users, but particularly on children and adolescents. According to this view the Internet exposes children and adolescents to inaccurate information, potentially harmful content, and personally dangerous situations. Moreover, time online, from the dystopian perspective, is time away from family, friends, and other potentially more useful and healthy pursuits such as reading books, doing schoolwork, and engaging in sports and recreational activities.

What does the research have to say about the effects of Internet use on adolescents? Does it support the utopian perspective that good things happen to adolescents when they use the Internet? Or does it support the dystopian perspective that bad things happen? We turn next to evidence of the effects of Internet use on adolescents.

### Social Effects of Internet Use

Nowhere has the utopian–dystopian debate played out more vehemently than in discussions of the social effects of Internet use. From the utopian perspective Internet use should contribute to social development by providing opportunities for social connectedness, expansion of social networks, and exposure to people and information that enhance political awareness and civic engagement. From the dystopian perspective Internet use should undermine social development by detracting from real-life social connectedness and activities, including civic activities. Social effects of Internet use are of particular concern for adolescents because adolescence is a period of rapid social transformation and expansion of social networks and civic participation.

SOCIAL RELATIONSHIPS

Research on the effects of adolescents' Internet use on their relationships with family and friends provides more support for the utopian perspective than the dystopian perspective (ANN, 2004, 2006; Bargh & McKenna, 2004; Craig, 2003; Gross et al., 2002; Katz & Rice, 2002; McKenna & Bargh, 2000; McKenna, Green, & Gleason, 2002; PEW, 2006a, 2007; Wellman & Haythornthwaite, 2002). National surveys by the Pew Internet & American Life Project consistently find that adolescents use the Internet to communicate with family and friends, primarily via e-mail and instant messaging, but more recently via blogs and social networking Web sites. Moreover, adolescents believe that social networking Web sites help them to manage their offline friendships. In support of this view, adolescents who use social networking Web sites are more socially active offline, participating in more clubs and organizations than do nonusers (ARCI, 2005).

Findings of small-scale studies are consistent with those of national surveys. Internet use has been positively related to the size of one's real-life social network, and to the frequency of face-to-face interactions with friends (Kraut et al., 2002; Uslaner, 2004). Not surprisingly, frequency of Internet use is positively related to number of online friendships (Peter, Valkenburg, & Schouten, 2005; Wolak et al., 2002).

On the other hand there is also support for the dystopian perspective that using the Internet has negative effects on adolescents' social relationships. An early national survey conducted by the Stanford Institute for the Quantitative Study of Society found that hours of Internet use, like hours of television use, were negatively related to time spent with family and friends (Nie & Erbring, 2000). In one small-scale study adolescent Internet users reported feeling less close to persons with whom they communicated mostly by e-mail (Cummings, Butler, & Kraut, 2002). Another small-scale study found an increase in weak online ties and decrease in strong offline ties with increased Internet use (LaRose, Eastin, & Gregg, 2001; Kraut et al., 2002). Still other studies have found no differences between Internet users and nonusers in the number of strong and weak social ties (PEW, 2006c, 2007).

One of the earliest and most publicized studies of home Internet use initially found support for the dystopian perspective. Adolescents who used the Internet more were more likely to report being lonely and depressed than those who used it less (Kraut et al., 1998). However, a follow-up study by these same investigators qualified these findings (Kraut et al., 2002). It turned out that extroverted adolescents who used the Internet more felt more socially connected, whereas introverted adolescents who used the Internet more became more depressed and withdrawn.

Other studies have similarly found that adolescent characteristics interact with the nature of Internet use to influence the social effects of use (Gross et al., 2002). According to the "rich get richer" hypothesis, Internet use benefits adolescents who already have strong social skills and whose Internet activities add more social resources to an already impressive social network (Kraut et al., 2002; Walther, 1996). In contrast, the "social compensation" hypothesis argues that Internet use benefits adolescents lacking social resources, such as the socially anxious adolescent. For the socially anxious or introverted adolescent the anonymity and absence of visual and auditory cues on the Internet encourage more self-disclosing and intimate interactions online, interactions that facilitate social skills and development (McKenna et al., 2002).

Studies examining the role of adolescent characteristics such as loneliness, introversion, and social anxiety in understanding the social effects of Internet use have thus far supported the rich get richer hypothesis (Amichai-Hamburger, Wainapel, & Fox, 2002; Kraut et al., 2002; Moody, 2001; Peter et al., 2005; Waestlund, Norlander, & Archer, 2001; Weiser, 2001), although there is some evidence supporting the social compensation hypothesis (Amichai-Hamburger & Ben-Artzi, 2003) and still other evidence supporting neither hypothesis (Amichai-Hamburger, 2005; Amichai-Hamburger et al., 2002; Jackson et al., 2004, 2006b; Leung, 2002; Scealy, Phillips, & Stevenson, 2002). For example, one study (Heitner, 2002) found that adolescents who used the Internet to connect with others in real-time social exchanges (e.g., instant messaging) had higher peer status, greater social skills, and greater social integration than their more socially introverted and withdrawn peers. The latter group of adolescents spent most of their Internet time engaged in solitary activities. Additionally, adolescents who used chat rooms had lower peer status and were less socially skilled than those who did not.

## CIVIC ENAGAGEMENT

Research on the effects of Internet use on adolescents' civic engagement has been more supportive of the utopian than dystopian perspective. In a nationally representative survey of over 1,000 young people ages 14 to 22, those who used the Internet more were more politically aware and civically engaged than those who used it less (Pasek, Kenski, Romer, & Jamieson, 2006). Similar findings were obtained in other research (Kenski & Stroud, 2006; Uslaner, 2004).

The positive relationship between Internet use and civic engagement has been used to explain the eleven percentage point increase in voting among persons younger than age 25 in the 2004 presidential election (Lopez,

Kirby, & Sagoff, 2005; Patterson, 2005). Indeed the potential of the Internet to promote civic engagements has sparked optimism about the participation of future generations in the political system.

## AGGRESSION

Perhaps more than any other aspect of social behavior, aggression has received the most research attention with respect to the effects of technology use. Most of this research has focused on the effects of playing violent video games on aggression. Nearly half of "heavy gamers" are under 17 years old (Walsh, Gentile, Walsh, & Bennett, 2006).

Evidence overwhelmingly supports the conclusion that playing violent video games contributes to aggressive thought and behavior. Moreover, it desensitizes the player toward violence, both immediately and in the long run (Anderson et al., 2003; Anderson, Gentile, & Buckley, 2007). Since 81% of adolescents say they play games online (PEW, 2006a) these findings suggest that Internet use may be increasing the level of aggressive behavior in youth, to the extent that youth are playing violent games online.

## SUMMARY: SOCIAL EFFECTS OF INTERNET USE

Overall, research on the social effects of Internet use provides more support for the utopian than dystopian perspective. However, it also suggests that the social effects of Internet use depend on characteristics of the adolescent user and the nature of Internet use. Adolescents who are already social engaged in the real world have more and better social relationships when they use the Internet. Adolescents who are not may become more socially isolated with Internet use, most likely because they use the Internet in ways that further isolate them. Moreover, the dystopian perspective finds strong support in research on the effects of playing video games. The more adolescents play violent video games, the greater their aggressive thought and behavior.

## Cognitive Effects of Internet Use

Surprisingly few studies have examined the cognitive effects of Internet use. From the utopian perspective Internet use should enhance cognitive development by providing instant access to a wealth of information about every conceivable topic and by providing an engaging, multimedia, interactive environment for learning in new and potentially superior ways. From the dystopian perspective Internet use should undermine cognitive development by distracting adolescents from more substantive intellectual pursuits, such as reading and writing. Findings thus far provide a rather mixed picture of the effects of Internet use—and computer use in general—on cognitive development (National Science Foundation Report, 2001).

## ACADEMIC PERFORMANCE

Most of the research on the effects of technology use on academic performance has focused on computer use. An early review of research on school learning with computer-based technology, which included five meta-analytic reviews, came to the unsatisfying conclusion that findings are inconclusive (Roschelle, Pea, Hoadley, Gordon, & Means, 2000). Studies that did find a relationship between technology use and academic performance failed to establish the causal direction of this relationship (Blanton, Moorman, Hayes, & Warner, 1997; Cole, 1996; Rocheleau, 1995). For example, several studies found that the presence of educational resources in the home, including computers, was a strong predictor of academic success in mathematics and science (National Center for Educational Statistics, 2000). But a variety of factors related to both having educational resources in the home and to academic success, such as family income and parental education, may account for their relationship.

A recent longitudinal study of low-income children and home Internet use suggests a positive causal relationship between the two (Jackson et al., 2006c). In this study, children who used the Internet more had higher scores on standardized tests of reading achievement and higher grade point averages six months, one year, and sixteen months later than did children who used the Internet less.

Large-scale national surveys have examined perceived relationships between Internet use and academic performance. In a 2004 survey (ANN, 2004), more than 60% of students ages 18 and under said that the Internet was very important or extremely important to doing schoolwork. However, most parents claimed that having the Internet at home had no effect on their children's school grades.

In the UK, one large-scale evaluation project tested the hypothesis that computer and Internet availability in school was related to improved test scores (BECTA, 2003). Contrary to this hypothesis no relationship was found between computer or Internet availability in school and students' test scores. Nor is there evidence elsewhere in the literature that Internet use has any academic benefits.

## VISUAL SKILLS

As noted earlier, 81% of adolescents play games online (PEW, 2006a). Early reviews of the relationship between video game playing and cognitive skills suggested positive effects on visual skills, such as spatial, iconic, and image representation skills (Subrahmanyam et al., 2000; Subrahmanyam, Green-field, Kraut, & Gross, 2001). More recent studies provide stronger evidence of a causal link between video game playing and visual skills (Green & Bavelier, 2003, 2006, 2007).

SUMMARY: COGNITIVE EFFECTS OF INTERNET USE

Although research is scant, there is as yet no evidence that Internet use has any cognitive benefits, contrary to both the utopian and dystopian perspectives. Adolescents who use the Internet more do no better in school than those who use it less or not at all, after controlling for sociodemographic characteristics that influence both Internet use and school performance (e.g., parental education and income). There are two notable exceptions to this conclusion. Low-income children may benefit academically from home Internet use, although only one study to date has observed this effect. Playing video games, online or offline, improves visual-spatial skills, skills that are consider by many to be the "training wheels" for performance in mathematics, science, and engineering.

## Psychological Effects of Internet Use

Efforts to establish a link between Internet use and psychological well-being (as distinct from social well-being) have been scattered throughout the literature (Caplan, 2003; Gross et al., 2002; Van, Huang, Qui, & Han, 2006; Wartella, Caplovitz, & Lee, 2004). According to the utopian perspective, Internet use should enhance psychological well-being by providing opportunities for self-expression, social support, and identity development within an anonymous and "safe" environment. According to the dystopian perspective Internet use should undermine psychological well-being by exposing adolescents to potentially harmful content and experiences, including support for maladaptive and/or socially unaccept-able behavior.

PSYCHOLOGICAL WELL-BEING

Only a handful of studies have examined the relationship between Inter-net use and overall psychological well-being. Most find no relationship between time online and either dispositional or daily well-being (Amichai-Hamburger, 2005; Amichai-Hamburger & Ben-Artzi, 2003; Amichai-Hamburger et al., 2002). A longitudinal study of low-income adolescents similarly found no effects of Internet use on a variety of psychological outcomes, including self-esteem and affective well-being (Jackson et al., 2006b).

Other research indicates that adolescents use the Internet to find help for psychological and emotional problems (Gould, Munfakh, Lubell, Kleinman, & Parker, 2002). How helpful this information is to them is rarely reported, the single exception finding that online help was viewed as the least helpful among a variety of help sources (e.g., parents; ARCI, 2005).

## IDENTITY DEVELOPMENT

Proponents of the utopian perspective have argued that the Internet provides powerful tools that allow for creative approaches to identity development (Calvert, 2002; Cheung, 2000; Donath, 2003; Mazzarella, 2005; Simpson, 2005; Slater, 2002). Chat rooms, in particular, may serve as playgrounds where young people can try on new and alternative identities. Most of the research in this area has been qualitative and limited to small and select samples of adolescents. Thus, broad generalizations about the effects of Internet use on adolescent identity development are not yet possible.

Some of the earliest research on identity development online was conducted by Sherri Turkle (1995). Her ethnographic interviews of adolescents interacting in virtual environments provide rich accounts of how the Internet may be used to construct and alter identity. Qualitative research by Suler (2002) has also examined the construction of identity online, and whether online identities differ from identities in real life. His findings provide some support for the view that Internet activities have the potential to positively impact adolescent identity development.

Other research has focused on identity development as revealed in personal Web pages. These findings suggest that adolescents present as well as construct their identities in these pages (Suler, 2002). A study of identity presentation in online teen chat rooms found that adolescents communicate identity information online, particularly information about gender (Subrahmanyam, Smahel, & Greenfield, 2006), presumably to compensate for the text-based environment of the chat room by providing information that is typically available in face-to-face interactions.

## INTERNET ADDICTION

In contrast to the paucity of research on the positive psychological effects of Internet use, there is an abundance of research on one specific negative effect—Internet addiction. Unfortunately, much of this research has been plagued by conceptual and methodological issues, rendering conclusions difficult to draw (Brenner, 1997; Chou, Condron, & Belland, 2005; Griffiths, 2000; Morahan-Martin, 2005; Morahan-Martin & Schumacker, 2000). Moreover, despite media attention to this topic, Internet addiction appears to afflict only a small percentage of adolescents, with estimates ranging from as little as 3% (U.S. females; Morahan-Martin & Schumacker, 2000) to as much as 12% (Asian males; Chou & Hsiao, 2000).

Research on susceptibility to Internet addiction suggests that some adolescents may be at greater risk than others. Low self-esteem, poor motivation, fear of rejection, and high need for approval—all factors associated with depression—are also associated with susceptibility to Internet addiction (Young & Rogers, 1998). Internet addiction has been related to a variety of problematic behaviors, such as lack of sleep, missing meals, missing work or school, and to social isolation and depression (Morahan-Martin & Schumacker, 2000), although some studies find no relationship between addiction and emotional or personality problems (Cao & Su, 2006).

TIME DISPLACEMENT

One of the major arguments of the dystopian perspective is that time on the Internet is time taken away from other activities that contribute to psychological well-being, such as interacting with family and friends, reading books, and participating in sports and leisure activities. As discussed later, time online does appear to detract from time spent in physical activity. However, there is no evidence that time online takes time away from any other activity except one—watching TV (ANN, 2004, 2006). Adolescents who use the Internet more spend less time watching TV.

SUMMARY: PSYCHOLOGICAL EFFECTS OF INTERNET USE

Contrary to both the utopian and dystopian perspectives, there is no compelling evidence that Internet use either helps or hurts the psychological development of adolescents. However, it may adversely affect subgroups of adolescents who overuse particular Internet tools, such as chat, or overuse the Internet itself (i.e., Internet addicts).

## Physical Effects of Internet Use

Does using the Internet contribute to or detract from physical well-being? From the utopian perspective Internet use should benefit physical health by providing a wealth of information, 24/7, at no cost. From the dystopian perspective Internet use should detract from physical health by taking time away from physical activity and, possibly, by providing false, erroneous, or misleading information about health.

## HEALTH INFORMATION

Results of a large-scale national survey indicate that 31% of adolescents have searched the Internet for information about health, dieting, and physical fitness (PEW, 2006b). One-fifth (21%) have looked for information about "a health topic that's hard to talk about, like drug use, sexual health or depression" (Borzekowski & Rickert, 2001a, 2001b; Johnson-Vickberg, Kohn, Franco & Criniti, 2003; Rideout, 2001). However, very little is known about the consequences of this behavior (Gould et al., 2002; Gray, Klein, Noyce, Sesselberg, & Cantrill, 2005). Thus, we do not know how successful searchers are, or whether adolescents are satisfied with the information they find. We do not know whether adolescents use the information they find online or whether this information contributes to or detracts from their actual physical health.

## OBESITY

Estimates are that 16% of adolescents in the United States are obese, triple the rate of just two decades ago (American Obesity Association, 2005). The causes of adolescent obesity are many and include poor eating habits, soft drink consumption, lack of physical exercise, and too much time in front of a screen (Adams, 2006). Between the ages of 8 and 18, youth spend more time in front of computer, television, and game screens than in any other activity except sleeping (44.5 hours per week; Kaiser Family Foundation, 2005).

Research indicates that adolescents who use computers are more likely to be overweight than nonusers (Subrahmanyam et al., 2000). Youth who play video games are more likely to be overweight or obese than nonplayers, especially if they play video games in their bedroom rather than in shared family space (Vandwater, Shim, & Caplovitz, 2004; Walsh et al., 2006). Moreover, it is the lack of physical activity associated with screen time that is responsible for the relationship between time online and obesity (Vandwater et al., 2004).

## SUMMARY: PHYSICAL EFFECTS OF INTERNET USE

Contrary to the utopian perspective, although adolescents use the Internet to search for information about health, there is no evidence that Internet use contributes in any way to their actual health. On the other hand, in support of the dystopian perspective, the more time spent online the greater the likelihood of adolescents' becoming overweight or obese.

## Internet Exposure to Potentially Harmful Content and Experiences

### INAPPROPRIATE SEXUALLY EXPLICIT MATERIAL

The fact that inappropriate sexually explicit material is available on the Internet, often anonymously and at low or no cost, has fueled public concern about adolescents' Internet use (Runkel, 2005). This concern is understandable in light of the evidence that adolescents use the Internet frequently (as discussed earlier), are curious about sexuality, and often seek out and find sexual material and stimulation (Savin-Williams & Diamond, 2004). However, like the effects of offline exposure, the effects of exposure to inappropriate sexually explicit material online—cyberporn—are unclear, especially when intentionality and intensity of exposure are taken into account (Bauserman, 1996; Fisher & Barak, 2001; Greenfield, 2004; Gunter, 2002; Mitchell, Finkelhor, & Wolak, 2003; Peter & Valkenburg, 2005; Valkenburg & Soeters, 2006).

Estimates of the extent and intensity of exposure to inappropriate sexually explicit material online (cyberporn) vary among surveys and samples. A survey sponsored by the Kaiser Family Foundation (2000) found that 70% of U.S. adolescents ages 15 to 17 said they have "accidentally" encountered pornography online. In the UK more than half (57%) of online youth said they had encountered "pornography" online (i.e., cyberporn). More than half (54%) were not bothered by it and only 14% said "I do not like it," the most negative response option available to them.

Research on intentional exposure to sexually explicit material online has produced a mixed picture of the extent of this activity. A study of U.S. adolescents in 1999 and 2000 found that only 8% of 10- to 17-year-olds intentionally sought sexually explicit material on the Internet (Ybarra & Mitchell, 2005). Much higher rates were observed in a study of U.S. college students: 59% of men and 33% of women said they intentionally accessed sexually explicit material on the Internet, although the majority said they rarely did so (Goodson, McCormick, & Evans, 2000). Nearly one-third (38%) of Taiwanese adolescents sought sexually explicit material online (Lo & Wei, 2005). Low-income adolescents in the United States, particularly males, accessed pornography Web sites frequently, but only during the first three months of home Internet access (Jackson et al., 2006a).

The effects of exposure to inappropriate sexually explicit material online are even less clear than the extent of exposure, intentional or unintentional. One study of a large sample of 12- to 14-year-olds found a positive relationship between consumption of sexual content in six media and sexual activity and intentions to become sexually active (Pardun, L'Engle, & Brown, 2005). However, the strongest relationships were for movie and music exposure, not for Internet exposure. A report by the National Research Council concluded that difficulties in defining what constitutes inappropriate sexually explicit material has rendered the task of determining its effects and formulating public policy difficult at best (Thornburgh & Lin, 2002).

SEXUAL PREDATORS

The prevalence of sexual predators online is impossible to estimate, although public concerns about them loom large—and understandably so (DiMarco, 2003; Ost, 2003; Palmer & Stacey, 2004; Potter & Potter, 2001). The National Center for Missing & Exploited Children (2006) reported that about 4% of children ages 10 to 17 have received "distressing sexual solicitations" online within the previous year. There is no question that the Internet allows child sexual predators (pedophiles) instant and continual access to potential victims, primarily through chat rooms and social networking Web sites. Predators can disguise their true identities (e.g., pretend to be a teen), build long-term Internet relationships with potential victims, and conduct open discussions with other predators (e.g., sexual desires, ideas about ways to lure victims; see National Center for Missing and Exploited Children, 2006).

Research sponsored primarily by the law-enforcement community has developed profiles of Internet sexual predators and guides for parents on how to monitor their children's Internet use (Crisis Connection, 2007). Demographically, sexual predators are almost always male (94 to 96%), range in age from 13 to 65 years old, and are single (86%). Beyond these broad demographic characteristics predators have been categorized into four major groups based on predatory characteristics and behaviors.

The group labeled "collectors" consists of predators who focus on collecting child pornography online. Most have no prior contact with law enforcement or any known illegal contact with children. The second group, labeled "travelers," engages in online chat with children and, through manipulation and coercion, attempts to meet them in person for sexual purposes. Most travelers are also collectors of child pornography.

"Manufacturers" are the third group of sexual predators online. They distribute child pornography, usually by way of videotapes or CD-ROMs. Manufacturers are often sexually involved with children in real life and are likely to have criminal records of sex offending. "Chatters," the fourth group of Internet sexual predators, pretend to be mentors to children in Internet chat rooms. Their innocent "teaching" quickly escalates to conversations about sex.

Research indicates that 100% of the children molested by a sexual predator they met online went willingly to meet with him, often believing that they were meeting with a peer.[1] About 25% of U.S. adolescent girls report meeting in person a stranger they first met online. One in seven adolescent boys admits to doing this. While most "Internet friends" do turn out to be peers, some are sexual predators and the consequences of such encounters can be horrific.

As discussed earlier in examining the nature of Internet use, youth are twice as likely to encounter strangers online if they use social networking Web sites than if they go online for other purposes, such as instant messaging or information search. About 60% of adolescents say they visit social networking Web sites and 80% do so daily, regardless of sex, age, urban–rural location, region of the country, race/ethnicity, grades in school, and neighborhood income. Although not all strangers online are sexual predators, the rise in popularity of social networking Web sites such as MySpace and Facebook may inadvertently be increasing the likelihood that youth will one day encounter a sexual predator online.

## CYBERBULLYING

Wikipedia defines cyberbullying as the use of electronic information and communication devices such as e-mail, instant messaging, text messages, and blogs to bully or otherwise harass an individual or group through personal attacks or other means. Cyberbullying can be as simple as continuing to send e-mails to someone who has indicated she wants no further contact to as serious as issuing threats, sexual remarks, and pejorative labels (i.e., hate speech). Some forms of cyberbullying may even constitute a computer crime (Hinduja, 2007).

Cyberbullying has attracted a great deal of research attention in part because its real-world counterpart, schoolyard bullying, is so familiar and in part because youth are typically both the perpetrators and victims of this behavior (Swartz, 2005). Most of the research on cyberbullying has focused on documenting its prevalence and nature (e.g., Li, 2005, 2006). Less attention has been given to the consequences of cyberbullying for either the victim or perpetrator.

Studies of the prevalence and nature of cyberbullying have produced mixed results. One study of approximately 1,500 adolescent Internet users found that over 33% had been victims of cyberbullying and 16% had been cyberbullies (Patchin & Hinduja, 2006). Most instances of cyberbullying involved relatively minor behaviors (40% were disrespected, 18% were called names) but about 12% involved physical threats and about 5% of victims reported being concerned for their physical safety.

Another study of over 3,000 girls ages 8 to 17 found that 38% had been cyberbullied (Burgess-Proctor, Patchin, & Hinduja, 2006). The two most common bullying behaviors were being ignored (46%) and being disrespected (43%). Serious behaviors like being threatened were relatively infrequent (11%). Cyberbullying was most likely to occur in chat rooms (26%), followed by computer text messaging (22%), and e-mail (14%). The majority of victims (79%) knew their cyberbully, who was usually a friend from school (31%), someone else from school (36%), or someone they met in a chat room (28%).

This same study examined victims' responses to being cyberbullied (Burgess-Proctor et al., 2006). The most common behavioral response was to retaliate or cyberbully back (27%). Few victims informed a parent (13%) or other adult (7%). Almost half of the victims told an online buddy about the event (47%) and about half that many told another friend (18%). Some victims felt forced to stay offline for a while (17%), while others did nothing different as a result of being cyberbullied (25%). A significant number of victims did not respond at all to event; they told no one (36%) and did nothing (25%). Contacting law enforcement was never mentioned, even when cyberbullying was as severe as a death threat. About one-fourth of victims said that victimization had affected them at home (27%) or school (23%). The most common emotional response was frustration (41%), followed by anger (35%), and sadness (30%). However, being cyberbullied had no adverse effects on over half (55%) of its victims.

Results of a recent Internet-based survey of 384 youth, boys and girls (Patchin & Hinduja, 2006), found that 29% had been victims of cyberbullying and 11% had been perpetrators. Other results where quite similar to findings for girls in the Burgess-Proctor et al. (2006) study just discussed.

A survey by the National Children's Home Charity (2005) examined cyberbullying prevalence and responses to it among 856 British youth ages 11 and 19 years old. One-quarter (25%) had been victims of cyberbullying and almost three-fourths (73%) of victims knew their cyberbully. Less than half (42%) told a friend about the incident, 32% told a parent, and 19% told no one.

Other surveys have reported different levels of cyberbullying victimization, attributable in part to different definitions of cyberbullying. A 2003 phone survey of 1,500 online youth ages 10 to 17 years old found that 19% had received or sent an aggressive communication during the previous year (Ybarra & Mitchell, 2005). The vast majority (84%) of perpetrators knew their victims and almost one-third (31%) of victims knew their perpetrators.

An earlier survey by the Work and Family Institute found that 12% of the 1,000 youth sampled, grades five to twelve were victims of five or more cyberbullying instances during the previous month (Galinski & Salmond, 2002).

Overall, cyberbullying appears to be a relatively common experience for online adolescents, with far more victims than perpetrators. Most cyberbullying is of the mild variety, expressed as ignoring or disrespecting behaviors. Most reponses to cyberbullying are mild emotional reactions and, less frequently, modest changes in online behavior. However, the extent of severe cyberbullying and its negative consequences for adolescent victims may be underestimated in the research. Adolescents may be reluctant to admit to severe victimization and even more reluctant to admit to severe cyberbullying.[2]

### SUMMARY: INTERNET EXPOSURE TO POTENTIALLY HARMFUL CONTENT AND EXPERIENCES

Adolescents who use the Internet are potentially exposed to inappropriate sexually explicit material (cyberporn), sexual predators, and cyberbullying. The evidence in this regard is unequivocal, thus supporting the dystopian perspective regarding the "evils of the Internet." On the other hand, the incidence of intentional exposure to cyberporn is relatively low (8% to 59%, the latter for college males), reactions to accidental exposure are relatively mild (I don't care for it) and the harmful consequences of exposure uncertain. Cyberbullying is a more frequent occurrence but mostly in its mildest forms (e.g., ignoring) with the mildest of consequences (e.g., not bothered by it). Estimates of the prevalence of sexual predators online are difficult to obtain. Although these uncertainties do not mean the Internet is a safe place for adolescents, the findings do suggest that the potential harms of Internet use need to be weighed against the potential benefits of use in decisions about adolescents' use of this ubiquitous technology.

## Internet Use to Support Maladaptive Behavior

Characteristics of the Internet make it particularly well-suited to supporting maladaptive behavior. The accessibility and anonymity of the Internet, the relative ease with which socially deviant or unacceptable behaviors can occur online, the absence of adult supervision, and the 24/7 availability of the Internet all contribute to its appeal as a platform for supporting maladaptive behavior. The Internet may be especially appealing to marginalized adolescents (i.e., adolescents who exhibit depressive symptomatology) who are more likely than other adolescents to engage in maladaptive behavior. For marginalized adolescents the Internet provides an anonymous venue for sharing actual and fabricated aspects of identity within a community of (presumably) similar marginalized peers (McKenna et al., 2002).

Supporting the view that marginalized adolescents are particularly at risk on the Internet are findings that they are more likely to talk with strangers and disclose personal information online (Ybarra, Alexander, & Mitchell, 2005). Although such conversations and disclosures can provide much-needed support and cathartic sharing for the marginalized adolescent, they can also provide a means for spreading and deepening maladaptive behaviors. Two examples are illustrative.

## CUTTING

Cutting is a form of self-injurious behavior that involves intentional carving or cutting of the skin and subdermal tissue, scratching, burning, ripping or pulling skin or hair, swallowing toxic substances, bruising, and breaking bones. Although not typically a suicidal gesture, self-injury is statistically associated with suicide and can result in unanticipated severe harm or fatality (Claes, Vandereycken, & Vertommen, 2003; Favazza, 1999).

Estimates of the prevalence of cutting vary widely, from as little as 4% to as high as 38% of adolescents and young adults (Briere & Gil, 1998; Favazza, 1999; Gratz, Conrad, & Roemer, 2002; Muehlenkamp & Gutierrez, 2004). Large-scale studies in the UK estimate that approximately 10% of youth ages 11 to 25 have engaged in cutting. A British report on the national scope of the problem documents a dramatic increase in disclosures of cutting to national children's help lines—a 65% increase between 2002 and 2004 (Young People and Self Harm, 2004). Adolescent cutting behavior appears to be on the rise in the United States as well (Welsh, 2004; Yates, 2004).

One recent study (Whitlock, Powers, & Eckenrode, 2006) used observational data from Internet message boards to investigate how adolescents solicit and share information online related to cutting. More than 400 self-injury message boards were identified, most populated by females who described themselves as between 12 and 20 years old. Findings indicated that online interactions clearly provided positive social support for ending this maladaptive behavior. However, participation in these message boards also exposed these vulnerable adolescents to a subculture in which cutting was normalized and even encouraged. For example, discussions found on these message boards included how to conceal cuts and techniques for cutting.

## ANOREXIA NERVOSA

In a news commentary on anorexia nervosa Reaves (2001) remarked that developing an eating disorder is no easy task. It requires "months, even years, of obsessive, destructive tunnel vision and single-minded dedication." The Internet potentially contributes to this pathological effort by providing pro-anorexic Web sites that support this maladaptive and self-destructive behavior. For example, proanorexic Web sites describe how to conceal weight loss, how to "diet" (i.e., starve) more effectively, and how to deal with the reactions of others to changes in one's appearance (Jackson & Elliott, 2004). Moreover, Internet support is 24/7, anonymous, and free.

Research on the actual impact of proanorexic Web sites has yet to emerge. Thus, while it is reasonable to expect that the very existence of such Web sites is contributing to maladaptive behavior, there is yet no evidence to support this claim. Moreover, it is important to note that the overwhelming majority of Web sites aimed at anorexics provide information and social support for ending this behavior and restoring self-esteem and a positive body image (e.g., WebMD[3]).

### SUMMARY: INTERNET USE TO SUPPORT MALADAPTIVE BEHAVIOR

In support of the dystopian perspective, the Internet has the potential to provide information and social support for continuing maladaptive behavior. However, in support of the utopian perspective, it also has a greater potential to provide information and social support for ending maladaptive behavior.

## ADOLESCENTS AND THE DIGITAL DIVIDE

Whether or not one concludes there is a digital divide in adolescents' Internet use depends on how one defines *digital divide* (Bradbrook & Fisher, 2004; Compaine, 2001; Drori, 2005; Fong Wellman, Kew, & Wilkes, 2004; Katz & Rice, 2002; Livingstone, 2003; Murdock, 2002; Norris, 2001; PEW, 2000b, 2002, 2003, 2005d, 2006c, 2006d; Rice 2002; Selwyn, 2004; Van Dijk, 2003, 2005; Warschauer, 2003). In the United States and the UK, adolescents' access to the Internet from school is nearly universal. About 99% of schools in the United States have Internet access and 92% of UK youth report having accessed the Internet from school. However, a digital divide persists in both countries in terms of home Internet access and how users connect to the Internet. Moreover, a divide of a different sort is emerging in how adolescents use the Internet once access is no longer an issue.

In the United States 13% of adolescents do not use the Internet at all. About half (47%) of these nonusers have been online but dropped off for a variety of reasons, including bad experiences, parental restrictions, or not feeling safe online. Adolescents who never used the Internet say that lack of interest, time, and access are the major reasons for not using it. In the UK

16% of youth make little or no use of the Internet. Reasons are lack of access, interest, computer skills, and time.

Home Internet access in the United States is less likely for adolescents whose parents have less education and income and for African American adolescents (Hoffman, Novak, & Schlosser, 2001; Jackson, Ervin, Gardner, & Schmitt, 2001b; PEW, 2006e). And a new divide is developing between those who have broadband access at home and those who have dial-up access, a divide based largely but not exclusively on parental income (PEW, 2006e). This new divide may have implications as widespread as the original access divide because broadband changes dramatically the users' relationship with the Internet, including how often they go online, how long they stay online, and what they do online (Livingstone, 2003; PEW, 2006e).

In the United States and the UK the gender gap in Internet access, once huge, has essentially disappeared (PEW, 2003, 2005d). But a gender gap persists worldwide; males are more likely to have Internet access than females (Chen & Wellman, 2004; Norris, 2001; van Dijk, 2005). Moreover, national surveys in the United States consistently report gender differences in the intensity and nature of Internet use and knowledge about the Internet (PEW, 2000a, 2003, 2005d). Males use the Internet more intensely than do females, going online more often and for longer periods of time. Males are more likely than females to use the Internet for commercial transactions whereas the reverse is true for staying in touch with family and friends. Males are more knowledgeable about the Internet than are females (Boneva et al., 2006; PEW, 2006c, 2006d; Van Dijk, 2003).

In a report on Internet use by youth in the UK Livingstone (2003) discussed a new type of digital divide that is developing between youth who use the Internet as a rich, diverse, engaging, and stimulating resource and those who use it as a narrow, unengaging, if occasionally useful resource of lesser significance. This divide is structured primarily along ethnic, gender, socioeconomic, age, and urban–rural lines (Drori, 2006; Livingstone, 2003; Van Dijk, 2005).

Some researchers have argued that disparities in the nature of Internet use have potentially huge consequences for deepening social and economic divides. Essentially, their arguments support the "rich get richer" hypothesis because these disparities, which are based primarily on income and education, result in further disparities in digital skills and literacy, which contribute to continued disparities in income and education (van Dijk, 2005). However, other researchers have argued in favor of the "social compensation" hypothesis. They believe that through technology diffusion, contagion, and adoption perspective, existing disparities will continue to shrink and the digital divide will be eventually disappear (van Dijk, 2005).

## ADOLESCENTS, INTERNET USE, AND PUBLIC POLICY

What implications do findings about the frequency, nature, and effects of adolescents' Internet use have for public policy? Do clear recommendations about encouraging or discouraging Internet use, types of use, and responsibility for adolescents' Internet use follow from these findings?

First, evidence of both the frequency and nature of adolescents' Internet use leaves no room for doubt that today's adolescents are indeed the "Net generation." Their day-to-day lives rely increasingly on Internet access for communication and information. Entertainment is also gravitating away from unidirectional broadcast media to the interactive online world. Thus, adolescents who are without access to the Internet—the digital "have nots"—are lacking an important resource that is available to their peers. In the United States this divide continues to be based primarily on income, education, and race. Adolescents whose parents have less education and income and African American adolescents remain the digital "have nots."

Public policy is needed to address the digital divide issue in ways that recognize its complexity. The digital divide goes beyond mere access to the Internet. It includes the nature of access and how the Internet is used once access is obtained. Adolescents who access the Internet using broadband have significant advantages over those who have dial-up or no access. Adolescents who use the Internet in creative and engaging ways have advantages over those who use it in mundane and unengaging ways. This digital "use" divide has the potential to exacerbate existing inequalities and produce new forms of exclusion among adolescents that will be based primarily on parental education, income, and race. And this divide will persist into adulthood.

Second, there is currently little evidence that Internet use benefits adolescents' cognitive development. Thus, neither the utopian perspective that promised benefits nor the dystopian perspective that promised liabilities finds much support in the research. The only exception is the evidence that playing video games—on the Internet or elsewhere—enhances visual-spatial skills, skills that are important in learning science, technology, engineering, and mathematics.

One explanation for the failure to find benefits or liabilities of Internet use on cognitive development is the absence of experimental and longitudinal research needed to establish cause-effect relationships. Such research is difficult, costly, and time consuming but nevertheless critical to determining if and when using the Internet has an effect on cognitive development. Another explanation is that Internet use has been too broadly defined. Rather than global measures of frequency of use research needs to use more refined measures of the nature of Internet use. Where public policy enters the picture is in encouraging and supporting research on the relationship between specific types of Internet use and a variety of measures of cognitive development, academic performance being top among them. Also needed is support for educational interventions that teach adolescents, as well as their parents and teachers, how to use the Internet effectively, that is, in ways most likely to benefit academic performance and develop the skills needed for the twenty-first century workforce.

Third, public policy is needed to address the potential evils of the Internet. Two considerations are suggested by the research. First, some adolescents are more susceptible to Internet evils than are others. Marginalized adolescents—those most likely to be depressed, socially anxious, or withdrawn—may be more susceptible to Internet harm than are other adolescents. Second, some types of Internet use are more likely to result in harm than are other types of use. Chat rooms and Web sites that facilitate contact with strangers are potentially more harmful than Internet activities that focus on existing social ties and information search. Time spent in Internet activities may be another signal to potential harm. Public policy that takes adolescent characteristics and nature and extent of Internet use into account is more likely to be effective in minimizing harm than policy that paints a broad stroke of the Internet as either good or evil.

## NOTES

1. See http://www.wiredsafety.org/internet_predators/index.html
2. See http://www.cybertipline.com
3. See http://www.webmd.com

## REFERENCES

Adams, C. K. (2006). Childhood and adolescent obesity: A winning way to fight a "losing battle." *Northeast Florida Medicine, 57,* 47–48.

Adolescent Risk Communication Institute (ARCI), Annenberg Public Policy Center at the University of Pennsylvania. (2005). *Treating and preventing adolescent mental health disorders: What we know and what we don't know.* New York: Oxford University Press.

Adolescent Risk Communication Institute (ARCI). (2006, September). *Stranger contact in adolescent online social networks common but likelihood of contact depends on type of website.* Annenberg Public Policy Center at the University of Pennsylvania.

American Obesity Association. (2005, May). *Fact sheet: Obesity in youth.* Retrieved from http://obesity1.tempdomainname.com/subs/childhood

Amichai-Hamburger, Y. (Ed.). (2005). *The social net: Human behavior in cyberspace.* New York: Oxford University Press.

Amichai-Hamburger, Y., & Ben-Artzi, E. (2003). Loneliness and Internet use. *Computers in Human Behavior, 19*, 71–80.

Amichai-Hamburger, Y., Wainapel, G., & Fox, S. (2002). "On the Internet no one knows I'm an introvert:" Extroversion, neuroticism, and Internet interaction. *Cyberpsychology & Behavior, 5*, 125–128.

Anderson, C. A., Berkowitz, L., Donnerstein, E., Huesmann, L. R., Johnson, J. D., Linz, D., et al. (2003). The influence of media on youth. *Psychological Science in the Public Interest, 4*, 81–110.

Anderson, C. A., Gentile, D. A., & Buckley, K. E. (2007). *Violent video game effects on children and adolescents: Theory, research and public policy.* New York: Oxford University.

Annenberg Digital Future Project. (2004). *Surveying the digital future–Year 4: Ten years, ten trends.* Retrieved from http://www.digitalcenter.org/downloads/Digi talFutureReport-Year4-2004.pdf

Annenberg Digital Future Project. (2006). *Online world as important to Internet users as real world? 6th annual survey.* Press release, November 29. Retrieved from http://www.digitalcenter.org/pages/current_report.asp?intGlobalId=19

Bargh, J. A., & McKenna, K.Y.A. (2004). The Internet and social life. *Annual Review of Psychology, 55*, 573–590.

Bauserman, R. (1996). Sexual aggression and pornography: A review of correlational research. *Basic and Applied Psychology, 18*, 405–427.

BECTA. (2003). *Impact2–The impact of information and communication technology on pupil learning and attainment.* British Educational Communications and Technology Agency. Retrieved from http://www.becta.org.uk

Blanton, W. E., Moorman, G. B., Hayes, B. A., & Warner, M. L. (1997). Effects of participation in the fifth dimension on far transfer. *Journal of Educational Computing Research, 16*, 371–396.

Boneva, B. S., Quinn, A., Kraut, R. E., Kiesler, S., & Shklovski, I. (2006). Teenage communication in the instant messaging era. In R. Kraut, M. Brynin, & S. Kiesler (Eds.), *Computers, phones, and the Internet: Domesticating information technology* (pp. 201–218). New York: Oxford University Press.

Borzekowski, D. L. G., & Rickert, V. I. (2001a). Adolescents, the Internet, and health: Issues of access and content. *Journal of Applied Developmental Psychology, 22*, 49–59.

Borzekowski, D. L. G., & Rickert, V. I. (2001b). Adolescent cybersurfing for health information: A new resource that crosses barriers. *Archives of Pediatric and Adolescent Medicine, 155*, 813–817.

Bradbrook, G., & Fisher, J. (2004, March). *Digital equality: Reviewing digital inclusion activity and mapping the way forwards.* Citizens Online: A new society for the 21st century. Retrieved from http://www.citizensonline.org.uk/site/media/documents/939_DigitalEquality1.pdf

Brenner, V. (1997). Psychology of computer use: Parameters of Internet use, abuse and addiction: The first 90 days of the Internet usage survey. *Psychological Reports, 80*, 879–882.

Briere, J., & Gil, E. (1998). Self-mutilation in clinical and general population samples: Prevalence, correlates, and functions. *American Journal of Orthopsychiatry, 68,* 609–620.

Burgess-Proctor, A., Patchin, J. W., & Hinduja, S. (2006, October). *Cyberbullying: The victimization of adolescent girls.* Retrieved from http://www.cyberbullying.us/cyberbullying_girls_victimization.pdf

Calvert, S. L. (2002). Identity construction on the Internet. In S. L. Calvert, A. B. Jordan, & R. R. Cocking (Eds.), *Children in the digital age: Influences of electronic media on development* (pp. 57–70). Westport, CT: Praeger.

Cao, F., & Su, L. (2006). Internet addiction among Chinese adolescents: Prevalence and psychological features. *Child: Care, Health and Development, 33,* 275–281.

Caplan, S. E. (2003). Preference for online social interaction: A theory of problematic Internet use and psychosocial well-being. *Communication Research, 30,* 625–648.

Chen, W., & Wellman, B. (2003). *Charting and bridging digital divides: Comparing socio-economic, gender, life stage, and rural–urban Internet access and use in eight countries.* AMD Global Consumer Advisory Board. Retrieved from http://www.amd.com/us-en/assets/content_type/DownloadableAssets/Final_Report_Charting_Digi_Divides.pdf

Cheung, C. (2000). A home on the web: Presentations of self in personal homepages. In D. Gauntlett (Ed.), *Web studies* (pp. 43–51). London: Arnold.

Chou, C., Condron, L., & Belland, J. C. (2005). A review of the research on Internet addiction. *Educational Psychology Review, 17,* 363–388.

Chou, C., & Hsiao, M. C. (2000). Internet addiction, usage, gratifications, and pleasure experience: The Taiwan college students' case. *Computer Education, 35,* 65–80.

Claes, L., Vandereycken, W., & Vertommen, H. (2003). Eating-disordered patients with and without self-injurious behaviours: A comparison of psychopathological features. *European Eating Disorders Review, 11,* 379–396.

Cole, M. (1996). *Cultural psychology: A once and future discipline.* Cambridge, MA: Harvard University Press.

Compaine, B. (2001). (Ed.). *The digital divide: Facing a crisis or creating a myth?* Cambridge, MA: MIT Press.

Craig, D. (2003). Instant messaging: The language of youth literacy. Retrieved from http://www.stanford.edu/group/pwr/publications/Boothe_0203/PWR%20Boothe-Craig.pdf

Crisis Connection: Internet sexual predators. (2007). Retrieved from http://www.crisisconnectioninc.org/sexualassault/internetchild_sexual_predators.htm

Cummings, J. N., Butler, B., & Kraut, R. (2002). The quality of online social relationships. *Communications of the Association of Computer Machinery, 45,* 103–108.

DiMarco, H. (2003). The electronic cloak: Secret sexual deviance in cyberspace. In Y. Jewkes (Ed.), *Dot.coms: Crime, delinquency and identity on the Internet.* Devon, UK: Willan.

Donath, J. S. (2003). Identity and deception in the virtual community. In M. A. Smith & P. Kollock (Eds), *Communities in cyberspace*. New York: Taylor & Francis.

Drori, G. S. (2005). *Global e-litism: Digital technology, social inequality and transnationality*. New York: Worth.

Favazza, A. R. (1999). Self-mutilation. In D. G. Jacobs (Ed.), *The Harvard Medical School guide to suicide assessment and intervention* (pp. 125–145). San Francisco: Jossey-Bass.

Fisher, W. A., & Barak A. (2001). Internet pornography: A social psychological perspective on Internet sexuality. *Journal of Sex Research, 38*, 5–20.

Fong, E., Wellman, B., Kew, M., & Wilkes, R. (2004, June). *Correlates of the digital divide: Individual, household and spatial variation*. Report to the Office of Learning Technologies, Human Resources Development, Canada (pp. 1–84).

Galinski, E., & Salmond, K. (2002). *Youth and violence: Colorado students speak out for a more civil society*. Family and Work Institute: Ask the Children Series, New York.

Goodson, P., McCormick, D., & Evans, A, (2000). Sex and the Internet: A survey instrument to assess college students' behavior and attitudes. *Cyberpsychology and Behavior, 3*, 129–149.

Gould, M. S., Munfakh, J. L. H., Lubell, K., Kleinman, M., & Parker, S. (2002). Seeking help from the Internet during adolescence. *Journal of the American Academy of Child and Adolescent Psychiatry, 41*, 1182–1189.

Gratz, K. L., Conrad, S. D., & Roemer, L. (2002). Risk factors for deliberate self-harm among college students. *American Journal of Orthopsychiatry, 72*, 128–140.

Gray, N. J., Klein, J. D., Noyce, P. R., Sesselberg, T. S., & Cantrill, J. A. (2005). Health information-seeking behaviour in adolescence: The place of the Internet. *Social Science & Medicine, 60*, 1467–1478.

Green, C. S., & Bavelier, D. (2003). Action video games modify visual attention. *Nature, 423*, 534–537.

Green, C. S., & Bavelier, D. (2006). Effects of video game playing on the spatial distribution of visual selective attention. *Journal of Experimental Psychology: Human Perception and Performance, 32*, 465–478.

Green, C. S., & Bavelier, D. (2007). Action video experience alters the spatial resolution of vision. *Psychological Science, 18*, 88–94.

Greenfield, P. M. (2004). Inadvertent exposure to pornography on the Internet: Implications of peer-to-peer file-sharing networks for child development and families. *Journal of Applied Developmental Psychology, 24*, 741–750.

Griffiths, M. D. (2000). Does Internet and computer "addiction" exist? Some case study evidence. *Cyberpsychology and Behavior, 3*, 211–218.

Gross, E. F. (2004). Adolescent Internet use: What we expect, what teens report. *Journal of Applied Developmental Psychology, 25*, 633–649.

Gross, E. F., Juvonen, J., & Gable, S. L. (2002). Internet use and well-being in adolescence. *Journal of Social Issues, 58*, 75–90.

Gunter, B. (2002). *Media sex: What are the issues?* Mahwah, NJ: Erlbaum.

Hartman, J. B., Shim, S., Barber, B., & O'Brien, M. (2006). Adolescents' utilitarian and hedonic web-consumption behavior: Hierarchical influence of personal values and innovativeness. *Psychology & Marketing, 23*, 813–839.

Heitner, E. (2002). *The relationship between use of the Internet and social development.* Unpublished doctoral dissertation, Pace University, New York.

Hinduja, S. (2007). Computer crime investigations in the United States: Leveraging knowledge from the past to address the future. *International Journal of Cyber Crimes and Criminal Justice, 1,* 1–26.

Hoffman, D., Novak, T., & Schlosser, A. (2001). The evolution of the digital divide: Examining the relationship of race to Internet access and usage over time. In B. Compaine (Ed.), *The digital divide* (pp. 47–72). Cambridge, MA: MIT Press.

Jackson, M., & Elliott, J. (2004, August). *Dangers of pro-anorexia websites,* BBC News Online. Retrieved from http://news.bbc.co.uk/2/hi/health/3580182.stm

Jackson, L. A., Ervin, K. S., Gardner, P. D., & Schmitt, N. (2001a). Gender and the Internet: Women communicating and men searching. *Sex Roles, 44,* 363–380.

Jackson, L. A., Ervin, K. S., Gardner, P. D., & Schmitt, N. (2001b). The racial digital divide: Motivational, affective, and cognitive correlates of Internet use. *Journal of Applied Social Psychology, 31,* 2019–2046.

Jackson, L. A., Samona, R., Moomaw, J., Ramsay, L., Murray, C., Smith, A., et al. (2006a). What children do on the Internet: Domains visited and their relationship to socio-demographic characteristics and academic performance. *Cyber-Psychology and Behavior, 10,* 182–190.

Jackson, L. A., von Eye, A., Barbatsis, G., Biocca, F., Fitzgerald, H. E., & Zhao, Y. (2004). The social impact of Internet use on the other side of the digital divide. *Communications of the Association for Computing Machinery, 47*(7), 43–47.

Jackson, L. A., von Eye, A., Biocca, F. A., Barbatsis, G., Zhao, Y., & Fitzgerald, H. E. (2006b). Children's home Internet use: Predictors and psychological, social and academic consequences. In R. Kraut, M. Brynin, & S. Kiesler (Eds.), *Computers, phones and the Internet: Domesticating information technology* (pp. 145–167). New York: Oxford University Press.

Jackson, L. A., von Eye, A., Biocca, F. A., Barbatsis, G., Zhao, Y., & Fitzgerald, H. E. (2006c). Does home Internet use influence the academic performance of low-income children? Findings from the HomeNetToo project. *Developmental Psychology* [Special section on children, adolescents, and the Internet], *42,* 429–435.

Johnson-Vickberg, S. M., Kohn, J. E., Franco, L. M., & Criniti, S. (2003). What teens want to know: Sexual health questions submitted to a teen website. *American Journal of Health Education, 34,* 258–264.

Kaiser Family Foundation. (2000). U.S. adults and kids on new media technology. In C. von Feilitzen & U. Carlsson (Eds.), *Children in the new media landscape* (pp. 35–51). Göteborg, Sweden: Nordicom.

Kaiser Family Foundation. (2005). Generation M: Media in lives of eight to eighteen year olds. Retrieved from http://www.kff.org/entmedia/entmedia030905pkg.cfm

Katz, J. E., & Rice, R. E. (2002). *Social consequences of Internet use: Access, involvement, and interaction.* Cambridge, MA: MIT Press.

Kenski, K., & Stroud, N. J. (2006). Connections between Internet use and political efficacy, knowledge, and participation. *Journal of Broadcasting & Electronic Media, 50,* 173–192.

Kim, Y.-C., Cheong, P., Lin, W.-Y., & Jung, J.-Y. (2004, May 27). *Cultivating expectation and reproduction of social inequality: Human, social, and cultural capitals as factors in quality Internet connectedness among adolescents in East Asian cities.* Paper presented at the annual meeting of the International Communication Association, New Orleans, LA.

Kraut, R., Kiesler, S., Boneva, B., Cummings, J., Helgeson, V., & Crawford, A. (2002). Internet paradox revisited. *Journal of Social Issues, 51,* 49–74.

Kraut, R., Patterson, M., Lundmark, V., Kiesler, S., Mukophadhyay, T., & Scherlis, W. (1998). Internet paradox: A social technology that reduces social involvement and psychological well-being? *American Psychologist, 53,* 1017–1031.

LaRose, R., Eastin, M. S., & Gregg, J. (2001). Reformulating the Internet paradox: Social cognitive explanations of Internet use and depression. *Journal of Online Behavior, 1.* Retrieved from http://www.behavior.net/JOB/v1n2/paradox.html

Leung, L. (2002). Loneliness, self-disclosure and ICQ ("I Seek You") use. *Cyberpsychology and Behavior, 5,* 241–251.

Li, Q. (2005, April). *Cyberbullying in schools: Nature and extent of Canadian adolescents' experience.* Paper presented at the annual conference of AERA, Montreal, Canada.

Li, Q. (2006). Cyberbullying in schools: A research of gender differences. *School Psychology International, 27,* 157–170.

Livingstone, S. (2003). Children's use of the Internet: Reflections on the emerging research agenda. *New Media & Society, 5,* 147–166.

Livingstone, S., & Bober, M. (2005). *U.K. Children Go Online: Final report of key project findings.* Economic and Social Research Council (ESRC), London School of Economics and Political Science, London, WC2A 2AE. Retrieved from http://www.children-go-online.net

Lo, V., & Wei, R. (2005). Exposure to Internet pornography and Taiwanese adolescents sexual behavior and attitudes. *Journal of Broadcasting & Electronic Media, 49,* 221–237.

Lopez, M. H., Kirby, E., & Sagoff, J. (2005). The youth vote 2004. College Park, MD: Center for Information and Research on Civic Learning and Engagement. Retrieved from http://www.civicyouth.org/PopUps/FactSheets/FS_Youth_Voting_72–04.pdf

Mazzarella, S. R. (2005). (Ed.). *Girl wide web: Girls, the Internet and the negotiation of identity.* New York: Peter Lang.

McKenna, K. Y. A., & Bargh, J. A. (2000). Plan 9 from cyberspace: The implications of the Internet for personality and social psychology. *Personality and Social Psychology Bulletin, 4,* 57–75.

McKenna, K. Y. A., Green, A. S., & Gleason, M. E. J. (2002). Relationship formation on the Internet: What's the big attraction? *Journal of Social Issues, 58,* 9–31.

Media Awareness Network (2005). Internet use by Canadian youth, phase 2, ERIN research. Retrieved from http://www.media-awareness.ca/english/research/YCWW/index.cfm

Mitchell, K. J., Finkelhor, D., & Wolak, J. (2003). The exposure of youth to unwanted sexual material on the Internet: A national survey of risk, impact, and prevention. *Youth & Society, 34,* 330–358.

Moody, E. J. (2001). Internet use and its relationship to loneliness. *CyberPsychology & Behavior, 4,* 393–401.

Morahan-Martin, J. M. (2005). Internet abuse: Addiction? Disorder? Symptom? Alternative explanation? *Social Science Computer Review, 23,* 39–48.

Morahan-Martin, J. M., & Schumacker, P. (2000). Incidence and correlates of pathological Internet use. *Computers and Human Behavior, 16,* 13–29.

Muehlenkamp, J. J., & Gutierrez, P. M. (2004). An investigation of differences between self-injurious behavior and suicide attempts in a sample of adolescents. *Suicide & Life-Threatening Behavior, 34,* 12–24.

Murdock, G. (2002). Review article: Debating the digital divide. *European Journal of Communication, 17,* 385–390.

National Center for Educational Statistics. (2000, February). *Internet access in public schools and classrooms: 1994–99. Stats in brief.* Washington, DC: Department of Education, Office of Educational Research and Improvement.

National Center for Missing & Exploited Children. (2006). *Online victimization of youth: Five years later.* Retrieved from http://www.missingkids.com/en_US/publications/NC167.pdf

National Children's Home Charity. (2005). Child abuse, child pornography and the Internet. Retrieved April 8, 2008, from http://www.nch.org.uk/uploads/documents/children_internet_report_summ.pdf

National Research Council. (2003). *Youth, pornography and the Internet.* Washington, DC: National Academy Press.

National Science Foundation Report, Division of Science Resources Studies. (2001, February). The application and implications of information technologies in the home: Where are the data and what do they say? Retrieved March, 16, 2008, from http://www.eric.ed.gov/ERICWebPortal/recordDetail?accno=ED452050

Nie, N. H., & Erbring, L. (2000). *Internet and society: A preliminary report.* Stanford, CA: Stanford Institute for the Quantitative Study of Society.

Norris, P. (2001). *Digital divide: Civic engagement, information poverty, and the Internet worldwide.* New York: Cambridge University Press.

Ost, S. (2003). Getting to grips with sexual grooming: The new offense under the Sexual Offense Act 2003. *Journal of Social Welfare and Family Life, 26,* 147–159.

Palmer, T., & Stacey, L. (2004). *Just one click: Sexual abuse of children and young people through the Internet and mobile telephone technology.* London: Barnardo.

Pardun, C. J., L'Engle, K. L., & Brown, J. D. (2005). Linking exposure to outcomes: Early adolescents' consumption of sexual content in six media. *Mass Communication and Society, 8,* 75–91.

Pasek, J., Kenski, K., Romer, D., & Jamieson, K. H. (2006). America's youth and community engagement: How use of mass media is related to civic activity and political awareness in 14- to 22-year-olds. *Communication Research, 33,* 115–135.

Patchin, J. W., & Hinduja, S. (2006). Bullies move beyond the schoolyard: A preliminary look at cyberbullying. *Youth Violence and Juvenile Justice, 4,* 148–169.

Patterson, T. E. (2005). *Young voters and the 2004 election.* Cambridge, MA: Harvard University Press.

Peter, J., & Valkenburg, P. M. (2006). Adolescents' exposure to sexually explicit material on the Internet. *Communication Research, 33,* 178–204.

Peter, J., Valkenburg, P. M., & Schouten, A. P. (2005, May 26–30). *Talking with strangers on the Internet and its consequences.* Paper presented at the 55th annual conference of the International Communication Association (ICA), New York.

Pew Internet & American Life Project. (2000a). *Tracking online life: How women use the Internet to cultivate relationships with family and friends.* Retrieved March 16, 2008, from http://www.pewinternet.org/report_display.asp?r=11

Pew Internet & American Life Project. (2000b). *African-Americans and the Internet.* Retrieved March 16, 2008, from http://www.pewinternet.org/report_display .asp?r=25

Pew Internet & American Life Project. (2001). *Teenage life online: The rise of the instant-message generation and the Internet's impact on friendships and family relationships.* Retrieved March 16, 2008, from http://www.pewinternet.org/ report_display.asp?r=36

Pew Internet & American Life Project. (2002). *The digital disconnect: The widening gap between Internet savvy students and their schools.* Retrieved March 16, 2008, from http://www.pewinternet.org/report_display.asp?r=67

Pew Internet & American Life Project. (2003). *The ever-shifting Internet population: A new look at Internet access and the digital divide.* Retrieved March 16, 2008, from http://www.pewinternet.org/report_display.asp?r=88

Pew Internet & American Life Project. (2005a). *A decade of adoption: How the Internet has woven itself into American life.* Retrieved March 16, 2008, from http:// www.pewinternet.org/PPF/r/148/report_display

Pew Internet & American Life Project. (2005b). *Teens and technology: Youth are leading the transition to a fully wired and mobile nation.* Retrieved March 16, 2008, from http://www.pewinternet.org/PPF/r/162/report_display.asp

Pew Internet & American Life Project. (2005c). *Teen content creators and consumers.* Retrieved March 16, 2008, from http://www.pewinternet.org/PPF/r/166/ report_display.asp

Pew Internet & American Life Project. (2005d). *Digital divisions.* Retrieved March 16, 2008, from http://www.pewinternet.org/PPF/r/165/report_display.asp

Pew Internet & American Life Project. (2006a). *Teens and the Internet. Findings submitted to the House Subcommittee on Telecommunications and the Internet.* Retrieved March 16, 2008, from http://www.pewinternet.org/PPF/r/67/presentation_ display.asp

Pew Internet & American Life Project. (2006b). *Finding answers online in sickness and in health.* Retrieved March 16, 2008, from http://www.pewinternet.org/ report_display.asp?r=183

Pew Internet & American Life Project. (2006c). *Internet evolution, Internet penetration and impact.* Retrieved March 16, 2008, from http://www.pewinternet .org/PPF/r/182/report_display.asp

Pew Internet & American Life Project. (2006d). *Internet usage trends: Through the demographic lens.* Retrieved March 16, 2008, from http://www.pewinternet .org/presentation_display.asp?r=74

Pew Internet & American Life Project. (2006e). *Home broadband adoption 2006.* Retrieved March 16, 2008, from http://www.pewinternet.org/PPF/r/184/report_display.asp

Pew Internet & American Life Project. (2007). *Social networking websites and teens: An overview.* Retrieved March 16, 2008, from http://www.pewinternet.org/PPF/r/198/report_display.asp

Potter, R. H., & Potter, L. A. (2001). The Internet, cyberspace and sexual exploitation of children: Media, moral panics and urban myths for middle-class parents. *Sexuality and Culture, 5,* 31–48.

Reaves, J. (2001, July 31). *Anorexia goes high tech.* Retrieved from http://www.time.com/time/health/article/0,8599,169660,00.html

Rice, R., & Haythornthwaite, C. (2002). Perspectives on Internet use: Access, involvement, and interaction. In L. Lievrouw & S. Livingstone (Eds.), *The handbook of new media* (pp. 92–113). London: Sage.

Rideout, V. (2001). *Generation Rx.com: How young people use the Internet for health information.* Menlo Park, CA: Kaiser Family Foundation.

Roberts, D. F., Foehr, U., & Rideout, V. (2005). *Kids and media in America.* New York: Cambridge University Press.

Rocheleau, B. (1995). Computer use by school-age children: Trends, patterns and predictors. *Journal of Educational Computing Research, 1,* 1–17.

Roschelle, J. M., Pea, R. D., Hoadley, C. M., Gordon, D. N., & Means, B. M. (2000). Changing how and what children learn in school with computer-based technologies. *Children and Computer Technology, 10,* 76–101.

Runkel, J. (2005, March 22). When teens find porn online. *San Jose Mercury News,* p. 8E.

Savin-Williams, R. C., & Diamond, L. M. (2004). Sex. In R. M. Lerner (Ed.), *Handbook of adolescent psychology* (pp. 189–231). Hoboken, NJ: Wiley.

Scealy, M., Phillips, J. G., & Stevenson, R. (2002). Shyness and anxiety as predictors of patterns of Internet use. *Cyberpsychology & Behavior, 5,* 507–515.

Seiter, E. (2005). *The Internet playground: Children's access, entertainment and miseducation.* New York: Peter Lange.

Selwyn, N. (2004). Reconsidering political and popular understandings of the digital divide. *New Media & Society, 6,* 341–362.

Simpson, B. (2005). Identity manipulation in cyberspace as a leisure option: Play and the exploration of self. *Information and Communications Technology Law, 14,* 115–131.

Slater, M. D. (2002). Social relationships and identity online and offline. In L. Lievrouw & S. Livingstone (Eds.), *The handbook of new media* (pp. 534–547). London: Sage.

Subrahmanyam, K., Kraut, R. E., Greenfield, P. M., & Gross, E. F. (2000). The impact of home computer use on children's activities and development. *Future of Children, 10,* 123–144.

Subrahmanyam, K., Greenfield, P., Kraut, R., & Gross, E. (2001). The impact of computer use on children's and adolescents' development. *Applied Developmental Psychology, 22,* 7–30.

Subrahmanyam, K., Smahel, D., & Greenfield, P. (2006). Connecting developmental constructions to the Internet: Identity presentation and sexual exploration in online teen chat rooms. *Developmental Psychology* [Special section: Children, adolescents, and the Internet], *42*, 395–406.

Suler, J. R. (2002). Identity management in cyberspace. *Journal of Applied Psychoanalytic Studies, 4*, 455–460.

Swartz, A. (2005, March 7). "Schoolyard bullies get nastier online." *USA Today*, page 1a.

Tapscott, D. (1998). *Growing up digital: The rise of the net generation.* New York: McGraw-Hill.

Thornburgh, D., & Lin, H. S. (Eds.). (2002). *Youth, pornography, and the Internet.* Washington, DC: National Academic Press.

Turkle, S. (1995). *Life on the screen: Identity in the age of the Internet.* New York: Simon & Schuster.

UCLA Internet Project. (2003). Surveying the digital future: Year 3. UCLA Center for Communication Policy. University of California, Los Angeles. Available at http://www.digitalcenter.org/pdf/InternetReportYearThree.pdf

Uslaner, E. M. (2004). Trust, civic engagement, and the Internet. *Political Communication, 21*, 223–242.

Valkenburg, P. M., & Soeters, K. (2001). Children's positive and negative experiences with the Internet. *Communication Research, 28*, 653–676.

Valkenburg, P. M., & Soeters (2006). Adolescents' exposure to sexually explicit material on the Internet. *Communication Research, 33*, 178–204.

Van, B., Huang, M., Qui, B., & Han, Y. (2006). Relationship between Internet behavior and subjective well-being of teenagers. *Chinese Journal of Clinical Psychology, 14*, 68–69.

van Dijk, J. (2003). The digital divide as a complex and dynamic phenomenon. *The Information Society, 19*, 315–326.

van Dijk, J. (2005). *The deepening divide: Inequality in the information society.* Thousand Oaks, CA: Sage.

Vandwater, E. A., Shim, M., & Caplovitz, A. G. (2004). Linking obesity and activity level with children's television and video game use. *Journal of Adolescence, 27*, 71–85.

Waestlund, E., Norlander, T., & Archer, T. (2001). Internet blues revisited: Replication and extension of an Internet paradox study. *Cyberpsychology & Behavior, 4*, 385–391.

Walsh, D., Gentile, D. A., Walsh, E., & Bennett, N. *11th Annual Video Game Report Card.* Available at http://www.mediafamily.org/research/2006_Video_Game_Report_Card.pdf

Walther, J. B. (1996). Computer-mediated communication: Impersonal, interpersonal and hyperpersonal interaction. *Communication Research, 23*, 342–369.

Warschauer, M. (2003). *Technology and Social Inclusion: Rethinking the digital divide.* Cambridge, MA: MIT Press.

Wartella, E., Caplovitz, A. G., & Lee, P. (2004). Internet use and well-being in adolescence. *Journal of Social Issues, 58*, 75–90.

Weiser, E. B. (2001). The functions of Internet use and their psychological consequences. *Cyberpsychology & Behavior, 4*, 723–744.

Wellman, B., & Haythornthwaite, C. (Eds.). (2002). *The Internet in everyday life*. New
York: Blackwell.

Welsh, P. (2004, June 28). Students' scars point to emotional pain. *USA Today*,
p. A11.

Whitlock, J., Powers, J., & Eckenrode, J. (2006). The virtual cutting edge: The Internet and adolescent self-injury. *Developmental Psychology* [Special section: Children, adolescents, and the Internet], *42*, 407–417.

Wolak, J., Mitchell, K. J., & Finkelhor, D. (2002). Close online relationships in a national sample of adolescents. *Adolescence, 37*, 441–445.

Wolak, J., Mitchell, K. J., & Finkelhor, D. (2003). Escaping or connecting? Characteristics of youth who form close online relationships. *Journal of Adolescence,
26*, 105–119.

Yates, T. M. (2004). The developmental psychopathology of self-injurious behavior:
Compensatory regulation in posttraumatic adaptation. *Clinical Psychological Review, 24*, 35–74.

Ybarra, M. L., & Mitchell, K. J. (2005). Exposure to Internet pornography among
children and adolescents: A national survey. *Cyberpsychology and Behavior, 8*,
473–486.

Ybarra, M. L., Alexander, C., & Mitchell, K. (2005). Depressive symptomatology,
youth Internet use, and online interactions: A national survey. *Journal of Adolescent Health, 36*, 9–18.

Young People and Self Harm (2004). *A national inquiry: What do we already know?
Prevalence, risk factors, and models of intervention*. Retrieved from http://www
.selfharmuk.org

Young, K. S., & Rogers, R. C. (1998). The relationship between depression and Internet addiction. *Cyberpsychology and Behavior, 1*, 25–28.

# Part IV

# Policy Implications for Healthy
# Adolescent Development

# 14

## Policy Interventions

C. EDWIN BAKER

Ripe for governmental policy intervention is any arena where societal practices systematically produce bad results or fail in their potential for good results. This book considers changes in media portrayal of youth and presentations to youth over the last fifty years. Any report that these portrayals or presentations of or to youth lead increasingly to negative consequences pushes the issue of policy interventions to the fore. Even lack of change is consistent with a continuing need for interventions if possible positive changes are available. Moreover, new social science knowledge can emphasize (or dispel the belief in) this need.

Despite the general propriety of addressing possible policy interventions, the media context is special. Unlike matters of occupational safety, environmental degradation, health care, labor standards, capital market efficiency, or even carriage of communicative content, this context involves communicative content itself, a realm of special constitutional and democratic concern. At this point in the discussion someone routinely introduces the First Amendment, often playing "the heavy"—the factor that would block otherwise desirable regulation and makes the discussion of regulation seem pointless.

This role for the First Amendment should be resisted. Historically, interpretations of the First Amendment have varied dramatically. If governmental interventionist policies are in fact desirable, the First Amendment can and should be interpreted to allow them—though in making this claim one must be careful with the notion of "desirable." At its (occasional) best, First Amendment doctrine represents historical learning. Many purportedly justified and widely popular speech policy proposals embody underlying evils that their advocates did not recognize but that should have caused their rejection by a wise democratic polity. The wise counsel that First Amendment doctrine embodies—if and when that is what it embodies, not the mere constitutional roadblock created by judicial protection of free speech—also provides the proper reasons to reject some illiberal policy proposals and, instead, to seek other responses to apparent problems. Of course, most new policies concerning the media, if adopted, would be predictably challenged on First Amendment grounds and some would be struck down, wisely or unwisely. Nevertheless, the sole concern of this chapter is with the merits of the proposals. References herein to the First Amendment, even if frequent, are not meant to block further thinking but are mostly offered merely either as illustrative historical reports or as shorthand for rationales for not taking particular interventionist approaches.

## A NEED FOR GOVERNMENTAL INTERVENTION?

Whether there is *any* need for new government policies could be doubted. This book describes media presentations of and to youth over time. In contrast to common "sky is falling" sentiments, although with some variations, most chapters do not identify significant changes in media presentations of and to youth that suggest *new* urgency for intervention. Some trends have even been favorable—greater portrayal of African Americans in some media, and less portrayal of tobacco products. Often, available research is simply inadequate for observing changes that may or may not have occurred. Of course, even without changes, a continuation of longstanding problems can call for policy responses. Certainly, media portrayals of youth and media presentations made available to youth have consequences that merit assessment. Given my assignment of writing a chapter on governmental or legal intervention, I simply assume that some forms of governmental interventions may be valuable. Since this book has focused primarily on change in portrayal, not "effects," I also will not try to offer any assessment of the social science evidence of need for policies. Rather, I simply provide a summary account and evaluative comments about generic forms that interventions might take if a need for intervention were found. Before engaging in this primary task, however, I comment critically on four reasons for doubts about an interventionist project: (1) an objection to the paternalism of regulation, (2) a doubt that government is the right entity to respond, (3) the problem of unintended consequences, and (4) a worry about the diversion of interventionist energies.

First, if research shows that youth consume media content that negatively affects only their *own* lives, the issue is whether this evidence about some statistically limited number of people justifies what might be negatively labeled as "paternalistic" governmental intervention. Generally, if people choose to watch sex and violence, drinking and smoking, and other forms of self-destructive behavior that leaves them ill-informed and with less fulfilled lives, the liberal view is still that the choice is and should be their own. What justifies policy makers trying to prevent this? Why not trust people to make their own media choices? Children often are more like adults and more capable of evaluation than advocates of intervention admit (Levesque, 2007). Worse, often these advocates really wish generally to suppress what they consider undesirable media content but, feeling thwarted by society's liberal traditions, adopt a concern for children primarily as a convenient excuse for censorious policies that affect the content available to everyone.

The term *paternalism* even suggests a counter: paternalism is (sometimes) the right response of adults to children. Precisely the age of the people involved justifies the policies. Some evidence suggests the age group's particular vulnerability to certain messages, perhaps about the appeal of smoking or other advertisements that exploit adolescent anxiety over body image. Still, plausible qualms persist. Even if these facts justify "paternalism" by parents or even certain paternalistic practices by schools, as is often implicitly recognized in chapters in this book, direct interventions in the media realm by the government can be questioned. Despite finding troubling aspects of media portrayals, many chapters offer no suggestion that government intervention related to the media makes sense. For example, Harrison's chapter (Chapter 6) on body image begins with the huge health problem created by our epidemic of obesity and then, in a quick switch to a seemingly opposite problem, also strongly criticizes the media's constant portrayal of the thin body ideal, a criticism justified largely because that image encourages imitative efforts that sometimes take the form of potentially life-threatening anorexia. The policy responses, though, that Harrison offers—and that I consider quite sensible—relate only to the behavior of audiences, parents, and schools.

Other, better arguments justify putting aside the antipaternalists' objections to interventions. Often their key premises are wrong. For example, the often negative behavioral effects of media violence accrue to persons other than those choosing to consume the media content, in which case interventions could aim to protect these persons whose interests are ignored, for example, by the market and often by the individual media consumer. Moreover, people's media consumption does not merely reflect individuals' own choices, as the antipaternalist would have it. Their choices reflect both their preferences—which themselves are not simply self-authored but are largely socially created by many forces including education, peer group relations, and advertising—*and by what is available and at what cost*. More pointedly, availability and cost is nowhere a natural (or "unregulated") occurrence but results from society's communicative structure that itself necessarily depends on the collectively created legal structures—that is, it is necessarily affected by either self-conscious or unexamined media policy. Elsewhere I have described how the market is hugely dysfunctional at providing people with the content they want, whether "want" is measured by what they would actually pay (a market measure) or by what they would pay if they had equal income (an arguably more democratic or egalitarian measure) (Baker, 2002). As long as the market systematically and predictably creates a huge gap between what people want and what is made available to them at a price they will bear, legal structural choices to correct at least these market failures should not be considered paternalistic; rather, they may reflect people's political efforts to get what they want when it is not provided by the market.

Second is the point mentioned above about parents versus the state. If certain media content or usage has systematic negative consequences, this calls for a response, just not necessarily a government response. To the extent the research described in this book and elsewhere identifies negative consequences, this information can be useful to parents, other adults in caretaking or guidance positions, social movements directed either at personal behavior or media practices, or youth themselves. Information can arm all these actors to make better decisions. Moreover, these "responders" are, as compared to the state operating through general legal interventions, better able to individualize their responses to the particular youth involved, to make more sensitive evaluations of particular content, and to make the responses educationally productive. In a recent book emphasizing what the authors conclude is the unquestionable and huge role of violent video games as a causal agent in producing violence by users, one of the few factors identified as possibly reducing—in fact, in this case, significantly reducing—this effect is parent involvement in the adolescents' media practices (Anderson, Gentile, & Buckley, 2007, pp. 67, 121–22).

Third, caution is merited due to the possibility that interventions will have (usually unintended) consequences that are worse than any benefit that they purport to provide. The discussion below of censorship provides one illustration, but the point should be kept in mind more generally. Any intervention responding to one problem is likely to have multiple, often unpredicted, and sometimes negative consequences. Especially where the subject is media content, concerns that interventions will limit individually valued and collectively valuable freedom should impose a special burden of care on policy makers before recommending interventions. An obvious counter, however, is that, although humans inevitably make mistakes in adopting legal measures, that fact hardly justifies not responding to identifiable problems or evils but rather calls for intelligence, sensitivity, and a fallibilistic attitude in dealing with problems. Application of humans' even limited intelligence to formulating responses—and often, most effectively, legal responses—are usually better than abdicating responsibility and doing nothing.

Fourth are possibly the most important reasons for caution here about interventions. Some people, certainly including myself, believe that there are huge problems with today's media—problems that new technologies such as the Internet will certainly not fully solve and in some respects will exacerbate. For example, despite adding to the contributions of "voluntaristic" citizen journalism, the Internet's effect on the overall distribution of audience attention and advertising money negatively affects the number of employed professional journalists on whom society depends greatly for much resource-intensive, quality investigative reporting, and the production and editing of more routine news. Intelligent, public-serving media interventions require considerable use of two scarce resources—legislative or administrative policy makers' time and attention and public interest media advocates' energy. Different areas of potential intervention should be prioritized in terms of both their importance and the likelihood of appropriate interventions occurring, either now or in the long run. It would be easy to conclude—I will not attempt the argument—that while the portrayal of youth by the media presents in some respects a serious "public health" problem, for the most part this arena gets unjustifiably more attention than many other areas of either public health or media policy. In fact, attention to this area may be overdone precisely because of the less controversial nature of concerns for children, the popularity of portraying unappealing speech as a major problem, and the belief that intelligent paternalism is possible and justifiable. This arena may present a serious distraction from other more controversial areas which urgently merit policy making attention.

I certainly do not want to end the discussion with this point about the diversionary quality of policy making here—hence I offer the rest of the chapter with thoughts about the merits of possible interventions. I do believe some forms of interventions, such as insisting that broadcasters provide more educational content directed at youth, or regulating the content and maybe the amount of advertising directed at youth, are merited. Still, it would be wise to keep in mind this caveat about the use of reformist energies. Finally, however, as a caveat to this caveat, some of the best policy responses to issues suggested by this book's concern with youth might, at the same time, be among the most useful responses to other major problems with the media. If and when this is so, identification of problems by this book merely reinforces other policy arguments for these forms of intervention.

Despite these cautions, the rest of this chapter surveys and comments on possible interventions. In the following sections, I consider seven general categories of such policies: (1) censorship or prohibited content and then two subcategories of censorship—(2) differential availability (i.e., censorship for some audiences) and (3) regulation or prohibition of categories of advertising; other content-related interventions, such as (4) forced media internalization of costs caused by media content, (5) mandatory content, and (6) incentives for, or sponsored promotion of, content or practices serving various objectives; and, finally, (7) various structural interventions relating to ownership or decision-making control. Although this categorization and the placement of different policy possibilities into a category are to some extent arbitrary, this list allows discussion of the merits and demerits of different approaches. In what follows I say something about each approach, both in general and in the context of the issues raised by this book.

## REGULATORY METHODS—GENERAL AND RESTRICTED CENSORSHIP

### Censorship Generally

In Chapter 8, discussing violence in TV programming, James Potter is clear that it presents a problem but quickly rejects censorship—that is, rejects legal suppression of the harm-causing content. But he rightly observes that this response usually comes to mind first when the public identifies the problem. The First Amendment generally forbids censorship—but that constitutional doctrine could change, and in some contexts the present judicial position as to some censorship is not so clear. Certainly, present understandings of the First Amendment encompass protection of fiction and entertainment, but some serious scholars—including Alexander Meiklejohn, a liberal educator and political philosopher, and Robert Bork, a conservative Yale law professor and Supreme Court nominee—have argued that the First Amendment should only protect political or politically-salient speech (Bork, 1971; Meiklejohn, 1960). Or, to give another example, the question of whether video games should be viewed as communications or as mere paraphernalia for use in activities could easily be disputed—although lower courts currently clearly put it into the protected speech category. But change has taken place and can again. Not until roughly fifty years ago did the Supreme Court first strike down any federal law on First Amendment grounds (*Lamont v. Postmaster General*, 1965). Judicial deference to governmental regulation could return—although it is fair to say that, despite ebbs and flows, the general trend for most of the country's history has been in the direction of expanding First Amendment protection. Still, some forms of censorship, especially when less than a complete ban as discussed below, have been adopted by legislative bodies and upheld by courts. Thus, censorship as a regulatory approach to media content that social science shows has antisocial "effects" is surely worth consideration. Rather than mechanically invoke the First Amendment, it is important to consider why (or whether) policy makers should reject censorship. With caveats suggested in the next two sections, I believe they should.

In my view, possibly the worst aspect of censorship is the attitude toward social problems that it embodies and encourages. Censorship is not a surprising impulse among people who regularly respond to any objectionable behavior with prohibitions, repression, and punishment rather than by seeking to change the conditions that generate the behavior. The proportion of the population that the United States presently has in prison (738 per 100,000), which is the highest in the world and compares to 107 per 100,000 in Canada, and fewer than 100 in most European countries including all the Scandinavian countries, illustrates this country's tendency to respond with suppression (Wolmsley, 2007). An impulse toward use of punitive power is clearly implicated in the catastrophe created by our Iraq invasion and the failure of our "war" on terror. The failure of repression to achieve improvement is often entirely predictable, as it was in Iraq, while its costs are often inadequately recognized. The day I wrote this section, the *New York Times* editorialized that the Los Angeles area had spent billions using repressive means to combat gangs with the result that the problem had become worse there than anywhere in the country. Meanwhile, in New York, prevention programs had successfully prevented street gangs from being near the problem they once were (*New York Times*, 2007). Of course, programs responding to underlying conditions or aimed at enabling or encouraging better behavior require careful thought and, as the *New York Times*'s editorial noted, are often much harder to sell to legislators.

Research identifies various types of media entertainment as causing real negative effects. Although both private and public response to these harms may be appropriate, multiple considerations counsel likely failure or suggest serious (often underappreciated) costs of censorship as a response. Below I describe seven such considerations, the first three related primarily to likely failure, the last four to serious costs.

To be effective, censorship requires identifying problematic content and then effectively suppressing meaningful amounts of this content. It is doubtful that this project would succeed for the following reasons.

1.  Identification will be difficult and inevitably contested, whether it relies on a prior approval system as states once used for movies,

which they reviewed prior to licensing for public presentation, or merely prohibitions providing standards for courts to enforce, the system traditionally relied upon in respect to print versions of obscenity. Problematic content inevitably will escape identification (and, as emphasized below, the censorship system will surely cover or chill socially valuable content). For example, although many feminists, including many of the most radical, rejected the censorship strategy, procensorship feminists who wished to outlaw pornography in part because of the message it communicated about women usually ignored mainstream commercial advertising, which often communicates and "normalizes" roughly the same invidious messages.

2.   To succeed, the legal order must actually suppress the problematic content to a significant extent. (I say "significant" rather than complete suppression, which would be impossible, because significant reduction of the content may provide much of the purported benefits of censorship.) It is doubtful whether the government will muster sufficient levels of enforcement to achieve this result. If, however, content is pushed underground—or even into alternative media—the level of its consumption may be reduced enough to achieve a real benefit. Nevertheless, empirically, the opposite could occur. Ineffective attempts to suppress could simply add to the materials' allure. Many people want to see what was "Banned in Boston," a rebellious instinct that may be particularly strong among adolescents. Still, a plus favoring a ban could be that it provides a symbolic form of disapproval that may have beneficial cuing or educational effects.

3.   Finally, to be a meaningful policy, suppression must be designed so as not to be circumvented by invigorating creation and distribution of other comparably injurious content.

These three difficulties provide real reasons to doubt the efficacy of many censorship systems. The more serious objections to censorship, however, are its costs—specifically, those beyond the often heavy use of administrative, police, and judicial resources necessary to implement the censorship system.

4.   Importantly, the same material that has bad effects on some people may also have good effects on other (and sometimes even the same) audiences, effects that could be lost due to effective censorship. Television shows, movies, and songs that have been part of the causal chain that lead some people to commit

some unknown number of murders, rapes, suicides, or other harmful acts have also provided valued entertainment for millions and are often the stimulus of productive self-reflection and sometimes strengthened prosocial attitudes. To put the point more provocatively, should society censor content that predictably would lead some people to violence—for example, if that material included Tom Paine's *Common Sense* or pre–Civil War abolitionist literature? Or, maybe more relevant to this book, if, as described in Chapter 2, youth use music to explore and debate, often in rebellious manner, their identity and values, should this crucially important function be stunted by censoring content that leads to life-ending behavior by a few vulnerable young people? Would the same argument provide a justification to suppress automobiles? Would that position be taken in respect to adults or should responsibility be placed on, that is, placed only on, agents who respond illegally or self-destructively? Even admitting as one must that some media content sometimes leads to horrific results, the fact that this same content is often valuable for other people provides a primary reason to look beyond censorship for alternative responses to antisocial or criminal behavior.

5.  Even if some materials were justifiably suppressed, history teaches clearly that officials regularly abuse regimes of censorship, limiting valuable freedom and often propping up unjust regimes or culturally oppressive practices. First, even if the law were written to ban only properly suppressed (harmful) content, the law must be applied—and some improper application, limiting socially valuable content is inevitable, and historically has been common. For example, whatever problem obscene, sexually explicit content creates, it seems quite clear that applying the corresponding censorious laws at the end of the nineteenth century to feminists' provision of birth control information to other women was not an evil worthy of the law. Relatedly, even if properly formulated bans on particular content were otherwise defensible, reliance on them is likely to make censorious responses seem more plausible where not merited. The real-world danger of this so-called slippery slope should not be ignored even if, in principle, some communicative content is not worthy of defense. Finally, even if not precisely outlawed, any practice of censorship will inevitably chill some creative communicative efforts that could contribute meaningfully to a richer as well as a freer culture.

6. A real cost of any censorship regime relates to creating a culture of (that is, creating work lives devoted to) censorship. A society can be evaluated in part by the types of jobs it makes available. It can be questioned whether censorship—spending time examining and then suppressing offensive communications in order to stop other people from being able to receive them when they want—is an activity to which society should ask people (and pay people) to devote their lives. Justice Hugo Black commented that unlike other Justices whose view of the constitutional protection permissibility of suppressing particular sexual materials depended on their personal evaluation of the content, his "absolutist" view that all speech was protected under the First Amendment relieved him from spending his time on the debasing activity of studying purportedly obscene content. (Justice Douglas agreed with Black's absolutist views but rumor has it that he did not mind examining the material at issue.) A more systemic evil from the perspective of freedom of communication is that any requirement of prior approval of speech involves the creation of a work culture in which those who must give approval will find their work meaningless unless they identify categories and specific cases of content to which they then refuse approval. Acceptance of censorship as a practice necessarily encourages attitudes—a culture of censorship, both among those who enforce the laws and those who politically support the regime—that ought to be assessed for their impact on society, an evaluation that most people who believe in freedom are likely to find turns out quite negative.

7. I believe, most important, political and activist efforts to legislate and effectively to implement censorship are likely to divert attention from, or otherwise undermine, better alternative responses. Already mentioned is the diversion from policy interventions needed for multiple reasons in the general media sphere. To be noted here is diversion from other responses, mostly discussed below, specifically related to a concern with youth. These responses include more parental guidance, media literacy programs, and popular demands and government financial support for the creation and effective distribution of better media content. Also worth considering are legally mandated structural changes that aim at increasing control within media industries of people whose choices reflect either their own creative vision or the needs of youth and other audiences rather than solely bottom-line profits.

Each of these seven considerations merits more exploration. Each may supply an independent and sufficient ground to reject censorship. Cumulatively, I believe, their force is overwhelming. The underlying thought that tilts away from censorship is probably that in a free society the government generally should assume that each person should be free to make choices about specifically self-regarding behavior, certainly choices about which communications to receive or to make, even though these choices eventually have huge consequences for society. Of course, people make mistakes, sometimes very harmful mistakes. Overall, the democratic faith must be that this freedom, and our respect for this freedom, eventually leads to a stronger and better society.

## Differential or Restricted Availability

Courts and popular (adult) opinion often accept restrictions on the content made available to particular audiences, especially youth. Regulation of sales practices or physical or time "zoning" are typically used to achieve this aim. Many states prohibit the sale of sexually explicit magazines or books to minors. In some media arenas various media products are first rated by industry groups, and then their sale to youth is restricted by voluntary industry practice—although often against a threat of imposed regulation if the industry fails to act "voluntarily." Also, sometimes portions of the scheme—for instance, devices on television sets—are mandated while other aspects are voluntary. The film industry, for example, against a backdrop of actual or potential regulation, limits youth in their access to some movies.

Early on the Supreme Court approved a so-called variable obscenity standard that allowed restrictions of the sale of material to minors that it constitutionally protects in relation to adults (*Ginsberg v. New York*, 1968). Then in 1978, the Supreme Court famously upheld a prohibition of "indecency"—speech that is constitutionally protected but that is offensive to many and thought by some to be harmful to children—in broadcasting as applied to a George Carlin monologue containing seven dirty words when aired on a weekday at 2 P.M. (*FCC v. Pacifica*, 1978). The Court specifically left open the possibility of reaching a different result at different times during the day. Subsequently, lower courts read the decision to approve only time "channeling" of "adult" or indecent material, allowing it in late evening time slots. The Court originally gave various rationales for its holding, but most subsequent justifications focus solely on reducing access by minors to such "indecent" content (or, more legitimately, as aiding those parents who want to limit their children's access) (Baker, 1996). In 2004, Congress asked the Federal Communications Commission (FCC) to consider the merits of applying the *Pacifica* approach to excessively violent programming and in 2007 the FCC indicated such an approach might be permissible. This idea of constitutional permissibility provides the logic of laws recently adopted in many states (but uniformly struck down in the face of First Amendment challenges by lower courts) restricting the availability to minors of violent video games (*Video Software Dealers Association v. Schwarzenegger*, 2007).

At this writing, *Pacifica* still stands—or maybe teeters—as a Supreme Court decision upholding restrictive regulation of indecency in broadcasting. As a matter of history, *Pacifica* was given limited application long after being decided. Then during Republican administrations in the 1980s, the FCC and Congress made renewed efforts to restrict broadcast indecency (defined legally in terms of offensive references to sexual and excretory matters and organs). The FCC again reinvigorated enforcement efforts under President George W. Bush, although lower courts have questioned and limited these moves (*Fox Television v. FCC*, 2007). Congress has also tried to restrict sexual content's availability to children by imposing various restraints on cable, telephone dial-a-porn, and the Internet—with the Supreme Court striking down each attempt (with the exception of partial approval of a restriction on youth access in libraries that receive federal funding for Internet access) (*United States v. American Library Association*, 2003). Some predict that the Court will uphold a limited version of such a restriction that will be decided by the time this book is published. In most cases the Court's objection to these laws is either that the restriction seemed unnecessary to accomplish the government's aim, or that the law excessively restricted the availability of content to adults. Both objections have major practical importance for efforts to provide for differential availability, but the second has special theoretical significance. Repeatedly and emphatically, the Court has been clear that in a free society any restriction justified out of concern for youth must not (significantly) reduce the availability of the quarantined content to adults—that is, the state cannot "reduce the adult population … to reading only what is fit for children" (*Butler v. Michigan*, 1957).

Certainly, there can be no policy complaint about parents trying to exercise judgment about their children's access to various media material or about the appropriate level of freedom their children should exercise at various ages. Likewise, it is reasonable to wish that media producers and distributors of media material would responsibly consider these issues rather than focus solely on the economic bottom line. Some existing legal restrictions on the availability of certain sexually oriented media content may have aided some parents in their efforts, wise or not, to restrict access by their children. On the other hand, it is very doubtful these governmental restrictions will be sensitive enough to accurately identify sexual or violent media portrayals that individual parents actually wish to restrict; or, for that matter, media portrayals that actually have negative effects on some youth. It is likely that government efforts will restrict both content and youth for which limitations are not useful while not covering material that does in fact contribute to harmful consequences. More fundamentally, such regulation is likely to be a diversionary salve that allows policy makers to ignore more useful interventions. While this type of regulation cannot be universally condemned, its merits seem distinctly limited, and its costs, especially taking into account predictable side effects, are considerable.

## Restrictions on Advertising

Several chapters identify advertising content that arguably has negative effects on youth. Advertising for high caloric, often fatty foods during a time of an epidemic of obesity in the country and for tobacco products were noted, but other, sometimes controversial, examples could be offered. Of course, the media in its self-authored content (that is, authored by the writers and producers or chosen by media editors) or an individual in her speech can always present the exact same message content as presented in an advertisement. Media creators are, however, likely to choose a more diverse set of perspectives than the single-minded, continuously repeated, proconsumption content of advertisements. A society can reasonably conclude that, although people (and presumably the media) should be able to express whatever message they want—about food or smoking, for example—this social discourse is perverted by the participation of advertisers whose message content merely reflects an economic entity's market-dictated profit orientation rather than a person's view that the advocated activity is actually desirable. This point was made long ago by John Stuart Mill, who argued that the principles explicated in *On Liberty* (1863) did not apply to or justify protection of commercial promotion of behavior. Mill's view could justify restricting particular speakers—namely, the business that is promoting itself—from sponsoring or promoting messages that society considers harmful even as it decides, as Mill argued it should (at least in respect to adults), to allow the production and sale of the not-to-be-promoted product and to allow unrestricted discourse on the merits of the product's use by all those other than the seller. The thought is that a free society is well served by a free media and must respect the autonomous speech freedom of individuals and voluntary associations, but that the market and its enterprises, with their own structural incentives, is only (although hugely important) an instrumentally valued institution that should be subject to regulation to further collectively approved goals.

In this view, the only question about regulation of commercial advertising is the effectiveness of the restraint in furthering a sensible public goal. This might, as some governmental policy makers have concluded, suggest the merits of regulating tobacco advertising directed at children. However, two reasons—one related to scope and the other to effectiveness—to pause at this form of the conclusion should be noted. Adolescence is an especially vulnerable period during which addictions, if they are to occur, to substances like tobacco are particularly likely to begin and in which dietary habits and other identity-related behaviors are forming or solidifying. Still, if smoking is really bad and if other behaviors should not be justified merely in behalf of larger bottom lines (or waistlines), there is little reason to conclude that these behaviors should be commercially promoted to adults. Even if more powerful in relation to youth, there is no reason to believe tobacco advertising, for example, is more desirable or worthy when directed at adults. The same point applies to almost any advertising message that a concern with children would identify as objectionable.

Second, young people hardly live in a self-contained universe. Almost any advertising directed at adults is likely to reach them, too. They are in cars with their parents (or older teens) seeing billboards both close to school and farther away. Massachusetts's effort to protect young people by requiring that outdoor tobacco advertising be far removed from schools and indoor tobacco advertising within a store be five feet off the floor seemed to assume that young people seldom traveled except from home to school or lifted their eyes off the ground—ludicrous notions, as the Court recognized in invalidating this legislation (*Lorillard Tobacco v. Reilly*, 2001). The arguments for why advertising should be subject to regulation suggest, however, that a more general ban would make sense and should be accepted.

Concerns about the integrity of media content justify other general regulation of advertising, regulations that could also influence the messages received by youth. Existing laws require that when newspapers or magazines (that use second-class postal rates), broadcasters, and sometimes cable programmers, include paid-for content, the included content be clearly identified as an advertisement. These laws quite clearly apply to "product placements"—although how much the law is ignored or underenforced is a substantial question and some current controversy exists over the precise nature the identification should take. Still, there are substantive arguments for the benefit of applying these requirements more generally across the range of mass media entities (Baker, 1994; Goodman, 2006; Piety, 2001).

It must be noted that the Supreme Court's view on this issue of regulation of advertising is both unclear and subject to considerable change over the years. When the Court first faced the issue, it reached the same conclusion as did Mill and most American First Amendment "absolutists"—

commercial speech should receive *no* constitutional protection (*Valentine v. Chrestensen*, 1942). That view had changed in 1976 or slightly before (*Virginia State Board of Pharmacy v. Virginia Citizens Consumer Council*, 1976). Since 1976, commercial speech has consistently received some First Amendment protection, with both the legal doctrines (judicial tests) and the stringency of their application varying over time, with the precise degree of protection and possibly the judicial tests likely to change further, possibly soon. The currently official test, however, is that the First Amendment permits regulation not only if the commercial speech is false or misleading or promotes an illegal product but also as long as the state's interest in the regulation is substantial, the regulation directly advances the interest, and the regulation is no more extensive than necessary to advance it (*Central Hudson v. Public Service Commission*, 1980). Given the serious problems of obesity and smoking, for example, under this test the Court should uphold any ban that directly (significantly) reduces promotion of problematic behavior (smoking or eating various high caloric, low nutritional foods) and this is apparently true even if the product itself has various beneficial qualities. Certainly, as a policy matter, carefully crafted laws along these lines make sense.

## OTHER CONTENT-RELATED REGULATORY RESPONSES

### Internalization of Costs

Economists often note that commercial enterprises are less likely to engage in harm-causing behavior if forced to pay the costs of the harm. This deterrent effect of being forced to pay, as well as the reasonable goal of compensating victims, provides a major justification for much of the tort law system as applied to the commercial realm. If law could identify media content that contributed to specifically harmful conduct, the producer could be made civilly liable for the harms related to its content and distribution decisions. (Alternatively, if harm–cost estimates could be assigned different categories of content, producers who choose to produce those categories could be taxed accordingly, both to discourage the content choice and to raise money for a compensation fund.) Although this approach is routine in some industries, when civil litigants have attempted to impose these costs on the media, courts routinely reject their claims, often on common law tort grounds but also sometimes on the First Amendment ground that imposing liability could be described as form of censorship or punishment for speech content.

After watching Oliver Stone's *Natural Born Killers*, two teenagers killed several people in apparent imitation of action in the movie. After watching and discussing a nationally televised made-for-television network movie, several assailants in apparent imitation of the movie used a bottle to rape a nine-year-old girl. In these and many similar cases, courts have rejected liability in suits against the filmmakers or broadcasters, usually either because the media content did not fit the legal definition of "incitement" or because of the court's interpretation of the First Amendment (*Byers v. Edmundson,* 2002; *Olivia N. v. National Broadcasting Co.,* 1981). Underlying this conclusion is the apparent view that a free society must protect producers of art and fiction from liability for the consequences of their audiences' reactions; thus responsibility for criminal or harmful acts properly lies with the audience member even when harm-causing or criminal responses to the communications are reasonably predictable.

This result is analogous to the law in the context of defamation. People are unjustly hurt by defamatory falsehoods. The Court invokes the First Amendment to restrict governmental power to impose liability on the media (and on individuals), with restrictions on liability being greatest precisely in the context in which a person's reputation among strangers (and, thus, where injury by the media's falsehoods) is likely to be especially significant to her—particularly if she is a public figure, a person whose reputation is among her most important assets. In these cases, while liability would internalize the cost and, thus, predictably lead to more cautious media behavior, the Court understands the First Amendment to deny imposition of liability on the speaker for negligently false speech.

Attempting to use tort standards to impose cost internalization generally seems unwise for many of the same reasons that more direct censorship is unwise. In the news context, liability would be too restrictive, discouraging press exposés and comprehensive reporting, and would be inadequately responsive to speech harms. In more culturally oriented media aimed at youth, the tort remedy would be a blunderbuss technique that would chill cultural creativity and inevitably catch up content that also produces positive externalities. Moreover, it would miss the more serious problems. Antisocial responses mostly reflect repeated exposures to problematic content, not viewing, hearing, or reading an individual violent or sexist or otherwise problematic media presentation. For example, the constant diet of media content is what generates increased aggressive behavior, increased levels of anxiety-producing or otherwise dysfunctional fears, or desensitization of attitudes toward violence (see Chapter 8), the undue narrowing of gender scripts and sexism (see Chapter 5), and most other problems discussed in this book. These problems seldom if ever can be pinned on individualized media contents. For that reason, use of tort law to respond, which only focuses on reception of particular items, will miss the most serious target.

The wisest policy conclusion in respect to communications is probably, given the ubiquity of both harms caused (and not paid for by media producers) and benefits produced for culture and the polity (but without full compensation being captured by the speakers, by the media), to generally insulate speakers from liability, respond to harmful occurrences by other social policies, and seek more structural methods to change media practices. Policy should try to create structures or contexts where media speakers are most likely to choose to use their freedom responsibly and to enhance the likelihood that individual media consumers and media targets will protect themselves from harms. Certainly, existing law largely embodies this pro–free press, free speech protective half of this recommendation, rejecting this form of cost internalization. It does less, however, than it might in furthering the more affirmative policy half, a point discussed below.

## Mandatory Content

Two broad forms of mandated content—one related broadly to scripts the other to warnings or speaker identification—aim at different goals: pro–social education (or propaganda) and audience empowerment. As a matter of policy, the first form is inconsistent with speaker freedom while the second is less obviously so. The second arguably could contribute to audiences' capacity to make intelligent choices.

Chapter 11 emphasizes the typical lack of safe-sex practices in media portrayals of sex, noting that in some countries media entertainment features content that successfully encourages family planning and other pro-health consequences. Chapter 5, after describing negative consequences of overwhelmingly stereotypical presentation of gender roles, especially of girls and women, describes benefits that result from counterstereotyping content. Chapter 8 notes that the specific form of television portrayal of violence—including greater realism and failure to emphasize pain and suffering in victims—increases the risk of negative consequences. There surely can be no objection to encouraging media creators and distributors to take these effects into account in changing their creative and commercial practices. However, no author in this book proposed governmental mandates to include the favored type of content, a response that would have been inconsistent with expressive or creative freedom. As a constitutional as well as a policy matter, mandating content within the script of an entertainment program should be seen (and courts would likely see it) as an interference with communicative freedom. The choice of content to include or exclude inherently affects the message; even mandates of arguably benign content can often distort story lines. Public health advocates would like communicators to include messages or portray practices (such as safe sex) that these advocates consider desirable. Requiring these portrayals, however, interferes with authorial freedom and potentially with societal diversity—as the Supreme Court concluded when it invalidated New York's statutory mandate that movies' presentation of adultery always show it as undesirable (*Kingsley Int'l Pictures v. Regents*, 1959). Like censorship, such mandates seem inconsistent with the idea of a free society and, in any event, accept a quite dangerous role for government power over communications.

Laws mandating labeling that characterize specific features of the media content, usually features related to portrayal of sex, violence, or adult language, raise different issues. The legitimate justification is that labeling does not interfere with authorial freedom but gives audiences an improved capacity to know whether they want to read, hear, or view the content; that is, labeling does not censor but rather empowers informed consumer choice. To that extent, labeling closely resembles requirements that food or drug producers list ingredients or include warning labels. It also resembles a law adopted at the end of the nineteenth century and upheld by the Supreme Court (but before the development of modern First Amendment theory) that, in order to inform the public, required newspapers that used the mail to publish the names of its owners at least twice a year and to identify paid sponsorship of content as "advertising" (*Lewis Publ'g Co. v. Morgan*, 1913). Nevertheless, two policy-related differences that could be raised but would probably lose in constitutional challenges to mandatory labeling of media content are worth noting.

First, whether the labeling would make a useful and informative contribution to consumers is a much debated matter and the answer is likely to be contextual. Will youth or other consumers favor rather than avoid material because of its being labeled as containing explicit sex or violence? Alternatively, would the vast majority of people simply ignore the labeling—maybe not caring or maybe already knowing any information it provides—so that the contentious labeling categorizations and the apparatus required to make and implement them would amount to a huge effort signifying nothing? Before policy makers mandate any intrusive, expensive regulation, *especially in the communication sphere*, they should have some basis for confidence that the regulation will serve a useful purpose. Unlike drug labeling, which is done once and then included on each package, media labeling requires a new judgment for each "product." Failure to have a justifiable basis for confidence in its utility can result in regulation that not only increases the expense of communication but also contributes to widespread antagonism toward overbearing government.

Second, unlike the comparatively uncontroversial bases to identify the amount of sodium or trans fat a cracker contains, placing media content into varying categories requires an inevitably contestable examination, evaluation, and characterization of its content. If government makes or even supervises (by making accurate performance a legal requirement) this determination, reasons for concern about potential ideological abuse immediately arise. (The law could leave the judgment entirely to the media producer and leave "enforcement" to the possibility of public retaliation against, and reputational injury to, those producers who overtly abused their discretion.) Certainly this danger was obvious when, in a much criticized opinion, a divided Supreme Court upheld a mandate that American exhibitors of certain governmentally identified foreign films apply a "political propaganda" label to films (*Meese v. Keene*, 1987).

Imagine a law, purportedly designed not to limit freedom but to aid consumers, that required the media to identify its content as R for reactionary, P for progressive, or U for unbiased or ideologically neutral—with government monitoring and enforcement in the background. Is this the type activity that a free society wants its government to use its power to mandate and enforce? Will the government even choose the right categories for its mandated labels—that is, ones a consuming public has an interest in having foreknowledge about—or will the labels instead primarily, although only implicitly, teach what categories the government considers important? In contrast, if the information really serves the interests of substantial numbers of the media's audience, would there not be market pressure that could be intensified by activist organizing to provide the labeling voluntarily? (Of course, this voluntary solution did not work so well in respect to foods, drugs, securities, or real estate, and there may be reasons to doubt that it would work better here.) Probably most troubling from the perspective of media and artistic freedom—will the labeling turn out to distort story line and creative choices due to efforts to obtain the commercially most advantageous rating for the content? In sum, reasoned judgments are likely to vary about the policy merits of mandatory labeling, although information about empirical issues noted above could affect these judgments. Hence, I recommend nothing more than voluntary labeling of film and television content.

## Content-Related Incentives

Media content and distribution reflect the interaction of abilities and values of writers or producers and their employers on the one hand and the incentives to produce and distribute one or another type of content on the other. Government influence on incentives occurs in roughly two ways: first, directly by payments for, purchases of, or elimination of the costs of desired behavior and, second, more indirectly by influencing the structure in which the media operate. The second I leave for the next section, considering here only a few cases of the more direct method.

Government pays to influence public sphere communicative content in at least three generic ways. First, the government pays its own employees (or contracts with outsiders) to produce and publish content in a form and manner that its policy requires. Although the practice is ubiquitous and hugely relevant to the communications sphere generally (Herman & Chomsky, 1988; Shiffrin, 1980), I suspect this method of influence has marginal relevance to the general concerns of this book related to young people's consumption of media material. Second, the government funds individual independent projects that create (or distribute) content. If expanded, programs like those of the National Endowment for the Humanities and the National Endowment for the Arts could contribute substantially to the quality of the cultural realm in a manner that could have a significant impact on youth. Similar forms of subsidies could encourage pro-social content involving and consumed by youth. Nevertheless, except when the funding encourages creation of different media institutions, to be considered in the next section, these practices too are likely to have limited benefits in relation to the concerns of this book and the history of this type of content has not been a subject in this book.

Finally, the most obvious way to influence general media content is to pay for inclusion of content in existing commercial media. Advertising is the paradigm example. When the identified problem with the media content is simply the availability of objectionable content—Carlin's monologue was (probably wrongly) said to be capable of expanding a child's vocabulary in an instant—this type of intervention accomplishes very little except by being competitive for audience attention. Thus, this strategy seems ill-suited to problems related to too much violence, portrayals of gender relations, or many of the other negative aspects of media content discussed in this book. Sometimes, however, the problem is that youth are not adequately offered particular messages or information. Some chapters identified lack of sexual health information in media programming and, at a more massive level, lack of variation in sexual role portrayals or gender scripts (Chapters 11 and 5, respectively). Payments to add to this content could be plausible policies.

Expenditures for desired content can take various forms. Consider here differences along two dimensions—the nature of payment and the identification of sponsorship. First, expenditures can range from direct payment to media creators or purveyors for including the favored content—the standard advertising model—to free provision of often expensive-to-produce, appealing, useable program or informational content that eliminates a major expense for the media: producing (or buying) their own content. Both government and private entities use the latter form of expenditure to great effect—it is often called "public relations"—but in certain hard-to-define circumstances it could be problematic. It includes practices ranging from offering press or "video news" releases, which are to some extent essential for keeping the public informed, to providing free cartoons for children that feature the providers' products. The FCC once struggled with the characterization of the last example, given rules restricting the permissible amount of advertising time in children's television programming (*National Association for Better Broadcasting v. FCC*, 1987). The children's advocates claimed that these cartoons, which the stations used instead of creating or purchasing its own programming and which featured characters whose models and related paraphernalia the company sold to children as branded products, amounted to advertising. More generally, media critics have explained that one reason establishment viewpoints—that is, government and corporate sources—so dominate media news is that these entities are able to design and time their press releases and press conferences to be much easier (i.e., cheaper) for the media to integrate into stories than outsider voices which require expensive reporting in order for the media to access (Herman & Chomsky, 1988).

Provision of free content largely cuts the media out of the creative or journalistic process, for example, in relation to video news releases or other prepackaged programs on topics of interest to the corporate or governmental provider. This displacement raises normative issues related to a free society's commitment to a media or press valued as a "fourth estate"—an independent source (or filter) of judgment about the information or culture that merits public attention. A ministry of propaganda hardly satisfies the values justifying press freedom. Although society is well served by a government (and corporate realm) that provides the public with information, often most effectively through providing the information to an intermediary (the mass media), there is a hard-to-define point when this process arguably turns into objectionable propaganda and manipulation.

Second, the media's presentation of government (or corporate) messages varies in whether they identify the sponsor/payer. The government may want antidrug messages—or favored messages on a wide variety of issues—included in media content but reasonably conclude that identification of the government as sponsor undermines the effectiveness of the message. Nevertheless, Congress has legislated against use of government funds to pay the media to include content unless the government is identified as its source, thus converting the message into a traditional advertisement by which the government forthrightly uses the press to communicate with the public. Covert presentation is barred as propaganda. In my view, for the government to pay for inclusion of content without having itself identified as the source causes this practice to violate the First Amendment by undermining the integrity of the press as an independent entity that plays a special fourth estate role in a free society. Nevertheless, despite public outcries whenever the practice is exposed, the Government Accounting Office (GAO) has found that various administrations disregard these laws (and possible constitutional norm), a contempt for law that the GAO found escalated greatly during the recent Bush presidency.

In any event, despite objections to payments for covert influence on media content, a policy response to young people's need for particular information can sometimes be met by government providing the information—through press releases or government publications—or by paying for and sponsoring media provision of the information, for example, by paid public service announcements or other overt forms of advertising.

## STRUCTURAL CHANGES

From both the perspectives of freedom and usually of predictable positive societal results, government steps to enable or encourage desirable behavior generally produce more beneficial results than does seeking to identify and punish bad behavior. A method to enable the former would be to create or change institutional structures in a way that either changes who makes decisions, changes their mandate, or changes the incentive framework under which they operate. While less direct than the policy approaches aimed directly at media content discussed above, and not even intended to be fully effective (on the premise that diversity in media valuably serves different audiences and exposes social complexity), structural interventions, broadly defined, may be the most legitimate and, in the long run, most effective way of responding to many of the problems identified in this book. As noted, media content and distribution necessarily result from the interaction of the skills and inclinations of the creators and their structural context—a context that creates both incentives and opportunities. Attempts to regulate coercively the creator's expression are extraordinarily problematic in a free society—a point repeatedly made above, most emphatically in objecting to censorship. The government, however, is necessarily and inevitably largely responsible for creating (in combination with the reactive choices of individuals) the structure in which the media operate.

The outcome of a so-called free market, for example, is entirely dependent on governmental policy choices about the laws it adopts. Even in its most extreme libertarian forms, both the nature of media entities and the outcomes of the market reflect government choices about the particular content and methods of enforcement of property, contract, and tort laws, the content of corporate law, tax law, and government educational and other policies that influence the distribution of wealth and education and the existence of preferences among the population. When the government chooses one or another set of these laws and policies, the structure—and hence media content—changes. Of course, the government can make these choices with or without being influenced by some thought about the impact on the media order, but given the government's necessary involvement, there is little argument against their making their decisions as thoughtfully and, hence, as conscious about their effects on the media as possible.

Thus, no objection can be raised generically to government involvement in creation of institutional structures. If, under current arrangements, the media produces and distributes content that has problematic features or content lacking desirable features, any good policy analysis should consider how the structure exacerbates or alleviates these problems. Of course, the task of engaging in such an analysis, even in respect to the limited domain of issues raised in this book, is immense, certainly beyond the scope of this chapter.

Nevertheless, the admonition "think structural" is probably the most meaningful (and most often disregarded) advice that one can give in relation to media policy issues. Structural interventions are where intellectual, reformist, and activist energy most often should be placed because (or at least so I believe) they are the form that is both most legitimate and, in the long run, most effective. A careful analysis requires at least three general categories of inquiry: (1) What media content is problematic? (2) How does structure contribute to the pervasiveness of this content? (3) What changes would usefully reduce these problematic results without introducing new, presumably unintended, problems that outweigh any gain from the change? Here, without the needed full evaluation, I give a few examples related to the issues raised in this book.

## Media Literacy

Mass media produces consequences due to the behavior of both sides of the equation—the media and its audience. Each provides a context for the other. Maybe in part due to well-placed skepticism about censorious approaches, Chapter 8 argues for media literacy as the most promising policy response related to media presentations of violence. Although the author does not develop the point (and I will not try to describe the precise meaning) of goals or methods of media literacy, in principle this form of education could limit negative consequences in two ways—either by favorably changing reactions to media content or by favorably changing preferences and consumption choices, thereby, also changing the incentives placed on media creators. As kids develop—and in a sense become more media literate—their knowledge of how advertisements seek to manipulate their behavior increases and, consequently, to some degree their responsiveness to this attempted manipulation also changes. Although one hardly expects any real-world presence of "debriefing" subsequent to viewing violent sex films, one experimental study found not only evidence of various antisocial effects of viewing of "aggressive erotic" films but also found that when those who saw the films were debriefed, they "revealed *less* acceptance of the standard rape myths than those in a control group who had not seen the films"[1] (Donnerstein & Berkowitz, 1981). In a sense, intuitive or reflexive debriefing represents a goal of media literacy. Media literacy can also influence the value people place on different media content, thereby changing their consumption inclinations—a hoped-for consequence more generally of teaching the literary canon in school. I offer here nothing about the appropriate form of expenditures or governmental and educational policies related to media literacy. And although advantages of greater media literacy are obvious, a proper assessment of any proposal must consider its predictable costs, including student time, in relation to its predictable benefits. Still, unless it takes financial, educational, or activist resources and time away from more urgent matters, there are no obvious general reasons to criticize media literacy as a meaningful policy measure except on the ground of effectiveness of particular proposals.

## Market Structures

George Gerbner long ago observed that while television programming emphasizing violence is less popular than other programming, it relies less on culturally bound content, which thereby makes its exportability easier (e.g., Gerbner, 1996). Given the high proportion of media earnings attributable to the export market, this translatability effect increases the incentive to produce this violent content. The obvious implication is that success of U.S. trade policy, which pushes hard to reduce all barriers for American audio-video products, would have the nefarious effect of increasing the pressure to produce and, given the low or zero copy costs of whatever has initially been produced, to make available domestically a type of content this book finds problematic. Elsewhere I have described as "weak protectionism" those policies, justifiable primarily in countries that are net importers of media content, that, without aiming to keep out any particular content, impose some burden on media imports. Ideally, these countries should use the payments collected from imports to subsidize local media content that is valuable in support of both democratic and local cultural development and preservation. This weak protectionism imposed by non-American countries could have a number of desirable effects including greater prevalence in America of content that places less emphasis on violence and that better addresses cultural and political issues salient in America (Baker, 2002).

Legal policy influences the market in many other ways that affect content. Strong copyright protection, for example, generally favors commodified production of communications and specifically favors ownership and control by conglomerate firms (Benkler, 1999). Both effects influence the nature of content produced and consumed. Similarly, apparently benign choices about whether to apply sales taxes to the media product itself or to advertisers' purchase of space or time affect content, with the former choice increasing the incentive for a media company to respond to preferences of advertisers and the latter choice favoring preferences of the public (Baker, 1994). Thought might usefully be given to whether copyright and tax law, or other forms of legal structuring of the market, significantly affect the content that is the subject of this book.

## Structural Specification of Media-Content Decision Makers

Not only the market but also the identity of empowered decision makers within the media realm can favorably or unfavorably influence media content. In Chapter 5, the authors report that although male artists dominate in music videos, those featuring women artists were distinctly less sexist. This result, though, likely reflects the demand of the consumers of these videos rather than the artists' choices (or, if it reflects the artists' choices, consumers' demand may explain the popularity of these artists). On the other hand, clearly the availability of high operating profits for most successful communication products—an economic effect that reflects the nature of media products (Baker, 2002)—leaves room for those in decision-making control to significantly influence content (Baker, 2007). This fact justifies the authors' suggestion in Chapter 5 that increases of women in control of production decisions could have benefits to adolescents by helping reduce the stereotypical presentation of women. As a policy matter, absent evidence to the contrary, one can expect that greater efforts to increase the sexual, racial, and ethnic diversity of the media workforce, particularly at the content decision-making level—for example, editors, producers, writers, and higher level decision makers—would influence content, for instance by increasing its diversity in identity-scripts, in ways that this book recommends.

One reason often given for local ownership of broadcast stations is the greater likelihood that local owners will be perceived by themselves and by others with whom they daily interact as responsible for providing a product that reflects community needs and other pro-social values rather than that merely maximizes profits. Thus, local owners have refused to air national network programming that they considered unsuitable for their community. While sometimes this produces a troublesome parochialism, more often it results in greater responsibility in providing news and entertainment.

Policies restricting ownership concentration is a structural measure that could also affect the nature of diversity in media content as more, and more often local, owners make key decisions. Policies more explicitly promoting a greater diversity along racial, sexual, and ethnic lines could also favorably influence media content. This expectation provided the key justification for Justice William Brennan's last decision for the Supreme Court, a decision upholding explicit racial preferences favoring minority ownership of a broadcast station. While the decision's treatment of affirmative action has since been repudiated by a more conservative Supreme Court, its specific holding still stands (*Metro Broadcasting v. FCC*, 1990).

Sociological reasons exist to expect that ownership by those professionally closer to the creative process as well as by smaller, perhaps family firms will have less strictly monetary and more often creative or socially responsible ambitions for their products. In contrast, large publicly traded corporate firms have profitability legally mandated as their responsibility to their shareholders. Personal rewards of managers in such firms are usually similarly structured. These facts support arguments for policies that favor dispersal of media ownership and disfavor ownership of media, especially news media, by publicly traded firms. Beyond merely justifying concerns with conglomerate firms, no matter what their genesis, this structural goal of reducing the sway of profit considerations also justifies a more pointed rationale to restrict media mergers. The highest bidder is not the party who necessarily believes that it can produce the most quality or most value[2] in owning the purchased entity, but the party who believes it can produce the most profit, an expectation that it can then capitalize into the high bid, a result that locks the new owner into the necessity to produce that profit to pay off the purchase price.

These concerns with the identity of the relevant decision makers support a wide array of structural policies (Baker, 2007). Both general antitrust and, as a crucial addition, media specific ownership rules should restrict media mergers and favor ownership dispersal. Cross-ownership of different types of local media presents special evils of dominance by a single firm and should be barred. Both civil rights laws restricting institutional bias against minorities and women in ownership and employment and affirmative action policies could have favorable effects. More innovatively, the United States could follow and expand on the treatment that legal rules (as well as contractual provisions, especially in effectively unionized contexts) give to the distribution of power within media firms in ways that favor greater control by editors and journalistic or creative personnel. The media entity's employees could also be given explicit power to veto various decisions ranging from replacement of editors to the sale of the company.

## Influence of Advertisers

Advertisers both directly constitute a major portion of the content and hugely influence the nonadvertising content in some media—broadcasting, newspapers, and magazines most obviously. Advertisers can be shown to have different interests in media content than do consumers so their influence constitutes one reason that media content often diverges from what audiences want and would otherwise purchase (Baker, 1994). For example, advertisers' interest in not being associated with content that offends some potential customers disfavors diverse content desired by other potential audience members. Similarly, competition with low-priced advertising-supported products, designed with the goal of attracting a particular audience of potential customers, could make it uneconomical for another producer to offer media products more valued by those who are not potential customers. A relevant research question from the perspective of the concerns of this book is whether systematic differences exist in the quantity and, equally important, the quality—for example, the type of scripts—of portrayals of adolescents in the nonadvertising content of media that are and are not dominantly advertising-supported. How, for example, do movies compare with television serial programming or magazines in their portrayal of violence or gender scripts? To what extent are differences related to the influence of advertisers rather than, for example, FCC policy that restricts some graphic sexuality on broadcast television? Although policies are imaginable to reduce advertiser influence on nonadvertising content, this book has not investigated ways in which their influence contributes to particular problems discussed here or has changed over time, so I put the issue aside.

## Alternative Nonmarket or Less Market-Oriented Institutions

Possibly more important than the identity of the owners in a market setting is the extent that structural factors lead, sometimes force, owners, no matter who they are, to be almost exclusively market or profit oriented. This is important to the extent that a major, maybe the dominant, reason for the extent of the problematic portrayal of violence and gender reported in this book reflect judgments about profitability. If maximizing profits were a less dominant concern, decision makers could make media content choices on the basis of their own views of creative quality or of social responsibility. In the news media, the increasing structural dominance of profit concerns contributes to laying off journalists even when society greatly benefits from their reporting but whose work, after deducting the expense of their employment, does not add net profits to the bottom line. In the entertainment media, reducing the sway of the bottom line may expand the amount and range of culturally challenging and variable content that the media entity offers. It would allow for the exercise of greater editorial or creator responsibility for the entity's messages, responsibility that could well be exercised in ways consistent with the implicit content recommendations found in this book.

Earlier, I noted the possibility of government subsidization of desirable content. Even more to the point could be a structural policy of subsidizing or otherwise promoting nonprofit media entities. For example, in addition to direct subsidies, the government could enact tax or inheritance laws, legal rules relating to the sale of media entities, broadcast licensing rules, and laws related to the operation of nonprofits that favor ownership by nonprofit foundations or nonprofit community groups. More fine-grained support for community cultural creation and presentations, required cable cross-subsidization of cable access channels, licensing and/or subsidies for lower power or community radio could also affect the overall media environment.

Provision for entirely different financial bases of some media entities can leave them less focused on maximizing profit. Such entities are freer to consider the possible benefits and costs of their content choices that do not show up in the bottom line. In Chapter 4, the authors note that frequent TV viewing is associated with more stereotypical beliefs, while exposure to nontraditional characters and educational television is associated with the reverse. Public broadcasting is possibly the most developed option. Relative small audience share of public broadcasting, especially in the United States, does not show lack of interest in its preferred content but rather its inadequate financial support. In various countries, the audience share attracted by public broadcasting reflects various factors, including the entity's remit and the nature and extent of commercial competition that the country allows. The most significant factor, however, appears to be the extent (and to some extent the source) of financial resources the public broadcaster has. Greater financial resources allow creation (or purchase) of higher quality productions that attract larger audiences. Given evidence and defensible predictions that the public broadcast and other nonprofit media producers systematically will or do offer content with more varied gender scripts and with more responsible use and varied portrayals of violence, more cultural variability, and possibly greater responsibility in portrayals ranging from body image to substance abuse and eating habits, concerns raised in this book could be significantly advanced by greater governmental support of a public broadcasting service that is given an appropriate mandate.

## CONCLUSION

The future, we are often told, lies with today's youth. Support for that future provides probably the most popular and easiest justification for an active government. When that leads to greater support for education, there is no basis for objection. But fears of how the mass media leads youth astray are also historically common. The point that the media serve youth inadequately, particularly when they are too young to be highly valued by (or to resist) advertisers, is a well-taken observation. It justifies one of the FCC's least controversial, even if inadequate, content regulations—its requirement that broadcasters provide each week a few hours of "educational" programming aimed at children. Nevertheless, the inclination to solve purported problems with more censorious measures is equally ubiquitous, as illustrated by constant proposals and occasional efforts to restrict youth access to materials available to adults. As an initial point, as a matter of principle, this inclination should not be allowed to reduce the availability of cultural or entertainment products to adults. Whether these efforts significantly contribute to desirable results in respect to youth is at best doubtful.

The quality of both our democracy and our culture may depend on new policy interventions concerning the media. This issue should be high on the country's policy agenda. Certainly media content consumed by youth affects their development. We know enough to identify some content that has generally negative effects on youth as an aggregate (although this same content may often have, although this may be less clear, positive effects for at least some youth). Still, whether this arena media directed at youth justifies the efforts necessary to activate governmental interventions beyond the government's traditional responsibility for education, and which should include media literacy, is unclear. If there is one claim that this chapter advances, however, it is that if there is to be intervention it should not take the form of a blanket censorship of any media content and generally is best when broadly structural. Possibly, the primary structural reforms that promise the most improvement in the media content directed at youth are the same (certainly the same type) interventions that are also justified on independent grounds related to the overall quality of the communications environment.

## NOTES

1. Obviously, the postdebriefing attitudes may have been cued by viewing the experimental debriefers, but the general point remains that both context of reception and discursive evaluation of reception likely influences impact effects.
2. Much of the value of media products go to those other than the immediate purchases, so the owning firm does not capture this portion of the value of what they produce. The same is true for disvalue—the people harmed by media-stimulated violence or sexism. The result is systematic divergence between production of value and the production of profits—the latter not being advanced by the positive externalities nor harmed by the negative externalities of the content they sell.

## REFERENCES

Anderson, C. A., Gentile, D. A., & Buckley, K. E. (2007). *Violent video game effects on children and adolescents.* New York: Oxford University Press.

Baker, C. E. (1994). *Advertising and a democratic press.* Princeton, NJ: Princeton University Press.

Baker, C. E. (1996). The evening hours during Pacifica standard time. *Villanova Sports & Entertainment Law Journal, 3,* 45.

Baker, C. E. (2002). *Media, markets, and democracy.* New York: Cambridge University Press.

Baker, C. E. (2007). *Media concentration and democracy: Why ownership matters.* New York: Cambridge University Press.

Benkler, Y. (1999). Free as the air to common use: First Amendment constraints on enclosure of the public domain. *New York Law Review, 74,* 354–446.

Bork, R. (1971). Neutral principles and some First Amendment problems. *Indiana Law Review, 47,* 1–35.

Donnerstein, E., & Berkowitz, L. (1980). Victim reactions in aggressive erotic films as a factor in violence against women. *Journal of Personality and Social Psychology, 41,* 710–724.

Gerbner, G. (1996). The hidden side of television violence. In G. Gerbner, H. Mowlana, & H. Schiller (Eds.), *Invisible crises: What conglomerate control of media means for America and the world* (pp. 27–34). Boulder, CO: Westview Press.

Goodman, E. P. (2006). Stealth marketing and editorial integrity. *Texas Law Review, 85,* 83–152.

Herman, E. S., & Chomsky, N. (1988). *Manufacturing consent.* New York: Pantheon Books.

Levesque, R. J. R. (2007). *Adolescents, media, and the law.* New York: Oxford University Press.

Meiklejohn, A. (1960). *Political freedom: The constitutional powers of the people.* New York: Harper.

Mill, J. S. (1863). *On liberty.* Boston: Ticknor and Fields. (Original work published 1859)

*New York Times*. (2007, July 19). Editorial: The wrong approach to gangs. Retrieved from http://www.nytimes.com/2007/07/19/opinion/19thur3.html?_r=1&oref=slogin

Piety, T. R. (2001). Merchants of discontent: An exploration of the psychology of advertising, addiction, and the implications for commercial speech. *Seattle University Law Review, 25*, 377–450.

Shiffrin, S. H. (1980). Government speech. *UCLA Law Review, 27*, 565–655.

Wolmsley, R. (2007). *World prison population list* (7th ed.). King's College, London: International Centre for Prison Studies. Retrieved November 1, 2007, from http://www.apcca.org/stats/7th%20Edition%20(2007).pdf

## CASES CITED

Butler v. Michigan, 352 US 380 (1957).

Byers v. Edmundson, 826 So. 2d 551 (2002).

Central Hudson v. Public Service Commission, 447 U.S. 557 (1980).

FCC v. Pacifica, 438 US 726 (1978).

Fox Television v. FCC, 489 F.3d 444 (2rd Cir. 2007).

Ginsberg v. New York, 390 US 629 (1968).

Kingsley Int'l Pictures v. Regents, 360 U.S. 684 (1959).

Lamont v. Postmaster General, 381 US 301(1965).

Lewis Publ'g Co. v. Morgan, 229 U.S. 288 (1913).

Lorillard Tobacco v. Reilly, 533 US 525 (2001).

Meese v. Keene, 481 US 465 (1987).

Metro Broadcasting v. FCC, 497 US 547 (1990).

National Association for Better Broadcasting v. FCC, 830 F2d 270 (1987).

Olivia N. v. National Broadcasting Co., 126 Cal. App.3d 488 (1981).

United States v. American Library Association, 539 U.S. 194 (2003).

Valentine v. Chrestensen, 316 US 52, 54 (1942).

Video Software Dealers Association v. Schwarzenegger, 2007 U.S. Dist. LEXIS 57472 (Cal.D.C., August 6, 2007).

Virginia State Board of Pharmacy v. Virginia Citizens Consumer Council, 426 US 748 (1976).

# 15

# Conclusions

PATRICK E. JAMIESON, AMY JORDAN, AND DANIEL ROMER

Mass media play important roles in the lives of adolescents. As noted in Chapter 1, the rise of the teenager as a marketing target following World War II placed the needs and concerns of adolescents on the agenda of advertisers and the media. Several chapters in this volume, especially Chapters 2, 3, and 13, note the important and evolving role that the media have played in the postwar period for adolescent self-expression, while others have focused on the role of the media in socializing youth to adult norms and identity: Chapter 11 for sex, Chapter 5 for gender roles, Chapter 6 for body image, and Chapter 7 for ethnicity.

Some authors (e.g., Johnson, 2005) have also noted that media entertainment has become more complex over time (e.g., television plots) and may actually be engendering greater cognitive flexibility in youth, especially in the evolution of video games (Chapter 12). Johnson (2005) claims that our popular culture is actually making us smarter, and he attributes some of the steady increase in youth IQ over the past fifty years (the Flynn effect) to the increasing complexity of the media. Flynn agrees (2007). Furthermore, the new and exciting opportunities for adolescent expression and learning on the Internet may open new vistas for the socialization and development of youth (see Chapters 11 and 13).

Despite these favorable trends, the same opportunities that the media provide for positive socialization also include many sources of risk to healthy development. The ever-present use of violence in fictional media portrayals on television (Chapter 8) and in film (Chapter 4) increases risks of similar behavior in young people. Marketing of alcohol (Chapter 10) and tobacco (Chapter 9) has not declined, and youth are often the target of such efforts.

Body ideals as represented in both advertising and entertainment encourage unhealthy self-images in adolescents that are inconsistent with food advertising which encourages overeating (Chapter 6). Furthermore, the media often portray behaviors that are impulsive but dysfunctional, such as unprotected sex with casual partners (Chapter 11), that may encourage risk taking. Hence, the goal of our conclusion is to find ways to encourage the positive effects of the media on adolescent development while curbing, as much as possible, the unfavorable consequences.

## THE CULTURE OF CONSUMPTION AND ADOLESCENTS

One of the most pervasive influences of the media results from the industry's dependence on advertising. Advertising helps to promote consumer spending which is a major engine of economic prosperity. Many commentators have noted, however, that the growth of the media during the postwar era encouraged an ethos of immediate gratification. Indeed, this hedonistic ethos embodies one of the major contradictions in our culture between the need to invest time and resources to achieve success while continuously being reminded that immediate gratification is the source of happiness. As noted in Chapter 1, one consequence of this contradiction has been the creation of a youthful hedonism in adults that is promoted by advertising and marketing.

The culture of youthful hedonism poses conflicts for adolescents who are held in limbo by ever-increasing demands for continued education and delay of adult responsibility, a condition that effectively extends adolescence into the third decade of life. The extension of adolescence exposes young people to all of the influences of the culture of consumption with few of the responsibilities of adulthood. Our culture wants youth to mature into adults, but wants adults to remain youthful. The cultural blurring between adulthood and adolescence poses challenges for young people that are exacerbated by media portrayals. Because adolescents are more impulsive than adults, they are more likely to take up potentially harmful behaviors, such as use of tobacco and alcohol, unprotected sex, and violent behavior (Chambers, Taylor, & Potenza, 2003; Moffitt, 1993). In view of the often glamorous portrayal of these behaviors in the media, adolescents would be expected to be more subject to the disinhibiting effects of these media influences, despite society's expectation to the contrary.

Given a culture of youthful hedonism, it is also not surprising that young people are increasingly represented in the entertainment media, including top-ranking television programs (Introduction) and films (Chapter 4). The increased presence of young people in the media is encouraging because it gives them greater recognition in the culture. But it also allows for greater portrayal of risk taking, such as violence, alcohol and tobacco use, and unprotected sex. Indeed, as suggested in the Introduction and more clearly seen in the analysis of film content in Chapter 4, many of the trends toward increased adolescent engagement in risky behavior in the postwar period have coincided with the overall increase in explicit portrayal of behaviors such as sex, suicide, and violence. Although the portrayal of smoking and alcohol use has declined in general, this is not the case among youthful characters.

## GENDER PORTRAYAL IN THE MEDIA

A major concern about the effects of the media on adolescent socialization is the continued unequal representation of gender in both TV and film. Gendered content in magazines still encourages traditional roles for both sexes; indeed, a taskforce of the American Psychological Association (2007) found that alluring and sexual images of women and girls have increased in magazine advertising. There is evidence that such images inhibit the perceived professional competence of women. Although the evidence regarding mental health consequences is less clear, these portrayals may continue to support gender roles that stereotype women as caregivers, sexual objects, and dependent on men (see Chapter 5). Given the growing representation of women at all levels of the workforce, military, and politics, this pattern of portrayal is surprising and clearly out of step with societal realities.

The cultural confusion between adulthood and adolescence is nowhere more evident than in the treatment of women in advertising and marketing. Recent analyses of advertising and marketing trends find that preteen girls (often called "tweens") are increasingly socialized to act as adults with sexy clothing lines and stores that cater to this demographic (Cook & Kaiser, 2004). Newly created magazines, such as *Teen Vogue, Cosmo Girl!,* and *Elle Girl* enable them to learn of the latest styles in the same way their older siblings and parents do. At the same time, adult women are increasingly portrayed as youthful and even childlike as in the clothing ad from Bloomingdales shown in Figure 15.1 (see also Merskin, 2004). Again, we see how advertising and marketing are working to merge adolescence and adulthood, despite the obvious lack of experience and maturity that go with sexuality at this young age.

Media critic Jeane Kilbourne (1999) depicts the problem facing girls between expectations that they simultaneously appear mature and innocent in these terms:

> What is new is that girls are now supposed to embody both within themselves. This is symbolic of the central contradiction of

Figure 15.1. Ad in the New York Times for an adult "baby-doll" outfit with hair style and ribbon to match. (*Source*: *New York Times*, November 11, 2007, p. 34.)

the culture—we must work hard and produce and achieve success and yet, at the same time, we are encouraged to live impulsively, spend a lot of money, and be constantly and immediately gratified. This tension is reflected in our attitudes toward many things, including sex and eating. Girls are promised fulfillment both through being thin and through rich foods, just as they are promised fulfillment through being innocent and virginal and through wild and impulsive sex. (p. 145)

## POLICY DIRECTIONS

### School Interventions

Our discussion of the conflicts posed by the media for young people suggest that adolescents need help to cope with the culture of youthful hedonism that is pervasive in our media culture as they make the transition to adulthood. Schools can play a role in helping young people to develop healthy lifestyles. One approach is through curricula that encourage mature social problem solving. Such programs encourage youth to consider alternative solutions to social conflicts and help them to resist impulsive options that produce short-term gain at the expense of long-term costs. A recent meta-analysis indicates that school-based programs aimed at encouraging conflict resolution succeed in reducing violence and aggression in youth (Centers for Disease Control and Prevention, 2007). Similar programs have been found to help prevent use of alcohol, tobacco, and other drugs (Romer, 2003).

Schools that encourage healthy decision making also may encounter more success than approaches that attempt to control behavior through the use of drug testing and other coercive measures (LaRusso, Romer, & Selman, 2007). The major challenge for health educators is to find ways to combine these interventions so that they are efficient and cost effective. Programs that build on healthy decision making as a base with content-specific material directed toward different risks should be able to accomplish this objective. Some examples of this approach have been found to be successful (Botvin, Griffin, & Nichols, 2006; Griffin, Botvin, & Nichols, 2004; Lonczak, Abbott, Hawkins, Kosterman, & Catalano, 2002).

Another educational approach is to help youth to recognize those influences of media portrayals that encourage impulsive and unhealthy solutions to life problems. There are already increasing attempts to teach curricula that improve media literacy (Hobbs, 2004), and three chapters in our volume support this approach to reducing harmful media effects (Chapters

6, 8, and 14). However, media literacy approaches have not necessarily focused on building healthy lifestyles. Some progress has been made in developing new interventions to inoculate youth from the harmful influences of the media on violent and other unhealthy behaviors (Cantor & Wilson, 2003; Evans et al., 2006; Goldberg, Niedermeier, Bechtel, & Gorn, 2006; Reichert, LaTour, Lambiase, & Adkins, 2007; Wilksch, Tiggemann, & Wade, 2006). However, these programs have only been tested in their pilot stages. To date, the most effective component appears to be instruction that helps young people recognize the unrealistic aspects of media portrayals (Carney, 2006). More research will be needed to test the long-term effects of these programs. In addition, media literacy programs that can be combined with nutrition curricula are needed to help youth recognize the harmful effects of foods high in calories and low in nutrients that are often promoted in advertising.

If media literacy approaches could be combined with healthy problem-solving and decision-making curricula, we would have powerful interventions that could help to insulate youth from the harmful effects of media influence. Most problem-solving curricula focus only on harmful peer influences. However, media influence may be just as strong a factor and may influence individuals through peer leaders (Katz & Lazarsfeld, 2006). Research is clearly needed to identify effective curricula for integrating media literacy skills into problem-solving training, especially for healthy nutrition.

## Improving Mental Health

We have argued that adolescents are vulnerable to the pervasive influence of the media in promoting a culture of consumption and risk taking. It is also likely that some adolescents are more vulnerable to this influence than others. One source of vulnerability is mental illness. It is estimated that 10% of youth suffer from a mental disorder that interferes with normal functioning and that another 10% are at risk for similar conditions (U.S. Department of Health and Human Services, 1999). Major depression, the most common of these disorders, puts adolescents at increased risk for suicidal ideation and media contagion (Gould, Jamieson, & Romer, 2003). Other conditions that increase impulsive behavior, such as ADHD and bipolar disorder, may also increase the risks of unfavorable media influences.

Many youth who suffer from mental health conditions end up in the juvenile justice system, where treatment services are less than optimal. It is estimated that nearly two-thirds of male youth and three-fourths of female youth in detention at any time suffer from at least one diagnosed mental disorder (Teplin et al., 2006). This also suggests that youth with mental health conditions may be more vulnerable to the disinhibiting effects of the media. Poor youth are also less likely to receive adequate mental health care, potentially increasing their chances for exposure to the juvenile justice system. Greater efforts to improve the mental health of youth as outlined in a recent Annenberg-Sunnylands initiative (Evans et al., 2005) may contribute significantly to reducing adolescent vulnerability to impulsive media influences.

## CONTROL OF MEDIA CONTENT

### Voluntary Content Ratings

Chapter 14 reviews the many arguments against censorship of the media, including mandatory rating of media content. One way in which the United States has obviated the need for censorship is by having the media industry "self-regulate." Television shows, movies, video games, and computer games each have a system of ratings that were developed by the media makers and are applied by either the producers or by an industry-funded board. The success of industry-provided ratings depends on one's perspective. In one study, researchers recruited fifty-five parents to rate the content of computer and video games, movies, and television programs (Walsh & Gentile, 2001). Raters felt that industry labels were "too lenient" when compared with what parent coders would find suitable for children.

Nor are ratings well understood. Perhaps because of rating inconsistencies, or because parents are not fully aware of the information offered by media, many parents do not consistently use the ratings to guide their children. A recent Kaiser Family Foundation survey (Rideout, 2007) found that although 78% of parents say they have used movie ratings to direct children's movie viewing, only about half say they use music advisories, video game ratings, and television program ratings (54%, 52%, and 50%, respectively). Even among parents who reported using industry-provided ratings and advisories, most did not find them to be "very useful."

Research has also found that a government-mandated television blocking device, known as the V-Chip, has also been underutilized. Widely seen as a way to avoid censorship in the face of rising levels of sex and violence on TV, the V-Chip would allow parents to program the sets so that shows with objectionable content never appear on the screen. A study conducted by the Annenberg Public Policy Center in the year following implementation of the V-Chip mandate found that less than 10% of parents consistently used the device, even when they were shown how to use it (Scantlin & Jordan, 2006). Why? Postexperiment interviews with mothers revealed that many found the device difficult to locate (it was buried five menus into the RCA model provided) and confusing to program. Research at the Kaiser Family Foundation also suggests that the TV ratings used to program the V-Chip are too complex to be effective for parents (Rideout, 2007). A full decade after the ratings were introduced, only 11% of parents know that "FV" is an indicator of violent content in children's programming.

Despite these challenges, voluntary rating systems provide information for consumers and may help to reduce exposure to extremely violent content. Although ratings have not worked well for television, they may have worked better for films, perhaps by reducing access to sensitive sexual content in theaters (see Chapter 4). Better use of these ratings should be considered for restricting access to violence on TV and in films. The film industry has recently agreed to consider use of tobacco in determining its ratings. The same should be done on a consistent basis for violence.

## Voluntary Expansion of Content

We do not argue a position of censorship, nor do we argue that media only present images of a fantasyland in which all characters are healthy, vice-free, peaceful, and asexual. Instead, we argue that media should do a better job of reflecting a reality that includes healthy alternatives to the negative portrayals of many behaviors that are so prevalent in today's content. Producers who decide not to include risky behaviors do not necessarily compromise profits. The major Hollywood blockbuster film, *The Devil Wears Prada*, about a young woman who finds herself morally compromised as a new employee of a fashion magazine, did exceedingly well at the box office and in rentals. This was despite (or because of) the fact that there were no portrayals of smoking, even though the content (fashion and models) and settings (New York and Paris) would easily include such behavior. Similarly, we encourage the media industry to challenge conventional wisdom that only certain plotlines or characters "sell." As pointed out in Chapters 4 and 5, neither television nor top-grossing films feature women as often as men in major roles. When they do, they can be enormously successful. *Grey's Anatomy*—a popular and critical television success—centers on a female medical resident's (Meredith Grey) perspective on relationships and doctoring. *The Devil Wears Prada* featured both a strong female executive (Meryl Streep) and her young assistant (Anne Hathaway) in starring roles. The entertainment industry is encouraged to develop more products that recognize women as lead characters. There is no reason to assume that men should receive more attention in films and on TV in leading roles.

We also encourage the entertainment industry to consider producing more films and TV shows that do not rely heavily on violence to attract large audiences. In order to identify films that meet this criterion, we analyzed the film database from the Annenberg-RWJ CHAMP. Table 15.1 lists seventeen films from the past two decades that contained the lowest scores on our indices of violence. These highly successful films, ranked in the top fifteen for gross sales in a year, range across a variety of genres, from comedy to drama, romance to adventure, and biography to sci-fi. It should also be noted that this small sample of films was awarded over twenty-five Oscar nominations and won seven. Their success indicates that it is possible to produce money-making films that appeal to a wide range of audience interests without relying on violence. These films still become blockbusters and allow artistic expression regardless of genre without perpetuating the expectation of sensationalistic violence. Good stories will always be admired as long as we have good storytellers.

Table 15.1. Highly Successful Films That Contained Low Levels of Violence, 1985 to 2004

| Title | Release Date | Rating | Genre |
|---|---|---|---|
| Star Trek IV | 1986 | PG | Adventure / Comedy / Mystery / Sci-Fi |
| Moonstruck | 1987 | PG | Comedy / Romance / Drama |
| Field of Dreams | 1989 | PG | Drama / Family / Fantasy / Sport |
| Honey, I Shrunk the Kids | 1989 | PG | Family / Adventure / Comedy / Sci-Fi |
| A Few Good Men | 1992 | R | Crime / Drama / Thriller |
| Free Willy | 1993 | PG | Family / Adventure / Drama |
| Indecent Proposal | 1993 | R | Drama / Romance |
| Mrs. Doubtfire | 1993 | PG-13 | Comedy / Drama / Family |
| Sleepless in Seattle | 1993 | PG | Comedy / Romance / Drama |
| Apollo 13 | 1995 | PG | Adventure / Drama / History |
| The First Wives Club | 1996 | PG | Comedy |
| Twister | 1996 | PG-13 | Action / Adventure / Drama / Thriller |
| Contact | 1997 | PG | Drama / Mystery / Sci-Fi / Thriller |
| Deep Impact | 1998 | PG-13 | Drama / Sci-Fi / Thriller |
| Cast Away | 2000 | PG-13 | Adventure / Drama |
| Erin Brockovich | 2000 | R | Drama / Biography |
| American Pie 2 | 2001 | R | Comedy / Romance |

## Research on Portrayals That Promote Healthy Development

If producers of entertainment can be persuaded to include more healthy content in their products, it will be increasingly important to evaluate the success of such efforts. A good example of this type of research is a study done by Rebecca Collins and her colleagues (Collins, Elliot, Berry, Kanouse, & Hunter, 2003), who examined adolescents' recall and interpretation of an episode of the television show *Friends*. In the episode, Rachel discovers that she is pregnant even though she and her partner Ross used a condom. Their national telephone survey, conducted immediately after the program aired, found that youth who watched with a parent were more likely to recall the condom storyline and, more importantly, those who discussed the program with a parent were more likely to understand the true efficacy of condoms in preventing sexually transmitted infections and pregnancy.

Collins and colleagues knew in advance that this program was airing and had funding with which to carefully study the reception of a health-related message. This study highlights the value of industry–researcher partnerships in not only crafting prosocial, healthy messages in the media that youth consume, but also in designing efficient, timely, and effective interventions. Initiatives such as this have been increasingly undertaken to develop better content for youth. Hollywood, Health & Society, for example—an initiative housed at the Norman Lear Center at the University of Southern California and funded by a variety of government and philanthropic organizations— makes experts available to television and movie series to ensure that writers "get it right" when weaving health content into their narratives.[1] More research is needed to understand the efficacy of these efforts, although early evaluations are promising (Huang et al., 2007).

## Voluntary Restrictions on Advertising

Further restrictions on advertising for tobacco and alcohol should be considered. Tobacco advertising is still permitted in magazines that reach youth, and alcohol advertising reaches young people in both electronic and print formats. The 30% rule used by the alcohol industry for youth audience thresholds appears to be too liberal. The tobacco industry already subscribes to a 15% rule, and a recent report by the Academy of Science (2004) recommends the same threshold for alcohol advertising.

The author of Chapter 14 also suggests that the regulatory structure of the media may be modified to encourage more local (versus corporate) ownership, a move that may be more sensitive to community interests and that may insulate owners from sole concerns for profit. Expansion of public- and foundation-financed television may also be worth considering to reduce the influence of market demands and advertising on entertainment and news programming. These arrangements should be studied to see if they provide more diverse representation of gender and racial/ethnic identities as well as more effective portrayal of the risks of violence, sex, and drug use.

## EXPANSION OF YOUTHFUL EXPRESSION

Continued development of media outlets such as the Internet and hand-held devices will enable greater opportunities for youthful expression. It is an understatement to say that the media are undergoing dramatic transformation. The eventual convergence of television and the Internet will surely create a new media landscape. The transfer of analog broadcast to digital and high-definition signals will also provide new opportunities for innovation. One possibility may be that the new media will engender less reliance on advertising and other forms of marketing to provide youth with greater opportunities for expression. The review in Chapter 13 suggests that early concerns about the dystopic effects of the Internet have not materialized. To the extent that youth can communicate with each other with fewer constraints of advertising and marketing, they may be able to develop a voice of their own that is more representative of all ethnic/racial identities and of both genders. The evolution of the music video (Chapter 3) provides some lessons for how marketing constraints can subvert youthful expression. Perhaps the continued evolution of this genre on the Internet will permit young people to disseminate their musical expression with less interference from adults.

The media reflect who we are as a culture and how we want our young people to mature into adults. If the media unnecessarily accentuate dysfunctional attitudes and behavior in adolescents, we will all bear the costs.

## NOTE

1. See http://www.learcenter.org/html/projects/?cm.hhs

## REFERENCES

American Psychological Association. (2007). *Report of the APA task force on the sexualization of girls.* Washington, DC: Author.

Botvin, G., Griffin, K. W., & Nichols, T. D. (2006). Preventing youth violence and delinquency through a universal school-based prevention approach. *Prevention Science, 7*, 403–408.

Cantor, J., & Wilson, B. J. (2003). Media and violence: Intervention strategies for reducing aggression. *Media Psychology, 5*, 363–403.

Carney, M. E. (2006). *Using media literacy education for health promotion: A qualitative meta-analysis of effective program components.* Washington, DC: Cable in the Classroom.

Centers for Disease Control and Prevention. (2007). The effectiveness of universal school-based programs for the prevention of violent and aggressive behavior: A report on recommendations of the task force on community preventive services. *Morbidity and Mortality Weekly Report, 56*(RR-7).

Chambers, R. A., Taylor, J. R., & Potenza, M. N. (2003). Developmental neurocircuitry of motivation in adolescence: A critical period of addiction vulnerability. *American Journal of Psychiatry, 160*, 1041–1052.

Collins, R. L., Elliot, M. N., Berry, S. H., Kanouse, D. F., & Hunter, S. B. (2003). Entertainment television as a healthy sex educator: The impact of a condom-efficacy information episode of *Friends. Pediatrics, 112*, 1115–1121.

Cook, D. T., & Kaiser, S. B. (2004). Betwixt and between. *Journal of Consumer Culture, 4*, 203–227.

Evans, A. E., Dave, J., Condrasky, M., Wilson, D., Griffin, S., Palmer, M., et al. (2006). Changing the home nutrition environment: Effects of a nutrition and media literacy pilot intervention. *Family and Community Health, 29*, 43–54.

Evans, D., Foa, E. B., Gur, R. E., Hendin, H., O'Brien, C. P., Seligman, M. E. P., et al. (2005). *Treating and preventing adolescent mental health disorders: What we know and what we don't know.* New York: Oxford University Press.

Flynn, J. R. (2007). *What is intelligence?* New York: Cambridge University Press.

Goldberg, M. E., Niedermeier, K. E., Bechtel, L. J., & Gorn, G. J. (2006). Heightening adolescent vigilance toward alcohol advertising to forestall alcohol use. *Journal of Public Policy and Marketing, 25*, 147–159.

Gould, M., Jamieson, P. E., & Romer, D. (2003). Media contagion and suicide among the young. *American Behavioral Scientist, 46*, 1269–1284.

Griffin, K. W., Botvin, G., & Nichols, T. D. (2004). Effects of a school-based drug abuse prevention program for adolescents on HIV risk behaviors in young adulthood. *Prevention Science, 7*, 103–112.

Hobbs, R. (2004). A review of school-based initiatives in media literacy education. *American Behavioral Scientist, 48*, 42–59.

Huang, G., Murphy, S., Hether, H., Beck, V., Phillips, Z., & Valente, T. (2007). *Health disparities in primetime television: Evaluating content and impact of popular medical shows on minority viewers.* Paper presented at the American Public Health Association, Washington, DC.

Johnson, S. (2005). *Everything bad is good for you: How today's popular culture is actually making us smarter.* New York: Riverhead Books.

Katz, E., & Lazarsfeld, P. F. (2006). *Personal influence: The part played by people in the flow of mass communications.* New Brunswick, NJ: Transaction Publishers.

Kilbourne, J. (1999). *Deadly persuasion: Why women and girls must fight the addictive power of advertising.* New York: Free Press.

LaRusso, M. D., Romer, D., & Selman, R. L. (2007). Teachers as builders of respectful school climates: Implications for adolescent drug use norms and depressive symptoms in high school. *Journal of Youth and Adolescence, 37,* 386–398.

Lonczak, H. S., Abbott, R. D., Hawkins, J. D., Kosterman, R., & Catalano, R. F. (2002). Effects of the Seattle social development project on sexual behavior, pregnancy, birth, and sexually transmitted disease outcomes by age 21 years. *Archives of Pediatric and Adolescent Medicine, 156,* 438–447.

Merskin, D. (2004). Reviving Lolita? A media literacy examination of sexual portrayals of girls in fashion advertising. *American Behavioral Scientist, 48,* 119–129.

Moffitt, T. E. (1993). Adolescence-limited and life-course-persistent antisocial behavior: A developmental taxonomy. *Psychological Review, 100,* 674–701.

Reichert, T., LaTour, M. S., Lambiase, J. J., & Adkins, M. (2007). A test of media literacy effects and sexual objectification in advertising. *Journal of Current Issues and Research in Advertising, 29,* 81–92.

Rideout, V. (2007). *Parents, children & the media: A Kaiser Family Foundation survey.* Menlo Park, CA: Kaiser Family Foundation.

Romer, D. (2003). *Reducing adolescent risk: Toward an integrated approach.* Thousand Oaks, CA: Sage.

Scantlin, R., & Jordan, A. (2006). Families' experiences with the v-chip: An exploratory study. *Journal of Family Communication, 6,* 139–159.

Teplin, L. A., Abram, K. M., McClelland, G. M., Mericle, A. A., Dulcan, M. K., & Washburn, J. J. (2006). *Psychiatric disorders of youth in detention.* Washington, DC: Office of Juvenile Justice and Delinquency Prevention.

U.S. Department of Health and Human Services. (1999). *Mental health: A report of the Surgeon General.* Rockville, MD: U.S. Department of Mental Health and Human Services.

Walsh, D., & Gentile, D. (2001). A validity test of movie, television and video game ratings. *Pediatrics, 107,* 1302–1308.

Wilksch, S. M., Tiggemann, M., & Wade, T. D. (2006). Impact of interactive school-based media literacy lessons for reducing internalization of media ideals in young adolescent girls and boys. *International Journal of Eating Disorders, 39,* 385–393.

# Index

adolescence, extended, 6

adolescent portrayal in the media, evolution of, 18–20, 46–47

advertisers, influence of, 441

advertising, 434–35. *See also* alcohol use, in television advertising; beer advertising; tobacco advertising
  body size in, 177–82
  and impulsive behavior, 15–18
  magazine, 149–51
  obesity and, 16–18
  restrictions on, 427–29
  treatment of women in, 448–50
  voluntary restrictions on, 455–56

African Americans, 6, 39, 49
  music and, 71–73
  music videos and, 84, 86
  presented on TV in minor and low-status occupational roles, 202–3
  self-concept, 210–11

African Americans, Latinos, Asians, and Native Americans (ALANAs) in media, 198, 214–15
  and adolescent socialization, 198–200
  media exposure and adolescent development, 209–10
    potential negative effects, 210–11
    potential positive effects, 211–13
  portrayal of adolescence and adolescents in the media, 206–9
  portrayals in prime-time TV, 200–205
  research agenda, 213–14

AIP (American International Pictures) films, 44

ALANAs. *See* African Americans, Latinos, Asians, and Native Americans (ALANAs) in media

alcohol use
  in music videos, 88–90, 271
  in television advertising, 284–86. *See also* beer advertising
    a focus on narrative, 286–87
    policy implications, 307–8
  and tobacco use in TV shows, 269–71
  trends in, 305, 306

animated commercials, 300–301

animated films, 273–74

anorexia nervosa, 175, 397–98. *See also* eating disorders

Asia, growth of teen market in, 41–43

Asian Americans. *See* African Americans, Latinos, Asians, and Native Americans (ALANAs) in media

Austin, Joe, 28

Australia, 42–43

Bandura, Albert, 11–13, 106

beer advertising, 284–86. *See also* alcohol use, in television advertising
  beer, animals, and the MTV lifestyle, 298

beer advertising (*continued*)
   beer as achievement/reward, 292–97
   beer as boundary between work and
      leisure, 296
   beer as reaffirming friendship
      (reconciliation), 296
   "beer is precious" narrative, 302–4
   black comedy, 301–4
   and the changing legal drinking
      environment, 288, 291
      1950s and 1960s, 288–91
      1970s, 291–94
      1980s, 294–97
      1990s, 298–301
      2000s, 301–4
   a focus on narrative, 286–87
   "Miller Time," 292, 295
   overcoming barriers to beer, 304–8
   risk, achievement, and parody, 298–301
   sociable transfer of beer from one
      person to another, 292–93
   spending on, 285
   themes of masculinity and work, 287,
      292
Bernard, Jessie, 40
bhangra, 74
body change strategies, unhealthful,
   184–85
   smoking in, 184
body image, 17–18, 90–91. *See also* eating
   behavior; ideal body
body image disturbance
   defined, 166
   prevalence, 166–67
body mass index (BMI), 169. *See also*
   body image; ideal body
Bourdieu, Pierre, 48–49, 53n20
Bowie, David, 67–68
Britain, growth of teen market in,
   40–41
Bud Light, 302–4. *See also* beer
   advertising
Bulman, R. C., 318
Butcher, Melissa, 42–43

California, 46
Cantor, J., 234–35
censorship, 245
   culture of, 424
   general, 420–25
      problems with and costs of, 421–25
   restricted, 425–29
Center for Media and Child Health
   (CMCH), 82

chat rooms, online, 333–34, 389
Chibnall, Steve, 41
China, 42
civil rights movement, 6
Cobain, Kurt, 70
college students, 29–31
commercial youth market, rise of, 28–31
consumer culture, adolescents in, 46–47
   media role in, 9–11
consumer pleasure, as theme in 1960s,
   47–49
consumption, 35. *See also* culture of
   consumption; spending
contagion theory, 106, 107
content ratings. *See* labeling of media
   content
corporations, 5
counterculture of 1960s, 47–49, 64.
   *See also* hippie movement
Country Music Television (CMT), 143
crime. *See also* violence
   "juvenile crime wave," 43–45
cross-dressing, 67
cultivation theory, 11, 83, 86–87, 106–7,
   199, 239
cultural imperialism, 41
culture of consumption. *See also*
   consumption
   adolescents and, 46, 47, 447–48
   media influence in the new, 9–11
      desensitization and normalization, 13
      disinhibition, 11–13. *See also*
         impulsive behavior
      learning new rules of behavior,
         13–15
      postwar prosperity and the, 5–6
   "culture wars," 10
cutting (self-mutilation), 397
cyberbulling, 394–96
   defined, 394
cyberporn. *See* pornography, online

Dayton, Abraham, 28, 29
Depression. *See* Great Depression
*Devil Wears Prada, The* (film), 453
digital divide in adolescents' Internet use,
   398–99
disco, 49
disinhibiting effects of media portrayals,
   11–13, 232. *See also* impulsive
   behavior
Disney Channel, 206–7
Dominick, J. R., 323, 324
drug culture, 65

drug use. *See also* alcohol use
in music videos, 88–90

eating behavior, portrayals of
and body size in advertisements,
177–78
body size and eating behavior by age
group, 178–79
body size and eating behavior by
gender, 178–79
nutritional breakdown of foods
associated with teen characters,
180–82
misguided perceptions of link between
size and eating behaviors, 185
research and policy suggestions
audience strategies, 190
caregiver and educator strategies,
189–90
family/peer strategies, 189
health issues, 186
maturational issues, 187
media strategies, 188–89
outstanding questions and problems,
186–87
recommendations for policy makers
and caregivers, 188–90
social issues, 186–87
research on, 176–77
eating disorders, 175, 183–84
definitions and prevalence,
166–67
education, expansion of higher, 29–30
Erikson, Erik H., 199–200
*Esquire* magazine, 30–31, 36, 45
"ethic of fun," 49
ethnic identities. *See also* African
Americans, Latinos, Asians, and
Native Americans (ALANAs) in
media
music's representation of, 71
Europe, growth of teen market in,
40–41

fashion, 30–31
Fass, Paula, 30
Federal Communications Commission
(FCC), 329–30, 425–26
Feixa, Carles, 42
feminist movement, 5
Fiji, 18, 183–84
film criticism and adolescent gender roles,
145–46
films. *See* movies/films

First Amendment, 7–8, 415–16,
420–21, 428–30. *See also*
Supreme Court
food advertisements. *See under* eating
behavior
food consumption, 15–18
percent of disposable income spent on,
15, 16
Frank, Thomas, 48
Freed, Alan "Moondog," 37, 60

gay culture, 67, 68
gender, 5
beliefs about, 152, 153
gender boundaries, blurring of, 67–68
gender development in adolescence,
132–34
gender differences, 154. *See also* movies/
films; *specific topics*
in eating behavior, 178–79
in eating disorders, 166
in Internet use, 399
music videos and, 84
in smoking, 270
gendered reality, perceptions of, 152
gender ideology, 152
gender role portrayals in media,
adolescent, 448–50
changes in, 134
difficulty determining, 155
in magazine advertising, 149–51
in magazines, 146–49
in movies, 108–10, 144–46
in music videos, 141–44, 153.
*See under* music video(s)
in television commercials, 138–41
in television programming, 134–38
directions for future research and
policy, 155–56
effects on adolescents, 151–54
film criticism and, 145–46
gender roles, attitudes and stereotypes
about, 152, 153
gender socialization, 133
Gerbner, G., 11, 106. *See also* cultivation
theory
Germain, Richard, 29
Gilbert, Eugene, 36–37
Gilbert, James, 43–44, 46
girls. *See also* gender; *specific topics*
expectations to appear both mature
and innocent, 448–50
global teen market, growth of, 40–43
Gordy, Berry, Jr., 49

Gould, M., 122
government intervention. *See* policy
	interventions and directions;
	*specific institutions*
Great Depression, 30
"grunge," 70

Hays Code, 7–8, 316
health. *See also* food consumption; obesity
	media effects on, 209–10, 255–60,
	355–56
health information provided by media, 17,
	212, 214, 391, 455. *See also* sexual
	health information Web sites
Hebdige, D., 72–73
Hechinger, Fred, 45
Hechinger, Grace, 45
hedonism, youthful, 10, 47, 447. *See also*
	culture of consumption
hip-hop music, 49, 73
hippie movement, 64–66. *See also*
	counterculture of 1960s
HIV/AIDS prevention information, 212
Hollander, Stanley, 29
Hollywood Production Code, 120, 316.
	*See also* Hays Code
homosexuality, 67, 68
Horton, Donald, 321–22

ideal body, trends in portrayal of, 168
	for adolescent boys and young men
		lean body ideal, 172–73
		muscular body ideal, 173–75
	for adolescent girls and young women
		portrayals of fatness, the anti-ideal,
			171–72
		the thin ideal in electronic media,
			170–71
		the thin ideal in print media, 168–
			70
ideal-body media, 167
ideal body portrayals. *See also* ideal body
	effects of concern for adolescents,
		182–83
	on Internet, 175–76
identity development, 199–200, 389. *See
	also* self-concept/self-definition;
	socialization
imitation, 242, 429–30. *See also* modeling
impulsive behavior
	advertising and, 15–18
	disinhibition and, 11–13
Internet, impact on music videos, 95–96
Internet relay chat (IRC), 95

Internet use
	cognitive effects, 386–88, 400–401
		on academic performance, 387
		on visual skills, 387–88
	digital divide in adolescents', 398–99
	exposure to harmful content and
		experiences, 396
		cyberbulling, 394–96
		sexually explicit material, 392–93
		sexual predators, 393–94
	frequency, 377–79
	nature of, 378, 380–82
	physical effects, 390–92
	psychological effects, 388, 390
		identity development, 389
		Internet addiction, 389–90
		psychological well-being, 388–89
		time displacement, 390
	public policy and, 400–401
	social effects, 383, 386
		aggression, 386
		civic engagement, 385–86
		social relationships, 384–85
	to support maladaptive behavior, 396–98
		anorexia nervosa, 397–98
		cutting, 397
	utopian and dystopian perspectives,
		383–98

Jam, The, 69–70
Jamieson, K. H., 107
Jamieson, Patrick E., 107, 122, 123
juvenile delinquency (JD), 43–45.
	*See also* violence

Katz, E., 7
Kilbourne, Jeane, 448, 450
Koop, C. Everett, 298

labeling of media content. *See also*
		media content; Motion Picture
		Association of America (MPAA)
		rating system
	mandatory, 432–33
Lamont, Michèle, 53n20
Latinos. *See also* African Americans,
		Latinos, Asians, and Native
		Americans (ALANAs) in media
	presented on TV in minor and low-
		status occupational roles, 202–3
	self-perceptions, 211
Lazarsfeld, P. F., 7
lean body ideal. *See also* ideal body;
		thin body ideal

for adolescent boys and young men, 172–73
ways to communicate the, 171–72
"leisure class," 40
*Life* magazine, 32–33
LSD, 65

Macdonald, Dwight, 27–28, 40, 44–45, 52
magazine advertising. *See also* advertising
  changes in gender role portrayals in, 149–51
magazines. *See also specific magazines*
  changes in gender role portrayals in, 146–49
  gender representation, 147–48
mainstreaming, 154
mandatory content, 431–33
  forms of, 431
marketing, 27–28
market research, 36
market structures, 438–39
Marley, Bob, 72
May, Kirse, 46
media content, control of. *See also* labeling of media content; Motion Picture Association of America (MPAA) rating system; policy interventions and directions
  research on portrayals that promote healthy development, 455
  voluntary content ratings, 452–53
  voluntary expansion of content, 453–54
  voluntary restrictions on advertising, 455–56
media literacy, 437–38. *See also* television violence
Miles, Steven, 51–52
Mill, John Stuart, 427
modeling, 13–14, 429–30. *See also* imitation; movies/films
Motion Picture Association of America (MPAA) rating system, 124–25, 316
Motown, 49
Movie Production Code, 120, 316. *See also* Hays Code
movies/films
  alcohol in, 111, 112, 115–16, 128
  animated, 273–74
  changes in gender role portrayals in, 144–45
  film criticism, 145–46
  juvenile delinquency (JD), 44
  MPAA rating system, 124–25, 316

portion of characters under age 21, 108, 109
portrayal of ALANA adolescence and adolescents, 207–8
in postwar era, 7–8
risk behaviors in, 109–23, 125–27
  content and sales rank, 124–25
  measures of violence and sex, 124–25
sex in, 111, 112, 117–19, 124–28
suicide in, 121–24, 129
tobacco in, 109–16, 128
trends in representation of age and gender, 108–10
  portion of male characters, 108–10
violence in, 111, 112, 114, 120–21, 124–26, 128–29, 429–30
  successful films with low levels of violence, 454
muscular body ideal, 173–75
music, representation of youth in popular, 37–39, 49, 59–60, 74–75. *See also* radio
  blurring of gender boundaries, 67–68
  developments during 1960s, 63–66
  gender bending, 67–68
  a soundtrack for youth, 60–62
  "stand up for your rights," 71–74
  teenagers in love, 62–63
  "teenage wasteland," 68–71
Music Television Network (MTV), 78, 94, 141–43, 298. *See also* music video(s)
music video(s), 78, 96
  changes in gender role portrayals in, 141
    gender representation, 141–42
    gender roles, 90–92, 142–44
  content, 85
    body image, gender roles, and sexual violence, 90–92
    sex, 84, 92–93, 323–24
    tobacco, alcohol, and other drug use, 88–90, 271–72
    violence, weapon-carrying, and suicide, 85–88
  as a distinct medium, 79–82
  effects on youth, 83
    unique influence on youth, 84–85
  historical predecessors, 79
  impact of Internet and radio on, 94–96
  as media of youth, 79–82
  methods of finding the content and influences of, 82–85
  who is watching, and why, 82

music video(s) (*continued*)
  portrayal of ALANA adolescence and
      adolescents, 207–8
  the short, happy life of, 93–96
music video viewers, youth as, 83–84
  gender and racial differences, 84
"My Generation" (The Who), 63–64

Native Americans. *See* African Americans,
      Latinos, Asians, and Native
      Americans (ALANAs) in media
Nilan, Pam, 42
9/11 terrorist attacks, 302
Nirvana, 70

obesity. *See also* body image
  advertising and, 16–18
  Internet use and, 391
  video games and, 356

Pepsi-Cola, 46–47
*Playboy* magazine centerfold subjects
      (Playmates), 168–71
pleasure. *See* consumer pleasure
policy interventions and directions,
      155–56, 400–401, 415–16, 443.
      *See also under* alcohol use; eating
      behavior; Internet use
  improving mental health, 451–52
  paternalism of regulation, 416–18
  pros and cons of government
      intervention, 416–20
  regulatory methods
  availability, differential or restricted,
      425–27
    content-related incentives, 433–36
    general and restricted censorship,
      420–29
    internalization of costs, 429–31
    mandatory content, 431–33
  school interventions, 450–51
  structural changes, 436–37
    alternative nonmarket or less market-
        oriented institutions, 441–43
    influence of advertisers, 441
    market structures, 438–39
    media literacy, 437–38, 450–51
    structural specification of
        media-content decision
        makers, 439–41
pornography
  child, 393–94
  online, 332–33, 392–94

postwar America, teenage spending in,
      27–28
postwar era, mass media in, 3–10
postwar optimism and America's
      youth, 32–33
postwar prosperity and the culture
      of consumption, 5–6. *See also*
      consumption
Presley, Elvis, 38, 62, 80, 325
Production Code, 7. *See also* Movie
      Production Code
product placement
  defined, 265
  laws regarding, 428
  origins, objectives, and effectiveness,
      265–66
  for tobacco products, 266–67
protectionism, "weak," 439
punk rock music, 67–70

racial and ethnic differences, 6, 84. *See
      also* African Americans, Latinos,
      Asians, and Native Americans
      (ALANAs) in media
racism, 6, 39
radio
  in postwar era, 8, 31, 32, 60, 68
  satellite, 96
Ramones, 69
rap music, 49, 73, 87
Rastafarian religion & Rasta culture, 72–73
rebellion against parent culture, 61. *See
      also* punk rock music
reggae, 72
rhythm and blues (R & B), 37–38, 60
"rich get richer" hypothesis (Internet use),
      385, 399
risk behaviors. *See under* beer advertising;
      movies/films
rock and roll, 37–39, 60–62, 64–66. *See
      also* music; music video(s)
rock stars who died young, 70
role models. *See* modeling
Romer, Daniel, 107, 122
Russia, growth of teen market in, 41

San Francisco, 65
school interventions, 450–51
Schrum, Kelly, 29
segregation, 6
self-complexity, 213
self-concept/self-definition, 199–200,
      210–11, 213, 355

self-mutilation. *See* cutting
self-regulation of media industry. *See*
    media content
September 11, 2001, terrorist attacks, 302
*Seventeen* magazine, 33, 34, 147–48, 170,
    183
Sex Pistols, 69
"sex romp" films, 317–19
sexual boundaries, blurring of, 67–68
sexual health information Web sites,
    334–35
sexual information, media as sources of,
    212, 314–15, 334–35, 337, 455
sexuality in media, 313–15, 335–38. *See
    also under* movies/films
  future research, 336–38
  on Internet, 331–35
  in music, 67–68, 321–23
  in music videos, 84, 90–93, 323–24
  in prime-time television, 324–30
    trends in 1990s, 327–28
  in soap operas, 330–31
sexually explicit material. *See*
    pornography
sexual predators, Internet, 393–94
sexual violence in media, 90–92, 338
Shary, T., 145, 319, 321
Sherman, B. L., 323, 324
Sinatra, Frank, 33
smoking. *See under* movies/films; tobacco
    use
soap operas, sexuality in, 330–31
social cognitive theory (of mass
    communication), 11, 106. *See also*
    social learning theory
"social compensation" hypothesis
    (Internet use), 385, 399
socialization. *See also* identity
    development
  adolescent, and the media, 198–200
  gender, 133
social learning theory, 239–40. *See also*
    social cognitive theory
soul music, 49
Soviet Union, growth of teen market in,
    41
spending, teenage, 35. *See also*
    consumption
  in postwar America, 27–28
  as "the last merchandising frontier,"
    49–52
*Sports Illustrated for Kids*, 150
Spuds MacKenzie, 298

suicidal content and themes
  in movies, 121–24, 129
  in music videos, 86–88
Supreme Court, 7–8, 425, 426, 428–30,
    440
symbolic annihilation, 168

"Teen-Age Boys" (*Life* magazine), 32–33
teenage culture, symbolic resonance of,
    43–47
"teenager," origin and early use of the
    term, 46
"Teen-Age Tide, The," 35, 39
*Teen-Age Tyranny* (Hechinger &
    Hechinger), 45
"teenage wasteland," 50
*Teens Market in the U.S., The*, 52
television, 38–39
  portrayal of ALANA adolescence and
    adolescents, 206–7
  portrayals of ALANAs in prime time,
    200–201
    presentation in minor and low-status
      occupational roles, 202–3
    stereotyping and negative
      connotations, 203–5
    underrepresentation, 201–2
  in postwar era, 8–10
television commercials, changes in gender
    role portrayals in, 138–41
television programming, changes in gender
    role portrayals in, 134–38
television violence, 10–11, 14, 221, 225,
    242–43
  and aggressive behavior, 233–36
  content analysis literature, 222, 231–33,
    244
    adolescents in violent actions on TV,
      222–25
    patterns of consequences and
      characteristics of violence, 227–31
    patterns of seriousness of violence,
      225–27
    types of violent acts, 226, 227
  desensitization effect, 236
  factors influencing a disinhibition
    effect, 232
  fear effect, 234–36, 241
  frequency of exposure to, 237–39
  imitation of, 242
  justification, 229
  pattern of portrayal, 239–41
  portrayed in humorous context, 230

television violence (*continued*)
  profiles of characters involved
    with, 229
  recommendations for scholars, 244
  recommendations for the public,
    244–46
  shift from serious to minor acts,
    241–42
  shown in fantasy context of unrealistic
    pattern, 230
  standard formula for presenting
    violence on TV, 228–29
  trends in the amount of, 224–25
  what constitutes a negative effect,
    236–42
thin body ideal, 168. *See also* ideal body
  in electronic media, 170–71
  in print media, 168–70
Thomas, Mandy, 42–43
tobacco advertising, 251–54, 274–76
  content analysis studies assessing,
    254–55
    content appealing to youth and
      women, 260–62
    health/smoking controversy events
      and broadcast advertising ban,
      255–60
    shifts in tobacco industry
      promotional spending, 262–64
tobacco marketers and the relevance of
    youth consumers, 251–54
tobacco use representation in
    entertainment media, 250–51,
    264, 274–76. *See also* smoking
  content analysis studies assessing, 267
  frequency in movies, 272–74
  frequency in TV shows, 267–72
  in music videos, 88–90
  product placement for tobacco
    products, 266–67
transgender. *See* gender boundaries
transglobal media flows, 42. *See also*
    global teen market

V-Chip, 452–53
video games, 347–48, 365–67, 367n1
  interface and play control, 360–63
  popularity among youth, 348–49
  potential effects on youth, 349–50,
    357–58
    addiction and displacement of other
      activities, 354–55

changes over time and, 358–65
  educational and learning outcomes,
    356–57
  physical fitness, physical skills,
    and health, 355–56
  self-perception, 355
  violent content and aggressive/
    antisocial behavior, 14, 350–53
  violent/sexual content and
    perceptions of reality, 353–54
  social interaction and representation,
    363–65
  technical fidelity and realism, 358–60
violence, 386. *See also* juvenile
    delinquency; movies/films,
    violence in; music video(s);
    television violence
  sexual, 90–92, 338
  television and, 11
  video games and, 14, 350–54
virtual reality (VR) devices in video
    games, 360–62

Ward, L. M., 327–28
"weak protectionism," 438–39
weapon-carrying in music videos, 86
weapons used in violent acts on TV, 230
Willard, Michael, 28
Willis, Paul, 51
women. *See also* gender
  treatment in advertising and marketing,
    448–50
"Woodstock" (Joni Mitchell), 65–66
Woodstock Music and Art Fair, 65–66
World War II. *See also* postwar era
  youth culture in wartime, 31–32
World Wide Web (WWW). *See* Internet

youth cultures, modern
  "hybridized"/"syncretic" character, 43
"youth," definitions and connotations of
    the term, 46, 48
youthful expression, expansion of, 456
youthful hedonism, 10, 47, 447. *See also*
    culture of consumption
"youth market," 48
  and media during 1950s and early
    1960s, 33–40
Youth Marketing Co., 36
YouTube, 95–96

zoot suits and "zoot suit riots," 31–32